MINDS on MATH ▶8

ONTARIO EDITION

Robert Alexander
Formerly with the
Toronto Board of Education
Toronto, Ontario

Katie Pallos-Haden
Memorial Composite High School
Stony Plain, Alberta

Ron Lancaster
St. Mildred's Lightbourn School
Oakville, Ontario

Fred Crouse
Kings County District School Board
Kentville, Nova Scotia

David DeCoste
Dr. J.H. Gillis Regional High School
Antigonish, Nova Scotia

Brendan Kelly
University of Toronto
Toronto, Ontario

Florence Glanfield
Consultant
Edmonton, Alberta

Paul Atkinson
Waterloo County Board of Education
Kitchener, Ontario

Jane Forbes
E.C. Drury High School
Milton, Ontario

Addison
Wesley

Toronto

DEVELOPMENTAL EDITORS
Lesley Haynes
Sarah Mawson

EDITORS
Maurice Barry
Mei Lin Cheung
Santo D'Agostino
Anna-Maria Garnham
Lee Geller
Lynne Gulliver
Helen Nolan
Rajshree Shankar
Anita Smale

RESEARCHER
Louise MacKenzie

DESIGN/PRODUCTION
Pronk&Associates

ART DIRECTION
Pronk&Associates/Joe Lepiano

ELECTRONIC ASSEMBLY & TECHNICAL ART
Pronk&Associates/Steve Doinidis, Marcela Grant,
Aleksandar Janicijevic, Linda Stephenson, Craig Swistun,
Stanley Tran.

COVER DESIGN
Pronk&Associates

Acknowledgments appear on pages 539 and 540.

Canadian Cataloguing in Publication Data

Main entry under title:
    Minds on math 8
Ontario ed.
Includes index.
ISBN 0-201-51270-X

1. Mathematics — Juvenile literature.
I. Alexander, Bob, 1941 —

QA107.M55 1998a   510   C98-931781-1

ISBN 0-201-51270-X
This book contains recycled product and is acid free.
Printed and bound in Canada.

REVIEWERS/CONSULTANTS
Professor Andrew Adler
Department of Mathematics
University of British Columbia

Anne Boyd
Curriculum Consultant
School District 72
Campbell River, British Columbia

Edna M. Dach
Supervisor, Programs
Instructional Services
Elk Island Public Schools
Sherwood Park, Alberta

Liliane Gauthier
Educational Consultant – Instructions
Mathematics & Science - K-8
Saskatoon Board of Education, Saskatchewan

Rita C. Janes
Mathematics Coordinator
St. John's Roman Catholic School Board
St. John's, Newfoundland

Dr. Arthur Jorgensen
Education Consultant
Edson, Alberta

Richard J. Kopan
Coordinator
Calgary Board of Education, Alberta

Peter Saarimaki
Coordinator of Mathematics
Toronto Board of Education, Toronto

Elaine Simmt
University of Alberta
Edmonton, Alberta

Elizabeth Wood
National Sport School
Calgary, Alberta

CONTENTS

CHAPTER 1: REPRESENTING WHOLE NUMBERS

CHAPTER 2: FRACTIONS

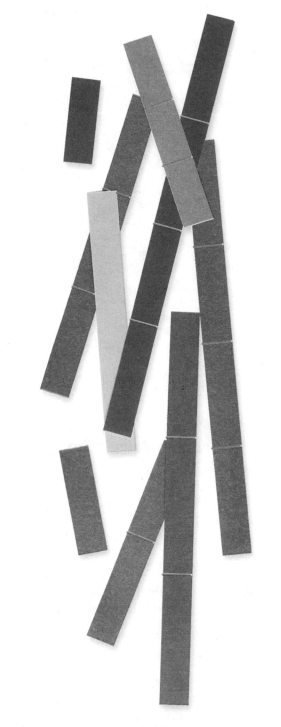

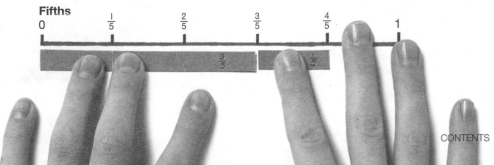

CHAPTER 3: THINKING PROPORTIONALLY

CHAPTER 4: PERCENT

CHAPTER 7: MEASUREMENT

CHAPTER 8: ALGEBRA

CHAPTER 9: TWO-DIMENSIONAL GEOMETRY

WELCOME TO *MINDS ON MATH 8*

We hope this book helps you see that mathematics can be useful, interesting, and enjoyable. We wish you every success.

This book is about…

…Problem Solving

Learning to solve problems is the main reason for studying mathematics. You will find that all the parts of this book are designed to help you improve your problem-solving skills.

…Math in the Real World

This book describes many new ways you can use mathematics to understand your everyday world. You will also learn about how people use mathematics in their careers.

…Calculators and Computers

Technology is a tool you will be using often in your life, and in your study of mathematics. You will need a calculator to complete some of the activities and exercises in this book. You will also want to use a computer and some popular software to work with Draw programs, spreadsheets, and databases. This book will help you add these tools to the paper and pencil you already use every day.

Take a few moments to read the following pages. They explain how this book is organized and how you will be using it.

CHAPTER CONTENTS

Each chapter begins with a magazine-style Contents. This gives you an idea of what you will be studying and what problems the mathematics can help you solve.

WHAT'S COMING UP?

This is a list of the mathematics topics covered in the chapter.

DEPARTMENTS

Most chapters contain five departments. You will get to know the departments as you use the book. For example, a Quest always offers you an interesting opportunity to build your problem-solving skills — and to discover something new.

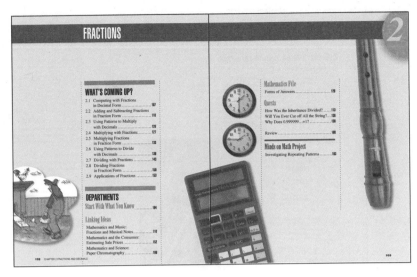

START WITH WHAT YOU KNOW

Each chapter begins with Start With What You Know. These questions and activities give you a chance to review so that you can be successful with the new material.

For example, this Start With What You Know describes the demise of the cod in Atlantic Canada. The questions help you review interpreting graphs.

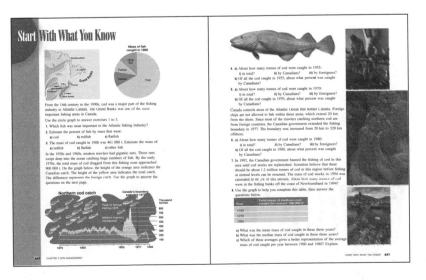

DEVELOPING THE IDEAS

The mathematics in this book is developed in a variety of ways.
Two or more of these ways are often used in the same lesson.

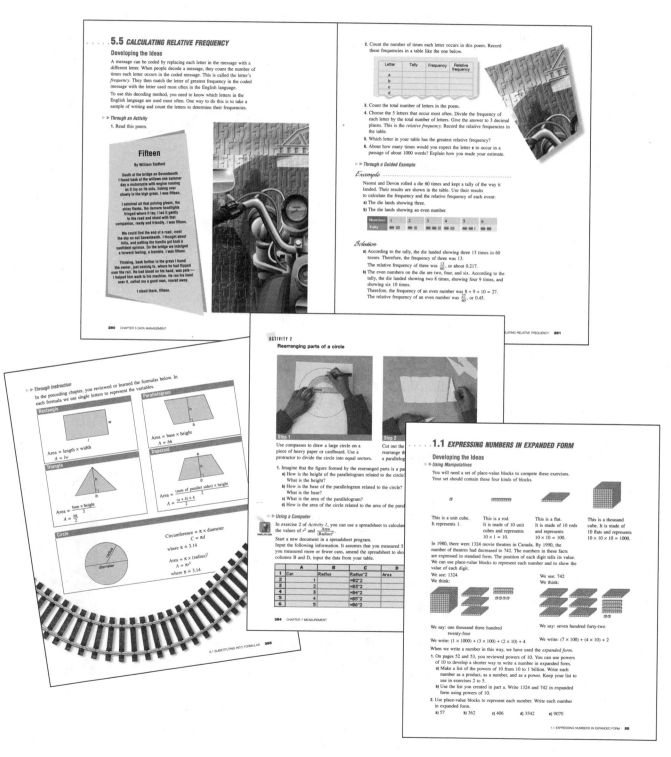

▶▶ Through Activities

I hear and I forget.
I see and I remember.
I do and I understand.

One of the best ways to learn anything new is to become actively involved with it. This is true whether you are learning to play a musical instrument, learning a new sport, or learning to use a computer.

The same is also true of mathematics. When you use this book you will be actively doing mathematics. Many ideas are developed through activities you can do with a partner or in a small group.

▶▶ Using Manipulatives

Some ideas are best understood using concrete materials, called manipulatives. This is an excellent way to develop new ideas in algebra and to help you see the connections between arithmetic and algebra.

▶▶ Through Discussion

New ideas are often introduced through discussion with a partner, in a small group, or as a class.

▶▶ Through Instruction

Some Through Instruction sections help you consolidate the ideas you learned through activities or discussion. In other cases, ideas are easiest to understand when you can read a straightforward explanation of the concepts involved.

▶▶ Through Guided Examples

After you have learned some new ideas through an activity or discussion, it helps to see examples showing how to use the ideas. The examples in this book are called guided examples because they usually contain explanations of the steps in the solution.

▶▶ Using a Computer

A computer can be used to create graphs and to explore concepts in geometry.

WORKING WITH MATHEMATICS

There are five different kinds of exercises in the lessons in this book.

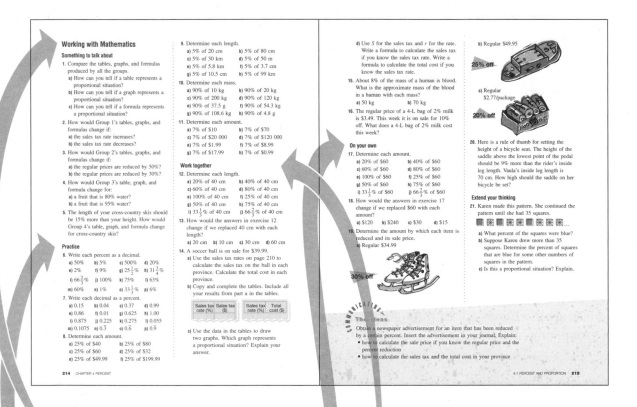

Something to talk about
These exercises will get you talking. They give you and your classmates a chance to check your understanding together before you begin to solve problems on your own.

Practice
Learning anything new requires practice. These exercises let you practise the new skills you have learned.

On your own
After you have gained confidence working with a partner, these exercises should be completed on your own.

Work together
You will probably want to complete these exercises with a partner or in a group. Talking with other students helps you learn because you see how they make connections between the new ideas and what they already know. There are two more advantages:

- Other students can sometimes explain new ideas to you in ways that make sense.
- Explaining something you understand to someone else can help you to understand it better.

Technology

The computer is a tool for learning and doing mathematics in ways that were not possible just a few years ago. Some of the computer exercises give you a chance to work with popular computer applications, such as spreadsheets and Draw programs. These exercises are labelled with logos. The *Minds on Math Template Disk* lets you get started right away.

For other computer activities, you will need to use a computer database. The *Minds on Math Data Disk* provides a vast amount of data you can use to answer questions and to understand and present information.

Using ClarisWorks® or Microsoft Works™ for your applications software will make it easiest for you to do the spreadsheet and Draw program exercises in this book. You will need one of these programs to use the *Minds on Math Template Disk* and the *Minds on Math Data Disk*.

Extend your thinking

These exercises are extensions of the ideas in the lesson. Some of these exercises may require you to think about what you have been doing and to apply your thinking to related ideas. Others may be more challenging than the previous exercises.

DATA DISK   TEMPLATE DISK

Be sure you have correct solutions in your notebook for the exercises in the **Work together** *and* **On your own** *sections of each lesson. To study for a test or examination, try these exercises again. If you have difficulty, refer to the solutions in your notebook.*

That's all there is to it!

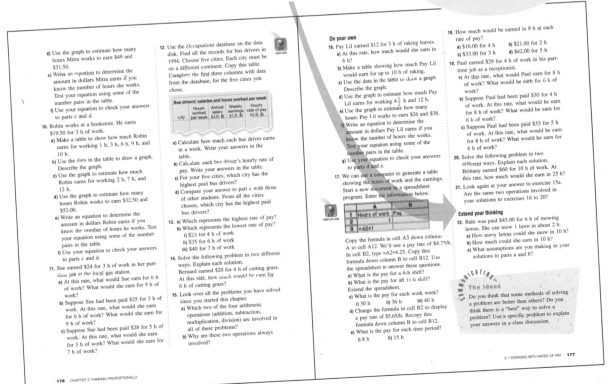

COMMUNICATING THE IDEAS

Communicating your knowledge about a concept or skill can help you learn mathematics. Also, when you learn something interesting or puzzling or exciting, it makes sense to talk about it! In this book you will be asked to communicate your ideas in a variety of ways, such as:

- writing in your journal
- explaining to a friend
- writing a report
- designing a poster

19. Find the measure of each angle marked e.
a)
b)
c)
d)

22. Construct a right triangle ABC like that below. Construct altitude AD. Measure the angles in each of the three triangles. Describe any patterns you discover.

Extend your thinking

23. Kelly and Sook-Yin were discussing the triangle below. Kelly said, "That's neat. One angle is double another, and one angle is triple another. This must only be true for a triangle with angles of 30°, 60°, and 90°." After thinking for a moment, Sook-Yin replied, "No, that's not true. I can draw a triangle with different angles from this one that has this same property." Is Sook-Yin correct? If so, what are the measures of the angles in her triangle? If not, explain how you know she is wrong.

20. Find the measures of the angles marked r and s.
a)
b)
c)
d)

21. Find the measures of the angles marked w and x.
a)
b)

The Ideas

In your journal, draw diagrams and explain how we use the sum of the angle measures of a triangle to find the sum of the angle measures of a quadrilateral, and of a pentagon

444 CHAPTER 9 TWO-DIMENS

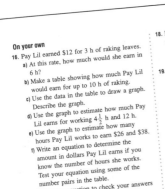

On your own

16. Pay Lil earned $12 for 3 h of raking leaves.
   a) At this rate, how much would she earn in 6 h?
   b) Make a table showing how much Pay Lil would earn for up to 10 h of raking.
   c) Use the data in the table to draw a graph. Describe the graph.
   d) Use the graph to estimate how much Pay Lil earns for working $4\frac{1}{2}$ h and 12 h.
   e) Use the graph to estimate how many hours Pay Lil works to earn $26 and $38.
   f) Write an equation to determine the amount in dollars Pay Lil earns if you know the number of hours she works. Test your equation using some of the number pairs in the table.
   g) Use your equation to check your answers to parts d and e.

17. We can use a computer to generate a table showing the hours of work and the earnings. Start a new document in a spreadsheet program. Enter the information below.

TEMPLATE DISK

	A	B
1	Hours of work	Pay
2		1
3	=A2+1	

   Copy the formula in cell A3 down column A to cell A12. We'll use a pay rate of $4.25/h. In cell B2, type =A2*4.25. Copy this formula down column B to cell B12. Use the spreadsheet to answer these questions.
   a) What is the pay for a 6-h shift?
   b) What is the pay for an 11-h shift? Extend the spreadsheet.
   c) What is the pay for each work week?
      i) 30 h   ii) 36 h   iii) 40 h
   d) Change the formula in cell B2 to display a pay rate of $5.65/h. Recopy this formula down column B to cell B12.
   e) What is the pay for each time period?
      i) 8 h   ii) 15 h

18. How much would be earned in 8 h at each rate of pay?
   a) $16.00 for 4 h   b) $21.00 for 2 h
   c) $33.00 for 3 h   d) $42.00 for 5 h

19. Paul earned $29 for 4 h of work in his part-time job as a receptionist.
   a) At this rate, what would Paul earn for of work? What would he earn for 6 h work?
   b) Suppose Paul had been paid $30 for of work. At this rate, what would he for 8 h of work? What would he ea 6 h of work?
   c) Suppose Paul had been paid $33 for of work. At this rate, what would he for 8 h of work? What would he ea 6 h of work?

20. Solve the following problem in two different ways. Explain each solution Brittany earned $60 for 10 h of work this rate, how much would she earn

21. Look again at your answer to exerci Are the same two operations involv your solutions to exercises 16 to 20

Extend your thinking

22. Bahi was paid $45.00 for 6 h of m lawns. She can mow 1 lawn in ab
   a) How many lawns could she mo
   b) How much could she earn in 1
   c) What assumptions are you mak solutions to parts a and b?

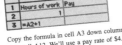

The Ideas

Do you think that some methods of solving a problem are better than others? Do you think there is a "best" way to solve a problem? Use a specific problem to explain your answers in a class discussion.

3.1 WORKING WITH RATES OF PAY **177**

Keep a Journal.

A journal helps you explore ideas and keep a record of what you have learned. This book gives you many suggestions for what to write about in your journal. If you keep your journal up to date, you'll discover that it can help you review your thinking when you're studying for tests or exams.

QUESTS

Most chapters contain one or two Quests. Each Quest is a significant problem for you to solve.

You will want to approach Quests in a thoughtful way. You can use the four-step problem solving plan built into each Quest to help you. As you work, you will be finding interesting answers to meaningful questions and learning how to be a successful problem solver.

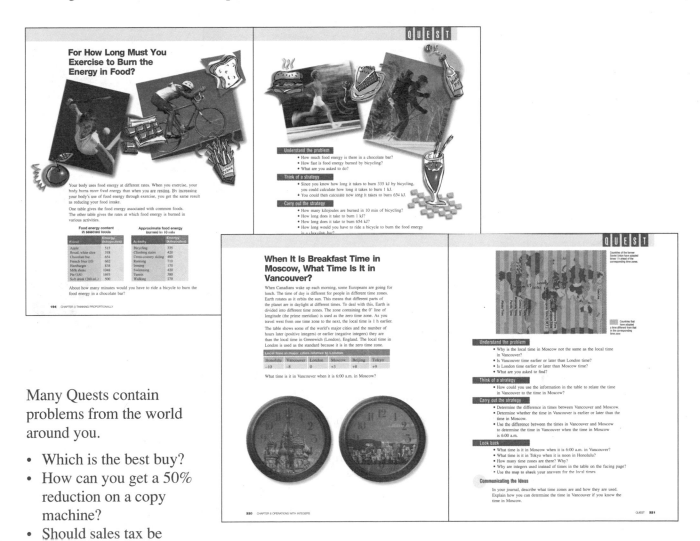

Many Quests contain problems from the world around you.

- Which is the best buy?
- How can you get a 50% reduction on a copy machine?
- Should sales tax be applied before or after a discount?

Other Quests involve patterns in arithmetic or geometry.

- Will you ever cut off all the string?
- Can you visualize the hidden faces of a cube?

LINKING IDEAS

In the Linking Ideas department, you'll find activities that help you explore connections between mathematics and other subject areas, or between strands in mathematics.

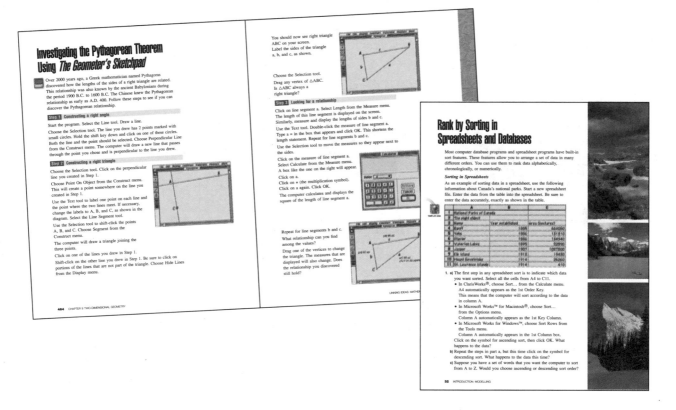

Links with Technology

The computer lets you investigate problems that would be too difficult or involve too much computation to solve with paper and pencil, or even with a calculator. You can also use a computer to explore geometry in a dynamic way that is impossible without a computer.

Other examples of links with technology

- Using Simulations to Calculate Probability
- How Long Can You Talk for $25?
- Using Data for Investigations

Links with Science

Several linking features show mathematics at work in different fields of science.

Other examples of links with science

- Did We See What Destroyed the Dinosaurs?
- Contaminants in the Great Lakes

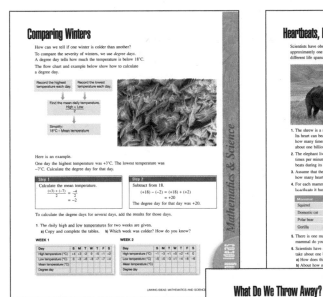

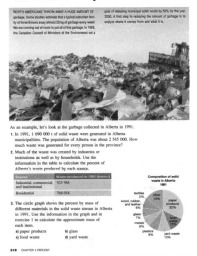

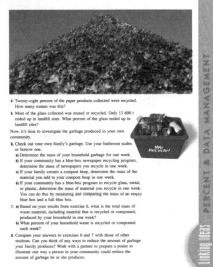

Other Links

- Mathematics and the Consumer
- Mathematics and Music
- Linking strands within mathematics

MATHEMATICS FILES

Mathematics Files provide opportunities for you to develop your mathematical understanding. These pages may help you see why many people believe mathematics is a fascinating and even beautiful field of study all on its own, with no need for "uses" or "connections" to make it important.

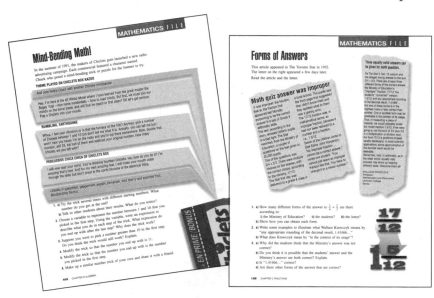

Other examples of Mathematics Files

- Working with Scales
- What Percent of a Newspaper Is Advertising?
- The Poggendorf Effect
- Networks
- How Big is One Billion?

BOGGLE YOUR MIND

Many problems involving interesting facts and questions occur throughout the text. These give you more opportunities to practise your problem-solving skills. Often the answers you reach will boggle your mind.

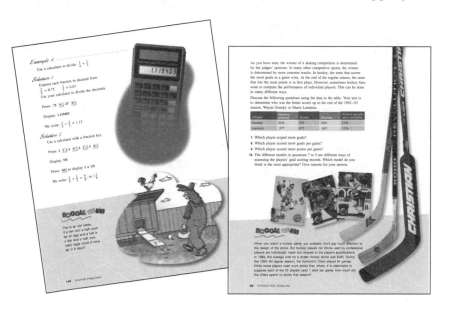

Other Boggle Your Mind topics

- The volume of soft drinks purchased by Canadians in one year
- The number of species of life on Earth
- The world champion pumpkin grower
- The daily amount spent by Canadian teenagers on snack food

MINDS ON MATH PROJECT

Each chapter ends with a project or investigation that gives you freedom to use and develop mathematics in your own way. You will need to plan, research, experiment, and make choices and decisions. Probably your project will take a few weeks to complete.

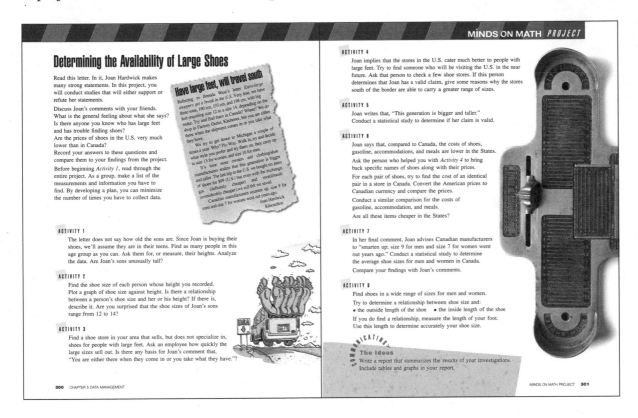

- Each project contains several related activities for you to do over a period of time.
- You can work alone or with a partner.
- The projects are open-ended. This means that there may be more than one answer, or that students doing the same project may get different results.
- You will be asked to write a report or to make a presentation so that you can share your thinking and results with others.

Other topics to explore in Minds on Math Projects

- Exploring how maps and globes represent Earth
- Investigating enlargements of photographs
- Comparing what you eat to the recommendations in Canada's Food Guide
- The Consumer Price Index
- Reducing heating, lighting, and water costs in your home

MODELLING

Modelling in mathematics means to apply mathematics to solve realistic problems. In this introductory section, you will find activities involving modelling. These activities will help you review concepts and skills you learned in previous grades. You will need to use these skills as you work through the chapters in this book.

WHAT'S COMING UP?

DEPARTMENTS

Start With What You Know

Linking Ideas

Quest

Minds on Math Project

Start With What You Know

In each case below, you are given some information and asked to make a comparison. Describe how you would use the given information to answer each question.

1. Which of these two animals is larger?

Giraffe
Height: 5.5 m
Mass: 1000 kg

Elephant
Height: 3.4 m
Mass: 2800 kg

2. Which of these two containers would hold more liquid?

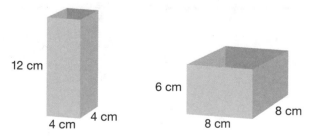

12 cm

4 cm   4 cm

6 cm

8 cm   8 cm

3. From 1943 to 1954, there was a women's professional baseball league in the United States. Compare the batting statistics from the 1944 season for Merle Keagle and Faye Dancer. Which of these women do you think was the better batter that season?

Player	Times at bat	Number of hits	Home runs
Merle Keagle	406	107	7
Faye Dancer	329	90	2

4. Which city, Vancouver or Ottawa, is closer to Winnipeg?

NUMERICAL MODELS

Developing the Ideas

▶ ▶ *Through Discussion*

When you hear the word *model*, you may think of a person who appears in fashion magazines. In mathematics, a model is a set of data or a diagram that describes an object or a situation.

Numerical models are widely used in competitive sports to compare performance. To evaluate figure skaters in international competitions, nine judges rate each performance on a scale of 0 to 6. A mark of 6 is perfect. Numbers such as 5.8 and 5.9 are assigned to near perfect performances. Each skater receives one mark for technical merit and another for artistic impression. These combine to give a mark out of 12.

More important than the actual mark is the rank assigned to the skater by each judge. The numerical equivalent of the rank is called an *ordinal*. To understand how ordinals work, think of arranging the skaters according to the marks they receive from a judge. The skater who receives the highest mark receives an ordinal of 1 from that judge, the second highest receives a 2, and so on. If one skater receives five or more first-place ordinals, she or he is the winner. If no one has five or more firsts, the second-place votes are added as well. If there is still no one with five or more votes, the person with the lowest ordinal total wins.

1. Why do you think numerical ratings are used instead of ratings such as these?

| poor | fair | good | very good | excellent | outstanding |

2. Why do you think 9 judges are used instead of 1? Instead of 10?

At the 1994 Olympic Winter Games, there was controversy over who should have won the gold medal in women's figure skating. Read the following excerpt from an article published in the Winnipeg Free Press on Saturday, February 26, 1994, and discuss the questions below.

Ukrainian skater edges past Kerrigan

By Neil Stevens

Canadian Press

Hamar, Norway — Oksana Baiul, a tiny teenager from the Ukraine who had to be shot full of pain killers one hour before performing, won the women's gold figure skating medal in one of the closest decisions in Olympic history yesterday.

It could not have been closer between Baiul and Nancy Kerrigan in the judges' eyes: it was a 5–4 split. Judge No. 9, Jan Hoffman of Germany, gave Kerrigan 5.8 for technical merit and 5.8 for artistic impression and gave Baiul 5.7 and 5.9.

The marks gave each skater an 11.6 total, but ties are broken by impression marks, so Baiul got the ninth and deciding verdict.

3. Here are the marks received by each skater.

Free skating		-1- GBR	-2- POL	-3- CZE	-4- UKR	-5- CHN	-6- USA	-7- JPN	-8- CAN	-9- GER
BAIUL Oksana	Technical merit	5.6	5.8	5.9	5.8	5.8	5.8	5.8	5.5	5.7
	Artistic impression	5.8	5.9	5.9	5.9	5.9	5.8	5.8	5.9	5.9
KERRIGAN Nancy	Technical merit	5.8	5.8	5.8	5.7	5.7	5.8	5.8	5.7	5.8
	Artistic impression	5.9	5.8	5.9	5.9	5.9	5.9	5.9	5.8	5.8

a) Determine the mark out of 12 each skater received from each judge.

b) Without including Judge No. 9, how many first-place ordinals did each skater receive?

4. Judge No. 9 gave both skaters exactly the same mark. Who received the first-place ordinal from this judge? Do you think this was fair?

5. a) Suppose the marks were totalled and the skater with the greater total were awarded the gold medal. Who would have won?

b) Do you think this would have been a fair way to award the medal? Explain.

6. If you were an official, how would you decide who should win the gold medal in a case like this? Explain why you think your method is fair.

As you have seen, the winner of a skating competition is determined by the judges' opinions. In many other competitive sports, the winner is determined by more concrete results. In hockey, the team that scores the most goals in a game wins. At the end of the regular season, the team that has the most points is in first place. However, sometimes hockey fans want to compare the performance of individual players. This can be done in many different ways.

Discuss the following questions using the data in the table. Your aim is to determine who was the better scorer up to the end of the 1992–93 season, Wayne Gretzky or Mario Lemieux.

Player	Games played	Goals	Assists	Points (goals plus assists)
Gretzky	1044	765	1563	2328
Lemieux	577	477	697	1174

7. Which player scored more goals?

8. Which player scored more goals per game?

9. Which player scored more points per game?

10. The different models in questions 7 to 9 are different ways of assessing the players' goal scoring records. Which model do you think is the most appropriate? Give reasons for your answer.

BOGGLE YOUR MIND

When you watch a hockey game, you probably don't pay much attention to the design of the sticks. But hockey players do! Sticks used by professional players are individually made and shaped to the player's specifications. In 1994, the average cost for a dozen hockey sticks was $280. During the 1993–94 regular season, the Edmonton Oilers played 84 games. While some players used more sticks than others, it is reasonable to suppose each of the 25 players used 1 stick per game. How much did the Oilers spend on sticks that season?

Working with Mathematics

Something to talk about

1. On a scale of 0 to 10, what rating would correspond to:

    a) a perfect score?   **b)** an average score?

Give reasons for your answers.

2. Why are numerical models used to compare preferences and performances?

3. a) How do Canadians determine which candidates should represent us in government?

    b) In what way is this a numerical model?

Work together

4. List five of your favourite television programs. Interview 7 students and ask them to rate each program on a scale of 1 to 10. Explain that the more they like a program, the closer their rating should be to 10.

    a) Calculate the total rating for each program.

    b) For each program, divide the total rating by 7. This is the mean rating for that program.

    c) Draw a number line labelled 1 to 10. Use the mean rating to place each program on this line.

    d) Which program is most liked?

    e) Which program is least liked?

5. Refer to the data you collected in exercise 4.

    a) For each program, list the 7 ratings in order. The median rating is the rating that appears in the middle of the list. What is the median rating for each program?

    b) Draw a number line labelled 1 to 10. Use the median rating to place each program on the line.

    c) Which program is most liked?

    d) Which program is least liked?

    e) Does the popularity of the programs change when you use the median scores instead of the mean scores? Explain.

    f) Do you think the popularity of the programs would change if you interviewed adults as well as students? Explain your answer.

6. Before some movies are distributed, they are shown to groups of people to judge the audience reaction. This is called a preview.

    a) At one movie preview, 100 people were asked to rate the movie on a scale of 1 to 10. When the responses were tallied, it was found that the median rating was 4. Did most of the people in the audience like the movie? Explain your answer.

    b) What do you think a movie studio might do with the information collected at a preview?

DATA DISK

7. The *Box Office Hits* database on the data disk provides information about the top 5 movies for each year from 1939 to 1993. Look through the database. Use the Find feature of your database program to find the records for *Dances with Wolves* and *Home Alone*, which were both released in 1990.

    a) How much money did each movie earn?

    b) How many academy awards did each movie win?

    c) Decide what it means for a movie to be successful. Which movie is more successful according to your model? Justify your model.

Box Office Hits

    Title Dances with Wolves
    Year 1990
    Studio Orion
    Money made 81537971
    Director(s) Kevin Costner

    Cast Kevin Costner, Mary McDonnell, Graham Greene, Rodney A. Grant, Floyd Red Crow Westerman, Tantoo Cardinal, Robert Pastorelli, Charles Rocket,

Academy Award nominations 12
    Academy Award wins 7

8. The prices of food, housing, and services increase over the years. To compare what an item cost in one year with its cost in another year, we use a model called a *Consumer Price Index* (CPI). It compares current prices to prices in 1986. This CPI table shows that items with a total cost of $100 in 1986 cost $130.20 in 1993.

Year	1986	1987	1988	1989
CPI	100	104.4	108.6	114.0
Year	1990	1991	1992	1993
CPI	119.5	126.2	128.1	130.2

a) An item cost $100 in 1986. Estimate its cost in 1991.

b) An item cost $200 in 1986. Estimate its cost in 1991.

c) An item cost $114 in 1989. Estimate its cost in 1986.

d) An item cost $228 in 1989. Estimate its cost in 1986.

9. In the 1927 baseball season, Babe Ruth hit a record 60 home runs. This record remained until Roger Maris hit 61 home runs in the 1961 season.

a) Who had more home runs in a single season?

b) Babe Ruth hit 60 home runs in 154 games. When Roger Maris hit his 61st home run he had played 162 games. Who had more home runs per game played?

c) Babe Ruth had come to bat 547 times when he hit his 60th home run. Roger Maris had come to bat 588 times when he hit his 61st home run. Who had more home runs per time at bat?

d) Which model in parts a to c would you use to decide the better home run hitter? Explain.

On your own

10. Describe how much you enjoy each sport by rating it on a scale of 0 to 10. Give a rating of 0 to a sport you do not enjoy playing or watching. Give a rating of 10 to the sport you enjoy most.

- gymnastics
- swimming
- skiing
- lacrosse
- basketball
- baseball
- hockey
- soccer
- volleyball

Explain how you could combine the ratings of all the students in the class to determine which of these sports students like best.

11. Nutritionists suggest that we restrict our consumption of fat and cholesterol. Harvey's publishes a table of nutrition facts for its products. Part of the table is shown here.

	Energy (Cal)	Protein (g)	Total fat (g)	Choles-terol (mg)
Hamburger	357	18.4	17.5	45.0
Superburger	518	24.4	28.9	72.2
Chicken sandwich	375	19.7	16.0	35.5
Fish sandwich	393	15.3	14.9	16.8

a) Which item has the highest cholesterol content? Which has the lowest?

b) Which item has the highest fat content? Which has the lowest?

c) Which item has the most protein? Which has the least?

d) How might the information in this table help a person make a choice? Explain.

12. Doctors warn of the health dangers of excessive exposure to the sun. They recommend that you use a sunscreen when you are outdoors. But what lotion should you use? Scientists have created a numerical model for comparing the protection we get from different sunscreens. It is called a *sun protection factor*, or SPF. A sunscreen with SPF 6 allows you to be in the sun 6 times as long as if you were unprotected.

a) Suppose you could stay in the sun unprotected for 30 minutes without burning. How long could you stay in the sun without burning if you were using a sunscreen with SPF 8?

b) Suppose you are using a sunscreen with SPF 30. Your sister who has the same colouring as you is using a sunscreen with SPF 10.

   i) Who could stay in the sun longer without burning?

   ii) How many times as long could this person stay in the sun?

c) Why don't doctors or sunscreen manufacturers publish a table showing, for each SPF value, how long you can stay in the sun without burning?

Extend your thinking

13. To compare the loudness of sounds, scientists have devised a model that measures intensity of sound in decibels (db). A sound that exceeds another by 10 db is 10 times as loud. The chart below shows the decibel rating of a variety of sounds.

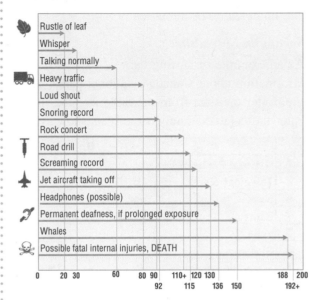

a) What is the sound intensity of a jet aircraft during takeoff?

b) What is the sound intensity of the record for the loudest scream?

c) How many times as loud as the record for screaming is a jet aircraft during takeoff?

d) How many times as loud as talking normally is heavy traffic?

e) How many times as loud as heavy traffic is the record for screaming?

f) Permanent deafness occurs from prolonged exposure to sounds of 150 db. How many times as loud as the sound of a rock concert is a sound of 150 db?

g) How many times as loud as a jet engine during takeoff is a sound of 150 db?

The Ideas

Look back at the questions you answered on pages 24 and 25. In your journal, describe how you used models to answer the questions.

Rank by Sorting in Spreadsheets and Databases

Most computer database programs and spreadsheet programs have built-in sort features. These features allow you to arrange a set of data in many different orders. You can use them to rank data alphabetically, chronologically, or numerically.

Sorting in Spreadsheets

As an example of sorting data in a spreadsheet, use the following information about Canada's national parks. Start a new spreadsheet file. Enter the data from the table into the spreadsheet. Be sure to enter the data accurately, exactly as shown in the table.

TEMPLATE DISK

	A	B	C
1	National Parks of Canada		
2	The eight oldest		
3	Name	Year established	Area (hectares)
4	Banff	1885	664080
5	Yoho	1886	131310
6	Glacier	1886	134940
7	Waterton Lakes	1895	52590
8	Jasper	1907	1087800
9	Elk Island	1913	19430
10	Mount Revelstoke	1914	26260
11	St. Lawrence Islands	1914	410

1. **a)** The first step in any spreadsheet sort is to indicate which data you want sorted. Select all the cells from A4 to C11.
   - In ClarisWorks®, choose Sort… from the Calculate menu. A4 automatically appears as the 1st Order Key. This means that the computer will sort according to the data in column A.
   - In Microsoft Works™ for Macintosh®, choose Sort… from the Options menu. Column A automatically appears as the 1st Key Column.
   - In Microsoft Works for Windows™, choose Sort Rows from the Tools menu. Column A automatically appears in the 1st Column box.

   Click on the symbol for ascending sort, then click OK. What happens to the data?
   b) Repeat the steps in part a, but this time click on the symbol for descending sort. What happens to the data this time?
   c) Suppose you have a set of words that you want the computer to sort from A to Z. Would you choose ascending or descending sort order?

d) Suppose you have a set of numbers that you want the computer to sort from least to greatest. Would you choose ascending or descending sort order? Test your idea by sorting the data in your spreadsheet according to the data in column B. To do this, follow the steps in part a, but enter B4 as the 1st Order Key in ClarisWorks, enter B as the 1st Key Column in Microsoft Works for Macintosh, and enter B in the 1st Column box in Microsoft Works for Windows. List the 8 parks in order from first established to most recently established.

2. Use the sort feature to list the 8 parks in order from largest area to smallest area.

3. Use the sort feature to display the list of parks in the same order as it appears on page 32.

Sorting in Databases

Open the *Mammals of Canada* database on the data disk. This database contains information about 160 Canadian mammals. Each record contains information about one mammal. The information is organized into 10 categories called fields. One record is shown here. Depending on the type of computer you use, the field names may be different from those shown here. Browse through the database.

DATA DISK

Mammals of Canada

Name	Woodland Vole
Group	Rodents
Average mass (kg)	0.028
Average total length (cm)	12.1
Average tail length (cm)	2
Gestation period (days)	22
Number of young	5
Longevity (yrs)	1
Diet	nuts, seeds, bark, bulbs, tubers, green leaves; insects
Habitat	deciduous forests
Predators	snakes, short-tailed shrew; fox, racoon, opossum, skunk, mink, weasel, coyote, domestic dog and cat

4. a) One of the fields tells you the average mass of the animal. Use the sorting feature of the database to find the Canadian mammal with the greatest average mass. Follow the steps described below for your program.

- In ClarisWorks, choose Sort Records… from the Organize menu. A list of all the field names appears.
  Double click on Average mass (kg) since this is the field you want to sort by.
  Choose either Ascending order or Descending order.
  Click OK.
  Each time you want to sort by a new field, begin by clearing the Sort Order list.

Mathematics & Technology

Linking Ideas

- In Microsoft Works for Macintosh, choose Sort… from the Data menu.

  Scroll down the list of field names until you find Mass in kg, since this is the field you want to sort by.

  The program will sort in ascending order unless you click on the box labelled Descending.

  Click Sort.

- In Microsoft Works for Windows, choose Sort Records… from the Tools menu.

  Under 1st field, scroll down the list of field names until you find Mass in kg since this is the field you want to sort by.

  Choose either the Ascend or Descend option.

  Click OK.

  To sort by a different field, replace the field name in the 1st field box.

  Which Canadian mammal has the greatest average mass?

  b) Which is the lightest mammal in the database?

5. a) Sort the database by the field that gives the total length. Which is the longest Canadian mammal? Which is the shortest?

b) Gestation period is the amount of time that a mammal is pregnant. Sort the database by the field that gives the gestation period. Which mammal has the longest gestation period? Which has the shortest?

DATA DISK

6. Open the *Box Office Hits* database from the data disk. This database contains information about the 5 movies released each year that earned the most money. Sort the database to find which of the movies in the database:

a) had the greatest total earnings

b) was nominated for the most academy awards

c) won the most academy awards

7. Which studio has the most movies included in the database?

.....STATISTICAL MODELS

Developing the Ideas

▶ ▶ *Through Instruction*

We display data on a graph or a chart. How do we display the measures of central tendency? Are there other numbers that can be used to represent data? Can we display these numbers as well?

Recall that the *median* is the number located at the halfway point when the data are arranged in increasing order.

There are other numbers that are useful to know. The number located at the one-quarter point is called the *lower quartile*. The number located at the three-quarters point is called the *upper quartile*.

Suppose, for 11 days, the manager of a local coffee shop counted the numbers of people eating lunch. Here are the numbers:

9, 16, 37, 28, 32, 18, 30, 21, 40, 33, 12

We will find the median and the quartiles for these data. To do this, we arrange the data in increasing order.

9   12   16   18   21   28   30   32   33   37   40

Since there are 11 numbers, the halfway point is the sixth number. The one-quarter point is the third number, and the three-quarters point is the ninth number.

The median is 28.

The lower quartile is 16.

The upper quartile is 33.

The least and greatest numbers in the data are called the *extremes*. The difference between the extremes, $40 - 9 = 31$, is called the *range*.

We use a *box-and-whisker plot* to display these data.

The box and the whiskers are drawn to scale. The lower quartile is marked at the left end of the box. The upper quartile is marked at the right end. The median is shown as a vertical line inside the box. The median is closer to the upper quartile since 28 is closer to 33 than to 16. We draw line segments from the ends of the box to the extremes.

Example ....

The stem-and-leaf diagram at the right shows the tonnes of household garbage taken to a landfill each day for a month. Use the stem-and-leaf diagram to draw a box-and-whisker plot to display these data.

```
28 | 1 4 5
29 | 3 6 8 9
30 | 4 7 9 9
31 | 2 3 4 5 6 7
32 | 1 3 4 8
33 |
34 | 0 2
```

28 | 1 represents 281 t.

Solution

There are 23 numbers.

The median is the number at the halfway point, 312.

The lower quartile is the number at the one-quarter point: it is the sixth number, 298.

The upper quartile is the number at the three-quarters point: it is the eighteenth number, 321.

The extremes are 281 and 342.

We use these numbers to draw the box-and-whisker plot.

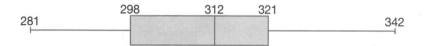

The mean can also be marked on the box-and-whisker plot. Draw a vertical line to scale at the appropriate location.

For the landfill site data, the mean is the sum of the numbers:

$281 + 284 + 285 + 293 + \cdots + 328 + 340 + 342$, divided by 23. The mean is 310.

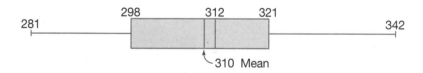

When you are working with a lot of data, you could input them in a spreadsheet or a database program and use the Sort feature. This makes it easier to create a stem-and-leaf diagram or a box-and-whisker plot.

Recall that to find the median when there is an even number of numbers, we arrange the data in order and find the mean of the two middle numbers. Similarly, to find the quartiles when there is an even number of numbers in the first and second halves of the ordered data, we find the mean of the two middle numbers in each half.

Working with Mathematics

Something to talk about

1. This box-and-whisker plot shows the marks of students on a recent examination. Explain the meaning of each number shown.

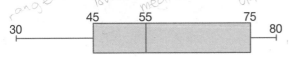

2. The heights of grade 8 students are summarized by this box-and-whisker plot. What information does it display?

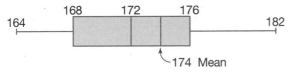

Practice

3. For each set of numbers below, state the:
  i) mean   ii) median
  iii) lower quartile   iv) upper quartile
  v) extremes   vi) range
  - **a)** 1, 1, 2, 3, 5, 6, 6, 7, 8, 8, 8
  - **b)** 3, 3, 3, 4, 4, 6, 10, 10, 10, 15, 20
  - **c)** 20, 21, 12, 14, 14, 12, 15, 21, 13, 23, 22

4. For each stem-and-leaf diagram below, state the:
  i) mean   ii) median
  iii) lower quartile   iv) upper quartile
  v) extremes   vi) range

  a)

1	2266
2	0555
3	444

  b)

3	005
4	0555
5	0003

On your own

5. For each set of numbers below, state the:
  i) mean   ii) median
  iii) lower quartile   iv) upper quartile
  v) extremes   vi) range
  - **a)** 10, 12, 13, 14, 17, 21, 25
  - **b)** 52, 56, 63, 59, 61, 52, 48, 62, 61, 60, 31

6. Display each set of numbers in exercise 5 on a box-and-whisker plot.

7. For each stem-and-leaf diagram below, state the:
  i) mean   ii) median
  iii) lower quartile   iv) upper quartile
  v) extremes   vi) range

  a)

3	01579
4	00588
5	8

  b)

20	1
21	00257
22	0335799
23	00

8. Two groups of students wrote the same mathematics test and obtained the following marks out of 20.

A	16	17	18	20	11	18	20	19	15
	15	20	15	15	17	12	19	8	
	13	16	17	14	19	14	20	12	
B	12	11	18	15	12	6	9	11	
	11	11	16	14	11	17	12	13	
	9	8	10	10	7	11	18	5	

  - **a)** For each group, calculate the mean, the median, the quartiles, and the range.
  - **b)** For each group, display this information on a box-and-whisker plot.
  - **c)** For the two groups taken together, calculate the mean, the median, the quartiles, and the range.
  - **d)** Display this information on a box-and-whisker plot.

Work together

9. a) Determine a set of 15 numbers which have a mean of 70, a lower quartile of 50, an upper quartile of 80, a lower extreme of 32, and a range of 60.
  b) Display your numbers on a stem-and-leaf diagram.
  c) Draw a box-and-whisker plot for these data.

10. The box-and-whisker plots below show the distribution of masses for the 28 members of the Toronto Blue Jays and the Philadelphia Phillies baseball teams. These teams met in the World Series in 1993.

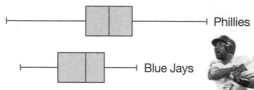

70 kg   80 kg   90 kg   100 kg   110 kg   120 kg

Phillies

Blue Jays

a) Use the plots to determine which team has:
  i) the heaviest player
  ii) the lightest player
  iii) the greater median mass
  iv) more players over 100 kg
  v) at least 6 players under 85 kg

b) It was reported in the media that the Blue Jays were fitter than the Phillies. If a smaller mass were an indication of fitness, do you think this report was true?

11. Sixteen words were written on the board. A class of 18 students was asked to look at them for two minutes. The words were then erased. The students had to write as many words as they remembered. The number of words remembered by each student is listed below. Display the information on a box-and-whisker plot.

8, 11, 9, 14, 5, 14,

10, 12, 13, 16, 11, 13,

12, 11, 14, 15, 14, 14

12. The table lists the average life expectancy for females in 30 countries. Display the data on a box-and-whisker plot.

Average life expectancy for females in 30 countries			
Albania	77	Argentina	75
Australia	81	Belgium	80
Bosnia	78	Brazil	67
Chile	78	China	69
Croatia	78	Czech Republic	77
Egypt	63	Ethiopia	52
France	82	Germany	80
Greenland	72	India	60
Iraq	68	Ireland	79
Israel	80	Italy	81
Japan	82	Mexico	77
Namibia	65	Nicaragua	68
North Korea	73	Pakistan	59
Russia	74	Somalia	56
South Korea	74	United States	80

Extend your thinking

13. Quartiles divide a set of data into four parts. *Percentiles* divide a set of data into 100 parts. For example, the 90th percentile is the number in a set of data below which 90% of the data lie. If a person scores at the 90th percentile on an aptitude test, then she has scored above 90% of all other students writing the test.

a) Express the median, the lower quartile, and the upper quartile as percentiles.

b) Suppose a girl's height is at the 78th percentile among all Canadian girls her age. What percent of Canadian girls are taller than she is?

The Ideas

How would you explain to a friend who has missed class why it is useful to arrange data in increasing (or decreasing) order? Which statistical measures require this? Why?

GEOMETRIC MODELS

Developing the Ideas

▶ ▶ *Through an Activity*

Work in a group or with a partner. Your goal is to determine the height of a tree in your schoolyard using a geometric model.

The first step is to construct a *clinometer*, which is an instrument used to measure angles of objects from a base level. The clinometer you make will measure the angles of objects from your eye level. Most commercial clinometers measure angles from ground level. You will need the following materials:

- enlarged photocopy of a protractor
- cardboard
- scissors
- one drinking straw
- glue and adhesive tape
- a washer or other object to use as a weight
- about 20 cm of string

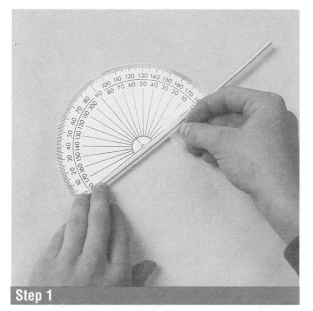

Step 1

Glue the paper protractor to the cardboard and cut it out. Attach the straw along the flat side of the protractor. Tie the washer to one end of the string.

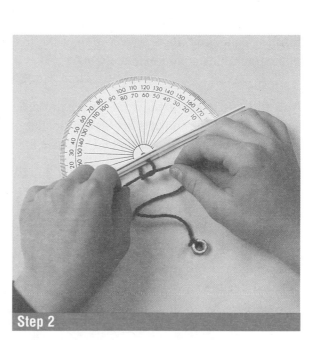

Step 2

Make a hole at the centre mark of the protractor. Put the other end of the string through the hole and tie a knot, as shown.

For the next part of the activity you will need a measuring tape.

Choose a tree in the schoolyard.

Measure and mark a point on the ground 10 m from the base of the tree. One group member should stand at this point and look up at the top of the tree through the straw on the clinometer.

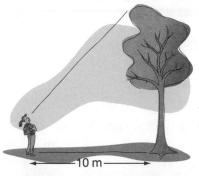

10 m

When the clinometer is tilted, the string indicates the angle (in degrees) between the line joining the viewer's eye to the top of the tree, and the line of the tree. Observe and record this measure. Subtract the measure from 90°. The result is called the *angle of elevation* of the treetop. In the photograph, this is approximately 90° − 57° = 33°.

Also measure and record the height of the viewer's eye from the ground. Once you have made these measurements return to class.

You will now construct a *scale drawing* to determine the height of the tree. In a scale drawing, objects are shown smaller or larger than in real life. For your drawing, use a scale of 1 cm to 2 m.

This means that an object with a length of 1 cm on your drawing is really 2 m long.

You stood 10 m away from the tree. Since $\frac{10\text{ m}}{2\text{ m}} = 5$, begin by drawing a horizontal line 5 cm long. Label one end **Viewer** and the other **Tree**.

Use a protractor to draw a 90° angle at the end labelled **Tree**.

Use a protractor to draw an angle at the end labelled **Viewer** equal to the angle of elevation you calculated.

Extend these two lines until they meet. You now have a triangle. Measure the length in centimetres of the side of the triangle that represents the tree.

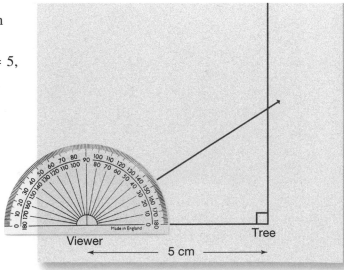

Viewer

Tree

5 cm

Since 1 cm on the diagram represents 2 m, multiply this measure by 2 to find the height of the tree (in metres) from the level of the viewer's eye to the top.

Add the distance from the ground to the viewer's eye.

1. What is the height of the tree?

2. How do you know that the angles in the model triangle have the same measures as the angles in the triangle formed by the tree and the viewer?

3. How did the model triangle help you calculate the height of the tree?

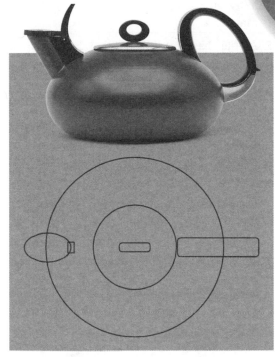

▶▶ *Through Instruction*

Engineers, mechanics, and draftspeople sometimes represent three-dimensional objects in two-dimensional drawings. These drawings are geometric models. It is important that someone looking at a drawing will be able to interpret it correctly. Usually, the relative sizes of objects in the drawings match those in real life.

Technical drawings and plans often show top, side, or front views of an object.

Consider the object shown here.

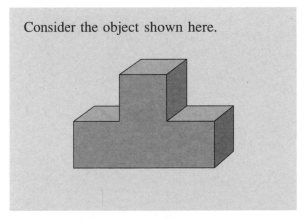

To sketch its top view, look at it directly from above.

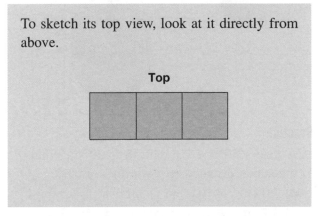

To sketch its side view, look at it directly from the side.

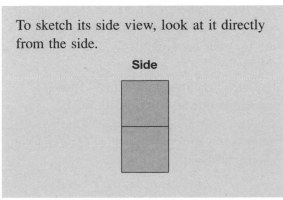

To sketch its front view, look at it directly from the front.

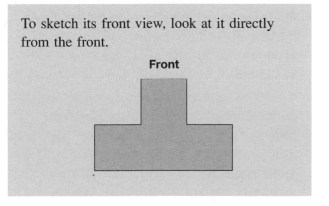

Working with Mathematics

Something to talk about

1. Why do we use scale drawings such as maps?

2. A map has a scale such that 1 cm represents an actual distance of 10 km. What is the actual distance between two towns that are 3 cm apart on the map?

3. An actual distance of 20 m in the school-yard is represented by a distance of 2 cm on a scale drawing. What is the scale?

4. The first diagram below shows a design. The second diagram shows an enlargement of the design.
a) Measure something on the small diagram.
b) Measure the same thing on the large diagram.
c) What is the scale of the enlargement?

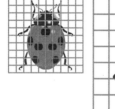 

Practice

5. A map scale is 1 cm represents 20 km. Find the actual distance for each map distance.
a) 2.0 cm   **b)** 10.0 cm   **c)** 3.0 cm   **d)** 5.5 cm
e) 3.7 cm   **f)** 2.4 cm   **g)** 8.9 cm   **h)** 6.3 cm

6. A map scale is 1 cm represents 20 km. Find the map distance for each actual distance.
a) 40 km   **b)** 50 km   **c)** 117 km   **d)** 360 km
e) 154 km   **f)** 33 km   **g)** 79 km   **h)** 441 km

7. A map distance and the corresponding actual distance are given. Find the scale of each map.
a) 1 cm, 50 km   **b)** 2 cm, 60 km
c) 0.5 cm, 50 km   **d)** 1.5 cm, 60 km
e) 3.7 cm, 185 km   **f)** 2.4 cm, 360 km

Work together

8. This square is a model of a baseball diamond.

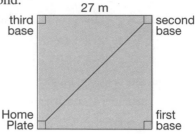

a) Measure the side length of the square.
b) What is the side length of a baseball diamond?
c) What is the scale of this drawing?
d) About how far is it from home plate to second base?

9. In this scale drawing, a person was 60 m from the base of a cliff. A clinometer showed the top of the cliff at an angle of elevation of 56°.
a) What is the scale of the drawing?
b) How high is the cliff?

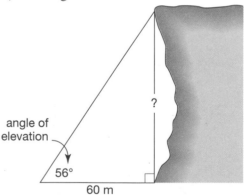

10. Use the clinometer you made. Determine the height of your school. What scale did you use for your drawing? How did you choose this scale?

11. Use the clinometer you made. Determine the height of one other object in your schoolyard or neighbourhood. What scale did you use for your drawing? How did you choose this scale?

12. The three views of an object depend on how it is placed. For example, suppose the object shown on page 41 were placed, as shown below. Sketch the front, top, and side views.

a)

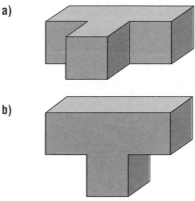

b)

13. The diagrams in parts a to d show top views of different nuts used by mechanics. Match each top view with the corresponding side view in the box. What clues in the drawings helped you to find matching pairs?

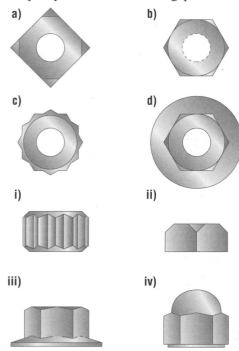

a)

b)

c)

d)

i)

ii)

iii)

iv)

14. Cut a strip of paper 50 cm long and 8 cm wide. Twist the strip once then glue it to form a loop as shown.

Draw a centre line along the strip parallel to its edges. Cut the strip along the line. Into how many pieces have you cut the paper strip?

15. In this scale drawing, a person was 20 m from the base of a tree. A clinometer showed the top of the tree at an angle of elevation of 34°.
  a) What is the scale of the drawing?
  b) How high is the tree?

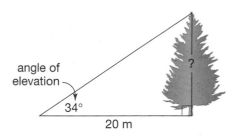

angle of elevation

34°

20 m

16. Six homes in a neighbourhood are connected with information cables. Each house is connected directly to each of the other five houses.
  a) Draw a diagram that shows all the connections.
  b) How many connections are there in all?

17. A student measures the length of a picture of a snowmobile. It is 50 cm. The student uses a tape measure to find the length of the snowmobile, which is 300 cm.
  a) What is the scale of the drawing?
  b) A ski in the drawing is 18 cm long. What is the actual length of the ski?

18. A scale diagram of the fourteenth hole at Whispering Pines Golf Club is shown. The scale in the diagram is 1 cm represents 40 m.
   a) What is the distance over the pond from the men's tee to the hole?
   b) What is the distance over the pond from the women's tee to the hole?

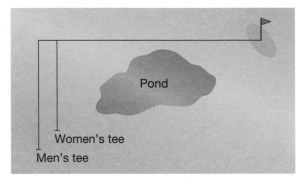

19. The scale drawing shows a balloon floating.

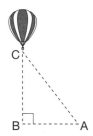

   a) The actual distance BA is 75 m. Measure BA in the drawing. Determine the scale of the drawing.
   b) Measure BC in the drawing. Use your answer to part a to find the balloon's altitude.

20. a) Construct an object using 8 cubes. Draw the front, top, and side views of your object.

   b) Give 8 cubes and the drawings to a classmate. Challenge her or him to construct an object with those front, top, and side views. Check whether the object she or he creates matches your drawings. Is the object the same as yours?
   c) Do you think it is it possible for two different objects created with the cubes to have the same top, front, and side views?

Extend your thinking

21. This enlargement of a 50¢ Canadian stamp has a scale where 1 cm on the stamp is 1.4 cm on the enlargement.

   a) How long is the enlargement?
   b) How long is the stamp?
   c) How wide is the enlargement?
   d) How wide is the stamp?
   e) How many times as great as the area of the stamp is the area of the enlargement?

22. The front, top, and side views of an object are shown below. Sketch the object.

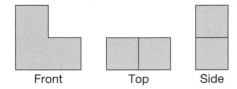

Front   Top   Side

The Ideas

Describe what is meant by a *geometric model*. Give some examples that show how a geometric model can be used to calculate unknown lengths using known or measured lengths.

Can You Visualize the Hidden Faces of a Cube?

Perhaps when you were younger you played the "One of these things is not like the other" game on *Sesame Street*. Or maybe you have a younger sister or brother who plays the game now. This Quest involves a similar, but more challenging, task. Three of the photographs below are of the same cube. The fourth photograph is of a different cube. Can you figure out which photograph it is? Each letter appears on only one face.

Understand the problem

- What are you being asked to do?
- Do all the photos show the cube from the same side?
- What clues does each photo give about the letters on faces with a common edge?
- If the cube is rotated, will the letters on adjacent faces change?

Think of a strategy

- Use a small wooden or plastic cube. Try to place the letters on the cube using one or more of the photos. Check whether you can rotate the cube to match the other photos.

Carry out the strategy

- Place letters on your cube to match one photo.
- Check whether you can rotate your cube to match the other photos.
- Which photo does not belong to the set?

Look back

- How could you have found the photo that didn't match without making a model?
- What are the advantages and disadvantages of constructing a model?

Communicating the Ideas

In your journal, describe how you were able to determine which photograph was of a different cube. Illustrate with diagrams.

Review

1. The credit rating of a country or province is important. A better credit rating means that the country or province can borrow money at better rates of interest.
   a) Find out what kind of scale is used to measure the credit rating of a country or province.
   b) How is the scale like a numerical model? How is it different?

2. Use the data below to make comparisons.

Country	1990 population	1990 population under 15 years of age
Canada	26 521 000	5 543 000
Chile	13 173 000	4 031 000
China	1 139 060 000	301 851 000
Congo	2 271 000	1 000 000

   a) Rank the four countries according to the number of people under 15.
   b) For each country, calculate the fraction of the population under 15. Write each fraction in decimal form, to the nearest hundredth.
   c) Rank the four countries according to the fraction of the population under 15.
   d) Which country would you say has the "youngest" population? Explain.

3. The Consumer Price Index for December 1994 was 131.6. This means items that cost $100 in 1986 cost $131.60 in 1994.
   a) An item cost $200 in 1986. Estimate its cost in December 1994.
   b) An item cost $526 in December 1994. Estimate its cost in 1986.

4. A soft-drink company conducted an opinion poll. It asked participants to sample its new product, and rank it by giving it a number from 1 to 5. A ranking of 1 meant "poor," and 5 meant "excellent." The table below lists the responses from 15 participants.

4	4	1	5	1
1	1	2	2	2
1	2	4	3	2

   a) Did the participants generally like or dislike the product?
   b) Find the mean response and the median response. Give the answer to one decimal place where necessary.
   c) Suppose you wanted to show the soft drink was popular. Which measure of central tendency would you use?
   d) Suppose you wanted to show the soft drink was unpopular. Which measure of central tendency would you use?

5. For the set of numbers, and the stem-and-leaf diagram below, state the:
   i) mean   ii) median
   iii) lower quartile iv) upper quartile
   v) extremes   vi) range
   a) 9, 10, 12, 10, 14, 10, 14, 10, 15, 19, 11, 10
   b)

10	1445
11	0066
12	3356
13	002

6. Display the set of numbers and the stem-and-leaf diagram in exercise 5 on box-and-whisker plots.

7. The owner of a chain of video rental outlets surveyed her stores to determine how busy each was. She telephoned the manager of each outlet to find the number of movies each store had rented out the previous Saturday night. The numbers of movies rented out for the stores are listed below. Display the information on a box-and-whisker plot.

110	190	160	205	207	168	155
195	325	177	164	158	200	185
165	157	160	172	165	179	180

8. Examine the box-and-whisker plots below. Find the statement that best describes each plot.

  i) smallest range

  ii) large range; the median is closer to the lower quartile

  iii) large range; the median is closer to the upper quartile

  iv) largest range

a)

b)

c)

d)

9. On a map, the distance between two towns is 9.25 cm. The actual distance between the towns is 37 km. What is the scale of the map?

10. On a scale drawing of a ship, 1 cm represents an actual distance of 4 m.

  a) The ship is 32 m long. What is the length of the ship on the drawing?

  b) On the drawing, the diameter of one propeller is 0.2 cm. What is the actual diameter of the propeller?

  c) On a cutaway diagram with the same scale, the propeller drive shaft is 1.3 cm. What is the actual length of the shaft?

11. This scale drawing shows a hang-glider flying.

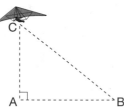

  a) The horizontal distance AB is 80 m. Measure AB on the diagram. Determine the scale of the drawing.

  b) Measure AC. Use your answer to part a to determine the altitude AC.

12. A map has a scale where 1 cm on the map represents a distance of 100 km. What is the distance between two cities that are 4.5 cm apart on the map?

13. Use this drawing of a tower.

  a) What is the scale of the drawing?

  b) How high is the tower?

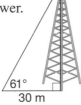

61°

30 m

14. Four objects are shown below.

  a) Which objects have these top views?

  i)   **ii)**

  b) Which objects have these side views?

  i)   **ii)**

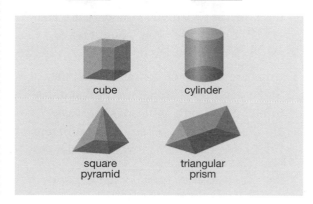

cube   cylinder

square pyramid   triangular prism

Models for Our World

People have been constructing and using maps for many centuries. A map provides an efficient model to communicate information about cities, countries, or regions.

ACTIVITY 1

Use the city map below to explore map scales and grids. To describe a particular square on the map, you state the letter and number that label the square. These are called the *coordinates* of the square.

1. Name one street or point of interest that is located within each square.

   a) C-3   **b)** D-1   **c)** B-2

   d) E-1   **e)** D-2

2. Name the coordinates of the squares containing these items:

   a) each of the four bridges

   b) each of the seven municipal parking lots

3. Use the scale to determine these measurements:

   a) the width of the area shown on the map

   b) the length and width of each small square on the grid

   c) the area of each small square on the grid

4. Obtain a map of the capital city of your province or territory. From the index of points of interest, choose four attractions you would like to visit. Use the map reference to locate each attraction. Plan the order in which you would visit them. Describe the routes you would take to travel from one to the other.

5. Compare the use of coordinates on the Saskatoon map with the use of coordinates to plot points on a grid. In what ways are the coordinates on city maps different from those on grids? In what way are they similar?

Downtown Saskatoon

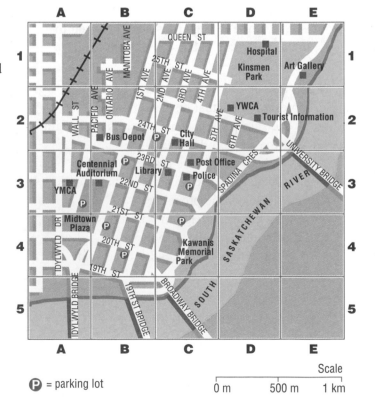

P = parking lot

Scale

0 m   500 m   1 km

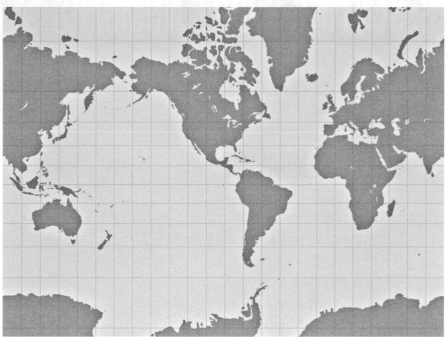

Mercator projection

ACTIVITY 2

This map of the world can be found in many atlases and geography books.

1. Compare the shapes of the continents on the map with their shapes on a globe.
    a) Find a continent that looks much different on the map than it looks on the globe.
    b) Find a continent that looks about the same on the map as it looks on the globe.

2. Why do you think some continents look so different on the map than on the globe? Why do others look about the same?

3. In an almanac or an atlas, find some maps of the world that look different from the one above. Compare each one you find with your globe. What parts of Earth's surface look different? What parts look the same?

4. Do you think it is possible for a flat map to show all parts of Earth's surface without any distortions? Explain your answer.

The Ideas

Write a report describing what you investigated in this project. Include an explanation of how we describe a particular location on a map. Describe some of the similarities and differences between maps and globes.

REPRESENTING WHOLE NUMBERS

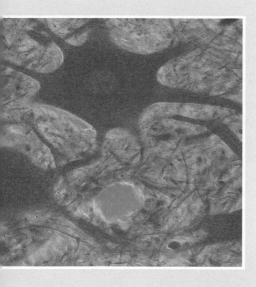

WHAT'S COMING UP?

DEPARTMENTS

Quests

Minds on Math Project

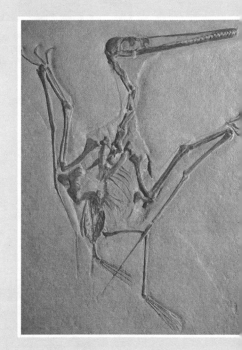

Start With What You Know

A generation ago, populations of countries were expressed in millions. Today, we express the population of China in billions. To write large numbers in a convenient form, we can use powers of 10.

In words	As a numeral	As a power
one thousand	1000	10^3
one million	1 000 000	10^6
one billion	1 000 000 000	10^9
one trillion		
one quadrillion		

1. Write each product or number as a power of 10.
   a) 10×10
   b) $10 \times 10 \times 10 \times 10$
   c) $10 \times 10 \times 10 \times 10 \times 10 \times 10$
   d) 10 000
   e) 100 000
   f) 10 000 000

2. The table on page 52 reviews how we use exponents to express one thousand, one million, and one billion. Look at the patterns in the table. Write the numbers *one trillion* and *one quadrillion* as a numeral and as a power.

3. The table on the right shows the 1990 populations of six countries.

Country	1990 Population
Australia	17 052 000
Brazil	150 360 000
Canada	26 521 000
China	1 139 960 000
Italy	57 620 000
Nigeria	108 542 000

   a) Order the countries from smallest population to largest population.
   b) The power of 10 that is closest to the population of Australia is 10^7, or 10 000 000. Write the power of 10 that is closest to the population of each country in the table.
   c) Which country has a population about 10 times as great as that of Australia?
   d) Which country has a population about 10 times as great as that of Nigeria?
   e) Does the closest power of 10 give a precise description of a population? Explain.

4. By 1979, the population of China was one billion. To reduce the rapid growth in population, the Chinese government passed a law allowing families to have only one child. This slowed the population growth for a while, but by 1992 the population of China had reached 1.2 billion.
   a) The world population in 1992 was 5.6 billion. What percent of the world's population lived in China in 1992?
   b) What power of 10 is closest to 5.6 billion?

5. Multiply.
   a) 4.5×10
   b) 4.5×100
   c) 4.5×1000
   d) $4.5 \times 10\ 000$
   e) $4.5 \times 100\ 000$
   f) $4.5 \times 1\ 000\ 000$
   g) 38.257×10
   h) 38.257×100
   i) 38.257×1000
   j) $38.257 \times 10\ 000$
   k) $38.257 \times 100\ 000$
   l) $38.257 \times 1\ 000\ 000$

6. a) What do you notice about the second number in each product in exercise 5?
   b) Describe the pattern formed by your answers to exercise 5.

7. a) Describe what it means for a number to be *prime*.
   b) Describe what it means for a number to be *composite*.
   c) Identify each number as prime or composite.
      i) 8
      ii) 13
      iii) 19
      iv) 35
      v) 41
      vi) 51

Forming Expressions with 1, 4, 8, and 9

Using the digits 1, 4, 8, and 9, can you write an expression for each whole number from 1 to 100?

Understand the problem

Study the examples on the right.
Discuss these questions with a partner.
- Does each digit have to be used?
- Do the digits have to be in numerical order?
- What mathematical symbols can you use?
- Can you use 2-digit numbers?

$$6 = 4 + 9 - 8 + 1$$

$$35 = 9(4 - 1) + 8$$

$$40 = 4 \times 8 - 1 + 9$$

$$54 = 18 + 4 \times 9$$

Think of a strategy

- Study the patterns formed by the operations in each example above.
- Use these patterns and other patterns like them to help you create your expressions.

Carry out the strategy

- In the first example, $4 + 9 - 8 + 1$ was used. In this expression there are two additions and one subtraction: ■ + ■ − ■ + ■

  Think of the shaded boxes as places to write the digits. Write the digits in this pattern in as many different ways as you can.
- Think of other patterns similar to the one above. For each pattern, write the digits in as many different ways as you can.
- Repeat these steps using the patterns in the other examples.

  ■(■ − ■) + ■   ■ × ■ − ■ + ■

  ■■ + ■ × ■

Look back

- Can you think of any other patterns for the operations? Each pattern you come up with gives you another opportunity to get more numbers.

Communicating the Ideas

Write a description of this problem in your journal. Include a list of the numbers from 1 to 100. As you obtain an expression, write it beside the appropriate number.

Plan to work on this problem for a few minutes each day. In a few days you will probably have expressions for many of the numbers from 1 to 100.

····· 1.1 *EXPRESSING NUMBERS IN EXPANDED FORM*

Developing the Ideas

▶▶ *Using Manipulatives*

You will need a set of place-value blocks to compete these exercises.
Your set should contain these four kinds of blocks.

This is a unit cube.
It represents 1.

This is a rod.
It is made of 10 unit
cubes and represents
$10 \times 1 = 10$.

This is a flat.
It is made of 10 rods
and represents
$10 \times 10 = 100$.

This is a thousand
cube. It is made of
10 flats and represents
$10 \times 10 \times 10 = 1000$.

In 1980, there were 1324 movie theatres in Canada. By 1990, the
number of theatres had decreased to 742. The numbers in these facts
are expressed in standard form. The position of each digit tells its value.
We can use place-value blocks to represent each number and to show the
value of each digit.

We see: 1324
We think:

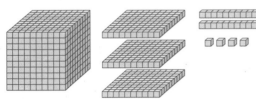

We say: one thousand three hundred
        twenty-four

We write: $(1 \times 1000) + (3 \times 100) + (2 \times 10) + 4$

We see: 742
We think:

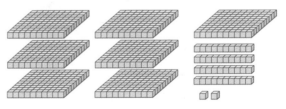

We say: seven hundred forty-two

We write: $(7 \times 100) + (4 \times 10) + 2$

When we write a number in this way, we have used the *expanded form*.

1. On pages 52 and 53, you reviewed powers of 10. You can use powers
   of 10 to develop a shorter way to write a number in expanded form.
   a) Make a list of the powers of 10 from 10 to 1 billion. Write each
   number as a product, as a number, and as a power. Keep your list to
   use in exercises 2 to 5.
   b) Use the list you created in part a. Write 1324 and 742 in expanded
   form using powers of 10.

2. Use place-value blocks to represent each number. Write each number
   in expanded form.
   a) 57   **b)** 362   **c)** 406   **d)** 3542   **e)** 9070

3. Look at this set of place-value blocks.

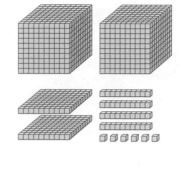

   a) How many thousand cubes are there? What product do they represent?

   b) How many flats are there? What product do they represent?

   c) How many rods are there? What product do they represent?

   d) How many unit cubes are there? What number do they represent?

   e) Use your answers to parts a to d. Write the number represented by the set of blocks in expanded form and in standard form.

4. What number is represented by each set of place-value blocks? Write each number in expanded form and in standard form.

a)

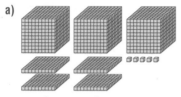

b)

c)

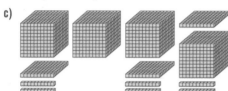

d)

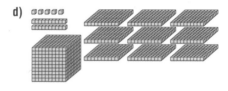

We cannot use place-value blocks to represent very large numbers. We use a place-value chart instead. For example, in 1990, the population of Canada was about 26 521 000.

We see: 26 521 000

We think:

Millions			Thousands					
H	T	O	H	T	O	H	T	O
10^8	10^7	10^6	10^5	10^4	10^3	10^2	10	1
	2	6	5	2	1	0	0	0

We say: twenty-six million five hundred twenty-one thousand

We write:

$(2 \times 10\ 000\ 000) + (6 \times 1\ 000\ 000) + (5 \times 100\ 000) + (2 \times 10\ 000) + (1 \times 1000)$,
or $(2 \times 10^7) + (6 \times 10^6) + (5 \times 10^5) + (2 \times 10^4) + (1 \times 10^3)$

5. Refer to the table in exercise 3 on page 53. Use a place-value chart to write each population in expanded form.

Working with Mathematics

Something to talk about

1. What does *expanded form* mean?

2. Do you think every whole number can be written in expanded form? Explain.

3. Explain what powers of 10 are. How are they useful when writing numbers in expanded form?

4. What is the value of 8 in each number?
   a) 3485   **b)** 5869   **c)** 7 852 079
   d) 8 406 319   **e)** 987 342   **f)** 108 753

Practice

5. What number is represented by each set of place-value blocks? Write your answers in expanded form, in standard form, and in words.

   a)

   b)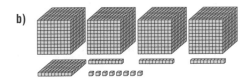

   c)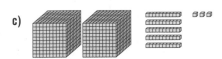

6. Use place-value blocks to represent each number. Write each number in expanded form and in words.
   a) 87   **b)** 360   **c)** 725
   d) 1377   **e)** 5206   **f)** 7438

7. Suppose you use a calculator to add these numbers. Write the number on the calculator's display.
   a) 40 000 + 4000 + 500 + 30 + 3
   b) 90 000 + 7000 + 20 + 9
   c) 500 000 + 6000 + 200 + 80 + 2

   d) 2 000 000 + 300 000 + 50 000 + 6000
   e) 1000 + 40 000 + 8 + 200 + 700 000 + 50
   f) 600 000 + 8 000 000 + 300 + 9000 + 7

8. Which number replaces ■ to make each statement true?
   a) 63 819 = 60 000 + 3000 + ■ + 10 + 9
   b) 4902 = 4000 + 900 + ■
   c) 872 100 = 800 000 + ■ + 2000 + 100
   d) ■ = 90 000 + 1000 + 600
   e) 3898 = 3000 + 800 + ■ + 8
   f) ■ = 4 000 000 + 50 000 + 8000 + 20

Work together

9. What is the common name for each number? Write each number as a product of tens and as a power of 10.
   a) 1000   **b)** 10 000
   c) 10 000 000   **d)** 1 000 000 000
   e) 10 000 000 000   **f)** 100 000 000 000

10. Write each number in expanded form using powers of 10.
    a) 7000   **b)** 80 000
    c) 5 000 000   **d)** 800 000
    e) 90 000   **f)** 500
    g) 3 000 000 000   **h)** 40 000

11. Write each sum in exercises 7 and 8 in expanded form using powers of 10.

12. Use a place-value chart to write each number in expanded form.
    a) 19 604   **b)** 127 300
    c) 5 084 000   **d)** 600 049
    e) 92 738   **f)** 328 923 500
    g) 3 750 000 000   **h)** 21 495 000 000

13. Write each number in standard form.
    a) $(9 \times 10\ 000) + (7 \times 1000) + (6 \times 10)$
    b) $(2 \times 1\ 000\ 000) + (8 \times 1000) + 4$
    c) $(6 \times 100\ 000) + (3 \times 1000) + (9 \times 10)$
    d) $(3 \times 10^3) + (2 \times 10^2) + 1$
    e) $(6 \times 10^5) + (2 \times 10^4) + (6 \times 10^2)$
    f) $(8 \times 10^2) + (5 \times 10^3) + 8$
    g) $(6 \times 10^7) + (2 \times 10^5) + (6 \times 10^3)$
    h) $(5 \times 10^4) + (9 \times 10^6) + (7 \times 10)$

14. Here are some facts about Canada. Write each number in standard form and in expanded form.
   a) Canada is one of the largest countries in the world. Its area is just under 10 million square kilometres.
   b) In 1991, there were almost four hundred twelve thousand births in Canada, and one hundred ninety-six thousand deaths.
   c) In January 1995, the Canadian national debt was almost $600 billion.
   d) In 1990, Canadian department stores sold over $14 billion worth of goods.

15. Rearrange each set of digits to form the greatest number.
   a) 2109   b) 5734   c) 63 275
   d) 400 672   e) 2 611 825   f) 30 194 856

On your own

16. Use place-value blocks to represent each number. Write each number in expanded form and in words.
   a) 45   b) 921   c) 330
   d) 2877   e) 4303   f) 6059

17. Use a place-value chart to write each number in expanded form.
   a) 315 075   b) 91 426
   c) 1 239 000   d) 897 484
   e) 41 690 300   f) 126 452 918

18. Read these facts about space exploration. Write each number in standard form and in expanded form.
   a) The space suits worn by shuttle astronauts cost about three million four hundred thousand dollars each, in U.S. dollars.
   b) The greatest altitude reached by a rocket was five billion nine hundred million kilometres. This was reached by Pioneer 10 in 1972.
   c) The first woman in space was Valentina Tereshkova from the former Soviet Union. In 1963, she orbited Earth forty-eight times and travelled one million nine hundred thousand kilometres.

19. Earth takes one year to orbit the sun. In that time, Earth travels about 938 221 900 km. Write the number that is:
   a) 10 000 greater   b) 1 000 000 less

20. Recall the meanings of the words *trillion* and *quadrillion*. Look up the meaning of *quintillion*. Write these numbers in standard form and in expanded form.
   a) 2 trillion   b) 30 trillion
   c) 5 quadrillion   d) 7 quintillion

Extend your thinking

21. You have been using powers of 10 to write numbers in expanded form. You can also write numbers in expanded form using other powers.
   a) Write each product in standard form and as a power of 2.
      i) 2×2 ii) $2 \times 2 \times 2$
      iii) $2 \times 2 \times 2 \times 2$ iv) $2 \times 2 \times 2 \times 2 \times 2$
   b) Write each number as a sum. In your sum, use only the number 1 and powers of 2. Use each power of 2 only once. For example, you would write
      $28 = 16 + 8 + 4$, or $28 = 2^4 + 2^3 + 2^2$.
      i) 12   ii) 21   iii) 26   iv) 38   v) 54

The Ideas

Explain what it means to write a number in standard form and in expanded form. Give examples of each form. Explain how they are alike and how they are different.

1.2 ESTIMATING WITH LARGE NUMBERS

Developing the Ideas

▶ ▶ *Through an Activity*

Work in a group.

You will need a telephone book, a ruler, a measuring tape, and a calculator.

Estimating the number of telephone numbers

1. How many telephone numbers do you think there are in your telephone book? Don't try to calculate the number—just look through the book and estimate roughly how many telephone numbers you think it contains.

2. Discuss with your partner how you could determine approximately how many telephone numbers there are in your telephone book. Carry out your ideas. What answer do you get? Do you think the actual number is more or less than this?

Estimating the number of telephones

3. **a)** Do you think the number of telephones in the region served by your telephone book would be more than or less than the number of telephone numbers? Give reasons for your answer.

   b) About how many telephones do you think there might be in the region served by your telephone book?

Estimating the number of telephone books

4. About how many telephone books do you think were printed for your community?

5. If all these telephone books were stacked one on top of another, about how high would the pile be?

6. **a)** About how many telephone books would you need to cover the floor of your classroom?

   b) If all the telephone books were to be stored in your empty classroom, how many layers would there be?

   c) How high would the stacks of telephone books be? How does this compare with the height of your classroom?

Estimating the number of trees used to produce the books

7. **a)** Measure or estimate the mass of 1 telephone book.

   b) What is the approximate mass of all the telephone books printed for your community?

   c) It takes about 17 trees to produce 1 t of newsprint. Suppose none of the paper in the telephone books was made from recycled material. About how many trees would have been used to produce the telephone books for your community?

Canada Post Delivers!
Canada Post processes an average of 120 million pieces of mail every month. If all the mail processed in one month were placed in a line, it would reach more than halfway around the world.

We frequently hear or read trivia items like this one. Do you think it is possible that 120 million pieces of mail are processed every month in Canada? Do you think it is possible that this many pieces of mail would reach halfway around the world?

You can't determine exactly how many pieces of mail are processed in Canada in one month. But you can estimate the answer based on some common knowledge and some reasonable assumptions.

1. Check the amount of mail processed.

a) Compare the number of items processed with the population of Canada. On average, about how many pieces of mail would every person in Canada have to send to total 120 million in one month?

b) Do you think this is reasonable?

c) If your answer to part b was no, then how many pieces of mail do you think would be processed in Canada in one month?

Common knowledge:
Population of Canada

Reasonable assumption:
Average number of pieces of mail sent per person in one month

Some populations useful for estimation:

	10 000 000 000	World	5.6 billion
1 billion	1 000 000 000	United States	250 million
	100 000 000	Canada	28.9 million
	10 000 000		
1 million	1 000 000	Vancouver	1.6 million
	100 000	Football stadium	60 000
	10 000		
1 thousand	1 000	High school	1000
	100	Family reunion	100
	10		
	1		

Items of many different sizes are sent in the mail. So, no one knows exactly how far 120 million pieces of mail would reach if they were placed in a line. But you can use some common knowledge and some reasonable assumptions to check the statement that the mail would reach halfway around the world.

2. Check the distance the mail would reach.

a) About how long do you think an average envelope is?

b) If all the envelopes were this long, how far would 120 million pieces of mail reach?

c) How does this compare with the distance around the world shown below?

d) Do you think that the statement about the distance the mail would reach is reasonable?

e) If your answer to part d was no, then how would you describe the distance that 120 million pieces of mail would reach?

Reasonable assumption:
Average size of an envelope

Common knowledge:
Distance around the world at the Equator

Some distances useful for estimation:

1 trillion	1 000 000 000 000		
	100 000 000 000	Distance to sun	150 000 000 000 m
	10 000 000 000		
1 billion	1 000 000 000	Distance to moon	376 000 000 m
	100 000 000	Earth circumference	40 000 000 m
	10 000 000	Distance across Canada	5 500 000 m
1 million	1 000 000		
	100 000		
	10 000		
1 thousand	1 000		
	100	Length of a football field	100 m
	10	Height of a door	2 m
	1		

Working with Mathematics

Something to talk about

1. Use common knowledge and some reasonable assumptions. Can you choose the number that is closest to the answer to each question? Explain your choice. Use the information on pages 60 and 61. How could you determine if your answer is reasonable? Where could you find the information?

   a) What is the population of Halifax?
   32 050
   320 500
   3 205 000

   b) The peregrine falcon is the fastest animal. What is its speed?
   3.5 km/h
   35 km/h
   350 km/h

   c) How many people were granted Canadian citizenship in 1990?
   1040
   104 000
   104 000 000

   d) What is the population of China?
   11 500 000
   115 000 000
   1 150 000 000

   e) How many compact discs were sold in Canada in 1992?
   2 600 000
   26 000 000
   260 000 000

   f) What is the total length of the Canada-U.S. border, including the part between Yukon and Alaska?
   8890 km
   88 900 km
   889 000 km

   g) How high is the world's highest waterfall?
   80.7 m
   807 m
   8070 m

   h) How many households in Canada have at least one telephone?
   99 000
   990 000
   9 900 000

2. On July 20, 1990, a statement about blue boxes appeared in three different editions of The Toronto Star newspaper:

   - 200 million Ontario households have blue boxes for recycling bottles and cans.
   - 200 000 Ontario households have blue boxes for recycling bottles and cans.
   - 2 million Ontario households have blue boxes for recycling bottles and cans.

   Which number do you think is correct? Give a reason for your answer.

Practice

3. **a)** How many days are in a week? In a month? In a year?

   b) Jasmine estimates that she drinks about 300 mL of apple juice every day. About how much apple juice does she drink in a week? In a month? In a year? Express each answer in millilitres and litres.

4. **a)** How many minutes are in an hour? In a day? In a year?

   b) There are about 150 people born in the world every minute. About how many are born every hour? Every day? Every year?

Work together

Make measurements to help you estimate each number. Include calculations as needed.

5. About how many times will your heart beat in your lifetime?

6. About how many hours of television have you watched in your lifetime?

7. About how far do you walk in a day?

8. About how many words do you speak in a day? In a week? In a month? In a year?

On your own

9. In keyboarding, a character refers to a letter, space, or punctuation mark. Look at a page in a novel. Estimate the number of characters in each line and on the page. Estimate the number of characters in the novel. What assumptions are you making?

10. **a)** Refine your estimate in exercise 9 using a word processing program. Input 100 characters. Copy these and paste them 9 times to make 1000 characters. Copy the 1000 characters and paste to make 10 000. How many pages of print does this represent? Refine your original estimate based on this information.

   b) How many characters can you input in 5 min? If you were to keep inputting at this rate, about how long would it take you to input a novel?

Extend your thinking

11. In two different ways, these magazine excerpts express the rate at which the tropical rainforests are disappearing.

> The tropical rainforests are disappearing at 30 ha per minute.
>
> *E Magazine*

> The tropical rainforests are disappearing at 3.7 million ha per year.
>
> *Scientific American*

   a) The symbol 'ha' is the metric symbol for a unit of area called a hectare. Do you need to know what a hectare is to determine if the two rates are the same? If so, find out this information.

   b) Carry out calculations to compare the two rates. Try to think of an explanation for any difference in the rates.

   c) How do you think scientists estimate the rate of disappearance of the tropical rainforests?

COMMUNICATING
The Ideas

About how many hours will you spend eating in your lifetime? Include with your final answer an explanation of the assumptions you made.

How Big Is One Billion?

The exercises below will help you visualize how big a number one billion is. Work with a partner.

Estimating one million seconds

1. How many days, months, or years do you think it would take to equal one million seconds? Don't try to calculate this. Just think about one million seconds and estimate how long you think they are.

2. Use your calculator to calculate how many seconds there are in:
   a) one hour   **b)** one day   **c)** one year

3. Have you reached one million yet? How many days does it take to equal one million seconds?

Estimating one billion seconds

4. How many days, months, or years do you think equal one billion seconds?

5. Calculate approximately how many years equal one billion seconds.

6. Use a ruler to draw a line segment 10 cm long. Make this a number line by marking the left end 0 and the right end 1 000 000 000. Where would you put the number 1 000 000 on this number line?

7. Read the caption describing the photograph below. Is Loring's claim reasonable? Include some calculations to support your answer.

CBC Radio's Barbara Smith wipes away tears as newsreader Rex Loring signs off after 35 years with the network. Loring has delivered "World Report" for more than 20 years, and claims to have spoken 7 billion on-air words.

1.3 POSITIVE EXPONENTS

Developing the Ideas

▶▶ *Through Instruction*

On pages 55 and 56, you learned about place value. The development of place value was important because it provided a way to write large numbers using a few symbols. Another way to write certain large numbers is to use exponents. It was only in the 1600s that people began to use exponents to write large numbers.

You have used exponents to express powers of 10…

We see: 10^3

The base, 10, tells the number that is to be multiplied repeatedly. The exponent, 3, tells the number of 10s that are to be multiplied.

We think: $10 \times 10 \times 10 = 1000$

We say: 10 cubed is one thousand,
or 10 to the power 3 is one thousand.

The base is 10. → 10^3 ← The exponent is 3.

10^3 is called a *power*.

…and you can use exponents to express powers with bases other than 10.

We see: 2^4

We think: $2 \times 2 \times 2 \times 2 = 16$

We say: 2 to the fourth is sixteen,
or 2 to the power 4 is sixteen.

The base is 2. → 2^4 ← The exponent is 4.

2^4 is called a *power*.

▶▶ *Through Activities*

ACTIVITY 1

Use a piece of writing paper.

1. Fold your paper in half. Open it and draw a line along the fold. In a table, record the number of sections into which the paper is divided. Write this as a power of 2.

2. Fold your paper into quarters. Open it and draw a line along the new fold. Record the number of sections into which the paper is divided.

Number of folds	Number of sections	Sections as power of 2
1	2	2^1
2	$4 = 2 \times 2$	2^2
3		
4		
5		
6		

3. Fold your paper into eighths. Open it and draw a line along the new fold. Record the number of sections into which the paper is divided.

4. Continue to fold and draw lines until you have made as many folds as possible.

5. Each time you folded the paper, what happened to the number of sections?

6. Suppose you could fold a piece of paper 10 times. How many sections would you create? Write your answer as a power and as a numeral.

Work with a partner to construct models of powers of 2 and powers of 3. You will need about 60 centimetre cubes.

1. Use the cubes to model 2. Sketch your model.

2. a) Use the cubes to model 2×2. To do this, make two copies of your model from exercise 1. Place them side by side to form a square. Sketch your model.

   b) How many centimetre cubes did you use in part a? Write 2×2 as a numeral and as a power.

3. a) Use the cubes to model $2 \times 2 \times 2$. To do this, make two copies of your model from exercise 2. Place one on top of the other to form a cube. Sketch your model.

   b) How many centimetre cubes did you use in part a? Write $2 \times 2 \times 2$ as a numeral and as a power.

4. a) Use the cubes to model 3. Sketch your model.

   b) Use the cubes to model 3×3. How many rows do you need? How many cubes are in each row? Sketch your model. Write 3×3 as a numeral and as a power.

   c) Use the cubes to model $3 \times 3 \times 3$. How many layers do you need? How many cubes are in each layer? Sketch your model. Write $3 \times 3 \times 3$ as a numeral and as a power.

5. Suppose you used cubes to model 4, 4×4, and $4 \times 4 \times 4$. How would the models be similar to those you made for powers of 2 and powers of 3? How would they be different?

6. a) Why do you think a power with an exponent of 2 is called a square?

   b) Why do you think a power with an exponent of 3 is called a cube?

7. Look at the models you made for 2^2 and 2^3. Describe models you could make for 2^4, 2^5, and 2^6. Make each model if you have enough cubes. Sketch each model if you do not have enough cubes. Compare your models with those of other students. Did all of you make the same models?

Eight million bolts of lightning strike Earth daily. How many strike Earth each second? How many would strike Earth each year?

Working with Mathematics

Something to talk about

1. Explain the meaning of each power.

    a) 10^4 **b)** 4^2 **c)** 6^3 **d)** 13^2

2. a) Name the exponent and the base for each power in exercise 1.

    b) What does the exponent tell you?

    c) Explain how to use the exponent to evaluate a power.

Practice

3. Express each power in exercise 1 as a numeral.

4. Express the number of small squares in each large square as a power.

a)

b)
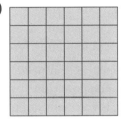

c)
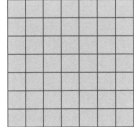

5. Write each product as a power.

    a) $5 \times 5 \times 5 \times 5 \times 5 \times 5 \times 5$

    b) $100 \times 100 \times 100 \times 100 \times 100$

    c) $116 \times 116 \times 116 \times 116$

    d) $67 \times 67 \times 67 \times 67 \times 67$

    e) $825 \times 825 \times 825$

    f) $1 \times 1 \times 1 \times 1 \times 1 \times 1 \times 1 \times 1$

6. Write each power as a product, then write each product as a numeral.

    a) 10^7 **b)** 11^3 **c)** 2^6

    d) 1^9 **e)** 5^4 **f)** 25^2

Work together

7. a) Write a product to show how many centimetre cubes are in each layer.

    b) How many layers are in each cube?

    c) Write a product to show how many centimetre cubes are in each large cube. Write each product as a power.

    i)

    ii)

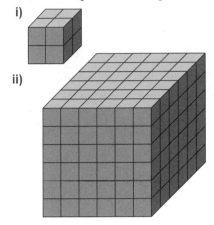

8. Use a calculator to evaluate each power.

    a) 7^3 **b)** 13^2 **c)** 5^4 **d)** 12^3

9. What is the area of a square tile with sides 18 cm long? Write your answer as a power and as a numeral.

10. The semi-finals of the 1994 World Cup Soccer tournament were played at Giants Stadium in New Jersey. After the game, the stadium owners sold fans squares of turf from the field. A square with an area of 10 cm^2 sold for $1 U.S. How much would the stadium owners receive if they sold all the turf from the field measuring about 110 m by 75 m?

11. Refer to the Quest on page 54. Use powers in your expressions for the numbers from 1 to 100. For example, if you need an expression for 88, you can write $89 - 1^4$. In this expression, the pattern is: ■■ − ■■.

    a) Use this pattern. Write the digits 1, 4, 8, and 9 in as many ways as you can.

    b) Think of other patterns using powers. For each pattern, write the digits in different ways. Can you get all the numbers from 1 to 100 now?

On your own

12. Write each power as a numeral.

    a) 10^5 **b)** 3^3 **c)** 4^3 **d)** 13^4 **e)** 8^3

TEMPLATE DISK

13. Start a new spreadsheet file. Type the numbers 2, 3, and 5 in cells A1, B1, and C1. You can use formulas to make a table of powers like the one below.

	A	B	C
1	2	3	5
2	4	9	25
3	8	27	125

    a) Enter the formula =A1*2 in cell A2. What does the formula do?

    b) Copy the formula down to cell A15. What does the computer display?

    c) Enter a formula in cell B2 to display the square of 3. Copy your formula down to cell B15. Does the computer display powers of 3? If not, modify your formula and copy it down again.

    d) Use a formula to display powers of 5 in column C.

    e) Look at the completed table. How is the row number related to the exponent of the powers in that row?

14. Which is the greater number in each pair? Explain your answers.

    a) $2^6, 6^2$ **b)** $3^4, 4^3$ **c)** $5^4, 4^5$

    d) $6^8, 8^6$ **e)** $7^3, 3^7$ **f)** $9^{10}, 10^9$

15. A baseball diamond is a square with sides approximately 27 m long. Is the area of a baseball diamond greater or less than 1000 m²?

16. **a)** What is the value of a 3 by 3 block of Canadian 50¢ postage stamps?

    b) What is the value of a 6 by 6 block of these stamps?

17. **a)** What is the volume of a cube with edge length 3.5 cm?

    b) What is the volume of a cube with edge length 7 cm?

    c) The cube in part b has edges twice as long as the cube in part a. How many times as great is its volume?

    d) Based on your answers to parts b and c, estimate the volume of a cube with edge length 14 cm. Calculate to check.

    e) What happens to the volume of a cube when its edge length is doubled?

18. Write a product to show how many centimetre cubes are needed to make one cubic metre. Write the product as a power and a numeral.

19. Suppose you invested $1 today and your investment doubled in value every year.

    a) Express as a power the value of your investment after each time.

        i) 1 year   **ii)** 5 years   **iii)** 10 years

    b) Write each power in part a as a numeral.

    c) Approximately how many years does it take for the investment to become 1000 times as large?

    d) Use your answer to part c. Estimate how many years it would take your investment be worth one million dollars.

Extend your thinking

20. Areas of land are measured in hectares. One hectare is the area of a square with side length 10^2 m. Express the number of square metres in a hectare as a power.

COMMUNICATING
The Ideas

Write a paragraph to explain how exponents are useful in expressing the areas of squares and volumes of cubes.

Can You Out-Think Your Calculator?

When the answers to mathematical calculations become too large, calculators show an error message — they just can't cope! However, the human mind has problem-solving abilities that provide solutions to problems that elude calculators. Try this one!

What is the last digit of 7^{22}?

Understand the problem

- Explain what 7^{22} means.
- What are you asked to find?
- Do you need to know all the digits in 7^{22}?
- If you have a calculator with a y^x key, enter
  7 y^x 22 = . What shows on the display?
- If you have a calculator without a y^x key, what happens when you attempt to multiply 22 sevens together?

Think of a strategy

- Calculate the first 8 powers of 7. Look for a pattern in the last digits.

Carry out the strategy

- Copy and complete this table.

Power of 7	Last digit
7^1	7
7^2	
7^3	
7^4	
7^5	
7^6	
7^7	
7^8	

- What is the pattern in the sequence of the last digits?
- Use this pattern to predict the last digit of 7^{12}, 7^{16}, and 7^{20}.
- Look at the last digit of 7^{20} and determine the last digit of 7^{22}.

Look back

- Investigate similar patterns in the last digits of other powers.

Communicating the Ideas

In your journal, state what the last digit of the number 7^{22} is. Describe how you were able to use patterns to determine this digit.

1.4 *SCIENTIFIC NOTATION*

Developing the Ideas

▶ ▶ *Through Discussion*

Scientific notation is used to express a large number as a product of a number between 1 and 10 and a power of 10. Some examples are shown below.

The human brain is composed of more than 5×10^{10} active brain cells called *neurons*.

Mercury is the planet nearest the sun. The mean distance from Mercury to the sun is 5.8×10^7 km.

1. Write the number of neurons in the brain as a numeral.

2. How many billions of neurons are there in the human brain?

3. Multiply 5.8 by 10^7 on your calculator. Record what you see on the calculator display.

4. Write as a numeral the mean distance from Mercury to the sun.

The earliest dinosaurs first appeared on Earth about 2.6×10^6 years ago.

5. Write as a numeral how long ago the dinosaurs first appeared on Earth.

6. Were the dinosaurs on Earth 2.5×10^7 years ago? Give a reason for your answer.

▶ ▶ *Through Instruction*

• • • • • • • • • •

To express a number in scientific notation, follow these steps:
- Place a decimal point after the first non-zero digit. This gives a number between 1 and 10.
- Starting where you placed the decimal point, count the number of places to the original position of the decimal point. Use this number as the exponent of 10.

For example, to express 28 000 000 in scientific notation:

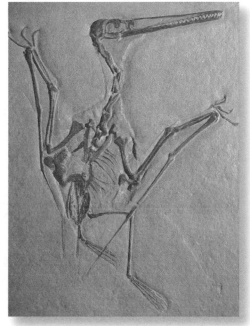

$$28\ 000\ 000$$

Place the decimal point after the 2.

The original position was 7 places to the right.

Think: 2.8×10^7

Large numbers in newspapers or magazines have usually been rounded to the nearest thousand, million, billion, or trillion. This is because we do not need to know the actual numbers for most purposes. Suppose we know there are exactly 557 246 words in a particular dictionary. We might round this number to the nearest thousand and say there are about 557 000, or 5.57×10^5 words.

If we round to the nearest hundred thousand, we say there are about 600 000 or 6×10^5 words. The number 5.57×10^5 gives more precise information than 6×10^5.

▶ ▶ **Through Guided Examples**

Example 1 ···

Write 67 500 000 000 in scientific notation.

Solution

Place the decimal point after the 6 in 67 500 000 000 to get 6.750 000 000 0.

The original position of the decimal point was 10 places to the right.
So, multiply by 10^{10}.

67 500 000 000 = 6.750 000 000 0 $\times 10^{10}$, or 6.75×10^{10}

Example 2 ···

Express each product as a numeral.

a) 6×10^5 **b)** 3.7×10^6

Solution

a) $6 \times 10^5 = 6 \times 100\ 000$
$= 600\ 000$ ◀ The decimal point moves 5 places.

b) $3.7 \times 10^6 = 3.7 \times 1\ 000\ 000$
$= 3\ 700\ 000$ ◀ The decimal point moves 6 places.

If your calculator has a $\boxed{y^x}$ key, use it to check the answers to *Example 2*.

To check part a, enter:
6 $\boxed{\times}$ **10** $\boxed{y^x}$ **5** $\boxed{=}$ to obtain 600 000

To check part b, enter:
3.7 $\boxed{\times}$ **10** $\boxed{y^x}$ **6** $\boxed{=}$ to obtain 3 700 000

Working with Mathematics

Something to talk about

1. We express a number in scientific notation as a product of two numbers. Describe these two numbers.

2. Write each number in scientific notation.
   a) one thousand   b) one million
   c) one billion   d) ten thousand
   e) ten million   f) ten billion

3. Is each number written in scientific notation? Explain.
   a) 4.3×10^7 b) 2.5×5^4 c) 1×10^6
   d) 1.284×10^9 e) 0.8×10^5 f) 24.1×10^9

Practice

4. To make each equation true, what number replaces $\blacksquare$?
   a) $9000 = 9 \times 10^{\blacksquare}$
   b) $420\ 000 = 4.2 \times 10^{\blacksquare}$
   c) $7\ 000\ 000 = 7 \times 10^{\blacksquare}$
   d) $6\ 400\ 000 = 6.4 \times 10^{\blacksquare}$
   e) $81\ 000\ 000 = 8.1 \times 10^{\blacksquare}$
   f) $3\ 570\ 000\ 000 = 3.57 \times 10^{\blacksquare}$

5. To make each equation true, which number replaces $\blacksquare$?
   a) $9400 = \blacksquare \times 10^3$ b) $40\ 000 = \blacksquare \times 10^4$
   c) $70\ 200 = \blacksquare \times 10^4$ d) $\blacksquare = 5.49 \times 10^5$
   e) $670 = \blacksquare \times 10^2$ f) $\blacksquare = 1.311 \times 10^8$

6. To express each product as a numeral, how many places to the right must you move the decimal point? Express each product as a numeral.
   a) 5.9×10^8 b) 6.35×10^4
   c) 9.01×10^6 d) 1.12×10^3
   e) 8.3×10^5 f) 4.592×10^{11}

7. Write in scientific notation.
   a) $1\ 470\ 000$ b) $680\ 000$
   c) $31\ 750\ 000$ d) $11\ 800$
   e) $95\ 870\ 200$ f) $4\ 698\ 500\ 000$

8. Write as a numeral.
   a) 1.3×10^5 b) 3.97×10^4 c) 2.175×10^9
   d) 3.0×10^6 e) 7.94×10^7 f) 9.3×10^8

Work together

9. Here are some data about four planets.

Planets	Distance from sun (km)	Mass (t)
Earth	1.5×10^8	5.976×10^{21}
Mercury	5.8×10^7	3.3×10^{23}
Neptune	4.5×10^9	1.02×10^{23}
Saturn	1.43×10^9	5.69×10^{23}

   a) Express each planet's mass and distance from the sun as numerals, and in expanded form using powers of 10.
   b) Order these planets by distance from the sun, from closest to farthest.
   c) Order these planets by mass, from least to greatest.
   d) Do you think it is appropriate to express the data in the table in scientific notation? Explain.

10. Pluto is the smallest planet. It has a mass of about 12 000 000 000 000 000 000 000 kg. Pluto is about 5 900 000 000 km from the sun.
    a) Express Pluto's mass and distance from the sun in expanded form using powers of 10, and in scientific notation.
    b) Convert Pluto's mass to grams. Express your answer in standard form and in scientific notation.
    c) Convert Pluto's distance from the sun to metres. Express your answer in standard form and in scientific notation.

11. The human body has some remarkable measurements. For example, the inside surface of your blood vessels covers an area of about 8 000 000 cm^2. The total length of your blood vessels is about 100 000 km.
    a) Express the area and length of blood vessels in scientific notation.
    b) Convert the total length of blood vessels from kilometres to metres. Express your answer in standard form and in scientific notation.

12. The table lists some amazing facts from the world of science. What numbers complete the table?

	Numeral	Scientific notation
a) Number of known insect species		7.51×10^5
b) Number of known species of all other animals, including mammals	281 000	
c) Estimated age of Earth		4.6×10^9 years
d) Area of Earth's largest ocean, the Pacific		1.65×10^6 km²
e) Distance from Earth to the moon	384 700 km	
f) Mass of Earth		5.976×10^{21} t

13. The painting *Mona Lisa* has an estimated value of $\$10^8$. In 1990 a painting, *Portrait of Dr. Gachet*, sold for $\$8.25 \times 10^7$. Which painting has the higher value? Explain.

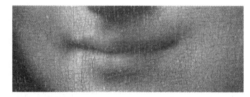

14. Arrange each set of numbers in order from smallest to largest. Explain your reasoning.
   a) $5.2 \times 10^4, 5.5 \times 10^4, 5.4 \times 10^4$
   b) $2.9 \times 10^7, 2.79 \times 10^7, 2.7 \times 10^7$
   c) $3.68 \times 10^5, 3.62 \times 10^5, 3.6 \times 10^5$
   d) $7.215 \times 10^9, 7.21 \times 10^9, 7.211 \times 10^9$
   e) $6.9 \times 10^4, 6.9 \times 10^5, 6.7 \times 10^4$
   f) $4.25 \times 10^8, 5.24 \times 10^7, 5.42 \times 10^7$

15. You can use a spreadsheet to make a chart of powers of 10.
   a) Start a new spreadsheet file. Make sure column A is wide enough to display at least 20 digits. Type the number 1 in cell A1. In cell A2, type =A1*10.

	A	B	C
1	1		
2	=A1*10		

Copy this formula down to row 16. What does the formula do? What does the computer display?
   b) Copy the text and formulas in cells A1 to A16 to column B. Format column B to show numbers in scientific notation. You now have a chart of powers of 10 expressed as numerals and in scientific notation.
   c) In column C, type the words thousand, million, billion, trillion, and quadrillion in the cells where they belong.
   d) Print your spreadsheet. Glue it in your journal. Use it as a reference when completing other exercises.

On your own

16. Write in scientific notation.
   a) 750 000   b) 8 500 000
   c) 27 600 000   d) 781 000 000

17. Express each large number in scientific notation.
   a) France was the most popular tourist destination in 1992. That year, about 59 million tourists visited France.
   b) The population of the world is estimated to reach 6228 million by the year 2000.
   c) In 1993, the government of the United States had a budget of $1.4 trillion.
   d) By the end of 1993, the U.S. national debt had reached $4351 billion.
   e) Some scientists estimate the age of the universe to be about 14 billion years.
   f) Except for the sun, the nearest star to Earth is Proxima Centauri. This faint star is about 40 trillion kilometres away.
   g) The greatest speed travelled by a human is just under forty thousand kilometres per hour. This speed was reached by the Apollo 10 crew in 1969.
   h) The greatest altitude reached by humans was four hundred thousand kilometres. This was reached by the Apollo 13 crew in 1970.

18. The table lists some amazing facts from the world of entertainment, as recorded in *The Guinness Book of Records*. What numbers complete the table?

	Numeral	Scientific notation
a) Number of copies sold of the single *White Christmas* by Bing Crosby		1.71×10^8
b) Number of copies sold of the album *Thriller* by Michael Jackson	47 000 000	
c) Attendance at the 1983 US Rock Festival in California		7.25×10^5
d) Box office gross of *E.T. The Extra Terrestrial* (including videos)	700 000 000	
e) Audience for the television broadcast of 1990 World Cup soccer finals		2.65×10^{10}

19. The table lists the amount of money made by movies the year they were released. Write each amount as a numeral. Order the movies from the least money made to the most.

Movie	Money earned in $U.S.
Dick Tracy	6.061×10^7
Jurassic Park	2.08×10^8
The Fugitive	9.26×10^7
Mrs. Doubtfire	1.098×10^8
Sister Act	6.242×10^7

20. Use a reference such as an encyclopedia or *The Guinness Book of Records*. Find an interesting fact that involves a large number. Use this fact and the large number it involves as a basis for a poster. Your poster should help the viewer understand the significance of the large number.

21. Use the *Canadian Agriculture* database on the data disk. Select the records for 1991. For each province, record the population, area, and total provincial farm income. Round each population to the nearest hundred thousand. Round each area to the nearest hundred thousand hectares. Round each income to the nearest million dollars. Express each rounded amount in scientific notation.

DATA DISK

Extend your thinking

22. The Sahara Desert in North Africa is the world's largest desert. It is roughly rectangular and measures about 5×10^3 km across from east to west and 1.8×10^3 km from north to south.

  a) Write the approximate area of the Sahara Desert in square kilometres using scientific notation.

  b) Recall that one hectare is the area of a square with side length 10^2 m.

   i) How many hectares are in one square kilometre?

   ii) Express your answer from part a in hectares using scientific notation.

23. Write in scientific notation,

   a) 452×10^3 **b)** 76.5×10^3

   c) 824×10^4 **d)** 93.1×10^4

The Ideas

In your journal, explain how you can tell whether a number is expressed in scientific notation. Write two numbers in scientific notation. Write one number that includes a power of 10, but is not in scientific notation. Ask a friend to identify the number that is not in scientific notation.

In July 1994, Did We See What Destroyed the Dinosaurs?

WHY DID THE DINOSAURS SUDDENLY VANISH FROM Earth 65 million years ago after ruling Earth for 175 million years?

One theory is that a large meteor or comet smashed into the Yucatan Peninsula in Mexico 65 million years ago. The impact was so powerful that huge clouds of dust and debris were sent into Earth's atmosphere, blocking the sun's rays. The reduced heat and light from the sun chilled the climate and destroyed the plants that fed the plant-eating dinosaurs. As their numbers were reduced, the food supply of the meat-eating dinosaurs also disappeared.

Until recently, there was no way to check this theory or to assess what kind of damage such a collision might create. However, in July 1994, something occurred never before seen by humans — a comet collided with the planet Jupiter.

Jupiter is the largest planet in our solar system, with a diameter of approximately 143 000 km compared to Earth's diameter of 12 756 km. The comet, called Shoemaker-Levy 9, was discovered by Canadian scientist David Levy and American scientists Carolyn and Eugene Shoemaker. In 1992, it was pulled into Jupiter's gravitational field. The comet entered the atmosphere of Jupiter and, on July 16, 1994, the first fragment of the comet smashed into the planet at a speed of 216 000 km/h.

The collision, viewed by the Hubble telescope, revealed an explosion that soared 965 km into the atmosphere. As one scientist exclaimed,

It produced a fireball like that which was predicted. That means that the energy created was equivalent to 200 000 megatonnes of TNT or more!

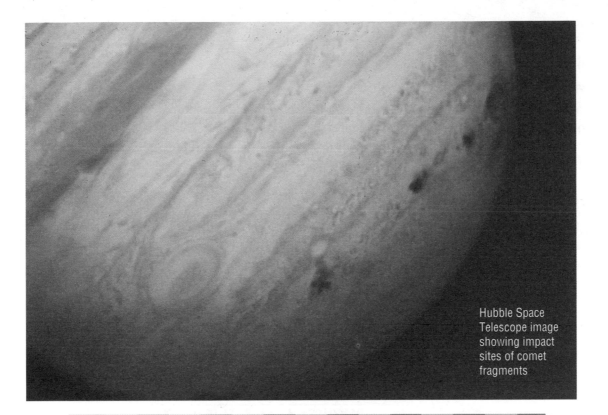

Hubble Space Telescope image showing impact sites of comet fragments

1. Write each number on page 76 in scientific notation.

2. *Weight* is a measure of the force of gravity on an object. To determine your weight on Earth, multiply your mass by 9.8. The gravitational pull on Jupiter is 2.65 times Earth's gravitational pull. This means that you would weigh about 2.65 times as much on Jupiter as you do on Earth. How much would you weigh if you could stand on Jupiter?

3. a) How many times as great as the diameter of Earth is the diameter of Jupiter?
   b) The mean distance from the sun to Jupiter is 7.50×10^8 km. The mean distance from the sun to Earth is 1.50×10^8 km. How many times as great as the distance to Earth is the distance to Jupiter?

4. The mass of Jupiter is 1.899×10^{27} kg. The mass of Earth is 5.976×10^{24} kg. Explain how you know Jupiter has a greater mass even though 1.899 is less than 5.976.

5. a) How fast was the comet travelling when it collided with Jupiter?
   b) A typical speed limit for cars driving on city streets is 50 km/h. How many times as great as this was the speed of the comet?
   c) Express the speed of the comet in kilometres per second.

6. One megatonne is 1 000 000 t. Write, in scientific notation, the energy in tonnes of TNT that was generated by the collision.

Mathematics & Science

Linking Ideas

1.5 DIVISIBILITY RULES

Developing the Ideas

▶ ▶ *Through Activities*

Ms. Farley, the physical education teacher, often divides her students into two equal teams. When she counts the students, she knows immediately whether this is possible. In *Activity 1*, you will discover Ms. Farley's rule for determining whether a number is divisible by 2.

ACTIVITY 1

Finding a Rule for Divisibility by 2

Look at the 100-square on the right. All the numbers that are multiples of 2 are shown in colour.

1	2	3	4	5	6	7	8	9	10
11	12	13	14	15	16	17	18	19	20
21	22	23	24	25	26	27	28	29	30
31	32	33	34	35	36	37	38	39	40
41	42	43	44	45	46	47	48	49	50
51	52	53	54	55	56	57	58	59	60
61	62	63	64	65	66	67	68	69	70
71	72	73	74	75	76	77	78	79	80
81	82	83	84	85	86	87	88	89	90
91	92	93	94	95	96	97	98	99	100

1. Explain how you know that all the numbers in the 100-square that are divisible by 2 are coloured.

2. Describe any patterns you see in the 100-square.

3. Make a list of the last digits of the first 15 numbers that are divisible by 2. What do you notice?

4. Do you think the pattern in exercise 3 is true for numbers greater than 100? Check a few numbers.

5. Numbers that are divisible by 2 are called *even numbers*. Write a rule to explain how to determine whether a number is even.

ACTIVITY 2

Finding a Rule for Divisibility by 9

1. Obtain a 100-square.
   a) Colour all the multiples of 9.
   b) Explain how you know that you have coloured all the numbers in the 100-square that are divisible by 9.

2. Describe any patterns you see in the 100-square.

3. a) What is the sum of the digits of each number you have coloured?
   b) Write a rule to explain how to determine whether a number less than 100 is divisible by 9.

4. a) Does your rule work for numbers greater than 100? To check, use your calculator to multiply a large whole number by 9. Add the digits of the product.

b) Repeat part a for a few different large numbers. What do you notice about the sum of the digits for each product?

c) Write a rule to explain how to determine whether a number is divisible by 9.

Finding a Rule for Divisibility by 3

Look at the 100-square on the right. All the numbers that are multiples of 3 are shown in colour.

1	2	3	4	5	6	7	8	9	10
11	12	13	14	15	16	17	18	19	20
21	22	23	24	25	26	27	28	29	30
31	32	33	34	35	36	37	38	39	40
41	42	43	44	45	46	47	48	49	50
51	52	53	54	55	56	57	58	59	60
61	62	63	64	65	66	67	68	69	70
71	72	73	74	75	76	77	78	79	80
81	82	83	84	85	86	87	88	89	90
91	92	93	94	95	96	97	98	99	100

1. Explain how you know that all the numbers in the 100-square that are divisible by 3 are coloured.

2. Describe any patterns you see in the 100-square.

3. a) Make a list of the sum of the digits of the first 15 numbers that are divisible by 3. What do you notice?

b) Write a rule to explain how to determine whether a number is divisible by 3.

4. Does your rule work for numbers greater than 100? Use your calculator to check for a few different numbers.

▶ ▶ *Through Instruction*

In *Activities 1* to *3*, you should have discovered these divisibility rules.

• • • • • • • • •

A number is divisible by 2 if its last digit is 0 or is divisible by 2.

A number is divisible by 9 if the sum of its digits is divisible by 9.

A number is divisible by 3 if the sum of its digits is divisible by 3.

In the following exercises, you will discover rules for divisibility by 4, by 5, by 6, and by 10.

Working with Mathematics

Something to talk about

1. Explain the meaning of each statement. Is each statement true?
   a) 1638 is divisible by 9.
   b) 1638 is a multiple of 9.

2. Is there a number that is a multiple of 9 but is not divisible by 9? Explain.

3. Explain how to determine whether a number is:
   a) even   b) odd

4. You are asked to determine whether 1 234 567 is divisible by 9, without using a calculator.
   a) What is the sum of the digits in this number?
   b) Suppose you do not know whether your answer to part a is divisible by 9. How could you check?

5. Is there a number that is divisible by 9 but not divisible by 3? Explain.

6. What is the remainder when an odd number is divided by 2?

Practice

7. State whether each number is divisible by 2. Do not use a calculator.
   a) 29   b) 68   c) 399
   d) 232   e) 513   f) 875
   g) 9750   h) 80 532   i) 1 000 003

8. List the numbers in exercise 7 that are not divisible by 2. Change these numbers to make them divisible by 2.

9. a) Write 3 even numbers between 545 and 567.
   b) Write 3 odd numbers between 18 748 and 18 756.

10. State whether each number in exercise 7 is divisible by 3. Do not use a calculator.

11. State whether each number in exercise 7 is divisible by 9. Do not use a calculator.

Work together

12. There are 9 players on a baseball team. Can 426 players who joined the league be exactly divided into teams of 9?
    a) Use a divisibility rule to decide without dividing.
    b) Represent the 426 people with place-value blocks. Think about the remainder when you divide a flat or a rod by 9. Explain why the rule for divisibility by 9 works.

13. Replace each ■ with a digit so that each number is divisible by 9.
    a) 5■38   b) 2■634   c) ■9 067
    d) 7■65   e) 90 48■   f) 875 4■6

14. a) Colour all the multiples of 10 in a 100-square.
    b) Describe any patterns you see on the 100-square.
    c) Write a rule to explain how to determine whether a number is divisible by 10.
    d) Colour all the multiples of 5 in a different colour. Write a rule to explain how to determine whether a number is divisible by 5.

15. a) State whether each number in exercise 7 is divisible by 10.
    b) State whether each number in exercise 7 is divisible by 5.

16. a) Colour all the multiples of 6 in a 100-square.
    b) Compare your 100-square to the one in *Activity 1* on page 78. Are there any multiples of 6 that are not multiples of 2?
    c) Compare your 100-square to the one in *Activity 3* on page 79. Are there any multiples of 6 that are not multiples of 3?
    d) State a rule that explains how to determine whether a number is divisible by 6.

17. State whether each number in exercise 7 is divisible by 6. Do not use a calculator.

18. **a)** On a 100-square, colour all the multiples of 4.
   b) Copy this table. Use a calculator and your 100-square to help you complete the table. The first row is completed for you.

Number	Divisible by 4?	Last two digits	Divisible by 4?
2 367	no	67	no
4 982		82	
34 592		92	
15 674		74	
34 690		90	
236 876		76	
54 864		64	

   c) Compare your answers in the second column with your answers in the last column. What do you notice?
   d) State a rule that explains how to determine whether a number is divisible by 4.

19. State whether each number in exercise 7 is divisible by 4. Do not use a calculator.

20. What is the smallest number that is divisible by 4, 5, and 6?

21. **a)** A box of chocolates can be divided equally among 3, 5, or 6 friends with none left over. What is the smallest number of chocolates the box can contain?
   b) Suppose the box in part a could also be divided equally between 2 friends. Does this change your answer to part a? Explain.

On your own

22. Only one number in this list is divisible by 2. Which number is it?
   111, 18, 27, 49, 1175, 99, 10 563, 89, 373

23. Only five numbers in exercise 22 are divisible by 3. Which numbers are they?

24. Only one number in this list is divisible by 9. Which number is it?
   1241, 1502, 5632, 20 175, 24 714, 33 499

25. Which of the numbers in exercise 24 are divisible by 3?

26. Write a number that is divisible by both 5 and 9.

27. **a)** Mayumi has a bag of 48 cookies to share with her brother and sister. Can the bag be divided equally among the three children? Explain.
   b) When Mayumi opens the bag, she discovers that her father has eaten two cookies. Show that the remaining cookies cannot be divided equally among the 3 children. How could the children resolve this problem?

28. **a)** Determine how many ways your class could be divided into equal groups.
   b) Suppose 2 students are absent. In how many ways could the remaining students be divided into equal groups?

Extend your thinking

29. Without using your calculator, replace each ■ with a digit so that each number is divisible by 3.
   a) $3^4 + 3^2 +$ ■ $+ 1$
   b) $9^4 + 6^2 +$ ■
   c) $666\ 666 + 7 +$ ■

The Ideas

In your notebook, record the rules for divisibility by 2, 3, 4, 5, 6, 9, and 10. Include examples. Describe a situation in everyday life when a divisibility test can be helpful.

1.6 EXPRESSING NUMBERS AS PRODUCTS OF POWERS OF PRIMES

Developing the Ideas

▶ ▶ *Through Activities*

ACTIVITY 1

Finding the Primes between 1 and 100

Recall that a prime number has exactly two factors; itself and 1.

Around 250 B.C., the Greek mathematician Eratosthenes made a list of prime numbers by following these steps. Follow these steps to create your own list of prime numbers up to 100.

1. Make a 100-square containing the numbers 1 to 100. Cross out 1 because it is not a prime number.

1	2	3	4	5	6	7	8	9	10
11	12	13	14	15	16	17	18	19	20
21	22	23	24	25	26	27	28	29	30
31	32	33	34	35	36	37	38	39	40
41	42	43	44	45	46	47	48	49	50
51	52	53	54	55	56	57	58	59	60
61	62	63	64	65	66	67	68	69	70
71	72	73	74	75	76	77	78	79	80
81	82	83	84	85	86	87	88	89	90
91	92	93	94	95	96	97	98	99	100

2. Circle 2; it is a prime number. Cross out all the multiples of 2.

3. Circle 3; it is a prime number. Cross out all the multiples of 3.

4. Explain why the multiples of 4 are already crossed out.

5. Circle the first remaining number; it is a prime number. Cross out all its multiples.

6. Repeat Step 5 until every number has been either circled or crossed out.

The circled numbers are the prime numbers less than 100.

This method of identifying prime numbers is called the *sieve of Eratosthenes* because it is like placing the numbers in a sieve and filtering out those that had factors other than 1 and themselves.

Drawing Factor Trees

Recall that a composite number has more than two factors. You can use a factor tree to write any composite number as a product of two or more prime numbers.

A factor tree begins with a composite number at the top. Express this number as a product of factors. Write these factors in the circles below the number.

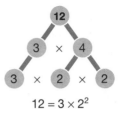

$12 = 3 \times 2^2$

Next, if possible, express each factor in the product as a product of factors. Again, write these factors in the circles below the number. Continue until the factors in the products are all prime numbers. These are called *prime factors*.

As a final step, check whether any prime factor occurs more than once. If it does, express it as a power.

1. Complete each factor tree. Use the tree to write each composite number as a product of powers of prime factors.

a)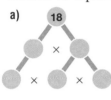

b)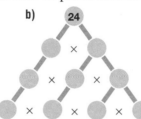

c)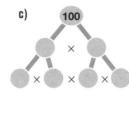

2. Draw a factor tree for each number.

a) 28   b) 66   c) 91

▶▶ *Through a Guided Example*

Example ···

Draw a factor tree for 48. Write 48 as a product of prime numbers.

Solution

Write 48 as a product of two factors other than 1 and 48.
We know that $6 \times 8 = 48$.

6 is a composite number, so write it as 2×3.

8 is a composite number, so write it as 2×4.

2 and 3 are prime numbers, so leave them as they are.

4 is a composite number, so write it as 2×2.

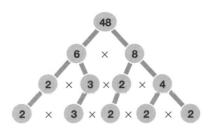

Since all the factors are prime numbers, the factor tree is complete. Use the bottom row to write 48 as a product of prime numbers.

$48 = 2 \times 2 \times 2 \times 2 \times 3$, or $48 = 2^4 \times 3$

Working with Mathematics

Something to talk about

1. Explain the difference between a prime number and a composite number.

2. Explain what is meant by a *factor* of a number.

3. How many factors has a prime number? Name them.

4. Is the number 2056 a prime number? Explain how you know.

5. Is the number 57 a prime number? Give a reason for your answer.

6. Do prime numbers have factor trees? Explain.

Practice

7. List all the factors of each number.
   a) 25   b) 32   c) 49   d) 60   e) 64
   f) 15   g) 36   h) 54   i) 71   j) 100

8. Complete the factor tree for each composite number. Write each number as a product of prime factors. Use powers in your product where appropriate.

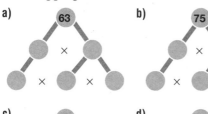

a) 63   b) 75

c) 99   d) 50

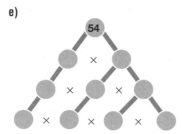

e) 54

Work together

9. Draw a factor tree for each number. Write each number as a product of prime factors. Use powers in your product where appropriate.
   a) 16   b) 42   c) 85   d) 96   e) 120
   f) 74   g) 108   h) 125   i) 176   j) 400

10. Do you think a number can have factor trees with different branching patterns? Compare the factor trees you drew in exercise 9 with those of other students. Did the factor trees all of you drew for each number have the same branching pattern?

11. Find a number whose factor tree can have the branching pattern shown below.

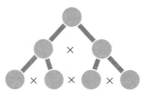

12. Compare your answers to *Activity 2* and exercises 8 and 9 with those of other students. Do you think there is more than one way to write a number as a product of prime factors? Explain.

13. Write each product as a single number.
    a) 2×7^2 b) $3^3 \times 2^3$ c) $5^2 \times 3^2$

14. Find a number between 75 and 100 whose prime factors are 2, 3, and 5. Write this number as a product of powers of primes. Describe the method you used to find the number.

On your own

15. Examine the results of exercise 7.
    a) For each number, how many factors are there?
    b) Which numbers have an odd number of factors? What kind of numbers are these?
    c) Do you think all numbers of this kind have an odd number of factors? Make up some examples to check your answer.

16. Complete the factor tree for each number. Write each number as a product of prime factors. Use powers in your product, where appropriate.

a)
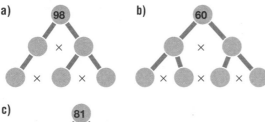

b)

c)

17. Draw a factor tree for each number. Write each number as a product of prime factors. Use powers in your product, where appropriate.
    a) 45   b) 56   c) 102   d) 144   e) 200

18. Write each product as a single number.
    a) $2^2 \times 3^2$ b) $5^2 \times 2^3$
    c) $7^2 \times 2^3$ d) $7^2 \times 2^2 \times 3^2$

19. Two consecutive odd numbers that are prime are called *twin primes*. List all the twin primes you can find between 1 and 100.

Extend your thinking

20. What is the largest prime factor that a number between 120 and 130 could have? Use your list of prime numbers between 1 and 100 and your calculator to find all the prime numbers between 120 and 130.

21. About 300 years ago, a monk named Marin Mersenne calculated $2^p - 1$ for different prime number values of p. He wanted to determine for which values of p this expression was prime. Prime numbers formed in this way are called Mersenne primes in his honour.
    a) Calculate 2^p for $p = 2$, $p = 3$, $p = 5$, and $p = 7$. Are any of these numbers prime? Explain.
    b) To find some Mersenne primes, make a table like the one below. Use your calculator to compute the numbers in the last column. Which of these numbers are prime?

Prime exponent	Power of 2	Subtract 1	Result
2	2^2	$2^2 - 1$	
3	2^3	$2^3 - 1$	
5	2^5	$2^5 - 1$	
7	2^7	$2^7 - 1$	

    c) Is every prime number a Mersenne prime? Explain.

The Ideas

In this section, you completed several activities involving prime and composite numbers. In your journal, describe each of these types of numbers. Explain how you can use a factor tree to express any composite number as a product of prime numbers.

According to *The Guinness Book of Records*, the largest known prime number can be expressed as $2^{859\ 533} - 1$. This number has 258 716 digits. It is not printed here because it would take too much space. Estimate the number of pages it would take to print the number in this book.

·······1.7 ORDER OF OPERATIONS WITH EXPONENTS

Developing the Ideas

▶ ▶ *Through Instruction*

Every day, we make choices about the order in which we perform tasks. Some of these tasks require us to follow a specific order, as you can see in this cartoon.

When we simplify a mathematical expression involving several operations, we could choose the order in which we perform the operations. To ensure that we all get the same answer, mathematicians have agreed on rules for the order to perform operations.

For example, are these two expressions the same?

$$3 \times 10^2 \text{ and } (3 \times 10)^2$$

If we show 10^2 as a 10 by 10 layer of centimetre cubes, then 3×10^2 is the number of cubes in 3 layers.

THE FAR SIDE By GARY LARSON

First pants, THEN your shoes

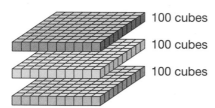

100 cubes

100 cubes

100 cubes

There are $3 \times 100 = 300$ cubes

To evaluate 3×10^2, we calculated 10^2 first to get 100, then multiplied by 3.

$(3 \times 10)^2$ is the number of cubes in a layer with 3×10 cubes on each side.

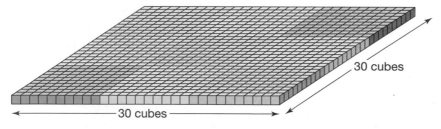

30 cubes

30 cubes

There are $30 \times 30 = 900$ cubes

To evaluate $(3 \times 10)^2$, we calculated 3×10 first to get 30, then squared it.

 **Through a Guided Example**

Recall that when we simplify an expression with more than one operation, it is important to follow the correct order.

To ensure that we all get the same answer, we agree on rules for the order in which the operations are performed.

- Do all operations in brackets first.
- Do exponents next, and simplify powers.
- Do multiplication and division in the order they occur.
- Do addition and subtraction in the order they occur.

Example

Simplify.

a) $3^2 + 5$ **b)** $3 \times 10^5 \div 5$

c) $(4 + 6)^2 \div 3$ **d)** $9^2 - 7^2$

Solution

a) There are no brackets, so do the exponent first.

$3^2 + 5 = 9 + 5$
Add.
$\quad\quad = 14$

b) There are no brackets, so do the exponent first.

$3 \times 10^5 \div 5 = 3 \times 100\ 000 \div 5$
Do the multiplication next, since it comes before the division.
$\quad\quad = 300\ 000 \div 5$
Divide.
$\quad\quad = 60\ 000$

c) Do the operation in brackets first.

$(4 + 6)^2 \div 3 = 10^2 \div 3$
Do the exponent next.
$\quad\quad = 100 \div 3$
Divide.
$\quad\quad = \frac{100}{3}$

d) Do the exponents first.

$9^2 - 7^2 = 81 - 49$
Subtract.
$\quad\quad = 32$

Working with Mathematics

Something to talk about

1. Why must we know the order in which operations should be performed?

2. a) List the order of operations to evaluate each expression.

   i) $4^3 + 1$ **ii)** $(4 + 1)^3$

   b) How is the order changed when brackets are used?

3. Pick a number between 1 and 9. Apply the operations described in parts a and b to that number. Compare the results.
   a) Square the number and add 4.
   b) Add 4 and square the number.

4. a) Simplify $6^2 - 6 \div 3$ and $(6^2 - 6) \div 3$.
   b) Do both expressions give the same answer? Explain.

Practice

5. Simplify.

   a) $2^2 + 1$ **b)** $2^2 - 1$ **c)** $(2 + 1)^2$

   d) $(2 - 1)^2$ **e)** $4 + 2^2$ **f)** $4^2 - 2$

   g) $(4 + 2)^2$ **h)** $(4 - 2)^2$ **i)** $4 - 2^2$

6. Simplify.

   a) 2×3^2 **b)** $2^3 \times 3$ **c)** $(2 \times 3)^2$

   d) $(2 \times 3)^3$ **e)** $4 \div 2^2$ **f)** $4^3 \div 2$

   g) $(4 \div 2)^2$ **h)** $(4 \div 2)^3$ **i)** $4 \div 2^3$

Work together

7. Pick two numbers between 1 and 20. Apply the operations described in parts a and b to these numbers. Compare the results. Which gives the greater number, part a or part b?
   a) Square each number and then add.
   b) Add the numbers and then square.

8. Simplify each expression.

   a) $2^5 - 3^2$ **b)** $(10 - 2)^2$

   c) 2×7^2 **d)** $5 + 6^2 \div 3^2$

   e) $10^2 - (9 - 3)^2$ **f)** $8 + (9 \times 2 - 6)^2$

9. Copy this table.
   a) Complete column A and column B.

Column A	Column B	Column A – Column B
$(1 + 3)^2 =$	$1^2 + 3^2 =$	
$(3 + 2)^2 =$	$3^2 + 2^2 =$	
$(2 + 4)^2 =$	$2^2 + 4^2 =$	
$(3 + 5)^2 =$	$3^2 + 5^2 =$	

   b) Complete the third column.
   c) Compare each number in the third column with the two numbers that were added in column A. Describe any pattern you see.
   d) Use your pattern to predict the value of $(10 + 17)^2 - (10^2 + 17^2)$.

10. Use a calculator to simplify each expression using both methods described below. Compare your answers using the two methods. If the answers are different, try to figure out why they are different and which one is correct.

Method 1
Do the calculation one step at a time, recording each result. Use the result from one step in the next calculation.

Method 2
Complete the calculations in such a way that you need not record any numbers until all the calculations are done.

    a) $3.15^2 - 17.40 \div 2$
    b) $17.8^3 - 4 \times (8.2 - 4.5)$
    c) $(3.5 - 2.4)^2 \div (7.8 - 4.1)$

11. Replace each ■ with one of the operations $+, -, \times,$ or $\div$ to make each equation true.
    a) $6^2 \ ■ \ 3 \ ■ \ 2^4 = 84$
    b) $(4 \ ■ \ 3)^2 \ ■ \ 5^2 = 24$
    c) $(8 \ ■ \ 2)^2 \ ■ \ 7^2 = 65$

12. How many different answers can you get by using brackets with the expression $4^3 + 2 \times 3^2 - 7$?

On your own

13. Simplify.
    a) $80 - 6^2$
    b) $4^3 + 50$
    c) $8^2 - 2^3$
    d) $7^2 - 7 \div 7$
    e) $5 \times 4^2 - 7^2$
    f) $6 \div (5 - 3)$
    g) $(7 + 3)^2 \div 5$
    h) $3^4 + 6 + 7 \times 2$

14. Which expression is larger, $1^2 + 2^2 + 3^2$ or $(1 + 2 + 3)^2$? Show your solution.

15. Simplify.
    a) $40 - 8 \div 2 + 4^2$
    b) $(40 - 8) \div 2 + 3^2$
    c) $(40 - 8 \div 2 + 4)^2$
    d) $40 - (8 \div 2 + 4^2)$

16. a) Complete the pattern.
$$1^3 = 1^2$$
$$1^3 + 2^3 = \blacksquare^2$$
$$1^3 + 2^3 + 3^3 = \blacksquare^2$$
    b) Use the pattern to simplify.
    i) $1^3 + 2^3 + 3^3 + 4^3$
    ii) $1^3 + 2^3 + 3^3 + 4^3 + 5^3$

17. a) Complete the pattern.
$$3^2 - 1^2 = \blacksquare^3$$
$$6^2 - 3^2 = \blacksquare^3$$
$$10^2 - 6^2 = \blacksquare^3$$
    b) Use the pattern to simplify.
    i) $15^2 - 10^2$
    ii) $21^2 - 15^2$

18. Using brackets, write the expression so that it equals the number in colour.
    a) $2 + 3^2 \times 5 - 1$ 38
    b) $36 \div 4 + 2^2 + 1$ 4
    c) $10 + 5 + 3^3 \div 4$ 18
    d) $2 + 3^2 \times 7 - 4$ 33

19. Write an expression with exponents and with brackets. Simplify the expression. Ask a classmate to simplify the expression. Check to see if both of you follow the same order of operations.

Extend your thinking

20. a) Apply each series of operations in the table below to the number 4. Record your answers.

Description in words	Using a variable
i) Cube the number and add 5.	$x^3 + 5$
ii) Subtract the square of a number from its cube.	$y^3 - y^2$
iii) Add 17 to a number and divide the square of the sum by 3.	$(z + 17)^2 \div 3$

   b) Apply each series of operations to a variable.
   i) Add 13 to a number and square the sum.
   ii) Add 9 to a number and divide the cube of the sum by 6.
   iii) Add 3 to a number and multiply by the number that is 3 less than the number you started with. Divide this product by 3 and then square it.
   c) What are the advantages of applying a series of operations to a variable rather than describing it in words?
   d) Write a series of operations of your own. Give it to a friend. Ask her or him to apply it to a variable.

COMMUNICATING The Ideas

In your journal, make a list showing the order in which operations in a mathematical expression should be completed.

A stack of one trillion Canadian $20-bills would reach over 110 000 km high. Estimate the thickness of a Canadian $20-bill in millimetres.

1.8 SQUARE ROOTS

Developing the Ideas

▶ ▶ *Through Discussion*

The *perfect squares* (sometimes called *squares*) are a set of numbers that
have special properties.

These are the numbers: 1, 4, 9, 16, …

They are formed by squaring the natural numbers: 1, 2, 3, 4, …

One property of a perfect square is that it can be represented by a square
array. The arrays for the first four perfect squares are shown:

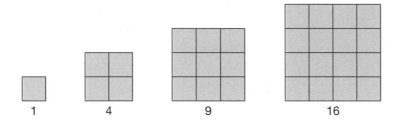

Look at the last array above.

If each small square has a side length of 1 cm, then the large square
has a side length of 4 cm and an area of 4 cm × 4 cm = 16 cm².
The number 4 is called a *square root* of 16.

We say: A square root of 16 is 4.

We write: $\sqrt{16} = 4$

We think: 4 is a square root of 16 because $4^2 = 16$.

1. What are the next three perfect squares after 16?

2. What is a square root of 100?

Numbers such as 2, 3, 5, and 6 are not perfect squares. They do not have
whole-number square roots. In *Activity 2*, you will discover how to find
square roots of some numbers that are not perfect squares.

ACTIVITY 1

What is a square root of 25?

To answer this question, we ask:

"What is the length of a side of a square with area 25 square units?"

1. Get 25 square tiles. Use them to make the largest square possible.
   a) Did you use all the tiles?
   b) What are the dimensions of this square?
   c) Use the result of part b to determine $\sqrt{25}$.
2. Use this method to determine $\sqrt{9}$ and $\sqrt{49}$.

BOGGLE YOUR MIND

The video game rental market in North America generates $1.5 billion a year, according to industry estimates. Sales of video games total another $6 billion. What is the ratio of rentals to sales? What fraction of the total market is for rentals?

What is the square root of 30?

To answer this question, we ask:

"What is the length of a side of a square with area 30 square units?"

To determine an approximate square root of 30, complete the steps below.
You will need a supply of square tiles and unit grid paper.

Step 1

Get 30 square tiles. Use them to make the largest square possible. What are the dimensions of this square? How many squares are left over?

Step 2

Use the grid paper. Cut out a square to match the square you made in Step 1. Cut a strip of 5 squares to represent 5 leftover tiles.

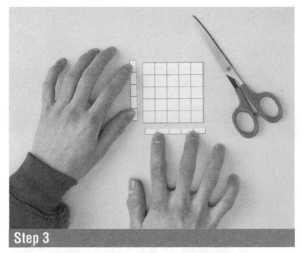

Step 3

Cut the strip into 2 narrow strips. Place them against the square.

1. Use the result in Step 3 to estimate $\sqrt{30}$. Use your calculator to determine the approximate value of $\sqrt{30}$. Compare the calculated value with your estimate. How close was your estimate to the calculated value?

2. Use the method in Steps 1 to 3 to estimate $\sqrt{31}$. What change is there in the way the strips fit against the square in Step 3? Use your square and strips to estimate $\sqrt{31}$. Use your calculator to determine $\sqrt{31}$. Compare your estimate with the calculator result.

Recall that when we square a number, we multiply it by itself:

$$7^2 = 49$$

Since $7 \times 7 = 49$, we say that 7 is a square root of 49, and we write $\sqrt{49} = 7$.

All positive numbers have square roots. Those that have square roots which are natural numbers are called *perfect squares*. For example, 25 is a perfect square because one of its square roots is 5.

Number, n	0	1	4	9	16	25	36	49	64	81	100
Square root, $\sqrt{n}$	0	1	2	3	4	5	6	7	8	9	10

You can estimate the square roots of numbers that are not perfect squares. To estimate $\sqrt{50}$ and $\sqrt{75}$, think of the perfect squares near 50 and 75:

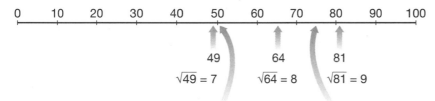

50 is between 49 and 64, and is much closer to 49.
Hence, $\sqrt{50}$ is between 7 and 8, and is probably much closer to 7.
We estimate $\sqrt{50}$ to be about 7.1.

75 is between 64 and 81, and is a little closer to 81.
Hence, $\sqrt{75}$ is between 8 and 9, and is probably a little closer to 9.
We estimate $\sqrt{75}$ to be about 8.6.

BOGGLE YOUR MIND

The Hermitage art gallery in St. Petersburg, Russia has nearly 3 million works of art and historical artifacts on display. What if it takes an average of 15 s to look at each item? How many days would it take to view the entire collection?

Working with Mathematics

Something to talk about

1. Explain the meaning of the term *square root*.

2. Which natural numbers have square roots that are natural numbers?

3. a) What is the side length of a square with an area of 64 cm^2?
   b) What is a square root of 64?

4. Do all natural numbers have square roots? Explain your answer.

5. Explain how $\sqrt{\frac{4}{9}}$ can be determined from this diagram.

1 unit

Work together

6. Use the method of *Activity 1*. Determine each square root.
   a) $\sqrt{4}$ b) $\sqrt{36}$ c) $\sqrt{64}$ d) $\sqrt{100}$

7. Is the product of two perfect squares also a perfect square? Give reasons for your answer.

8. Use the method of *Activity 2*. Estimate each square root. Explain your method. Compare your estimate with a calculator result.
   a) $\sqrt{20}$ b) $\sqrt{21}$ c) $\sqrt{42}$ d) $\sqrt{43}$
   e) $\sqrt{56}$ f) $\sqrt{57}$ g) $\sqrt{72}$ h) $\sqrt{132}$

9. Here is another way to estimate the square root of a number that is not a perfect square. To estimate $\sqrt{28}$, think of the perfect squares that are close to 28.

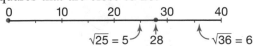

28 is between 25 and 36, and is much closer to 25. So, $\sqrt{28}$ is between 5 and 6, and is probably much closer to 5. We estimate $\sqrt{28}$ to be about 5.2.
Which square roots are between 5 and 6?
   a) $\sqrt{40}$ b) $\sqrt{34}$ c) $\sqrt{26}$ d) $\sqrt{20}$

10. Use the method in exercise 9 to estimate each square root.
    a) $\sqrt{13}$ b) $\sqrt{19}$ c) $\sqrt{28}$ d) $\sqrt{41}$
    e) $\sqrt{52}$ f) $\sqrt{63}$ g) $\sqrt{70}$ h) $\sqrt{85}$

11. Which letter on the number line corresponds to each square root?
    a) $\sqrt{20}$ b) $\sqrt{15}$ c) $\sqrt{4}$ d) $\sqrt{33}$
    e) $\sqrt{3}$ f) $\sqrt{8}$ g) $\sqrt{12}$ h) $\sqrt{38}$

12. Some paint comes in 1-L and 4-L cans. The label contains the following information:

> Coverage: 1 litre will cover up to 12 square metres—4 litres will cover up to 48 square metres.

   a) Suppose you used all the paint in the 1-L can to paint a square. Estimate the length of its side.
   b) Suppose you used all the paint in the 4-L can to paint a square. Estimate the length of its side.
   c) How are the areas of the squares in parts a and b related? How are the side lengths related?

13. a) Enter 18 in your calculator. Press $\boxed{\sqrt{\ }}$. If your calculator has an $\boxed{x^2}$ key, press it. If your calculator does not have an $\boxed{x^2}$ key, press $\boxed{\times}$ then the number in the display, then $\boxed{=}$. Explain the results.
    b) Repeat part a with some other numbers.

14. Use a calculator to simplify. Express each answer to the nearest tenth.
    a) $\sqrt{17}$ b) $\sqrt{72}$ c) $\sqrt{119}$ d) $\sqrt{1000}$

15. Use these diagrams to help you find each square root.
    a) $\sqrt{\frac{1}{4}}$ b) $\sqrt{\frac{9}{16}}$

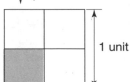

1 unit   1 unit

On your own

16. a) What is the side length of a square field with an area of 900 m²?

b) How many metres of fencing would be needed to fence the field described in part a?

17. Kofi has a piece of construction paper 45 cm by 20 cm. He cuts it into parts that can be rearranged to form a square.

a) How long is a side of the square?

b) What is the least number of cuts he could have made?

18. Use a calculator to simplify. Express each answer to the nearest tenth.

a) $\sqrt{29}$ **b)** $\sqrt{148}$ **c)** $\sqrt{249}$ **d)** $\sqrt{357}$

19. Set up a "square root estimator" on a spreadsheet. It will help you judge how close your estimates are. Start a new file. Enter the text and formulas shown below. Select cells A5 and A6. Format them to show numbers as fixed decimals with 5 places.

TEMPLATE DISK

	A	B	C	D
1		The number		
2		My estimate of the square root of the number		
3				
4				
5	=A2*A2	My estimate squared		
6	=A5−A1	How close my estimate squared is		

a) What do the formulas in cells A5 and A6 do? If you are not sure, enter numbers in cells A1 and A2. Check the numbers shown in cells A5 and A6.

b) To use the estimator in cell A1, enter the number whose square root you want to know. Enter your estimate of the square root in cell A2. Look at the numbers in cells A5 and A6. Revise your estimate until its square is within 0.1 of the value in cell A1. Use the spreadsheet to help estimate each square root.

i) $\sqrt{43}$ ii) $\sqrt{117}$ iii) $\sqrt{183}$ iv) $\sqrt{546}$

20. Emily is fencing a section of her property for her eight dogs to use. She wants the fenced area to be large enough so that there are 4 m² of space for each dog.

a) What should the area of the fenced section be?

b) Emily would like the fenced section to be square. Use your square root estimator to determine the side length of the square.

c) How many metres of fencing should Emily buy?

Extend your thinking

21. A cube can be used to demonstrate cube roots. The base 10 cube shown has an edge length of 10 units. Its volume is 1000 cubic units. We say that $\sqrt[3]{1000} = 10$. Obtain some 1-cm cubes. Arrange them to find:

a) $\sqrt[3]{8}$ **b)** $\sqrt[3]{27}$ **c)** $\sqrt[3]{125}$ **d)** $\sqrt[3]{64}$

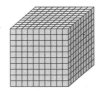

22. a) What is the edge length of a cube with a volume of 125 cm³?

b) What is the area of each face of the cube?

c) What is the total surface area of the cube?

23. José is adding a bulk food section to his store. He is designing storage boxes to hold the bulk products. He wants the boxes to be cubes. Each cube must hold 25 000 cm³. Determine the edge length of the boxes.

COMMUNICATING

The Ideas

In your journal, explain how to calculate the length of the side of a square if you know its area. Describe how this enables you to calculate the perimeter of a square if you know its area.

Review

1. Find the value of ■ that makes each equation true.
   a) $27\ 685 = 20\ 000 + 7000 + ■ + 80 + 5$
   b) $9801 = 9000 + 800 + ■$
   c) $■ = 400\ 000 + 70\ 000 + 8000 + 200 + 60 + 3$
   d) $■ = 100\ 000 + 7000 + 40$
   e) $1\ 006\ 497 = 1\ 000\ 000 + ■ + 400 + 90 + 7$
   f) $■ = 600\ 000 + 9000 + 800 + 30 + 2$

2. Find the value of ■ that makes each equation true.
   a) $8000 = ■ \times 10^3$
   b) $■ = 2 \times 10^5$
   c) $3\ 000\ 000 = 3 \times 10^■$
   d) $■ = 6 \times 10^4$
   e) $700 = ■ \times 10^2$
   f) $90\ 000\ 000 = 9 \times 10^■$

3. Write each number in standard form.
   a) $(7 \times 10^4) + (6 \times 10^3) + (9 \times 10^2) + (8 \times 10) + 5$
   b) $(4 \times 10^2) + (3 \times 10^4) + 5 + (6 \times 10)$
   c) $(1 \times 10^3) + (2 \times 10^7) + (4 \times 10^5) + 1$
   d) $(8 \times 10^2) + (5 \times 10^6) + (9 \times 10^4) + 7 + (6 \times 10^3)$

4. Write each number in expanded form using powers of 10.
   a) 2547   b) 39 675
   c) 358 200   d) 80 603
   e) 785 426   f) 10 674 900

5. Explain the meaning of each power, then write each power as a numeral.
   a) 16^2 b) 5^3 c) 6^4
   d) 7^4 e) 10^6 f) 9^5

6. a) Without calculating, predict which number is greater, 8^4 or 4^8.
   b) Evaluate each power in part a using a calculator. Was your prediction correct?

7. A square tile has a side length of 5 cm.
   a) What is its area?
   b) What is the area when the side length is doubled?

c) What is the area when the side length is tripled?
d) What is the area when the side length is multiplied by 4?
e) Record your answers to parts b to d in a table like the one below. What conclusion can you make about how the area of a square changes when the side length is doubled? Tripled? Multiplied by 4?

Side length (cm)	Area (cm²)	side length / original side length	area / original area
5	25	1	1
10			
15			
20			

8. a) What is the value of a 2 by 2 block of Canadian 45¢ stamps?
   b) What is the value of a 4 by 4 block of these stamps?

9. To make each equation true, which number replaces ■?
   a) $3\ 150\ 000 = 3.15 \times 10^■$
   b) $22\ 000 = 2.2 \times 10^■$
   c) $664\ 000 = 6.64 \times 10^■$
   d) $57\ 800\ 000 = 5.78 \times 10^■$

10. Write in scientific notation.
    a) 4 235 000   b) 140 000
    c) 13 700   d) 19 710 000
    e) 608 000   f) 8 136 000 000

11. Write as a numeral.
    a) 2.9×10^2 b) 3.72×10^6
    c) 4.306×10^8 d) 7×10^{11}
    e) 5.794×10^4 f) 9.51×10^9

12. Arrange each set of numbers in order from smallest to largest. Explain your reasoning.
    a) $4.9 \times 10^3, 4.4 \times 10^3, 4.5 \times 10^3$
    b) $6.3 \times 10^6, 6.3 \times 10^8, 6.3 \times 10^5$
    c) $8.42 \times 10^5, 8.56 \times 10^5, 8.53 \times 10^5$
    d) $7.013 \times 10^9, 7.92 \times 10^8, 7.113 \times 10^9$
    e) $6.4 \times 10^5, 6.4 \times 10^6, 4.8 \times 10^7$

13. Write, in scientific notation, all the numbers in the following passage.

> Some scientists suggest that the human species, like the dinosaurs, may one day become extinct. The modern human is believed to have come into existence about 2 million years ago. Humans belong to a family of species called *mammals*. Rodent-like mammals appeared on Earth about 200 million years ago. These mammals co-existed with the dinosaurs in small numbers for about 140 million years. When the dinosaurs became extinct 65 million years ago, the mammals became dominant and began to flourish. Some scientists believe that the insects with their ability to reproduce quickly in large numbers and to adapt to changing conditions may become the survivors in a post-human era. It is estimated that there are over 30 million different species of insects today.

14. The table lists the approximate ages of some of the meteorite craters in Canada. Which numbers complete the table? Which crater is the oldest?

| | Age in years | |
Location of crater	Numeral	Scientific notation
a) Carswell, SK	485 000 000	
b) West Hawk Lake, MN		1.0×10^8
c) Sudbury, ON		1.84×10^9
d) Steen River, AB	95 000 000	
e) Deep Bay, SK	100 000 000	
f) Haughton, NWT		1.5×10^7

15. Write each fact about coins using a numeral instead of scientific notation.
    a) In 1992, a group in the U.K. made the longest ever line of coins. It consisted of about 1.887×10^6 coins and stretched a distance of about 4.81×10^4 m.
    b) The American penny showing Lincoln's head is the most common coin ever made. Since 1909, about 2.5×10^{11} have been made. If placed end-to-end, they would stretch a distance of 4.16×10^4 m.
    c) In 1980, Terry Fox ran 5373 km to raise money for cancer research. He raised the

equivalent of 2.47×10^7 loonies. If placed end-to-end, this number of loonies would stretch a distance of 6.42×10^5 m.

16. State whether each number is divisible by 2. Do not use a calculator.
    a) 57   b) 95   c) 114
    d) 538   e) 8063   f) 15 780

17. Suppose you were to replace ■ with the digit 6, 7, or 8. Would the number be divisible by 3?
    a) 7■   b) 2■3   c) 35■
    d) 22■5   e) 1■211   f) 11■116

18. Replace each ■ with a digit so that the number is divisible by 6.
    a) 6■30   b) 5■614   c) ■9 086
    d) 7■08   e) 71 48■   f) 895 0■6

19. Replace each ■ with a digit so that the number is divisible by 9.
    a) 9■   b) 6■5   c) 1■25
    d) ■760   e) 87 11■   f) 3■1 011

20. There are 344 people in a golf tournament. Can they be grouped exactly into foursomes? Explain.

21. Complete the factor tree for each number. Write each number as a product of prime factors. Use powers in your product.

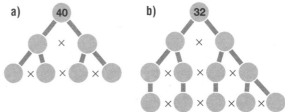

22. Draw a factor tree for each number. Write each number as a product of prime factors. Use powers in your product where appropriate.
    a) 92   b) 90   c) 110   d) 126
    e) 65   f) 88   g) 136   h) 175

23. Write each product as a single number.
    a) $2^2 \times 7^2$ b) $5^2 \times 2^2$
    c) $7^2 \times 3^2$ d) $2^3 \times 3^2 \times 7^2$

Polygonal Numbers

In this project, you will investigate numbers that can be described using geometric figures.

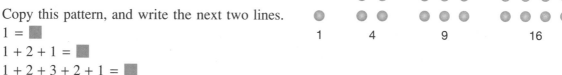

1   4   9   16

ACTIVITY 1

These are the first four *square numbers*.

1. Write the first twelve square numbers.

2. a) Copy this pattern, and write the next two lines.

   1 = ▪

   1 + 2 + 1 = ▪

   1 + 2 + 3 + 2 + 1 = ▪

   b) Predict this sum, without adding.

   1 + 2 + 3 + 4 + 5 + 6 + 7 + 8 + 9 + 10 + 9 + 8 + 7 + 6 + 5 + 4 + 3 + 2 + 1 = ▪

3. Do you think it is possible for two square numbers to add to another square number? Find an example to support your claim.

4. There are five different ways to write 100 as the sum of four square numbers. Here is one way:

   100 = 81 + 9 + 9 + 1

   Find the other four ways.

5. Try to find a number that cannot be written as a sum of four square numbers. Show your number to a friend. Have that person try to write it as a sum of four square numbers.

6. To find the sum of the first four odd numbers, you can draw L-shaped partitions on a square number to make sets of 1, 3, 5, and 7.

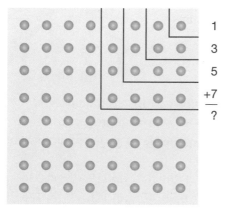

1
3
5
+7
___
?

These sets together form a 4 by 4 array of 16 dots.

1 + 3 + 5 + 7 = 16

Use this method to find the sum of the first 6 odd numbers.

What is the sum of the first 20 odd numbers?

ACTIVITY 2

These are the first four *triangular numbers*.

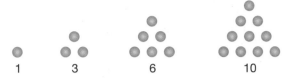

1   3   6   10

1. Write the first twelve triangular numbers.

2. Do you think it is possible for two triangular numbers to add to another triangular number? Find an example to support your claim.

3. The number 1 is both a square number and a triangular number. Can you find another number that is both square and triangular?

4. A square number can always be written as the sum of two triangular numbers.

   a) Make up some examples to show this.

   b) Use diagrams to illustrate why a square number can be written as the sum of two triangular numbers.

ACTIVITY 3

These are the first three *pentagonal numbers*.

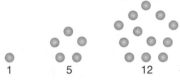

1   5   12

1. Draw the next three pentagonal numbers.

2. Look at the six pentagonal numbers. Can you find a way to get the 7th pentagonal number without drawing a diagram?

3. Do you think it is possible for a square number and a triangular number to add to make a pentagonal number? Write down any sums you find.

4. The number 1 is both a square number and a pentagonal number. Can you find another number that is both square and pentagonal?

5. The number 1 is both a triangular number and a pentagonal number. Can you find another number that is both triangular and pentagonal?

6. Apart from the number 1, are there any other numbers that are square, triangular, and pentagonal?

The Ideas

Write a report to explain what you found out about the three types of numbers.

Cumulative Review

1. For the set of numbers, and the stem-and-leaf diagram below, state the:

    i) mean   ii) median

    iii) lower quartile   iv) upper quartile

    v) extremes   vi) range

    a) 133, 151, 166, 135, 137, 141, 128, 130, 140, 136, 132

    b)
    ```
    1 | 3
    2 | 0 1 3 3 4 6 7 9
    3 | 3 4 7 7 6
    4 | 9
    ```

2. Display the set of numbers and the stem-and-leaf diagram in exercise 1 on box-and-whisker plots.

TEMPLATE DISK

3. Start a new document in a spreadsheet program. Type what is shown below.

	A	B
1		
2		
3	Lower quartile	12
4		
5		
6	Median	43
7		
8		
9	Upper quartile	62
10		
11		
12	----------	------------
13	Mean	

In cell B13, type a formula to calculate the mean of the numbers in cells B1 to B11.

In ClarisWorks, cell B13 is =AVERAGE(B1..B11)

In Microsoft Works, cell B13 is =AVERAGE(B1:B11)

Input any numbers you choose in cells B1, B2, B4, B5, B7, B8, B10, and B11. Ensure that the numbers are sorted from least to greatest. Use the quartiles and the median shown in the chart.

a) Enter numbers so the mean and median are both 43.

b) Enter numbers so the mean equals the upper quartile.

c) Can you enter numbers so that the mean is equal to the lower quartile?

4. Suppose a robot were designed to pick up objects for a child with disabilities. The computer in the robot must recognize an object the child requests. One way to do this might be to equip the robot with a camera. The top, front, and side view of each object are stored in the computer's memory. When the child requests a particular object, the robot can look at the top, front, and side views of this object in its memory. It can then scan the selection of objects looking for one with a view that matches.

a) Two of the objects are a baseball cap and a mug. Draw top, front, and side views of each object.

b) Do you think just one view of each object could be stored in the computer's memory instead of three? Explain.

5. Write each number in standard form.

a) 60 000 + 2000 + 400 + 90 + 5

b) 8 000 000 + 500 000 + 8000 + 70 + 3

c) 1000 + 40 000 + 8 + 200 + 700 000 + 50

d) 30 000 + 1 000 000 + 200 000 + 90 + 700

e) 4 000 000 + 300 + 70 000 + 8

f) 60 000 + 900 + 4 + 20 000 000

g) 100 000 + 50 + 30 000 + 200

6. What is the value of the 3 in each number?
   a) 3541
   b) 139 000
   c) 178 430
   d) 923 608 605
   e) 35 297 000
   f) 10 321 940

7. Express each power as a product and as a numeral.
   a) 9^3
   b) 2^6
   c) 3^5
   d) 15^2
   e) 11^5
   f) 13^2
   g) 5^3
   h) 1^8

8. Which is the greater number in each pair? Explain.
   a) $3^5, 5^3$
   b) $9^2, 2^9$
   c) $6^4, 4^6$
   d) $3^8, 8^3$

9. A square tile has a side length of 4 cm.
   a) What is the area of the tile?
   b) What is the area of a square tile with double the side length?
   c) What is the area of a square tile with one-half the side length?

10. To make each equation true, which number replaces ▪ ?
   a) $3\ 150\ 000 = 3.15 \times 10^{▪}$
   b) $22\ 000 = 2.2 \times 10^{▪}$
   c) $664\ 000 = 6.64 \times 10^{▪}$
   d) $57\ 800\ 000 = 5.78 \times 10^{▪}$

11. Write in scientific notation.
   a) 200 000
   b) 39 800
   c) 11 300 000
   d) 8 790 000
   e) 17 040 000
   f) 10 600 000 000
   g) 33 500
   h) 9 610 000

12. Write as a numeral.
   a) 2.21×10^5
   b) 8.02×10^3
   c) 9.0×10^6
   d) 4.51×10^8
   e) 7.37×10^4
   f) 1.063×10^7
   g) 1.05×10^{12}
   h) 3.2×10^6

13. Arrange each set of numbers in order from least to greatest.
   a) $2.5 \times 10^3, 2.3 \times 10^4, 2.2 \times 10^4$
   b) $1.05 \times 10^7, 1.06 \times 10^7, 1.052 \times 10^7$
   c) $5.49 \times 10^8, 5.5 \times 10^8, 5.65 \times 10^6$
   d) $9.133 \times 10^5, 9.311 \times 10^5, 9.131 \times 10^6$

14. The table lists the approximate land areas of 7 countries. Which numbers complete the table?

Country	Land area in hectares	
	Numeral	Scientific notation
a) Australia	761 800 000	
b) Canada		9.221×10^8
c) Fiji		1.827×10^6
d) French Polynesia	366 000	
e) Hong Kong		9.9×10^4
f) Iceland	10 030 000	
g) Netherlands	3 392 000	

15. Do not use a calculator. State whether each number is divisible by 3. Explain your reasoning.
   a) 31
   b) 49
   c) 87
   d) 176
   e) 977
   f) 11 220

16. Suppose you replace the ▪ with 3, 4, or 5. Would the number be divisible by 2? Explain.
   a) 9▪3
   b) ▪02
   c) 76▪
   d) 4▪05
   e) 51 0▪0
   f) 322 63▪

17. Simplify.
   a) $2^5 - 17$
   b) $63 + 5^3$
   c) $9^2 - 4^3$
   d) $7 + 10^2 \div 2^2$
   e) $35 - 21 \div 3 + 2^2$
   f) $(6 + 5)^2 - 7 \times 3^2$

18. Replace each ▪ with one of the operations $+, -, \times,$ or $\div$ to make each equation true.
   a) $15 ▪ 2^2 ▪ 3 ▪ 8 = 11$
   b) $(8 ▪ 2)^2 ▪ 4 ▪ 9 = 16$

19. Arrange 10 squares of paper to help you estimate $\sqrt{10}$.

20. Use the diagram to help you determine $\sqrt{\dfrac{16}{49}}$.

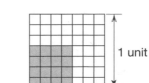

1 unit

FRACTIONS

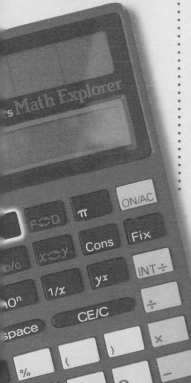

Linking Ideas

Mathematics File

Quests

Minds on Math Project

Start With What You Know

You have used fraction strips and number lines to work with fractions. Use the number lines shown here to complete the exercises below.

Equivalent Fractions

1. Find some fractions on these number lines that lie in a line one above another. Why are they called equivalent fractions?

2. Express in simplest form.

   a) $\frac{4}{6}$
   b) $\frac{9}{12}$
   c) $\frac{16}{12}$
   d) $\frac{12}{8}$

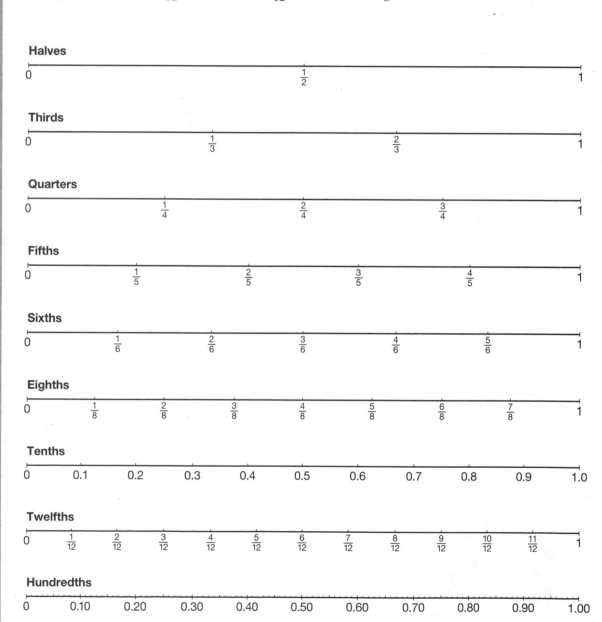

Halves

0 $\frac{1}{2}$ 1

Thirds

0 $\frac{1}{3}$ $\frac{2}{3}$ 1

Quarters

0 $\frac{1}{4}$ $\frac{2}{4}$ $\frac{3}{4}$ 1

Fifths

0 $\frac{1}{5}$ $\frac{2}{5}$ $\frac{3}{5}$ $\frac{4}{5}$ 1

Sixths

0 $\frac{1}{6}$ $\frac{2}{6}$ $\frac{3}{6}$ $\frac{4}{6}$ $\frac{5}{6}$ 1

Eighths

0 $\frac{1}{8}$ $\frac{2}{8}$ $\frac{3}{8}$ $\frac{4}{8}$ $\frac{5}{8}$ $\frac{6}{8}$ $\frac{7}{8}$ 1

Tenths

0 0.1 0.2 0.3 0.4 0.5 0.6 0.7 0.8 0.9 1.0

Twelfths

0 $\frac{1}{12}$ $\frac{2}{12}$ $\frac{3}{12}$ $\frac{4}{12}$ $\frac{5}{12}$ $\frac{6}{12}$ $\frac{7}{12}$ $\frac{8}{12}$ $\frac{9}{12}$ $\frac{10}{12}$ $\frac{11}{12}$ 1

Hundredths

0 0.10 0.20 0.30 0.40 0.50 0.60 0.70 0.80 0.90 1.00

Expressing Fractions in Decimal Form

3. How can you use the number lines to express fractions in decimal form?

4. Use the number lines to express each fraction in decimal form.

  a) $\frac{1}{4}$ **b)** $\frac{2}{3}$ **c)** $\frac{3}{2}$ **d)** $3\frac{5}{8}$

5. What other way is there to express a fraction in decimal form?

6. Express in decimal form.

  a) $\frac{3}{7}$ **b)** $\frac{10}{7}$ **c)** $\frac{5}{9}$ **d)** $2\frac{1}{9}$

7. Replace each ▉ with < or >.

  a) $1\frac{5}{8}$ ▉ $1\frac{5}{6}$ **b)** $2\frac{5}{12}$ ▉ $1\frac{3}{8}$ **c)** $2\frac{4}{5}$ ▉ $2\frac{3}{4}$

  d) $1\frac{5}{8}$ ▉ $1\frac{2}{3}$ **e)** $1\frac{3}{8}$ ▉ 1.4 **f)** 2.6 ▉ $2\frac{7}{12}$

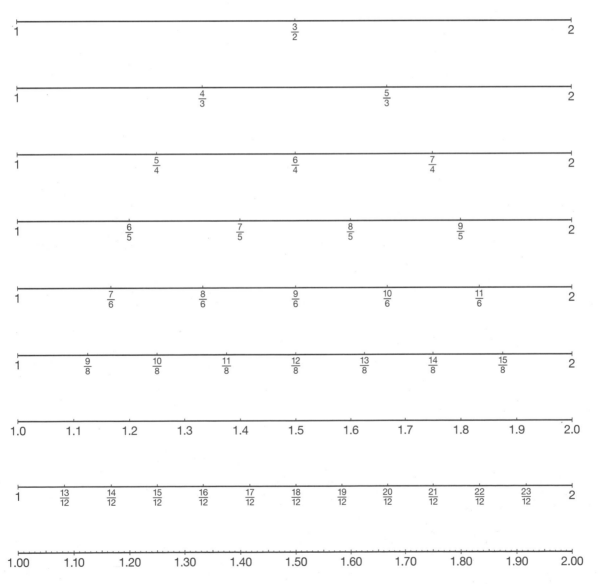

Adding Fractions

To add two fractions such as $\frac{1}{2} + \frac{2}{5}$, use the fifths line to mark the distance $\frac{2}{5}$ on the edge of a piece of paper. Place this with its left end at $\frac{1}{2}$ on the halves line.

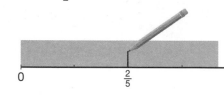

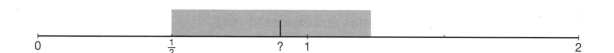

8. a) What number line should you use instead of the halves line? How would you express the fractions $\frac{1}{2}$ and $\frac{2}{5}$ on this line?

   b) What is the answer to $\frac{1}{2} + \frac{2}{5}$?

9. Use the number lines to add.

   a) $\frac{3}{4} + \frac{1}{2}$ b) $\frac{2}{3} + \frac{5}{6}$ c) $\frac{1}{4} + \frac{1}{3}$

Subtracting Fractions

To subtract two fractions such as $\frac{5}{4} - \frac{2}{3}$, use the thirds line to mark the distance $\frac{2}{3}$ on the edge of a piece of paper. Place this with the mark at $\frac{5}{4}$ on the quarters line.

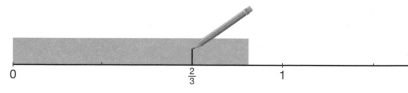

10. a) What number line should you use instead of the quarters line? How would you express the fractions $\frac{5}{4}$ and $\frac{2}{3}$ on this line?

    b) What is the answer to $\frac{5}{4} - \frac{2}{3}$?

11. Use the number lines to subtract.

    a) $\frac{3}{4} - \frac{1}{8}$ b) $\frac{4}{5} - \frac{1}{2}$ c) $2 - \frac{3}{5}$

2.1 COMPUTING WITH FRACTIONS IN DECIMAL FORM

Developing the Ideas

▶▶▶ *Through Guided Examples*

You can always work with fractions by expressing them in decimal form and using the decimals. If you use a fraction calculator, there is a key that converts a fraction to an equivalent decimal. When you use this method, the answer will be in decimal form.

You can use a calculator, unless the decimals are very simple ones such as 0.25 and 0.6.

Approximate populations of Earth's continents and regions in 1992

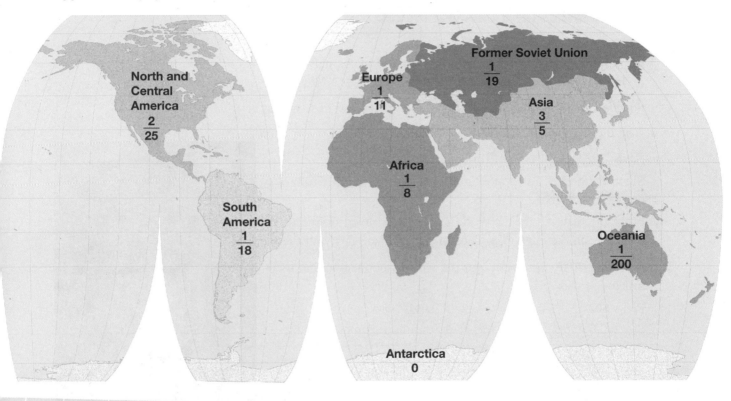

BOGGLE YOUR MIND

The country with the world's youngest population is Kenya. In 1992, about $\frac{1}{2}$ of the 26 164 000 people living in Kenya were under 15 years old. Only $\frac{17}{500}$ were 65 years or older. In contrast, Sweden has the world's oldest population. In 1992, $\frac{23}{100}$ of the 8 602 000 people living in Sweden were 65 years or older, while only $\frac{9}{50}$ were under 15 years old. Calculate the number of people in each age group living in each country.

Example 1

Use the information in the table to check the fractions of the world population shown on the map on page 107 for these continents.

a) Asia **b)** Europe

Continent or region	1992 Population (millions)
Africa	682
Antarctica	uninhabited
Asia	3233
Europe	504
North and Central America	436
Oceania	28
South America	304
Former Soviet Union	293
Total world population	5480

Solution

a) From the table, the population of Asia was 3233 million and the total world population was 5480 million.

So, the fraction of the world's population that lived in Asia was $\frac{3233}{5480}$.

Use your calculator to express $\frac{3233}{5480}$ in decimal form.

Press: **3233 ÷ 5480 =** to obtain **0.5899635**

Since 0.589 963 5 is approximately 0.6, the fraction on the map is reasonable.

b) From the map, $\frac{1}{11}$ of the world's population lived in Europe.

Press: **1 ÷ 11 =** to obtain **0.0909091**

From the table, the fraction of the world's population that lived in Europe was $\frac{504}{5480}$.

Press **504 ÷ 5480 =** to obtain **0.0919708**

Since 0.090 909 1 and 0.091 970 8 are approximately equal, the fraction on the map is reasonable.

Example 2

What fraction of the world's population lived in North, Central, and South America? Express the answer in decimal form to the nearest hundredth.

Solution

From the map, $\frac{2}{25}$ of the world's population lived in North and Central America and $\frac{1}{18}$ lived in South America.

Express the fractions $\frac{2}{25}$ and $\frac{1}{18}$ in decimal form.

Press: **2 ÷ 25 =** to obtain **0.08**

Press: **1** ÷ **18** = to obtain **0.0555556**

Add the numbers in decimal form. The display still shows 0.0555556.

Press: **+** **0.08** = to obtain **0.1355556**

To the nearest hundredth, the fraction of the world's population living in North, Central, and South America was 0.14.

Calculators display more digits than we usually need. From now on, we will show only the first five digits from the display unless stated otherwise.

Example 3 ....

Use your calculator to determine each answer in decimal form to the nearest hundredth.

a) $\frac{5}{6} + \frac{2}{7}$ b) $\frac{5}{6} - \frac{2}{7}$ c) $\frac{5}{6} \times \frac{2}{7}$ d) $\frac{5}{6} \div \frac{2}{7}$

Solution

Express the fractions $\frac{5}{6}$ and $\frac{2}{7}$ in decimal form.

Press: **5** ÷ **6** = to obtain **0.8333**

Write this number on a piece of paper, because you will need to enter it again.

Press: **2** ÷ **7** = to obtain **0.2857**

Write this number on a piece of paper also.

a) Press: .8333 **+** .2857 = to obtain **1.119**

To the nearest hundredth, $\frac{5}{6} + \frac{2}{7} = 1.12$

b) Press: .8333 **−** .2857 = to obtain **0.5476**

To the nearest hundredth, $\frac{5}{6} - \frac{2}{7} = 0.55$

c) Press: .8333 **×** .2857 = to obtain **0.2380**

To the nearest hundredth, $\frac{5}{6} \times \frac{2}{7} = 0.24$

d) Press: .8333 **÷** .2857 = to obtain **2.9166**

To the nearest hundredth, $\frac{5}{6} \div \frac{2}{7} = 2.92$

If you have a calculator with a fraction key, you can use it to compute with fractions. The next two examples are solved with a calculator that has a fraction key. *Example 5* is the same as *Example 3*. The key strokes are for the *TEXAS INSTRUMENTS Math Explorer*™. If you have a different fraction calculator, the key strokes may be different.

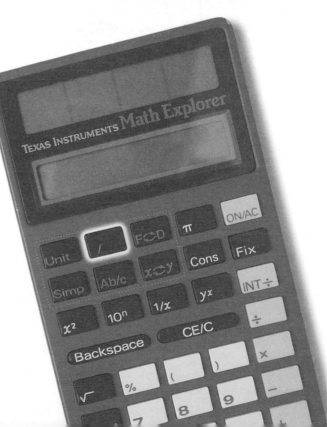

Example 4

Use a calculator with a fraction key to determine the fraction of the world's population that lives in Asia and Africa.

Solution

$\frac{3}{5}$ of the world's population lives in Asia.

$\frac{1}{8}$ of the world's population lives in Africa.

Add the fractions to find the fraction of the world's population that lives in Africa and Asia.

Use a calculator with a fraction key.

Press: **3** / **5** + **1** / **8** =

Display: **29/40**

$\frac{29}{40}$ of the world's population lives in Asia and Africa.

Example 5

Use a calculator with a fraction key to determine each answer in fraction form:

a) $\frac{5}{6} + \frac{2}{7}$ **b)** $\frac{5}{6} - \frac{2}{7}$ **c)** $\frac{5}{6} \times \frac{2}{7}$ **d)** $\frac{5}{6} \div \frac{2}{7}$

Solution

a) Press: **5** / **6** + **2** / **7** = to display: **47/42**

Press: **Ab/c** to display **1 u 5/42**

$\frac{5}{6} + \frac{2}{7} = \frac{47}{42}$, or $1\frac{5}{42}$

b) Press: **5** / **6** − **2** / **7** = to display: **23/42**

$\frac{5}{6} - \frac{2}{7} = \frac{23}{42}$

c) Press: **5** / **6** × **2** / **7** = to display: **10/42**

Press: **Simp** = to display **5/21**

$\frac{5}{6} \times \frac{2}{7} = \frac{5}{21}$

d) Press: **5** / **6** ÷ **2** / **7** = to display: **35/12**

Press: **Ab/c** to display **2 u 11/12**

$\frac{5}{6} \div \frac{2}{7} = \frac{35}{12}$, or $2\frac{11}{12}$

Working with Mathematics

Something to talk about

1. **a)** From the table in *Example 1*, what was the total world population in 1992? From the map, what fraction of the population lived in Asia?

   b) Use your answers to part a to solve *Example 1* in a different way.

2. **a)** From the table in *Example 1*, what was the total population of North, Central, and South America?

   b) Use your answer to part a to solve *Example 2* in a different way.

3. In *Example 3*, the answer was needed only to the nearest hundredth.

   a) In the solution, do you think the fractions $\frac{5}{6}$ and $\frac{2}{7}$ could have been expressed to the nearest hundredth before you calculated? Try it to see if you get the same answers.

   b) Could the fractions have been expressed to the nearest thousandth before you calculated? Try it to see if you get the same answers.

4. Use your calculator to express the answers to *Example 5* in decimal form. Compare the results with the answers to *Example 3*.

5. If your calculator has a memory, how could you solve *Example 3* a different way?

Practice

6. Express each fraction in decimal form.

   a) $\frac{1}{2}$ **b)** $\frac{1}{4}$ **c)** $\frac{1}{5}$ **d)** $\frac{1}{10}$ **e)** $\frac{3}{4}$

   f) $\frac{3}{5}$ **g)** $\frac{4}{10}$ **h)** $\frac{4}{5}$ **i)** $\frac{7}{10}$ **j)** $\frac{2}{5}$

7. Use your calculator to express each answer in decimal form to the nearest hundredth.

   a) $\frac{1}{3}$ **b)** $\frac{5}{6}$ **c)** $\frac{3}{8}$ **d)** $\frac{2}{9}$ **e)** $\frac{2}{3}$

   f) $\frac{3}{11}$ **g)** $\frac{5}{7}$ **h)** $\frac{7}{12}$ **i)** $\frac{4}{13}$ **j)** $\frac{5}{9}$

8. Use your calculator to express each answer in decimal form to the nearest hundredth.

   a) $\frac{1}{2} + \frac{2}{7}$ **b)** $\frac{3}{5} - \frac{1}{6}$ **c)** $\frac{2}{3} \div \frac{3}{8}$

   d) $\frac{2}{7} \times \frac{5}{8}$ **e)** $\frac{3}{5} \times \frac{1}{6}$ **f)** $\frac{3}{11} + \frac{1}{10}$

   g) $\frac{5}{8} - \frac{3}{7}$ **h)** $\frac{3}{5} \div \frac{1}{6}$ **i)** $\frac{1}{3} \times \frac{6}{7}$

9. If you have a calculator with a fraction key, use it to obtain the answers to exercise 8 in fraction form.

Work together

10. Use your calculator to express each answer in decimal form to the nearest hundredth.

    a) $\frac{6}{7} + \frac{2}{9}$ **b)** $\frac{6}{7} - \frac{2}{9}$ **c)** $\frac{6}{7} \times \frac{2}{9}$

    d) $\frac{6}{7} \div \frac{2}{9}$ **e)** $\frac{4}{5} + \frac{2}{3}$ **f)** $\frac{3}{4} - \frac{1}{7}$

    g) $\frac{5}{6} \times \frac{2}{7}$ **h)** $\frac{2}{3} \div \frac{5}{6}$ **i)** $\frac{2}{7} \div \frac{3}{5}$

11. If you have a calculator with a fraction key, use it to obtain the answers to exercise 10 in fraction form.

12. The map gives the approximate population of each province or territory as a fraction of Canada's population. In 1994, the population of Canada was about 29 248 100. Use the information on the map to calculate the population of each province in 1994. Express your answers to the nearest thousand.

Population of Canada

Yukon $\frac{1}{982}$

Northwest Territories $\frac{1}{474}$

British Columbia $\frac{3}{25}$

Alberta $\frac{3}{32}$

Saskatchewan $\frac{1}{28}$

Manitoba $\frac{1}{25}$

Ontario $\frac{10}{27}$

Quebec $\frac{1}{4}$

Newfoundland & Labrador $\frac{1}{48}$

P.E.I. $\frac{1}{210}$

New Brunswick $\frac{1}{38}$

Nova Scotia $\frac{1}{30}$

13. **a)** What do you think the sum of the populations in exercise 12 should be?

   b) Do you think this sum would be exact or only approximate?

   c) Check your answer in two ways:
   i) by expressing the fractions in decimal form and adding the results
   ii) by adding the answers you obtained

14. What fraction of Canada's population lives in each region below? Express each answer in decimal form to the nearest hundredth.

   a) the Maritime Provinces

   b) the Prairie Provinces

On your own

15. Use your calculator to express each answer in decimal form to the nearest hundredth.

   a) $\frac{5}{8} + \frac{3}{7}$　　**b)** $\frac{5}{8} - \frac{3}{7}$　　**c)** $\frac{5}{8} \times \frac{3}{7}$

   d) $\frac{5}{8} \div \frac{3}{7}$　　**e)** $\frac{1}{6} + \frac{3}{8}$　　**f)** $\frac{2}{3} - \frac{1}{8}$

   g) $\frac{3}{4} \times \frac{5}{13}$　　**h)** $\frac{7}{9} \div \frac{3}{11}$　　**i)** $\frac{3}{4} \times \frac{7}{9}$

16. If you have a calculator with a fraction key, use it to obtain the answers to exercise 15 in fraction form.

17. **a)** Determine the saving on each item in the table.

   b) What is the sale price of each item?

Item	Regular price ($)	Reduction
Slacks	33.75	$\frac{1}{3}$ off
Jacket	78.50	$\frac{1}{2}$ off
Shirt	19.50	$\frac{2}{3}$ off
Shoes	45.95	$\frac{1}{5}$ off

DATA DISK

18. Open the *Olympic Winter Games* database on the data disk. Browse through the records.

   a) Find all the records for the three figure skating events included in the database. How many records are there?

   b) Sort the figure skating records in alphabetical order by winner's country. What fraction of the gold medals in the three events were won by each country? Sort the fractions from greatest to least.

19. The total area of the world's land is about 148 million km². Calculate the area of each region to the nearest million square kilometres.

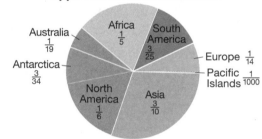
Approximate world land areas

Extend your thinking

20. We can express fractions in fraction form or in decimal form. Look at the problems in this section. What is a disadvantage of using the fraction form in applied problems? Is there a disadvantage of using the decimal form?

21. Find four different fractions that have a sum of 1.

The Ideas

If two or more fractions have the same denominator and different numerators, how can you tell which is the largest and which is the smallest? If two or more fractions have the same numerator and different denominators, how can you tell which is the largest and which is the smallest? Illustrate your answer with examples.

How Was the Inheritance Divided?

Here is a puzzle. Can you figure it out?

An elderly woman had 17 rings. Her will stipulated that upon her death the eldest daughter should receive one-half of her rings, the second daughter one-third, and the youngest daughter one-ninth. When the woman died, the three daughters tried as hard as they could, but they could not figure out a way to divide the 17 rings according to her wishes.

The daughters decided to ask their mother's wise old friend for help. "That's easy," she said. "Just borrow one of my rings. Include that one with your mother's rings when you divide them up. When you have finished, you will have one left over, and I'll take my ring back."

How many rings did each daughter receive?

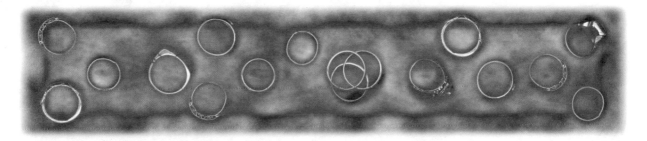

Understand the problem

- Why did the three daughters have trouble dividing up the 17 rings?
- What are you asked to do?

Think of a strategy

- Work out the arithmetic, following the wise woman's suggestion.

Carry out the strategy

- When the wise woman's ring was included, how many rings were there to be divided?
- How many of these should the eldest daughter receive? The second daughter? The youngest daughter?

Look back

- Why is it possible to solve the puzzle by adding one ring, then taking it away later?
- Add the three fractions $\frac{1}{2}$, $\frac{1}{3}$, and $\frac{1}{9}$. Do you see why the puzzle works?
- Create another problem like this one using 7 rings instead of 17 rings.

Communicating the Ideas

In your journal, describe how you decided how many rings each daughter should receive.

Fractions and Musical Notes

To create a piano score, a composer uses whole notes and fractions of notes.

whole $\dfrac{1}{2}$ $\dfrac{1}{4}$ $\dfrac{1}{8}$ $\dfrac{1}{16}$

The musician must understand fractions and operations with fractions to produce the rhythm and sound that the composer intended.

The skills we learn when studying fractions, especially addition of fractions and equivalent fractions, are useful in understanding music.

A *note tree* shows the relationships among the values of the notes.

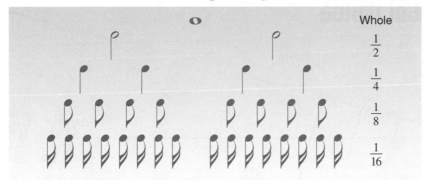

is equal in value to: $\frac{1}{2}$ $\frac{1}{2}$ or $\frac{1}{4}$ $\frac{1}{4}$ $\frac{1}{4}$ $\frac{1}{4}$

1. Write two notes that have the same value as each note.

a)   b)   c)

2. ♪♪ are often written, and ♪♪ are written

Write one note that has the same value as each group of notes.

a)   b)   c)   d)   e)   f)

3. In $\frac{4}{4}$ time, the sum of the values of the notes in a bar is 1.

List the note or notes that would complete each bar.

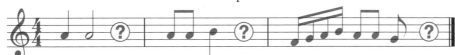

4. In $\frac{3}{4}$ time, the sum of the values of the notes in a bar is $\frac{3}{4}$.

List the note or notes that would complete each bar.

5. In $\frac{6}{8}$ time, the sum of the values of the notes in a bar is $\frac{3}{4}$.

List the note or notes that would complete each bar.

Mathematics & Music

Linking Ideas

2.2 ADDING AND SUBTRACTING FRACTIONS IN FRACTION FORM

Developing the Ideas

▶ ▶ *Through Instruction*

Consider adding the fractions $\frac{1}{4}$ and $\frac{1}{3}$. You can use the twelfths line to complete the addition.

On the twelfths line: $\frac{1}{4}$ is represented by $\frac{1 \times 3}{4 \times 3}$, or $\frac{3}{12}$

$\frac{1}{3}$ is represented by $\frac{1 \times 4}{3 \times 4}$, or $\frac{4}{12}$

We write …

$$\frac{1}{4} + \frac{1}{3} = \frac{1 \times 3}{4 \times 3} + \frac{1 \times 4}{3 \times 4}$$
$$= \frac{3}{12} + \frac{4}{12}$$
$$= \frac{7}{12}$$

Consider subtracting $\frac{4}{3} - \frac{3}{4}$. You can use the twelfths line to do the subtraction.

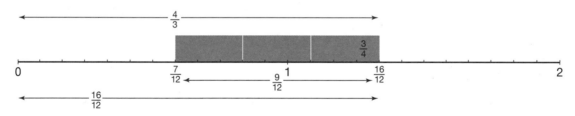

On the twelfths line: $\frac{4}{3}$ is represented by $\frac{4 \times 4}{3 \times 4}$, or $\frac{16}{12}$

$\frac{3}{4}$ is represented by $\frac{3 \times 3}{4 \times 3}$, or $\frac{9}{12}$

We write …

$$\frac{4}{3} - \frac{3}{4} = \frac{4 \times 4}{3 \times 4} - \frac{3 \times 3}{4 \times 3}$$
$$= \frac{16}{12} - \frac{9}{12}$$
$$= \frac{7}{12}$$

You discovered previously that when you add or subtract fractions, the fractions must have the same denominator. If the denominators are not the same, first express the fractions as equivalent fractions with the same denominator.

Example 1

Add: $\frac{2}{5} + \frac{4}{5}$

Solution

The denominators are the same. Add the numerators.

$$\frac{2}{5} + \frac{4}{5} = \frac{6}{5}$$

Example 2

Add: $\frac{1}{2} + \frac{7}{10}$

Solution

Express the first fraction with denominator 10.

$$\frac{1}{2} + \frac{7}{10} = \frac{1 \times 5}{2 \times 5} + \frac{7}{10}$$
$$= \frac{5}{10} + \frac{7}{10}$$
$$= \frac{12}{10}, \text{ or } \frac{6}{5}$$

In *Example 2*, the denominators of the fractions are 2 and 10. Notice that the second denominator is a multiple of the first. It is easy to express both fractions with denominator 10. In the next example, neither denominator is a multiple of the other.

Example 3

Subtract: $\frac{7}{6} - \frac{3}{4}$

Solution

The multiples of 6 are: 6, **12**, 18, 24, …

The multiples of 4 are: 4, 8, **12**, 16, 20, 24, …

The *least common multiple* of 6 and 4 is 12 since it is the smallest number that appears in both lists.

Express both fractions with denominator 12.

$$\frac{7}{6} - \frac{3}{4} = \frac{7 \times 2}{6 \times 2} - \frac{3 \times 3}{4 \times 3}$$
$$= \frac{14}{12} - \frac{9}{12}$$
$$= \frac{5}{12}$$

Working with Mathematics

Something to talk about

1. a) In *Example 2*, what other denominators could have been used? Why was the denominator 10 chosen?

   b) In *Example 3*, what other denominators could have been used? Why was the denominator 12 chosen?

2. When you add or subtract two fractions, do you always have to change both denominators?

Practice

3. Add.

   a) $\frac{1}{2} + \frac{1}{2}$ b) $\frac{1}{4} + \frac{1}{4}$ c) $\frac{1}{5} + \frac{4}{5}$

   d) $\frac{1}{10} + \frac{7}{10}$ e) $\frac{3}{8} + \frac{5}{8}$ f) $\frac{3}{4} + \frac{3}{4}$

   g) $\frac{9}{7} + \frac{5}{7}$ h) $1\frac{1}{3} + 2\frac{1}{3}$ i) $1\frac{3}{5} + \frac{2}{5}$

4. Subtract.

   a) $\frac{2}{3} - \frac{1}{3}$ b) $\frac{5}{6} - \frac{1}{6}$ c) $\frac{7}{8} - \frac{3}{8}$

   d) $\frac{8}{9} - \frac{2}{9}$ e) $\frac{5}{3} - \frac{2}{3}$ f) $\frac{14}{11} - \frac{3}{11}$

   g) $\frac{10}{7} - \frac{2}{7}$ h) $1\frac{11}{12} - \frac{5}{12}$ i) $2\frac{9}{10} - 1\frac{1}{10}$

5. Add or subtract.

   a) $\frac{1}{2} + \frac{1}{4}$ b) $\frac{4}{5} - \frac{3}{10}$ c) $\frac{2}{3} + \frac{1}{6}$

   d) $\frac{8}{9} - \frac{2}{3}$ e) $\frac{3}{4} + \frac{3}{8}$ f) $2\frac{4}{9} + \frac{1}{3}$

   g) $3\frac{7}{10} - \frac{2}{5}$ h) $1\frac{5}{12} + \frac{1}{3}$ i) $2\frac{7}{8} - \frac{1}{4}$

6. Simplify.

   a) $\frac{1}{2} + \frac{1}{2} + \frac{3}{2}$ b) $\frac{1}{3} + \frac{2}{3} + \frac{1}{3}$

   c) $\frac{11}{12} - \frac{7}{12} - \frac{1}{12}$ d) $\frac{9}{10} - \frac{3}{10} - \frac{1}{10}$

Work together

7. Add.

   a) $\frac{2}{7} + \frac{4}{7}$ b) $\frac{1}{6} + \frac{3}{6}$ c) $\frac{2}{3} + \frac{1}{9}$

   d) $\frac{1}{6} + \frac{1}{3}$ e) $\frac{3}{16} + \frac{5}{8}$ f) $\frac{1}{12} + \frac{5}{4}$

   g) $\frac{3}{5} + \frac{1}{2}$ h) $2\frac{3}{4} + \frac{4}{3}$ i) $1\frac{3}{5} + 3\frac{2}{3}$

8. Subtract.

   a) $\frac{4}{5} - \frac{1}{5}$ b) $\frac{7}{9} - \frac{4}{9}$ c) $\frac{5}{6} - \frac{2}{3}$

   d) $\frac{9}{8} - \frac{1}{4}$ e) $\frac{10}{7} - \frac{5}{14}$ f) $\frac{9}{10} - \frac{9}{20}$

   g) $\frac{3}{5} - \frac{6}{25}$ h) $4\frac{1}{4} - \frac{1}{5}$ i) $2\frac{5}{6} - 1\frac{5}{8}$

9. Simplify.

   a) $\frac{1}{2} + \frac{1}{4} + \frac{1}{8}$ b) $\frac{1}{2} + \frac{2}{3} + \frac{3}{4}$

   c) $\frac{11}{15} - \frac{2}{3} + \frac{1}{5}$ d) $\frac{9}{10} - \frac{2}{5} - \frac{1}{6}$

10. Copy and complete each line of this pattern, writing each sum in decimal form. Include the next two lines in your pattern.

$$\frac{1}{10} = \blacksquare$$

$$\frac{1}{10} + \frac{1}{100} = \blacksquare$$

$$\frac{1}{10} + \frac{1}{100} + \frac{1}{1000} = \blacksquare$$

11. These portions of each type of large pizza remained after a class party: $\frac{1}{2}, \frac{3}{4}, \frac{3}{8}, \frac{1}{4}$, and $2\frac{1}{2}$. One pizza fits in each box. What is the smallest number of pizza boxes needed to store the leftover pizza?

On your own

12. Add.

   a) $\frac{1}{8} + \frac{3}{8}$ b) $\frac{2}{6} + \frac{7}{6}$ c) $\frac{2}{15} + \frac{3}{5}$

   d) $\frac{5}{21} + \frac{4}{7}$ e) $\frac{5}{18} + \frac{1}{2}$ f) $\frac{4}{15} + \frac{4}{3}$

   g) $\frac{1}{10} + \frac{2}{5}$ h) $5\frac{1}{6} + 3\frac{3}{4}$ i) $\frac{9}{10} + 6\frac{3}{4}$

13. Subtract.

   a) $\frac{7}{8} - \frac{1}{8}$ b) $\frac{11}{12} - \frac{5}{12}$ c) $\frac{9}{10} - \frac{3}{5}$

   d) $\frac{13}{18} - \frac{1}{3}$ e) $3 - \frac{5}{6}$ f) $\frac{5}{4} - \frac{3}{8}$

   g) $\frac{17}{25} - \frac{2}{3}$ h) $7\frac{8}{9} - 2\frac{5}{6}$ i) $2\frac{3}{5} - \frac{3}{8}$

14. Add or subtract.

   a) $\frac{3}{4} + \frac{1}{5}$ b) $\frac{5}{18} + \frac{2}{3}$ c) $\frac{14}{15} - \frac{1}{2}$

   d) $\frac{13}{12} + \frac{5}{8}$ e) $\frac{7}{6} - \frac{3}{4}$ f) $\frac{7}{27} + \frac{5}{9}$

   g) $\frac{11}{12} - \frac{5}{9}$ h) $\frac{1}{4} - \frac{2}{15}$ i) $\frac{13}{10} - \frac{2}{3}$

15. Simplify.

   a) $\frac{1}{2} + \frac{1}{3} + \frac{1}{6}$ b) $\frac{9}{10} - \frac{2}{5} + \frac{5}{4}$

   c) $\frac{9}{4} + \frac{5}{6} - \frac{2}{3}$ d) $\frac{5}{6} + \frac{4}{3} - \frac{7}{8}$

16. a) Which of these products uses the greatest fraction of wood cut?

Forestry consumption	
Product	Fraction of total wood cut
Lumber	$\frac{1}{10}$
Pulp and paper	$\frac{1}{4}$
Veneer and plywood	$\frac{2}{5}$

b) What fraction of the total wood cut is used by these three products together?

c) What total fraction do other products consume?

17. a) What fraction of those surveyed preferred each subject?

i) drama   ii) action   iii) comedy

b) What is the difference between the fraction who preferred comedy and the fraction who preferred westerns?

c) What fraction did not prefer:

i) westerns?   ii) action and comedy?

d) Which combinations of movies were preferred by each following fraction of those surveyed?

i) $\frac{3}{4}$ ii) $\frac{2}{3}$ iii) $\frac{1}{3}$

Movie preferences

18. Diane's chocolate bar had 12 equal sections. She ate 2 sections. Her brother ate 6 sections. What fraction of the bar did each person eat? What fraction remained?

19. Before lunch, the recycle bin was about $\frac{1}{4}$ full. After lunch, it was about $\frac{7}{8}$ full.

a) What fraction of the bin was empty before lunch? After lunch?

b) What fraction of the bin was filled during lunch?

20. The Lui family started a trip with the fuel gauge reading $\frac{3}{4}$ full. After 5 h, the gauge read $\frac{1}{8}$ full. What fraction of a tank was used?

21. A pitcher of milk is half full. After one-half of a litre of milk is added, the pitcher is three-quarters full. How much milk does the pitcher hold when it is full?

Extend your thinking

22. Each fraction in the triangle is equal to the sum of the two nearest fractions in the line below.

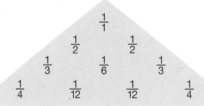

a) Check that the third and fourth rows of the triangle are correct.

b) What are the first and last fractions in the fifth row of the triangle?

c) Complete the fifth row of the triangle.

COMMUNICATING

The Ideas

Tanya's teacher asked her to add the fractions $\frac{1}{2}$ and $\frac{2}{3}$. She thought that she could do this by adding the numerators and adding the denominators. Her answer was $\frac{3}{5}$.

a) How could you convince Tanya that this answer is not correct?

b) In your journal, write an explanation of how to add $\frac{1}{2}$ and $\frac{2}{3}$. Be sure to include a reason why your method works.

2.3 USING PATTERNS TO MULTIPLY WITH DECIMALS

Developing the Ideas

▶ ▶ *Through Activities*

ACTIVITY 1

1. You can use patterns to multiply by 10, 100, 1000, and so on. Copy and complete these patterns.

   a) $2.8 \times 10 =$ ■
       $2.8 \times 100 =$ ■
       $2.8 \times 1000 =$ ■
       $2.8 \times 10\ 000 =$ ■

   b) $3.67 \times 10 =$ ■
       $3.67 \times 100 =$ ■
       $3.67 \times 1000 =$ ■
       $3.67 \times 10\ 000 =$ ■

2. You can also use patterns to multiply by 0.1, 0.01, 0.001, and so on. Copy and complete these patterns.

   a) $2.8 \times 0.1 =$ ■
       $2.8 \times 0.01 =$ ■
       $2.8 \times 0.001 =$ ■
       $2.8 \times 0.0001 =$ ■

   b) $3.67 \times 0.1 =$ ■
       $3.67 \times 0.01 =$ ■
       $3.67 \times 0.001 =$ ■
       $3.67 \times 0.0001 =$ ■

3. **a)** When you multiply a number by 10, 100, 1000, 10 000, and so on, is the product larger or smaller than the original number?

   b) When you multiply a number by 0.1, 0.01, 0.001, 0.0001, and so on, is the product larger or smaller than the original number?

4. How can your answers to exercises 1 to 3 help you multiply numbers by 10, 100, 1000, 10 000, or by 0.1, 0.01, 0.001, 0.0001?

5. Multiply.

   a) 5.7×10 **b)** 61.34×100 **c)** 72×0.01 **d)** $87\ 400 \times 0.1$

ACTIVITY 2

1. **a)** Copy and complete this pattern.

   $15 \times 360 =$ ■
   $15 \times 36 =$ ■
   $15 \times 3.6 =$ ■
   $15 \times 0.36 =$ ■

   b) How does the second number in each line compare with the second number in the line above it?

   c) How does the product in each line compare with the product in the line above it?

2. **a)** Copy and complete this pattern.

$150 \times 36 = \blacksquare$

$15 \times 36 = \blacksquare$

$1.5 \times 36 = \blacksquare$

$0.15 \times 36 = \blacksquare$

   b) How does the first number in each line compare with the first number in the line above it?

   c) How does the product in each line compare with the product in the line above it?

3. **a)** Multiply 42×23. Does the result seem reasonable? Explain.

   b) Consider the product 4.2×23.

   i) How does this compare with the product in part a?

   ii) Use your answer in part a to determine the product 4.2×23. Does the result seem reasonable? Explain.

   c) Consider the product 4.2×2.3.

   i) How does this compare with the product in part b?

   ii) Use your answer in part b to determine the product 4.2×2.3. Does the result seem reasonable? Explain.

4. Multiply to determine the first product. Use your answer to determine the other two products.

   a) $46 \times 18, 4.6 \times 18, 4.6 \times 1.8$

   b) $125 \times 32, 125 \times 3.2, 12.5 \times 3.2$

▶▶ *Through Guided Examples*

Example 1 ....

Christa has a part-time job that pays $6.75/h. She usually works 15 h a week.

a) What are her weekly earnings? Use estimation to check your answer.

b) One week Christa works only 9.5 h. What are her earnings that week?

Solution

a) Since Christa earns $6.75 in 1 h, multiply 6.75 by 15.

First estimate. This will help place the decimal point in the correct place.

If she earns $6/h, in 15 h she earns $6 \times 15 = \$90$.

If she earns $7/h, in 15 h she earns $7 \times 15 = \$105$.

The amount she earns per hour is between $6 and $7, and closer to $7.

So, the answer is between $90 and $105, and closer to $105.

Now, multiply 6.75×15. Follow the steps on the next page.

<table>
<tr><td>

Step 1

Multiply as with whole numbers.

$$
\begin{array}{r}
675 \\
\times\ 15 \\
\hline
3375 \\
6750 \\
\hline
10125
\end{array}
$$

</td><td>

Step 2

Place the decimal point in the product.

$$
\begin{array}{r}
6.75 \quad \leftarrow \text{2 decimal places} \\
\times\ 15 \quad \leftarrow \text{0 decimal places} \\
\hline
3375 \\
6750 \\
\hline
101.25 \quad \leftarrow \begin{array}{l}\text{2 decimal places}\\\text{in the product}\end{array}
\end{array}
$$

</td></tr>
</table>

In one week, Christa earns $101.25. This is reasonable since it is close
to our estimate.

b) First estimate. This will help place the decimal point in the correct place.

If she works 10 h, she earns $6.75 \times 10 = \$67.50$.

The answer is close to, but less than, $67.50.

Now, multiply 6.75 by 9.5.

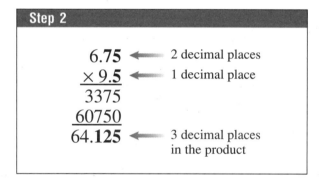

<table>
<tr><td>

Step 1

$$
\begin{array}{r}
675 \\
\times\ 95 \\
\hline
3375 \\
60750 \\
\hline
64125
\end{array}
$$

</td><td>

Step 2

$$
\begin{array}{r}
6.75 \quad \leftarrow \text{2 decimal places} \\
\times\ 9.5 \quad \leftarrow \text{1 decimal place} \\
\hline
3375 \\
60750 \\
\hline
64.125 \quad \leftarrow \begin{array}{l}\text{3 decimal places}\\\text{in the product}\end{array}
\end{array}
$$

</td></tr>
</table>

In that week, Christa earns $64.13. This is reasonable since it is close
to our estimate.

Example 2 ....

At the bulk food store, Halloween caramels cost $6.49 per kilogram.
Bruce has $14.00 and wants to purchase 1.75 kg of caramels.

a) Estimate to check whether Bruce has enough money.

b) Calculate the cost of 1.75 kg of caramels.

Solution

a) 1.75 kg of caramels cost 6.49×1.75.
Round both numbers up: $\$6.50 \times 2 = \$13.00$.
2 kg of caramels cost less than $13.00.
So, Bruce has enough money.

b) Use a calculator to multiply 6.49 by 1.75.
Press: **6.49** $\boxed{\times}$ **1.75** $\boxed{=}$ to display **11.3575**
The caramels cost $11.36.

Working with Mathematics

Something to talk about

1. Suppose 24.5 is multiplied by each number below. Which products are *less* than 24.5?
   a) 10   b) 0.1   c) 0.01
   d) 1000   e) 0.001   f) 100

2. Use estimation to determine where the decimal point is in each product.

   a)   6.48   b)   16.82
      $\times\ \ 22$ $\times\ \ \ 47$
       14256   79054

   c)   79.3   d)   8.78
      $\times\ 8.4$ $\times\ 9.6$
       66612   84288

   e)   48.7   f)   139.2
      $\times\ 0.35$ $\times\ 0.04$
       17045   5568

3. Estimate which products are:
   a) greater than 2000
   b) less than 1000

   Use a calculator to check your estimates.
   i) 95×42 ii) 58×34
   iii) 26×32 iv) 45.2×33
   v) 225×9.8 vi) 38.96×2.4
   vii) 14.8×96.5 viii) 41.2×4.16

4. Compare the method of multiplying in *Example 1* with the method of multiplying in *Activity 1*, exercise 5, page 120. In what ways are they similar? In what ways are they different?

Practice

5. Multiply.
   a) 5.7×10 b) 61.34×100
   c) 72×0.01 d) $87\,400 \times 0.1$
   e) 4.25×1000 f) 0.87×10
   g) 35×0.001 h) 0.25×0.01
   i) 48×100 j) 12.43×1000
   k) 6.3×0.1 l) 53×0.001
   m) 2.38×10 n) 0.75×100
   o) 1.29×0.01 p) 0.45×0.001

6. Multiply to determine the first product. Use the answer to determine the other two products.
   a) $51 \times 18, 5.1 \times 18, 5.1 \times 1.8$
   b) $136 \times 32, 136 \times 3.2, 13.6 \times 3.2$
   c) $39 \times 12, 3.9 \times 12, 3.9 \times 1.2$
   d) $247 \times 21, 247 \times 2.1, 24.7 \times 2.1$
   e) $64 \times 178, 6.4 \times 178, 6.4 \times 17.8$
   f) $205 \times 11, 20.5 \times 11, 20.5 \times 1.1$
   g) $84 \times 47, 84 \times 4.7, 8.4 \times 4.7$

7. Determine the missing number.
   a) $7.34 \times \blacksquare = 73.4$
   b) $0.374 \times \blacksquare = 374$
   c) $4.29 \times \blacksquare = 0.0429$
   d) $137.8 \times \blacksquare = 137.8$
   e) $25.6 \times \blacksquare = 0.0256$
   f) $85.04 \times \blacksquare = 8.504$

8. Suppose each number below is multiplied by 64.8. Which products are *greater* than 64.8?
   a) 1.23   b) 0.3   c) 1.03
   d) 0.0016   e) 0.18   f) 0.97

9. Pluto orbits the sun at a speed of 4.66 km/s. Mercury's speed is about 10 times as great. What is Mercury's speed?

10. The diameter of Saturn, the second largest planet, is about 120 000 km. The diameter of Venus is about 0.1 times that of Saturn. What is the diameter of Venus?

11. To find food, a giant anteater flicks its long tongue into an insect nest about 2.5 times a second. How many times would it flick its tongue in 10 s? In 100 s?

Work together

12. From the six numbers given below, find two with a product closest to:
    a) 10   b) 20   c) 30

7.9	6.3	3.8
8.8	2.8	7.2

13. Estimate each product. Use a calculator to check your estimates.

a) $2.20
× 58

b) $4.30
× 91.1

c) $5.75
× 7.36

d) $7.12
× 94.3

e) $9.44
× 8.07

f) $19.62
× 3.25

14. Multiply.

a) 5.15
× 16

b) 4.20
× 24

c) 7.90
× 0.7

d) 9.75
× 5.6

e) 22.4
× 0.37

f) 43.75
× 6.5

15. Certain lichens in Alaska grow only 3.4 mm in 100 years. At this rate, how much would they grow in 1000 years?

16. Fred earns $5.85/h cutting grass. How much will he earn in 3.5 h? Use estimation to check your answer.

17. The cost of painting a median line on a highway is $82.50/km. The highway distance from Calgary to Edmonton is 301.3 km. Calculate the cost of painting a median line on this highway. Use estimation to check your answer.

18. Electrical wire costs $0.29 per metre. Hong has $3.00. She wants to purchase 7.25 m of wire.
a) Estimate to check whether Hong has enough money.
b) Calculate the cost of 7.25 m of wire.

19. Each issue of the monthly magazine *Computer Games* sells for $4.75. A one-year subscription costs $38.50.
a) How much would you save in one year by buying a subscription?

b) Do you think it would be a good idea to buy a subscription? Explain your answer.

20. Sarah is making a quilt. She has purchased the supplies listed below. Calculate the total cost of the supplies, before tax.

Fabric	
1.2 m at $9.99/m	1 bag of stuffing at $6.98
2.2 m at $5.99/m	
2.8 m at $3.99/m	3 spools of thread at $0.89 each
8.8 m at $4.99/m	

On your own

21. Multiply.
a) 8.3×1.6
b) 94.2×12
c) 53.5×1.2
d) 0.97×6.4
e) 768×1.5
f) 24.6×4.3
g) 1.29×0.6
h) 0.59×3.7

22. From the numbers given, choose the most reasonable estimate for each product.

50	300	600	1300

a) 317.4
× 1.9

b) 58.37
× 0.87

c) 68.37
× 17.5

d) 70.93
× 4.22

e) 74.1
× 8.3

f) 105.8
× 12.7

23. Bones make up 0.18 of our body mass. Dimitri's mass is 58.3 kg. What is the mass of his bones? Use estimation to check your answer.

24. Potatoes cost $1.69 per kilogram. Amanda has $5.00. She wants to purchase a 3.25-kg bag of potatoes.
a) Estimate to check whether Amanda has enough money.
b) Calculate the cost of a 3.25-kg bag of potatoes.

25. There are 24 grapefruit in a box. The mass of the empty box is 1.75 kg. The average mass of one grapefruit is 0.35 kg. Calculate the total mass of the box packed with grapefruit. Use estimation to check your answer.

26. Calculate the cost of building a fence around the pool at $15.75/m. Use estimation to check your answer.

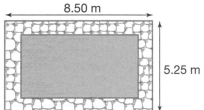

8.50 m

5.25 m

27. Bamboo is the fastest growing plant in the world. Some species grow up to 0.91 m per day. At this rate, how much would a plant grow in 1 year? Why do you think bamboo plants do not reach such heights?

Extend your thinking

28. A ball is dropped from a height of 2.30 m. After each bounce, it reaches 0.40 of its height before the bounce.

   a) What height does it reach after each of the first four bounces?

   b) After how many bounces does the ball reach a height of about 1 cm?

29. In the women's 100-m world-class hurdle competition, the first hurdle is 13 m from the starting line. The remaining 9 hurdles are 8.5 m apart.

   a) What is the distance between the last hurdle and the finishing line?

   b) Why do you think the distance from the starting line to the first hurdle is greater than the distances between the other hurdles?

COMMUNICATING

The Ideas

Two numbers are multiplied to form a product. Suppose one of the numbers is divided by 10 and the numbers are multiplied again. What happens to the product? What happens if both of the numbers are divided by 10? Answer these questions in your journal. Illustrate your answers with examples.

BOGGLE YOUR MIND

Prince Edward Island's oldest resident died on January 30, 1995. Baselice Gallant would have been 110 on March 25. She is survived by 8 of 14 children, 94 grandchildren, 205 great grandchildren and 89 great-great grandchildren. How many direct descendants does she have?

Forms of Answers

This article appeared in The Toronto Star in 1992. The letter on the right appeared a few days later.

Read the article and the letter.

Math quiz answer was improper

It was improper; the fraction, that is; the fraction that appeared last Monday purporting to be the correct answer in a test of Grade 8 arithmetic skills.

The test, according to the story, showed Ontario pupils in a bad light. The Star reprinted, from the Ministry of Education, a couple of questions on the test given to 20,000 pupils.

One of the questions was 3/4 + 2/3. There were multiple choices for the answer, with the correct choice, according to the ministry, 17/12.

The Star that day was delivered to a grade 8 class in a local school. The pupils saw the front page that suggested they didn't know math and they spotted what to them was a glaring error.

The 17/12 fraction was, in mathematical terms, an improper fraction, because it had not been reduced to a number and a fraction, i.e., 1 5/12.

Seven of the children wrote to Star Editor John Honderich. "An improper fraction ... cannot be a correct answer," wrote one student. "You cannot just leave an improper fraction like that. You have to change it to a mixed number."

Three equally valid answers can be given for math question.

Re The Star's Feb. 15 column and the alleged wrong answer to the sum 3/4 + 2/3. There are at least three different forms of the correct answer: the Ministry of Education's "improper" fraction, 17/12; the students' "corrected" version, 1 5/12; and any appropriate rounding of the decimal result, 1.41666 ...

Not one of these forms is in the slightest more or less correct than another. One or another form may be preferable in the context of its usage.

Thus, in measuring a piece of material, we would probably prefer the mixed fraction 1 5/12. If we were going to use the sum of 3/4 plus 2/3 in a multiplication or division next, the form 17/12 is preferred (indeed usually necessary). In most scientific applications, some approximation of the decimal result would be desirable.

Remember, kids: in arithmetic, as in the wider world, equally valid answers may show up wearing different faces. Welcome them all!

WALLACE KRAWCZYK
Professor
Mathematics and Electronics
Lambton College
Sarnia

1. **a)** How many different forms of the answer to $\frac{3}{4} + \frac{2}{3}$ are there according to:

    i) the Ministry of Education?   **ii)** the students?   **iii)** the letter?

   b) Show how you can obtain each form.

2. **a)** Write some examples to illustrate what Wallace Krawczyk means by "any appropriate rounding of the decimal result, 1.41666..."

   b) What does Krawczyk mean by "in the context of its usage"?

3. **a)** Why did the students think that the Ministry's answer was not correct?

   b) Do you think it is possible that the students' answer and the Ministry's answer are both correct? Explain.

   c) Is "1.41666..." correct?

   d) Are there other forms of the answer that are correct?

....2.4 MULTIPLYING WITH FRACTIONS

Developing the Ideas

▶▶ *Using Manipulatives*

You will need your fraction strips and number lines.

Multiplying a natural number by a fraction

You can use the meaning of multiplication to multiply a natural number by a fraction.

1. Consider the multiplication $3 \times \frac{2}{5}$.

   a) Use your green $\frac{2}{5}$-strip. Start at 0 on the fifths line. Count 3 groups of $\frac{2}{5}$ along the line.

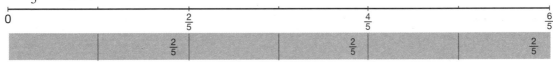

   Where do you get to? What is the answer to $3 \times \frac{2}{5}$?

   b) Determine each product in the same way.

   i) $2 \times \frac{2}{5}$ **ii)** $4 \times \frac{2}{5}$ **iii)** $5 \times \frac{2}{5}$

2. Use your fraction strips and number lines to multiply.

   a) $3 \times \frac{1}{3}$ **b)** $3 \times \frac{2}{3}$ **c)** $3 \times \frac{4}{3}$ **d)** $5 \times \frac{1}{3}$ **e)** $5 \times \frac{4}{3}$ **f)** $2 \times \frac{5}{3}$

▶▶ *Through Guided Examples*

Multiplying a fraction by a natural number or by a fraction

When you multiply with fractions you often encounter expressions such as $\frac{3}{4} \times 2$ and $\frac{4}{3} \times \frac{3}{4}$. To give meaning to these expressions we extend the definition of multiplication. Think of how we use fractions with time.

"I'll be $\frac{1}{2}$ an hour early." We think: $\frac{1}{2}$ *of* 60 min	"It'll take me $\frac{3}{4}$ of an hour to get there." We think: $\frac{3}{4}$ *of* 60 min

Separate 60 min into 2 equal parts. Each part is 30 min. Take 1 of the parts.

We write: $\frac{1}{2} \times 60$ min = 30 min

Separate 60 min into 4 equal parts. Each part is 15 min. Take 3 of the parts.

We write: $\frac{3}{4} \times 60$ min = 45 min

The following examples use these ideas to multiply $\frac{3}{4} \times 2$ and $\frac{4}{3} \times \frac{3}{4}$.

Example 1 ....

Multiply: $\frac{3}{4} \times 2$

Solution

We think: $\frac{3}{4}$ of 2

That is, separate 2 into 4 equal parts. $\frac{3}{4} \times 2$

Take 3 of the parts.

Look for a number line that has 2 separated into 4 equal parts.
Each part is $\frac{1}{2}$.

```
|-----------|-----------|-----------|-----------|
0           1/2         1           3/2         2
```

Take 3 of those parts.
We write: $\frac{3}{4} \times 2 = \frac{3}{2}$, or $1\frac{1}{2}$

Example 2 ....

Multiply: $\frac{1}{4} \times \frac{2}{3}$

Solution

We think: $\frac{1}{4}$ of $\frac{2}{3}$

That is, separate $\frac{2}{3}$ into 4 equal parts. $\frac{1}{4} \times \frac{2}{3}$
Take 1 of the parts.

Start with the blue $\frac{2}{3}$-strip. But it does not have 4 equal parts.

$\frac{2}{3}$

Replace it with an equivalent strip with 4 equal parts.
This is the purple $\frac{4}{6}$-strip.

$\frac{4}{6}$

Separate $\frac{4}{6}$ into 4 equal parts. Each part is $\frac{1}{6}$.

$\frac{1}{6}$

We write: $\frac{1}{4} \times \frac{2}{3} = \frac{1}{6}$

Example 3

Multiply: $\frac{4}{3} \times \frac{3}{4}$

Solution

We think: $\frac{4}{3}$ *of* $\frac{3}{4}$

That is, separate $\frac{3}{4}$ into 3 equal parts.  $\frac{4}{3} \times \frac{3}{4}$

Take 4 of the parts.

Start with the red $\frac{3}{4}$-strip.

$\boxed{ \frac{3}{4}}$

Separate $\frac{3}{4}$ into 3 equal parts. Each part is $\frac{1}{4}$.

$\boxed{\frac{1}{4}}$

Take 4 of those parts. They are equivalent to the white 1-strip.

$\boxed{}$

$\boxed{ 1}$

We write: $\frac{4}{3} \times \frac{3}{4} = 1$

We say that $\frac{4}{3}$ and $\frac{3}{4}$ are *reciprocals*.

BOGGLE YOUR MIND

From a pile of coins, Jamie took half the amount, and then put back 50¢.
He then took half of what was left, and put back 50¢ again.
Jamie again took half of what was left, and put back 50¢.
There was then $2 in the pile.
How much was in the pile at the beginning?

Example 4

Use a calculator to multiply: $\frac{3}{4} \times \frac{3}{2}$

Solution 1

Express each fraction in decimal form.

$\frac{3}{4} = 0.75 \qquad \frac{3}{2} = 1.5$

Use your calculator to multiply the decimals.

Press: .75 ⊠ 1.5 ⊟

Display: **1.125**

We write: $\frac{3}{4} \times \frac{3}{2} = 1.125$

Solution 2

Use a calculator with a fraction key.

Press: 3 / 4 ⊠ 3 / 2 ⊟

Display: **9/8**

Press: Ab/c to display: **1 u 1/8**

We write: $\frac{3}{4} \times \frac{3}{2} = \frac{9}{8}$, or $1\frac{1}{8}$

BOGGLE YOUR MIND

The mass of a running shoe is 170 g plus
half the mass of the running shoe.
What is the mass of a pair of running shoes?

Working with Mathematics

Something to talk about

1. Why can't we use the first meaning of multiplication on page 127 to multiply $\frac{3}{4} \times 2$ and $\frac{4}{3} \times \frac{1}{2}$?

2. a) Without multiplying, decide if $\frac{3}{2} \times \frac{1}{2}$ is greater than $\frac{1}{2}$ or less than $\frac{1}{2}$. Also, decide if $\frac{3}{2} \times \frac{1}{2}$ is greater than $\frac{3}{2}$ or less than $\frac{3}{2}$.

    b) Which of these products is greater than $\frac{1}{2}$?

$$\frac{3}{5} \times \frac{1}{2} \qquad \frac{5}{4} \times \frac{1}{2} \qquad \frac{4}{5} \times \frac{1}{2}$$

    c) Which of these products is greater than $\frac{3}{2}$?

$$\frac{3}{2} \times \frac{3}{4} \qquad \frac{3}{2} \times \frac{3}{2} \qquad \frac{3}{2} \times \frac{1}{3}$$

Practice

3. Use your fraction strips and number lines to multiply.

    a) $\frac{1}{2} \times \frac{1}{4}$ **b)** $\frac{1}{3} \times \frac{1}{4}$ **c)** $\frac{3}{2} \times \frac{1}{4}$

    d) $\frac{1}{4} \times 2$ **e)** $\frac{1}{5} \times \frac{1}{2}$ **f)** $\frac{1}{3} \times 2$

    g) $\frac{1}{2} \times \frac{14}{8}$ **h)** $3 \times \frac{3}{5}$ **i)** $\frac{1}{2} \times \frac{1}{6}$

4. Use your fraction strips and number lines to multiply.

    a) $5 \times \frac{3}{8}$ **b)** $\frac{1}{6} \times 6$ **c)** $\frac{1}{12} \times 12$

    d) $\frac{3}{2} \times \frac{1}{5}$ **e)** $\frac{5}{4} \times \frac{1}{3}$ **f)** $\frac{6}{5} \times \frac{1}{2}$

    g) $\frac{1}{2} \times \frac{7}{6}$ **h)** $\frac{5}{3} \times \frac{1}{2}$ **i)** $\frac{3}{2} \times \frac{1}{6}$

Work together

5. Use your fraction strips and number lines to determine each answer. Then write the multiplication statement.

    a) $\frac{1}{4} \times \frac{1}{2}$ **b)** $\frac{1}{2} \times \frac{1}{2}$ **c)** $\frac{3}{4} \times \frac{1}{2}$

    d) $1 \times \frac{1}{2}$ **e)** $\frac{5}{4} \times \frac{1}{2}$ **f)** $\frac{3}{2} \times \frac{1}{2}$

6. Use your fraction strips and number lines to multiply.

    a) $3 \times \frac{1}{4}$ **b)** $\frac{2}{3} \times 2$ **c)** $\frac{2}{5} \times \frac{1}{2}$

    d) $\frac{1}{3} \times \frac{1}{2}$ **e)** $\frac{3}{2} \times \frac{2}{5}$ **f)** $\frac{4}{3} \times \frac{3}{4}$

7. In *Example 1* we found that $\frac{3}{4} \times 2 = \frac{3}{2}$. Two related multiplications are shown below.

$$\frac{3}{2} \times 2 \qquad \frac{3}{8} \times 2$$

    a) Which is greater than $\frac{3}{2}$? Why? What is the answer to this multiplication?

    b) Which is less than $\frac{3}{2}$? Why? What is the answer to this multiplication?

8. In *Example 2* we found that $\frac{1}{4} \times \frac{2}{3} = \frac{1}{6}$. Two related multiplications are shown below.

$$\frac{1}{4} \times \frac{1}{3} \qquad \frac{1}{4} \times \frac{4}{3}$$

    a) Which is greater than $\frac{1}{6}$? Why? What is the answer to this multiplication?

    b) Which is less than $\frac{1}{6}$? Why? What is the answer to this multiplication?

9. Use a calculator to multiply.

    a) $\frac{2}{5} \times \frac{3}{2}$ **b)** $\frac{3}{4} \times \frac{1}{2}$ **c)** $\frac{2}{3} \times \frac{1}{2}$

10. a) Use your fraction strips and number lines to multiply.

    i) $3 \times \frac{1}{3}$ **ii)** $\frac{1}{4} \times 4$ **iii)** $2 \times \frac{1}{2}$

    iv) $\frac{1}{10} \times 10$ **v)** $\frac{1}{8} \times 8$ **vi)** $5 \times \frac{1}{5}$

    b) Two numbers whose product is 1 are *reciprocals*. One number is the reciprocal of the other. List the reciprocals in part a.

11. Copy and complete a multiplication table like this. Describe any patterns you see.

×	$\frac{1}{4}$	$\frac{1}{2}$	$\frac{3}{4}$	1	$\frac{5}{4}$	$\frac{3}{2}$
$\frac{1}{4}$						
$\frac{1}{2}$						
$\frac{3}{4}$						
1						
$\frac{5}{4}$						
$\frac{3}{2}$						

12. In *Example 2*, why did we replace $\frac{2}{3}$ with the equivalent fraction $\frac{4}{6}$ and not the equivalent fraction $\frac{8}{12}$?

On your own

13. Cobs of corn are sold by the dozen. Customers who want less than one dozen cobs buy fractions of a dozen. How many cobs of corn are in each purchase?

 a) $\frac{1}{2}$ a dozen **b)** $\frac{1}{4}$ of a dozen

 c) $1\frac{1}{2}$ dozen **d)** $\frac{3}{4}$ of a dozen

 e) $\frac{2}{3}$ of a dozen **f)** $3\frac{1}{4}$ dozen

14. Use your fraction strips and number lines to determine each answer. Then write the multiplication statement.

 a) $\frac{1}{2} \times \frac{1}{3}$ **b)** $\frac{1}{2} \times \frac{2}{3}$ **c)** $\frac{1}{2} \times 1$

 d) $\frac{1}{2} \times \frac{4}{3}$ **e)** $\frac{1}{2} \times \frac{5}{3}$ **f)** $\frac{1}{2} \times 2$

15. In *Example 3* we found that $\frac{4}{3} \times \frac{3}{4} = 1$. Use this result to determine each product.

 a) $\frac{2}{3} \times \frac{3}{4}$ **b)** $\frac{8}{3} \times \frac{3}{4}$

16. In *Example 4* we found that $\frac{3}{4} \times \frac{3}{2} = 1\frac{1}{8}$, or $\frac{9}{8}$. Use this result to determine each product.

 a) $\frac{3}{2} \times \frac{3}{2}$ **b)** $\frac{3}{8} \times \frac{3}{2}$

17. a) Use your fraction strips and number lines to multiply.

 i) $\frac{5}{10} \times \frac{10}{5}$ **ii)** $\frac{3}{2} \times \frac{2}{3}$ **iii)** $\frac{4}{6} \times \frac{6}{4}$

 iv) $\frac{8}{5} \times \frac{5}{8}$ **v)** $\frac{6}{5} \times \frac{5}{6}$ **vi)** $\frac{4}{8} \times \frac{8}{4}$

 b) How would you describe each pair of numbers in part a? Explain your answer.

18. Use a calculator to multiply.

 a) $\frac{3}{4} \times \frac{5}{2}$ **b)** $\frac{3}{4} \times \frac{3}{5}$ **c)** $\frac{4}{3} \times \frac{3}{2}$

19. Find two fractions whose product is close to 1, but not equal to 1. Start a new document in a spreadsheet program.

 a) What formula should you type in cell C1 to multiply fractions in cells A1 and B1?

 b) Input two fractions. How close to 1 is their product?

 c) How can you get closer to 1?

TEMPLATE DISK

20. Cecile can walk to school in $\frac{3}{4}$ of an hour. She can ride her bike to school in $\frac{1}{3}$ of that time.

 a) What fraction of an hour does it take Cecile to ride her bike to school?

 b) How many minutes does it take Cecile to ride her bike to school?

Extend your thinking

21. Here is a different meaning for a product such as $\frac{2}{3} \times \frac{3}{4}$.

 Take 2 groups of $\frac{3}{4}$. $\frac{2}{3} \times \frac{3}{4}$

 Separate them into 3 equal parts. The product is one of these parts.

 a) Use manipulatives or a diagram to carry out the multiplication as indicated above. Is the result the same as it is using the second meaning of multiplication on page 127?

 b) Try the examples on pages 129 and 130 using this meaning of multiplication.

 c) Why does multiplication have two meanings?

22. Use your fraction strips and number lines to explain each statement.

 a) $4 \times \frac{2}{5} = \frac{2}{5} \times 4$ **b)** $\frac{3}{4} \times \frac{1}{2} = \frac{1}{2} \times \frac{3}{4}$

The Ideas

In your journal, explain what it means to multiply a fraction by a fraction. Use an example to illustrate your explanation.

2.5 MULTIPLYING FRACTIONS IN FRACTION FORM

Developing the Ideas

▶▶ Through an Activity

On page 128, you used fraction strips to multiply $\frac{1}{4}$ by $\frac{2}{3}$. You obtained the answer $\frac{1}{6}$. In this section, you will discover a pattern to multiply fractions without using the number lines and fraction strips.

Work in a group or with a partner.

1. Get the exercises and answers for exercises 5 and 6 on page 131.

2. Use number lines to multiply.

   a) $\frac{1}{2} \times \frac{1}{4}$ b) $\frac{1}{2} \times \frac{3}{5}$ c) $\frac{3}{2} \times \frac{2}{3}$

   d) $\frac{5}{3} \times \frac{3}{4}$ e) $\frac{5}{4} \times \frac{4}{5}$ f) $\frac{2}{3} \times \frac{2}{3}$

3. In each part of exercises 1 and 2, compare your answer with the numbers in the expression. Try to find a pattern that applies in every example. You can use the pattern to multiply fractions.

4. Use your pattern to determine each answer. Check your answer using the number lines.

   a) $\frac{1}{2} \times \frac{5}{6}$ b) $\frac{5}{2} \times \frac{3}{4}$ c) $\frac{5}{6} \times \frac{3}{4}$

▶▶ Through Guided Examples

You should have discovered this pattern for multiplying by a fraction.

The product of these two numbers ...   ... is the numerator of the result.

$$\frac{5}{2} \times \frac{3}{4} = \frac{15}{8}$$

The product of these two numbers ...   ... is the denominator of the result.

To multiply fractions, multiply the numerators and multiply the denominators.

Since any natural number can be written as a fraction with a denominator of 1, we can use this method to determine any product involving fractions.

Example 1

Multiply: $\frac{2}{9} \times \frac{5}{4}$

Solution

$$\frac{2}{9} \times \frac{5}{4} = \frac{2 \times 5}{9 \times 4}$$
$$= \frac{10}{36}$$
$$= \frac{5}{18}$$

Example 2

Multiply: a) $\frac{5}{2} \times 8$ b) $7 \times \frac{2}{3}$

Solution

a) $\frac{5}{2} \times 8 = \frac{5}{2} \times \frac{8}{1}$ b) $7 \times \frac{2}{3} = \frac{7}{1} \times \frac{2}{3}$

         $= \frac{40}{2}$ $= \frac{14}{3}$

         $= 20$

Working with Mathematics

Something to talk about

1. By expressing the fractions in decimal form, explain why $\frac{4}{5} \times \frac{3}{2} = \frac{12}{10}$.

2. "Multiplication makes numbers larger." Do you agree with this statement? Give examples to support your answer.

3. In *Example 1*, is the answer:
   a) greater than $\frac{5}{4}$ or less than $\frac{5}{4}$?
   b) greater than $\frac{2}{9}$ or less than $\frac{2}{9}$?

Practice

4. Multiply.
   a) $\frac{1}{7} \times \frac{1}{2}$ **b)** $\frac{2}{7} \times \frac{1}{2}$ **c)** $\frac{3}{7} \times \frac{1}{2}$
   d) $\frac{4}{7} \times \frac{1}{2}$ **e)** $\frac{5}{7} \times \frac{7}{5}$ **f)** $\frac{6}{7} \times \frac{1}{2}$
   g) $\frac{7}{7} \times \frac{1}{2}$ **h)** $\frac{8}{7} \times \frac{1}{2}$ **i)** $\frac{9}{7} \times \frac{1}{2}$

5. Multiply.
   a) $3 \times \frac{1}{3}$ **b)** $\frac{1}{2} \times \frac{2}{9}$ **c)** $\frac{7}{8} \times \frac{3}{7}$
   d) $\frac{8}{9} \times \frac{3}{8}$ **e)** $\frac{5}{3} \times \frac{2}{3}$ **f)** $\frac{1}{5} \times \frac{5}{2}$
   g) $\frac{5}{6} \times \frac{6}{5}$ **h)** $\frac{3}{4} \times \frac{8}{3}$ **i)** $\frac{5}{6} \times \frac{1}{10}$

6. Multiply.
   a) $\frac{1}{2} \times 2$ **b)** $\frac{10}{3} \times \frac{3}{10}$ **c)** $\frac{3}{2} \times \frac{1}{6}$
   d) $\frac{8}{3} \times \frac{3}{4}$ **e)** $\frac{5}{4} \times \frac{4}{10}$ **f)** $\frac{4}{9} \times \frac{9}{4}$
   g) $\frac{15}{2} \times \frac{2}{5}$ **h)** $\frac{11}{3} \times \frac{2}{11}$ **i)** $4 \times \frac{7}{8}$

Work together

7. Multiply.
   a) $\frac{1}{5} \times \frac{1}{4}$ **b)** $\frac{2}{5} \times \frac{1}{4}$ **c)** $\frac{3}{5} \times \frac{1}{4}$
   d) $\frac{4}{5} \times \frac{1}{4}$ **e)** $\frac{5}{5} \times \frac{1}{4}$ **f)** $\frac{6}{5} \times \frac{1}{4}$

8. Multiply.
   a) $\frac{2}{3} \times \frac{4}{3}$ **b)** $\frac{1}{8} \times \frac{4}{5}$ **c)** $\frac{3}{2} \times 6$
   d) $4 \times \frac{5}{8}$ **e)** $\frac{5}{6} \times \frac{2}{3}$ **f)** $\frac{3}{2} \times \frac{5}{2}$
   g) $\frac{1}{6} \times \frac{12}{7}$ **h)** $\frac{8}{5} \times \frac{3}{16}$ **i)** $\frac{7}{4} \times \frac{28}{35}$

9. **a)** Simplify each expression in this pattern.
   $$\frac{1}{2} = \blacksquare$$
   $$\frac{1}{2} \times \frac{2}{3} = \blacksquare$$
   $$\frac{1}{2} \times \frac{2}{3} \times \frac{3}{4} = \blacksquare$$
   b) Write the products for the next two rows.
   c) What is the product in the tenth row?

10. Use the information on pages 107 and 111. Canada's population is approximately $\frac{4}{61}$ of the population of North America.
    a) About what fraction of North America's population lives in each province?
    i) Quebec   **ii)** Saskatchewan   **iii)** Alberta
    b) About what fraction of the world's population lives in Canada?

11. Do a Big Mac and Fries cost the same everywhere in the world they are sold? With the *International Prices* database and your knowledge of fractions, you can find out.
    a) Open the database. Look at the record for Montreal for 1994.
    i) How many minutes did a person have to work to buy a Big Mac and Fries? What fraction of an hour is this?
    ii) What was the average hourly wage?
    iii) Use your answers to parts i and ii. How much did a Big Mac and Fries cost?
    b) Repeat part a for another city. How does the price compare to that in Montreal?

12. A sweater originally cost $30. It was on sale for $\frac{1}{3}$ off. The sweater was then tagged with: "Take $\frac{1}{2}$ off the lowest ticket price."
    a) How much did the sweater cost before it was tagged with this ticket?
    b) How much did the sweater cost after it was tagged?

13. Lauren had $\frac{2}{3}$ of a chocolate bar. She gave Harry $\frac{1}{4}$ of what she had.
    a) Did Harry receive more or less than one chocolate bar?
    b) Did Harry receive more or less than $\frac{1}{3}$ of the chocolate bar? Explain your answer.

DATA DISK

On your own

14. Multiply.

a) $\frac{3}{4} \times \frac{1}{3}$ b) $\frac{3}{4} \times \frac{2}{3}$ c) $\frac{3}{4} \times \frac{3}{3}$

d) $\frac{3}{4} \times \frac{4}{3}$ e) $\frac{3}{4} \times \frac{5}{3}$ f) $\frac{3}{4} \times \frac{6}{3}$

15. Multiply.

a) $\frac{1}{2} \times \frac{1}{2}$ b) $\frac{5}{6} \times \frac{3}{10}$ c) $\frac{2}{3} \times 5$

d) $3 \times \frac{11}{6}$ e) $\frac{3}{5} \times \frac{3}{5}$ f) $\frac{2}{7} \times \frac{9}{2}$

g) $\frac{5}{18} \times \frac{9}{10}$ h) $\frac{4}{5} \times \frac{25}{32}$ i) $\frac{3}{8} \times \frac{24}{21}$

16. Complete the multiplication exercises in exercises 10 and 15 on pages 111 and 112. Express the answers in fraction form. Compare your answers with those you obtained previously.

17. Determine.

a) $\frac{2}{3}$ of $15 b) $\frac{2}{3}$ of $21 c) $\frac{3}{4}$ of $16

d) $\frac{2}{5}$ of $62 e) $\frac{3}{5}$ of $48 f) $\frac{3}{10}$ of $125

18. a) Copy and complete each pattern.

i) $4 \times 6 = $ ■
$ 4 \times 3 = $ ■
$ 4 \times \frac{3}{2} = $ ■
$ 4 \times \frac{3}{4} = $ ■
$ 4 \times \frac{3}{8} = $ ■

ii) $4 \times \frac{3}{8} = $ ■
$ 2 \times \frac{3}{8} = $ ■
$ 1 \times \frac{3}{8} = $ ■
$ \frac{1}{2} \times \frac{3}{8} = $ ■
$ \frac{1}{4} \times \frac{3}{8} = $ ■

b) In the products in part a, how do the numbers that are multiplied change from one row to the next? How do the answers change from one row to the next?

c) Write the products for the next three rows.

19. About $\frac{5}{6}$ of the class participated in a Walk-A-Thon for charity. About $\frac{2}{5}$ of these people raised over $100 each.

a) What fraction of the class raised over $100?

b) What fraction of the class participated and raised less than $100?

20. a) Simplify each expression in this pattern.

$\frac{3}{2} = $ ■

$\frac{3}{2} \times \frac{4}{3} = $ ■

$\frac{3}{2} \times \frac{4}{3} \times \frac{5}{4} = $ ■

b) Write the products for the next two rows.

c) What is the product in the tenth row?

21. Dana took $\frac{2}{3}$ of her weekly allowance to the rock concert. She spent $\frac{3}{4}$ of her money on souvenirs. What fraction of her allowance did she spend on souvenirs?

22. Multiply.

a) $\frac{1}{2} \times \frac{1}{3} \times \frac{1}{4}$ b) $\frac{1}{2} \times \frac{2}{3} \times \frac{3}{4}$

c) $\frac{3}{2} \times \frac{4}{3} \times \frac{5}{4}$ d) $\frac{5}{4} \times \frac{8}{9} \times \frac{4}{5}$

e) $\frac{5}{4} \times \frac{1}{2} \times \frac{5}{4}$ f) $\frac{3}{2} \times \frac{3}{4} \times \frac{3}{8}$

Extend your thinking

23. a) Determine the products in this pattern. Write the products for the next three rows:

$\frac{1}{2} \times \frac{3}{2} = $ ■

$\frac{2}{3} \times \frac{4}{3} = $ ■

$\frac{3}{4} \times \frac{5}{4} = $ ■

b) Find as many patterns in the results as you can.

ᶜᴼᴹᴹᵁᴺᴵᶜᴬᵀᴵᴺᴳ

The Ideas

In your journal, explain why we can multiply two fractions by multiplying the numerators and multiplying the denominators. Explain why we cannot add two fractions by adding the numerators and adding the denominators.

Will You Ever Cut off All the String?

Cut a piece of string 1 m long. Cut it in half, and discard one piece. Cut the other piece in half, and discard one piece. Continue cutting in half and discarding one piece. If you continue doing this, will you ever cut off all the string?

Understand the problem

- What are you asked to do?

Think of a strategy

- At each step, keep track of the length of string cut off and of the total length of string cut off up to that time.
- Also keep track of the length of string that remains.
- Illustrate the results with graphs.

Carry out the strategy

- Make a table like the one below. Continue the table.

Step	Length of string cut off (m)	Total length cut off so far (m)	Length of string remaining (m)
Start	0	0	1
1			
2			
3			

- Use the data in your table to draw two graphs like these:

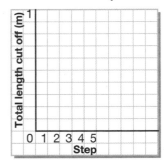

Look back

- How many cuts did you make to have less than 0.01 m of string remaining?
- How many cuts would you need to have less than 0.001 m of string remaining?
- One fibre of cotton in the string is about 0.0001 m across. Suppose you could continue cutting the string. How many cuts would you need to have this much string left?
- What would happen to the numbers in your table and to your graphs if you had started with a piece of string 2 m long? 3 m long? 4 m long? As long as your classroom?

Communicating the Ideas

In your journal, describe how you decided whether you would ever cut off all the string.

2.6 USING PATTERNS TO DIVIDE WITH DECIMALS

Developing the Ideas

▶▶ *Through Activities*

ACTIVITY 1

1. You can use patterns to divide by 10, 100, 1000, and so on. Copy and complete these patterns.

   a) $425 \div 10 = $ ■
   $425 \div 100 = $ ■
   $425 \div 1000 = $ ■
   $425 \div 10\ 000 = $ ■

   b) $18 \div 10 = $ ■
   $18 \div 100 = $ ■
   $18 \div 1000 = $ ■
   $18 \div 10\ 000 = $ ■

2. You can also use patterns to divide by 0.1, 0.01, 0.001, and so on. Copy and complete these patterns.

   a) $425 \div 0.1 = $ ■
   $425 \div 0.01 = $ ■
   $425 \div 0.001 = $ ■
   $425 \div 0.0001 = $ ■

   b) $18 \div 0.1 = $ ■
   $18 \div 0.01 = $ ■
   $18 \div 0.001 = $ ■
   $18 \div 0.0001 = $ ■

3. **a)** When you divide a number by 10, 100, 1000, and so on, is the quotient larger or smaller than the original number?
   b) When you divide a number by 0.1, 0.01, 0.001, and so on, is the quotient larger or smaller than the original number?

4. How can your answers to exercises 1 to 3 help you divide numbers by 10, 100, 1000, 10 000, or by 0.1, 0.01, 0.001, 0.0001?

5. Divide.
   a) $84 \div 10$ **b)** $425.3 \div 100$ **c)** $34 \div 0.01$ **d)** $43.5 \div 0.1$

ACTIVITY 2

1. **a)** Copy and complete this pattern.

   $\dfrac{800}{400} = $ ■

   $\dfrac{80}{40} = $ ■

   $\dfrac{8}{4} = $ ■

   $\dfrac{0.8}{0.4} = $ ■

   $\dfrac{0.08}{0.04} = $ ■

   b) Why are all the quotients in part a the same?

2. a) Use your calculator to divide.

$$\frac{810}{250} = \blacksquare$$

$$\frac{81}{25} = \blacksquare$$

$$\frac{8.1}{2.5} = \blacksquare$$

$$\frac{0.81}{0.25} = \blacksquare$$

b) Why are all the quotients in part a the same?

3. a) Divide. $48 \div 24$

b) Consider the expression $4.8 \div 2.4$.

   i) How does this compare with the expression in part a?

   ii) How should the quotient compare with the quotient in part a?

   iii) What is the quotient of $4.8 \div 2.4$? Does the result seem reasonable? Explain.

c) Consider the expression $0.48 \div 0.24$.

   i) How does this compare with the expression in part b?

   ii) How should the quotient compare with the quotient in part b?

   iii) What is the quotient of $0.48 \div 0.24$? Does the result seem reasonable? Explain.

4. Determine each quotient.

a) $36 \div 12, 360 \div 120, 3.6 \div 1.2$

b) $44 \div 8, 440 \div 80, 4.4 \div 0.8$

▷ ▶ *Through Guided Examples*

When we divide one number by another, the numbers are named as follows.

$$\text{Divisor} \longrightarrow 2.8 \overline{)11.67}$$

$$\text{Dividend} \underline{\hspace{4cm}}$$

In the preceding activities, you should have discovered that if we multiply both the divisor and the dividend by the same number we do not change the quotient. That is, the quotients of these two divisions are the same:

$$2.8 \overline{)11.67} \qquad 28 \overline{)116.7}$$

So, to divide a number by a decimal, we can always make the divisor a whole number.

Example 1

For the class barbecue, Jari bought 2.8 kg of ground beef for $11.67.
What was the cost per kilogram? Use estimation to check your answer.

Solution

To find out how much 1 kg costs, divide 11.67 by 2.8.

Step 1
Multiply divisor and dividend by 10 to make the divisor a whole number.

$$28 \overline{)116.7}$$

Step 2
Complete the division to 3 decimal places; add zeros to the dividend where necessary.

$$
\begin{array}{r}
4.167 \\
28 \overline{)116.700} \\
112 \downarrow \\
4\,7 \\
2\,8 \\
1\,90 \\
1\,68 \\
220 \\
196 \\
24
\end{array}
$$

The cost per kilogram was $4.17.

To check, think:
3 kg cost about $12.00.
1 kg would cost about $4.00.
So, $4.17 is reasonable.

Example 2

Andrea bought 1 CD priced at $12.95 and 3 equally priced tapes. The
total cost before tax was $33.20. How much did each tape cost? Check
by estimating.

Solution

Total cost of all items:	$33.20
Cost of the CD:	−$12.95
Cost of the 3 tapes:	$20.25

To determine the cost of 1 tape, divide by 3.
Use your calculator.

Cost of one tape: $\frac{\$20.25}{3} = \$6.75$

Check: 3 tapes at $7 cost:	$21
1 CD costs:	+$13
Total cost:	$34

Working with Mathematics

Something to talk about

1. Suppose 32.6 is divided by each number below. Which quotients are *greater* than 32.6?

   a) 10   **b)** 0.1   **c)** 0.01

   d) 1000   **e)** 0.001   **f)** 100

2. Estimate each quotient.

   a) $73.2 \div 7$ **b)** $79.6 \div 5$

   c) $330.2 \div 6$ **d)** $359.50 \div 8$

3. Compare the method of dividing in *Example 1* with the method of dividing in *Activity 2*, exercise 4, page 139. In what ways are they similar? In what ways are they different?

Practice

4. Divide.

   a) $6.5 \div 10$ **b)** $32.4 \div 100$

   c) $4.7 \div 0.1$ **d)** $2.34 \div 0.001$

   e) $85 \div 100$ **f)** $5.3 \div 1000$

   g) $29 \div 0.01$ **h)** $0.62 \div 0.1$

   i) $94 \div 10$ **j)** $94 \div 0.1$

   k) $94 \div 100$ **l)** $94 \div 0.01$

   m) $7 \div 10$ **n)** $2.3 \div 100$

   o) $4.2 \div 0.1$ **p)** $64.5 \div 0.01$

5. A package of 10 hockey cards costs $1.60. How much does each card cost?

6. Wilma Rudolph, who had polio as a child, set a women's world record in 1961. She ran 100 m in 11.2 s. At this speed, how long would it take her to run 1 m?

7. Johnny Weismuller, who played Tarzan in the movies, was one of the fastest swimmers of all time. He was the first man to swim 100 m in 58.6 s. At this speed, how long would it take him to swim 1 m?

8. Suppose 24 is divided by each number below. Which quotients are *greater* than 24?

   a) 3.2   **b)** 0.5   **c)** 1.08

   d) 0.02   **e)** 30.4   **f)** 0.98

9. Rewrite each division with a whole number divisor. Divide.

   a) $0.8\overline{)36.16}$ **b)** $0.13\overline{)1.131}$

   c) $3.4\overline{)66.64}$ **d)** $7.5\overline{)39.3}$

   e) $0.49\overline{)0.735}$ **f)** $5.3\overline{)6.466}$

Work together

10. Divide. Round each quotient to the nearest tenth.

    a) $0.7\overline{)12.52}$ **b)** $0.4\overline{)2.96}$

    c) $3.6\overline{)47.2}$ **d)** $7.1\overline{)9.228}$

11. Divide. Round each quotient to the nearest hundredth.

    a) $0.5\overline{)3.901}$ **b)** $0.6\overline{)26.45}$

    c) $2.3\overline{)2.81}$ **d)** $8.4\overline{)31.66}$

12. Li Yen has $4.62. How many tiger fish can she buy? Assume there is no sales tax. Use estimation to check your answer.

13. Eva saves $5.50 a week. About how many weeks will it take her to save enough to buy a bicycle that costs $149.50? Use estimation to check your answer.

14. To raise funds, winter carnival buttons were sold at $0.75 each. Three hundred eighty-four dollars were raised. How many buttons were sold?

15. Sue bought 1 tape priced at $4.95 and 3 equally priced CDs. The total cost before tax was $31.80. What was the cost of each CD? Use estimation to check your answer.

16. Fred bought 1 film priced at $5.95 and 4 batteries. The total cost before tax was $9.71. What was the cost of each battery?

17. There are 24 oranges in a box. The mass of the empty box is 1.75 kg. The total mass of the box packed with oranges is 8.47 kg. Calculate the average mass of an orange.

18. Four students are going on a camping trip. As well as their personal supplies, they will take the equipment listed below. They have agreed to divide the load so that each person carries about the same mass of equipment.

> • 2 tents ——— 2.42 kg each
> • 4 sleeping bags – 1.70 kg each
> • Stove + fuel ——1.65 kg
> • Cooking utensils 2.24 kg
> • Food ——— 5.95 kg
> • First aid kit and water filter 1.63 kg
> • Axe ————— 2.45 kg

a) What is the total mass of the equipment?

b) Suppose it were possible to divide the mass equally among the 4 students. How much would each student have to carry? Why might it not be possible to do this?

c) Try to determine 4 fair loads.

d) By the end of the trip, which supplies will have decreased in mass? What could the students do to redistribute the load at the end of the trip?

On your own

19. Divide.

a) $0.7\overline{)30.03}$ b) $0.6\overline{)7.518}$

c) $1.3\overline{)56.121}$ d) $2.6\overline{)144.82}$

e) $0.08\overline{)13.28}$ f) $2.3\overline{)9.499}$

g) $0.12\overline{)0.5436}$ h) $0.005\overline{)0.041\ 05}$

20. Divide. Round each quotient to 2 decimal places.

a) $15\overline{)0.645}$ b) $2.796 \div 2.4$

c) $0.4\overline{)0.155\ 35}$ d) $0.113\ 75 \div 1.2$

e) $3.924 \div 0.8$ f) $52 \div 0.15$

g) $1.895 \div 2.5$ h) $8.477 \div 0.09$

COMMUNICATING

The Ideas

Two numbers are divided to form a quotient. Suppose both numbers are multiplied by 10. What happens to the quotient? Answer this question in your journal, and illustrate your answers with examples.

21. Which two numbers in the box below have:

a) the greatest possible quotient?

b) the least possible quotient?

c) the quotient that is closest to 3?

7.9	6.3	3.8
8.8	2.8	7.2

22. Calculate the cost per case for each item in this bill.

> WALLY'S
> DISCOUNT WAREHOUSE
> 1.5 CASES OF TUNA $28.44
> 6 CASES OF JUICE $71.28
> 3.5 CASES OF CEREAL $83.72

23. The world's smallest egg is laid by the bee hummingbird. The average mass of the egg is 0.5 g. An ostrich egg, which is the largest in the world, has a mass of 1650 g. How many hummingbird eggs would have the same mass as one ostrich egg?

24. Giant kelp is a fast-growing ocean plant. It may grow 0.67 m in a day. Kelp plants have been found that are 61 m tall. About how many weeks would it take to grow this tall?

Extend your thinking

25. Use the information in exercises 6 and 7. Determine how many times as fast as Johnny Weismuller swam did Wilma Rudolph run.

26. A year on Mars is about 1.9 years on Earth.

a) Calculate how many years on Mars each of these times represents.

  i) 28.5 years on Earth

  ii) a decade on Earth

  iii) a century on Earth

b) What is your age in Mars years?

.... 2.7 DIVIDING WITH FRACTIONS

Developing the Ideas

▶ ▶ *Using Manipulatives*

In earlier grades you learned two meanings of division with natural numbers.

Division as sharing in equal parts

We see: $12 \div 3$

We think: Divide 12 into 3 equal parts.

We write: $12 \div 3 = 4$

Division as how many groups?

We see: $12 \div 3$

We think: How many 3s are there in 12?

We write: $12 \div 3 = 4$

When you divide with fractions you use the same meanings. You will need your fraction strips and number lines.

1. Consider the division $\frac{3}{4} \div 3$.

   a) Use your red $\frac{3}{4}$-strip. Use one meaning of division to determine the answer to $\frac{3}{4} \div 3$. Could you have used the other meaning to do this?

   b) Determine each quotient in the same way.

   i) $\frac{3}{2} \div 3$ ii) $\frac{3}{4} \div 6$ iii) $\frac{1}{2} \div 2$

2. Consider the division $2 \div \frac{1}{2}$.

   a) Locate 2 on your number lines. Use one meaning of division to determine the answer to $2 \div \frac{1}{2}$. Which number line is easiest to use? Could you have used the other meaning to do this division?

   b) Determine each quotient in the same way.

   i) $1 \div \frac{1}{2}$ ii) $\frac{3}{2} \div \frac{1}{2}$ iii) $\frac{3}{4} \div \frac{1}{8}$

3. Use your fraction strips and number lines to divide.

   a) $\frac{5}{8} \div 5$ **b)** $\frac{3}{2} \div 6$ **c)** $2 \div \frac{1}{3}$ **d)** $\frac{2}{3} \div \frac{1}{6}$ **e)** $3 \div \frac{1}{4}$ **f)** $\frac{3}{8} \div \frac{1}{4}$

4. Use exercises 1 to 3 as a guide. How can you tell which meaning of division to use when you divide with fractions?

Through Guided Examples

To divide with fractions, use one of the meanings of division.

- If the divisor is a natural number, use the meaning of sharing into equal parts.
- If the divisor is a fraction, find how many groups there are of this size in the first number.

In a division statement such as $12 \div 3 = 4$, the numbers are named as follows.

$$12 \div 3 = 4 \longleftarrow \text{quotient}$$

dividend   divisor

Example 1

Divide: $\frac{3}{4} \div 2$

Solution

The divisor is 2. This is a natural number.

We think: Divide $\frac{3}{4}$ into 2 equal parts.

Start with the red $\frac{3}{4}$-strip. It does not have 2 equal parts.

$$\frac{3}{4}$$

Replace it with an equivalent strip. This is the orange $\frac{6}{8}$-strip.

$$\frac{6}{8}$$

Divide $\frac{6}{8}$ into 2 equal parts. Each part is $\frac{3}{8}$.

$$\frac{3}{8}$$

We write: $\frac{3}{4} \div 2 = \frac{3}{8}$

Example 2

Divide: $2 \div \frac{1}{4}$

Solution

The divisor is the fraction $\frac{1}{4}$.

We think: How many $\frac{1}{4}$s are there in 2?

Use the red $\frac{1}{4}$-strip and the quarters number line.

Starting at 0, count how many $\frac{1}{4}$s there are in 2.

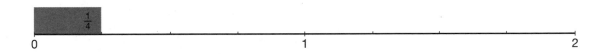

There are eight $\frac{1}{4}$s in 2.

We write: $2 \div \frac{1}{4} = 8$

Example 3

Divide: $\frac{4}{3} \div \frac{2}{3}$

Solution

The divisor is the fraction $\frac{2}{3}$.

We think: How many $\frac{2}{3}$s are there in $\frac{4}{3}$?

Use the blue $\frac{2}{3}$-strip and the thirds number line.

Starting at 0, count how many $\frac{2}{3}$s there are in $\frac{4}{3}$.

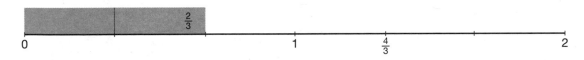

There are two $\frac{2}{3}$s in $\frac{4}{3}$.

We write: $\frac{4}{3} \div \frac{2}{3} = 2$

Example 4

Use a calculator to divide: $\frac{3}{4} \div \frac{2}{3}$

Solution 1

Express each fraction in decimal form.

$\frac{3}{4} = 0.75$ $\frac{2}{3} \doteq 0.67$

Use your calculator to divide the decimals.

Press: **.75** ÷ **.67** =

Display: **1.119403**

We write: $\frac{3}{4} \div \frac{2}{3} \doteq 1.12$

Solution 2

Use a calculator with a fraction key.

Press: **3** / **4** ÷ **2** / **3** =

Display: **9/8**

Press: Ab/c to display **1 u 1/8**

We write: $\frac{3}{4} \div \frac{2}{3} = \frac{9}{8}$, or $1\frac{1}{8}$

BOGGLE YOUR **MIND**

This is an old riddle. If a hen and a half could lay an egg and a half in a day and a half, how many eggs could 6 hens lay in 6 days?

Working with Mathematics

Something to talk about

1. Use your fraction strips and number lines to check the answer to *Example 4*.

2. Do you think it would be a good idea always to use a calculator for multiplying and dividing fractions? Explain your answer.

Practice

3. Use your fraction strips and number lines to divide.

    a) $1 \div 2$ b) $1 \div 3$ c) $2 \div 6$

    d) $\frac{1}{2} \div 6$ e) $\frac{7}{8} \div 7$ f) $\frac{3}{2} \div 3$

    g) $\frac{10}{12} \div 5$ h) $\frac{5}{6} \div \frac{1}{2}$ i) $\frac{5}{8} \div \frac{1}{4}$

4. Use your fraction strips and number lines to divide.

    a) $\frac{4}{5} \div 2$ b) $\frac{2}{3} \div \frac{1}{3}$ c) $\frac{9}{10} \div \frac{1}{5}$

    d) $1 \div \frac{2}{3}$ e) $\frac{7}{6} \div \frac{1}{2}$ f) $\frac{3}{4} \div \frac{1}{4}$

    g) $\frac{8}{5} \div \frac{2}{5}$ h) $\frac{2}{3} \div \frac{1}{12}$ i) $\frac{7}{10} \div \frac{1}{2}$

5. Use your fraction strips and number lines to divide.

    a) $2 \div \frac{1}{5}$ b) $\frac{3}{2} \div \frac{1}{6}$ c) $2 \div \frac{2}{3}$

    d) $\frac{3}{2} \div \frac{1}{8}$ e) $\frac{7}{4} \div \frac{1}{12}$ f) $\frac{5}{4} \div \frac{1}{8}$

    g) $\frac{11}{10} \div \frac{1}{5}$ h) $\frac{7}{12} \div \frac{1}{6}$ i) $\frac{7}{6} \div \frac{1}{12}$

Work together

6. Use your fraction strips and number lines to determine each answer. Then write the division statement.

    a) $2 \div 4$ b) $2 \div 2$ c) $2 \div 1$

    d) $2 \div \frac{1}{2}$ e) $2 \div \frac{1}{4}$ f) $2 \div \frac{1}{8}$

7. Divide using your fraction strips and number lines.

    a) $\frac{3}{8} \div 3$ b) $\frac{3}{2} \div 2$ c) $1 \div \frac{1}{3}$

    d) $\frac{3}{4} \div \frac{1}{8}$ e) $\frac{5}{6} \div \frac{1}{3}$ f) $\frac{1}{2} \div \frac{1}{3}$

8. In *Example 1* we found that $\frac{3}{4} \div 2 = \frac{3}{8}$. Two related divisions are shown below.

    $\frac{3}{8} \div 2$ $\frac{3}{2} \div 2$

a) Which is greater than $\frac{3}{8}$? Why? What is the answer to this division?

b) Which is less than $\frac{3}{8}$? Why? What is the answer to this division?

9. In *Example 2* we found that $2 \div \frac{1}{4} = 8$. Use this result to divide.

    a) $2 \div \frac{1}{2}$ b) $2 \div \frac{1}{8}$

10. Use a calculator to divide.

    a) $\frac{5}{8} \div \frac{3}{8}$ b) $\frac{1}{3} \div \frac{5}{6}$ c) $\frac{3}{5} \div \frac{2}{3}$

11. a) i) How many hundredths in 0.5?
       ii) Write the division statement.
    b) i) How many hundredths in $1\frac{1}{4}$?
       ii) Write the division statement.
    c) i) How many hundredths in $\frac{3}{4}$?
       ii) Write the division statement.

12. Copy this division table. Use your fraction strips and number lines to complete the table. The side column fractions are the divisors. The top row fractions are the dividends.

$\div$	1	$\frac{5}{6}$	$\frac{4}{6}$	$\frac{3}{6}$	$\frac{2}{6}$	$\frac{1}{6}$
1						
$\frac{5}{6}$						
$\frac{4}{6}$						
$\frac{3}{6}$						
$\frac{2}{6}$						
$\frac{1}{6}$						

On your own

13. Use your fraction strips and number lines to determine each answer. Then write the division statement.

    a) $\frac{1}{2} \div 4$ b) $\frac{1}{2} \div 2$ c) $\frac{1}{2} \div 1$

    d) $\frac{1}{2} \div \frac{1}{2}$ e) $\frac{1}{2} \div \frac{1}{4}$ f) $\frac{1}{2} \div \frac{1}{8}$

14. Divide using your fraction strips and number lines.

    a) $\frac{2}{3} \div 2$ b) $\frac{2}{3} \div 4$ c) $3 \div \frac{3}{4}$

    d) $\frac{3}{2} \div \frac{1}{4}$ e) $\frac{3}{4} \div \frac{3}{8}$ f) $\frac{7}{8} \div \frac{1}{4}$

15. In *Example 3* we found that $\frac{4}{3} \div \frac{2}{3} = 2$.

Three related divisions are shown below.

$$\frac{8}{3} \div \frac{2}{3} \qquad \frac{2}{3} \div \frac{2}{3} \qquad \frac{2}{3} \div \frac{1}{3}$$

a) Which is greater than 2? Why? What is the answer to this division?

b) Which is less than 2? Why? What is the answer to this division?

c) What is the answer to the other division? Explain why this is so.

16. In *Example 4* we found that $\frac{3}{4} \div \frac{2}{3} = 1\frac{1}{8}$, or $\frac{9}{8}$. Use this result to divide.

a) $\frac{3}{4} \div \frac{1}{3}$ **b)** $\frac{3}{4} \div \frac{4}{3}$

17. Find two fractions whose quotient is close to 1, but greater than 1. Start a new document in a spreadsheet program. Refer to exercise 19 on page 132.

a) What formula should you type in cell C1 to divide a fraction in cell A1 by a fraction in cell B1?

b) Input two fractions. How close to 1 is their quotient?

c) How can you get closer to 1?

d) How can you get closer to 1, but less than 1?

18. Use a calculator to divide.

a) $\frac{7}{8} \div \frac{1}{2}$ **b)** $\frac{7}{4} \div \frac{2}{5}$ **c)** $\frac{10}{3} \div \frac{5}{4}$

19. a) i) How many hundredths in 1.5?
     ii) Write the division statement.

b) i) How many hundredths in 0.60?
     ii) Write the division statement.

c) i) How many hundredths in $1\frac{4}{5}$?
     ii) Write the division statement.

20. Bonita has 6 tins of dog food. Her dog eats $\frac{1}{2}$ a tin of food every day. How many days will it take Bonita's dog to eat the 6 tins of dog food? Draw a diagram to support your answer.

21. There was $\frac{3}{4}$ of a pizza left after the class party. The 4 people on the clean-up crew shared the pizza equally. What fraction of the whole pizza did each person get? Draw a diagram to support your answer.

Extend your thinking

22. Determine each answer without using a calculator. Write each division statement.

a) $\frac{2}{3} \div \frac{1}{4}$ **b)** $\frac{1}{4} \div \frac{2}{3}$

c) $\frac{3}{4} \div \frac{1}{3}$ **d)** $\frac{1}{3} \div \frac{3}{4}$

23. The tallest iceberg ever sighted towered 168 m into the air. About $\frac{8}{9}$ of it was under water. What was the total height of the iceberg?

COMMUNICATING The Ideas

In your journal, make up an example of dividing:

a) a natural number by a fraction   **b)** a fraction by a natural number

c) a fraction by a fraction

Explain what each means and how to get the answer using manipulatives or a diagram.

Estimating Sale Prices

Estimate the sale prices of the items in the advertisements.

1.

VIDEO GAMES

$\frac{1}{2}$ OFF PRICES MARKED

$39.99

$58.85

$44.99

$69.99

$84.99

$77.77

2.

Going out of business — all sporting equipment at bargain prices!

$\frac{1}{3}$ OFF

Running Shoes
Cross Trainers

$29.99 to $84.99

Baseball Gloves

$14.98 to $64.98

Bicycle Helmets		18-Speed Mountain Bikes		In Line Skates	
Infant/Child	$24.98			Youth	$79.99
Youth	$34.98	Youth	$149.98	Adult	$99.99
Adult	$56.98	Adult	$274.98		

3. **End-of-season sale on all camping equipment!**

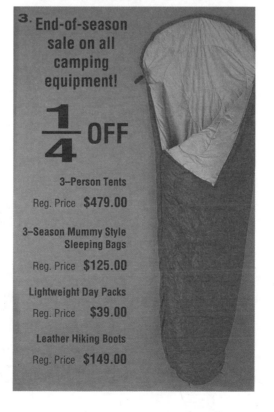

$\frac{1}{4}$ OFF

3–Person Tents

Reg. Price **$479.00**

3–Season Mummy Style Sleeping Bags

Reg. Price **$125.00**

Lightweight Day Packs

Reg. Price **$39.00**

Leather Hiking Boots

Reg. Price **$149.00**

2.8 *DIVIDING FRACTIONS IN FRACTION FORM*

Developing the Ideas

▶▶ *Through an Activity*

On page 145, you used number lines to divide $\frac{4}{3}$ by $\frac{2}{3}$. You obtained the answer 2. In this section, you will discover a pattern to divide fractions without using the number lines.

Work in a group or with a partner.

1. Get the exercises and answers for exercises 6 and 7 on page 147.

2. Use number lines to divide.

    a) $2 \div \frac{1}{4}$ **b)** $\frac{3}{2} \div \frac{3}{4}$ **c)** $\frac{3}{4} \div 2$

    d) $\frac{2}{3} \div \frac{1}{3}$ **e)** $\frac{2}{3} \div 4$ **f)** $3 \div \frac{3}{4}$

3. In each part of exercises 1 and 2, compare your answer with the numbers in the expression. Try to find a pattern that applies in every example and use it to divide fractions.

4. Use your pattern to determine each answer. Check your answer using the number lines.

    a) $\frac{3}{4} \div \frac{1}{8}$ **b)** $\frac{3}{2} \div \frac{5}{8}$ **c)** $\frac{1}{2} \div \frac{2}{3}$

▶▶ *Through Guided Examples*

You should have discovered this pattern for dividing by a fraction.

The product of these two numbers ...   ... is the numerator of the result.

$$\frac{3}{2} \div \frac{5}{8} = \frac{24}{10}$$

The product of these two numbers ...   ... is the denominator of the result.

We can express this division as a multiplication:

$$\frac{3}{2} \times \frac{8}{5} = \frac{24}{10}$$

That is, to determine $\frac{3}{2} \div \frac{5}{8}$, we multiply $\frac{3}{2}$ by $\frac{8}{5}$ instead.

The numbers $\frac{5}{8}$ and $\frac{8}{5}$ have a product of 1.

Recall that two numbers with a product of 1 are reciprocals.

    $\frac{5}{8}$ and $\frac{8}{5}$ are reciprocals because $\frac{5}{8} \times \frac{8}{5} = \frac{40}{40} = 1$.

    $\frac{1}{3}$ and 3 are reciprocals because $\frac{1}{3} \times 3 = 1$.

• • • • • • • • • •

    To divide by a fraction, multiply by its reciprocal.

Example 1

Divide: $\frac{9}{10} \div \frac{3}{4}$

Solution

The reciprocal of $\frac{3}{4}$ is $\frac{4}{3}$.

Instead of dividing by $\frac{3}{4}$, multiply by $\frac{4}{3}$.

$$\frac{9}{10} \div \frac{3}{4} = \frac{9}{10} \times \frac{4}{3}$$
$$= \frac{36}{30}$$
$$= \frac{6}{5}$$

Example 2

Divide: **a)** $12 \div \frac{2}{3}$ **b)** $\frac{3}{5} \div 4$

Solution

a) The reciprocal of $\frac{2}{3}$ is $\frac{3}{2}$.

$$12 \div \frac{2}{3} = 12 \times \frac{3}{2}$$
$$= \frac{36}{2}, \text{ or } 18$$

b) The reciprocal of 4 is $\frac{1}{4}$.

$$\frac{3}{5} \div 4 = \frac{3}{5} \times \frac{1}{4}$$
$$= \frac{3}{20}$$

BOGGLE YOUR **MiND**

An official Olympic-size swimming pool measures 50 m by 25 m and must be filled to a depth of at least 2 m. How many Olympic-size swimming pools could be filled with the 2 952 894 000 L of soft drinks purchased by Canadians in 1993?

Working with Mathematics

Something to talk about

1. "Division makes numbers smaller." Do you agree with this statement? Give examples to support your answer.

2. In *Example 1*, is the answer greater than $\frac{9}{10}$ or less than $\frac{9}{10}$?

3. What is the reciprocal of each number?
   a) $\frac{1}{5}$ b) $\frac{1}{7}$ c) $\frac{3}{5}$
   d) $\frac{3}{2}$ e) 4   f) 0.1

4. Which pairs of numbers are reciprocals?
   a) $\frac{2}{9}, \frac{9}{2}$ b) $6, \frac{1}{6}$ c) $\frac{3}{4}, \frac{3}{4}$
   d) $\frac{8}{3}, \frac{3}{8}$ e) $2, 0.2$ f) $2\frac{1}{3}, 3\frac{1}{2}$

5. Is it possible for a number and its reciprocal to be the same? If you think the answer is no, explain why. If you think the answer is yes, give an example of a number that is the same as its reciprocal.

Practice

6. What is the reciprocal of each number?
   a) $\frac{1}{2}$ b) $\frac{2}{7}$ c) $\frac{1}{9}$
   d) $\frac{4}{5}$ e) 3   f) $\frac{5}{2}$
   g) 5   h) 0.25   i) $1\frac{3}{4}$

7. Which pairs of numbers are reciprocals?
   a) $3, \frac{1}{3}$ b) $\frac{1}{2}, \frac{1}{2}$ c) $\frac{7}{8}, \frac{8}{7}$
   d) $\frac{8}{9}, \frac{9}{8}$ e) $\frac{5}{3}, \frac{3}{2}$ f) $\frac{1}{5}, 5$
   g) $6, \frac{6}{5}$ h) $\frac{10}{4}, 0.4$ i) $\frac{3}{4}, 1\frac{1}{3}$

8. Divide.
   a) $\frac{1}{9} \div \frac{1}{3}$ b) $\frac{2}{9} \div \frac{1}{3}$ c) $\frac{3}{9} \div \frac{1}{3}$
   d) $\frac{4}{9} \div \frac{1}{3}$ e) $\frac{5}{9} \div \frac{1}{3}$ f) $\frac{7}{9} \div \frac{1}{3}$
   g) $\frac{8}{9} \div \frac{1}{3}$ h) $1 \div \frac{1}{3}$ i) $\frac{10}{9} \div \frac{1}{3}$

9. Divide.
   a) $\frac{1}{2} \div \frac{1}{2}$ b) $\frac{1}{2} \div 2$ c) $4 \div \frac{1}{2}$
   d) $\frac{1}{5} \div \frac{3}{5}$ e) $\frac{5}{4} \div \frac{1}{5}$ f) $\frac{9}{10} \div 9$
   g) $\frac{3}{4} \div \frac{3}{2}$ h) $\frac{5}{12} \div \frac{1}{6}$ i) $6 \div \frac{5}{6}$

Work together

10. Divide.
    a) $\frac{1}{5} \div \frac{1}{2}$ b) $\frac{2}{5} \div \frac{1}{2}$ c) $\frac{3}{5} \div \frac{1}{2}$
    d) $\frac{4}{5} \div \frac{1}{2}$ e) $\frac{5}{5} \div \frac{1}{2}$ f) $\frac{6}{5} \div \frac{1}{2}$

11. Divide.
    a) $6 \div \frac{1}{2}$ b) $20 \div \frac{1}{8}$ c) $\frac{3}{4} \div 9$
    d) $\frac{1}{5} \div \frac{3}{7}$ e) $\frac{8}{9} \div \frac{1}{10}$ f) $\frac{9}{8} \div \frac{3}{16}$
    g) $\frac{3}{16} \div \frac{5}{4}$ h) $\frac{5}{12} \div \frac{25}{5}$ i) $\frac{21}{10} \div \frac{27}{5}$

12. a) Suppose a number became larger and larger. What happens to its reciprocal?
    b) Suppose a number were doubled. What happens to its reciprocal?
    Use some examples to support your answers.

13. Roy wants to cut a piece of gold ribbon $1\frac{3}{4}$ m long into $\frac{1}{4}$-m lengths. How many $\frac{1}{4}$-m lengths of ribbon can he cut?

14. A roller coaster ride lasts for about $\frac{3}{4}$ min. How many roller coaster rides could you take in each time period?
    a) 3 min   b) $4\frac{1}{2}$ min   c) $7\frac{1}{2}$ min

15. The width of a seat in a hall is $\frac{3}{5}$ m.
    a) How many seats can be placed in a row 12 m long?
    b) How many seats can be placed in a row 9 m long?
    c) Suppose a seat was $\frac{3}{8}$ m wide instead of $\frac{3}{5}$ m. Could you fit more or fewer seats in each row? Explain.
    d) Repeat parts a and b for seats $\frac{3}{8}$ m wide.

16. Ruja wants to trim the edge of her gardens with decorative bricks. Each brick is $\frac{1}{5}$ m long. Her gardens have edge lengths of $2\frac{1}{4}$ m, $4\frac{1}{2}$ m, and $5\frac{1}{4}$ m. How many bricks would she need for each garden?

17. Is it possible for both a positive number and its reciprocal to be:
    a) less than 1?   b) greater than 1?
    Explain your answers.

On your own

18. Divide.

a) $\frac{2}{3} \div \frac{1}{5}$ b) $\frac{2}{3} \div \frac{2}{5}$ c) $\frac{2}{3} \div \frac{3}{5}$

d) $\frac{2}{3} \div \frac{4}{5}$ e) $\frac{2}{3} \div \frac{5}{5}$ f) $\frac{2}{3} \div \frac{6}{5}$

19. Divide.

a) $9 \div \frac{1}{3}$ b) $8 \div \frac{3}{2}$ c) $\frac{1}{2} \div \frac{3}{5}$

d) $\frac{5}{3} \div 4$ e) $\frac{7}{8} \div \frac{3}{4}$ f) $\frac{5}{6} \div \frac{7}{12}$

g) $\frac{11}{12} \div \frac{3}{4}$ h) $\frac{15}{8} \div \frac{25}{4}$ i) $\frac{7}{27} \div \frac{28}{3}$

20. a) Copy and complete each pattern.

i) $4 \div 4 = \blacksquare$ ii) $4 \div \frac{1}{4} = \blacksquare$

    $4 \div 2 = \blacksquare$

    $4 \div 1 = \blacksquare$ $2 \div \frac{1}{4} = \blacksquare$

    $4 \div \frac{1}{2} = \blacksquare$ $1 \div \frac{1}{4} = \blacksquare$

    $4 \div \frac{1}{4} = \blacksquare$ $\frac{1}{2} \div \frac{1}{4} = \blacksquare$

                    $\frac{1}{4} \div \frac{1}{4} = \blacksquare$

b) In the products in part a, how do the divisors, then dividends change from one row to the next? How do the quotients change from one row to the next?

c) Add three additional lines to each pattern.

21. Which graph illustrates the relationship between a number and its reciprocal? Explain how you know.

a)

b)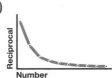

c)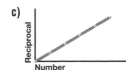

22. Fauzia has a case of 12 tins of cat food. Her cat eats $\frac{1}{2}$ a tin of food every day. How many days will it take the cat to eat the case of cat food?

23. How many times can a video be shown in 3 h if it runs for each time?

a) $\frac{1}{4}$ h   b) $\frac{1}{2}$ h   c) $\frac{3}{4}$ h

24. A $\frac{3}{4}$-full jug of lemonade can fill 9 glasses. How many glasses can a full jug fill?

25. About $\frac{1}{3}$ of a fence post should be underground. How long should a post be if you want it to have a height of 1.6 m above ground?

Extend your thinking

26. The example below illustrates another way to divide fractions.

To determine $\frac{5}{4} \div \frac{2}{3}$, write:

$$\frac{\frac{5}{4}}{\frac{2}{3}} = \frac{\frac{5}{4}}{\frac{2}{3}} \times \frac{12}{12}$$

$$= \frac{\frac{5}{4} \times 12}{\frac{2}{3} \times 12}$$

$$= \frac{15}{8}$$

a) Explain each step in this solution.

b) Try this method on a couple of other examples.

c) Could this method of dividing fractions be used to explain the rule "multiply by the reciprocal"? Explain.

COMMUNICATING

The Ideas

In your journal, summarize the rules for adding, subtracting, multiplying, and dividing fractions in fraction form. Use the expressions in *Example 5* on page 110 as examples.

Why Does 0.999999... = 1?

When we express fractions in decimal form we frequently encounter repeating decimals, as in $\frac{1}{3} = 0.333\,333\ldots$ and $\frac{2}{3} = 0.666\,666\ldots$

When we add $\frac{1}{3}$ and $\frac{2}{3}$ we get $\frac{3}{3}$, or 1.

When we add $0.333\,333\ldots$ and $0.666\,666\ldots$, we get $0.999\,999\ldots$
So, $0.999\,999\ldots = 1$

Some people have trouble believing that $0.999\,999\ldots$ can equal 1.
What are some other reasons why $0.999\,999\ldots = 1$?

Understand the problem

- What do the three dots mean in $0.999\,999\ldots$?
- What are you asked to do?

Think of some strategies

- You could try to get $0.999\,999\ldots$ when you use long division to express $\frac{3}{3}$ in decimal form.
- Or, you could try subtracting $0.333\,333\ldots$ from $1.000\,000\ldots$

Carry out the strategies

- Dividing 3 by 3 using long division is simple when you do it this way:

$$3\overline{)\begin{array}{l} 1 \\ 3 \\ \underline{3} \\ 0 \end{array}}$$

- Suppose you don't subtract the greatest multiple of 3 from the dividend each time. Start it this way, and continue doing the division:

$$3\overline{)\begin{array}{l} 0.9 \\ 3.0 \\ \underline{2\,7} \end{array}}$$

- For another strategy, observe what happens when you subtract a terminating decimal from 1:

$$\begin{array}{r} 1.0000 \\ -0.4657 \\ \hline \end{array}$$

Think... $\longrightarrow$

$$\begin{array}{r} 0\ \ 9\ 9\ 9\ 10 \\ 1.0000 \\ -0.4657 \\ \hline 0.5343 \end{array}$$

Rename the first 0 at the right as 10. Rename all the other 0s as 9s. Rename the 1 as 0.

- When you subtract $0.333\,333\ldots$ from $1.000\,000\ldots$, there is no first 0 at the right to rename as 10. Can you do the subtraction if you rename $1.000\,000\ldots$ as $0.999\,999\ldots$?

Look back

- We say that 1 is another name for $0.999\,999\ldots$
- What is another name for $1.999\,999\ldots$?
- What is another name for $1.499\,999\ldots$?

Communicating the Ideas

In your journal, write a description of this problem and your solution.

2.9 APPLICATIONS OF FRACTIONS

Developing the Ideas

▶ ▶ *Through Instruction*

The importance of computation with fractions is changing. There are now fewer applications of fractions than there were in the past. Two important reasons are described below.

- Before the metric system was introduced in Canada in the 1970s, people used imperial units. Since the imperial system of measurement is not based on 10, 100, 1000,… as is the metric system, fractions occurred in many computations involving measurement.
- In the past people did not have electronic calculators, and all computations were done mentally or with paper and pencil.

Although Canada converted to the metric system in the seventies, many people still use imperial units. You can tell this by looking at newspaper advertisements.

BOGGLE YOUR MIND

Here is an exercise from an arithmetic textbook used about 100 years ago.

Simplify $\dfrac{8\frac{3}{5} - 7\frac{3}{4} + 5\frac{2}{3} - 4\frac{1}{2}}{13\frac{3}{5} - 11\frac{9}{10} + 10\frac{7}{9} - 9\frac{17}{20}} \times \dfrac{2}{11}$ of 365

In those days, students had to do this exercise using only paper and pencil. Although this is very difficult, you should be able to estimate the answer fairly easily if you think about it carefully. Discuss the problem with a group to develop a way to estimate the answer.

If you have a calculator with a fraction key, use it to determine the answer.

The following examples show some applications of fraction operations that are still in use today. In applications like these, some people write fractions with the numerator and denominator beside each other, separated by a slanted line. People develop their own methods of calculating with these fractions, which are variations of the rules you learned in earlier sections of this chapter.

Many people still use fractions for cooking. For this reason, the recipes in some cookbooks are given in fractions of cups and spoons.

Example 1 ....

The ingredients for making waffles are shown on the right.

a) For only two people, this recipe makes too many waffles. Change the recipe to make one-half the number of waffles.

b) For some families, this recipe might not make enough waffles. Change the recipe to make one-and-one-half times as many waffles.

Waffles	
Flour	2 cups
Baking powder	3 tsp.
Salt	$\frac{1}{2}$ tsp.
Eggs	2
Milk	$1\frac{1}{4}$ cups
Shortening	$\frac{1}{2}$ cup

Solution

a) Flour: $\frac{1}{2}$ of 2 cups = $\frac{1}{2} \times 2$ cups = 1 cup

Baking powder: $\frac{1}{2}$ of 3 tsp. = $\frac{1}{2} \times 3$ tsp. = $1\frac{1}{2}$ tsp.

Salt: $\frac{1}{2}$ of $\frac{1}{2}$ tsp. = $\frac{1}{2} \times \frac{1}{2}$ tsp. = $\frac{1}{4}$ tsp.

Eggs: $\frac{1}{2}$ of 2 eggs = $\frac{1}{2} \times 2$ eggs = 1 egg

Milk: $\frac{1}{2}$ of $1\frac{1}{4}$ cups= $\frac{1}{4} \times \frac{5}{4}$ cups = $\frac{5}{8}$ cup ◀ To multiply by $1\frac{1}{4}$, change $1\frac{1}{4}$ to quarters.
That is, $1\frac{1}{4}$ is 5 quarters = $\frac{5}{4}$

Shortening: $\frac{1}{2}$ of $\frac{1}{2}$ cup = $\frac{1}{2} \times \frac{1}{2}$ cup = $\frac{1}{4}$ cup

b) To multiply by $1\frac{1}{2}$, change $1\frac{1}{2}$ to halves.

That is, $1\frac{1}{2}$ is 3 halves = $\frac{3}{2}$

Flour: $1\frac{1}{2} \times 2$ cups = $\frac{3}{2} \times 2$ cups = $\frac{6}{2}$, or 3 cups

Baking powder: $1\frac{1}{2} \times 3$ tsp. = $\frac{3}{2} \times 3$ tsp. = $\frac{9}{2}$, or $4\frac{1}{2}$ tsp.

Salt: $1\frac{1}{2} \times \frac{1}{2}$ tsp. = $\frac{3}{2} \times \frac{1}{2}$ tsp. = $\frac{3}{4}$ tsp.

Eggs: $1\frac{1}{2} \times 2 = \frac{3}{2} \times 2 = \frac{6}{2}$, or 3 eggs

Milk: $1\frac{1}{2} \times 1\frac{1}{4}$ cups = $\frac{3}{2} \times \frac{5}{4}$ cups = $\frac{15}{8}$, or $1\frac{7}{8}$ cups

Shortening: $1\frac{1}{2} \times \frac{1}{2}$ cup = $\frac{3}{2} \times \frac{1}{2}$ cup = $\frac{3}{4}$ cup

Fractions are used extensively on the stock exchange to describe amounts of money. For example, the price of a stock selling at \$15.50 is often written as $\$15\frac{1}{2}$.

Example 2

One AMC preferred share was purchased in 1990 at $\$17\frac{7}{8}$ and sold in 1994 at $\$24\frac{1}{4}$.

a) How much profit was earned on one share?

b) How much profit was earned on 250 shares?

Solution

a) The profit earned per share was $\$24\frac{1}{4} - \$17\frac{7}{8}$.
From $17\frac{7}{8}$ to 18 is $\frac{1}{8}$. From 18 to 24 is 6. From 24 to $24\frac{1}{4}$ is $\frac{1}{4}$.

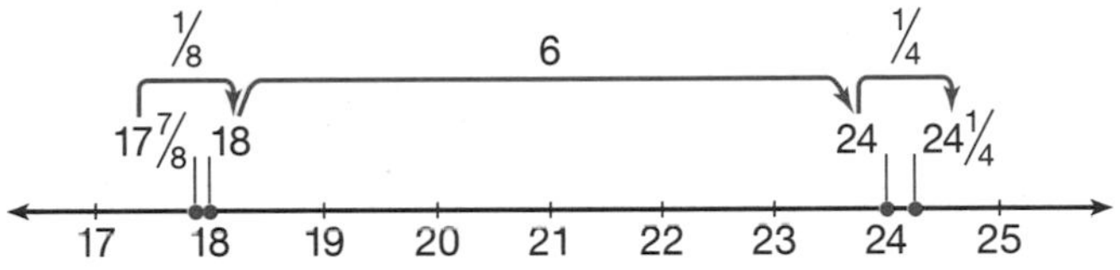

$\frac{1}{8} + 6 + \frac{1}{4} = 6\frac{3}{8}$

The profit earned per share was $\$6\frac{3}{8}$.

b) The profit earned on 250 shares was $250 \times \$6\frac{3}{8}$.

Think… $250 \times 6 = 1500$

$$250 \times \frac{3}{8} = \frac{750}{8}, \text{ or } 93.75.$$

The total profit earned was \$1500 + \$93.75 = \$1593.75.

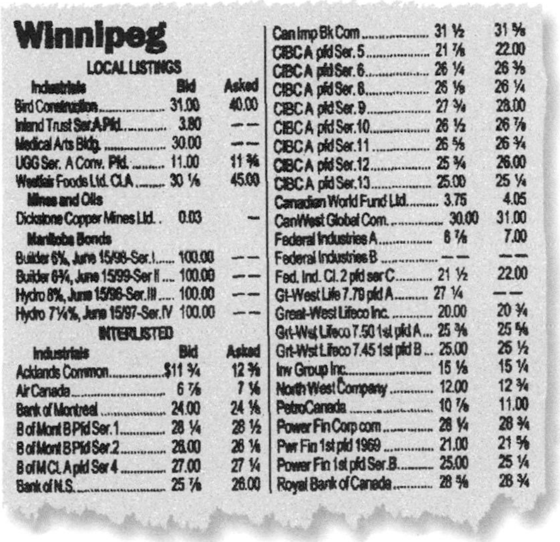

Winnipeg

LOCAL LISTINGS

Industrials	Bid	Asked
Bird Construction	31.00	40.00
Inland Trust Ser.A Pfd.	3.80	--
Medical Arts Bldg.	30.00	--
UGG Ser. A Conv. Pfd.	11.00	11 3/8
Westfair Foods Ltd. Cl.A	30 1/8	45.00
Mines and Oils		
Dickstone Copper Mines Ltd.	0.03	-
Manitoba Bonds		
Builder 6%, June 15/98-Ser.I	100.00	--
Builder 6¾, June 15/99-Ser II	100.00	--
Hydro 8%, June 15/96-Ser.III	100.00	--
Hydro 7¼%, June 15/97-Ser.IV	100.00	--

INTERLISTED

Industrials	Bid	Asked
Acklands Common	\$11 3/4	12 3/8
Air Canada	6 7/8	7 1/8
Bank of Montreal	24.00	24 1/8
B of Mont B Pfd Ser.1	28 1/4	28 1/2
B of Mont B Pfd Ser.2	28.00	28 1/8
B of M Cl. A pfd Ser 4	27.00	27 1/4
Bank of N.S.	25 7/8	26.00
Can Imp Bk Com	31 1/2	31 5/8
CIBC A pfd Ser. 5	21 7/8	22.00
CIBC A pfd Ser. 6	26 1/4	26 3/8
CIBC A pfd Ser. 8	26 1/8	26 1/4
CIBC A pfd Ser. 9	27 3/4	28.00
CIBC A pfd Ser.10	26 1/2	26 7/8
CIBC A pfd Ser.11	26 5/8	26 3/4
CIBC A pfd Ser.12	25 3/4	26.00
CIBC A pfd Ser.13	25.00	25 1/4
Canadian World Fund Ltd.	3.75	4.05
CanWest Global Com.	30.00	31.00
Federal Industries A	6 7/8	7.00
Federal Industries B	--	--
Fed. Ind. Cl. 2 pfd ser C	21 1/2	22.00
Gt-West Life 7.79 pfd A	27 1/4	--
Great-West Lifeco Inc.	20.00	20 3/4
Grt-West Lifeco 7.50 1st pfd A	25 3/8	25 5/8
Grt-Wst Lifeco 7.45 1st pfd B	25.00	25 1/2
Inv Group Inc.	15 1/8	15 1/4
North West Company	12.00	12 3/4
PetroCanada	10 7/8	11.00
Power Fin Corp com	28 1/4	28 3/4
Pwr Fin 1st pfd 1969	21.00	21 5/8
Power Fin 1st pfd Ser.B	25.00	25 1/4
Royal Bank of Canada	28 5/8	28 3/4

BOGGLE YOUR MIND

Here is one way to write 100 using each of the digits from 0 to 9 once. Confirm that this expression is equal to 100. Try to find two other ways to write 100 using all the digits from 0 to 9.

$$87 + 9\frac{4}{5} + 3\frac{12}{60}$$

Working with Mathematics

Something to talk about

1. Some people would solve a problem like *Example 2a* this way:

$$24\tfrac{1}{4} - 17\tfrac{7}{8} = 23\tfrac{5}{4} - 17\tfrac{7}{8}$$
$$= 23\tfrac{10}{8} - 17\tfrac{7}{8}$$
$$= 6\tfrac{3}{8}$$

In the first step, how was $23\tfrac{5}{4}$ obtained from $24\tfrac{1}{4}$? Some years ago, you learned a step in arithmetic similar to this one. What was it?

2. Here is another solution to *Example 2a*:

$$24\tfrac{1}{4} - 17\tfrac{7}{8} = \frac{97}{4} - \frac{143}{8}$$
$$= \frac{194}{8} - \frac{143}{8}$$
$$= \frac{51}{8}, \text{ or } 6\tfrac{3}{8}$$

Compare this solution with the one in exercise 1 and the one in *Example 2*. Do you think anyone would prefer to calculate this way?

3. Do the calculation in *Example 2a* by writing the prices in decimal form.

Practice

4. Add or subtract.

a) $\dfrac{5}{9} + \dfrac{1}{3}$ b) $\dfrac{6}{7} - \dfrac{1}{2}$ c) $\dfrac{9}{4} - \dfrac{2}{3}$

d) $1\tfrac{3}{8} + \dfrac{7}{8}$ e) $2\tfrac{2}{5} - \dfrac{1}{10}$ f) $3\tfrac{3}{4} - 2\tfrac{1}{2}$

g) $12 + 3\tfrac{5}{8}$ h) $10 - \dfrac{2}{3}$ i) $120 + 15\tfrac{7}{11}$

5. Multiply or divide.

a) $12 \times \dfrac{1}{3}$ b) $12 \div \dfrac{1}{3}$ c) $\dfrac{9}{4} \times \dfrac{2}{3}$

d) $\dfrac{9}{4} \div \dfrac{2}{3}$ e) $100 \div \dfrac{2}{5}$ f) $100 \times \dfrac{2}{5}$

g) $\dfrac{3}{7} \div 30$ h) $\dfrac{6}{5} \times 40$ i) $50 \times \dfrac{3}{5}$

6. Calculate.

a) $2\tfrac{5}{8} + \dfrac{1}{4}$ b) $10 - \dfrac{3}{4}$ c) $\dfrac{13}{9} \div \dfrac{1}{3}$

d) $\dfrac{10}{11} \times \dfrac{4}{5}$ e) $\dfrac{13}{7} \div \dfrac{13}{7}$ f) $15\tfrac{7}{8} - 1\tfrac{1}{4}$

g) $\dfrac{7}{9} + \dfrac{1}{3} + 18$ h) $120 \div \dfrac{2}{3}$ i) $240 \times \dfrac{3}{5}$

Work together

7. Here is a cake recipe from an old cookbook.

> **Busy–Day Cake**
>
> $\tfrac{1}{3}$ cup shortening
> $1\tfrac{3}{4}$ cups sifted cake flour
> $\tfrac{3}{4}$ cup sugar
> $2\tfrac{1}{2}$ teaspoon baking powder
> $\tfrac{1}{2}$ teaspoon salt
> 1 egg
> $\tfrac{3}{4}$ cup milk
> $1\tfrac{1}{2}$ teaspoon vanilla
>
> Stir shortening just to soften. Sift in dry ingredients. Add egg and half the milk; mix until all flour is dampened. Beat 2 minutes at medium speed on electric mixer. Add remaining milk and vanilla; beat 2 minutes longer. Bake in paper-lined 9x9x2–inch pan in moderate oven (375˚) about 25 minutes or until done.

a) According to the recipe, only half the milk is used at first. How much milk is this?

b) List the amount of each ingredient you would need if you wanted to double the recipe.

8. Solve *Example 2* by converting the fractions to decimal form before doing the calculations.

9. Nelson bought stocks for $12\tfrac{1}{4}$ per share. After one week, each share gained $1\tfrac{5}{8}$. After two weeks, each share fell $2\tfrac{1}{2}$. After three weeks, each share gained $5\tfrac{5}{8}$.

a) Did Nelson's stocks increase or decrease in value over the three weeks? By how much?

b) What was the value of each share after one week? After two weeks? After three weeks?

c) Nelson sold his stocks four months later for $14\tfrac{5}{8}$ per share. What was his profit per share?

10. For each stock listed, how much profit was earned:

   a) on each share?

   b) on 100 shares?

   c) on 250 shares?

	Stock	Purchase price per share ($)	Selling price per share ($)
i)	BAPL Corp.	$6\frac{1}{2}$	9
ii)	ISB Ltd.	$33\frac{1}{8}$	$40\frac{3}{4}$
iii)	MacPherco	$83\frac{3}{4}$	$106\frac{1}{2}$

11. In the 1993 World Series Baseball Championship, Duane Ward pitched $4\frac{2}{3}$ innings and allowed 1 earned run. His *earned run average* (ERA) is the number of earned runs he would have allowed in 9 innings at the same rate.

   a) In $4\frac{2}{3}$ innings Ward allowed 1 earned run. At this rate, how many earned runs would Ward have allowed in 1 inning?

   b) How many earned runs would Ward have allowed in 9 innings? Express your answer in decimal form to the nearest hundredth. This is Ward's ERA.

   c) Why do you think a period of 9 innings is used in this calculation?

12. In a lottery for a local charity, only 2000 tickets are available for sale. One-thousandth of these tickets will win $100, $\frac{1}{400}$ will win $50, $\frac{1}{200}$ will win $20, $\frac{1}{100}$ will win $10, and $\frac{1}{40}$ will win $1.

   a) How many tickets will win each prize: $100, $50, $20, $10, and $1?

   b) How many tickets will not win a prize?

   c) Each ticket sells for $1. How much profit will the charity earn?

13. In a class of 24 students, $\frac{1}{3}$ of the students took a school bus, $\frac{1}{4}$ took a city bus, $\frac{1}{12}$ were driven by parents, and the rest walked to school.

   a) How many students were in each group?

   b) What fraction of students in the class walked to school?

Extend your thinking

14. Suppose you wanted to make the cake in exercise 7. You cannot use the imperial units in that recipe because you have metric measuring utensils. In another cookbook you found the table below.

Conventional		Metric Measure
Spoons	1/4 tsp.	1 mL
	1/2 tsp.	2 mL
	1 tsp.	5 mL
Cups	1/4 cup	50 mL
	1/3 cup	75 mL
	1/2 cup	125 mL
	2/3 cup	150 mL
	3/4 cup	175 mL
	1 cup	250 mL

   a) Use the table to convert the recipe in exercise 7 to metric units.

   b) Suppose 1/4 tsp. were exactly 1 mL and 1/2 tsp. were exactly 2 mL. What should 1 tsp. be? Why do you think 1 tsp. is shown as 5 mL in the table?

   c) Suppose 1 tsp. were exactly 5 mL. What should 1/4 tsp. and 1/2 tsp. be?

   d) The figures in the table are approximate. Some are closer than others to the exact values. The closest approximation is 1/3 cup. This is very close to 75 mL. Assume that 1/3 cup = 75 mL. Calculate the metric measures for the other cup measures, to the nearest millilitre.

The Ideas

Ask an adult to give you an example of a situation in which he or she calculates with fractions. Make up a problem based on this situation and solve the problem.

Review

1. Express in simplest form.

   a) $\dfrac{6}{9}$ b) $\dfrac{8}{20}$ c) $\dfrac{16}{36}$ d) $\dfrac{35}{49}$

2. Express each fraction as a decimal.

   a) $\dfrac{1}{5}$ b) $\dfrac{2}{3}$ c) $\dfrac{5}{4}$ d) $\dfrac{3}{8}$

   e) $\dfrac{4}{7}$ f) $\dfrac{7}{11}$ g) $\dfrac{13}{8}$ h) $\dfrac{23}{48}$

3. a) Two fractions have the same denominator but different numerators. Explain how to determine which fraction is larger.

   b) Two fractions have the same numerator but different denominators. Explain how to determine which fraction is larger.

4. a) Express $\dfrac{4}{15}$ in decimal form.

   b) Use the result of part a to express each fraction in decimal form.

   i) $\dfrac{40}{15}$ ii) $\dfrac{400}{15}$ iii) $\dfrac{4}{150}$ iv) $\dfrac{4}{1500}$

5. a) Write each number in decimal form.

   i) $\dfrac{1}{7}\ \dfrac{2}{7}\ \dfrac{3}{7}$ ii) $\dfrac{6}{7}\ \dfrac{5}{7}\ \dfrac{4}{7}$

   iii) $\dfrac{3}{7}\ \dfrac{3}{6}\ \dfrac{3}{5}$ iv) $\dfrac{3}{8}\ \dfrac{3}{9}\ \dfrac{3}{10}$

   b) Does a fraction increase or decrease if:

   i) the numerator is increased?

   ii) the denominator is increased?

6. Use your fraction strips and number lines to add.

   a) $\dfrac{1}{10} + \dfrac{1}{10}$ b) $\dfrac{2}{5} + \dfrac{4}{5}$ c) $\dfrac{1}{2} + \dfrac{3}{4}$

   d) $\dfrac{1}{4} + \dfrac{1}{3}$ e) $\dfrac{3}{2} + \dfrac{2}{5}$ f) $\dfrac{1}{3} + \dfrac{1}{4} + \dfrac{1}{5}$

7. Add.

   a) $1\dfrac{2}{3} + 2\dfrac{1}{6}$ b) $3\dfrac{3}{4} + 4\dfrac{1}{2}$

   c) $2\dfrac{7}{8} + 5\dfrac{3}{4}$ d) $6\dfrac{1}{3} + 2\dfrac{7}{12}$

8. Add by expressing the fractions in decimal form.

   a) $\dfrac{1}{2} + \dfrac{1}{5}$ b) $\dfrac{3}{4} + \dfrac{7}{8}$

   c) $\dfrac{7}{4} + \dfrac{3}{5}$ d) $\dfrac{1}{4} + \dfrac{1}{5} + \dfrac{1}{8}$

9. Use a calculator to add.

   a) $\dfrac{3}{4} + \dfrac{5}{6}$ b) $\dfrac{2}{7} + \dfrac{5}{9}$

   c) $\dfrac{2}{3} + \dfrac{6}{5} + \dfrac{8}{11}$ d) $\dfrac{7}{4} + \dfrac{13}{6} + \dfrac{4}{9}$

10. Replace each ■ with a number so that the sum is close to 1.

    $\dfrac{■}{7} + \dfrac{■}{11}$

11. Use your fraction strips and number lines to subtract.

    a) $\dfrac{3}{5} - \dfrac{1}{5}$ b) $\dfrac{7}{8} - \dfrac{3}{4}$ c) $\dfrac{3}{2} - \dfrac{3}{4}$

    d) $\dfrac{1}{3} - \dfrac{1}{4}$ e) $\dfrac{3}{2} - \dfrac{2}{5}$ f) $\dfrac{1}{2} - \dfrac{1}{3} - \dfrac{1}{12}$

12. Subtract.

    a) $4\dfrac{2}{3} - 2\dfrac{1}{6}$ b) $3\dfrac{3}{4} - 1\dfrac{1}{2}$

    c) $7\dfrac{7}{8} - 5\dfrac{3}{4}$ d) $6\dfrac{5}{12} - 2\dfrac{1}{3}$

13. Subtract by expressing the fractions in decimal form.

    a) $\dfrac{1}{2} - \dfrac{1}{5}$ b) $\dfrac{7}{4} - \dfrac{7}{8}$

    c) $\dfrac{7}{4} - \dfrac{3}{3}$ d) $\dfrac{3}{2} - \dfrac{1}{4} - \dfrac{1}{5}$

14. Use a calculator to subtract.

    a) $\dfrac{3}{4} - \dfrac{1}{6}$ b) $\dfrac{5}{7} - \dfrac{4}{9}$

    c) $\dfrac{11}{3} - \dfrac{6}{5} - \dfrac{8}{11}$ d) $\dfrac{13}{4} - \dfrac{7}{6} - \dfrac{8}{9}$

15. Replace each ■ with a number so the difference is close to 0.

    $\dfrac{■}{3} - \dfrac{■}{13}$

16. Three baseboards are to be cut to lie along a wall. The first board covers $\dfrac{1}{2}$ of the distance. The second board covers $\dfrac{2}{5}$ of the distance. What fraction of the distance remains to be covered?

17. Use your fraction strips and number lines to multiply.

    a) $4 \times \dfrac{3}{2}$ b) $6 \times \dfrac{2}{3}$ c) $\dfrac{1}{2} \times \dfrac{3}{5}$

    d) $\dfrac{4}{5} \times \dfrac{5}{8}$ e) $\dfrac{5}{4} \times \dfrac{2}{3}$ f) $\dfrac{2}{3} \times \dfrac{3}{2}$

18. Multiply.

    a) $\dfrac{4}{6} \times \dfrac{3}{4}$ b) $\dfrac{3}{2} \times \dfrac{2}{5}$ c) $\dfrac{4}{5} \times \dfrac{4}{3}$

    d) $\dfrac{1}{2} \times \dfrac{1}{4}$ e) $\dfrac{2}{3} \times 5$ f) $\dfrac{5}{6} \times \dfrac{8}{10}$

19. Replace each ■ with a number so that the product is close to 0.23.

    $\dfrac{■}{5} \times \dfrac{■}{7}$

20. Two-thirds of the class is in the school choir.
   a) On Monday, only $\frac{3}{4}$ of those students went to choir practice. What fraction of the class went to choir practice on Monday?
   b) There are 30 students in the class. How many students went to choir practice on Monday?

21. There are 30 students in a grade 8 mathematics class. One-third of these are boys.
   a) How many boys are there?
   b) Half of the boys attended a concert. How many boys attended the concert?
   c) Three-quarters of the girls attended the concert. How many girls attended the concert?

22. Use your calculator to express each result in decimal form to the nearest hundredth.
   a) $\frac{2}{3} + \frac{3}{5}$ **b)** $\frac{4}{7} - \frac{3}{11}$ **c)** $\frac{34}{7} \div \frac{2}{10}$
   d) $\frac{2}{5} \times \frac{4}{9}$ **e)** $\frac{7}{9} + \frac{3}{5}$ **f)** $\frac{7}{9} - \frac{3}{5}$
   g) $\frac{7}{9} \times \frac{3}{5}$ **h)** $\frac{7}{9} \div \frac{3}{5}$ **i)** $\frac{4}{5} \div \frac{3}{7}$

23. If you have a calculator with a fraction key, use it to obtain the results of exercise 22 in fraction form.

24. a) Determine the saving on each item in the table.
   b) What is the sale price of each item?

Sale on summer sports equipment		
Item	**Regular price ($)**	**Reduction**
i) Croquet sets	44.99	$\frac{1}{3}$ off
ii) Baseball gloves	39.77	$\frac{1}{4}$ off
iii) 5-speed all-terrain bikes	124.98	$\frac{1}{5}$ off
iv) Fishing rods	36.98	$\frac{1}{2}$ off

25. Determine the least common multiple of each pair of numbers.
   a) 2 and 5   **b)** 4 and 6   **c)** 4 and 5
   d) 6 and 8   **e)** 9 and 12   **f)** 6 and 15

26. Add.
   a) $\frac{2}{5} + \frac{4}{5}$ **b)** $\frac{3}{11} + \frac{6}{11}$ **c)** $\frac{1}{6} + \frac{3}{8}$
   d) $\frac{1}{3} + \frac{4}{9}$ **e)** $\frac{5}{12} + \frac{3}{8}$ **f)** $\frac{5}{6} + \frac{4}{15}$
   g) $\frac{3}{7} + \frac{2}{3}$ **h)** $\frac{2}{9} + \frac{1}{5}$ **i)** $1\frac{2}{9} + 3\frac{1}{12}$

27. Subtract.
   a) $\frac{5}{7} - \frac{2}{7}$ **b)** $\frac{4}{9} - \frac{1}{9}$ **c)** $\frac{1}{3} - \frac{2}{9}$
   d) $\frac{3}{4} - \frac{5}{12}$ **e)** $\frac{5}{8} - \frac{7}{20}$ **f)** $\frac{7}{12} - \frac{4}{15}$
   g) $\frac{1}{2} - \frac{2}{5}$ **h)** $\frac{3}{7} - \frac{1}{3}$ **i)** $2\frac{5}{6} - 1\frac{3}{8}$

28. The table shows the fraction of oil consumed by the world's three largest consumers of oil.
   a) What fraction of the total world consumption do these three consume together?
   b) What fraction do all the other countries consume together?

Country or region	Fraction of world oil consumption
United States of America	$\frac{3}{10}$
Former Soviet Union	$\frac{3}{20}$
Japan	$\frac{1}{12}$

29. Add or subtract.
   a) $\frac{3}{4} + \frac{4}{7}$ **b)** $\frac{3}{4} - \frac{4}{9}$ **c)** $\frac{11}{7} - \frac{4}{5}$
   d) $\frac{13}{6} + \frac{4}{5}$ **e)** $4\frac{3}{8} - 1\frac{1}{4}$ **f)** $3\frac{3}{5} + 1\frac{2}{3}$

30. Simplify.
   a) $\frac{1}{2} + \frac{2}{3} + \frac{5}{6}$ **b)** $\frac{3}{4} + \frac{2}{3} - \frac{1}{2}$
   c) $\frac{11}{4} - \frac{5}{6} - \frac{2}{3}$ **d)** $\frac{1}{6} + \frac{5}{3} - \frac{3}{8}$

31. A grain elevator is half full. After one-half of a tonne of wheat is added, the elevator is two-thirds full. How much grain does the elevator hold when it is full?

32. The circle graph shows the results of a survey conducted by a group of students.

    a) What is the difference between the fraction who preferred butterscotch ripple and the fraction who preferred buttered almond?

    b) What fraction did not prefer:
      i) vanilla?
      ii) chocolate or chocolate chip?

    c) Which combinations of flavours were preferred by each fraction of those surveyed?
      i) $\frac{1}{2}$ **ii)** $\frac{3}{4}$

Favourite ice cream flavours

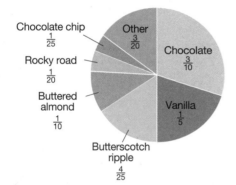

33. Multiply.

    a) $\frac{1}{3} \times \frac{1}{2}$ **b)** $\frac{2}{5} \times \frac{3}{4}$ **c)** $\frac{2}{3} \times \frac{4}{3}$

    d) $5 \times \frac{2}{3}$ **e)** $\frac{2}{5} \times \frac{10}{7}$ **f)** $\frac{15}{8} \times \frac{12}{25}$

    g) $\frac{6}{7} \times \frac{35}{9}$ **h)** $\frac{3}{4} \times \frac{21}{25}$ **i)** $4 \times \frac{3}{10}$

34. Determine.

    a) $\frac{1}{3}$ of \$57   **b)** $\frac{2}{3}$ of \$87   **c)** $\frac{3}{4}$ of \$76

    d) $\frac{3}{5}$ of \$43   **e)** $\frac{5}{8}$ of \$72   **f)** $\frac{7}{10}$ of \$91

35. About $\frac{8}{9}$ of an iceberg is below the water. How tall is an iceberg that extend 6.5 m above the water?

36. Shankar buys 1000 shares of Intl Hi-Tech at \$6¾ per share. He later sells them for \$9⅞ per share.

    a) How much profit did he earn per share?

    b) How much profit did he earn altogether?

37. Each week, Nicole drains one-fifth of the water in her 50-L aquarium and replaces it with fresh water.

    a) How much of the original water remains after each time?
      i) 1 week   **ii)** 2 weeks   **iii)** 3 weeks

    b) How long will it take for less than 10 L of the original water to remain?

38. What is the reciprocal of each number?

    a) $\frac{1}{7}$ **b)** $\frac{2}{3}$ **c)** 5   **d)** 0.4

39. Divide.

    a) $\frac{1}{3} \div \frac{1}{2}$ **b)** $10 \div \frac{1}{4}$ **c)** $\frac{5}{9} \div \frac{3}{7}$

    d) $\frac{5}{16} \div \frac{3}{4}$ **e)** $\frac{9}{10} \div \frac{12}{5}$ **f)** $\frac{21}{8} \div \frac{9}{4}$

    g) $\frac{14}{12} \div \frac{35}{8}$ **h)** $\frac{22}{9} \div \frac{7}{3}$ **i)** $\frac{5}{3} \div 6$

40. Multiply or divide.

    a) $3 \times \frac{1}{3}$ **b)** $3 \div \frac{1}{3}$ **c)** $\frac{2}{3} \times \frac{1}{2}$

    d) $\frac{2}{3} \div \frac{1}{2}$ **e)** $\frac{1}{4} \times 6$ **f)** $\frac{1}{4} \div 6$

41. a) Compare the results of parts a and b of exercise 40. Which is larger? Explain.

    b) Compare the results of parts c and d of exercise 40. Which is larger? Explain.

    c) Compare the results of parts e and f of exercise 40. Which is larger? Explain.

BOGGLE YOUR **MIND**

According to Statistics Canada, Canadians consume 80 849 kg of peanut butter every day. Of this, 20 212 kg are chunky and 60 637 kg are smooth. Based on these data, about what fraction of Canadians prefer chunky peanut butter? Survey your classmates to determine how many eat peanut butter and their preference. How do the preferences of your classmates compare to those of Canadians?

Investigating Repeating Patterns

ACTIVITY 1

 If you have access to a computer with a Draw program, you can use it to create the diagrams for this activity.

1. a) On 1-cm grid paper, draw a large square like the one below. The steps will be easier if you make the square 16 cm long on each side.

b) What fraction of the square is shaded?

2. a) Draw another square inside the first one, as shown below.

b) How do the dimensions of the new square compare with those of the original square?

c) What fraction of the original square is shaded now?

3. Repeat Step 2 as many times as you can, until the squares become too small to draw.

4. a) Make a table showing the fraction of the original square that is shaded and the fraction that is white, after each step.

Step	Fraction shaded	Fraction white
1		
2		
3		
⋮		

b) Use the data in the table to draw graphs showing the fraction of the square that is shaded and the fraction that is white, after each step.

c) If you could continue the steps many times, what fraction of the original square would be shaded? What fraction would be white?

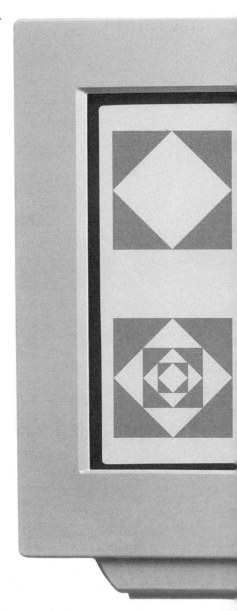

The next two activities are similar to *Activity 1*, but the diagrams are complicated to draw by hand. Use the diagrams provided or use a computer with a Draw program to create the diagrams. To complete the diagrams for *Activity 3*, you need a program that allows you to rotate objects through 60° and 120° angles. This feature can also help you draw an equilateral triangle for *Activity 2*. Draw a line segment and make two copies of it. Rotate one copy 60° and the other 120°. Form a triangle with the three line segments. Trace the triangle with the Polygon tool.

ACTIVITY 2

1. Start with an equilateral triangle.

2. Reduce the triangle by making each dimension half as long as before, and make 2 copies. Arrange the 3 triangles to form another triangle.

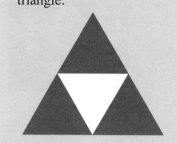

3. Repeat Step 2 with the new triangle.

4. Repeat.

5. Keep repeating many times.

1. a) Make a table showing the fraction of the triangle that is shaded and the fraction that is white, after each step.

b) How many steps would you need until the fraction of the triangle that is shaded is about: **i)** $\frac{1}{10}$?   **ii)** $\frac{1}{100}$?

c) Use the data in the table to draw graphs showing the fraction of the triangle that is shaded and white, after each step.

d) If you could continue the steps many times, how much of the triangle would be shaded, and how much would be white?

ACTIVITY 3

1. Start with three line segments 2 cm long connected like this. They form a broken line 6 cm long.

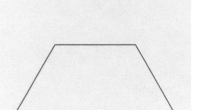

2. Reduce the diagram by making each segment half as long as before, and make 2 copies. Arrange the 3 objects like this. How long is the broken line now?

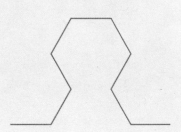

3. Repeat Step 2 with the new diagram.

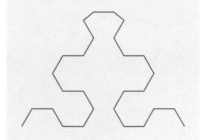

4. Repeat.

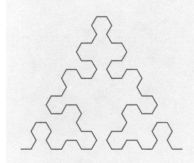

5. Keep repeating many times.

1. a) Make a table showing the length of the broken line after each step.

   b) How many steps would you need to have a broken line longer than:

     i) 1 m?   **ii)** 10 m?   **iii)** 100 m?   **iv)** 1 km?

   c) Use the data in the table to draw a graph showing the length of the broken line, after each step.

   d) If you could continue the steps many times, what would happen to the length of the broken line?

COMMUNICATING

The Ideas

Choose one activity you completed. Make a poster showing the pattern you investigated and your results. Explain what you discovered so that students who did not try the activity can understand your poster. Make a display with all the posters created by your classmates.

Paper Chromatography

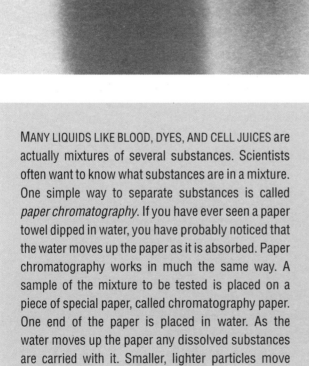

MANY LIQUIDS LIKE BLOOD, DYES, AND CELL JUICES are actually mixtures of several substances. Scientists often want to know what substances are in a mixture. One simple way to separate substances is called *paper chromatography*. If you have ever seen a paper towel dipped in water, you have probably noticed that the water moves up the paper as it is absorbed. Paper chromatography works in much the same way. A sample of the mixture to be tested is placed on a piece of special paper, called chromatography paper. One end of the paper is placed in water. As the water moves up the paper any dissolved substances are carried with it. Smaller, lighter particles move faster than larger, heavier particles. The particles in the mixture are separated according to the speed at which they travel.

Once this has been done, scientists use a ratio to identify the substances in the mixture. This is the ratio of the distance a substance travelled to the distance the water travelled. Because the edge of the water is called the front, this ratio is called the *ratio of fronts* or R_f value. This ratio is different for different substances. For any samples of the same substance, this ratio is the same. You can write this as a fraction:

$$R_f = \frac{\text{distance substance travelled}}{\text{distance water travelled}}$$

Inks are usually mixtures of several colours. You can separate the coloured substances in water-soluble felt-tip markers using paper chromatography. Gather the following materials:

- several strips of chromatography paper (2 cm by 15 cm strips of coffee filter paper will also work)
- several water-soluble felt-tip markers (black works well)
- a tall glass or graduated cylinder of water
- a ruler
- tape
- blocks or books
- scissors

Cut one end of the paper strip so it forms a point. Draw a line with a marker just above the pointed end. Keep a record of the colour and brand of the marker you used. Set up the blocks or books on each side of the glass of water. Place the ruler across the books. Tape the paper to the ruler so only the paper's point touches the water, as shown in the diagram. Let the water move up the paper until the water's edge (front) is close to the top of the paper. Remove the paper. Measure how far the water travelled.

1. a) How many different colours can you see in the separated marker ink?
   b) Choose one colour. Measure the distance it travelled. Calculate the R_f value for this colour.
   c) Repeat part b for each of the other colours in the ink.

2. Choose a different marker. Repeat the chromatography process. Answer exercise 1 for this marker.

3. Talk to another group who used the same colour and brand of marker for one sample. Compare R_f values for the coloured substances you found.

4. Talk with groups who used different marker colours or brands of marker.
   a) Were any of the component substances the same colour?
   b) Did they have the same R_f value?
   c) Do you think they were the same substance? Explain.

Mathematics & Science

Linking Ideas

THINKING PROPORTIONALLY

WHAT'S COMING UP?

DEPARTMENTS

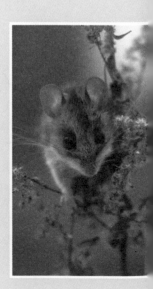

Quests

Minds on Math Project

Start With What You Know

When you exercise, your breathing rate and heartbeat change.

ACTIVITY 1

Breathing Rates

1. Determine about how many breaths you take in one minute. This is your breathing rate.

2. At this rate, find about how many breaths you will take in:
   a) one hour   **b)** one day   **c)** one year

3. Use your answer to exercise 2c. Determine the approximate number of breaths a person takes during a normal lifetime.

4. a) About how many seconds does each breath take?
   b) At this rate, find how long it will be until you have taken:
      i) 1000 breaths   **ii)** 1 000 000 breaths

5. With each breath, you inhale about 0.5 L of air. Use your breathing rate to calculate the volume of air you inhale in:
   a) one minute   **b)** one hour   **c)** one day   **d)** one year

6. About how many breaths have you taken in your life?

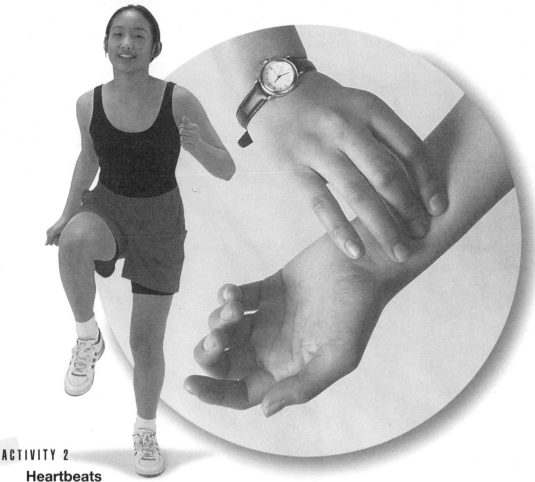

ACTIVITY 2

Heartbeats

1. To measure your pulse, press a finger on your wrist just below your thumb. Count the number of pulses you feel in 15 s. At this rate, find how often your heart will beat in:

   a) one minute **b)** one hour **c)** one day **d)** one year

2. Use your answer to exercise 1d. Determine approximately how often a human heart beats during a normal lifetime. What assumptions are you making?

3. **a)** About how many seconds does each heartbeat take?
   b) At this rate, find how long it will be until you have had:
     i) 1000 heartbeats   **ii)** 1 000 000 heartbeats

4. With each heartbeat, your heart pumps about 70 mL of blood through your arteries. Use your pulse rate to calculate the volume of blood your heart pumps in:

   a) one minute **b)** one hour **c)** one day **d)** one year

5. About how many heartbeats have you had in your life?

ACTIVITY 3

Comparing the Activities

1. About how many times does your heart beat for each breath you take?

3.1 WORKING WITH RATES OF PAY

Developing the Ideas

▶▶ *Through an Activity*

Work with a partner or in a group.

Clare baby-sat 5 h one evening and earned $25.

1. What was Clare's rate of pay, in dollars per hour?

2. At this rate, how much would she have earned after each number of hours?

   a) 2 h   **b)** 3 h   **c)** 4 h   **d)** 6 h   **e)** 7 h

3. Make a table like the one below. Insert your answers to exercises 1 and 2.

Number of hours	Clare's earnings in dollars
1	
2	
3	
4	
5	
6	
7	

4. Find as many patterns in the table as you can.

5. Use the data in the table to draw a graph.

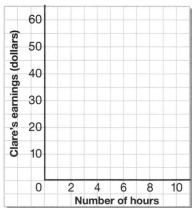

6. Write a short paragraph to describe the graph.

7. **a)** Write an equation to determine Clare's earnings if you know the number of hours she worked. Use E to represent the earnings in dollars and n to represent the number of hours.

   b) Test your equation using some of the number pairs in the table.

►► *Through Instruction*

Here is one pattern in the table.

Number of hours	Clare's earnings in dollars	Think...
1	5	$1 \times 5 = 5$
2	10	$2 \times 5 = 10$
3	15	$3 \times 5 = 15$
4	20	$4 \times 5 = 20$
5	25	$5 \times 5 = 25$
6	30	$6 \times 5 = 30$
7	35	$7 \times 5 = 35$

We see: In any row of the table, if the number of hours is multiplied by 5, the result is Clare's earnings in dollars.

We say: Clare's rate of pay for baby-sitting is $5 per hour.

We write: Clare's rate of pay is $5/h.

Using E to represent the earnings in dollars and n to represent the number of hours, we can write the equation: $E = 5n$

Is this the equation you wrote in exercise 7a on the previous page?

Here is another pattern in the table.

Choose any two rows and divide the numbers of hours.

Number of hours	Clare's earnings in dollars
1	5
2	10
3	15
4	20
5	25
6	30
7	35

Divide the corresponding earnings in these two rows.

$\frac{6}{3} = 2$ $\frac{30}{15} = 2$

We see: If the number of hours is doubled, the earnings are doubled. If the number of hours is tripled, the earnings are tripled, and so on.

We say: The ratio of the numbers of hours worked is the same as the ratio of the earnings.

We write: $\frac{6}{3} = \frac{30}{15}$ or $6 : 3 = 30 : 15$

Other examples: $\frac{4}{2} = \frac{20}{10}$ or $4 : 2 = 20 : 10$

                 $\frac{6}{2} = \frac{30}{10}$ or $6 : 2 = 30 : 10$

The graph you drew for exercise 5 on page 172 should look like the one on the right. You can use the graph to estimate Clare's earnings for numbers of hours not included in the table.

For example, suppose Clare worked $4\frac{1}{2}$ h. From $4\frac{1}{2}$ on the *Number of hours* axis, draw a vertical line to intersect the graph. From there, draw a horizontal line to the *Clare's earnings* axis. This indicates earnings halfway between \$20 and \$25. So, Clare would earn \$22.50 for working $4\frac{1}{2}$ h. You can check this by substituting 4.5 for n in the formula $E = 5n$.

To estimate how many hours Clare works to earn \$45, extend the graph to cross the horizontal line through \$45. From the point of intersection, draw a vertical line to the *Number of hours* axis. How many hours does Clare work? How could you check your answer?

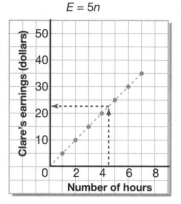

▶ ▶ *Through an Activity*

Work with a partner or in a group. Solve the problems below. Complete the exercises that follow.

Problem 1

Titus worked 4 h and earned \$24. At this rate, how much would he earn in 8 h?

Problem 2

Sabina worked 3 h and earned \$21. At this rate, how much would she earn in 5 h?

Problem 3

Betty worked 7 h and earned \$40. At this rate, how much would she earn in 14 h?

Problem 4

Gary worked 6 h and earned \$35. At this rate, how much would he earn in 11 h?

1. In what ways are these problems similar? In what ways are they different?

2. Which problem seemed easiest? Which seemed hardest? Why did some of the problems seem easier or harder than others?

3. Did you use the same method to solve each problem? If you did, explain why. If you did not, explain why not.

4. Choose one problem and solve it in a different way. Explain why you get the same answer as when you solved it the first time.

Working with Mathematics

Something to talk about

1. Refer to the table on page 173. How would the numbers in the table change for each situation below?
   a) Clare's rate of pay increased to $6/h.
   b) Clare's rate of pay decreased to $4/h.

2. Refer to the graph you drew to illustrate Clare's pay.
   a) Suppose you extend the line to the left. Does it pass through the origin? Explain why or why not.
   b) How would the graph change in each case?
      i) Clare's rate of pay increased to $6/h.
      ii) Clare's rate of pay decreased to $4/h.

3. The parts of exercise 2 on page 172 and the entries in the tables on page 173 are arranged from least to greatest. Suppose these had not been arranged this way. Would the patterns described on page 173 still apply?

Practice

4. The graph shows how much Randy earns baby-sitting.

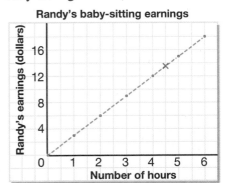

Randy's baby-sitting earnings

a) Use the graph to estimate how much Randy earns for baby-sitting 2 h, 4 h, and 5 h.
b) Use the graph to estimate how many hours Randy baby-sits to earn $18.
c) At the point marked X, how long did Randy baby-sit? Estimate how much he earned.

d) For each increase of one hour along the horizontal axis, how much more does Randy earn?
e) Write an equation to determine the amount in dollars Randy earns if you know the number of hours he baby-sits.

5. a) What is each person's rate of pay per hour?
   b) What would each person earn in 6 h at this rate of pay?
      i) Sophia earned $18 in 3 h.
      ii) Mario earned $20 in 4 h.
      iii) Mitsu earned $63 in 9 h.

6. a) Determine each rate of pay per hour.
   b) Order the rates of pay from lowest to highest.
   c) How much would you earn for working 5 h at each rate of pay?
      i) $12 for 4 h of work
      ii) $72 for 9 h of work
      iii) $65 for 13 h of work
      iv) $110 for 10 h of work
      v) $84 for 12 h of work

7. Calculate each person's rate of pay per hour.
   a) Henry earned $36 for working 8 h.
   b) Rosa earned $65.45 for working 7 h.
   c) Miguel earned $33.75 for working 5 h.
   d) Rachel earned $52 for working 8 h.
   e) Angie earned $71.50 for working 10 h.

8. How much would each person in exercise 7 earn for working 6 h?

Work together

9. Mitra works at a movie theatre. She earns $28 for 4 h of work.
   a) Make a table to show how much Mitra earns for working 1 h, 4 h, 5 h, and 9 h.
   b) Use the data in the table to draw a graph. Describe the graph.
   c) Use the graph to estimate how much Mitra earns for working 6 h, $8\frac{1}{2}$ h, and 11 h.

d) Use the graph to estimate how many hours Mitra works to earn $49 and $31.50.

e) Write an equation to determine the amount in dollars Mitra earns if you know the number of hours she works. Test your equation using some of the number pairs in the table.

f) Use your equation to check your answers to parts c and d.

10. Robin works at a bookstore. He earns $19.50 for 3 h of work.

a) Make a table to show how much Robin earns for working 1 h, 3 h, 6 h, 9 h, and 10 h.

b) Use the data in the table to draw a graph. Describe the graph.

c) Use the graph to estimate how much Robin earns for working 2 h, 7 h, and 12 h.

d) Use the graph to estimate how many hours Robin works to earn $32.50 and $52.00.

e) Write an equation to determine the amount in dollars Robin earns if you know the number of hours he works. Test your equation using some of the number pairs in the table.

f) Use your equation to check your answers to parts c and d.

11. Sue earned $24 for 3 h of work in her part-time job at the local gas station.

a) At this rate, what would Sue earn for 6 h of work? What would she earn for 9 h of work?

b) Suppose Sue had been paid $25 for 3 h of work. At this rate, what would she earn for 6 h of work? What would she earn for 9 h of work?

c) Suppose Sue had been paid $28 for 5 h of work. At this rate, what would she earn for 3 h of work? What would she earn for 7 h of work?

12. Use the *Occupations* database on the data disk. Find all the records for bus drivers in 1994. Choose five cities. Each city must be on a different continent. Copy this table. Complete the first three columns with data from the database, for the five cities you chose.

DATA DISK

Bus drivers' salaries and hours worked per week			
City	Hours worked per week	Annual salary (U.S. $)	Weekly earnings (U.S. $)	Hourly rate of pay (U.S. $)

a) Calculate how much each bus driver earns in a week. Write your answers in the table.

b) Calculate each bus driver's hourly rate of pay. Write your answers in the table.

c) For your five cities, which city has the highest paid bus drivers?

d) Compare your answer to part c with those of other students. From all the cities chosen, which city has the highest paid bus drivers?

13. a) Which represents the highest rate of pay?

b) Which represents the lowest rate of pay?
   i) $23 for 4 h of work
   ii) $35 for 6 h of work
   iii) $40 for 7 h of work

14. Solve the following problem in two different ways. Explain each solution.
Bernard earned $20 for 4 h of cutting grass. At this rate, how much would he earn for 6 h of cutting grass?

15. Look over all the problems you have solved since you started this chapter.

a) Which two of the four arithmetic operations (addition, subtraction, multiplication, division) are involved in all of these problems?

b) Why are these two operations always involved?

On your own

16. Pay Lil earned $12 for 3 h of raking leaves.

a) At this rate, how much would she earn in 6 h?

b) Make a table showing how much Pay Lil would earn for up to 10 h of raking.

c) Use the data in the table to draw a graph. Describe the graph.

d) Use the graph to estimate how much Pay Lil earns for working $4\frac{1}{2}$ h and 12 h.

e) Use the graph to estimate how many hours Pay Lil works to earn $26 and $38.

f) Write an equation to determine the amount in dollars Pay Lil earns if you know the number of hours she works. Test your equation using some of the number pairs in the table.

g) Use your equation to check your answers to parts d and e.

17. We can use a computer to generate a table showing the hours of work and the earnings. Start a new document in a spreadsheet program. Enter the information below.

TEMPLATE DISK

	A	B
1	Hours of work	Pay
2	1	
3	=A2+1	

Copy the formula in cell A3 down column A to cell A12. We'll use a pay rate of $4.25/h. In cell B2, type =A2*4.25. Copy this formula down column B to cell B12. Use the spreadsheet to answer these questions.

a) What is the pay for a 6-h shift?

b) What is the pay for an 11-h shift? Extend the spreadsheet.

c) What is the pay for each work week?

i) 30 h ii) 36 h iii) 40 h

d) Change the formula in cell B2 to display a pay rate of $5.65/h. Recopy this formula down column B to cell B12.

e) What is the pay for each time period?

i) 8 h ii) 15 h

18. How much would be earned in 8 h at each rate of pay?

a) $16.00 for 4 h **b)** $21.00 for 2 h

c) $33.00 for 3 h **d)** $42.00 for 5 h

19. Paul earned $29 for 4 h of work in his part-time job as a receptionist.

a) At this rate, what would Paul earn for 8 h of work? What would he earn for 6 h of work?

b) Suppose Paul had been paid $30 for 4 h of work. At this rate, what would he earn for 8 h of work? What would he earn for 6 h of work?

c) Suppose Paul had been paid $33 for 5 h of work. At this rate, what would he earn for 8 h of work? What would he earn for 6 h of work?

20. Solve the following problem in two different ways. Explain each solution. Brittany earned $60 for 10 h of work. At this rate, how much would she earn in 25 h?

21. Look again at your answer to exercise 15a. Are the same two operations involved in your solutions to exercises 16 to 20?

Extend your thinking

22. Bahi was paid $45.00 for 6 h of mowing lawns. She can mow 1 lawn in about 2 h.

a) How many lawns could she mow in 10 h?

b) How much could she earn in 10 h?

c) What assumptions are you making in your solutions to parts a and b?

COMMUNICATING

The Ideas

Do you think that some methods of solving a problem are better than others? Do you think there is a "best" way to solve a problem? Use a specific problem to explain your answers in a class discussion.

Which Is the Best Buy?

Yang Hsi's dad sent him to the grocery store to buy some watermelon and a box of cereal. For each item, which is the best buy?

Quarter watermelon
$1.60

Whole watermelon
$2.99

500 g $2.99   675 g $3.39   800 g $4.69

Understand the problem

- What choices does Yang Hsi have to make?
- What are you asked to do?
- What does "best buy" mean?

Think of a strategy

- You could determine a unit price for each item.
- For the watermelon, the unit price could be the price for a whole watermelon.
- For the cereal, the unit price would be the price for 100 g of cereal in each size of package.

Carry out the strategy

- One-quarter of a watermelon cost $1.60. At that price, how much would a whole watermelon cost?
- Which is the better buy for the watermelon?
- 500 g of cereal cost $2.99. At that price, how much would 100 g cost? Repeat this calculation for the other boxes.
- Which is the best buy for the cereal?

Look back

- The price of one-quarter of a watermelon is more than half the price of a whole watermelon. Is this reasonable? Explain your answer.
- When a product comes in different sizes, the unit price for a small size is often higher than for a large size. Is this reasonable? Explain.
- Can you be certain that the unit price for a small size is higher than the unit price for a large size?
- What other ways could you have compared the prices of the watermelon or the cereal?
- Do you want to change your decision about which is the better buy for the watermelon or the best buy for the cereal? Explain.

Communicating the Ideas

In your journal, describe what factors you would consider to determine the best buy or better buy in similar examples.

3.2 WORKING WITH UNIT PRICES

Developing the Ideas

▶ ▶ *Through an Activity*

Work with a partner or in a group.

Chai Kim bought 3 licorice sticks for 27¢.

1. Jim bought 5 licorice sticks at the same store. How much did Jim's licorice sticks cost?

   Think: 3 licorice sticks cost 27¢.

   How much would 1 licorice stick cost?

   How much would 5 licorice sticks cost?

2. How much would each cost?

   a) 6 sticks   **b)** 12 sticks   **c)** 10 sticks   **d)** 9 sticks

3. Copy and complete this table.

Number of licorice sticks	Cost in cents
3	
1	
5	
6	
12	
10	
9	

4. Find as many patterns in the table as you can.

5. Use the data in the table to draw a graph. Describe the graph.

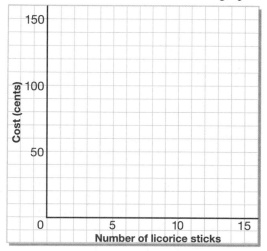

6. **a)** Extend the line on your graph to the right. Use it to estimate the cost of 7 sticks of licorice and 15 sticks of licorice.

   b) Use the graph to determine how many licorice sticks you can buy for $1.00.

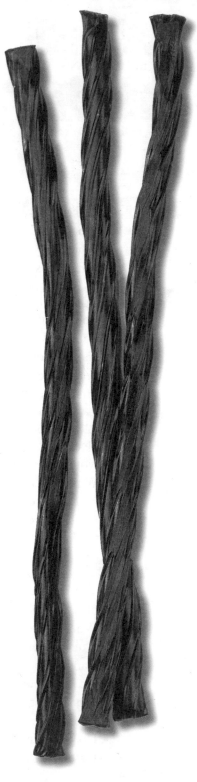

7. a) Write an equation to determine the cost if you know the number of licorice sticks. Use C for the cost in cents and n for the number of licorice sticks.

b) Test your equation using some of the number pairs in the table.

▶▶ *Through Instruction*

Here is one pattern in the table.

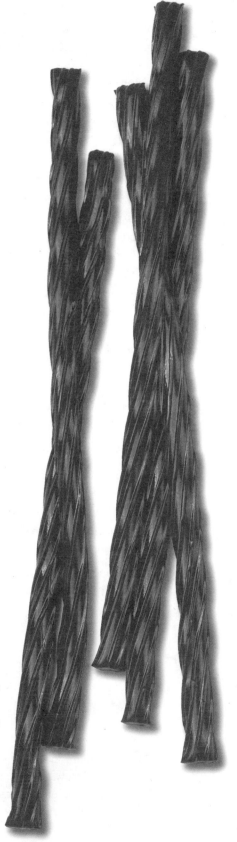

Number of licorice sticks	Cost in cents	Think...
3	27	$3 \times 9 = 27$
1	9	$1 \times 9 = 9$
5	45	$5 \times 9 = 45$
6	54	$6 \times 9 = 54$
12	108	$12 \times 9 = 108$
10	90	$10 \times 9 = 90$
9	81	$9 \times 9 = 81$

We see: In any row of the table, if the number of licorice sticks is multiplied by 9, the result is the cost in cents.

We say: The price is 9¢ per stick. This is called the *unit price*.

We write: The price is 9¢/stick.

Using C for the cost in cents and n for the number of licorice sticks, we can write the equation: $C = 9n$

Is this the equation you wrote in exercise 7a?

Here is another pattern in the table.

Divide the numbers of sticks in any two rows.

Number of licorice sticks	Cost in cents
3	27
1	9
5	45
6	54
12	108
10	90
9	81

$\frac{10}{5} = 2$

Divide the corresponding costs in these two rows.

$\frac{90}{45} = 2$

We see: If the number of sticks is doubled, the cost is doubled. If the number of sticks is tripled, the cost is tripled, and so on.

We say: The ratio of the numbers of sticks is the same as the ratio of the costs.

We write: $\frac{10}{5} = \frac{90}{45}$ or $10 : 5 = 90 : 45$

Other examples: $\frac{3}{6} = \frac{27}{54}$ or $3 : 6 = 27 : 54$

$\frac{9}{3} = \frac{81}{27}$ or $9 : 3 = 81 : 27$

Work with a partner or in a group. Solve the
problems below. Complete the exercises that follow.

Problem 1

Paul bought 3 cans of pop for $2.25.
At this price, how much would 6 cans of
pop cost?

Problem 2

Felicia bought 4 pieces of gum for 20¢.
At this price, how much would 6 pieces of
gum cost?

Problem 3

Manuel bought 4 kiwis for $1.09.
At this price, how much would 8 kiwis cost?

Problem 4

Wendy bought 4 grapefruits for $1.89.
At this price, how much would 7
grapefruit cost?

1. In what ways are these problems similar? In what ways are they different?

2. In what ways are these problems similar to the problems on page 174?

3. Which problem seemed easiest? Which seemed hardest? Why did some
   of the problems seem easier or harder than others?

4. Did you use the same method to solve each problem? If you did,
   explain why. If you did not, explain why not.

5. Solve one problem in a way that is different from the way you
   solved it the first time.

**BOGGLE**YOUR**MIND**

Each day, more than 75 million meteors enter Earth's
atmosphere. How many enter in one hour?
Use an almanac or an atlas to find the area of Earth.
Estimate how many meteors enter the atmosphere above
each square kilometre of Earth's surface in 10 years.

Working with Mathematics

Something to talk about

1. Refer to the table on page 181. How would the numbers in the table change for each situation below? Use numerical examples to illustrate your answers.
   a) The price of licorice sticks increased to 10¢.
   b) The price of licorice sticks decreased to 8¢.

2. Refer to the graph you drew to illustrate the price of licorice sticks.
   a) Why do the points on the graph lie on a straight line passing through the origin?
   b) How would the graph change for each situation in exercise 1?

Practice

3. For each food:
   a) What is the cost per kilogram?
   b) What is the cost for 2 kg?
      i) A 3-kg roast of beef costs $15.00.
      ii) A 4-kg chicken costs $8.40.
      iii) A 0.5-kg smoked salmon costs $4.00.
      iv) A 10-kg bag of potatoes costs $5.60.
      v) A 5-kg bag of apples costs $4.80.
      vi) An 8-kg turkey costs $27.75.

4. Which pricing has the lower unit price?
   a) pop at $5.99 for 2 dozen 355-mL cans or $0.59 for 750-mL bottle
   b) salsa at $2.49 for 375 mL or $3.99 for 750 mL
   c) cereal at $3.99 for 800 g, or $3.49 for 625 g
   d) milk at $3.20 for 4 L, or $2.40 for 2 L
   e) cheese at $5.00 for 350 g, or $3.50 for 250 g

Work together

5. Tom bought 4 popsicles for 60¢.
   a) What is the price of each popsicle?
   b) Make a table to show how much Tom pays for 4, 1, 2, 5, 10, and 13 popsicles.

c) Use the data in the table to draw a graph. Label the horizontal axis with numbers up to 20. Describe the graph.
d) Extend the graph to show costs for up to 20 popsicles. Use the graph to estimate the costs of 7, 15, and 18 popsicles.
e) Use the graph to determine how many popsicles Tom can buy for $1.00 and for $3.00.
f) Write an equation to determine the amount in cents Tom pays if you know the number of popsicles he buys. Test your equation using some of the number pairs in the table.
g) Use your equation to check your answers to parts d and e.

6. Markers are packaged in four different quantities.
   a) Calculate the price per marker for each package.
   b) What reasons might you have for not choosing the package with the lowest price per marker?

Markers

30 for	$9.75
24 for	$6.75
12 for	$4.25
8 for	$3.25

7. You can use a computer to complete exercise 6. Start a new document in a spreadsheet program. Enter the information from the table in exercise 6.

TEMPLATE DISK

	A	B	C
1	Marker prices		
2			
3	Quantity	for...	Unit price
4	30	9.75	
5	24	6.75	
6	12	4.25	
7	8	3.25	

a) Type a formula in cell C4 that calculates the cost of one marker. Copy the formula down to cell C7. Do the results agree with your results from exercise 6?

b) By changing the price in cell B5, determine the price this package should have so that it has the same unit price as the 30-marker package. Repeat for cells B6 and B7. How do the new prices compare with the old ones?

8. Solve the following problem in two different ways. Explain each solution.
Tom bought 4 popsicles. They cost 60¢. Brittany bought 20 popsicles at the same store. How much did Brittany's popsicles cost?

9. Look again at your answer to exercise 15a on page 176. Are the same two operations involved in your solutions to the problems on pages 182 and 183?

On your own

10. Umaa bought 3 pieces of gum for 21¢.
    a) At this price, how much would 6 pieces of gum cost?
    b) Make a table to show how much Umaa pays for 1, 3, 6, 8, and 12 pieces of gum.
    c) Use the data in the table to draw a graph.
    d) Use the graph to estimate the costs of 4, 7, and 10 pieces of gum.
    e) Write an equation to determine the amount in cents Umaa pays if you know the number of pieces of gum she buys. Test your equation using some of the number pairs in the table.
    f) Use your equation to check your answers to part d.

11. For each item, which pricing has the lower unit price?
    a) grapefruit at 3/99¢ or 5/$1.29
    b) flour at $3.21 for 2.5 kg or $2.65 for 2 kg
    c) sugar at 99¢ for 2 kg or $2.35 for 5 kg

12. Solve each problem in two different ways.
    a) Dobrilla bought 4 licorice sticks for 60¢. At this price, how much would 24 licorice sticks cost?
    b) At another store, Hakeem bought 4 licorice sticks for 70¢. At this price, how much would 6 licorice sticks cost?

13. **a)** Paper is packaged in four different quantities. List the packages in order from least expensive per sheet to most expensive.

Paper

50 sheets for	$1.24
100 sheets for	$1.77
200 sheets for	$3.32
250 sheets for	$3.99

b) Modify the spreadsheet in exercise 7 to use it to check your answers to part a.

Extend your thinking

14. Wilson was buying supplies for the class picnic for 30 people.

	Large size	Giant size
Paper plates	40/$2.44	100/$5.99
Paper cups	12/96¢	50/$4.50
Serviettes	50/65¢	300/$2.99
Fruit drinks	2 L/$1.49	8 L/$5.75

a) Which size of each item do you think he should buy? Explain your answers.
b) Make a list of the purchases you think he should make. Determine the total cost.

The Ideas

Cut out newspaper advertisements showing the prices and amounts of a few items. Calculate the unit price for each item. In your journal, include the advertisements and your calculations of the unit prices.

Heartbeats, Breathing, and Lifetimes

Scientists have observed that, on the average, most mammals live for approximately one billion heartbeats. This is true even though they have different life spans.

1. The shrew is a small creature that lives for approximately two years. Its heart can beat as many as 800 times per minute. Calculate about how many times a shrew's heart beats during its lifetime. Is the answer about one billion?

2. The elephant lives for approximately 65 years. Its heart beats about 25 times per minute. Calculate about how many times an elephant's heart beats during its lifetime. Is the answer about one billion?

White-footed mouse

3. Assume that the shrew and the elephant are typical mammals. About how many heartbeats do most mammals have in their lifetimes?

4. For each mammal in the table below, find approximately how many heartbeats it has in one minute.

Mammal	Average life span (years)
Squirrel	10
Domestic cat	12
Polar bear	25
Gorilla	43

Red squirrel

5. There is one mammal that is an exception to the pattern. Which mammal do you think this is? How do you know?

6. Scientists have also observed that all mammals, including humans, take about one breath for every four heartbeats.
   a) How does this rate compare with *Activity 3* on page 171?
   b) About how many breaths does a mammal take in its lifetime?
   c) Calculate the breathing rates, in breaths per minute, for the animals in exercises 1, 2, and 4.

3.3 *WORKING WITH SPEED*

Developing the Ideas

▶ ▶ *Through an Activity*

Work with a partner or in a group.

In January, 1992, Roberta Bondar was the first Canadian woman to orbit Earth in the space shuttle *Discovery*. The speed of the shuttle depends on its orbit. The average speed is about 28 000 km/h.

1. How far did Roberta travel in 1 h?

2. How far did Roberta travel in each time?
   a) 0.5 h   **b)** 1.5 h   **c)** 2 h   **d)** 2.5 h   **e)** 3 h

3. Copy and complete the table. Use the data from exercises 1 and 2.

Time in hours	Distance in kilometres
0	0
0.5	
1.0	

4. Find as many patterns in the table as you can.

5. Use the data in the table to draw a graph. Describe the graph.

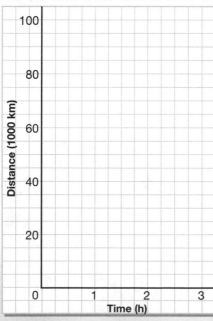

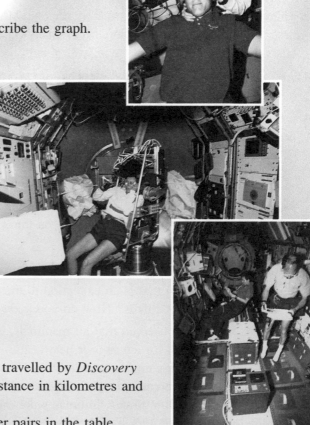

6. a) Write an equation to determine the distance travelled by *Discovery* if you know the time in hours. Use *d* for distance in kilometres and *t* for time.

   b) Test your equation using some of the number pairs in the table.

Work with a partner or in a group. Solve the problems below. Complete the exercises that follow.

Problem 1

After 2 h of flying, a plane had travelled 1600 km. At this speed, how far would it travel in 4 h?

Problem 2

In 4 h, a train travelled 800 km. At this speed, how far would it travel in 7 h?

Problem 3

After driving for 2 h, Marcia's mom had travelled 125 km. At this speed, how far would she travel in 6 h?

Problem 4

In 9 min, Abdul cycled 2 km. At this speed, how far could he cycle in 15 min?

1. In what ways are these problems similar? In what ways are they different?

2. In what ways are these problems similar to the problems on pages 174 and 182?

3. Which problem seemed easiest? Which seemed hardest? Why did some of the problems seem easier or harder than others?

4. Did you use the same method to solve each problem? If you did, explain why. If you did not, explain why not.

5. Solve one problem in a way that is different from the way you solved it the first time.

6. What assumption are you making about the speeds in your solutions to all of these problems? Do you think this assumption is reasonable?

BOGGLE YOUR MIND

In one second, the sun consumes about 4 million tonnes of its own matter. Use an almanac or a database to find the mass of the sun. How many years will the sun last before it burns out?

Working with Mathematics

Something to talk about

1. Refer to the table you completed on page 186. How would the numbers in the table change for each situation?
   a) The average speed of *Discovery* is 35 000 km/h.
   b) The average speed of *Discovery* is 20 000 km/h.

2. Refer to the graph you drew to illustrate the speed of *Discovery*.
   a) Why do the points on the graph lie on a straight line passing through the origin?
   b) From the graph, about how long would it take *Discovery* to travel 50 000 km?
   c) From the graph, about how far would *Discovery* travel in $2\frac{1}{4}$ h?
   d) How would the graph change for each situation in exercise 1?

Practice

3. a) What is the average speed of each vehicle below, in kilometres per hour?
   b) How far would it travel in 6 h?
   i) A car travels 120 km in 2 h.

   ii) A train travels 500 km in 3 h.

   iii) A plane travels 1000 km in 1.5 h.

   iv) A bicycle travels 3 km in 10 min.

   v) A space shuttle travels 500 km in 1 min.

Work together

4. Ashok cycles 34 km in 2 h.
   a) What is Ashok's average speed in kilometres per hour?
   b) Suppose he maintains this average speed. Make a table to show how far he cycles in 1 h, 2 h, 5 h, and 8 h.
   c) Use the data in the table to draw a graph. Describe the graph.
   d) Use the graph to estimate how far Ashok cycles in 3 h, 7 h, and 9 h.
   e) Use the graph to estimate how long it takes Ashok to cycle 60 km and 110 km.
   f) Write an equation to determine the distance cycled in kilometres if you know the time in hours. Test your equation using some of the number pairs in the table.
   g) Use your equation to check your answers to parts d and e.

5. One morning on their vacation, the Tsang family travelled 160 km in 2 h.
   a) At this speed, how far would they travel in 3 h? How far would they travel in 6 h?
   b) Suppose the Tsangs had travelled 170 km in 2 h. At this speed, how far would they travel in 3 h? How far would they travel in 6 h?
   c) Suppose the Tsangs had travelled 190 km in 3 h. At this speed, how far would they travel in 5 h? How far would they travel in 7 h?
   d) Compare the problems in parts a, b, and c with exercise 11 on page 176. In what ways are these problems similar? In what ways are they different?

6. For each distance and time below
   a) Which represents the highest average speed?
   b) Which represents the lowest average speed?
   i) 8 km in 5 min
   ii) 25 km in 15 min
   iii) 30 km in 8 min

7. This item appeared in *Science Digest* magazine in September 1986.

> Women walk faster and farther than men in everyday activities. In a study of 200 adults, it was found that women walked at 78.0 m/min; men walked at 74.7 m/min. On an average trip the women logged 890 m, the men lagged at 720 m.

a) About how long would it take the average woman to complete her average trip?

b) About how long would it take the average man to complete his average trip?

8. Solve the problem below in two different ways. Explain each solution.
A bus travelled 320 km in 4 h. At this speed, how far could it travel in 6 h?

9. Look again at your answer to exercise 15a on page 176. Are the same two operations involved in your solutions to the problems on pages 187 and 188?

On your own

10. How far would you travel in 6 h at each speed?

a) 160 km in 2 h **b)** 200 km in 3 h
c) 1000 km in 12 h **d)** 450 km in 5 h

11. a) A certain make of toy car travels 20 m in 10 s. At this speed, how far would it travel in 5 s? - In 15 s?

b) Copy and complete this table. It should show how far the car would travel for times up to one minute.

Time in seconds	Distance in metres
0	0
5	
10	
15	

c) Use the data in the table to draw a graph. Describe the graph.

d) Use the graph to estimate how far the car travels in 28 s and in 43 s.

e) Write an equation to determine the distance travelled in metres by the car if you know the time in seconds. Test your equation using some of the number pairs in the table.

f) Use your equation to check your answers to part d.

12. a) Suppose the car in exercise 11 could travel 24 m in 10 s. At this speed:
 i) How far would it travel in 20 s?
 ii) How far would it travel in 45 s?

b) Suppose the car could travel 19 m in 7 s. At this speed, how far would it travel in one minute?

13. Solve this problem in two different ways.
A plane travelled 5000 km in 8 h. At this speed, how far could it travel in 12 h?

Extend your thinking

14. To maintain an average speed of 40 km/h on her bicycle, Jane knows that she has to pedal constantly at 80 rotations per minute.

a) Suppose she does this for one hour. How many pedal rotations would she have completed?

b) How far does her bicycle move for each pedal rotation?

15. Refer to the table and graph on page 186. Notice that the time at the beginning was not stated. Could this have been at the start of the flight? Explain why or why not.

COMMUNICATING

The Ideas

In your journal, write an explanation of how you can calculate average speed. Use an example to illustrate your explanation.

3.4 RECOGNIZING PROPORTIONAL AND NON-PROPORTIONAL SITUATIONS

Developing the Ideas

▶ ▶ *Through Instruction*

The situations in the first three sections of this chapter have certain features in common. The tables and graphs from these sections are reproduced here to remind you of these features.

Clare's earnings

Number of hours	Clare's earnings in dollars
1	5
2	10
3	15
4	20
5	25
6	30
7	35

× 5

Cost of licorice

Number of licorice sticks	Cost in cents
3	27
1	9
5	45
6	54
12	108
10	90
9	81

× 9

***Discovery* space shuttle**

Time in hours	Distance in kilometres
0	0
0.5	14 000
1.0	28 000
1.5	42 000
2.0	56 000
2.5	70 000
3.0	84 000

× 28 000

$E = 5n$

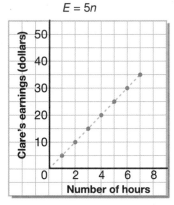

$C = 9n$

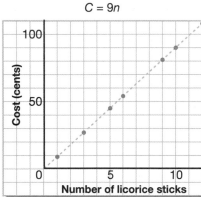

$d = 28\,000t$

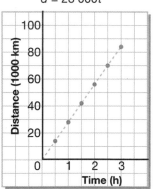

In each situation, two quantities are involved.
- The quantities involved are always related by multiplication or division.
- The points on each graph lie on a straight line passing through the origin.
- The graphs lean upwards to the right.

Any situation that has these properties is called a *proportional situation*. Solving problems about proportional situations involves a certain kind of thinking called *proportional thinking*. You have been using proportional thinking since you started this chapter.

To use proportional thinking effectively, you must be able to recognize proportional situations.

Group 1

Taxi fares are $2.00 plus 25¢ for each kilometre travelled.

Distance in kilometres	Cost in dollars
1	
2	
3	

Group 2

Two eggs make 3 slices of French toast.

Number of eggs	Number of slices
1	
2	
3	

Group 3

In a parking lot, the first hour is free. After that, the cost is $2/h.

Number of hours	Cost in dollars
1	
2	
3	

Group 4

A car used 10 L of gasoline to travel 90 km.

Number of litres of gas	Distance travelled in kilometres
10	
20	
30	

Work in a group, with one of 4 situations described above.

1. Make a table like the one shown. Include several pairs of values in your table.

2. Use the data in the table to draw a graph.

3. Is this a proportional situation? Explain your answer using the table and the graph.

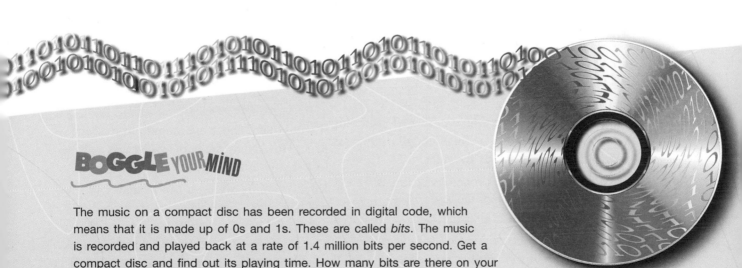

BOGGLE YOUR MIND

The music on a compact disc has been recorded in digital code, which means that it is made up of 0s and 1s. These are called *bits*. The music is recorded and played back at a rate of 1.4 million bits per second. Get a compact disc and find out its playing time. How many bits are there on your disc? How many are there on each track?

Working with Mathematics

Something to talk about

1. Which tables, graphs, and description represent proportional situations? Explain your answers. Explain why the others do not represent proportional situations.

a)

Number of quarters	Value in dollars
2	$0.50
8	$2.00
5	$1.25
20	$5.00
30	$7.50

b)

Degrees Celsius	Degrees Fahrenheit
−40	−40
−20	−4
0	32
20	68
40	104

c)

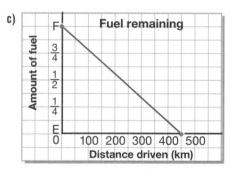

d)

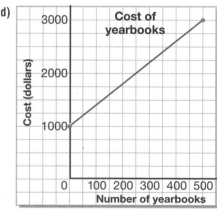

e) Five cartons of milk are needed for every 3 people. How many cartons are needed for 24 people?

Work together

Use tables or graphs to help you answer these questions.

Which problems below represent proportional situations? Explain how you know.

Why do the other problem(s) not represent proportional situations?

After you have answered these questions, solve each problem.

2. A space shuttle completes 2 orbits of Earth in 3 h. At this speed, how many orbits would it complete in 24 h?

3. Julie exchanged $7 Canadian for $5 U.S. How many Canadian dollars would she need to get $30 U.S.?

4. Tom and Kan Shu were running around a track at the same speed. When Tom had completed 10 laps, Kan Shu had completed 5 laps. When Tom had completed 30 laps, how many laps had Kan Shu completed?

5. The item below appeared in a one-page magazine advertisement for World Wildlife Fund.

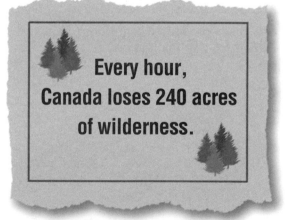

It would take about one minute to read the page. How many acres of wilderness will be lost in this time?

6. Kayla's family are on a trip in their car. The gas tank was $\frac{1}{2}$ full when they stopped to fill it up. They needed 30 L of gas to fill it. The next time they stopped for gas, the tank was $\frac{1}{4}$ full. How many litres did they need to fill it then?

On your own

Solve each problem. Which ones represent proportional situations?

7. To measure a patient's pulse, a doctor counts the number of beats in 10 s. Suppose there were 14 beats in this time. What is the patient's pulse rate in beats per minute?

8. Martin had a $2 bill. After purchasing 5 sour keys, he had $1.50 left. How much money would he have left if he had purchased 8 sour keys?

9. For every 50 swimmers there should be 2 lifeguards. How many lifeguards should there be for 200 swimmers?

10. Sue is 12 years old and her mother is 36 years old. How old will her mother be when Sue is 24 years old?

11. Some doctors prescribe the drug dimetane for children. The recommended daily dosage is 2 mg for every 5 kg of body mass. What is the daily dosage for a 30-kg child?

Extend your thinking

12. To promote energy conservation, a hydro-electric company prepared a booklet of tips. One tip is to replace light bulbs with bulbs having slightly lower wattages. This table appeared in the booklet.

Watts	100	90	60	52
Lumens	1650	1420	860	750

Watts measure the amount of electricity a light bulb uses, and lumens measure the amount of light you get from the bulb.

a) Is the relationship between watts and lumens a proportional situation? Explain how you know.

b) Do you think you would notice a difference if you used a 52-W light bulb instead of a 60-W light bulb, or if you used a 90-W light bulb instead of a 100-W light bulb?

c) If you painted a 100-W light bulb black, how many lumens of light would it produce? How many watts of electricity would it use?

13. An estimated 150 million viewers watched the 1994 Super Bowl on television.

Super Bowl ads snapped up at $900,000 for 30 seconds

NEW YORK (AP) — It's worth it.

That's not a marketing slogan, but it may be the refrain of advertisers forking over $900,000 (U.S.) for each 30 seconds of commercial time during next month's Super Bowl on NBC.

A month before the Jan. 30 contest, NBC has less than eight of 56 half-minute spots available. If they all sell at around the $900,000 price, the network would bring in $50.4 million in revenue, exceeding the approximately $41 million it paid for broadcast rights.

a) On the day the above article appeared in newspapers, $1 U.S. was worth about $1.3525 Canadian. What was the cost of a 30-s commercial in Canadian dollars?

b) Use the information in the newspaper article to calculate the cost per viewer (in Canadian dollars) that a company paid for one commercial. Do you agree with the statement in the article that "It's worth it."?

c) Which of parts a and b involve proportional thinking?

COMMUNICATING

The Ideas

Look up the word *proportional* in a dictionary. In your journal, write some examples that illustrate the use and meaning of this word. Why do you think "Thinking Proportionally" was chosen as the title for this chapter? Use specific examples to illustrate your answer.

For How Long Must You Exercise to Burn the Energy in Food?

Your body uses food energy at different rates. When you exercise, your body burns more food energy than when you are resting. By increasing your body's use of food energy through exercise, you get the same result as reducing your food intake.

One table gives the food energy associated with common foods. The other table gives the rates at which food energy is burned in various activities.

Food energy content in selected foods

Food	Energy (kilojoules)
Apple	515
Bread, white slice	318
Chocolate bar	654
French fries (10)	662
Hamburger	838
Milk shake	1048
Pie (1/6)	1693
Soft drink (280 mL)	500

Approximate food energy burned in 10 min

Activity	Energy (kilojoules)
Bicycling	335
Climbing stairs	420
Cross-country skiing	480
Running	710
Ironing	170
Swimming	420
Tennis	380
Walking	270

About how many minutes would you have to ride a bicycle to burn the food energy in a chocolate bar?

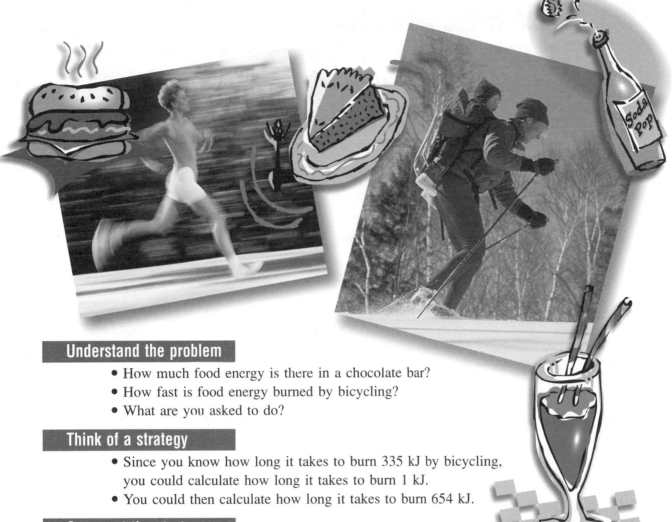

Understand the problem

- How much food energy is there in a chocolate bar?
- How fast is food energy burned by bicycling?
- What are you asked to do?

Think of a strategy

- Since you know how long it takes to burn 335 kJ by bicycling, you could calculate how long it takes to burn 1 kJ.
- You could then calculate how long it takes to burn 654 kJ.

Carry out the strategy

- How many kilojoules are burned in 10 min of bicycling?
- How long does it take to burn 1 kJ?
- How long does it take to burn 654 kJ?
- How long would you have to ride a bicycle to burn the food energy in a chocolate bar?

Look back

- To solve the problem, did you need to know what a kilojoule is?
- To burn the food energy in a chocolate bar, how long would you have to do each of the other activities listed?
- Use the data in the tables to make up a similar problem. Give it to a classmate to solve.

Communicating the Ideas

In your journal, write a description of this problem and your solution. Include solutions of the similar problems.

Unit Prices at the Donut Shop

each 60¢

dozen $4.⁴⁹

½ **dozen** $3.¹⁵

donuts

donuts

Work in a group or with a partner.

1. Joanne bought 9 donuts at the donut shop. She was charged $4.95.
   a) How did the clerk determine this price?
   b) According to the prices on the sign, do you think this was a fair price for 9 donuts? Explain your answer.
   c) What could Joanne do to get her 9 donuts more cheaply? Do you think this is reasonable?

2. **a)** Make a table showing the most economical prices for up to 30 donuts. Use your calculator to help you.

Number of donuts	Total price ($)
1	
2	
3	

   b) Use the data in the table to draw a graph. Describe the graph.
   c) Do the table and the graph represent a proportional situation? Explain your answer.

3. **a)** Add a column to your table for unit prices. Then determine the unit prices for purchases of up to 30 donuts.

Number of donuts	Total price ($)	Unit price ($)
1		
2		
3		

   b) Use the data in the table to draw a graph.
   c) Do the table and the graph represent a proportional situation? Explain your answer.

4. Find another situation like this one, in which it is cheaper to buy more of something than you really want or need.

.....3.5 *SOLVING PROBLEMS IN PROPORTIONAL SITUATIONS*

Developing the Ideas

▶ ▶ *Through Guided Examples*

Many problems in proportional situations can be solved in different ways.
We shall consider one method.

Example 1 ....

Carla has started an exercise program. The recommended
rate for doing push-ups is 3 in 15 s. At this rate, how
long should it take Carla to do 12 push-ups?

Solution

Carla can do 3 push-ups in 15 s.

She can do 1 push-up in $\frac{15 \text{ s}}{3} = 5$ s

She can do 12 push-ups in 12×5 s $= 60$ s

In *Example 1*, the ratio of push-ups to seconds is 3 : 15. Because the
quantities being compared in this ratio are measured in different units,
we call it a *rate*.

In *Example 1*, the ratio of the numbers of push-ups is equal to the ratio
of the times. We can write these ratios in fraction form or ratio form.

In fraction form

$\frac{3}{12} = \frac{15}{60}$

$\frac{3}{12}$ and $\frac{15}{60}$ are equivalent ratios.

In ratio form

3 : 12 = 15 : 60

3 : 12 and 15 : 60 are equivalent ratios.

You can obtain equivalent ratios by multiplying or dividing the terms of a
ratio by the same number (not 0).

The BiC company sells more than 12 million ball-point
pens a day worldwide. Each pen will produce more than
3.5 km of writing if it has a fine point, and 2.5 km if it
has a medium point. Suppose that all the pens sold in one
year are used to draw a line. How long would this line be?
How would the length of this line compare with the distance
from Earth to the sun?

Example 2

Write three equivalent ratios for 4 : 10.

Solution

Multiply or divide each term by the same number. For example, three ratios equivalent to 4 : 10 are:

$$4 : 10 = 12 : 30 \qquad \text{Multiplying each term by 3}$$
$$4 : 10 = 28 : 70 \qquad \text{Multiplying each term by 7}$$
$$4 : 10 = 2 : 5 \qquad \text{Dividing each term by 2}$$

In the ratio 2 : 5, the only common factor of the terms is 1. We say that 2 : 5 is in *simplest form*.

Example 3

Write the ratio 12 : 18 in simplest form.

Solution

The greatest common factor of 12 and 18 is 6.
Divide each term by 6. In simplest form, 12 : 18 = 2 : 3

In many problems in this chapter, the numbers divided exactly. This helps you to understand how to solve the problems. However, the numbers in problems often do not divide exactly. The same method can be used to solve any problems involving proportional thinking, no matter what numbers are involved.

Example 4

A car travelled 310 km on 42 L of gas. At this rate, how many litres of gas would be needed to travel 1000 km?

Solution

The car travelled 310 km on 42 L.

It travelled 1 km on $\frac{42 \text{ L}}{310} \doteq 0.1355 \text{ L}$

It can travel 1000 km on $1000 \times 0.1355 \text{ L} \doteq 136 \text{ L}$

Working with Mathematics

Something to talk about

1. Why did the question in *Example 1* begin with the words *At this rate*?

2. In *Example 1*, suppose the recommended rate had been 4 push-ups in 15 s. At this rate, how long should it take Carla to do 12 push-ups?

3. In *Example 1*, suppose the recommended rate had been 3 push-ups in 17 s. At this rate, how long should it take Carla to do 10 push-ups?

4. Explain what each statement means, without using the word *ratio*.

   a) Mrs. Adams and Mr. Singh divided the profits in the ratio 3 : 2.

   b) The ratio of girls to boys in the class is 7 : 5.

   c) The ratio of smokers to non-smokers is 3 : 7.

Practice

5. Write three equivalent ratios for each ratio.

   a) 2 : 5   b) 4 : 3   c) 7 : 4
   d) 3 : 8   e) 4 : 1   f) 1 : 5
   g) 10 : 3   h) 5 : 7   i) 2 : 11
   j) 8 : 4   k) 6 : 5   l) 3 : 15

6. Write each ratio in simplest form.

   a) 5 : 15   b) 21 : 18   c) 36 : 54
   d) 75 : 175   e) 32 : 72   f) 108 : 84
   g) 300 : 450 h) 360 : 90   i) 104 : 142
   j) 58 : 16   k) 24 : 33   l) 91 : 14

7. Sheila surveyed 60 students at her school to find out what sports they play. The table shows her results for some sports.

Sport	Number of students
Baseball	21
Basketball	24
Soccer	15
Volleyball	12

Write each ratio below. Express each ratio in simplest form.

   a) the number of students who play each sport to the number surveyed

   b) the number who play the most popular sport to the number who play each other sport

   c) the number who play the least popular sport to the number who play each other sport

8. Decide whether each situation involves a ratio or a rate. Write each ratio in simplest form. Write each rate as a number.

   a) For every metre of fabric you buy, you receive 2 m free.

   b) Moniika earned $35 for working 7 h.

   c) There are 35 girls in the school for every 30 boys.

   d) For $2.80 you can buy 500 g of chocolate chips.

   e) A train travelled 380 km in 4 h.

Work together

9. Patti did 60 sit-ups in 3 min. At this rate, how many could she do in 4 min?

10. In the first 4 games of the season, Renate scored 8 goals. At this rate, how many goals would she score in a 30-game season?

11. In 2 innings, Kovita threw 29 pitches. At this rate, about how many pitches would she throw in 9 innings?

12. Determine the goals per game average for each player. List the players in order from greatest average to least average goals per game.

	Player	Goals	Games
a)	Amy	5	2
b)	Elio	12	6
c)	Nadine	9	3

13. Car A went 96 km and used 12 L of gas. Car B went 165 km and used 15 L of gas. Which car went farther on 1 L of gas?

14. The energy burned in activities is measured in kilojoules. Determine the energy burned per hour for each activity in the table.

	Activity	Energy (kilojoules)	Time (min)
a)	Walking	135	5
b)	Running	1065	15
c)	Swimming	420	10
d)	Cross-country skiing	1440	30
e)	Ironing	340	20
f)	Bicycling	1005	30

15. Your body contains about 4 L of blood. With each heartbeat your heart pumps about 70 mL of blood.
   a) About how many heartbeats are needed to pump all your blood once through your heart?
   b) About how long would this take?

16. If you shop in the United States, you know that $20 U.S. is more than $20 Canadian. We can use a spreadsheet to convert U.S. dollars to Canadian dollars.

Look in the financial section of a newspaper to find out what $1 U.S. is worth in Canadian dollars. Suppose $1 U.S. is worth $1.3725 Canadian.

Start a new document in a spreadsheet program. Input the information below. Use the rate from the newspaper rather than $1.3725.

TEMPLATE DISK

	A	B
1	U.S. $	Canadian $
2	5	=A2*1.3725
3	=A2+5	=A3*1.3725

   a) For each cell, explain what the formula does.
      i) A3   ii) B2   iii) B3
   Copy the formulas in row 3 down to row 21. Select all the cells from A2 to B21 and format the numbers as currency.

   b) How much is $20 U.S. in Canadian dollars?
   c) Use the answer to part b to express each amount in Canadian dollars.
      i) $200   ii) $2000   iii) $2
   d) How much would you pay for each item in an American store?
      i) a jacket priced at $65 U.S.
      ii) a sweater priced at $80 U.S.
   e) Use the computer to graph the data. Describe the graph.
   f) Suppose the value of the U.S. dollar falls in comparison with the value of the Canadian dollar. What change would occur in the numbers in column B and in the graph?
   g) Is the conversion of U.S. dollars to Canadian dollars a proportional situation? Explain your answer.

17. For every 3 m of an iceberg above water, there are 25 m below water. What is the total height of an iceberg if its height above water is 50 m?

18. Here are three problems that test your ability to think proportionally. Solve each problem. The figure's name is Short.

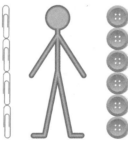

   a) Short's height is 4 paper clips or 6 buttons. There is another figure, named Tall, that is 6 paper clips high. What would Tall's height be in buttons?
   b) Suppose Short's height is 4 paper clips or 10 buttons. Tall's height is 12 paper clips. What is Tall's height in buttons?
   c) Suppose Short's height is 3 paper clips or 7 buttons. Tall's height is 5 paper clips. What is Tall's height in buttons?

19. Karl can do 40 toe touches in 2 min. At this rate, how many could he do in 3 min?

20. In the first 5 games of the season, Kwong Yeu had 30 min in penalties. At this rate, how many minutes in penalties would he get in 80 games?

21. During league play, Ann scored 9 goals in 14 games. Sharon played 12 games and scored 8 goals. Who had the better goals per game average?

22. The table shows the time in seconds for the number of heartbeats. Determine the number of heartbeats per minute for each animal.

		Heartbeats	Seconds
a)	Horse	2	3
b)	Hummingbird	15	1
c)	Lion	3	4
d)	Rabbit	5	2
e)	Sheep	5	4

23. Express each ratio in simplest form.
    a) 10 : 5   b) 6 : 15   c) 8 : 6
    d) 36 : 28   e) 27 : 18   f) 44 : 60

24. Which pairs of animals have average life spans in each ratio?
    a) 2 : 1   b) 3 : 2   c) 4 : 3   d) 5 : 1

Animal	Average life span (years)
Cat	12
Chipmunk	6
Cow	15
Deer	8
Dog	12
Elephant	65
Horse	20
Mouse	3
Polar bear	25
Squirrel	10

COMMUNICATING

The Ideas

Look up the words *ratio* and *rate* in a dictionary. In your journal, write examples that illustrate the uses and meanings of these words.

25. Which ratios are equivalent to 3 : 9?
    a) 1 : 3   b) 6 : 12   c) 15 : 45
    d) 18 : 6   e) 6 : 18   f) 2 : 6
    g) 9 : 3   h) 5 : 15   i) 9 : 18

26. A store sells its stock of 60 rolls of film. How many rolls were given free? What assumption did you make?

Colour Film

SPECIAL OFFER:
BUY 2 ROLLS—
GET 1 ROLL FREE

27. To make coffee, Corey's dad uses one more cup of water than measure of coffee. He normally uses 6 cups of water for 5 measures of coffee. To make extra coffee, he uses 7 cups of water for 6 measures of coffee. To make less coffee, he uses 5 cups of water for 4 measures of coffee. Will all these be the same strength? If you think they are, explain why. If you think they are not, which is strongest and which is weakest?

Extend your thinking

28. Scientists have found that the following statements apply to mammals.
    - The ratio of the mass of the heart to the mass of the body is about 1 : 200.
    - The ratio of the mass of the lungs to the mass of the heart is about 2 : 1.
    a) Write the statements above without using the word *ratio*.
    b) What is the ratio of the mass of the lungs to the mass of the body?

Review

1. a) What is each person's rate of pay per hour?
   i) Zenobia earns $28 in 4 h.
   ii) Koorosh earns $44 in 8 h.
   iii) Kajsa earns $51 in 6 h.

   b) Who has the highest rate of pay per hour?

   c) How much money would each person earn in 10 h?

2. Oonagh earned $112 for working 14 h.

   a) What was Oonagh's rate of pay, in dollars per hour?

   b) Copy and complete the table.

Number of hours	Oonagh's earnings ($)
1	
5	
8	
13	
14	
20	

   c) Use the data in the table to draw a graph. Describe the graph.

   d) Use the graph to estimate Oonagh's earnings when she works 6 h and 17 h.

   e) Suppose you know the number of hours Oonagh worked. Write an equation to determine her earnings. Test your equation using some of the number pairs in the table.

   f) Use your equation to check your answers to part d.

3. Jasper earns $6 per hour. On days when he works more than 7 h, he gets $10 for every hour that he works after the first 7 h.

   a) How much does Jasper earn each day?

Day	Time worked
Monday	6 h
Tuesday	7 h
Wednesday	5 h
Thursday	9 h
Friday	11 h
Saturday	13 h
Sunday	10 h

   b) Jasper's employer tells him that he may have to work up to 25 h next Saturday and Sunday, but it might be a lot less, depending on how busy it is. She offers Jasper a flat fee of $150 for the two days. Would you accept the offer if you were Jasper? Explain.

   c) Jasper is looking for a new job. He gets an offer that pays $8 per hour no matter how many hours he works per day. Would you take the job if you were Jasper? Explain.

4. Two friends have part-time jobs. Paloma works 15 h per week for $4.75/h. Raji works 6 h each Saturday and 5 h each Sunday for $6.00/h. Start a new document in a spreadsheet program. Generate a table showing the hours of work and earnings for the two girls. Use the spreadsheet in exercise 17 on page 177 as a model. Use column B for Paloma's pay and column C for Raji's pay.

   TEMPLATE DISK

   a) What formula should you type in each cell?
   i) B2   ii) C2

   b) i) After 11 h work, who has more money?
   ii) How much more does she have?

   c) i) Who earns more money in a week?
   ii) How much more does she earn?

   d) By changing the formulas in column B, determine Paloma's rate of pay if she earns in 15 h what Raji earns in 11 h.

   e) Change the formulas in column B back to what they were originally. By changing the formulas in column C, determine Raji's rate of pay if she earns in 11 h what Paloma earns in 15 h.

5. For each item, which pricing has the lower unit price?

   a) oats at $1.99 for 1.35 kg or $2.49 for 1.6 kg

   b) corn at 99¢ for 4 or $2.49 for one dozen

   c) mushrooms at $1.49 for a 227-g container or $4.99 per kilogram for loose mushrooms

6. Johanna is buying apples to make apple pies for a bake sale. The cost of the apples is 5 for 99¢.
   a) How much would it cost to buy 45 apples?
   b) A basket of apples costs $4.99 and contains 28 apples. Would it be better for Johanna to buy two baskets of apples? Explain.
   c) Find the cost per apple in parts a and b.
   d) Suppose Johanna has $14 to spend on apples. How many apples can she buy:
      i) in part a?   ii) in part b?

7. a) For each motion, what is the average speed in kilometres per hour?
   b) What distance would be covered in 4 h at this speed?
      i) A car travels 255 km in 3 h.
      ii) A person walks 10 km in 2.5 h.
      iii) A train travels 1.2 km in 1 min.
      iv) A tennis ball travels 5 m in 0.1 s.

8. A car travels 80 km in the first hour, 110 km in the second hour, and 65 km in the third hour.
   a) i) Find the total distance travelled in the first two hours.
      ii) Find the average speed for the first two hours.
   b) i) Find the total distance travelled in three hours.
      ii) Find the average speed for the three hours.

9. The fastest sprinters in the world can complete the 100-m sprint in about 10 s. The fastest marathon runners in the world can complete the 40-km marathon in about 2 h.
   a) What is the sprinter's average speed in metres per second?
   b) How many seconds are there in an hour?
   c) Suppose the sprinter could maintain her average speed for one hour. How far would she run?
   d) What is the sprinter's average speed in kilometres per hour?

e) What is the marathoner's average speed in kilometres per hour?
f) Compare and explain the results of parts d and e.

10. a) Which problems below represent proportional situations? Explain.
    b) Why do the other situations not represent proportional situations?
       i) A service station manager pays a mechanic $7.50 for every oil change she does. In one day, the mechanic earned $105. How many oil changes did she do?
       ii) A service station manager pays a mechanic $7.50 for every oil change she does. The mechanic gets a bonus of $25 if she does more than 15 oil changes in a day. In one day, the mechanic did 17 oil changes. How much money did she earn?
       iii) The wheels of a truck rotate 650 times for every kilometre that the truck travels. How many times do the wheels rotate when the truck travels 3.6 km?

11. Solve the problems in exercise 10 that represent proportional situations.

12. A printer charges $30 to set up the printing machine, then 6¢ per page printed.
    a) How much does it cost to print each number of pages?
       i) 100 pages   ii) 200 pages   iii) 300 pages
       iv) 500 pages   v) 1000 pages
    b) Which is cheaper: 2 print jobs of 500 pages each; or 1 print job of 1000 pages?
    c) Is this a proportional situation? Explain.

13. The Vancouver Sun costs 50¢ each day from Monday to Thursday, and $1.00 on Friday and Saturday. It does not publish on Sunday. Write each ratio in simplest form.
    a) the cost on Friday to the cost on Tuesday
    b) the cost on Saturday to the cost for one week
    c) the cost on Thursday to the cost for one week

Reducing Heating, Lighting, and Water Costs in Your Home

In this project, you will estimate how much money your family may be able to save in heating, lighting, and water costs.

ACTIVITY 1

Reducing Heating Costs

- At what temperature is your thermostat set during the winter? Would you still be comfortable if the temperature were set lower?
- If you can set it lower, by how many degrees during the day? At night?

Reducing the room temperature during the day by 2°C and at night by 5°C can reduce your heating bill by 15%.

- Ask your parent or guardian to look up the heating bills for last year. How much was paid for heating last year?
- Calculate 15% of that amount. How much money could your family save by reducing temperatures?

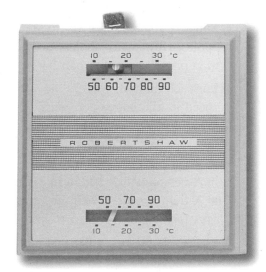

ACTIVITY 2

Reducing Lighting Costs

Ask your parent or guardian to look up the electrical bills for last year. What was your annual electricity cost?

- How many light bulbs are used in your home? What is the total wattage of all these light bulbs?
- For about how many hours daily are your lights on? How many hours would this be in one year?
- Find out from your hydro company how much one kilowatt-hour of electricity costs. This information may be contained with your hydro bill.
- How much does it cost to operate the lights in your home for one year?

You can reduce your lighting costs by replacing each light bulb with the next lower size. For example, a 100-W bulb could be replaced by a 75-W bulb.

- Suppose each light bulb were replaced by the next lower size. How much money could your family save in one year?

You could also reduce your lighting costs by using compact fluorescent bulbs. A 13-W fluorescent bulb gives as much light as a 60-W regular bulb, but uses much less electricity.

- Suppose you replaced each regular bulb with a fluorescent bulb. By how much would your family's hydro bill be reduced in one year?
- The fluorescent bulbs are much more expensive than regular bulbs. Find out the cost of a fluorescent bulb and a regular bulb.
- Regular bulbs last only about 6 months in the average home. The fluorescent bulbs can last ten times as long. How much money could your family save in 5 years by using fluorescent bulbs?

Billing Date	
Automatic Payment	Apr 18, 1995
DUE DATE May 09, 1995	
	$ 60.00
Account:	7741 10 7037723

EQUAL PAYMENT PLAN QUARTERLY BILL

750 kWh @19.900¢	
540 kWh @8.020¢	149.25
Rate Assistance	43.31
750 kWh @5.570¢	
GST #R119382901	41.78CR
TOTAL	10.56
	$161.34

ACTIVITY 3

Reducing Water Costs

Ask your parent or guardian to look up the water bills for last year. What was your annual water cost?

- Water is usually sold by the cubic metre. Find out from your utility company how much one cubic metre of water costs. This information may be contained with your water bill.

You can probably save water by taking a shower instead of a bath.

- When you take a bath, measure the length and width of the tub, and the depth of the water, in metres. About how many cubic metres of water did you use?
- When you take a shower, put the plug in the drain when you start. When you are finished, measure the depth of the water. About how many cubic metres of water did you use? Did you use less water than with the bath?
- How much less water would you use in one year by taking showers instead of baths? How much money would your family save?

You can also save water by using less water in the toilet tank. One way to do this is to put a brick in the tank.

- Take off the cover of your toilet tank and measure the length, width, and depth of the water, in metres. How many cubic metres of water are used with each flush?
- Why would you use less water if you put a brick in the tank?
- Measure a brick, and calculate its volume in cubic metres. How much less water would be used in one year if you put a brick in the tank?

COMMUNICATING

The Ideas

Prepare a report to illustrate the results of your investigations. Include any calculations you did.

Cumulative Review

1. For the set of numbers below, state the:
   - **i)** mean
   - **ii)** median
   - **iii)** lower quartile
   - **iv)** upper quartile
   - **v)** extremes
   - **vi)** range

   83, 74, 72, 77, 74, 81, 85

2. Display the set of numbers in exercise 1 on a box-and-whisker plot.

3. A bank distributed a map showing all its branches and automatic teller machines in town. The map's scale is 1 cm represents 500 m. Find the actual distance between two locations given each map distance. Express your answers in kilometres.
   - **a)** 3.0 cm
   - **b)** 7.5 cm
   - **c)** 11.0 cm
   - **d)** 4.5 cm
   - **e)** 1.5 cm
   - **f)** 6.6 cm

4. In this scale drawing, a person was 50 m from the base of a television antenna. A clinometer showed the top of the antenna at an angle of elevation of 22°.
   - **a)** What is the scale of the drawing?
   - **b)** How high is the antenna?

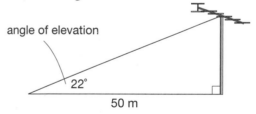

angle of elevation

22°

50 m

5. Sketch the front, top, and side views of each object.

   i)   **ii)**   **iii)**

   - **a)** For each object, which views are similar?
   - **b)** For all three objects, which views are similar?

6. Express each power as a product and as a numeral.
   - **a)** 10^3
   - **b)** 9^2
   - **c)** 2^5
   - **d)** 25^2
   - **e)** 3^4

7. Write as a numeral.
   - **a)** 1.71×10^4
   - **b)** 3.056×10^7
   - **c)** 2.975×10^9
   - **d)** 8.83×10^5
   - **e)** 9.04×10^3
   - **f)** 5.42×10^6

8. Do not use a calculator. State whether each number is divisible by 9. Explain your reasoning.
   - **a)** 71
   - **b)** 109
   - **c)** 456
   - **d)** 1305
   - **e)** 8811
   - **f)** 111 222

9. Here are some facts about birds from *The Guinness Book of Records*. Write each number in words and in expanded form.
   - **a)** The largest living bird is the North African ostrich. Some males are 2.74 m tall and have a mass of 156.5 kg.
   - **b)** The world's smallest bird is the bee hummingbird. The male is 5.7 cm long, including the beak and tail. It has a mass of 1.6 g.
   - **c)** In 1973, a Ruppell's vulture collided with a plane at an altitude of 11 277 m. This is the highest altitude ever recorded for a bird.
   - **d)** The red-billed quelea of Africa has one of the world's largest bird populations. There are about 1.5 billion adult quelea.

10. Complete the factor tree for each number. Write each number as a product of prime factors. Use powers in your product, where appropriate.

    a)   **b)**

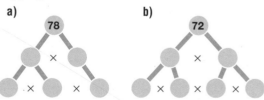

11. Draw a factor tree for each number. Write each number as a product of prime factors. Use powers in your product, where appropriate.
    - **a)** 30
    - **b)** 44
    - **c)** 84
    - **d)** 128

12. Write each product as a single number.
    - **a)** 7×3^3
    - **b)** $5^2 \times 7^2$
    - **c)** $3^3 \times 5^2$
    - **d)** $2^2 \times 5^2 \times 3^2$

13. Determine the side length of a square with each area.

   a) 36 cm^2 b) 64 cm^2 c) 81 cm^2 d) 121 cm^2

14. Estimate each square root, then use a calculator to find each square root to the nearest tenth.

   a) $\sqrt{31}$ b) $\sqrt{65}$ c) $\sqrt{83}$ d) $\sqrt{95}$

15. In 1938, the physicist Sir Arthur Eddington estimated that the number of particles in the universe is 33×2^{259}. This number is called the cosmical number.

   a) Use your scientific calculator to express this number in scientific notation.

   b) How many digits are in this number?

16. Estimate each square root to 1 decimal place.

   a) $\sqrt{18}$ b) $\sqrt{35}$ c) $\sqrt{85}$
   d) $\sqrt{105}$ e) $\sqrt{150}$ f) $\sqrt{210}$

17. Add.

   a) $\frac{5}{9} + \frac{2}{3}$ b) $\frac{4}{7} + \frac{1}{2}$

   c) $\frac{5}{4} + \frac{2}{3}$ d) $\frac{1}{12} + \frac{5}{4}$

   e) $1\frac{3}{8} + \frac{1}{4}$ f) $2\frac{3}{16} + \frac{5}{8}$

   g) $2\frac{3}{4} + 3\frac{1}{6}$ h) $\frac{1}{6} + \frac{2}{3} + \frac{5}{2}$

   i) $\frac{5}{6} + \frac{5}{8} + \frac{2}{3}$

18. Subtract.

   a) $\frac{7}{9} - \frac{1}{3}$ b) $\frac{5}{6} - \frac{1}{4}$

   c) $\frac{7}{4} - \frac{1}{3}$ d) $\frac{5}{2} - \frac{3}{8}$

   e) $\frac{11}{4} - \frac{3}{2}$ f) $3 - \frac{6}{7}$

   g) $10 - 2\frac{3}{4}$ h) $\frac{7}{6} - \frac{2}{3} - \frac{1}{6}$

   i) $2 - \frac{2}{5} - \frac{3}{2}$

19. Multiply.

   a) $\frac{5}{8} \times \frac{1}{5}$ b) $20 \times \frac{3}{10}$

   c) $\frac{13}{9} \times \frac{9}{13}$ d) $\frac{2}{7} \times \frac{7}{8}$

   e) $\frac{5}{6} \times 12$ f) $\frac{11}{8} \times \frac{2}{5}$

   g) $\frac{7}{2} \times \frac{4}{21}$ h) $\frac{1}{10} \times \frac{5}{3} \times \frac{2}{5}$

   i) $\frac{2}{3} \times \frac{3}{5} \times \frac{3}{4}$

20. Divide.

   a) $\frac{5}{9} \div \frac{2}{3}$ b) $\frac{6}{7} \div \frac{3}{14}$ c) $\frac{8}{5} \div \frac{3}{10}$

   d) $\frac{3}{16} \div \frac{5}{4}$ e) $\frac{7}{18} \div \frac{14}{3}$ f) $\frac{3}{4} \div \frac{4}{3}$

   g) $\frac{3}{4} \div 9$ h) $\frac{7}{8} \div \frac{3}{4}$ i) $12 \div \frac{3}{4}$

21. Only one of these statements is true. Which one is it? Give some examples to illustrate why the other statements are not true.

   a) Division always makes numbers smaller.

   b) Division always makes numbers larger.

   c) Division sometimes makes numbers smaller and sometimes makes them larger.

22. This sign is displayed in a taxi.

   Basic fare: $1.90 plus 10¢ per 130 m

   Wait time: 10¢ per 18 s or $20 per hour

   a) How much would it cost to travel each distance?
   i) 130 m   ii) 260 m   iii) 390 m

   b) How much would it cost to wait each time?
   i) 36 s   ii) 3 min
   iii) 6 min   iv) 30 min

23. The 60-storey Sunshine 60 building in Tokyo is 240 m tall. It has the world's fastest domestic passenger elevators, which travel at about 37 km/h.

   a) How long does it take to reach the top floor from the bottom floor, if there are no stops?

   b) How would your answer to part a change if the elevators were faster?

   c) Faster elevators can be found in mines. One of the fastest travels at 66 km/h. Suppose the elevators in the Sunshine 60 building could travel this fast. How long would it take to reach the top floor from the bottom floor?

PERCENT

WHAT'S COMING UP?

DEPARTMENTS

Start With What You Know

1. What percent of each circle is red?

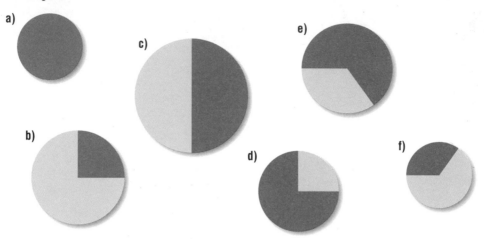

a)

c)

e)

b)

d)

f)

2. The map uses different colours to show average annual precipitation information for Canada. Use the map to estimate the percent of Canada that receives:
   a) less than 25 cm of precipitation a year
   b) 25–50 cm of precipitation a year
   c) 50–100 cm of precipitation a year
   d) more than 100 cm of precipitation a year

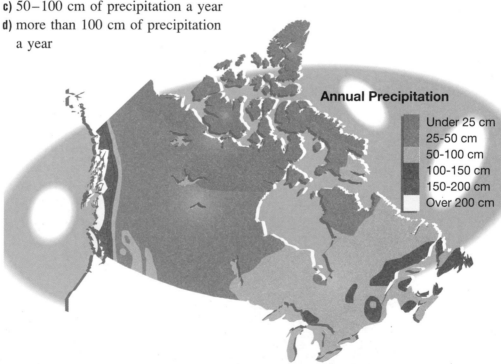

Annual Precipitation

Under 25 cm
25-50 cm
50-100 cm
100-150 cm
150-200 cm
Over 200 cm

3. What should the sum of your estimates be in exercise 2? Explain.

4. Express each percent as a decimal.
   a) 5%   b) 50%   c) 35%   d) 72%   e) 40%   f) 100%

5. In 1991, Canadians spent an average of $43 241 067 per week on take-out food. To the nearest dollar, how much was spent per week in each region of Canada?

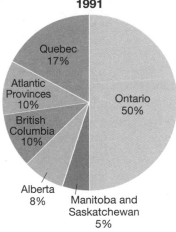

Take-out food sales 1991

- Quebec 17%
- Atlantic Provinces 10%
- British Columbia 10%
- Ontario 50%
- Alberta 8%
- Manitoba and Saskatchewan 5%

6. Write each fraction as a decimal.

   a) $\frac{5}{8}$ b) $\frac{3}{5}$ c) $\frac{7}{20}$ d) $\frac{4}{15}$

7. Write as a percent.

   a) $\frac{45}{100}$ b) $\frac{3}{100}$ c) 0.64   d) 0.01

8. Write each of these statistics about Canada using a percent.

   a) In 1990, $\frac{56}{100}$ of the people receiving a bachelor's degree from Canadian universities were women.

   b) According to the 1991 census, $\frac{3}{10}$ of Canadians were fluent in two or more languages.

   c) In 1851, only 13 out of 100 Canadians lived in urban areas. In 1992, 3 out of 4 Canadians lived in urban areas.

   d) In 1991, 4 out of 5 Canadians who were 100 years of age or older were women.

9. Simplify without using a calculator.

   a) 328×100 b) $328 \div 100$ c) 7.5×100 d) $7.5 \div 100$

   e) 0.43×100 f) $0.43 \div 100$ g) 0.07×100 h) $0.07 \div 100$

10. Suppose a number were given in decimal form, such as 5.29, 24.6, or 0.0851. Describe a shortcut for:

    a) multiplying the number by 100   b) dividing the number by 100

11. a) If you multiply a number by 0.6, is the product larger or smaller than the number?

    b) If you divide a number by 0.6, is the quotient larger or smaller than the number?

12. Use a calculator to simplify each expression. Round each answer to two decimal places.

    a) $\frac{15}{32} \times 100$ b) $4.95 \times \frac{100}{6.39}$ c) $\frac{47}{59} \times 100$

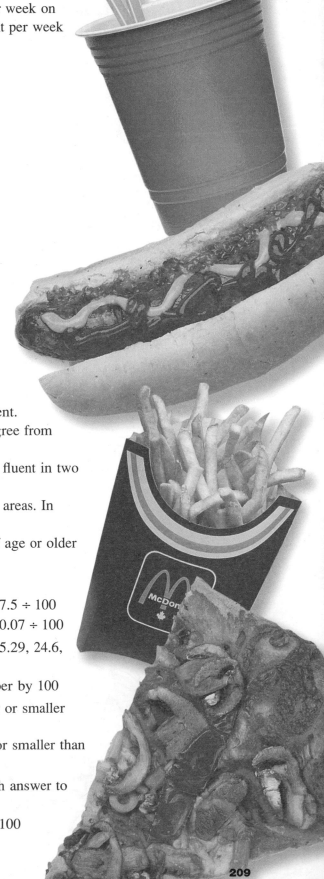

Estimating Sales Tax

You probably have made purchases and paid sales tax. The sales tax is determined by your province and is described as a percent. This is the amount you pay on each dollar you spend.

The federal government also collects a sales tax called the GST.

The table shows the sales tax rates in 1997. The 15% sales tax for 3 provinces is a harmonized sales tax, and includes GST. Use the current sales tax rate for your province or territory and the current GST rate to complete the exercises.

Province or territory	Sales tax %
Alberta	no tax
British Columbia	7
Manitoba	7
New Brunswick	15
Newfoundland and Labrador	15
Northwest Territories	no tax
Nova Scotia	15
Ontario	8
Prince Edward Island	10
Quebec	7.5
Saskatchewan	7
Yukon	no tax

1. Estimate the provincial sales tax and the GST on each item.

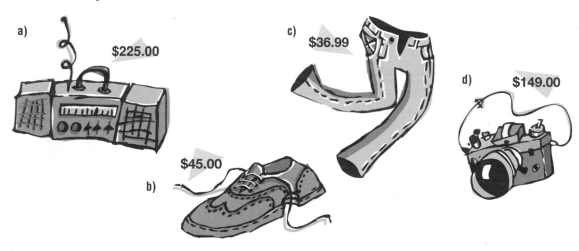

a) $225.00

b) $45.00

c) $36.99

d) $149.00

2. Estimate the total cost of each item including the provincial sales tax and the GST.

a) $29.89

b) $96.00

c) $8.75

d) $14.69

Mathematics & the Consumer

Linking Ideas

4.1 *PERCENT AND PROPORTION*

Developing the Ideas

▶▶ *Through an Activity*

Work in a group to complete one of the following activities.

Group 1

Use the sales tax rate for your province.

1. Calculate the sales tax on each amount.

  a) $2.00   **b)** $4.00   **c)** $6.00   **d)** $8.00   **e)** $10.00

2. Copy and complete the tables. Include the results from exercise 1 in the tables.

Price ($)	Sales tax ($)
0	
2	
4	

Price ($)	Total cost ($)
0	
2	
4	

3. Use the data in the tables to draw two graphs. Which graph represents a proportional situation, or do both graphs represent proportional situations? Explain your answer.

4. a) Write a formula to calculate the sales tax if you know the price. Use S for the sales tax and P for the price.

   b) Write a formula to calculate the total cost if you know the price.

Group 2

You are working in an electronics store. For a coming sale, the manager asks you to reduce the prices of the items below by 25%.

CD player	Reg. $200
Television	Reg. $400
Camcorder	Reg. $800
Laptop computer	Reg. $2800

1. Calculate the amount by which each item is reduced and its sale price.

REG. PRICE
$800.00
NOW 25% OFF

JVC

2. Copy and complete the tables. Include the results from exercise 1 in the tables.

Regular price ($)	Amount of reduction ($)
200	
400	

Regular price ($)	Sale price ($)
200	
400	

3. Use the data in the tables to draw two graphs. Which graph represents a proportional situation, or do both graphs represent proportional situations? Explain your answer.

4. **a)** Write a formula to calculate the amount by which a price is reduced if you know the regular price. Use *D* for the amount by which the price is reduced and *R* for the regular price.

   b) Write a formula to calculate the sale price if you know the regular price.

Group 3

About 90% of the mass of an apple is water.

1. You are given the mass of each apple below. Determine the mass of the water in each apple.

   a) 60 g   **b)** 80 g   **c)** 100 g   **d)** 120 g   **e)** 140 g

2. Copy and complete the table. Include the results from exercise 1 in the table.

Mass of the apple (g)	Mass of the water (g)
60	
80	

3. Use the data in the table to draw a graph. Does it represent a proportional situation? Explain your answer.

4. Write a formula to calculate the mass of the water if you know the mass of the apple. Use *W* for the mass of the water and *A* for the mass of the apple.

Here is a rule of thumb for choosing downhill skis. The length of your skis should be 5% more than your height.

1. Determine the length of the skis for a person with each height.

    a) 140 cm   **b)** 160 cm   **c)** 180 cm   **d)** 200 cm

2. Copy and complete the table. Include your results from exercise 1 in the table.

Height (cm)	Ski length (cm)
140	
160	

3. Use the data in the table to draw a graph. Does it represent a proportional situation? Explain your answer.

4. Write a formula to calculate the length of the skis if you know the person's height. Use L for the length of the skis and h for the person's height.

▷ ▷ **Through a Guided Example**

Example ···

    Determine 30% of 28 cm.

Solution

    To change from a percent to a decimal, divide by 100.
    30% = 0.30
    To find 30% of 28 cm, think:

$$\begin{aligned} 30\% \text{ of } 28 &= 0.30 \times 28 \\ &= 8.4 \end{aligned}$$

    30% of 28 cm is 8.4 cm.

Working with Mathematics

Something to talk about

1. Compare the tables, graphs, and formulas produced by all the groups.
   a) How can you tell if a table represents a proportional situation?
   b) How can you tell if a graph represents a proportional situation?
   c) How can you tell if a formula represents a proportional situation?

2. How would Group 1's tables, graphs, and formulas change if:
   a) the sales tax rate increases?
   b) the sales tax rate decreases?

3. How would Group 2's tables, graphs, and formulas change if:
   a) the regular prices are reduced by 50%?
   b) the regular prices are reduced by 30%?

4. How would Group 3's table, graph, and formula change for:
   a) a fruit that is 80% water?
   b) a fruit that is 95% water?

5. The length of your cross-country skis should be 15% more than your height. How would Group 4's table, graph, and formula change for cross-country skis?

Practice

6. Write each percent as a decimal.
   a) 50%   b) 5%   c) 500%   d) 20%
   e) 2%   f) 9%   g) $25\frac{1}{2}$%   h) $31\frac{3}{4}$%
   i) $66\frac{2}{3}$%   j) 100%   k) 75%   l) 63%
   m) 60%   n) 1%   o) $33\frac{1}{3}$%   p) 6%

7. Write each decimal as a percent.
   a) 0.15   b) 0.04   c) 0.37   d) 0.99
   e) 0.86   f) 0.01   g) 0.625   h) 1.00
   i) 0.875   j) 0.225   k) 0.275   l) 0.055
   m) 0.1075   n) $0.\overline{3}$ o) $0.\overline{6}$ p) $0.\overline{9}$

8. Determine each amount.
   a) 25% of $40   b) 25% of $80
   c) 25% of $60   d) 25% of $32
   e) 25% of $49.99   f) 25% of $199.99

9. Determine each length.
   a) 5% of 20 cm   b) 5% of 80 cm
   c) 5% of 30 km   d) 5% of 50 m
   e) 5% of 5.8 km   f) 5% of 3.7 cm
   g) 5% of 10.5 cm   h) 5% of 99 km

10. Determine each mass.
    a) 90% of 10 kg   b) 90% of 20 kg
    c) 90% of 200 kg   d) 90% of 120 kg
    e) 90% of 37.5 g   f) 90% of 54.3 kg
    g) 90% of 108.6 kg   h) 90% of 4.8 g

11. Determine each amount.
    a) 7% of $10   b) 7% of $70
    c) 7% of $20 000   d) 7% of $120 000
    e) 7% of $1.99   f) 7% of $8.99
    g) 7% of $17.99   h) 7% of $0.99

Work together

12. Determine each length.
    a) 20% of 40 cm   b) 40% of 40 cm
    c) 60% of 40 cm   d) 80% of 40 cm
    e) 100% of 40 cm   f) 25% of 40 cm
    g) 50% of 40 cm   h) 75% of 40 cm
    i) $33\frac{1}{3}$% of 40 cm   j) $66\frac{2}{3}$% of 40 cm

13. How would the answers in exercise 12 change if we replaced 40 cm with each length?
    a) 20 cm   b) 10 cm   c) 30 cm   d) 60 cm

14. A soccer ball is on sale for $39.99.
    a) Use the sales tax rates on page 210 to calculate the sales tax on the ball in each province. Calculate the total cost in each province.
    b) Copy and complete the tables. Include all your results from part a in the tables.

Sales tax rate (%)	Sales tax ($)

Sales tax rate (%)	Total cost ($)

    c) Use the data in the tables to draw two graphs. Which graph represents a proportional situation? Explain your answer.

d) Use *S* for the sales tax and *r* for the rate. Write a formula to calculate the sales tax if you know the sales tax rate. Write a formula to calculate the total cost if you know the sales tax rate.

15. About 8% of the mass of a human is blood. What is the approximate mass of the blood in a human with each mass?

  a) 50 kg   **b)** 70 kg

16. The regular price of a 4-L bag of 2% milk is $3.49. This week it is on sale for 10% off. What does a 4-L bag of 2% milk cost this week?

On your own

17. Determine each amount.

  a) 20% of $60   **b)** 40% of $60
  c) 60% of $60   **d)** 80% of $60
  e) 100% of $60   **f)** 25% of $60
  g) 50% of $60   **h)** 75% of $60
  i) $33\frac{1}{3}$% of $60   **j)** $66\frac{2}{3}$% of $60

18. How would the answers in exercise 17 change if we replaced $60 with each amount?

  a) $120   **b)** $240   **c)** $30   **d)** $15

19. Determine the amount by which each item is reduced and its sale price.

  a) Regular $34.99

b) Regular $49.95

c) Regular $2.77/package

20. Here is a rule of thumb for setting the height of a bicycle seat. The height of the saddle above the lowest point of the pedal should be 9% more than the rider's inside leg length. Vaula's inside leg length is 70 cm. How high should the saddle on her bicycle be set?

Extend your thinking

21. Karen made this pattern. She continued the pattern until she had 35 squares.

  a) What percent of the squares were blue?
  b) Suppose Karen drew more than 35 squares. Determine the percent of squares that are blue for some other numbers of squares in the pattern.
  c) Is this a proportional situation? Explain.

COMMUNICATING

The Ideas

Obtain a newspaper advertisement for an item that has been reduced by a certain percent. Insert the advertisement in your journal. Explain:
  • how to calculate the sale price if you know the regular price and the percent reduction
  • how to calculate the sales tax and the total cost in your province

What Do We Throw Away?

NORTH AMERICANS THROW AWAY A HUGE AMOUNT OF garbage. Some studies estimate that a typical suburban family of three throws away almost 20 kg of garbage every week! We are running out of room to put all of this garbage. In 1988, the Canadian Council of Ministers of the Environment set a goal of reducing municipal solid waste by 50% by the year 2000. A first step to reducing the amount of garbage is to analyze where it comes from and what it is.

As an example, let's look at the garbage collected in Alberta in 1991.

1. In 1991, 1 690 000 t of solid waste were generated in Alberta municipalities. The population of Alberta was about 2 545 000. How much waste was generated for every person in the province?

2. Much of the waste was created by industries or institutions as well as by households. Use the information in the table to calculate the percent of Alberta's waste produced by each source.

Source	Waste produced in 1991 (tonnes)
Industrial, commercial, and institutional	925 986
Residential	764 014

3. The circle graph shows the percent by mass of different materials in the solid waste stream in Alberta in 1991. Use the information in the graph and in exercise 1 to calculate the approximate mass of each item.

   a) paper products
   b) glass
   c) food waste
   d) yard waste

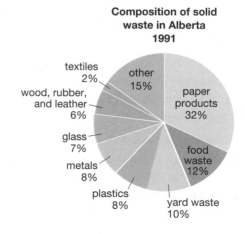

Composition of solid waste in Alberta 1991

textiles 2%
wood, rubber, and leather 6%
glass 7%
metals 8%
plastics 8%
other 15%
paper products 32%
food waste 12%
yard waste 10%

4. Twenty-eight percent of the paper products collected were recycled. How many tonnes was this?

5. Most of the glass collected was reused or recycled. Only 13 600 t ended up in landfill sites. What percent of the glass ended up in landfill sites?

Now, it's time to investigate the garbage produced in your own community.

6. Check out your own family's garbage. Use your bathroom scales or borrow one.
   a) Determine the mass of your household garbage for one week.
   b) If your community has a blue-box newspaper recycling program, determine the mass of newspapers you recycle in one week.
   c) If your family creates a compost heap, determine the mass of the material you add to your compost heap in one week.
   d) If your community has a blue-box program to recycle glass, metal, or plastic, determine the mass of material you recycle in one week. You can do this by measuring and comparing the mass of an empty blue box and a full blue box.

7. a) Based on your results from exercise 6, what is the total mass of waste material, including material that is recycled or composted, produced by your household in one week?
   b) What percent of your household waste is recycled or composted each week?

8. Compare your answers to exercises 6 and 7 with those of other students. Can you think of any ways to reduce the amount of garbage your family produces? Work with a partner to prepare a poster to illustrate one way a person in your community could reduce the amount of garbage he or she produces.

Linking Ideas

4.2 *SOLVING PROBLEMS USING PERCENT*

Developing the Ideas

▶ ▶ *Through Guided Examples*

Many percent problems involve proportional situations. You can solve them the same way you solve rate problems.

Example 1 ....

Brian had 6 hits in 20 at-bats. On what percent of his at-bats did he get a hit?

Solution

To find the percent 6 is of 20, think: 6 out of 20 is $\frac{6}{20}$.

To express this as a percent, multiply by 100%.

$$\frac{6}{20} \times 100\% = 0.3 \times 100\%$$
$$= 30\%$$

Brian gets a hit 30% of the time.

Example 2 ....

Ashley saved $30. This is 25% of her earnings. How much did she earn?

Solution

The amount Ashley earned is 100%.
25% of her earnings is $30.
Since we multiply 25 by 4 to get 100, we multiply $30 by 4 to get the total earnings.
100% of her earnings is $30 × 4 = $120
Ashley earned $120.

BOGGLE YOUR **MiND**

There are about 1 403 000 known species of life on Earth, including many varieties of animals, plants, bacteria, viruses, and fungi. The largest group is insects, of which 751 000 species are known. The smallest group is viruses, of which only 1000 are known. Humans belong to the mammal group, of which there are about 4000 known species. Calculate the percent each group represents of all known species.

Working with Mathematics

Something to talk about

1. Refer to *Example 1*. How would the percent change if:
   a) Brian had more than 6 hits in 20 at-bats?
   b) Brian had 6 hits in more than 20 at-bats?

2. In *Example 2*, how would the amount Ashley earned change if:
   a) her $30 represented less than 25% of her earnings?
   b) more than $30 represented 25% of her earnings?

Practice

3. Write as a percent.
   a) 0.45   b) 0.025   c) 0.244   d) $\frac{60}{100}$
   e) $\frac{51}{100}$ f) $\frac{6}{10}$ g) $\frac{15}{20}$ h) $\frac{1}{4}$
   i) $\frac{2}{5}$ j) $\frac{24}{40}$ k) $\frac{33}{60}$ l) $\frac{5}{6}$

4. Write as a decimal.
   a) 45%   b) 95%   c) 32.5%
   d) 14.5%   e) 5.25%   f) 9.75%

5. Determine each amount.
   a) 25% of 40 g   b) 50% of $70
   c) 60% of 40 books   d) 80% of 90 cars
   e) 10% of $30   f) 30% of $10

6. Determine the number.
   a) 2 is 50% of ■.   b) 5 is 50% of ■.
   c) 9 is 90% of ■.   d) 7 is 70% of ■.
   e) 2 is 25% of ■.   f) 5 is 25% of ■.

Work together

7. There are 30 students in Abdoulaye's class. Forty percent of the students received an A in mathematics. How many students received an A?

8. Winter boots regularly sell for $99.99. They were marked down by 25% in March. In April, the boots were further marked down by 15%.
   a) What was the selling price of the boots in April?
   b) What was the total amount by which the boots were reduced?
   c) What was this total amount as a percent of the original price?

9. Cases of pop are on sale at 25% off the regular price. The regular price for a case of 24 cans is $5.99. What is the sale price?

10. a) Penny received these marks on four mathematics tests:
   30 out of 40   40 out of 50
   15 out of 25   30 out of 60
   Determine her percent for each test.
   b) What is the mean of her percents for these four tests?

11. Who has the better batting record?
   Terry: 10 hits in 20 at-bats
   Saskia: 12 hits in 25 at-bats

12. What number am I if:
   a) 50% of me is 20?   b) 20% of me is 9?
   c) 10% of me is 5?   d) 25% of me is 30?

13. In Ms. Di Matteo's class there are 9 students who are First Nations people. This is 25% of the class. How many students are in Ms. Di Matteo's class?

On your own

14. Determine each amount.
   a) 50% of 80 cm   b) 75% of 200 m
   c) $33\frac{1}{3}$% of $120   d) $66\frac{2}{3}$% of $300
   e) 20% of 80 g   f) 80% of 20 g

15. A store reduced the price of its summer stock by 20% in July. In August, the store further reduced the price of its stock by 25%. Find the final sale price of each item.
   a) a pair of shorts originally selling for $35
   b) a T-shirt originally selling for $24
   c) a cotton skirt originally selling for $49.99
   d) a cotton jacket originally selling for $89.99

16. What is each number?
   a) 50% of the number is 6.
   b) 50% of the number is 15.
   c) 25% of the number is 7.

17. a) The mass of an animal's lungs is about 1% of the mass of its body. The mass of its heart is about 50% of the mass of its lungs. What is the mass of the heart of each animal?

i) a 900-kg giraffe

ii) a 9-kg two-toed sloth

iii) a 900-g hedgehog

iv) a 90-kg gorilla

DATA DISK

b) Open the *Mammals of Canada* database. Find and record the masses of the groundhog, the yellownose vole, and the northern long-eared bat. Calculate the mass of the groundhog's heart. Use your answer to predict the mass of each other animal's heart. Calculate to check your predictions.

18. Which items in the advertisement were reduced by 40%?

Reductions... up to 40% off!

Shirts	were $79.99	now $59.99
Dresses	were $149.99	now $89.99
Coats	were $249.99	now $149.99

19. Adrian received the test marks below. Express each mark as a percent.

a) Science: 40 out of 50

b) Music: 28 out of 40

c) Social studies: 8 out of 12

d) Language arts: 45 out of 60

e) Mathematics: 18 out of 25

20. In Ms. Bradley's class of 32 students, 24 are girls. What percent of the class are girls?

21. It is estimated that 9% of all humans who have ever lived are alive today. The world population is about 5.5 billion. Estimate the total number of humans who have ever lived.

22. The species of animals and plants now living on Earth represent only about 1% of the total number that have ever lived. The rest have become extinct. Estimate the numbers of species of animals and plants that have ever lived.

Species	Number living
Animals	1 400 000
Plants	500 000

Extend your thinking

23. In chess, the queen may move any number of squares in a straight line parallel to the sides of the board, or diagonally.

a) To how many squares can the queen move from the position shown? What percent of the board is this? This is the percent of the board the queen controls.

b) From which squares does the queen control:

i) the least percent of the board?

ii) the greatest percent of the board?

What are these percents?

COMMUNICATING

The Ideas

In your journal, write a sentence or two to explain the meaning of *percent*. Illustrate your explanation using two problems as examples. One of the problems should represent a proportional situation, and the other one should represent a non-proportional situation.

How Can You Get a 50% Reduction on a Copy Machine?

Some copy machines can make reductions. On many machines, three buttons allow you to select these sizes:

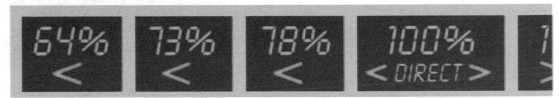

The percents shown on the buttons indicate the scale factors for the reductions. For example, if you use button 1, the scale factor is 78%. This means that every line segment on the reduction will be 78% as long as it is on the original.

Natasha's drawing is 25 cm long and 20 cm wide. She wants to make a 50% reduction of her drawing. How can she do it with this machine?

Understand the problem

- What are the dimensions of the reduction Natasha wants?
- What are you asked to do?

Think of a strategy

- None of the buttons gives Natasha a 50% reduction. She could make a reduction using one of the buttons, and then use the smaller drawing to make another reduction.
- For the second copy she could use the same button as before, or a different button.

Carry out the strategy

- Choose a button for the first copy and a button for the second copy.
- What are the dimensions of the first copy? What are the dimensions of the second copy?
- If the results are not 50% of the original dimensions, try other combinations of buttons.

Look back

- Is it possible to get a reduction that is exactly 50% of the original?
- Does it matter in what order the two buttons are used?
- What other sizes of reduction could Natasha make if she made a copy of a copy?

Communicating the Ideas

In your journal, write a description of this problem and your solution. Include diagrams to illustrate your conclusions.

4.3 DISCOUNT

Developing the Ideas

▶ ▶ *Through an Activity*

Work in a group or with a partner.

1. What do you think *20% OFF* means?

2. Suppose a hockey stick had a regular price of $1.00. By how much would the price of the hockey stick be reduced? How much would you pay for the hockey stick (ignore sales tax)?

3. Use the prices of the hockey sticks in the advertisement. For each stick:

   a) Determine how much the price of the hockey stick is reduced.

   b) Determine how much you would pay for the hockey stick.

▶ ▶ *Through a Guided Example*

Stores frequently reduce the prices of certain items. The difference between the regular price and the sale price of an item is called the *discount*.

Example

Hockey pads are regularly priced at $89.95. They are on sale for 30% off. Joanna, who lives in Manitoba, wants her mom to buy her the hockey pads. What is the sale price? Use the chart on page 210.

Solution 1

The discount is 30%. This means that for every dollar of the regular price, the discount is 30¢.

30% of $89.95 $= 0.30 \times \$89.95$
$= \$26.99$

Regular price:	$89.95
Less discount:	$26.99
Sale price:	$62.96
PST @ 7%	4.41
GST @ 7%	4.41
Total	$71.78

Solution 2

Since 100% − 30% = 70%, the sale price is 70% of the regular price.

70% of $89.95 $= 0.70 \times \$89.95$
$= \$62.97$

Sale price:	$62.97
PST @ 7%	4.41
GST @ 7%	4.41
Total	$71.79

Check if this is reasonable. The hockey pads cost about $90.00.

30% is almost $\frac{1}{3}$, and $\frac{1}{3}$ of $90.00 is $30.00. Hence, the discount is almost $30.00, and the pads should cost a little more than $60.00. The sales taxes total almost 15%, and 15% of $60.00 is $9.00. Hence, the total cost should be about $70.00.

The answer $71.78 is reasonable.

Working with Mathematics

Something to talk about

1. Why do you think stores offer discounts on certain items?

2. In the *Example*, why is there a 1¢ difference in the answers to Solution 1 and Solution 2?

3. What is the discount on each item?

a)

b)

Work together

4. Calculate the sale price of each item.

a)

b)

5. a) Why do you think the advertisement below says "up to 60% off"?
   b) Which items in the advertisement are reduced by 60%?
   c) Suppose all the items were reduced by 60%. What changes would be needed in the advertisement?
   d) Do you think the advertisement is misleading? Why?

On your own

6. Calculate the sale price of each item. Then calculate your provincial sales tax, the GST, and the total cost.

a)

b)

c)

d)

7. Is either of these advertisements misleading? Explain.

a)

b)

Extend your thinking

8. Murphy's Clothing Store had $199 men's suits marked down by 20% for a sale. After the sale, the sale price was marked up to the original price. What percent of the sale price would have to be added to return a suit to its original price?

COMMUNICATING

The Ideas

Does it make a difference to the total cost of an item if the discount is calculated after the sales taxes are added? Use an example to illustrate your answer.

Discount Coupons

U SAVE
Present this coupon and save $10.00
OFF any regularly priced item.
the **ULTIMATE** *saving*
VALID UNTIL MARCH 31

1. Tonisha and Shankar used the store's coupon above while shopping at U SAVE. Calculate the total cost of their bill. Use the provincial sales tax rate for your province.

U SAVE

2 pr. pants @ $27.95
1 sweater @ $50.00
3 pr. boots @ $34.99
Total
Discount
Subtotal
PST
GST
TOTAL BILL

2. Aisha used the Scratch'n'Save coupon (above right) to buy a pair of shoes for $68.95 and boots for $95.00. When the clerk scratched the coupon it showed 20% off. What was the total cost? Include provincial sales tax for your province and GST.

3. Use both discount coupons illustrated to determine the price of each item. Compare prices to find which store offers the better deal. Assume the Scratch'n'Save coupon shows a 20% discount.

a)

b)

c)

d)

4. For a particular item, the discount is the same for both coupons. What is the price of the item?

Developing the Ideas

▶ ▶ *Through an Activity*

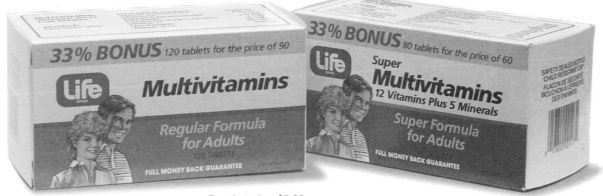

Regular price: $5.99
Sale price: $5.49

Regular price: $4.99
Sale price: $4.49

Work in a group or with a partner.

1. Explain why 80 tablets for the price of 60, and 120 tablets for the price of 90 are both a 33% bonus.

2. Suppose the bonus were 50%. How many tablets would you get for the price of 60? How many would you get for the price of 90?

3. Repeat exercise 2 for a bonus of 25%.

4. A box contains 72 tablets for the price of 60. What is the percent bonus?

5. Another box contains 150 tablets for the price of 90. What is the percent bonus?

▶ ▶ *Through Guided Examples*

You calculate percent increase and percent decrease as follows:

· · · · · · · · ·

$$\text{Percent increase} = \frac{\text{increase}}{\text{original amount}} \times 100\%$$

$$\text{Percent decrease} = \frac{\text{decrease}}{\text{original amount}} \times 100\%$$

In 1947, an investor bought Van Gogh's painting *Irises* for $84 000. In 1987, she sold it for $49 million. What was the percent increase in the value of the painting over the 40-year period?

Example 1

The price of a pair of jeans increased from $47.99 to $54.99.
What was the percent increase in price?

Solution

Round the prices to the nearest dollar.

Increase in price: $55 − $48 = $7

Percent increase: $\frac{7}{48} \times 100\% \doteq 14.6\%$

The price increased by about 14.6%.

Check: 14.6% of $48 = 0.146 × $48
$$\doteq \$7$$

Example 2

During a sale, the price of a pair of running shoes is reduced from $29.99
to $17.99. What is the percent decrease in price?

Solution

Round the prices to the nearest dollar.

Decrease in price: $30 − $18 = $12

Percent decrease: $\frac{12}{30} \times 100\% = 40\%$

There is a 40% decrease in price.

Check: 40% of $30 = 0.4 × $30
$$= \$12$$

Example 3

Last year Mr. Boichuk had 23 students in his class.
This year, he has 28 students.
What is the percent increase in class size?

Solution

Amount of increase: 28 − 23 = 5

Percent increase: $\frac{5}{23} \times 100\% \doteq 21.7\%$

The class size increased by about 21.7%.

Check: 21.7% of 23 = 0.217 × 23
$$\doteq 5$$

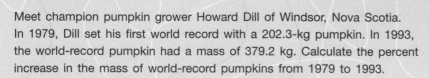

Meet champion pumpkin grower Howard Dill of Windsor, Nova Scotia.
In 1979, Dill set his first world record with a 202.3-kg pumpkin. In 1993,
the world-record pumpkin had a mass of 379.2 kg. Calculate the percent
increase in the mass of world-record pumpkins from 1979 to 1993.

Working with Mathematics

Something to talk about

1. a) Explain why 11 envelopes of instant hot chocolate for the price of 10 is 10% more.

   b) Another package is marked "15 envelopes for the price of 12." What is the percent bonus for this package?

2. a) In *Example 1*, why did we use $\frac{7}{48} \times 100\%$ and not $\frac{7}{55} \times 100\%$?

   b) In *Example 2*, why did we use $\frac{12}{30} \times 100\%$ and not $\frac{12}{18} \times 100\%$?

Practice

3. What is each percent increase?

   a) The price of bread rose from 99¢ to $1.15 a loaf.

   b) The length increased from 50 cm to 70 cm.

   c) Attendance increased from 8000 to 10 000.

   d) This year, Farah's height increased from 124 cm to 130 cm.

   e) The number of students in Carlo's class increased from 24 to 27.

   f) Joelle's hourly salary increased from $9.85 to $10.50.

4. What is each percent decrease?

   a) The price dropped from $1.00 to 75¢.

   b) The length decreased from 80 cm to 60 cm.

   c) Attendance fell from 10 000 to 8000.

   d) The regular price of a pair of hiking boots is $59.99. The sale price is $44.99.

   e) There were 20 people in Anna's aerobics class. Three people dropped out.

Work together

5. Refer to the photograph on page 225. Calculate the percent reduction in price for each kind of vitamins. Explain why the percent reductions are different, although there is a 50¢ savings on each.

6. Francine and her friends are forming a singing club at their school.

   a) Twelve people attend the first meeting. Eighteen people attend the second meeting. Calculate the increase and the percent increase in attendance from the first meeting to the second.

   b) Only 12 people attend the third meeting. Calculate the decrease and the percent decrease in attendance from the second meeting to the third.

   c) Compare your answers to parts a and b. Explain why the percents are different even though the amount of increase is the same as the amount of decrease.

7. A classmate tells you "An increase from 150 to 200 is a $33\frac{1}{3}\%$ increase. So, a decrease from 200 to 150 is a $33\frac{1}{3}\%$ decrease." Explain what is wrong with your classmate's reasoning.

8. What was the size of this 1-L bottle of syrup before it was changed to give a 33% bonus?

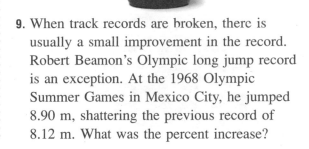

9. When track records are broken, there is usually a small improvement in the record. Robert Beamon's Olympic long jump record is an exception. At the 1968 Olympic Summer Games in Mexico City, he jumped 8.90 m, shattering the previous record of 8.12 m. What was the percent increase?

On your own

10. Calculate the percent saving on each item.

a)
Reg. $5.00
Sale price $4.00

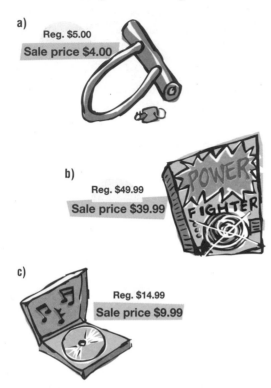

b)
Reg. $49.99
Sale price $39.99

POWER
FIGHTER

c)
Reg. $14.99
Sale price $9.99

11. Calculate the percent increase on each item.

a)
Was $89.99
Now $94.99

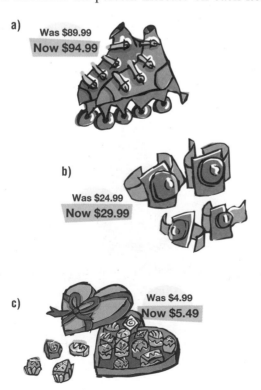

b)
Was $24.99
Now $29.99

c)
Was $4.99
Now $5.49

12. Calculate the sale price of each item.

a)
TORONTO
Reg. $26.99
Discount 10%

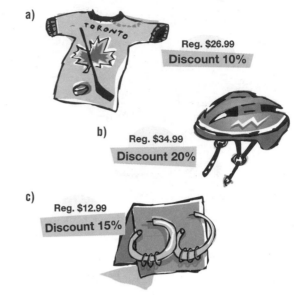

b)
Reg. $34.99
Discount 20%

c)
Reg. $12.99
Discount 15%

13. In 1972, hand-held calculators became available for $100. Today they can be purchased for about $5.00. Determine the percent decrease in the price of a hand-held calculator since 1972.

14. a) Calculate the percent bonus for this shampoo that offers 450 mL for the price of 350 mL.

b) If there were 200 mL more, would the percent bonus be twice as great? Explain.

c) Another kind of shampoo is labelled, "100 mL MORE, 550 mL for the price of 450 mL." How does the percent bonus for this shampoo compare with the one shown?

15. In 1980, the mass of a Canadian penny was decreased from 3.24 g to 2.80 g.
   a) What was the percent reduction in mass?
   b) Why do you think the mass of a penny was decreased?
   c) Some people think that the penny should be discontinued. Do you agree?

Extend your thinking

16. Ellen invested $1000 of her savings. Her investment increased by 10% in the first year and decreased by 10% in the second year.
   a) What is the value of her investment after the second year?
   b) By what percent has her investment increased or decreased?

17. Suppose your allowance were cut by 10% this week and then the new allowance was increased by 10% the next week. Would you be getting the same allowance as when you started? Set up a spreadsheet as shown below to investigate this idea.

	A	B	C
1	Original allowance	After 10% reduction	After 10% increase
2			
3			

a) Format columns A, B, and C to show numbers as currency. In cell A2, enter a starting allowance. In cell B2, enter a formula that calculates 10% of the number in cell A2 and subtracts it from the number in cell A2. This is the allowance after a 10% reduction. In cell C2, enter a formula that calculates 10% of the number in cell B2 and adds it to the number in cell B2. This is the final allowance after the 10% increase.

b) Is the final allowance greater or less than the original allowance? Explain why this happens.

c) Try to change the formula you enter in cell C2 so that the final allowance is equal to the original allowance. What percent increase was needed in cell C2 to restore the original allowance?

d) Enter a new amount in cell A2 as the original allowance. Does your formula from part c still restore the original allowance?

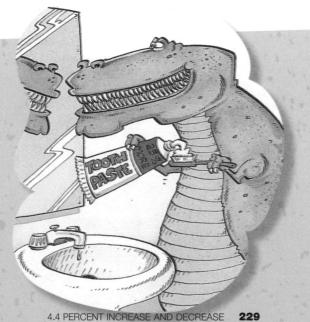

COMMUNICATING

The Ideas

Several exercises in this section involve packages that include an extra quantity of the product as a bonus. Find a package like this at home or in a store. In your journal, record the information about the package contents. If the label states a mass, volume, or number of items that you receive as a bonus, calculate the percent bonus. If the label states a percent bonus, verify the percent. Why do you think manufacturers include bonuses like these?

TEMPLATE DISK

. . . . . . 4.5 *INTEREST AND COMMISSION*

Developing the Ideas
▶▶ *Through Guided Examples*

Roshumba bought a $100 Canada Savings Bond. The interest rate, 6.5% per annum, means that after one year she will receive 6.5% of $100, or $6.50 more money. This money is called *interest*. The amount invested, $100 in this case, is called the *principal*.

Interest is money paid for the use of money. When you save money in a bank or trust company, you receive interest because the bank or trust company uses your money. When someone borrows money, the bank charges interest. The interest rate is usually quoted as a percent for one year.

Example 1 ....

Juan purchased a $500 Canada Savings Bond at an interest rate of 6.5% per annum.
a) How much interest did he receive after one year?
b) What was the value of the bond after one year?

Solution

a) 6.5% of $500.00 = 0.065 × $500.00
                                   = $32.50

He received $32.50 interest.

b) $500.00 + $32.50 = $532.50

The value of the bond after one year was $532.50.

Some sales personnel receive a percent of the price of any item they sell. This is called a *commission*.

Example 2 ....

Ms. Mikalu works as a real-estate agent. She is paid only when she sells a house, and then she receives 3% of the selling price. Last month she sold a house for $174 500. What was her commission?

Solution

3% of $174 500 = 0.03 × $174 500
                          = $5235.00

She received a commission of $5235.00.

Working with Mathematics

Each interest rate in the exercises is stated as a percent per annum.

Something to talk about

1. a) In *Example 1*, if the interest rate were doubled, would the interest be doubled?
   b) Suppose Juan bought a bond worth twice as much money. Would his bond be worth twice as much as the $500 bond is worth after one year?

2. Estimate the interest after one year.
   a) $123.50 at 5%   b) $68.30 at 7%
   c) $458.50 at 4%   d) $1015.60 at 6%

3. In *Example 2*, the seller of the house paid 6% commission. Part of this went to Ms. Mikalu, and the rest went to the real estate company.
   a) How much commission did the seller of the house have to pay?
   b) How much money did the seller receive for the house?

Practice

4. Calculate the interest for 1 year.
   a) $1000 at 6%   b) $500 at 5%
   c) $15 000 at 8%   d) $90 000 at 7%
   e) $600 at 6.5%   f) $1200 at 11.5%
   g) $21 000 at 10.5% h) $80 000 at 8.75%
   i) $200 at 8%   j) $140 at 12.5%
   k) $500 at $7\frac{3}{4}$%   l) $750 at 6%
   m) $60 at 9%   n) $250 at 11%
   o) $300 at $6\frac{1}{2}$%   p) $800 at $7\frac{1}{4}$%

5. Suppose you invest $1000 at 7%.
   a) Calculate the interest after 1 year.
   b) Calculate the balance after 1 year.

6. Suppose you borrow $800 at 15.5% for 1 year.
   a) Calculate the interest you owe after 1 year.
   b) Calculate the total amount you owe after 1 year.

7. A salesperson receives a commission of 4% on all sales. She sells a car for $20 000. What is her commission?

Work together

8. Mrs. Bateman has $987.00 in her account at the U-Save Trust Company. The trust company pays 6% per annum. She makes no further deposits or withdrawals. How much will Mrs. Bateman have in her account after the interest is credited one year later?

9. Mr. Gruder is paid a base salary of $1100 a month plus 4.5% commission on all sales. Calculate his total salary for each month.

Month	Sales ($)
September	22 300
October	21 900
November	19 500
December	26 000

10. Suppose you have $250 to invest for one year.
    a) Copy and complete tables like the ones below.

Interest rate (%)	Interest earned after one year ($)	Interest rate (%)	Total amount after one year ($)
0		0	
2		2	
4		4	
6		6	
8		8	
10		10	

    b) Use the data in the tables to draw two graphs. Which graph represents a proportional situation? Why does it represent a proportional situation? Why does the other graph not represent a proportional situation?

On your own

11. Choose a current interest rate for one-year investments.

a) Copy and complete these tables.

Amount invested ($)	Interest earned after one year ($)	Amount invested ($)	Total amount after one year ($)
100		100	
200		200	
300		300	
400		400	
500		500	

b) Use the data to draw two graphs.

c) Why are both these situations proportional, while only one situation in exercise 10 is proportional?

12. Josie borrowed $200, and repaid it with interest one year later. The interest was $20.

a) How much money did she repay?

b) What interest rate was she charged?

13. The commission is 5%. What would a salesperson receive for selling each item?

a) $160.00

b) $12 000

c) $159 000

14. In 1983, an 800-year-old book was sold for a record price of $13.1 million plus a 10% commission.

a) What was the commission on this sale?

b) What was the total cost of the book to the purchaser?

15. To get more clients, a financial agent reduced her commission from 8.5% to 5.0%. What is the saving to a customer who invests $7500?

Extend your thinking

16. When you purchase a Canada Savings Bond you can choose between these two types:

Regular bond

Interest is paid each year, either by cheque or by an automatic deposit to your account.

Compound interest bond

The interest earned each year is added to the principal. Hence, after the first year, you receive interest on the interest.

a) Stephen purchases $1000 worth of regular bonds at 6%. How much interest will he receive during the next three years?

b) Nasmin purchases $1000 worth of compound interest bonds at 6%. How much will the bonds be worth after three years?

c) Who received more interest, Stephen or Nasmin? How much more?

The Ideas

Look at the financial section of your newspaper. Find some articles or advertisements involving interest rates. What is the lowest rate you can find? What is the highest? Cut out these items and put them in your journal. In your journal, write your solution to this problem: Suppose you invested $250 at the lowest and highest rates found in the newspaper. How much would you have after one year?

Should Sales Tax Be Applied before or after a Discount?

Camping equipment is on sale at a 20% discount, but you must pay the sales tax. There are two possible ways to work out the bill.

Method 1	Method 2
Apply the 20% discount to the regular price, and then calculate the sales tax and the total cost.	Apply the sales tax to the regular price, and then calculate the discount and the total cost.

As a customer, which method would you prefer?
Would your answer be different if you were the merchant?
What if you were the tax collector?

Understand the problem

- What does a 20% discount mean?
- What is the sales tax rate in your province, including the GST?
- What are you asked to do?

Think of a strategy

- Try using a particular case.

Carry out the strategy

- Assume that you want to buy a tent with a regular price of $100.
- Use both methods to work out the bill. For each method, answer these three questions.

  What is the total amount you have to pay?
  How much does the merchant get?
  How much does the tax collector get?

- Based on this example, which method would you prefer if you were:
  a) the customer?   b) the merchant?   c) the tax collector?

  Explain your answers.

Look back

- Would it make any difference if another regular price had been used?
- Ask a few salespeople at local stores which method their stores use. Which method is more common? Why do you think this is the case?

Communicating the Ideas

In your journal, compare the results of calculating sales tax before and after applying a discount.

4.6 *PERCENTS GREATER THAN 100% AND LESS THAN 1%*

Developing the Ideas

We sometimes encounter percents greater than 100% or less than 1%. We solve problems involving these percents in the same way as before.

▶▶ *Through an Activity*

Work in a group. You will need a tape measure or metre stick marked in centimetres.

1. Measure each person's height.

2. Cross-country skis should be 115% of the skier's height. Use this rule and your results from exercise 1 to determine the length of cross-country skis for each person.

▶▶ *Through a Guided Example*

Example ·

Glen Forest School raised $5340 in the United Way campaign. Tom raised 0.3% of this amount. How much did Tom raise?

Solution

To change from a percent to a decimal, divide by 100.
0.3% = 0.003

Tom raised 0.3% of $5340 = 0.003 × $5340
                                      = $16.02

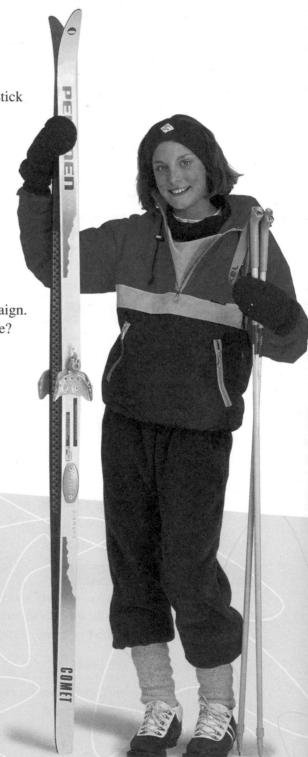

BOGGLE YOUR **MiND**

In 1993, companies in Canada spent about 10.2 billion dollars on advertising. The population of Canada was about 27.5 million. How much money was spent for every Canadian? Of the 10.2 billion dollars, 64% was spent on print, 19% on television, 8% on radio, and 9% on outdoor ads. How much money was spent on each type of ad?

Working with Mathematics

Something to talk about

1. a) As a decimal, $100\% = 1$. What decimals correspond to percents greater than 100%?
   b) As a decimal, $1\% = 0.01$. What decimals correspond to percents less than 1%?

2. Express as a decimal.
   a) 100%   b) 120%   c) 160%
   d) 180%   e) 200%   f) 0.4%
   g) 0.6%   h) 0.8%   i) 1.0%

3. Express as a percent.
   a) 1.3   b) 1.45   c) 2.7
   d) $\frac{3}{2}$ e) $\frac{5}{4}$ f) 0.005
   g) 0.003   h) 0.001   i) 0.025

Practice

4. Write each decimal as a percent.
   a) 0.20   b) 2.00   c) 0.002   d) 0.485
   e) 0.005   f) 0.0035   g) 1.48   h) 4.00
   i) 7.0   j) 8.6   k) $0.00\overline{3}$ l) 10.0
   m) $0.0\overline{3}$ n) 100.0   o) 0.75   p) $0.\overline{6}$

5. Write each fraction as a percent.
   a) $\frac{2}{100}$ b) $\frac{2}{1000}$ c) $\frac{2}{1}$ d) $\frac{3}{1}$
   e) $\frac{4}{1}$ f) $\frac{5}{4}$ g) $\frac{5}{3}$ h) $\frac{3}{500}$
   i) $\frac{3}{900}$ j) $\frac{2}{3000}$ k) $\frac{1}{100}$ l) $\frac{5}{2}$
   m) $\frac{1}{1000}$ n) $\frac{1}{10\,000}$ o) $\frac{2}{300}$ p) $\frac{10}{1}$

6. Write each percent as a decimal.
   a) 300%   b) 900%   c) 105%   d) 110%
   e) 0.1%   f) 0.9%   g) 0.35%   h) 108.75%
   i) 294.37%   j) 0.3%   k) 133%   l) 0.05%
   m) 166%   n) 0.08%   o) 250%   p) 0.25%

7. Write each percent as a decimal.
   a) $\frac{1}{2}\%$ b) $\frac{1}{4}\%$ c) $\frac{1}{3}\%$ d) $\frac{2}{3}\%$
   e) $666\frac{2}{3}\%$ f) $133\frac{1}{3}\%$ g) $\frac{3}{5}\%$ h) 108%
   i) $\frac{1}{10}\%$ j) $137\frac{1}{4}\%$ k) $105\frac{1}{2}\%$ l) $\frac{1}{5}\%$
   m) $\frac{3}{4}\%$ n) $100\frac{1}{10}\%$ o) $\frac{1}{6}\%$ p) $\frac{1}{9}\%$

8. Determine each amount.
   a) 200% of 70 kg   b) 110% of 50 s
   c) 107% of $10   d) 107% of $50
   e) 350% of 40 cm   f) 0.5% of 1200
   g) 0.22% of 52 000   h) 0.31% of $550 000
   i) $5\frac{1}{2}\%$ of 370 mL   j) $106\frac{2}{3}\%$ of 460 cm^2
   k) 300% of $175.36   l) 0.1% of 1000 km
   m) 100.1% of 375   n) 250% of 80 cm
   o) 0.2% of 150 g   p) $\frac{1}{4}\%$ of $358

Work together

9. Use a 100-square.
   a) Colour $\frac{1}{2}$ of the squares red.
      i) How many squares did you colour red?
      ii) Write the number of red squares as a fraction and as a percent of the 100-square.
   b) Colour $\frac{1}{4}$ of the squares blue.
      i) How many squares did you colour blue?
      ii) Write the number of blue squares as a fraction and as a percent of the 100-square.
   c) Colour $\frac{1}{8}$ of the squares yellow. Repeat parts i and ii above for the yellow squares.
   d) Colour $\frac{1}{16}$ of the squares green. Repeat parts i and ii above for the green squares.
   e) Colour $\frac{1}{32}$ of the squares black. Repeat parts i and ii above for the black squares.
   f) What pattern do you notice in the number of squares you coloured each time?

10. Use the 100-square you coloured in exercise 9, and two other 100-squares. How could you use these squares to show each percent?
    a) 150%   b) 225%   c) $112\frac{1}{2}\%$ d) $206\frac{1}{4}\%$
    e) $103\frac{1}{8}\%$ f) 200%   g) $212\frac{1}{2}\%$ h) $106\frac{1}{4}\%$

11. As a special offer, a magazine is selling a 10-issue subscription for $14.75.
    a) How much is this per issue?
    b) If you buy an issue of this magazine at a newsstand, you will pay 100% more than this special rate. How much does the magazine cost at a newsstand?

12. Determine.
    a) 120% of $40   **b)** 150% of $40
    c) 250% of $40   **d)** 0.5% of $40
    e) 0.7% of $40   **f)** 0.9% of $40

13. The cost price of a jacket is $40. The selling price of the jacket is 210% of the cost price. The jacket does not sell, so the manager marks down the selling price by 50%. What is the final selling price of the jacket?

14. The goal in a fund-raising drive was $4000, but $5000 was raised. What percent of the goal was raised?

15. When 3000 VCR tapes were tested, 0.2% were rejected. How many were rejected?

16. Earth's diameter is 12 740 km. Determine the diameter of each planet.

Planet's diameter as a percent of Earth's	
Saturn	941%
Jupiter	1120%
Pluto	18%

On your own

17. Use a 100-square.
    a) Colour $\frac{1}{3}$ of the squares red.
        i) How many squares did you colour red?
        ii) Write the number of red squares as a fraction and as a percent of the 100-square.
    b) Colour $\frac{2}{3}$ of the squares green.
        i) How many squares did you colour green?
        ii) Write the number of green squares as a fraction and as a percent of the 100-square.
    c) Use the 100-square you coloured in parts a and b, and two other 100-squares. How could you use these squares to show each percent?
        i) $66\frac{2}{3}\%$ **ii)** $33\frac{1}{3}\%$
        iii) $233\frac{1}{3}\%$ **iv)** $166\frac{2}{3}\%$

18. You can explore patterns on a spreadsheet to learn about fractions that represent percents greater than 100%. Begin by looking at eighths. Set up a spreadsheet that looks like the one below. Select column C by clicking on C at the top. Format the column to display numbers as percents.

TEMPLATE DISK

	A	B	C
1	Numerator	Denominator	Percent
2	1	8	=A2/B2
3	=A2+1	=B2	=A3/B3

Copy the formulas in row 3 down to row 20.
    a) Look down column C until you find 100%. What is the fraction for 100%?
    b) Look down column C until you find 200%. What is the fraction for 200%?
    c) What is the relationship between the fractions for 100% and 200%?
    d) What would you expect the fraction for 300% to be? Copy the formulas down for a few more rows to check your answer.
    e) Change the denominator to 12 by typing 12 in cell B2. Find the fractions for 100%, 200%, and 300% again. What is the relationship among the fractions?
    f) Change the denominator to 25 by typing 25 in cell B2. Change the starting number and the formulas in column A so the only percents that show are multiples of 100%.

19. You want to fly from Winnipeg to Vancouver. If you book 14 days in advance, you can get an economy ticket for $366. To fly sooner, you will have to buy a full fare economy ticket. A full fare ticket costs about 264% of the economy fare. How much would you have to pay for the full fare ticket?

20. The cost price of a suit is $75. The selling price of the suit is 240% of the cost price. The suit does not sell, so the manager marks down the selling price by 60%. What is the final selling price of the suit?

21. Determine.
    a) 110% of 25 cm b) 120% of 25 cm
    c) 200% of 25 cm d) 0.5% of 25 cm
    e) 0.2% of 25 cm f) 0.1% of 25 cm

22. The women's world record for the discus is 76.7 m.
    a) The record for the javelin is about 104% of this. What is the women's world record for the javelin?
    b) The record for the shot put is about 29% of the record for the discus. What is the women's world record for the shot put?

23. Express the amount of crackers in the 450-g box as a percent of the amount in the 250-g box.

24. Richview School raised $3870 for the Canadian Cancer Society. Sue raised 0.8% of this. How much did Sue raise?

25. Four hundred cassette tapes were tested. The rejection rate was 0.5%. How many cassette tapes were rejected?

26. The land area of Canada is 9 993 210 km². Calculate the area of each Maritime province, to the nearest square kilometre.

Province	Percent of Canada's area
Newfoundland and Labrador	4.0
New Brunswick	0.8
Nova Scotia	0.6
Prince Edward Island	0.06

27. About 7.5% of men and about 0.1% of women in Canada are colour blind. There were 14 242 800 men and 14 510 200 women in Canada in 1992. About how many men and women in Canada were colour blind in 1992?

28. The $100 Canadian gold coin contains 99.99% pure gold. The mass of the coin is 31.104 g. What is the mass of the other metals in the coin, to the nearest milligram?

Extend your thinking

29. The perimeter of a soccer field is 300% of its length. What is the ratio of its length to its width?

The Ideas

Sometimes it doesn't make sense to talk about more than 100% of something. Create an example to illustrate this statement. Explain your example. You can use exercises in earlier sections of this chapter to help you create the example.

What Percent of a Newspaper Is Advertising?

In some communities, people receive free newspapers.

Work in a group or with a partner. You will need a local newspaper. If the newspaper is large, use one section.

1. Calculate the print area of one page in your newspaper.

2. For each page:
   a) measure each advertisement and calculate its area
   b) calculate the percent of the page that is devoted to advertising

3. Calculate the percent of the newspaper that is devoted to advertising. Can you think of more than one way to do this?

4. Obtain the following information about the newspaper:
   • the cost of placing an advertisement in one issue of the newspaper
   • the number of copies of the newspaper that are printed
   a) Use this information to calculate the approximate amount of money the advertisers paid for the advertisements in the paper.
   b) How much would this be for each paper printed?

5. a) Why would a business pay for an advertisement?
   b) How would a business decide whether or not it is worth spending money for an advertisement?

6. If people receive free newspapers, how can the publisher make a profit from publishing the newspapers?

Many newspapers have a rate card, which lists sizes and costs of advertisements.

Review

1. Determine each length.

    a) 10% of 60 cm   **b)** 20% of 60 cm

    c) 30% of 60 cm   **d)** 40% of 60 cm

    e) 60% of 60 cm   **f)** 80% of 60 cm

    g) 25% of 60 cm   **h)** 50% of 60 cm

    i) 75% of 60 cm   **j)** 100% of 60 cm

2. How would the results of exercise 1 change if 60 cm is replaced by each length?

    a) 30 cm   **b)** 120 cm

    c) 15 cm   **d)** 90 cm

3. You are working in a clothing store. The manager asks you to reduce the prices of these items by 20%.

Leather coat	Reg. $599.99
Ski jacket	Reg. $299.99
Ski pants	Reg. $199.99
Toque	Reg. $19.99

    a) Calculate the discount and the sale price of each item.

    b) Copy and complete the tables. Include your results from part a in the tables.

Regular price ($)	Discount ($)

Regular price ($)	Sale price ($)

    c) Use the data in the tables to draw two graphs. Which graph represents a proportional situation? Explain.

    d) Write a formula to calculate the discount if you know the regular price. Write a formula to calculate the sale price if you know the regular price.

4. Determine the discount and the sale price of each item.

    a) Regular $49.99

    b) Regular $129.95

    c) Regular $79.99

5. A poster costs $12.99.

    a) Use the current sales tax rate for your province and the current GST rate. Calculate the sales tax and the GST on the poster. Calculate the total cost of the poster.

    b) The poster is on sale at a 10% discount. What is the sale price? Repeat part a for this sale price.

    c) In part b, does it matter whether the discount is applied before tax or after tax? Explain.

YOU STAND OUT IN A CROWD!

6. There are 600 students in Glenview School. Twenty percent of them are in grade 8. How many students are in grade 8?

7. There are 80 grade 8 students at Tecumseh Middle School. Find the number of grade 8 students in each category.

a) Fifty-five percent are girls and 45% are boys.

b) Thirty percent walk to school, 35% ride the bus, 20% get rides from their parents, and the rest travel in other ways.

c) Eighty percent of students eat their lunch at school, the rest eat their lunch at home.

d) About 93% like to watch movies at theatres.

e) About 37% say hockey is their favourite sport, 23% say baseball is their favourite sport, and the rest have other favourites.

8. In Mr. Cornwall's grade 8 class there are 30 students. Ten of these students were born in Asia, and 18 were born in Canada. What percent of the students in Mr. Cornwall's class were born:

a) in Asia?   b) in Canada?

c) elsewhere?

9. Talia earned these marks on five geography tests:

45 out of 50	34 out of 40
11 out of 25	28 out of 35
19 out of 25	

a) Calculate Talia's percent for each test.

b) What is the mean of her percents for the five tests?

10. Consider the following batting records for three baseball players.

Alina: 7 hits in 25 at-bats

Sophie: 6 hits in 20 at-bats

Dominique: 12 hits in 30 at-bats

a) Calculate the batting average (as a percent) for each player.

b) Suppose the three players formed a team.
   i) Find the total number of hits and at-bats for the team.
   ii) Find the batting average for the team.

c) In their next 10 at-bats, each player gets 3 hits. Calculate the new batting average for each player.

d) Compare the results in parts a and c for each player. Explain the changes in batting averages. Why did some increase and some decrease?

11. A karat is a unit used to specify the proportion of gold in an alloy. Pure gold is 24K. For example, the mark 18K on a ring means that the ring is 18 parts pure gold and 6 parts other metal.

a) Determine the percent of gold in each item.

Gold earrings	20K
Gold ring	18K
Gold bracelet	14K
Gold necklace	10K

b) Copy and complete the table. Include all your results from part a in the table.

Karats	Percent gold

c) Use the data in the table to draw a graph. Does it represent a proportional situation? Explain your answer.

d) Write a formula to calculate the percent of gold in an item if you know its number of karats.

12. You have probably heard of the legendary Loch Ness monster — a giant, dinosaur-like creature believed to be living in a lake in Scotland, preying on fish. Adrian Shine, the naturalist in charge of the Loch Ness project, uses mathematics to help decide whether the monster exists. To maintain a population, Shine believes there would have to be at least 10 monsters. According to a rule of thumb, the total mass of a predator population should be no more than 10% of the total mass of the available prey. Loch Ness contains 20 to 30 t of fish. What is the maximum mass of each of the 10 monsters? Compare this to the mass of some large mammals or fish. Is it a monster-sized mass?

13. Jonathon's mass is 56 kg, which is 70% of Trevor's mass. What is Trevor's mass?

14. There are four kinds of teeth. The number of different teeth most people have are shown in the table. What percent of the teeth are:

   a) incisors?   b) premolars?
   c) molars?   d) canines?

incisors	8
premolars	8
molars	12
canines	4

15. Jean was one of several partners who bought a winning lottery ticket. His share of the prize was 30%, and he won $1500. What was the total value of the prize?

16. A four-year-old car is worth 40% of its original value. It is worth $7000. What was the original value?

17. A salesperson earns 5.5% commission on all sales she makes. During one day she sold: 1 TV, 2 CD players, 1 pair of speakers, and 4 VCRs. Use the table below to calculate her commission.

Item	Price ($)	Item	Price ($)
VCR	320	Tape deck	220
TV	550	Camcorder	800
Camera	400	Speakers (pair)	450
Receiver	420	CD player	200

18. Calculate the interest for one year.
   a) $300 at 6%   b) $240 at 5%
   c) $215 at 7%   d) $295 at 11%
   e) $400 at 7.5%   f) $160 at 8.75%
   g) $325 at 6.25%   h) $158 at 4.125%

19. Frances purchased $1500 worth of Canada Savings Bonds at an interest rate of 8.5% per annum.
   a) How much interest did she receive after one year?
   b) What was the value of her bonds after one year?

20. Express as a decimal.
   a) 130%   b) 76%   c) 151%   d) 14.8%
   e) 1.79%   f) 0.45%   g) $\frac{2}{3}\%$ h) $\frac{1}{7}\%$
   i) $22\frac{1}{4}\%$ j) $5\frac{3}{4}\%$ k) $8\frac{2}{3}\%$ l) $107\frac{1}{3}\%$

21. Express as a percent.
   a) 0.53   b) 0.07   c) 0.004   d) 3.9
   e) 18.2   f) $\frac{7}{5}$ g) $\frac{4}{1200}$ h) $\frac{65}{12\ 500}$
   i) $\frac{146}{50}$ j) 0.0002   k) 4.887   l) 0.009 75

22. Determine.
   a) 140% of $60   b) 117% of $60
   c) 0.8% of $60   d) 0.15% of $60

23. When heated in the sun, a steel beam increases its surface area by 0.15%. The original area was 1.125 m². Find the new area.

24. A real-estate agent predicts the value of a house will increase by 0.7% during the next year. The house is currently worth $114 000. What will the value of the house be next year?

There are about 2.5 million teenagers in Canada. In a typical day, Canadian teenagers spend $2 071 428 on snack food. About how much does each teenager spend on snack food per day? How does your spending compare?

241

The Consumer Price Index

Every month Statistics Canada calculates the Consumer Price Index (CPI). The CPI is a way of measuring changes in prices. It expresses prices as a percent of the prices in a previous year, which we call the base year. The prices for the base year are represented by 100. The base year currently used is 1986.

For example, suppose that a 4-L bag of 2% milk, which in 1986 cost $2.79, now costs $3.59.

Think... Express the current price as a percent of the 1986 price.

Write... $\frac{\$3.59}{\$2.79} \times 100\% \doteq 1.287 \times 100\%$
$$= 128.7\%$$

The price index for 2% milk for the current month is 128.7. This means that the price of milk has risen by 28.7% since 1986.

Statistics Canada bases the CPI on a "market basket" of goods and services. These are the items the average Canadian urban family buys. The items range from cheese to T-shirts and from videos to bus tickets. Thousands of prices are collected every month and compared with the 1986 prices. The results are combined to determine the overall CPI for the month.

ACTIVITY 1

As the above example shows, if you know the price of an item in 1986 and the current price of a similar item, you can calculate its price index.

- From a newspaper flyer or some other source, determine a typical current price for each item listed in the table on the right. Use the 1986 prices to calculate the price index for each item.
- If the price index of an item is less than 100, what does that tell you about its price?
- If the price index of an item is greater than 200, what does that tell you about its price?

Item	1986 Price ($)
Large eggs (dozen)	0.99
Whole wheat bread (675 g)	0.89
Pasta (900 g)	0.79
Frozen peas (1 kg)	2.29
Flour (10 kg)	5.98
Apple juice (1.36 L)	0.79
Frozen orange juice concentrate (355 mL)	0.99
Potato chips (200 g)	0.99
Laundry detergent (12 L)	7.99
Shampoo (450 mL)	2.79
Toothpaste (100 mL)	1.19
Toothbrush	1.29

ACTIVITY 2

Use the *International Prices* database on the data disk. In this database, you will find the following information for 1982 and 1994 for many cities around the world:

City	Hong Kong
Year	1994
Net hourly earnings	4.4
Hours worked per year	2222
Local rent	1140
Cost of public transit ride	1.29
Cost of basket of food	307
Minutes worked to buy Big Mac and Fries	28
Minutes worked to buy 1 kg of bread	18

All dollar amounts are given in US dollars.

Local rent
Cost of public transit ride
Cost of basket of food

Each record in the database contains information about one city in one year. One record is shown above. Depending on the type of computer you use, the field names may be different from those shown here.

- Choose at least ten cities. Calculate the price index for each of the three items listed above and in the database. Use 1982 as the base year. Your price index should express the 1994 prices in terms of the 1982 prices.
- Observe that the prices are all given in U.S. dollars. If the prices were given in Canadian dollars, would the price indices be the same? Use some examples to illustrate your answer.

You can use a spreadsheet to do the calculations in this activity.

ACTIVITY 3

Prices have increased over the years, but so have wages and salaries. It is possible that an item whose price has increased seems less expensive than it used to be because people's wages and salaries have increased even more.

Use the *International Prices* database on the data disk. Complete the following for each city you chose in *Activity 2*.

- Obtain the net hourly earnings for 1982 and 1994.
- Suppose a person earned the net hourly earnings and paid the amount of rent listed in the record. Calculate the number of hours that person would have had to work to pay her or his rent in 1982 and in 1994.
- Would the rent have seemed less expensive to that person in 1994 than it did in 1982?

COMMUNICATING
The Ideas

Write a report that summarizes the results of your investigations. Include tables and graphs in your report.

DATA MANAGEMENT

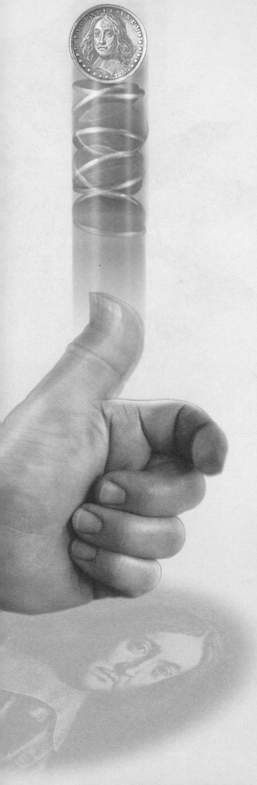

WHAT'S COMING UP?

DEPARTMENTS

Start With What You Know

Linking Ideas

Mathematics File

Quests

Minds on Math Project

Start With What You Know

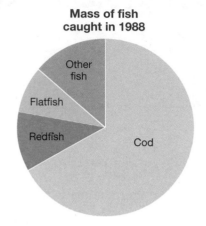

Mass of fish caught in 1988

From the 16th century to the 1990s, cod was a major part of the fishing industry in Atlantic Canada. The Grand Banks was one of the most important fishing areas in Canada.

Use the circle graph to answer exercises 1 to 3.

1. Which fish was most important to the Atlantic fishing industry?

2. Estimate the percent of fish by mass that were:

    a) cod   **b)** redfish   **c)** flatfish

3. The mass of cod caught in 1988 was 461 000 t. Estimate the mass of:

    a) redfish   **b)** flatfish   **c)** other fish

In the 1950s and 1960s, modern trawlers had gigantic nets. These nets swept deep into the ocean catching huge numbers of fish. By the early 1970s, the total mass of cod dragged from this fishing zone approached 900 000 t. On the graph below, the height of the orange area indicates the Canadian catch. The height of the yellow area indicates the total catch. The difference represents the foreign catch. Use the graph to answer the questions on the next page.

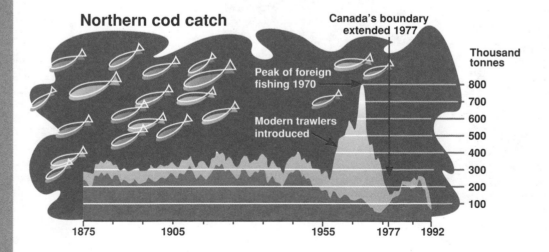

4. a) About how many tonnes of cod were caught in 1955:

   i) in total?   **ii)** by Canadians?   **iii)** by foreigners?

   b) Of all the cod caught in 1955, about what percent was caught by Canadians?

5. a) About how many tonnes of cod were caught in 1970:

   i) in total?   **ii)** by Canadians?   **iii)** by foreigners?

   b) Of all the cod caught in 1970, about what percent was caught by Canadians?

Canada controls areas of the Atlantic Ocean that border Canada. Foreign ships are not allowed to fish within these areas, which extend 20 km from the shore. Since most of the trawlers catching northern cod are from foreign countries, the Canadian government extended the fishing boundary in 1977. The boundary was increased from 20 km to 320 km offshore.

6. a) About how many tonnes of cod were caught in 1980:

   i) in total?   **ii)** by Canadians?   **iii)** by foreigners?

   b) Of all the cod caught in 1980, about what percent was caught by Canadians?

7. In 1992, the Canadian government banned the fishing of cod in this area until cod stocks are replenished. Scientists believe that there should be about 1.2 million tonnes of cod in this region before fishing at normal levels can be resumed. The mass of cod stocks in 1994 was estimated to be 2% of this amount. About how many tonnes of cod were in the fishing banks off the coast of Newfoundland in 1994?

8. Use the graph to help you complete this table, then answer the questions below.

Year	Total mass of northern cod caught (to nearest 100 000 t)
1960	
1970	
1980	

a) What was the mean mass of cod caught in these three years?

b) What was the median mass of cod caught in these three years?

c) Which of these averages gives a better representation of the average mass of cod caught per year between 1960 and 1980? Explain.

Using Data for Investigations

DATA DISK

How many are there? Which is the largest? Who makes the least money? What changes were there over five years?

These are examples of questions that come to mind as you examine a set of data. These are the types of questions that lead you to further and more detailed investigations. You can answer these questions by searching for and sorting data in an electronic database.

In this activity, you will create some questions and use a database program and an existing database to answer these questions. On the *Minds on Math 8* data disk, there are 10 databases. If you are not familiar with these databases, open each one and browse through the data.

Questions that can be answered using the Find or Search option

Some questions ask for a fact, a single piece of information. You can usually find the answers using the Find or Search option. If you are not familiar with the Find or Search option, refer to the tutorials that come with the data disk.

1. a) Open the *Olympic Winter Games* database. Find the names of the athletes who won the pairs figure skating gold medal at the 1968 Grenoble Winter Olympics.
   b) Describe the database processes you used to find this information. Could you have found this information some other way?
   c) Did you have the exact information to find the answer? Or, did you have too much or too little?

2. Select one database from the data disk. Make up three questions for another student to answer using the Find or Search option. Answer the questions yourself, then ask a classmate to answer those questions. Compare that classmate's answers with yours.

Questions that can be answered using the Sort option

If you are not familiar with the Sort option, refer to the activities on pages 33 and 34.

3. a) Open the *Mammals of Canada* database. Which Canadian mammal has the longest tail? How many Canadian mammals have tails between 40 cm and 50 cm long?
   b) Repeat exercise 1 parts b and c.

4. Select one database from the data disk. Make up three questions for another student to answer using the Sort option. Answer the questions yourself, then ask a classmate to answer those questions. Compare that classmate's answers with yours.

Questions that can be answered using both the Find or Search and Sort options

You can answer some questions by reducing a large set of data to a smaller set. You use the Sort option to organize or order the smaller set of data.

5. Open the *Box Office Hits* database. Find the movies released by Columbia studios. Sort these movies using the Money Made field. Is it true that the movies that made Columbia the most money also won the most Academy Awards? Explain your answer.

6. Select one database from the data disk. Make up a question for another student to answer using the Find or Search and Sort options together. Answer the question yourself, then ask a classmate to answer it.

If you do not have the data disk, you can complete the exercises below using the data provided.

The Moon and Planets					
Name	Distance from the sun (km)	Time of one orbit around the sun	Time of one rotation about its axis	Mean diameter (km)	Number of moons
Mercury	5.8×10^7	88.0 days	58.7 days	4 878.0	0
Venus	1.1×10^8	224.7 days	243.0 days	12 102.5	0
Earth	1.5×10^8	365.3 days	23.9 hours	12 734.9	1
Moon	1.5×10^8	365.3 days	27.3 days	3 476.0	0
Mars	2.3×10^8	1.9 years	24.6 hours	6 773.0	2
Jupiter	7.5×10^8	11.9 years	9.8 hours	138 262.0	16
Saturn	1.4×10^9	29.5 years	10.7 hours	114 632.0	18
Uranus	2.9×10^9	84.0 years	17.2 hours	51 118.0	15
Neptune	4.5×10^9	164.8 years	16.1 hours	49 104.0	8
Pluto	5.9×10^9	247.7 years	6.4 days	2 302.0	1

7. How many moons in total do Saturn, Uranus, and Neptune have?

8. Find the distance between each pair of planets, when they are on the same side of the sun and aligned with the sun.

  a) Earth and Pluto   **b)** Earth and Mercury

9. About how many Earth days does it take Saturn to rotate about its axis 10 times?

10. About how many times does Mercury orbit the sun in one Earth year?

11. Are the planets with the fewest moons closer to or farther from the sun than Earth?

12. Is the planet with the most moons also the largest planet?

13. Make up three questions for another student to answer using data on the moon and planets. Answer the questions yourself, then ask a classmate to answer these questions. Compare that classmate's answers with yours.

5.1 CONSTRUCTING GRAPHS

Developing the Ideas

▶▶ *Through an Activity*

Everywhere we look, in newspapers and magazines, on television and computers, data are presented as graphs. To understand graphs, we need to know how to read them and how to draw conclusions from them.

To present data graphically, we have to decide which type of graph is appropriate. We also need to know how to construct this graph. Graphs can be constructed using pencil, paper, rulers, protractors, and squared paper. You can also use graphing calculators and computers to generate graphs. In both cases, you begin by compiling your data in a table.

Many people find it easier to observe trends on a graph than in a table of numbers. In this activity, you will draw a broken-line graph to determine how the population in different regions of Canada has changed. The provinces and territories have been grouped into regions.

Grouping by region		
Western and Northern Canada	**Central Canada**	**Eastern Canada**
British Columbia	Manitoba	New Brunswick
Alberta	Ontario	Nova Scotia
Saskatchewan	Quebec	Prince Edward Island
Yukon and Northwest Territories		Newfoundland and Labrador

The table gives the populations of the three major regions in Canada in 1952 and every 10 years thereafter. The data were collected by Statistics Canada.

Population by region					
Region	**Year**				
Western and Northern	3 046 000	3 999 000	4 869 500	6 150 300	6 937 700
Central	9 760 000	12 658 000	14 855 300	16 198 400	18 120 900
Eastern	1 653 000	1 926 000	2 076 700	2 234 200	2 343 600

1. Copy the column and row headings in a new table. Round each number to the nearest hundred thousand, and write it in your table.

If you have a computer with a spreadsheet program, complete exercise 2 and then exercises 4 to 9. If you do not have access to a spreadsheet program, complete exercises 3 to 9.

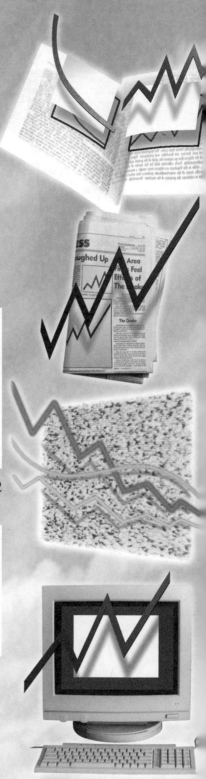

TEMPLATE DISK

2. Enter the data from the table in a new spreadsheet file like the one below.

A	B	C	D	E	F
1	1952	1962	1972	1982	1992
2 Western and Northern					
3 Central					
4 Eastern					

Highlight cells A1 to F4 since they contain the information you want
to graph.

- In ClarisWorks, choose Make Chart… from the Options menu.
  A gallery appears with a variety of chart types. Select Line. To
  the left of the gallery is a list of items you can modify. Click on
  General. On the screen that appears, click on the button on the
  lower right that tells the program to use the numbers from the
  first row as labels. Click OK.
- In Microsoft Works for Macintosh, choose New Chart… from the
  Chart menu. A bar chart of the data appears. Click twice on this
  chart and change the chart type to Line. Click OK.
- If you are using a different spreadsheet program, check your
  user's manual for instructions on creating a line graph.

3. a) Draw axes on grid paper. Label the vertical axis with the
  populations. Choose a scale to fit from 0 to 18 000 000 people.
  b) Label the horizontal axis with the years. Choose a scale to fit
  from 1952 to 1992.
  c) For each region in Canada:
  - Plot a point to represent each pair of values of year and
    population.
  - Use a ruler to join adjacent points with a straight line.
  - Label the broken-line graph with the name of the region.

4. From your graph, which region in Canada grew fastest between
1952 and 1992?

5. One interpretation of the graph could be "Central Canada outpaces
all other regions in population growth." Does the graph support this
statement? Why?

6. a) Write the 1992 population of Central Canada as a fraction of its
  1952 population.
  b) Write this fraction as a percent.
  c) Explain how the answer to part b illustrates that the population
  almost doubled in this period.

7. Write the 1992 population of Western and Northern Canada as a
percent of its 1952 population.

8. From the results of exercises 6 and 7, we might say "Western and Northern Canada outpaces all other regions in population growth." Would this interpretation be correct? Why?

9. Make up your own question about the graph you drew. Give it to your partner to answer.

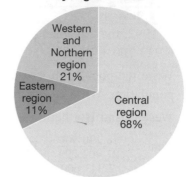

Location of Canadians by region –1952

▶ ▶ *Through a Guided Example*

We can also use circle graphs to compare the population changes in the three geographic regions of Canada. The circle graph shows the percent of the Canadian population that lived in each region in 1952. We shall draw a circle graph for the 1992 Canadian population and use the two graphs to make comparisons.

Example ....

a) Use the data in the table to draw a circle graph to show the percent of the Canadian population that lived in each region in 1992.

Population by region –1992	
Region	**Population**
Western and Northern	6 937 700
Central	18 120 900
Eastern	2 343 600

b) Did the population of Central Canada increase or decrease between 1952 and 1992?

c) Did the percent of the Canadian population in Central Canada increase or decrease between 1952 and 1992?

d) Did the population in Western and Northern Canada increase or decrease between 1952 and 1992?

e) Did the percent of the Canadian population in Western and Northern Canada increase or decrease between 1952 and 1992?

Western/Northern

Central

Eastern

f) Which statement in exercises 5 and 8 on pages 251 and 252 would you agree with? Why?

g) Has the population in Eastern Canada increased in 40 years? Has its share of the total Canadian population increased or decreased? Explain.

Solution

a) In 1992, the Canadian population was:

6 937 700 + 18 120 900 + 2 343 600 = 27 402 200

Write the population in each region as a percent of the total population. Write each percent to the nearest whole number.

Western and Northern: $\frac{6\ 937\ 700}{27\ 402\ 200} \times 100\% \doteq 25\%$

Central: $\frac{18\ 120\ 900}{27\ 402\ 200} \times 100\% \doteq 66\%$

Eastern: $\frac{2\ 343\ 600}{27\ 402\ 200} \times 100\% \doteq 9\%$

The area of the circle represents the population of Canada. All the angles at the centre of the circle add up to 360°. To find the angle for each region, change the percent to a decimal and multiply by 360°. Write each angle to the nearest degree.

Western and Northern, 25% : $0.25 \times 360° \doteq 90°$

Central, 66% : $0.66 \times 360° \doteq 238°$

Eastern, 9% : $0.09 \times 360° \doteq 32°$

Construct a circle. Use a protractor to construct the angle at the centre for each part. Start with the smallest angle.

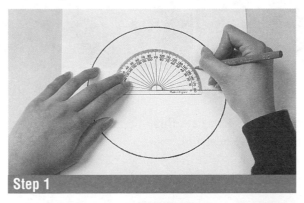
Step 1

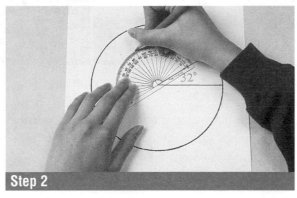
Step 2

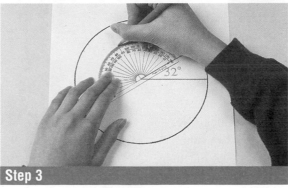
Step 3

Step 4

Label each sector of your graph with its name and percent. Write a title for your graph, as shown on the next page.

b) From the table on page 250, the population of Central Canada increased between 1952 and 1992.

c) From the circle graphs, the percent of the population in Central Canada decreased slightly, from 68% to 66%.

d) From the table on page 250, the population of Western and Northern Canada increased between 1952 and 1992.

e) From the circle graphs, the percent of the population in Western and Northern Canada increased from 21% to 25%.

f) It depends on whether the statements refer to the populations or the percents. Using populations, Central Canada increased by more than any other region. Using percents, Central Canada decreased while Western Canada increased.

g) From the tables, the population of Eastern Canada has increased by 750 000. From the graphs, this region's share of the total population has decreased from 11% to 9%.

Location of Canadians by region – 1992

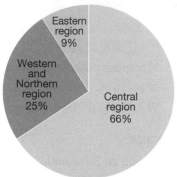

TEMPLATE DISK

▶ ▶ *Using a Computer*

We could have used a computer with a spreadsheet program to create this circle graph. Enter the data from the table into a new spreadsheet file, then follow the steps below.

	A	B
1		1992
2	Western	6937700
3	Central	18120900
4	Eastern and Northern	2343600

Highlight cells A2 to B4 since they contain the information we want to graph.

• In ClarisWorks, choose Make Chart… from the Options menu. A gallery appears with a variety of chart types. Select Pie. Click OK.

• In Microsoft Works for Macintosh, choose New Chart… from the Chart menu. A bar chart of the data will appear. Click twice on this chart and change the chart type to Pie. Click OK.

Working with Mathematics

Something to talk about

1. Why do we use graphs instead of tables to present data?

2. Describe each graph. Give an example of the data you might display using each graph.
   a) a double-bar graph
   b) a broken-line graph
   c) a double broken-line graph
   d) a circle graph

Practice

3. Round as indicated.
   a) Round 5400 to the nearest 1000.
   b) Round 186 400 to the nearest 1000.
   c) Round 17 100 to the nearest 10 000.
   d) Round 360 000 to the nearest 100 000.
   e) Round 1 433 000 to the nearest 100 000.

4. Write as a fraction in lowest terms.
   a) 13 out of 26   b) 3 out of 12
   c) 27 out of 135   d) 70 out of 119
   e) 105 out of 120   f) 114 out of 203

5. Write as a percent.
   a) 14 as a percent of 60
   b) 13 as a percent of 104
   c) 22 as a percent of 55
   d) 9.9 as a percent of 55
   e) 781 as a percent of 2200
   f) 462 as a percent of 4400

6. Write as a percent.
   a) $\dfrac{5200}{13\ 000}$ b) $\dfrac{1071}{6300}$ c) $\dfrac{1189}{2900}$
   d) $\dfrac{8325}{37\ 000}$ e) $\dfrac{40\ 000}{160\ 000}$ f) $\dfrac{32\ 000}{160\ 000}$

Work together

7. This table shows the number of record albums, cassettes, and CDs sold in Canada. The data were collected by Statistics Canada.

	1988	1990	1992
	15 400 000	4 400 000	700 000
	32 600 000	32 700 000	32 700 000
	5 400 000	9 500 000	27 100 000

a) Did the total purchase of records, cassettes, and CDs increase or decrease between 1988 and 1992?

b) Of the total number of records, cassettes, and CDs sold in 1988, what percent were:
   i) records?   ii) cassettes? iii) CDs?

c) Of the total number of records, cassettes, and CDs sold in 1992, what percent were:
   i) records?   ii) cassettes? iii) CDs?

d) For each year, draw a circle graph showing the numbers of records, cassettes, and CDs sold. How do the graphs help you see the share of each type of recording in the recorded music market? How have these shares changed over the 4-year period?

e) If you were a recording artist in 1992, would you sell your recording as a record, a cassette, or a CD?

f) Were people spending more money on records, cassettes, and CDs in 1992 than in 1988? Explain what additional information you might need to answer this question.

8. The table shows the mean price in dollars of a record, a cassette, and a CD.

	1988	1990	1992
	$5.24	$7.20	$7.14
	$5.21	$8.12	$7.37
	$13.88	$15.53	$11.88

a) Why do you think the mean price for compact discs changed so much from 1990 to 1992?

b) Use the information in exercise 7 and the table above. Determine the amount of money spent on recorded music in Canada for each year. Draw a graph of the data.

c) Were Canadians spending more or less on music recordings in 1992 than in 1988?

d) Make up your own question about the graph you drew. Give it to your partner to answer.

9. a) Explain what this table illustrates.

Year	World grain production (billions of kg)	World population (millions)
1950	500	2518
1980	1400	4400
2010	2000*	7200*
2040	1900*	9600*

b) Why do some numbers have asterisks?

c) How many millions are in one billion? Write the world grain production for each year in millions of kilograms.

d) For each year, calculate the number of kilograms of grain produced per person. To do this, divide the production in millions of kilograms by the population in millions.

e) Graph the data you calculated in part d. This will show the world grain production per person from 1950 to 2040.

f) What does your graph suggest about the future of the world grain supply for the 21st century?

10. Did you know that *Home Alone* earned more money than any other movie released in 1990? It earned over $140 million. This fact can be found in the *Box Office Hits* database on the data disk. The database provides information about the top 5 money-earning movies released each year from 1939 to 1993.

DATA DISK

a) Open the database. Find the movies that were released during or after 1989. Copy the earnings of these 25 movies into a new spreadsheet file.

b) Use the spreadsheet to calculate the total amount earned by the top 5 movies in each of these years.

c) Use the spreadsheet's charting options to draw a graph of the total earnings for each year. Describe the graph.

d) Based on your graph, do you think the top 5 movies from 1994 earned more or less than the top 5 movies from 1993? Explain. What further information might you want before you make a prediction?

On your own

11. The tables show the winning times for the 100-m sprint at the Olympic Summer Games.

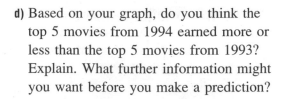

	Year		
	1972	1976	1980
Men	Borzov	Crawford	Wells
	U.S.S.R. 10.14 s	Trinidad 10.06 s	Great Britain 10.25 s
Women	Stecher	Richter	Kondratyeva
	E. Germany 11.07 s	W. Germany 11.08 s	U.S.S.R. 11.06 s

	Year		
	1984	1988	1992
Men	Lewis	Lewis	Christie
	U.S. 9.99 s	U.S. 9.92 s	Great Britain 9.96 s
Women	Ashford	Griffith-Joyner	Devers
	U.S. 10.97 s	U.S. 10.54 s	U.S. 10.82 s

a) Graph the winning times for the men's 100-m sprint.

b) On the grid in part a, graph the winning times for the women's 100-m sprint.

c) Use your graph to estimate the winning times for these events at the 1968 Olympic games. Use a computer database or almanac to see how close your estimate was.

d) Whose performance has improved most since 1972, the men's or the women's?

e) Would you expect both male and female athletes' performances to improve at these same rates in the future? Explain.

12. The table shows the percent of Canadians aged 10 and over who participated in certain recreational activities in two different years.

	Participation rate (%)	
Activity	**1981**	**1988**
Cycling	38	40
Dancing	13	33
Gardening	30	52
Home exercise	28	31
Jogging	31	18
Swimming	36	42
Walking	57	63

a) Draw a double-bar graph to represent the data.

b) Which two activities had the greatest increase in popularity?

c) Which activity decreased in popularity?

d) Based on these data, would you say Canadians were more or less active in 1988 than in 1981? Explain.

e) Write a question for a classmate to answer using your graph.

13. Use the population table below. The data were collected by Statistics Canada.

a) Graph the populations of Manitoba, Newfoundland and Labrador, and Yukon Territory for the period 1952 to 1992.

Population by province 1952 – 1992			
Province/Territory			
	Manitoba	Newfoundland and Labrador	Yukon Territory
1952	798 000	374 000	9 000
1962	936 000	468 000	15 000
1972	991 200	530 000	19 500
1982	1 033 300	566 200	23 900
1992	1 096 000	577 500	27 900

b) Which province or territory showed the greatest population increase between 1952 and 1992?

c) Which province or territory showed the greatest percent gain in population between 1952 and 1972?

d) If your answers to parts b and c are different, explain why.

TEMPLATE DISK

14. a) Start a new spreadsheet file. Enter the data from the table of population by region on page 250. Experiment with the charting option to make the computer draw the following chart. In some spreadsheet programs, you will need to draw five individual graphs.

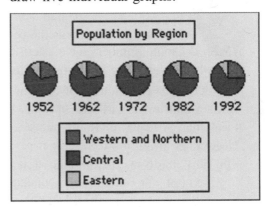

b) Describe how the chart shows the way the populations of the three regions have changed.

15. This circle graph was published by the student council of Eagle Valley Middle School.

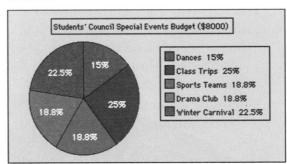

a) Without calculating how much money was spent on each type of event, rank the special events expenditures from least to greatest.

b) How much did the council spend on class trips? On dances?

c) Use the same total budget as the school council. Create a table of values in a spreadsheet file that shows the amount spent on each type of event. Use the spreadsheet's charting option to create a circle graph like the one above.

TEMPLATE DISK

16. In exercise 9, you calculated the amount of grain produced per person. Reports of such data use the term "per capita" to mean "per person." Calculate the per capita value for each statement below. The data were collected by Statistics Canada.

a) In January 1994, the Canadian population was 29 094 400. The Canadian debt was $500 000 000 000. What was the per capita Canadian debt?

b) In 1991, the Canadian population was 27 300 000. The number of litres of ice cream consumed was 535 344 000. What was the per capita consumption of ice cream, in litres?

c) In 1991, the Canadian population was 27 300 000. The number of kilograms of apples consumed was 416 180 000. What was the per capita consumption of apples, in kilograms?

d) In 1990, the Canadian population was 26 610 000. The total spent on magazines was $189 993 000. How much was spent per capita on magazines?

e) In 1990, the Canadian population was 26 610 000. The total spent on video tapes, games, and equipment was $44 503 000. How much was spent per capita on these items?

Extend your thinking

17. In exercise 9, you used estimates for the years 2010 and 2040 to make predictions about the future world grain supply. Suppose that the world population in the years 2010 and 2040 were only 70% of what was predicted in exercise 9. Suppose also that the world grain production were 1.5 times as great as predicted for those years.

a) Copy this table. Make new estimates for the grain production and population in 2010 and 2040 based on the information above. Use the new numbers to complete the table. Remember to convert the grain production to millions of kilograms before calculating the per capita production.

Year	World grain production (billions of kg)	World population (millions)	Grain per person (kg/person)
1950	500	2518	
1980	1400	4400	
2010			
2040			

b) Graph the per capita production of grain. What does your graph suggest about the world grain supply in the 21st century?

The Ideas

Look up the meaning of the expression, *per capita*, in the dictionary. Is the meaning the same as the one given in exercise 16? Write a sentence using the expression "per capita."

. . . . . 5.2 COLLECTING DATA

Developing the Ideas

▶ ▶ *Through an Activity*

1. As a class, make up a questionnaire to find answers to these questions. To make it easier to tally the responses to some questions, you may list several choices as answers. If you do this, you should include one choice, such as "none of these" or "other," in case none of the choices is appropriate for some students. A sample questionnaire on student music preferences is shown below.

   - How many hours of television does the average student in your school watch each week?
   - What is the average student's favourite television program?
   - What is the average student's favourite movie this year?
   - What is the average student's favourite food when he or she eats away from home?
   - What kind of pet, if any, does the average student have?
   - How many people are in the family of the average student?

Music Preferences Survey

1. What type of music do you most enjoy listening to?
   - □ Dance
   - □ Heavy Metal
   - □ Country
   - □ Reggae
   - □ World Music
   - □ Pop / Rock
   - □ Other: _____

2. How many hours do you spend listening to music in a typical week?
   - □ 3 or fewer
   - □ Between 3 and 6
   - □ Between 6 and 9
   - □ Between 9 and 12
   - □ 12 or more

3. Who is your favourite Canadian performer or group?
   - □ Blue Rodeo
   - □ Celine Dion
   - □ Spirit of the West
   - □ Crash Test Dummies
   - □ The Tragically Hip
   - □ Sarah McLachlan
   - □ Other: _____

2. Work with a partner or group. Use the class questionnaire to interview 10 students at your school. Tally their responses to each question.

3. Join with another group of students and combine your data.

4. Graph your data.

5. Answer each question in exercise 1.

6. Combine the data of all the groups in the class. Graph the class data.

7. Use the graph to determine:
   - the median number of hours of television watched per week
   - the favourite television program
   - the most popular movie
   - the most popular food when eating away from home
   - the most popular type of pet
   - the median number of people in a student's family

8. Did the results of exercise 7 differ from the results of exercise 5? Why?

9. Make up your own question for each graph drawn from the class data. Give it to another group to answer.

10. **a)** In your survey, you determined the favourite food to eat away from home of students at your school. Do you think your results are typical of all Canadians?

   b) The Canadian Restaurant and Food Services Association commissioned a survey to find out Canadians' top choices when they eat out. The six most popular items, in order, are listed below. Do the results surprise you? How do they compare with the results of your class survey? Explain why the results may be different from your class' results.
   - french fries
   - salads
   - hamburgers and cheeseburgers
   - bread, bagels, and toast
   - sweet baked goods such as muffins, Danish, and cinnamon buns
   - pizza

11. Use a database or an almanac to find out the average family size in Canada and the average number of hours of television watched by Canadians.

   a) Did the results of the class survey agree with the information for the average Canadian?

   b) Explain why any differences may have occurred. In what ways might the people in your class sample differ from average Canadians?

   c) Explain how you might change your sample to gather data for a better representation of the preferences of the average Canadian.

What do we know about the average Canadian? And how do we know it?

Most of the information about the practices and preferences of Canadians comes from *random samples* of Canadians. In this section, you will consider these questions:

- What is meant by a *random sample*?
- Why do we use a sample instead of gathering information from the entire Canadian population?
- Why must the sample be random?

According to "Are You an Average Canadian?", an article in the *Reader's Digest*, March 1994:

"The average Canadian female is older (34 years) than most women she sees in ads on television and in magazines … She gets about eight hours sleep per night, drives a 7-year-old white compact car and drives for half an hour to reach her office.

The average Canadian family owns a 7-room house built after 1969 and spends around a sixth of its income on shelter … it has two TV sets and the TV is on more than two hours a day."

Look at the information given above to answer these questions.

1. **a)** Which data do you think were obtained using a sample?
   b) Why do you think a sample was used?

2. **a)** Which data were collected from the entire Canadian population?
   b) How do you think this information was collected?

3. The term *average Canadian* could refer to the mean, the median, or the mode. You are already familiar with mean and median. The *mode* is the response that occurs most often in a set of responses. In each statement above, explain which average has been used.

4. What does it mean to say that the "average Canadian female drives a 7-year-old white compact car"?

Working with Mathematics

Something to talk about

1. Why are samples used to gather information about a population?

2. When the members of a sample are unlike most members of the population in some way, we say that the sample is *biased*. State how each of the following samples may be biased.

   a) To find out which hockey team is favoured by most Canadians, researchers interview 200 000 people in Vancouver.

   b) To determine the television preferences of the average Canadian, a questionnaire is sent to all junior high schools in Canada.

   c) To determine which political party Canadians prefer, the host of a phone-in radio show asks people to telephone their preferences, and then she tallies the results.

   d) To determine the average shoe size of Canadians, a data collection company tallies the number of shoes in each size sold by shoe stores across Canada.

   e) To determine the countries in which most Canadians vacation, a researcher records the destinations by country of all Canadian airline travellers.

3. How do statisticians try to ensure that the information gathered in a sample is also true for the entire population?

4. The article "Are You an Average Canadian?" states:

   "Like almost three-quarters of all Canadians, the average Canadian lives within 200 km of the American border."

   a) How do you think this information was obtained?

   b) What percent of Canadians live within 200 km of the American border?

   c) What fraction of Canadians live more than 200 km from the United States?

   d) Do you think this percent takes into consideration First Nations people such as the Inuit who live in the far north?

Work together

5. a) Have all the students in your class write the months of their birthdays on the board.

   b) Construct a graph to show how many students were born in each month. Which type of graph did you draw?

   c) Describe your graph. Are any months more common than others?

   d) The graph below shows the number of Canadians born each month in 1991.

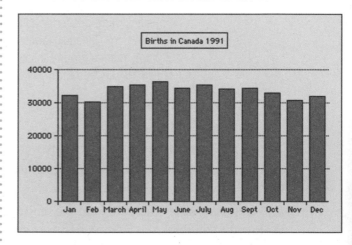

   i) Which season recorded the most births?

   ii) Which season recorded the fewest births?

   iii) How does the shape of the graph compare to that of your graph? Explain any differences.

e) Choose a year other than 1991. From a Statistics Canada publication or a database, find the number of Canadians born each month that year. Graph the data. How does the shape of the graph compare to the graphs in parts b and d? Compare your results with those of other groups. In general, which season recorded the most births? Which seasons recorded the fewest births?

f) Do you think the shape of a graph of the birth months of all the students in your school would be similar to the graph for all Canadians? Explain why or why not.

6. How do you think Canadians spend their time? You could conduct a survey to find out, or consult the *Time Spent* database on the data disk. The database provides information about people in a variety of age groups. One record is shown below as an example. It tells that 26% of females aged 25 to 34 each spends an average of 2.4 h a day on sports and hobbies.

DATA DISK

Activity	Sports and hobbies
Age group	25-34
Sex	F
Time spent on activity	2.4
Participation rate (%)	26

a) Compare the participation rate and time spent by males and females on domestic activities. In general, who does more chores around the house, men or women?

b) Information about four recreational activities is included in the database: reading, watching TV, sports and hobbies, and visiting with friends. Seventy percent of females aged 15 to 24 watch TV, which makes this the most popular of the four activities in this age group. Which activity do you think is most popular with females in other age groups? With men in the same age groups? Check using the database. Do the results surprise you?

c) For one week, keep track of how much time you spend on each activity listed in the database. Calculate the average time you spend on each activity per day. Do you think your results are typical for a person in your age group? Explain.

d) As a class, compile the results of part c for all students. Calculate participation rates and average time spent per day. How do your results compare with those listed in the database for the age group closest to your own?

7. Suppose you were hired to determine whether Canadians believe that students in grade 8 should spend more time studying mathematics.

a) Which of these sampling methods do you think would give the most representative results? Explain the advantages and disadvantages of each method.
   i) Interview 500 teachers and parents across Canada.
   ii) Set up two toll-free telephone numbers. Place advertisements in newspapers and on the radio to invite people across Canada to call one number if they agree or the other number if they disagree that grade 8 students should spend more time studying mathematics.
   iii) Telephone 500 randomly selected households across Canada. Ask an adult at the household for her or his opinion.
   iv) Interview 500 grade 8 students from across Canada.

b) Which of these questions would be the best to use in your study? Give reasons for your answer.
   i) Do you think Canadian students in grade 8 would perform better in mathematics if they spent more time learning mathematics in school?

ii) Should the Canadian school year be extended so that students can spend more time studying mathematics?

iii) In Canadian schools, is sufficient time devoted to the study of mathematics in grade 8?

8. Players are chosen for the major league baseball All-Star game from a survey of the fans. Survey cards are given out at the baseball games. Fans vote for the players on these cards. The players receiving the most votes are selected to play on the All-Star teams.

a) Do you think this method of selection is fair? Why or why not?

b) If you believe it is unfair, suggest a method that would be fair.

9. Suppose a door-to-door survey were conducted to determine how many times the average Canadian brushes her or his teeth per day. Suppose also that a similar survey were conducted using a questionnaire, which people completed anonymously. The results of these surveys would probably be very different. On which survey do you think Canadians would report to be brushing more frequently? Give reasons for your answer.

10. The manufacturer of a computer game uses magazine advertisements to sell its product. The advertisements promise a full refund to anyone who returns the game with a letter saying he or she is not satisfied. Only 4% of the games sold are returned. The company claims, "96% of those who purchased our product were satisfied." Is the company's claim misleading? Give reasons for your answer.

Extend your thinking

11. A researcher wanted to find out whether students learn mathematics better using a particular software program or a particular textbook. She divided a class of students into two randomly selected groups of equal size. Both groups studied mathematics for one hour every day. One group used only the software program and the other used only the book. When both groups were tested, the computer group had a higher mean score. Can the researcher conclude that the computer software produced the better performance? Explain.

The Ideas

In your journal, explain the difference between a sample and a population. What is a *random sample*? Why is a random sample useful? What is a *biased sample*? Give an example of a biased sample of a population and explain why it is biased.

The Poggendorf Effect

Answer this question without using a ruler or drawing a line.
If line *l* were extended, where do you think it would cross the line AB?

Copy this diagram. Just look at the diagram on your copy and mark the point on AB with an X. Make your decision quickly without experimenting.

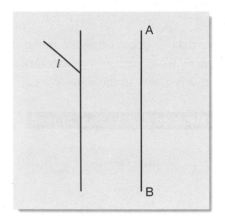

The diagram is an optical illusion. Most people tend to place their X too high on AB. Place a ruler along *l*. See how close your X is to the correct location.

This is known as the *Poggendorf effect*. To measure the magnitude or size of the effect, we measure the distance in millimetres from X to the correct location for *l* to cross AB.

Does the magnitude of the Poggendorf effect depend on:
a) the distance between the vertical lines?
b) the angle at which *l* meets the first vertical line?
c) whether *l* slopes up to the right or down to the left?

Conduct a survey to find answers to these questions. Organize your data by using the methods you have learned in this chapter. Write a report of your findings. What do you think is the cause of the Poggendorf effect?

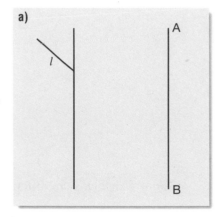

a)

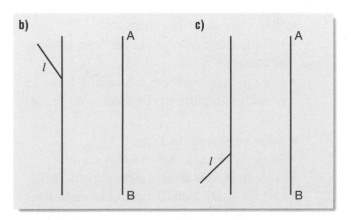

b)

c)

5.3 *MISUSES OF STATISTICS*

Developing the Ideas
▶ ▶ *Through Discussion*

Sometimes we see data or graphs that are misleading. It is very important for all of us to recognize errors and misrepresentations in data. We should ask questions to detect any flaws in the data. We call these *flaw-detector questions*.

Message that we hear or read	Flaw-detector questions
"Winter sale — 30% OFF"	• 30% off what? • Off the usual price? • Off all items or just some?
"40% fewer cavities"	• 40% fewer than whom? • Than people who don't brush? • Who was surveyed? Was it a random sample? How many people were sampled?
"250 000 in metro below the poverty line"	• How is the poverty line defined? Do two families with the same income and different numbers or ages of children have the same poverty line? • How is "metro" defined? • How was this information collected? Is it based on tax returns, door-to-door interviews, requests for assistance, or other information sources?
"7% of Canadians are illiterate."	• What do we mean by illiterate? • Does the 7% include children? If so, what ages? • How were the data collected? • Did the study involve people from all parts of Canada? • Does it include people whose first language is neither English nor French?
"Crime is up 28.2% over last year."	• What crimes are included? • Does this include only violent crimes? • Does it include crimes such as petty theft? • Did the study include urban and rural areas? • Who were sampled? How many people were in the sample?

For each of the messages on page 266, discuss:

1. What are the possible answers to the flaw-detector questions?

2. What other questions should we ask?

3. Rewrite the message to clarify the information presented.

▶▶ *Through Activities*

ACTIVITY 1

By 1992, the national debt was more than
$419 000 000 000. (That's 419 billion dollars!)
The Ministry of Finance published the graph
shown here. It was to illustrate that interest
on the debt from previous governments was
responsible for much of the country's current
debt. Complete the following exercises to
discover what is misleading about this graph
and how it could be changed to present the
information correctly.

Each rectangle in the graph represents an amount
of money.

1. In the graph, what does B represent?

2. a) In the graph, what is the height of the rectangle
representing $206 billion?

   b) Use the answer to part a to calculate the height
of a rectangle that represents $1 billion.

   c) Use the answer to part b to calculate the height
of a rectangle that represents $238 billion.

3. Measure the height of the rectangle in the graph
that represents $238 billion. How does it compare
with exercise 2c?

4. a) Use the answer to exercise 2b to calculate the
height of a rectangle that represents $419 billion.

   b) Measure the height of the rectangle in the graph
that represents $419 billion. How does it compare
with part a?

5. a) Why might the Ministry of Finance have wanted
to make the 1991–92 debt look smaller than it
actually was?

   b) Do you think this graph is misleading? Explain.

6. Draw a graph that correctly represents the amounts
given.

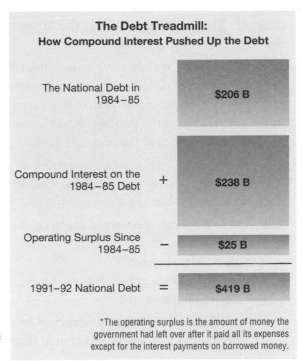

The Debt Treadmill:
How Compound Interest Pushed Up the Debt

The National Debt in 1984–85	$206 B
Compound Interest on the 1984–85 Debt +	$238 B
Operating Surplus Since 1984–85 −	$25 B
1991–92 National Debt =	$419 B

*The operating surplus is the amount of money the
government had left over after it paid all its expenses
except for the interest payments on borrowed money.

Sometimes the way a graph is drawn leads to misinterpretation. Often, the graph is drawn correctly, but the information is wrongly presented. This is the case in the following example. This graph appeared in The Toronto Star on February 27, 1994.

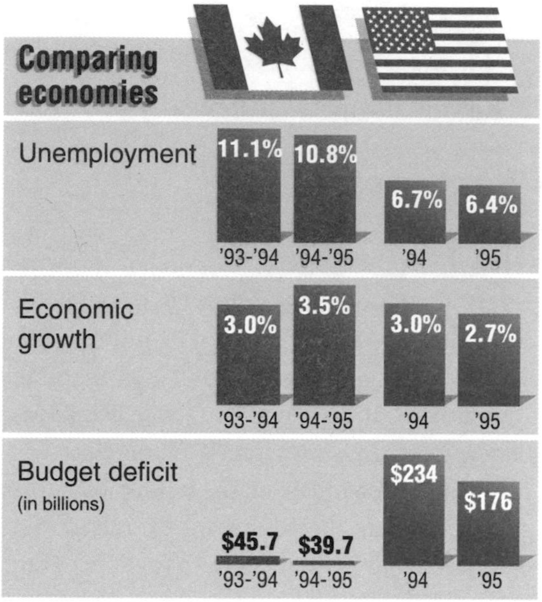

If the government spends more money than it takes in, it has a *budget deficit*. The *economic growth* of a country in a particular year is the increase in the total value of the goods and services it produces that year over the previous year.

We will ask some flaw-detector questions to determine if this graph is misleading. Use the graph to answer these questions.

Comparing economies

| Unemployment | 11.1% | 10.8% | 6.7% | 6.4% |
| | '93-'94 | '94-'95 | '94 | '95 |

| Economic growth | 3.0% | 3.5% | 3.0% | 2.7% |
| | '93-'94 | '94-'95 | '94 | '95 |

Budget deficit (in billions)			$234	$176
	$45.7	$39.7		
	'93-'94	'94-'95	'94	'95

Source: Canada Finance Dept. projections, U.S. Commerce Dept. projections

1. In 1993–94, which country, Canada or the United States, had:
   a) higher unemployment?
   b) higher economic growth?
   c) a higher budget deficit?

2. Copy both tables. Use the information for 1993–94 from the graph and the populations of Canada and United States to help you complete the tables.

	Canada (pop 27 000 000)		U.S. (pop 260 000 000)	
	Total number	As a percent of population	Total number	As a percent of population
Unemployed				

	Canada (pop 27 000 000)		U.S. (pop 260 000 000)	
	Total number	Per capita	Total number	Per capita
Budget deficit $				

3. a) Do the unemployment graphs compare the numbers of people unemployed in both countries or the percents unemployed?
   b) Why would it not make sense to compare the numbers of unemployed in each country?

4. a) How are the deficits compared in the graphs?
   b) Draw a bar graph that compares the per capita budget deficits. Which country's deficit appears to be lower?

5. How might a person be misled by looking at the three graphs and concluding that Canada has higher unemployment than the United States but better economic growth and lower debt?

Working with Mathematics

Something to talk about

1. a) What is a flaw-detector question?
   b) Describe the kinds of statements made in advertisements that contain misleading information.

2. For each statement, ask some flaw-detector questions to determine whether the information is accurate or misleading.
   a) Up to half price off the cost of brand name jeans if you buy today
   b) More teenagers buy Pepsi than any other beverage.
   c) The cost of living increased 14% last year.
   d) A recent study revealed that daily exposure to classical music helps plants grow more vigorously.
   e) A survey indicates that most people would rather go without a car than a television set.
   f) Scientists predict that next winter will be unusually cold.
   g) Greatly reduced holidays to the sunbelt, including free car rental and flight

3. Some advertisements for weight loss programs show pictures of people before and after they have participated in the program. Describe ways the "before" picture can be taken to make the person look overweight, and the "after" picture to make the person look slimmer.

Work together

4. To determine whether Canadians are concerned about crime, one polling company asked this question.
   "Are you concerned about the level of crime in Canada today?"
   Another polling company asked this question. "Are you concerned about your personal safety when walking in Canadian cities or towns?"

a) To which question do you think more people answered yes?
b) Conduct your own survey to find out if your answer to part a is correct.

5. a) Describe each graph below.

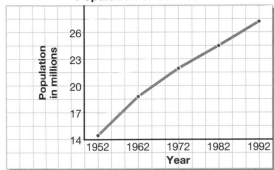

b) Which graph makes the population growth look more rapid? Why?
c) Which graph misrepresents the growth in the Canadian population? Why?

6. The graph shows the availability of office space in Metro Toronto between 1989 and 1993.

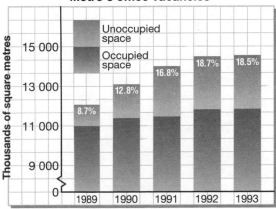

a) What do the green rectangles represent?

b) What do the purple rectangles represent?

c) Look at the green and purple rectangles in the bar for 1993. Without looking at the numbers in the graph, estimate the percent of the 1993 bar that shows unoccupied space.

d) Compare your estimate in part a with the 18.5% unoccupied space stated on the graph.

e) Explain why your answers to parts c and d are different.

f) Construct a bar graph so that the areas of the green and purple rectangles match the percents given on the original graph. Explain the design feature of the original graph that makes it easy to misinterpret the graph.

7. The graph below was part of an article published in The Vancouver Sun on December 18, 1993. The article described how the real income after tax of British Columbians was decreasing because of low wage increases and increased taxes.

a) Choose a year.
   i) What was the real income before tax?
   ii) What was the real income after tax?

iii) Express your answer to part ii as a percent of your answer to part i. What does this suggest about the percent of income that remains after taxes?

b) Use the same year as in part a.
   i) Measure the height of the point representing the income before tax.
   ii) Measure the height of the point representing the income after tax.
   iii) Express your answer to part ii as a percent of your answer to part i. What does this suggest about the percent of income that remains after taxes?

c) Compare your answers to parts a and b. Describe the way the graph is drawn that makes the answers so different. Which is the correct approximation of the percent of income that remains after taxes?

8. To find out whether people prefer Coke or Pepsi, a researcher presented the following question. "Do you prefer Coke over Pepsi?"

a) How would a person who prefers Coke answer this question?

b) How would a person who prefers Pepsi answer this question?

c) How do you think a person with no preference would answer the question?

d) Of the 1000 responses received, 525 replied no and 475 yes. The researcher concluded that most of the 1000 people preferred Pepsi. Was the researcher's conclusion valid? Explain your answer.

9. The graph shows a company's profits in its first three years of business. How does the graph misrepresent the data?

Extend your thinking

10. Read the following excerpt from an article that appeared in The Vancouver Sun on May 14, 1994.

a) According to the article, how many murders were reported in Canada in 1992?

b) The population of Canada was 18 265 300 in 1961 and 22 697 300 in 1975. The article states the number of reported murders per 100 000 people in 1961 and 1975. Use this information to calculate the number of murders reported in each of these years.

c) How could you use your answers to parts a and b to argue that the murder rate is increasing?

d) How could you use the number of reported murders per 100 000 people to argue that the murder rate is decreasing?

e) Which argument do you think is a fairer use of the statistics? Explain.

Perception crime is epidemic blamed on misuse of statistics

**DOUG FISCHER/Southam News
and NEAL HALL/Vancouver Sun**

OTTAWA – Has anything changed in the past year, the past decade, to warrant the huge public rallies and political demands for a new, tough approach to law and order?

The answer, according to most criminologists, is a resounding No. They say, police, Reformers and others leading the cry for a crackdown are being selective in their use of crime statistics.

And that – along with media pre-occupation with sensational crime – is wrongly feeding the perception that violence has reached epidemic levels, they say.

"You lie with statistics by using the statistics that work to your bias," says University of Toronto criminologist Anthony Doob. "I'm not any more at risk to violence today than I was 18 years ago but I am at more risk than I was 30 years ago."

The Canadian Centre for Justice Statistics says 730 murders were reported in 1992, about 2.7 homicides per 100 000 people and twice the 1.3 rate recorded in 1961.

But since the late 1970s, the murder rate has remained relatively stable and is, in fact, lower than it was in 1975, when it peaked at 3.09 per 100 000.

The Ideas

Look through magazines and newspapers. Find an example of a graph. Glue the graph in your journal. Describe whether or not the graph accurately represents the data.

Contaminants in the Great Lakes

CONTAMINANTS ARE TOXIC CHEMICALS OR OTHER unwanted substances released into the environment. How can we tell whether a lake is contaminated? Should we worry about contaminants?

Consider this study of how a group of toxic chemicals called PCBs have affected herring gull populations in the Great Lakes region.

PCBs, linked to cancer, birth defects, and other health problems, were used in electrical transformers, lubricating oils, and carbonless copy paper. In 1976, the United States discontinued the manufacture of PCBs. In 1977, Canada regulated their use. As of 1980, Canada disallowed electrical equipment containing PCBs.

In 1969, a biologist discovered that a colony of 100 herring gulls nesting on an island in Lake Ontario produced only 12 chicks, not 100 as expected. To discover what was wrong, Environment Canada monitored toxic chemicals in herring gull eggs from several islands in the Great Lakes. A few eggs were taken from each colony and analyzed. Of particular interest was the level of PCBs in the eggs.

PCBs get into the water from a variety of sources. Microscopic water plants absorb the chemicals. Fish eat the plants and the herring gulls, in turn, eat the fish. The adult birds pass on the chemicals to the eggs they produce. At each step of this process, the concentration of chemicals increases. Thus, it is easier to measure chemical levels in gull eggs than it would be in the water plants.

These graphs show the results of the study. The news is generally good. Levels of PCBs have decreased since the study started in the 1970s. The number of gulls born with deformities has also decreased. In addition, tests indicate that levels of most other contaminants, such as dioxins, have also decreased.

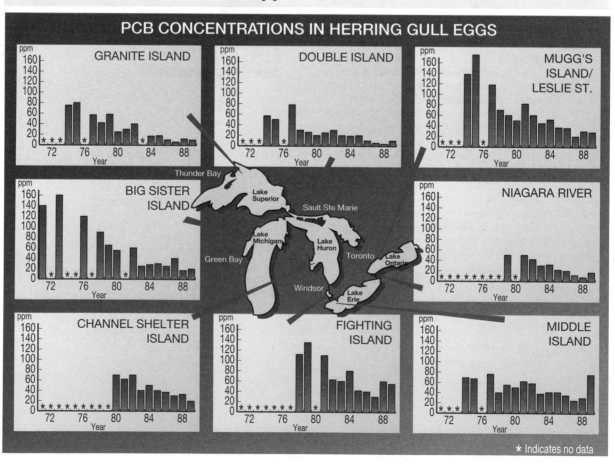

1. **a)** A few eggs were taken from each colony as a sample. Why was it necessary to use a sample in this study rather than to analyze the entire population?

   b) The results for the different locations were not combined. Why was it important to keep the results separate?

2. The concentration of contaminants is measured in ppm (parts per million). This is a very small unit. A concentration of 1 ppm means that for every million equal parts of the sample, there is 1 part that is PCB. To visualize how small this is, think of 1 cm in 1 000 000 cm. How many metres are 1 000 000 cm? How many kilometres are 1 000 000 cm?

3. **a)** Information from 1974 is provided for four lakes. Which lake had the highest level of PCBs that year?

   b) Why do you think this lake was more contaminated than the others? Check an atlas to see where large cities are located in the area around the Great Lakes.

4. **a)** Which lakes show the greatest decline in PCB concentrations over the course of the study?

   b) When did the periods of decrease occur? How does this relate to the changes in the production and use of PCBs during this time?

5. There is less industrial development around Lake Superior than there is around the other lakes. This means that fewer toxic chemicals are dumped directly into this lake. Most of the PCB contamination in Lake Superior comes from airborne sources. Try to explain why PCB levels in this lake were lower than those in other lakes at the beginnning of the study, and why the levels have not dropped as rapidly as in some of the other lakes.

Linking Ideas · *Mathematics & Science*

5.4 MEASURES OF CENTRAL TENDENCY

Developing the Ideas

▶ ▶ *Through Discussion*

Here are the pay scales for Winnipeg fire fighters and police constables.

Class of constable	Pay	Level of fire fighter	Pay
4th	$24 908	Trainee	$27 274
3rd	$28 756	1st	$29 562
2nd	$38 324	4th	$38 662
1st	$47 918	Senior	$47 658

Who earns more, police constables or fire fighters?

From the data given, it appears that fire fighters earn more.
- Would all police constables earn less than all fire fighters?
- Would some fire fighters earn less than some police constables?
- What single number best represents the income of all members of each occupation? What further information would you need to calculate this number?

Recall that there are three commonly used averages:

. . . .

The *mean* of a set of numbers is the sum of all the numbers divided by the number of numbers.

. . . .

The *median* of a set of numbers is the middle number when the numbers are arranged in order. If there is an even number of numbers, the median is the mean of the two middle numbers.

. . . .

The *mode* of a set of numbers is the most frequently occurring number. There may be more than one mode, or there may be no mode.

The mean, the median, and the mode are *measures of central tendency*. They tend to be located somewhere in the "centre" of the data. They give us information about the data. Often, large amounts of data are summarized by stating the values of the mean, the median, and the mode. The mode is seldom used as an average because it ignores all values except the most frequent.

Through Guided Examples

Example 1

The annual incomes for the people who work at the Beta Metal Works are shown below.

    1 Manager: $80 000   3 Mechanics: $35 000
    1 Supervisor: $45 000   5 Labourers: $25 000

a) Determine the mean, the median, and the mode for the payroll.

b) Which measure could be used to make the salaries look:

  i) high?   ii) low?

c) Which measure most fairly represents the average income?

d) Suppose the manager's salary were changed to $150 000.
   What changes would that make to the answers in part a?

Solution

a) The mean salary, in dollars, is given by:

$$\frac{80\ 000 + 45\ 000 + (3 \times 35\ 000) + (5 \times 25\ 000)}{10} = \frac{355\ 000}{10}$$
$$= 35\ 500$$

For the median, arrange the salaries in order:

80 000, 45 000, 35 000, 35 000, 35 000, 25 000, 25 000, 25 000, 25 000, 25 000

Since there is an even number of salaries, the median is the mean of the fifth and sixth values.

$$\frac{35\ 000 + 25\ 000}{2} = \frac{60\ 000}{2}$$
$$= 30\ 000$$

The mode is the salary that occurs most often, $25 000.
The mean is $35 500, the median is $30 000, and the mode is $25 000.

b) i) To make the salaries look high, the mean value of $35 500 would be chosen as being representative.

  ii) To make the salaries look low, the mode value of $25 000 would be chosen as being representative.

c) Only 2 of the 10 employees earn more that the mean value of $35 500. Therefore, as a representative value, it is too high. Since every employee earns at least the mode value of $25 000, as a representative value, this is too low. The median value of $30 000 probably best represents the average income.

d) If the manager's salary is increased to $150 000, the total payroll increases by $70 000. The mean increases by $\frac{\$70\ 000}{10}$, or $7000, to $42 500. The median does not change. It is not affected by large changes in extreme values. The mode does not change either.

$80 000

$45 000

$35 000

$25 000

Example 2

The number of tonnes of household garbage taken to a municipal landfill site each day of a month is shown below. The landfill site is closed on weekends.

304	312	285	328	316	309	315	293
340	314	299	281	323	309	324	313
307	296	342	321	284	317	298	

a) What are the mean and median masses of household garbage taken to the landfill site?

b) The landfill site can accommodate 500 000 t of garbage before it is full. When must a new site be found?

c) Suppose reducing, reusing, and recycling result in a 15% reduction in household garbage each year. How much longer would the municipality be able to use the landfill site?

Solution

a) The mean $= \dfrac{\text{sum of all the garbage}}{\text{number of days}}$

$$= \frac{304 + 312 + 285 + \cdots + 284 + 317 + 298}{23}$$
$$= \frac{7130}{23}$$
$$= 310$$

The mean mass is 310 t.

To find the median, we create a stem-and-leaf diagram. We arrange the leaves in numerical order.

28	1 4 5
29	3 6 8 9
30	4 7 9 9
31	2 3 4 5 6 7
32	1 3 4 8
33	
34	0 2

In this diagram,

 means 281 t.

The median is the middle value. There are 23 values. The median is the twelfth value from either 281 or 342. The median mass is 312 t.

b) Since the landfill site is closed on weekends, the 7130 t of garbage were collected in approximately one month.
In one year, approximately 12×7130 t, or 85 560 t are collected.
Since the capacity of the site is 500 000 t, a new site must be found in $\dfrac{500\ 000}{85\ 560}$ years, or approximately 6 years after this site is first used.

c) Suppose the amount of garbage collected in 1 year is reduced by 15%. The annual amount collected would then be 85% of 85 560, which is $0.85 \times 85\ 560 = 72\ 726$. A new site would have to be found in $\dfrac{500\ 000}{72\ 726}$ years, or approximately 7 years. A 15% reduction would enable the landfill site to be used for an additional year.

Working with Mathematics

Something to talk about

1. Which measure of central tendency is most suitable to describe each average? Why?
   a) the average volume of water used by a Canadian household in one day
   b) the average number of pages in a newspaper
   c) the average mark of a student on a test
   d) the average rainfall in Quebec city
   e) the average time you spend on homework each night
   f) the average size of shoes sold by a store

2. A random sample of 100 people were polled. They were found to have a mean income of $35 000. Does this mean that a random sample of 200 people would have a mean income of $70 000? Explain.

3. A student received a mean mark of 70% in his first three exams. After getting 90% on his next exam, he stated that his overall mean mark was 80%, because the mean of 70 and 90 is 80. Is his reasoning correct? Explain.

Practice

4. State the mean, median, and mode for the data in this stem-and-leaf diagram.

   ```
   2 | 3 3 5 7 8        2 | 3   means 23.
   3 | 0 1 2 2 5 7
   4 | 0 1 1 2 6 8 9
   5 | 1 4 4 6 8 9
   ```

5. State the mean and the median for each set of data. Give the answers to 1 decimal place where necessary.
   a) 1, 2, 4, 4, 9, 15
   b) 3, 5, 5, 7, 11, 15
   c) 7, 9, 22, 9, 13, 15, 18
   d) 70, 60, 24, 50, 24, 60
   e) 15, 18, 16, 21, 18, 14, 12, 19, 11, 16
   f) 1, 2, 2, 3, 4, 3, 4, 4, 4, 4, 4, 4, 5
   g) 9, 12, 7, 5, 18, 15, 5, 11

Work together

6. There are 5 numbers in a set. The mode is 2. The median is 2. The sum of the numbers is 15.
   a) Find the mean.
   b) One number is 4. What are the numbers?

7. Three grade 8 classes had these numbers of students and mean marks on a chapter test for mathematics.
   - Room 101 has 26 students, with mean mark 66%.
   - Room 107 has 23 students, with mean mark 71%.
   - Room 111 has 28 students, with mean mark 64%.

   What is the mean mark for the grade 8 students? Give the answer to one decimal place.

8. The mean mark on a quiz was 7. The median mark was 6 and the mode was 5. Fifteen students wrote the quiz. The lowest mark was 1, and the highest mark was 10.
   a) Write a possible set of marks.
   b) One student, who was absent, wrote the quiz later. Her mark was 10. How does this mark affect the mean, the median, and the mode?

9. a) Copy and complete the table below.

Type of plant	Number of plants	Height of each plant (cm)	Sum of heights of plants (cm)
A	1	26	
B	2	19	
C	2	14	
Total number of plants		Total height	

   b) Use the data in the table. Find the mean height of a plant.

10. For the numbers 2, 2, 4, 5, 7, 8, 10, 11:
    a) Find the mean, the median, and the mode.
    b) Double each number in the set. Find the mean, the median, and the mode.
    c) How does doubling the numbers affect the mean, the median, and the mode?

d) Triple each number in the set. Find the mean, the median, and the mode.

e) How does tripling the numbers in a set affect the mean, the median, and the mode?

f) Add 4 to each number in the set. Find the mean, the median, and the mode.

g) How does adding the same number to each number in a set affect the mean, the median, and the mode?

11. Pay Lil is the manager of a shoe store. She likes to maintain mean daily sales of $3500. The sales for the first 4 days of the week are $2795, $3150, $3630, and $2654. The store does not open on Sunday.

a) What sales does Pay Lil need on Friday and Saturday to attain mean daily sales of $3500?

b) Do you think this expectation is reasonable? Explain.

12. In one year, a person bought 3 CDs at $18.99 each, 5 CDs at $14.99 each, and 1 CD at $10.99. Find the mean and the median for the amounts spent.

13. The mean of the numbers 8, 12, 13, 14, and x is 13. What is the value of x?

DATA DISK

14. Use the *Olympic Winter Games* database on the data disk. Choose an event. Record the winning time for each year. Express each time in the same units. Create a stem-and-leaf diagram to represent these results. From the diagram, determine the mean and median times.

On your own

15. For the numbers 40, 42, 43, 44, 45, 46, 47, 48, 49, 50, and 52, find the effect on the mean and the median if:

a) each number is increased by 5

b) each number is doubled

c) the smallest number is increased by 2 and the largest number is decreased by 2

d) the number 1356 is included in the set

e) the number 2 is included in the set

16. Maurice has written 4 math tests this term. His mean mark is 69%. What mark does he need on his next test to raise his mean mark to 75%?

17. Write seven lengths, such that the median length is 3 m, the greatest length is 20 m, and the shortest length is 1 m.

18. Three grade 8 classes had these numbers of students and mean marks on the end-of-term exam.

- Ms. Cheung's class has 29 students, with mean mark 74%.
- Mr. Lewis' class has 25 students, with mean mark 72%.
- Ms. Shankar's class has 31 students, with mean mark 76%.

What is the mean mark for the grade 8 students? Give the answer to 1 decimal place.

19. The table shows the annual incomes of people who work for a CBC network current affairs show.

POSITION	SALARY ($)
1 executive producer	76 000
1 senior producer	65 000
2 hosts	63 000
4 producers	55 000
2 associate producers	44 500
4 researchers	33 000

a) Find the measures of central tendency for these salaries.

b) Which measure of central tendency most fairly represents the pay structure? Give reasons for your answer.

20. The mean mark on the end-of-term English exam was 64%. The median mark was 68%, and the mode was 72%. Ten students wrote the exam. The lowest mark was 24%. The highest mark was 82%.

a) Write a possible set of marks.

b) One student wrote the exam later. His mark was 80%. How does this mark affect the mean, median, and mode?

21. As an exercise, students were asked to measure the diameter of the same brass cylinder. Although all students measured the same cylinder, students were not told specifically what method or equipment to use. Various answers were reported by members of the class and are shown below.

1.8 m, 1.8 m, 2.0 cm, 180 cm, 19 cm, 18 cm, 2.0 cm, 1.8 cm, 1.8 cm, 1.9 cm, 18 m, 1.8 cm, 1.8 cm, 1.8 cm, 1.8 cm

Which measure of central tendency best describes the data? Why?

22. A sales department was split into three divisions. The mean income for each division is shown below.

Division	Number of people	Mean income ($)
A	3	13 500
B	10	15 000
C	7	20 500

a) Explain why the mean for the department cannot be found by adding the numbers in the third column and dividing by 3.
b) What is the mean income?

23. Determine each set of numbers.
a) Five numbers with range 11 and median 18
b) Six numbers with range 78 and median 56
c) Seven numbers with range 28 and mode 46
d) Eight numbers with range 2 and median 9
e) Seven numbers with range 1 and mode 6
f) Six numbers with range 0 and mean 4
g) Five numbers with mean and median 5

24. The number of passengers riding each bus in one day was recorded. The data were analyzed. The mean number of passengers was 43, and the median was 46.
a) The standard bus fare is $1.30. What are the mean and the median amounts of money collected?
b) Suppose there were 20 more passengers on each bus. What would have been the mean and the median number of passengers?

Extend your thinking

25. Determine 7 numbers that have a mean of:
a) 12 and a median of 13
b) 62 and a median of 65
c) 8, a median of 10, and a mode of 5
d) 15, a median of 12, and a mode of 15

The Ideas

Use a dictionary to find the meaning(s) of the word "median." In your journal, explain how the meaning in statistics is similar to the meanings in other uses, such as median of a highway.

BOGGLE YOUR MIND

In 1994, there were about 11.4 million cows in Canada. A single cow drinks about 55 L of water and eats about 14 kg of vegetation every day. How much water and vegetation would be consumed in one year by all the cows in Canada?

5.5 *CALCULATING RELATIVE FREQUENCY*

Developing the Ideas

A message can be coded by replacing each letter in the message with a different letter. When people decode a message, they count the number of times each letter occurs in the coded message. This is called the letter's *frequency*. They then match the letter of greatest frequency in the coded message with the letter used most often in the English language.

To use this decoding method, you need to know which letters in the English language are used most often. One way to do this is to take a sample of writing and count the letters to determine their frequencies.

▶ ▶ *Through an Activity*

1. Read this poem.

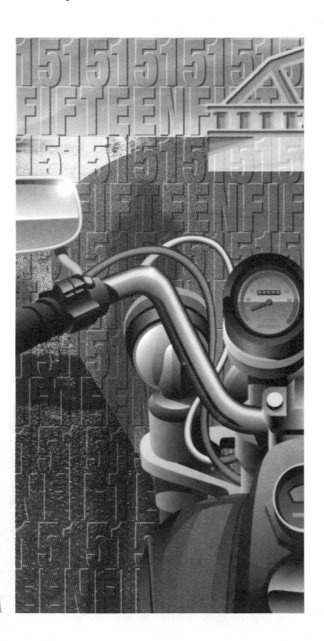

Fifteen

By William Stafford

South of the bridge on Seventeenth
I found back of the willows one summer
day a motorcycle with engine running
as it lay on its side, ticking over
slowly in the high grass. I was fifteen.

I admired all that pulsing gleam, the
shiny flanks, the demure headlights
fringed where it lay; I led it gently
to the road and stood with that
companion, ready and friendly. I was fifteen.

We could find the end of a road, meet
the sky on out Seventeenth. I thought about
hills, and patting the handle got back a
confident opinion. On the bridge we indulged
a forward feeling, a tremble. I was fifteen.

Thinking, back farther in the grass I found
the owner, just coming to, where he had flipped
over the rail. He had blood on his hand, was pale —
I helped him walk to his machine. He ran his hand
over it, called me a good man, roared away.

I stood there, fifteen.

2. Count the number of times each letter occurs in this poem. Record these frequencies in a table like the one below.

Letter	Tally	Frequency	Relative frequency
a			
b			
c			
d			

3. Count the total number of letters in the poem.

4. Choose the 5 letters that occur most often. Divide the frequency of each letter by the total number of letters. Give the answer to 3 decimal places. This is the *relative frequency*. Record the relative frequencies in the table.

5. Which letter in your table has the greatest relative frequency?

6. About how many times would you expect the letter **e** to occur in a passage of about 1000 words? Explain how you made your estimate.

▶ ▶ *Through a Guided Example*

Example ···

Naomi and Devon rolled a die 60 times and kept a tally of the way it landed. Their results are shown in the table. Use their results to calculate the frequency and the relative frequency of each event:

a) The die lands showing three.

b) The die lands showing an even number.

Number	1	2	3	4	5	6
Tally	₩ IIII	₩ III	₩ ₩ III	₩ IIII	₩ ₩ I	₩ ₩

Solution

a) According to the tally, the die landed showing three 13 times in 60 tosses. Therefore, the frequency of three was 13.

The relative frequency of three was $\frac{13}{60}$, or about 0.217.

b) The even numbers on the die are two, four, and six. According to the tally, the die landed showing two 8 times, showing four 9 times, and showing six 10 times.

Therefore, the frequency of an even number was $8 + 9 + 10 = 27$.

The relative frequency of an even number was $\frac{27}{60}$, or 0.45.

Working with Mathematics

Something to talk about

1. **a)** Explain what is meant by the "frequency" of a letter in a given passage.
   b) The frequency of the letter **a** in a poem is 18. The poem contains 100 letters. What is the relative frequency of the letter **a**?
   c) The relative frequency of the letter **e** in a newspaper article is 0.09. The article contains 1000 letters. How many times does the letter **e** occur?

2. What is the relative frequency of the letter **e** in the first line of the poem *Fifteen?* Is this the same as the relative frequency of the letter **e** in the entire poem? Explain.

3. A computer count revealed that the relative frequency of the letter **s** in a 50 250-word book was 0.072. Would you expect the relative frequency of **s** to be the same in a book containing twice as many words, if both books are in the same language? Explain your answer.

Work together

4. **a)** Find the frequencies and relative frequencies of the letters **a**, **e**, **s**, and **t** for the first two verses of the poem *Fifteen*. Record your answers in a table.
   b) Find the frequencies and relative frequencies of the letters **a**, **e**, **s**, and **t** for the third and fourth verses of the poem *Fifteen*. Record your answers in a table.
   c) Is the relative frequency of a letter in the first two verses of the poem the same as its relative frequency in the third and fourth verses? Explain.
   d) For a particular letter, would the relative frequencies in both halves of a poem be closer in value for short poems or for long poems? Explain.

5. **a)** Find the frequencies of the letters **a**, **e**, **s**, and **t** in this poem.

To the Mothers and Fathers Who Hover ...

By Jean Little

She is young to start through the wood,
To swim the ocean,
To cross the limitless desert, to climb
The impossible, beautiful mountain

Leave her alone.

She cannot carry so much equipment.
You did not start with as much.
She cannot follow so many different guides.

Give her a compass, yes.
But not the lessons.
Throw out the Tourist Guides.

Take down the signs.
She must find the way herself.
Your map is out of date. She must make her own.
Each of us finds this country unexplored
And the charts we make can never be handed on —
Although examining them we may remember
A little of what it was like.

She must follow a star
Which only her eyes can see,
Discover a route
As fresh as the furrow plowed
By the *Santa Maria.*

And her logbook is private.
Do not inquire so often.
Do not give her those postcards, stamped and addressed.

Let her waste time.
Hand her long hours of wonder.
Have faith in her sense of direction
And set her free.

And do not stand waving good-bys from the door forever.
Put a light in the window, but do not sit up.
If she had not gone, she would have grown away.
In time, in her own good time,
She will come home.

b) Calculate the relative frequencies of **a**, **e**, **s**, and **t** in this poem.

c) Compare these relative frequencies with the relative frequencies of those letters in the poem, *Fifteen*. Are the relative frequencies about the same in both poems for the same letter? If not, explain why they may differ.

6. a) Find the frequencies of the letters **a**, **e**, **s**, and **t** in the two poems combined.

b) Calculate the relative frequencies of these four letters in the two poems combined.

7. Toss a coin 100 times. Record the number of heads and the number of tails.

a) What was the frequency of heads?

b) What was the frequency of tails?

c) What was the relative frequency of heads? Of tails? Express the relative frequencies as percents.

d) Construct a bar graph showing the frequency of heads and of tails in the 100 tosses.

8. a) Two dice are rolled, and the numbers that show are added. What sums are possible?

b) Make a table with these headings. List the possible sums.

Sum	Tally	Frequency	Relative frequency

c) Roll two dice 50 times. Record the frequency of each sum. Calculate the relative frequency of each sum.

d) Construct a bar graph to show the frequency of each sum.

e) Which sum has the greatest frequency?

On your own

9. Personal Lettering Incorporated (PLC) produces weather-resistant letters. People fasten these letters to their mailboxes or houses to display their names.

a) Should PLC make the same number of each letter? Why or why not?

b) To determine which letters occur most frequently in people's names, follow these steps:

- Pick a page at random from a local telephone book. Close your eyes and point to a name. Record the name.
- Repeat this procedure for 20 names.
- Calculate the relative frequencies of the letters.
- Which letter has the greatest frequency?
- Which letter has the least frequency?

c) Which 6 letters should PLC manufacture in greatest quantity?

d) Which 6 letters should PLC manufacture in the least quantity?

e) Compare your answers to parts c and d with other students. Explain any differences.

Extend your thinking

10. A magazine article contains 80 560 letters. The letters **e**, **t**, and **s** were found to have relative frequencies of 0.131, 0.110, and 0.060 respectively.

a) About how many times did each letter occur in the article?

b) Do you think it is possible to say *exactly* how many times each letter occurred based on the information given? Explain.

The Ideas

Write a few sentences to explain why two or more poems or passages may have a letter occurring with different relative frequencies.

5.6 PROBABILITY

Developing the Ideas

When outcomes are equally likely, it is possible to estimate their relative frequencies without conducting an experiment.

▶ ▶ *Through an Activity*

Work in a group. Follow these steps to construct a spinner. You will need paper, compasses, scissors, red and green coloured pencils, and a paper clip.

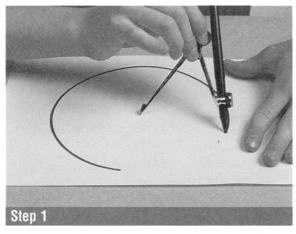

Step 1

Use compasses to draw a circle at least 10 cm in diameter. Cut out the circle.

Step 2

Fold the paper circle in half, then in half again to divide it into quarters.

Step 3

Colour one-quarter of the spinner red and three-quarters green.

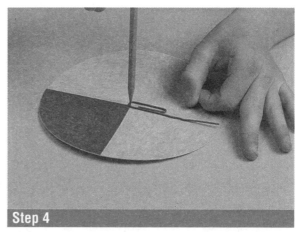

Step 4

Bend a paper clip into the shape of a pointer. Place a sharp pencil at the centre of the circle as shown, and spin the paper clip.

1. Suppose you were to spin the pointer 40 times. Predict how many times the pointer will land in the green area. That is, predict the frequency of the "green" outcome. How did you do this? Predict the relative frequency of the "green" outcome.

2. Spin the paper clip 40 times. Tally the outcomes. Record the frequency of the "green" outcome. Calculate its relative frequency.

3. Combine your results with those of all the groups in your class. Calculate the frequency and the relative frequency of the "green" outcome.

4. Compare the relative frequencies of the "green" outcome in exercises 2 and 3 with your predicted value. Which is closer to the predicted value? Do you think the predicted relative frequency and the calculated relative frequency would be closer if the number of spins were increased to 2000? Explain.

▶ ▶ *Through Discussion*

The spinner you made in the *Activity* is a circle divided into four equal regions. Three of these regions are green and one is red. Since it is equally likely that the pointer will stop in any of the four regions, we would expect that on a large number of spins it would land in each region about the same number of times.

1. One region is red. In 400 spins, about how many times would you expect the pointer to land in the red region?

2. Three regions are green. In 400 spins, about how many times would you expect the pointer to land in each green region? In all three green regions?

3. What relative frequency would you predict for each colour?

If the outcomes of an experiment arc equally likely, then the *probability* of an event is the number of outcomes favourable to the event divided by the total number of outcomes.

• • • • • • • • • •

> For an experiment where the outcomes are equally likely, the probability P of an event is given by
>
> $$P = \frac{\text{the number of outcomes favourable to the event}}{\text{the total number of outcomes}}$$
>
> If there are 2 equally likely outcomes, the probability of one outcome is $\frac{1}{2}$.
>
> If there are 6 equally likely outcomes, the probability of one outcome is $\frac{1}{6}$.

For example, when a coin is tossed, the outcomes are "land heads" and "land tails." The outcomes are equally likely, so the probability of landing heads, P(H), is equal to the probability of landing tails, $P(T) = \frac{1}{2}$.

When a die is rolled, there are 6 equally likely outcomes. The probability of showing a 2, P(2) is equal to the probability of showing a 5, $P(5) = \frac{1}{6}$.

There are many possible events when a die is rolled. For example, one event is "a number greater than 1." The outcomes favourable to this event are the numbers 2, 3, 4, 5, and 6. So, there are 5 outcomes favourable to this event. The probability of rolling a number greater than 1, $P(> 1) = \frac{5}{6}$.

The following examples show how we can use the definitions on the preceding page to calculate the probabilities of various events in a probability experiment.

▶ ▶ *Through Guided Examples*

Example 1

Write the probability of each event on a roll of a fair die.

a) number 6
b) a number less than 3
c) an odd number
d) either 3 or 6
e) a number greater than 2
f) number 7

Solution

In each case, the probability is the predicted relative frequency.
There are 6 equally likely outcomes. They are 1, 2, 3, 4, 5, and 6.

a) The die will show 6 about $\frac{1}{6}$ of the time. The probability is $\frac{1}{6}$.

b) The numbers less than 3 are 1 and 2.
There are 2 outcomes.
The probability is $\frac{2}{6}$, or $\frac{1}{3}$.

c) The odd numbers are 1, 3, and 5.
There are 3 outcomes.
The probability is $\frac{3}{6}$, or $\frac{1}{2}$.

d) To show 3 or 6, there are two outcomes.
The probability is $\frac{2}{6}$, or $\frac{1}{3}$.

e) The numbers greater than 2 are 3, 4, 5, and 6.
There are 4 outcomes.
The probability is $\frac{4}{6}$, or $\frac{2}{3}$.

f) The number 7 does not appear on a die.
The probability is 0.

Example 2

How many times would you expect the paper clip to land in the blue region in 100 spins?

Solution

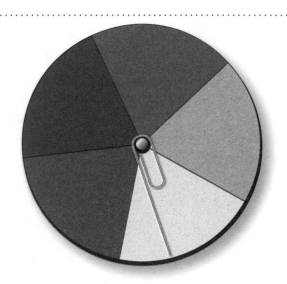

The spinner is divided into 5 equal regions.
Only one region is blue.
Therefore, the probability of the paper clip landing in the blue region on each spin is $\frac{1}{5}$.

In 100 spins, we would expect the paper clip to land in the blue region about $\frac{1}{5} \times 100 = 20$ times.

Working with Mathematics

Something to talk about

1. What is the *probability* of an event?

2. Explain the difference between the relative frequency of an outcome and its probability.

3. Why is it helpful to know the probability of an event?

4. a) What are the outcomes for the experiment in *Example 2?*
   b) Are the outcomes equally likely?

Practice

5. A coin is tossed.
   a) List the possible outcomes. How many are there?
   b) What is the probability of tossing heads?

6. A cube has A on 2 sides, B on 2 sides, and C on 2 sides. The cube is rolled.
   a) List the possible outcomes. How many are there?
   b) What is the probability of rolling A?

7. Two identical dice are rolled simultaneously.
   a) List the possible outcomes. How many are there?
   b) Are all the outcomes equally likely? Explain.

8. A deck of cards is shuffled. A card is randomly selected.
   a) How many outcomes are there?
   b) Are all the outcomes equally likely?

Work together

9. The spinner has 7 equal regions. The pointer on this spinner is spun.
   a) List the outcomes.
   b) Are the outcomes equally likely?
   c) Calculate the probability of each event.
      i) number 7   ii) a coloured space
      iii) an even number   iv) either 4 or 6
      v) a number greater than 4

10. The jar is shaken. A blindfolded person picks one ball from the jar.
    a) List the outcomes.
    b) Are the outcomes equally likely?
    c) Calculate the probability that the ball that was taken from the jar first is: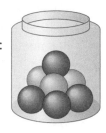
       i) blue
       ii) yellow
       iii) either blue or yellow
       iv) blue and yellow

11. a) Cut four matching cards from cardboard of different colours and place them in a bag. Pick one card from the bag without looking. Record the colour. Put the card back in the bag. Repeat until each colour has been picked at least once. How many cards did you have to pick before each colour had been picked at least once?
    b) Repeat the experiment several times. Were you surprised by the results?
    c) Compare your results with those of other groups. What was the mean number of cards that had to be picked?
    d) You have probably seen boxes of cereal that include small gifts. The label often encourages you to collect a whole set of similar items by buying more boxes of cereal. How is this situation similar to the experiment you completed? Based on your experimental results, how many boxes might you have to buy to collect a set of four different items?
    e) Do you think the number of items affects the result? Repeat the experiment using six different coloured cards.
    f) What else could a cereal company do to make collecting a whole set more of a challenge?

12. In a deck of cards, kings, queens, and jacks are called face cards.
    a) How many face cards are there in a deck?
    b) What is the probability of randomly selecting a face card from a deck?

On your own

13. The pointer on this spinner is spun.

a) List the outcomes.

b) Are the outcomes equally likely?

c) Calculate the probability of each event.

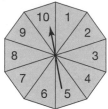

i) 10

ii) a number greater than 7

iii) an odd number

iv) either 5 or 10

v) neither 5 nor 10

14. The jar is shaken. A blindfolded person picks one ball from the jar.

a) List the outcomes.

b) Are the outcomes equally likely?

c) Calculate the probability of each event.

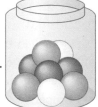

i) The ball is green.

ii) The ball is white.

iii) The ball is purple.

iv) The ball is not white.

v) The ball is neither purple nor white.

15. a) How many aces are there in a deck of cards?

b) What is the probability of randomly selecting an ace from a deck of cards?

16. a) Start a new spreadsheet file. In cell A1 enter a formula that randomly picks a natural number between 1 and 5. In ClarisWorks, the formula is =Rand(5). In Microsoft Works, the formula is =Int(Rand()*5)+1.

Copy this formula to cells A2 to A20. Recalculate the spreadsheet. Count the number of 3s that appear in the list. Record this number. Repeat this until you have 10 results.

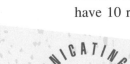

TEMPLATE DISK

i) How many numbers were shown in column A during the 10 trials?

ii) How many 3s were shown?

iii) What percent of the numbers shown were 3s?

b) Enter a formula in cell B1 that randomly picks a natural number between 1 and 10. The formula will be the same as that in column A with the 5 replaced with 10. Copy this formula to cells B2 to B20. Recalculate the spreadsheet. This time, record the number of 3s in column A separately from the number of 3s in column B.

i) How many numbers were shown in each column during the 10 trials?

ii) How many 3s were shown in each column?

iii) What percent of the numbers in column A were 3s?

iv) What percent of the numbers in column B were 3s?

v) What percent of the time should you see an 8 in column A? In column B? Explain.

Extend your thinking

17. Katrina answered three multiple-choice questions. Each question had five possible answers. She answered questions 1 and 2 correctly and guessed at question 3. What is the probability that:

a) all three of her answers are correct?

b) only two answers are correct?

18. Give some examples of situations for which it is not possible to calculate probabilities in the way you have done in this section. Explain why you cannot calculate the probability in each case.

COMMUNICATING
The Ideas

In your journal, explain how frequency is different from relative frequency. Which measure, the frequency or the relative frequency, of an outcome provides a useful estimate of its probability?

Is Anita's Idea Fair?

Anita, Kari, and Mitra want to play a game, but they can't decide who should go first. Anita suggests that they toss two coins. If both coins land showing heads, she will go first; if both coins land showing tails, Kari will go first; and if the coins land showing one head and one tail, Mitra will go first. Is Anita's idea fair?

Understand the problem

- When one coin is tossed, how can it land? Is it more likely to land one way than another?
- If you follow Anita's suggestion, what must happen for Anita to go first? For Kari to go first? For Mitra to go first?
- What are you asked to do?

Think of a strategy

- Calculate the probability that both coins will land showing heads; the probability that both coins will land showing tails; and the probability that one will land showing heads and the other showing tails. Compare the probabilities.

Carry out the strategy

- Suppose you toss a penny and a nickel. List the outcomes. To do this, write down the ways the penny could land. For each of these, write down the ways the nickel could land.
- Is each outcome you listed equally likely? Explain.
- In how many outcomes do both coins land showing heads? What is the probability of this?
- In how many outcomes do both coins land showing tails? What is the probability of this?
- In how many outcomes do the coins land in different ways? What is the probability of this?

Look back

- Is Anita's idea fair? If not, who has the greatest chance of going first?
- Check your answer by performing an experiment. Obtain two coins. Toss the coins 40 times. Record the number of times both coins land showing heads, both coins land showing tails, and the coins land in different ways. Calculate the relative frequency of each event. Compare them with the probabilities you calculated earlier.

Communicating the Ideas

In your journal, describe Anita's idea and explain whether or not it is fair. Include a description of the experiment you carried out in *Look back*.

Using Simulations to Calculate Probability

Suppose there are 3 children in a family. What is the probability that all the children are girls?

We can use a computer to conduct an experiment to calculate this probability. We say that the computer *simulates* the possible combinations of boys and girls.

The computer has a built-in random number generator. A list of digits, selected so that each of the digits from 0 to 9 has an equal chance of being selected, is called a list of *random numbers*. We use the random numbers generated by the computer to calculate probability.

Since it is equally likely to have a boy or a girl, we use the computer to generate a 1 or a 2. Let 1 represent a girl, and 2 a boy. Recall the formulas in exercise 16, page 288, for generating random numbers from 1 to 5. We change these formulas to generate the random numbers 1 and 2.

In ClarisWorks, the formula is =Rand(2).
In Microsoft Works, the formula is =Int(Rand()*2)+1

Start a new spreadsheet file. Enter the information below.

TEMPLATE DISK

	A	B	C
1	Families of three		
2			
3	1st child	2nd child	3rd child

In cells A4, B4, and C4, enter the ClarisWorks or Microsoft Works formula from above. These formulas generate the random numbers 1 and 2. The computer may display this:

	A	B	C
1	Families of three		
2			
3	1st child	2nd child	3rd child
4	2	2	1

A result of 2, 2, 1 was generated. This means, on the first trial, a family with 2 boys and 1 girl was selected. Select Calculate Now to get a second trial.

To look at a large number of trials at one time, highlight cells A4 to C13. Choose Fill Down to copy the formulas from row 4 to row 13. You are now looking at 10 families.

The family could have 3 girls, 2 girls and 1 boy, 1 girl and 2 boys, or 3 boys. Enter the text that describes the number of girls in cells E3 to E7. In cells F4 to F7, enter the number of each type of family for this set of data.

	A	B	C	D	E	F
1	Families of three					
2						
3	1st child	2nd child	3rd child		Family types	
4	2	2	1		3 girls	1
5	1	1	2		2 girls	2
6	1	2	2		1 girl	6
7	1	2	2		0 girls	1
8	2	1	1			
9	2	2	2			
10	1	2	2			
11	1	1	1			
12	2	2	1			
13	1	2	2			

Choose Calculate Now to get a new set of family data. Update the count of each type of family. Do this 10 times to obtain the results of 100 simulated families. Be sure the numbers in cells F4 to F7 add to 100.

1. Are the four family types equally likely?

2. If your answer to exercise 1 is no, which type of family is most likely?

3. Suppose a family has 3 children. What is the probability that these 3 children are girls?

4. Adapt the spreadsheet to show the possible family types with 4 children. Suppose a family has 4 children. What is the probability of there being exactly 3 boys?

5. Adapt the spreadsheet to calculate the probability that at least 2 of the 3 digits on a licence plate are the same.

6. Suppose you did not have a computer. How could you use 3 coins to simulate the possible combinations of boys and girls in a family with 3 children? Conduct an experiment with 3 coins to calculate the probability that these 3 children are girls. Compare your result with that of exercise 3. Explain any differences.

7. Use 4 coins to simulate the possible combinations of boys and girls in a family with 4 children. Conduct an experiment to calculate the probability that there will be exactly 3 boys in a family with 4 children. Compare your results with that of exercise 4. Explain any differences.

Mathematics & Technology

Linking Ideas

5.7 PROBABILITY OF COMPOUND INDEPENDENT EVENTS

Developing the Ideas

▶ ▶ *Through Discussion*

There is a coin-tossing game for two people (player A and player B) in which a coin is tossed twice.

Player A wins if a head appears on at least one of the two tosses. What is the probability that player A wins?

Legend has it that two 17th century mathematicians, Roberval and Fermat, discussed this game.

Roberval argued this way:
There are 3 possible outcomes.

First toss	Second toss	Result
H	No second toss because game ends	A wins
T	H	A wins
T	T	B wins

A wins on 2 out of 3 outcomes.
The probability that A wins is $\frac{2}{3}$.

Fermat argued this way:
There are 4 possible outcomes.

First toss	Second toss	Result
H	H	A wins
H	T	A wins
T	H	A wins
T	T	B wins

A wins on 3 out of 4 outcomes.
The probability that A wins is $\frac{3}{4}$.

Who was right, Roberval or Fermat?

ACTIVITY 1

We know that the probability of an event is very close to the relative frequency of the event if the experiment is conducted many times.

If we toss a coin many times we can get an idea of the probability of at least one head in every two tosses. In this way we can test the reasoning of Roberval and of Fermat.

It does not matter whether we toss the coins one after the other, or together. So, we can simulate the game by tossing two coins at the same time.

Work with a classmate. Select two different coins, such as a nickel and a quarter. Toss the coins 50 times. Tally the outcomes in a table like this:

Two heads	A head and a tail	Two tails	Number of tosses

- Calculate the relative frequency of the outcome a head and a tail.
- What do you think the probability of that outcome is?
- Combine your data with that of three other groups. Calculate the probability of the outcome a head and a tail.
- Whose argument, Roberval's or Fermat's, is better supported by these results?

Each event of this experiment is the combined outcomes of tossing a nickel and tossing a quarter. This result is called a *compound event* because it consists of two single events.

We can show the possible outcomes with a *tree diagram*.

There are 4 outcomes: H H, H T, T H, T T.

There are 3 events: two heads, two tails, a head and a tail.

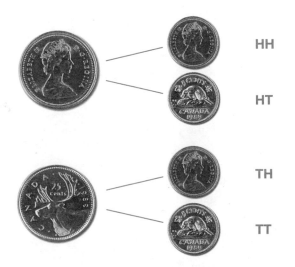

With a partner, toss a coin and roll a die.

1. How many different outcomes are there for one toss of the coin?

2. How many different outcomes are there for one roll of the die?

A tree diagram can represent the outcomes of this experiment.
Each branch of the tree shows one combined outcome of
tossing a coin and rolling a die.

3. How many branches should the tree diagram have?

4. Draw the tree diagram. Label each branch with the
combined outcomes.

5. Use the tree diagram to calculate each probability:

    a) a tail and a four   **b)** a head and an even number

    c) a tail and a number greater than two

    d) a head and a prime number

▶ ▶ *Through Instruction*

From your tree diagram, you should have found that:

The probability of a head and an even number, P(H and E), is $\frac{3}{12}$, or $\frac{1}{4}$.

The probability of a head, P(H), is $\frac{6}{12}$, or $\frac{1}{2}$.

The probability of an even number, P(E), is $\frac{6}{12}$, or $\frac{1}{2}$.

Notice how these fractions are related.

The probability of a head and an even number, P(H and E) = P(H) × P(E)

$$= \frac{1}{2} \times \frac{1}{2}, \text{ or } \frac{1}{4}$$

Similarly, from your tree diagram:

The probability of a tail and a number greater than 2, P(T and > 2), is $\frac{4}{12}$, or $\frac{1}{3}$.

The probability of a tail, P(T), is $\frac{6}{12}$, or $\frac{1}{2}$.

The probability of a number greater than 2, P(> 2), is $\frac{8}{12}$, or $\frac{2}{3}$.

We can write P(T and > 2) = P(T) × P(> 2)

$$= \frac{1}{2} \times \frac{2}{3}, \text{ or } \frac{1}{3}$$

These activities illustrate the following rule:

• • • • • • • • • •

> If P(A) is the probability of event A, and P(B) is the probability of event B, then the
> probability of the compound event A and B is P(A and B). P(A and B) = P(A) × P(B)

Since the outcome of tossing a coin does not depend on the outcome of
rolling a die, we say the events are *independent*. Similarly, the outcome
of selecting a particular card from a deck of cards is independent of the
outcome of a spinner. So, these are independent events.

Working with Mathematics

Something to talk about

1. Explain what is meant by a *compound event*. Give an example.

2. a) What is the probability of obtaining a head and a tail on the toss of a nickel and a dime?

   b) Does the probability change if the two coins are both nickels?

   c) Does the probability change if a single coin is tossed once, then tossed again?

Practice

3. List the outcomes for 2 coins being tossed.

4. List the outcomes for 2 dice being rolled.

5. List the outcomes for the toss of a coin and the roll of a die.

6. Describe the outcomes for the selection of a card from a deck and the toss of a coin.

7. Describe the outcomes for the selection of a card from a deck and the roll of a die.

Work together

8. One bag contains 1 red marble and 1 green marble. Another bag contains 1 yellow marble and 1 blue marble. From each bag, 1 marble is randomly selected.

   a) List all the possible outcomes. Are they equally likely?

   b) What is the probability of selecting 1 red and 1 blue marble?

9. The pointer of this spinner is spun twice. The product of the two outcomes is calculated. List all the possible outcomes. Are they all equally likely?

10. A bag contains 1 red, 1 blue, and 1 green marble. Another bag contains 1 black, 1 white, and 1 yellow marble. From each bag, 1 marble is randomly selected.

   a) List all the possible outcomes. Are they equally likely?

   b) What is the probability of removing 1 red marble from the first bag?

   c) What is the probability of removing 1 black marble from the second bag?

   d) Multiply your answers in parts b and c.

   e) What is the probability of randomly selecting 1 red marble and 1 black marble?

11. A spinner has 3 congruent sectors labelled A, B, and C. A jar contains 4 marbles — 1 red, 1 blue, 1 yellow, and 1 green. The pointer is spun. From the jar, 1 marble is randomly selected.

   a) List the possible outcomes.

   b) What is the probability of spinning A?

   c) What is the probability of choosing 1 red marble?

   d) What is the probability of spinning A and choosing 1 red marble?

   e) What is the probability of spinning A or B?

   f) What is the probability of spinning A or B and choosing 1 red marble?

   g) What is the probability of spinning A or B and choosing 1 red or 1 green marble?

12. Two dice are rolled. What is the probability of each event?

   a) The numbers total 8.

   b) The numbers total 12.

   c) Both dice display the same number.

   d) The sum of the numbers is greater than 10.

   e) The sum of the numbers is not 8.

13. Assume it is equally likely that a child be born a boy or a girl.

   a) Draw a tree diagram to show the possible outcomes for a family of 2 children.

   b) What is the probability that both children will be girls?

14. a) Extend the tree diagram in exercise 13. Show the possible outcomes for a family of 4 children.

   b) What is the probability that all the children will be boys?

On your own

15. To answer exercise 12, you could use a grid showing all possible outcomes when two dice are rolled. Suppose one die is red and the other is green. To show the outcome green 3 and red 5, circle the dot at the point (3, 5). Copy this grid.

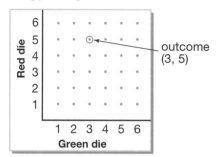

a) Circle all the outcomes for which both dice show the same number. Write the probability for rolling a double.

b) Circle all the outcomes for which the sum of the numbers is 7. Write the probability of obtaining 7 on the roll of two dice.

c) Repeat part b for the sum of the numbers being 9.

d) Is there a pattern in the points which correspond to outcomes with the same total? Explain your answer.

16. Two spinners are constructed as shown.

The pointers are spun. The numbers they land on are multiplied.

a) List the possible outcomes. How do you know you have not missed any outcomes?

b) Are the outcomes equally likely? Explain.

c) Calculate each probability.
  i) The product is less than 10.
  ii) The product is an odd number.
  iii) The product is a multiple of 3.
  iv) The product is less than 5.
  v) The product is greater than 5.

17. A die is rolled. From a deck of cards, 1 card is randomly selected.

a) How many possible outcomes are there?

b) What is the probability of selecting the ace of hearts and rolling a 6?

c) What is the probability of selecting an ace of any suit and rolling a 6?

d) What is the probability of selecting a heart and rolling an even number?

e) What is the probability of selecting a face card and rolling a 1 or a 2?

18. A bag contains 2 red, 2 blue, 2 white, and 2 black marbles. A die is rolled. From the bag, 1 marble is randomly selected.

a) How many possible outcomes are there?

b) What is the probability of rolling a 2 and selecting 1 red marble?

c) What is the probability of rolling an even number and selecting 1 red marble?

d) What is the probability of rolling a 1 or a 2 and selecting 1 red marble?

e) What is the probability of rolling an even number and selecting 1 red or 1 blue marble?

Extend your thinking

19. In basketball, a player given a one-and-one foul shot is given a second shot only if the first is successful. The player can score 0, 1, or 2 points in this situation.
The player shoots with 75% accuracy.
Find the probability that she will score:
  a) 0 points   **b)** 1 point   **c)** 2 points

The Ideas

In your journal, describe some limitations of a grid and of a tree diagram for listing the outcomes of an experiment.

Can You Calculate the Number of Black Jellybeans in a Jar?

Different numbers of coloured jellybeans are put in a jar. You pay to guess how many black jellybeans there are in the jar. There is a total of 1000 jellybeans in the jar. The person whose guess is closest to the actual number wins the jar of jellybeans.

Understand the problem

- Can you count all the black jellybeans by looking at the jar?
- Are the black jellybeans randomly distributed in the jar?
- How many beans are in the jar?

Think of a strategy

- Suppose you scoop a cupful of jellybeans from the jar. How could you use the total number of jellybeans in the cup and the black jellybeans in the cup to estimate the number of black jellybeans in the jar?
- How could you use proportional thinking to estimate the number of black jellybeans in the jar?

Carry out the strategy

- Suppose 40 jellybeans make a cupful, and 12 of these jellybeans are black.
- We assume that the ratio of black jellybeans in the cup to the total number of jellybeans in the cup is equal to the ratio of black jellybeans in the jar to the total number of jellybeans in the jar. That is, 12 : 40 = number of black jellybeans in the jar : 1000
- The ratios above are equivalent. Use this fact to calculate the approximate number of black jellybeans in the jar.

Look back

- Suppose the cupful of jellybeans contained 8 red jellybeans. About how many red jellybeans are in the jar?
- Suppose the cupful of jellybeans contained 7 yellow jellybeans. About how many yellow jellybeans are in the jar? Are there exactly this number of yellow jellybeans in the jar? Explain.
- A jar contains pennies, nickels, dimes, and quarters. There are 1750 coins in all. You remove a cupful of coins from the jar. The cup contains 110 coins, 17 of which are pennies. Estimate the number of pennies in the jar.

Communicating the Ideas

In your journal, explain how you estimated the number of black jellybeans in the jar. Make up your own problem like this one.

Review

1. This graph appeared in the Edmonton Journal in February 1994. The city of Edmonton had a population of about 460 000 in 1993. Use the graph and the figure for the population of Edmonton to complete this exercise.

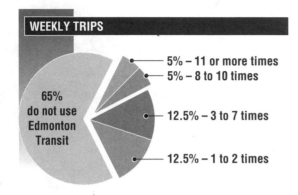

WEEKLY TRIPS

65% do not use Edmonton Transit

5% – 11 or more times
5% – 8 to 10 times
12.5% – 3 to 7 times
12.5% – 1 to 2 times

   a) How many people did not use public transit?

   b) How many people used public transit 1 to 2 times per week?

   c) How many people used public transit 11 or more times per week?

   d) Perform calculations to estimate the weekly ridership of the Edmonton public transit system. Explain your method.

2. a) If your community has public transit services, conduct a survey to determine how many times per week people from your community use public transit. Ask 10 people how often they use public transit in a typical week. Record their responses in a tally sheet like the one below.

How often do you use public transit in a typical week?				
Do not use	1 to 2 times	3 to 7 times	8 to 10 times	More than 11 times

   b) Combine your results with 4 other students so that you have 50 responses. Construct a graph to display the data.

   c) How do your results compare with the data for Edmonton in exercise 1?

3. The editor of a health food magazine wants to determine whether large doses of vitamin C reduce the number of colds a person gets. The editor asks her readers who take large doses of vitamin C to write in and report whether they have had fewer colds since they began taking vitamin C.

   a) Who do you think is more likely to respond?
   - people who have had fewer colds
   - people who have had the same number of colds or more colds

   b) Will this survey generate a random sample or a biased sample? Explain.

4. Consider the following graph showing a city's spending for a six-year period.

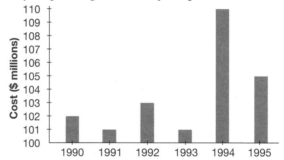

   a) Just by glancing at the graph, what is your first impression about the city's spending over the six-year period?

   b) Use your "flaw-detector" skills to explain what is misleading about the graph.

   c) Draw the graph in a way that eliminates the flaw in part b. What is your impression now about the city's spending?

5. a) Find the relative frequencies of the letters in this tongue-twister.

   How much wood could a woodchuck chuck
   If a woodchuck could chuck wood?

   b) Do you think the relative frequencies of letters **o** and **w** would be approximately the same if you randomly selected another passage? Give reasons for your answer.

6. a) What is the probability of each event on the roll of a fair die?

   i) number 4   ii) an odd number

b) Suppose you roll a die 30 times. How many times would you expect it to land:

   i) on 4?   **ii)** on an odd number?

c) Roll a die 30 times. Record the number of times it landed on each number.

   i) How many times did it land on 4?

   ii) How many times did it land on an odd number?

d) How do your answers to parts b and c compare? Why might they be different?

7. When Mario Pietrantoni moved from Italy to Canada as a teenager, he spoke no English. In school, he did not learn to read and write as well as he wished to. Literacy courses Mario took as an adult inspired him to write poetry. Read Mario's poem *Music*. Find the frequency and relative frequency of each of the letters **a**, **e**, **s**, and **t** in the poem.

> ## Music
>
> Music is the beat
> to my heart. I feel
> that the flow
> is into the air.
> It makes me move
> towards the stars
> in a pace so smooth
> that I feel honey
> running through my flesh.
> The shivering gets
> through my mind
> so alive when
> the music flows
> through my soul.

8. A jar contains ten marbles that are identical except for colour. One marble is red, two are blue, three are white, and four are black.

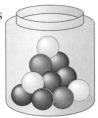

One marble is randomly selected from the jar by a blindfolded person. What is the probability of each event?

a) The marble is red.

b) The marble is blue.

c) The marble is either black or white.

d) The marble is not white.

e) The marble is neither black nor red.

f) The marble is purple.

9. Refer to exercise 8. Suppose ten purple marbles were added to the jar so that there are twenty marbles in the jar. Repeat the calculations of exercise 8.

10. Two coins are tossed simultaneously.

a) How many possible outcomes are there? List the outcomes.

b) Are all the outcomes equally likely?

c) What is the probability of the outcome 2 heads?

d) What is the probability of the outcome heads and tails?

11. A deck of cards is shuffled. One card is randomly selected.

a) What is the probability of the card being the king of diamonds?

b) What is the probability of the card being a king of any suit?

c) What is the probability of the card being a diamond?

12. A stack of cards contains 12 hearts, 3 diamonds, 3 spades, and 3 clubs. The cards are shuffled, and 1 card is randomly selected.

a) Are all the outcomes equally likely?

b) What is the probability of selecting a diamond?

c) What is the probability of not selecting a spade?

13. A spinner is constructed as shown. The pointer is spun.

a) How many outcomes are there?

b) Are all the outcomes equally likely? Explain.

c) What is the probability of the outcome being a 3?

Determining the Availability of Large Shoes

Read this letter. In it, Joan Hardwick makes many strong statements. In this project, you will conduct studies that will either support or refute her statements.

Discuss Joan's comments with your friends. What is the general feeling about what she says? Is there anyone you know who has large feet and has trouble finding shoes?

Are the prices of shoes in the U.S. very much lower than in Canada?

Record your answers to these questions and compare them to your findings from the project.

Before beginning *Activity 1*, read through the entire project. As a group, make a list of the measurements and information you have to find. By developing a plan, you can minimize the number of times you have to collect data.

Have large feet, will travel south

Referring to Brenda West's letter *Extra-large shoppers get a break in the U.S.* Very true, we have three sons, 190 cm, 193 cm, and 198 cm, with big feet requiring size 12 to a size 14, depending on the make. Try and find them in Canada? Where? We do shop in Factory Outlet, Kitchener, but you are either there when the shipment comes in or you take what they have.

We try to get down to Michigan a couple of times a year. Why? Pic-Way. Walk in, try and decide what style you prefer and try them on, they carry up to size 13 for women, and size 16 for men.

It's time store owners and clothing/shoe manufacturers realize that this generation is bigger and taller. The last trip to the U.S. we bought six pairs of shoes for $99 (U.S.) but even with the exchange, gas (definitely cheaper) and motel/meals (considerably cheaper),we still felt we saved.

Canadian manufacturers smarten up, size 9 for men and size 7 for women went out years ago.

Joan Hardwick
Kincardine

ACTIVITY 1

The letter does not say how old the sons are. Since Joan is buying their shoes, we'll assume they are in their teens. Find as many people in this age group as you can. Ask them for, or measure, their heights. Analyze the data. Are Joan's sons unusually tall?

ACTIVITY 2

Find the shoe size of each person whose height you recorded. Plot a graph of shoe size against height. Is there a relationship between a person's shoe size and her or his height? If there is, describe it. Are you surprised that the shoe sizes of Joan's sons range from 12 to 14?

ACTIVITY 3

Find a shoe store in your area that sells, but does not specialize in, shoes for people with large feet. Ask an employee how quickly the large sizes sell out. Is there any basis for Joan's comment that, "You are either there when they come in or you take what they have."?

ACTIVITY 4

Joan implies that the stores in the U.S. cater much better to people with large feet. Try to find someone who will be visiting the U.S. in the near future. Ask that person to check a few shoe stores. If this person determines that Joan has a valid claim, give some reasons why the stores south of the border are able to carry a greater range of sizes.

ACTIVITY 5

Joan writes that, "This generation is bigger and taller." Conduct a statistical study to determine if her claim is valid.

ACTIVITY 6

Joan says that, compared to Canada, the costs of shoes, gasoline, accommodations, and meals are lower in the States.

Ask the person who helped you with *Activity 4* to bring back specific names of shoes along with their prices.

For each pair of shoes, try to find the cost of an identical pair in a store in Canada. Convert the American prices to Canadian currency and compare the prices.

Conduct a similar comparison for the costs of gasoline, accommodation, and meals.

Are all these items cheaper in the States?

ACTIVITY 7

In her final comment, Joan advises Canadian manufacturers to "smarten up; size 9 for men and size 7 for women went out years ago." Conduct a statistical study to determine the average shoe sizes for men and women in Canada.

Compare your findings with Joan's comments.

ACTIVITY 8

Find shoes in a wide range of sizes for men and women.

Try to determine a relationship between shoe size and:
• the outside length of the shoe   • the inside length of the shoe

If you do find a relationship, measure the length of your foot. Use this length to determine accurately your shoe size.

The Ideas

Write a report that summarizes the results of your investigations. Include tables and graphs in your report.

Cumulative Review

1. For the set of numbers, and the stem-and-leaf diagram below, state the:

  i) mean   **ii)** median

  iii) lower quartile   **iv)** upper quartile

  v) extremes   **vi)** range

Give the answers to 1 decimal place where necessary.

  a) 4, 4, 3, 7, 3, 9, 6, 8, 5, 7, 6, 9, 3, 6, 2, 1, 1, 9, 2

  b) 18 | 1 1 4 8 8
       19 | 2 5
       20 | 3 6 7 7

2. Display the set of numbers and the stem-and-leaf diagram in exercise 1 on box-and-whisker plots.

3. A map scale is 1 cm represents 25 km. Find the actual distance for each map distance.

  a) 4.0 cm   **b)** 2.5 cm   **c)** 8.2 cm

  d) 6.8 cm   **e)** 3.2 cm   **f)** 5.1 cm

4. a) What is the scale of this diagram?

  b) How long is the ladder?

  c) How high above the ground does the top of the ladder meet the wall?

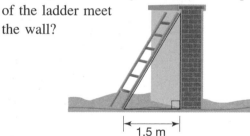

1.5 m

5. The front, top, and side views of two objects are shown below. Sketch each object.

a)

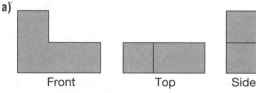

Front   Top   Side

b)

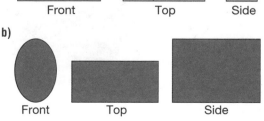

Front   Top   Side

6. Subtract by expressing the fractions in decimal form.

  a) $\frac{5}{9} - \frac{1}{3}$ **b)** $\frac{6}{7} - \frac{1}{2}$ **c)** $\frac{9}{4} - \frac{2}{3}$

  d) $1\frac{3}{8} - \frac{7}{8}$ **e)** $15 - \frac{5}{12}$ **f)** $3\frac{1}{4} - 2\frac{1}{8}$

  g) $\frac{10}{11} - \frac{1}{6} - \frac{3}{7}$ **h)** $\frac{8}{7} - \frac{2}{3} - \frac{1}{9}$ **i)** $8 - 1\frac{1}{2} - \frac{3}{4}$

7. Divide.

  a) $\frac{1}{6} \div \frac{2}{3}$ **b)** $\frac{2}{3} \div \frac{1}{6}$ **c)** $1 \div \frac{1}{5}$

  d) $\frac{1}{3} \div \frac{1}{4}$ **e)** $\frac{5}{8} \div \frac{3}{4}$ **f)** $\frac{3}{8} \div \frac{2}{5}$

8. Make each equation true by replacing ■ with a number.

  a) $8400 = 8.4 \times 10^{■}$

  b) $211\,000\,000 = 2.11 \times 10^{■}$

  c) $31\,040\,000 = 3.104 \times 10^{■}$

  d) $670\,000 = 6.7 \times 10^{■}$

  e) $1\,980\,000 = 1.98 \times 10^{■}$

  f) $43\,000 = 4.3 \times 10^{■}$

9. List all the possible digits that could replace each ■ so the number is divisible by 4. Use a calculator to check your answers.

  a) 5■   **b)** 24■   **c)** 386■

  d) 25 79■   **e)** 19■4   **f)** 641 18■

10. Multiply or divide.

  a) 4.2×7.5 **b)** 12.08×6.9

  c) 0.7×21.6 **d)** 27.4×18.2

  e) 125.6×5.8 **f)** 13.4×13.7

  g) $25 \div 6.25$ **h)** $86.8 \div 12.4$

  i) $16.2 \div 5.4$ **j)** $37 \div 7.4$

  k) $21.75 \div 8.7$ **l)** $73.96 \div 8.6$

11. Calculate the percent increase or decrease in price.

	Old price ($)	New price ($)
a)	8.99	10.79
b)	12.99	10.39
c)	10.39	12.99
d)	32.99	24.74
e)	79.99	51.99
f)	24.99	21.24

12. A hockey arena has a seating capacity of 7000. During a playoff game, the attendance was 108% of the seating capacity. What was the attendance during the playoff game?

13. In the Bingham School Sport-A-Thon, 80 students participated. Sixty percent of them played basketball. The rest played volleyball. How many students played each game?

14. There are 40 students in Ms. Kwok's grade 8 music class. Fifty percent of the students play the clarinet, 20% play the trumpet, and the rest play other instruments. None of the students plays more than one instrument. How many students play each instrument?
   a) the clarinet   b) the trumpet
   c) other instruments

15. Determine each amount.
   a) 4% of $20 000   b) 14% of 20 000 000
   c) 7% of $185 000   d) 35% of 95 000 kg

16. a) What percent of 200 s is 90 s?
   b) What percent of $4500 is $675?
   c) What percent of 350 000 kg is 42 000 kg?
   d) What percent of 22 000 km is 9900 km?

17. A student listed her daily activities in the table. Display the information as a circle graph.

Activity	Percent of day
eating	6
attending school	30
chores	14
recreation	20
sleeping	30

18. Suppose you were asked to determine the average Canadian's opinion on video games. State the disadvantages of each method of gaining your information.
   a) You carry out an in-depth study on the game-playing habits of a classmate.
   b) You ask all your classmates to write a paragraph on how they feel about video games.
   c) You design a questionnaire and post copies on the bulletin board. Members of the school are invited to complete a copy and return it to you.

   d) You randomly pick 50 people from the phone book and mail them your questionnaire, along with a stamped, self-addressed envelope.

19. There are 7 numbers in a set. The mean is 12, the modes are 10 and 14, and the median is 11. List 7 numbers that could be in the set.

20. The mean price for the sale of four new houses in a subdivision is $140 000. The fifth house was sold for $120 000. What is the new mean price per house?

21. The salaries of the employees at a company are shown in the table.

Position	Number of employees	Salary ($)
manager	1	120 000
foreperson	2	70 000
welder	3	45 000
carpenter	4	42 000
labourer	5	21 000

   a) Find the mean, median, and mode salary.
   b) Which measure of central tendency best describes the data?

22. A spinner is constructed as shown. The pointer is spun twice. The numbers on which it lands are added.

   a) List all the possible outcomes. Are they equally likely?
   b) If your answer to part a is no, which outcome is most likely?
   c) What is the probability of the sum 2?
   d) What is the probability of the sum 5?

23. A die is constructed with A on 3 sides, B on 2 sides, and C on 1 side. The die is rolled.
   a) How many possible outcomes are there? List the outcomes.
   b) Are all the outcomes equally likely?
   c) What is the probability of each outcome?
      i) an A   ii) a B   iii) a C

OPERATIONS WITH INTEGERS

WHAT'S COMING UP?

DEPARTMENTS

Mathematics File
Modelling the Multiplication
of Integers....................................322

Quests

Minds on Math Project
Graphing Population Shifts 338

Start With What You Know

Use the numbers in the pictures on these pages to complete the following exercises.

1. Explain the meaning of each type of number. Then find as many examples of each as you can.
   - **a)** multiples of 5
   - **b)** perfect squares
   - **c)** fractions
   - **d)** integers
   - **e)** powers of 2
   - **f)** consecutive numbers
   - **g)** prime numbers

2. Several pictures contain numbers that are factors of 30. Find as many of these numbers as you can.

3. Find a picture containing two numbers whose product is in another picture.

4. Find a picture containing a number such that when it is multiplied by itself, the product is in another picture.

5. Find the one-digit number such that when it is multiplied by itself, the product is a two-digit number. The sum of these two digits is equal to the original number.

6. Find a picture containing a number whose reciprocal is in another picture.

7. Find a number that is the number of degrees in a right angle.

8. Some of the numbers in the pictures are exact, and others are rounded. Find the numbers that you think have been rounded. Why do you think each one has been rounded?

North York

Welcome to the City with heart

Population 560,000

Ⓟ No Parking On City Streets
2AM To 6AM From Dec.1st To Mar.31st

Buying a souvenir hat? Make sure you choose the correct size.

Imperial							
$6\frac{5}{8}$	$6\frac{3}{4}$	$6\frac{7}{8}$	7	$7\frac{1}{8}$	$7\frac{1}{4}$	$7\frac{3}{8}$	$7\frac{1}{2}$
Continental							
54	55	56	57	58	59	60	61

Jasper Tramway, Alberta, Canada
Visited by over 150 000 people every year.
From the 2500m observation deck, you have a
breathtaking view of the majestic Rocky Mountains.
#SL-64-526   16/08/94

Dear Gita:
  Having a great vacation!
Today we took this cable car
ride. It was pretty exciting.
In less than 10 minutes we
went up 973 metres to the
top. The view was amazing.
We're staying in Jasper
2 more days before driving
to Edmonton. My cousin
promised she'll take me
to the West Edmonton
Mall. See you in 3 weeks,
              Julie

Gita Azarshahi
81 ½ Coronation Avenue
Halifax, Nova Scotia
B3N 2M5

S & R Productions

6.1 *MODELLING WITH INTEGERS*

Developing the Ideas

▶▶ *Through Discussion*

In the Second International Mathematics Study, thousands of grade 8 students from 23 different countries responded to statements such as these:

	strongly disagree	disagree	no opinion	agree	strongly agree
I think mathematics is easy.	strongly disagree	disagree	no opinion	agree	strongly agree
I think mathematics is fun.	strongly disagree	disagree	no opinion	agree	strongly agree

To calculate the score for each statement, we give each response an integer value.

Each *no opinion* response has a score of 0.
Each *disagree* response has a score of −1.
Each *strongly agree* response has a score of +2.

1. What score do you think was assigned to *strongly disagree*?

2. What score do you think was assigned to *agree*?

For each statement, the responses were added. The mean score was calculated and then multiplied by 10. The results for six countries are shown in the graphs below.

Graph 1 **I think mathematics is easy.**

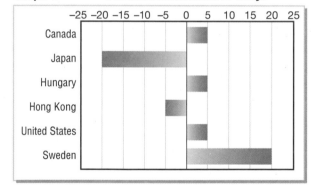

Graph 2 **I think mathematics is fun.**

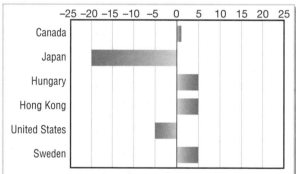

3. What is the meaning of a zero score in each graph?

4. What is the meaning of a positive score in each graph?
   a) graph 1   **b)** graph 2

5. What is the meaning of a negative score in each graph?
   a) graph 1   **b)** graph 2

6. In which countries do the students think that mathematics is:
   a) easy?   **b)** fun?

7. In which countries do students least enjoy mathematics?

8. Why is it useful to use positive and negative integers to show attitudes?

The area of the square on the hypotenuse is equal to the sum of the areas of the squares on the other two sides

Working with Mathematics

Something to talk about

1. Which integer is greater, −10 or −5? Give a reason for your answer.

2. Rate each experience on a scale from −10 to +10, where −10 indicates *displeasure* and +10 indicates *great pleasure*.
   a) receiving birthday presents
   b) doing homework
   c) going on vacation
   d) visiting the dentist
   e) doing chores at home
   f) sleeping
   g) stubbing your toe
   h) forgetting your money on pizza day

3. In exercise 2:
   a) Which experience is the most pleasant?
   b) Which experience is the most unpleasant?
   c) Order your rates from lowest to highest.

4. In the Second International Mathematics Study, grade 8 students responded to the following statement:

I think mathematics is important.				
strongly disagree	disagree	no opinion	agree	strongly agree

   The results for six countries are shown in this graph.

   I think mathematics is important.

   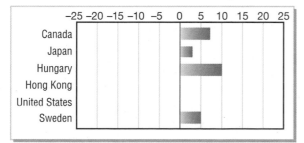

   a) In which country do students most strongly agree that mathematics is important?
   b) In which countries do students have no opinion about the importance of mathematics?

c) Compare this graph with those on page 306. Which countries have positive responses for all three statements?

5. A survey about mathematics homework contains the following statement:

I think the calculator should be allowed for mathematics homework.				
never	infrequently	no opinion	frequently	always

   Suppose each response is given an integer value. *No opinion* corresponds to 0. *Always* corresponds to +2. Which integer corresponds to each of the other responses?

Work together

6. Draw a number line from −15 to +10. Write the integer that is:
   a) halfway between −10 and −6
   b) 3 less than −9
   c) the mean of −5 and +5
   d) 4 more than −13

7. With your partner, list your five favourite singers or pop groups. Copy this survey sheet. Enter the names of your favourite singers or groups in the first column.

	How do you feel about these singers?				
Singer's name	strongly dislike	dislike	no opinion	like	strongly like

   Survey 10 of your classmates. Ask each one to choose an integer between −2 and +2 for each singer.
   a) Add the 10 integers for each singer.
   b) Divide each answer in part a by 10. This is the mean score for each singer.

c) Use your answer to part b to determine:
  i) the highest and lowest scores
  ii) the most popular singer
  iii) the least popular singer

d) Were there any singers who were not liked by most of those surveyed? If so, which ones?

8. The September 10, 1994, edition of The Financial Post displayed this graph. It shows the net earnings of *Avenor Inc.* in each quarter in 1993 and in the first six months of 1994.

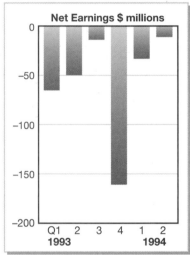

Avenor Inc.
Fiscal year-end Dec. 31

a) In this graph, what is meant by a *quarter*?

b) What is measured along the vertical axis of the graph?

c) Why do the bars in the graph begin at the top and reach downwards?

d) Q1 means the first 3 months of 1993. Which months are these?

e) About how much did *Avenor Inc.* earn or lose during the first quarter of 1993?

f) i) In which quarter did *Avenor Inc.* lose the most?
  ii) In which months did this loss occur?
  iii) About how much did the corporation lose in this quarter?

On your own

9. Use your number line from exercise 6. Write each statement replacing ■ with either > or <.
  a) +6 ■ −2   **b)** −6 ■ −7
  c) +12 ■ −13   **d)** −32 ■ −30

10. Carli made a time line of the first 13 years of her life. She ranked each event on a scale between −10 and +10. She used positive integers to represent happy experiences and negative integers to show sad experiences.

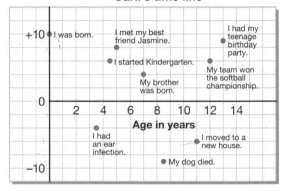

Carli's time line

a) To which event in her life did Carli give the highest rating?

b) What was the saddest event in Carli's life that she recorded on this graph?

c) i) What rating did Carli give her ear infection?
  ii) What rating did she give to moving house?
  iii) Which of these two events was rated worse by Carli?

d) Make a time line of your own. Mark at least 5 happy and 5 sad events on your time line.

e) i) Which event in your life do you rate as the most positive?
  ii) Which event do you rate as the most negative?

11. In August 1993, the Classic golf tournament was played in London, Ontario. The final leader board showed these scores for the top six golfers.

Player	Score
Brandie Burton	–11
Betsy King	–11
Dawn Coe-Jones	–10
Dottie Mochrie	–9
Kris Monaghan	–8
Vicki Fergon	–8

a) Who had the best score in the tournament?
b) Who took more strokes, Dawn Coe-Jones or Vicki Fergon?
c) The tournament was played over 4 days and 72 holes. Par for the tournament was 288. How many strokes did Brandie Burton take for the 72 holes?
d) What would Betsy King's score have been if she had taken 3 fewer strokes?

Extend your thinking

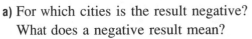

DATA DISK

12. Use the *International Prices* database on the data disk. Find the cost of rent in 1982 and 1994 in these twelve cities: Abu Dhabi, Bangkok, Bombay, Caracas, Copenhagen, Geneva, London, Manila, Montreal, Singapore, Sydney, and Tokyo. Subtract the 1982 cost from the 1994 cost.
a) For which cities is the result negative? What does a negative result mean?
b) For which cities is the result positive? What does a positive result mean?
c) Which city had the greatest decrease in rent cost? Which had the greatest increase?

13. In hockey statistics, there is a +/– statistic for each player. This statistic is calculated by subtracting the goals scored *against* the player's team while he is on the ice from the goals scored *by* the player's team while he is on the ice (not counting power play goals). The top five scoring leaders in the 1992–93 playoffs are named in the table below.

Player	Goals scored	Total points	+ / –
Wayne Gretzky	15	40	+6
Doug Gilmour	10	35	+16
Tomas Sandstrom	8	25	–2
Vincent Damphousse	11	23	+8
Luc Robitaille	9	22	–13

a) Which player had the best +/– record in the 1992–93 playoffs? Explain.
b) Was Luc Robitaille's team more likely to score or to be scored on when he was on the ice?
c) By how many points do the +/– statistics of Gretzky and Robitaille differ?

COMMUNICATING

The Ideas

In your journal, write several sentences to describe how integers are used in golf. If you know of other sports that use integers, describe how integers are used in these sports.

6.2 ADDING AND SUBTRACTING INTEGERS

Developing the Ideas
▶▶ *Through Instruction*

Anders Celsius

When Anders Celsius developed the Celsius thermometer in 1742, he assigned *zero degrees* (written 0°C) to the temperature at which water boils. He assigned 100°C to the temperature at which water freezes. The scale was later reversed by Carolus Linnaeus, but it was named for Celsius. When temperatures fall below the freezing point of water, we use negative integers to show how far below zero these temperatures are.

The temperature of most of Earth's surface is usually between −35°C and +35°C, depending upon the season and the latitude of the location. The weather map below appeared in an edition of a local newspaper.

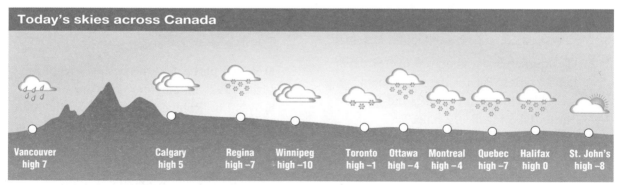

Today's skies across Canada

Vancouver	Calgary	Regina	Winnipeg	Toronto	Ottawa	Montreal	Quebec	Halifax	St. John's
high 7	high 5	high −7	high −10	high −1	high −4	high −4	high −7	high 0	high −8

When the temperature is a positive integer, it is often written without the positive sign. That is, 7°C means +7°C.

We can use the weather map to find out how much warmer it is in Vancouver than in St. John's.

We want the difference in temperatures in the two cities; that is, the difference between +7 and −8.

To find the difference, we can use a thermometer.

The temperature in St. John's is −8°C.
The temperature in Vancouver is +7°C.
To get from −8°C to +7°C, we count from −8 to 0
and then count another 7 degrees from 0 to +7.
In all, we count 15 degrees from −8°C to +7°C.

The difference in temperatures is +15.
We can write this as a subtraction statement.
The difference between +7 and −8 is (+7) − (−8) = +15
Vancouver is 15°C warmer than St. John's.

In earlier work with integers, you learned this rule.

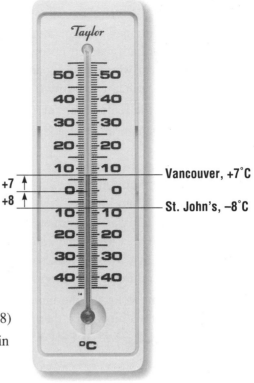

• • • • • • • • •

> To subtract an integer, add its opposite.

For this example, recall that (+7) − (−8) can be written as
(+7) + (+8) = +15

(or more simply as +7 + 8 = +15, since +8 can be written as 8)

If we want to know how much colder it is in St. John's than in
Vancouver, we want the difference between −8 and +7.

We write : (−8) − (+7) = (−8) + (−7)
$$= −15$$
St. John's is 15°C colder than Vancouver.

▶▶ *Through Guided Examples*

Example 1 ··

On one day in Calgary, the lowest temperature is 13°
below the highest temperature of +5°C.
a) What is the lowest temperature?
b) Write the situation as a subtraction statement.
c) Write the situation as an addition statement.

Solution

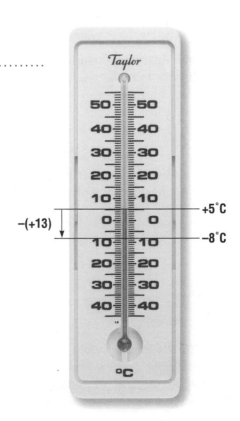

a) Think of a thermometer.
Start at +5.
Count down 13.
You end up at −8.
The lowest temperature is −8°C.
b) As a subtraction statement: (+5) − (+13) = −8
c) To subtract, add the opposite. (+5) + (−13) = −8

Example 2

At 9 a.m., Winnipeg's temperature was −19°C.
By 11 a.m., it had warmed up by 5°.
By noon, it had warmed up by another 4°,
but by 2 p.m. it had cooled by 6°.

a) What was the temperature at 2 p.m.?

b) Write the situation as an addition statement.

Solution

a) Think of a thermometer.
It was −19°C at 9 a.m.
By 11 a.m., it was 5° warmer, so move up 5° to reach −14°C.
By noon, it was 4° warmer, so move up 4° to reach −10°C.
By 2 p.m., it was 6° cooler, so move down 6° to reach −16°C.
The temperature at 2 p.m. was −16°C.

b) For each move up the thermometer, add a positive integer.
For each move down the thermometer, add a negative
integer. $(-19) + (+5) + (+4) + (-6) = -16$

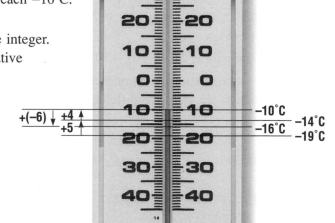

▶ ▶ **Through an Activity**

Work with a partner.

For each expression:

a) Describe it as a change in temperature.

b) Draw a thermometer to show the change.

c) Calculate the final temperature.

1. $(+5) + (+9)$ **2.** $(+5) + (-9)$

3. $(+5) - (+9)$ **4.** $(+5) - (-9)$

5. $(-5) + (+9)$ **6.** $(-5) + (-9)$

7. $(-5) - (+9)$ **8.** $(-5) - (-9)$

Check your results with another pair of students. If the results
are different, try to find out which is correct in each case.

BOGGLE YOUR MIND

According to *The Guinness Book of Records*, the greatest recorded
temperature ranges on Earth occur in Siberia. Temperatures in the Siberian
city of Verkhoyansk have reached highs of 37°C and lows of −68°C. What is
the difference between these temperatures?

Working with Mathematics

Something to talk about

Refer to the weather map on page 310 to answer exercises 1 to 6.

1. In which season of the year do you think this map appeared? Why?

2. Which city had the warmest temperature?

3. Which city had the coldest temperature?

4. How many degrees warmer was it in Calgary than in Ottawa?

5. Which city, Regina or Montreal, had the lower temperature?

6. The lowest temperature in Winnipeg was 11° less than its highest temperature of −10°C. What was the lowest temperature in Winnipeg?

Practice

7. Describe each expression as a change in temperature. Calculate the final temperature.
   a) $(-16) + (+4)$
   b) $(-10) - (+2)$
   c) $(-12) - (-2)$
   d) $(-13) + (-1)$
   e) $(+20) + (+3)$
   f) $(+30) - (+10)$
   g) $(+35) - (-7)$
   h) $(+17) + (-3)$

8. Simplify.
   a) $(+3) - (-20)$
   b) $(+2) + (-11)$
   c) $(+5) + (+12)$
   d) $(+1) - (+13)$
   e) $(-3) - (-19)$
   f) $(-2) + (-18)$
   g) $(-1) + (+14)$
   h) $(-7) - (-9)$
   i) $(-16) + (+4)$
   j) $(+8) - (-2)$
   k) $(-12) + (-9)$
   l) $(+16) - (-21)$
   m) $(-15) - (+17)$
   n) $(-8) + (-14)$

Work together

9. The Dead Sea is the world's saltiest lake. Its shore has an elevation of 400 m below sea level. At its deepest point, the lake has a depth of 328 m. Represent each of these facts using an integer. What is the lake's depth relative to sea level?

10. The world's largest underground lake is believed to be in the Drachenhauchloch cave in Namibia. Its surface is 66 m underground. At its deepest point, the lake has a depth of 84 m. Represent each of these facts using an integer. How far below ground is the deepest point in the lake?

11. The Great Lakes are among the world's largest freshwater lakes. The chart lists the elevation of the shore of each lake relative to sea level and its maximum depth relative to the shore.

Lake	Elevation (m)	Depth (m)
Superior	183	405
Michigan	176	281
Huron	176	229
Erie	174	64
Ontario	75	224

   a) Write a positive integer to represent each elevation relative to sea level.
   b) Write a negative integer to represent each depth relative to the shore.
   c) Determine the depth of each lake relative to sea level.

12. Look in a telephone book for a time zone map.
   a) What time is it in Montreal when it is noon in Vancouver?
   b) What time is it in Calgary when it is noon in Ottawa?
   c) The "red-eye" flight leaves Vancouver at 11:30 p.m. It arrives in Toronto 5 h 30 min later. What time is it in Toronto when the plane arrives?
   d) An aircraft from Toronto arrives in Halifax at 6:30 p.m. The flight took 2 h 30 min. The aircraft stays in Halifax for 1 h, and then flies to St. John's. The flight takes 1 h 30 min.
      i) What (local) time did the aircraft leave Toronto?
      ii) What (local) time did the aircraft land in St. John's?

On your own

13. Describe each expression as a change in temperature. Calculate the final temperature.

   a) $(-3) + (+10)$ **b)** $(-1) + (+15)$
   c) $(-4) - (-12)$ **d)** $(-5) + (-14)$
   e) $(+6) + (+16)$ **f)** $(+5) - (+20)$
   g) $(+2) - (-17)$ **h)** $(+7) + (-18)$

14. Simplify.

   a) $(+18) + (-5)$ **b)** $(+27) - (-3)$
   c) $(+33) - (+8)$ **d)** $(+21) + (+4)$
   e) $(-17) + (-3)$ **f)** $(-19) - (-1)$
   g) $(-23) - (+8)$ **h)** $(-18) + (+2)$

15. Simplify.

   a) $(+23) - (-21)$ **b)** $(+14) - (+19)$
   c) $(-32) - (-16)$ **d)** $(-28) + (-24)$
   e) $(-39) + (+18)$ **f)** $(+25) + (-26)$
   g) $(+19) + (-17)$ **h)** $(-25) - (-14)$

16. Copy this square. Fill in the empty squares with integers so that the sum of the numbers in each row is 0, the sum of the numbers in each column is 0, and the sum of the numbers along each diagonal is 0.

+1		
-4	0	
+3		

Extend your thinking

17. The table shows the prices in cents of some stocks at the Vancouver Stock Exchange on September 19, 1994. The second column shows the change in prices from the previous day.

Stock	Price on September 19	Change from September 18
Gerl Gld	35¢	-7¢
Booker Gld	205¢	-15¢
Greshm Rs	144¢	+19¢

   a) Write the price of each stock on September 18, 1994.
   b) For each stock:
     i) Write the change in price as a fraction of its value on September 18.
     ii) Write the fraction as a percent.
     iii) Write the percent change as a positive or negative integer.
   c) Which stock value showed the greatest percent change?

18. Replace each ■ with an integer.

   a) $(-2) + ■ = +31$ **b)** $(+23) - ■ = -3$
   c) $■ - (-21) = +25$ **d)** $(-22) + ■ = +37$
   e) $(+18) - ■ = -7$ **f)** $■ - (-25) = +21$

The Ideas

Look in *The Guinness Book of Records* or an almanac. Determine the coldest temperature on Earth ever recorded (in degrees Celsius). Research also the hottest temperature ever recorded. Find the difference between the two temperatures. Is this difference greater than the difference between the freezing and boiling points of water? Record your findings in your journal.

6.3 *MULTIPLYING INTEGERS*

Developing the Ideas

▶▶*Using Manipulatives*

We extend our investigation of integers by considering the product of two integers.

We will use our red and yellow tiles.

We can think of 2 as +2 and of 3 as +3.

Consider 2 sets of 3 yellow tiles.

We think: 2 sets of 3 yellow tiles

We write: $(+2) \times (+3)$

$(+2) \times (+3)$ means $2 \times (+3)$, or $(+3) + (+3)$

There are 6 yellow tiles, which represent +6.

We write: $(+2) \times (+3) = +6$

Consider 2 sets of 3 red tiles.

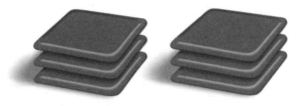

We think: 2 sets of 3 red tiles

We write: $(+2) \times (-3)$

$(+2) \times (-3)$ means $2 \times (-3)$, or $(-3) + (-3)$

There are 6 red tiles, which represent −6.

We write: $(+2) \times (-3) = -6$

1. For each group of tiles below:
   i) Describe the group using a multiplication expression.
   ii) Write the multiplication statement that describes the total number of tiles.
   a) 3 sets of 4 red tiles   b) 4 sets of 3 red tiles
   c) 3 sets of 4 yellow tiles   d) 4 sets of 3 yellow tiles
   e) 4 sets of 2 yellow tiles   f) 2 sets of 5 red tiles
   g) 6 sets of 2 red tiles   h) 5 sets of 3 yellow tiles

2. Compare your results to exercise 1 with your classmates. Did you all write the same statements?

3. What do you predict about the product of two positive integers?

4. What do you predict about the product of a positive integer and a negative integer?

▶ ▶ *Through Discussion*

We continue our investigation of the product of two integers by using patterns.

Study the following pattern:

$$(+4) \times (+3) = +12$$
$$(+3) \times (+3) = +9$$
$$(+2) \times (+3) = +6$$
$$(+1) \times (+3) = +3$$
$$(0) \times (+3) = 0$$
$$(-1) \times (+3) =$$
$$(-2) \times (+3) =$$
$$(-3) \times (+3) =$$
$$(-4) \times (+3) =$$

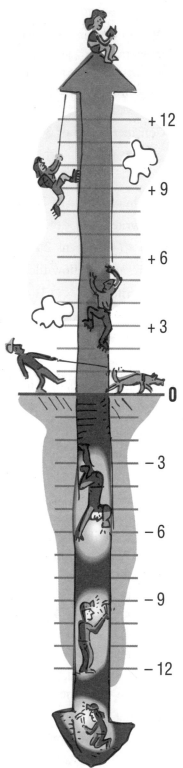

1. What number is the same in each multiplication statement?

2. How does the first number change from one line to the next?

3. How does the result change from one line to the next?

4. Use this pattern to state the sign of the product when multiplying two positive integers.

5. Copy and complete the pattern. Use this pattern to state the sign of the product when multiplying a negative integer by a positive integer.

Now look at this pattern.

$$(+4) \times (-3) = -12$$
$$(+3) \times (-3) = -9$$
$$(+2) \times (-3) = -6$$
$$(+1) \times (-3) = -3$$
$$(0) \times (-3) = 0$$
$$(-1) \times (-3) =$$
$$(-2) \times (-3) =$$
$$(-3) \times (-3) =$$
$$(-4) \times (-3) =$$

6. What number is the same in each multiplication statement?

7. How does the first number change from one line to the next?

8. How does the result change from one line to the next?

9. Use this pattern to state the sign of the product when multiplying a positive integer by a negative integer.

10. Copy and complete the pattern. Use this pattern to state the sign of the product when multiplying two negative integers.

▶ ▶ Using a Computer

EMPLATE DISK

We can use a spreadsheet to investigate the patterns when two integers are multiplied. Start a new document in a spreadsheet program. Input any integer in cell A1. Copy this number down to cell A12. Input any integer in cell B1. In cell B2, input the formula shown at the right. Copy this formula down to cell B12. In cell C1, input the formula shown at the right. Copy this formula down to cell C12.

	A	B	C
1			=A1*B1
2		=B1+1	
3			
4			
5			
6			
7			
8			
9			
10			
11			
12			

1. Explain what the formula in each cell does.

   a) B2   **b)** C1

2. Describe the sign of the integer in column C in each case.

   a) The integer in column A is positive and the integer in column B is:

   i) negative   **ii)** zero   **iii)** positive

   b) The integer in column A is negative and the integer in column B is:

   i) negative   **ii)** zero   **iii)** positive

If the integers in columns A and B do not enable you to complete any of exercise 2, change the integers in cells A1 and B1 until you can complete the exercise.

▶ ▶ Through a Guided Example

From the patterns investigated above, you should have discovered these facts.

• • • • • • • • •

   • If two integers have the same sign, their product is positive.
   • If two integers have different signs, their product is negative.

Example ....

Multiply.

   a) $(+3) \times (+9)$ **b)** $(-4) \times (-8)$ **c)** $(+5) \times (-7)$ **d)** $(-6) \times (+4)$

Solution

   a) $(+3) \times (+9)$ ⎯ The signs are the same so the product is positive.
   $(+3) \times (+9) = +27$

   b) $(-4) \times (-8)$ ⎯ The signs are the same so the product is positive.
   $(-4) \times (-8) = +32$

   c) $(+5) \times (-7)$ ⎯ The signs are different so the product is negative.
   $(+5) \times (-7) = -35$

   d) $(-6) \times (+4)$ ⎯ The signs are different so the product is negative.
   $(-6) \times (+4) = -24$

Working with Mathematics

Something to talk about

1. Is each product negative or positive?
   a) A negative integer is multiplied by a positive integer.
   b) A positive integer is multiplied by a negative integer.
   c) A negative integer is multiplied by a negative integer.
   d) A positive integer is multiplied by a positive integer.

2. What is the product when an integer is multiplied by 0?

Practice

3. Copy and complete each pattern. Extend each pattern for three more rows. Take turns to explain how you did it.

   a) $(+5) \times (+3) = +15$
   $(+5) \times (+2) = +10$
   $(+5) \times (+1) = +5$
   $(+5) \times (0) = 0$
   $(+5) \times (-1) =$
   $(+5) \times (-2) =$
   $(+5) \times (-3) =$
   $(+5) \times (-4) =$

   b) $(-4) \times (+2) = -8$
   $(-4) \times (+1) = -4$
   $(-4) \times (0) = 0$
   $(-4) \times (-1) =$
   $(-4) \times (-2) =$
   $(-4) \times (-3) =$
   $(-4) \times (-4) =$
   $(-4) \times (-5) =$

   c) $(+7) \times (-3) = -21$
   $(+7) \times (-2) = -14$
   $(+7) \times (-1) = -7$
   $(+7) \times (0) =$
   $(+7) \times (+1) =$
   $(+7) \times (+2) =$
   $(+7) \times (+3) =$

   d) $(-6) \times (-3) = +18$
   $(-6) \times (-2) = +12$
   $(-6) \times (-1) =$
   $(-6) \times (0) =$
   $(-6) \times (+1) =$
   $(-6) \times (+2) =$
   $(-6) \times (+3) =$

Work together

4. Complete the number statement for each product.
   a) $(+4) \times (+5) =$ b) $(+2) \times (-10) =$
   c) $(-7) \times (-2) =$ d) $(0) \times (-5) =$
   e) $(+7) \times (+3) =$ f) $(-6) \times (+8) =$
   g) $(+9) \times (+4) =$ h) $(-8) \times (+9) =$
   i) $(-1) \times (-9) =$ j) $(-2) \times (0) =$

5. Take turns to explain whether each statement is true or false.
   a) A positive integer multiplied by a positive integer will always equal a positive integer.
   b) A positive integer multiplied by a negative integer will always equal a positive integer.
   c) A negative integer multiplied by a positive integer will always equal a negative integer.
   d) A negative integer multiplied by a negative integer will always equal a positive integer.

6. Multiply.
   a) $(+11) \times (+3)$ b) $(-1) \times (+1)$
   c) $(-8) \times (-3)$ d) $(+4) \times (-2)$
   e) $(-3) \times (-10)$ f) $(-7) \times (+7)$

7. Describe the rule that is used to write each pattern. Write the next three numbers in each pattern.
   a) $-1, -4, -16, -64, \dots$
   b) $+3, -9, +27, -81, \dots$
   c) $-2, -10, -50, -250, \dots$
   d) $-3, +3, -3, +3, \dots$
   e) $+2, -14, +98, -686, \dots$
   f) $+1, +6, +36, +216, \dots$
   g) $+10, -100, +1000, -10\,000, \dots$

8. Multiply.

a) $(+1) \times (+2) \times (+3)$
b) $(-1) \times (+2) \times (+3)$
c) $(-1) \times (-2) \times (+3)$
d) $(-1) \times (-2) \times (-3)$
e) $(-2) \times (+1) \times (-3)$
f) $(-2) \times (+3) \times (-1)$
g) $(-3) \times (-1) \times (+2)$
h) $(+3) \times (+1) \times (-2)$

9. a) The temperature fell 5°C each hour for 3 hours. What was the total change in temperature?

b) The temperature fell 3°C each hour for 7 hours. What was the total change in temperature?

On your own

10. Complete the number statement for each product.

a) $(-6) \times (-3) =$ **b)** $(+3) \times (-9) =$
c) $(-11) \times (+4) =$ **d)** $(-4) \times (0) =$
e) $(-10) \times (+6) =$ **f)** $(-9) \times (-7) =$

11. Multiply.

a) $(-2) \times (+20)$ **b)** $(-6) \times (+7)$
c) $(-8) \times (-4)$ **d)** $(+9) \times (-6)$
e) $(+12) \times (+6)$ **f)** $(-13) \times (-5)$

12. Start a new document in a spreadsheet program.
In cell A1, type −8.
In cell A2, type =A1+1.
Copy this formula down to cell A17.

TEMPLATE DISK

	A	B	C
1	-8		
2	=A1+1		
3			
4			

a) In cell B1, type =A1*4. Copy this formula down to cell B17. Look at the numbers in columns A and B. Explain what happens when an integer is multiplied by a positive integer.

b) In cell C1, type =A1*(−4). Copy this formula down to cell C17. Look at the numbers in columns A and C. Explain what happens when an integer is multiplied by a negative integer.

13. Write a number statement for each expression.

a) Multiply +3 by −7.
b) Multiply −4 by −13.
c) Multiply +5 by +16.
d) Multiply −16 by −7.
e) Multiply −13 by +3.
f) Multiply +14 by −7.

14. Multiply.

a) $(+2) \times (+2) \times (+3)$
b) $(-2) \times (-2) \times (+3)$
c) $(-2) \times (-2) \times (-3)$
d) $(+1) \times (+5) \times (+4)$
e) $(-1) \times (+5) \times (+4)$
f) $(-4) \times (-5) \times (+1)$

Extend your thinking

15. a) Determine all of the pairs of integers that have a product of −24.

b) List the factors of −24.

16. Give an example of:

a) two integers with a product of 0
b) an integer that has a product greater than itself when multiplied by −1

COMMUNICATING

The Ideas

In your journal, explain how you know whether the product of two integers will be positive or negative.

When It Is Breakfast Time in Moscow, What Time Is It in Vancouver?

When Canadians wake up each morning, some Europeans are going for lunch. The time of day is different for people in different time zones. Earth rotates as it orbits the sun. This means that different parts of the planet are in daylight at different times. To deal with this, Earth is divided into different time zones. The zone containing the 0° line of longitude (the prime meridian) is used as the zero time zone. As you travel west from one time zone to the next, the local time is 1 h earlier.

The table shows some of the world's major cities and the number of hours later (positive integers) or earlier (negative integers) they are than the local time in Greenwich (London), England. The local time in London is used as the standard because it is in the zero time zone.

Local time in major cities relative to London					
Honolulu	Vancouver	London	Moscow	Beijing	Tokyo
−10	−8	0	+3	+8	+9

What time is it in Vancouver when it is 6:00 a.m. in Moscow?

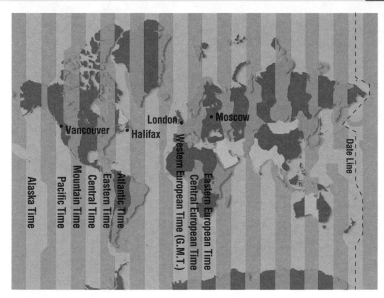

Countries of the former Soviet Union have adopted times 1 h ahead of the corresponding time zones.

Alaska Time
Pacific Time
Mountain Time
Central Time
Eastern Time
Atlantic Time
Western European Time (G.M.T.)
Central European Time
Eastern European Time

• Vancouver
London •
• Halifax
• Moscow

Date Line

Countries that have adopted a time different from that in the corresponding time zone

Understand the problem

- Why is the local time in Moscow not the same as the local time in Vancouver?
- Is Vancouver time earlier or later than London time?
- Is London time earlier or later than Moscow time?
- What are you asked to find?

Think of a strategy

- How could you use the information in the table to relate the time in Vancouver to the time in Moscow?

Carry out the strategy

- Determine the difference in times between Vancouver and Moscow.
- Determine whether the time in Vancouver is earlier or later than the time in Moscow.
- Use the difference between the times in Vancouver and Moscow to determine the time in Vancouver when the time in Moscow is 6:00 a.m.

Look back

- What time is it in Moscow when it is 6:00 a.m. in Vancouver?
- What time is it in Tokyo when it is noon in Honolulu?
- How many time zones are there? Why?
- Why are integers used instead of times in the table on the facing page?
- Use the map to check your answers for the local times.

Communicating the Ideas

In your journal, describe what time zones are and how they are used. Explain how you can determine the time in Vancouver if you know the time in Moscow.

Modelling the Multiplication of Integers

We can model the product of two integers by extending our model of red and yellow tiles. We shall use red and yellow boxes.

To multiply two integers, we place tiles in the boxes.

For our model to work, we have to agree on two conditions for the tiles.
- When a tile is placed in a yellow box, the tile does not change colour.
- When a tile is placed in a red box, the tile changes colour.
  For example, 2 red tiles placed in a red box become 2 yellow tiles.
  Two yellow tiles placed in a red box become 2 red tiles.

Consider the product: $(+2) \times (+3)$

The +3 is represented by 3 yellow tiles.

The +2 is represented by 2 yellow boxes.

To multiply +2 by +3, we place 3 yellow tiles in each of 2 yellow boxes.

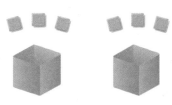

We have a total of 6 yellow tiles, +6.
So, $(+2) \times (+3) = +6$

Consider the product: $(-2) \times (+3)$

The +3 is represented by 3 yellow tiles.

The −2 is represented by 2 red boxes.

To multiply −2 by +3, we place 3 yellow tiles in each of 2 red boxes.

When yellow tiles are placed in red boxes, the tiles change colour.

We have a total of 6 red tiles, −6.

So, $(-2) \times (+3) = -6$

1. Use the model of yellow and red tiles and boxes. Find each product.
   a) $(+2) \times (-3)$ **b)** $(-2) \times (-3)$

2. For any product, does it affect the result if the first factor represents the number of tiles and the second factor represents the number of boxes?

BOGGLE YOUR **MIND**

The British airline, Virgin Atlantic Airways, donated $75 000 U.S. to charity in March 1995. The money was loose change that was left in airplane seats and foreign coins that passengers donated rather than take home. It was collected during the first 10 weeks of the year. The airline calculated that the amount represented 18¢ per passenger. How many passengers flew with Virgin Atlantic Airways in the first 10 weeks of 1995?

6.4 DIVIDING INTEGERS

Developing the Ideas

▶ ▶ *Through Discussion*

Division is the *inverse operation* of multiplication. This means that when we multiply two numbers and get a product, we can "undo" the multiplication with division.

For example, $50 \times 2 = 100$

To "undo" this operation, we write $100 \div 2 = 50$

Another way that $50 \times 2 = 100$ could be "undone" is by writing $100 \div 50 = 2$.

For any product, there are two related division statements. We can use these relationships to find the quotient of two integers.

We can use the products of integers we found in the preceding section to find quotients of integers.

1. Write the two division statements that are related to this product:
   $(+2) \times (+3) = +6$

2. For each product, write the two division statements that are related to it.
   a) $(+3) \times (+4) = +12$
   b) $(+6) \times (+8) = +48$
   c) $(+12) \times (+10) = +120$

3. What do you notice about the signs of all the quotients in exercise 2? Use your calculator to determine whether or not the result of dividing two positive integers is always a positive number.

4. Write a statement that describes the sign of the quotient when two positive integers are divided.

5. Write the two division statements that are related to this product:
   $(-2) \times (-3) = +6$

6. For each product, write the two division statements that are related to it.
   a) $(-3) \times (-4) = +12$
   b) $(-6) \times (-8) = +48$
   c) $(-12) \times (-10) = +120$

7. What do you notice about the signs of all the quotients in exercise 6? Use your calculator to determine whether or not the result of dividing a positive integer by a negative integer is always a negative number.

8. Write a sentence that describes the sign of the quotient when a positive integer is divided by a negative integer.

9. Write the two division statements that are related to this product:
$(+2) \times (-3) = -6$

10. Write the two division statements that are related to this product:
$(-2) \times (+3) = -6$

11. For each product, write the two division statements that are related to it.
    a) $(-3) \times (+4) = -12$
    b) $(+6) \times (-8) = -48$
    c) $(+12) \times (-10) = -120$
    d) $(-5) \times (+4) = -20$

12. What do you notice about the signs of the quotients in exercise 11? Use your calculator to determine whether or not the result of dividing a negative integer by a positive integer is always a negative number. Use your calculator to determine whether or not the result of dividing two negative integers is always a positive number.

13. Write a sentence that describes the sign of the quotient when a negative integer is divided by a positive integer.

14. Write a sentence that describes the sign of the quotient when two negative integers are divided.

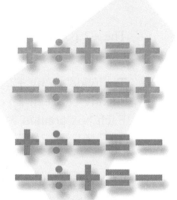

▶ ▶ *Through a Guided Example*

From the patterns investigated above, you should have described these facts.

• • • • • • • • •

- If two integers have the same sign, their quotient is positive.
- If two integers have different signs, their quotient is negative.

Example ⋯⋯⋯⋯⋯⋯⋯⋯⋯⋯⋯⋯⋯⋯⋯⋯⋯⋯⋯⋯⋯⋯⋯⋯⋯⋯⋯⋯⋯⋯⋯⋯⋯⋯⋯⋯

Divide.
   a) $(-12) \div (+4)$ b) $(+10) \div (-2)$ c) $(+20) \div (+2)$ d) $(-18) \div (-3)$

Solution

   a) $(-12) \div (+4)$ ◁ The signs are different so the quotient is negative.
      $(-12) \div (+4) = -3$

   b) $(+10) \div (-2)$ ◁ The signs are different so the quotient is negative.
      $(+10) \div (-2) = -5$

   c) $(+20) \div (+2)$ ◁ The signs are the same so the quotient is positive.
      $(+20) \div (+2) = +10$

   d) $(-18) \div (-3)$ ◁ The signs are the same so the quotient is positive.
      $(-18) \div (-3) = +6$

We shall use a model of red and yellow tiles and red and yellow boxes to model the division of integers.

For our model to work, we have the same conditions as on page 322.

Consider the quotient: (+6) ÷ (+2)

The +6 is represented by 6 yellow tiles.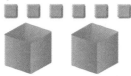

The +2 is represented by 2 yellow boxes.

To divide +6 by +2, we divide 6 yellow tiles
equally between 2 yellow boxes.
Each box contain 3 yellow tiles, +3.
So, (+6) ÷ (+2) = +3

Consider the quotient: (+6) ÷ (−2)

The +6 is represented by 6 yellow tiles.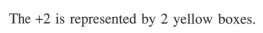

The −2 is represented by 2 red boxes.

To divide +6 by −2, we divide 6 yellow tiles
equally between 2 red boxes.
Recall that when tiles are placed into red boxes,
the colours of the tiles change.
The yellow tiles become red tiles.

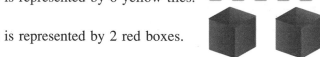

Each box contains 3 red tiles, −3.

So, (+6) ÷ (−2) = −3

1. Use the model of red and yellow boxes. Find each quotient.
   a) (−6) ÷ (+2)   b) (−6) ÷ (−2)

2. Explain what role the red and yellow boxes have in illustrating
   the division of integers.

Working with Mathematics

Something to talk about

1. Is each quotient negative or positive?
   a) A negative integer is divided by a positive integer.
   b) A positive integer is divided by a negative integer.
   c) A negative integer is divided by a negative integer.
   d) A positive integer is divided by a positive integer.

2. What is the result when 0 is divided by an integer?

Practice

3. Use tiles and the model of red and yellow boxes to find each quotient.
   a) $(-5) \div (+1)$ b) $(-5) \div (-1)$
   c) $(+5) \div (+1)$ d) $(+5) \div (-1)$
   e) $(+8) \div (+2)$ f) $(+8) \div (-2)$
   g) $(-8) \div (+2)$ h) $(-8) \div (-2)$
   i) $(+6) \div (+3)$ j) $(+6) \div (-3)$
   k) $(-6) \div (+3)$ l) $(-6) \div (-3)$

4. For each product, write the two division statements that are related to it.
   a) $(+4) \times (+8) = +32$
   b) $(+8) \times (+9) = +72$
   c) $(+3) \times (+7) = +21$
   d) $(-4) \times (-7) = +28$
   e) $(-6) \times (-9) = +54$
   f) $(+4) \times (-6) = -24$
   g) $(-5) \times (+3) = -15$
   h) $(+8) \times (-5) = -40$
   i) $(-10) \times (+1) = -10$

Work together

5. List the related multiplication statement for each division statement.
   a) $(-8) \div (-2) = +4$
   b) $(-21) \div (+3) = -7$
   c) $(+32) \div (+4) = +8$
   d) $(+30) \div (-5) = -6$
   e) $(-18) \div (+6) = -3$
   f) $(-42) \div (-7) = +6$
   g) $(+40) \div (-8) = -5$
   h) $(+18) \div (+9) = +2$
   i) $(-30) \div (-1) = +30$

6. Find each quotient.
   a) $(-36) \div (+6)$ b) $(+63) \div (-9)$
   c) $(-45) \div (-5)$ d) $(+91) \div (+7)$
   e) $(-27) \div (-3)$ f) $(+56) \div (+8)$
   g) $(+34) \div (-1)$ h) $(-28) \div (+4)$
   i) $(-72) \div (-2)$ j) $(-75) \div (+5)$
   k) $(-108) \div (-9)$ l) $(+29) \div (-1)$

7. Calculate negative quotients only.
   a) $(-15) \div (+3)$ b) $(+44) \div (+4)$
   c) $(-54) \div (-9)$ d) $(-60) \div (+12)$
   e) $(+36) \div (-6)$ f) $(-91) \div (+13)$
   g) $(+108) \div (-9)$ h) $(-112) \div (-8)$

8. Write a division statement for each expression.
   a) Divide $+52$ by -13.
   b) Divide -96 by -12.
   c) Divide $+108$ by $+6$.
   d) Divide -135 by $+9$.
   e) Divide -112 by -7.
   f) Divide $+126$ by -14.

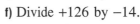

According to the estimates of Manitoba Agriculture, in his first 18 years a boy will eat $29 626 worth of food. This is almost $3000 more than a girl will eat in the same time.
What is the mean annual cost of food for a boy and for a girl?

9. **a)** The temperature fell 3°C each hour for a total change of −12°C. How many hours did this take?

  b) The temperature fell 2°C each hour for a total change of −14°C. How many hours did this take?

10. Describe the rule that is used to write each pattern. Write the next three numbers in each pattern.

  a) +64, +32, +16, …

  b) +243, −81, +27, …

  c) +160, +80, +40, …

  d) −972, −324, −108, …

  e) +4096, −1024, +256, …

  f) +384, −192, +96, …

  g) +100 000, −10 000, +1000, …

11. In each pair, which quotient is larger?

  a) (+56) ÷ (+7)   **b)** (−20) ÷ (+4)

  　 (+56) ÷ (−7)   　 (−20) ÷ (−4)

  c) (+60) ÷ (+5)   **d)** (+96) ÷ (−8)

  　 (+60) ÷ (+4)   　 (+96) ÷ (−12)

  e) (−90) ÷ (+6)   **f)** (−48) ÷ (−4)

  　 (−90) ÷ (+5)   　 (−48) ÷ (−6)

On your own

12. Find each quotient.

  a) (+55) ÷ (−5)   **b)** (−54) ÷ (−9)

  c) (−51) ÷ (+1)   **d)** (+88) ÷ (+8)

  e) (−48) ÷ (+2)   **f)** (+63) ÷ (−7)

  g) (+90) ÷ (+10)   **h)** (−75) ÷ (−3)

13. Find each quotient.

  a) (+84) ÷ (+12)   **b)** (+98) ÷ (−14)

  c) (−140) ÷ (−20)   **d)** (−78) ÷ (+13)

  e) (−105) ÷ (+15)   **f)** (+121) ÷ (+11)

  g) (+128) ÷ (−16)   **h)** (−300) ÷ (−50)

14. Calculate positive quotients only.

  a) (−42) ÷ (−7)   **b)** (+54) ÷ (+3)

  c) (−54) ÷ (−9)   **d)** (−99) ÷ (+9)

  e) (+75) ÷ (−5)   **f)** (−68) ÷ (−4)

  g) (+96) ÷ (+8)   **h)** (−121) ÷ (−11)

15. Write a division statement for each expression.

  a) Divide −16 by +4.

  b) Divide +49 by −7.

  c) Divide −56 by −8.

  d) Divide +45 by −3.

  e) Divide −72 by −8.

  f) Divide +169 by −13.

  g) Divide +180 by −12.

16. Describe the rule that is used to write each pattern. Write the next three numbers in each pattern.

  a) −3125, −625, −125, …

  b) +4096, −2048, +1024, …

  c) −32 768, −4096, −512, …

  d) +224, +112, +56, …

  e) +486, −162, +54, …

Extend your thinking

17. Find the value of ■ that makes each statement true.

  a) ■ ÷ (−4) = −5   **b)** (+63) ÷ ■ = −9

  c) ■ ÷ (−12) = +6   **d)** (+75) ÷ ■ = +15

  e) ■ ÷ (+9) = −8   **f)** (−144) ÷ ■ = +12

18. Find as many examples as you can of three different 1-digit numbers that are all divisible by +3 and have a sum of +6.

19. From this list of integers:

  0, −2, +3, −1, +1, +2, +4

  a) Which two have a quotient of −2?

  b) Which two have the greatest product?

  c) Which two have the least sum?

  d) Which two have a quotient less than −3?

COMMUNICATING

The Ideas

In your own words, explain how you know whether the quotient will be negative or positive when dividing two integers.

Operations with Integers

When we perform the four arithmetic operations on two integers, is the result always an integer?

Understand the problem

- What is an integer?
- What do we mean by "perform the four arithmetic operations on two integers"?
- List the four arithmetic operations.
- Rewrite the problem in your own words.

Think of a strategy

- Choose any two integers. Perform the arithmetic operations on these integers.

Carry out the strategy

- Write a number sentence that describes each operation.
- Repeat the strategy for different pairs of integers.
- Determine whether or not the result of each operation is an integer.

Look back

- Was there an operation for which the result was not always an integer?
- What type of number is the result?

Communicating the Ideas

In your journal, write a description of which operations always result in an integer and which operations do not always result in an integer. Give examples to support your conclusions.

Developing the Ideas

▶▶ *Through an Activity*

Read the conversation between Annette and Bernard.

Work with a partner.

Take turns to be Annette and Bernard.
Follow the steps to calculate each other's birthday.
Did you get the correct date?

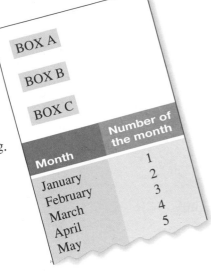

▶ ▶ *Through Instruction*

The formula for calculating the birthday might be written as:
Box A + Box C ÷ 10
We shall investigate whether it makes a difference to the
answer if we add before dividing, or if we divide before adding.

Consider someone who is born on November 9.
November is the eleventh month.
The product for box A is $11 \times 1010 = 11\ 110$

The number for box B is $(+9) - (+11) = -2$

The number for box C is $(-2) \times 10 = -20$

Substitute these numbers in the formula:
$$\text{Box A} + \text{Box C} \div 10 = 11\ 110 + (-20) \div 10$$

Add before dividing.
$= 11\ 090 \div 10$
$= 1109$
The birthday is November 9.

Divide before adding.
$= 11\ 110 + (-2)$
$= 11\ 108$
We cannot determine a birthday from
this number.

Addition, subtraction, multiplication, and division are all *operations*. To
avoid discrepancies like that above, there are rules for the order in which
operations are performed. These rules are called the *order of operations*.

• • • • • • • • • •

- Operations within brackets are performed first.
- Multiplication and division are performed next, in order
  from left to right.
- Addition and subtraction are performed last, in order from
  left to right.

For the formula above, to ensure that the addition is performed first,
we put brackets around the numbers involved in that operation.
The formula must be written as: (Box A + Box C) ÷ 10

The *TEXAS INSTRUMENTS Math Explorer* calculator is programmed
to follow the order of operations listed above. If you use a different
calculator, check to see if it follows the order of operations.

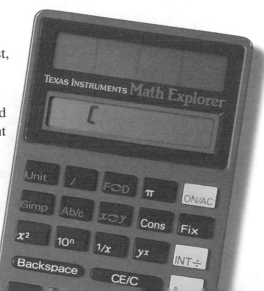

Example 1 ....

Simplify. $(-4)(+2) + (-5)(-3)$

Solution

$(-4)(+2) + (-5)(-3)$
Do the multiplications in order.
$= (-8) + (-5)(-3)$
$= (-8) + (+15)$
$= +7$

Example 2 ....

Simplify. $(-6)^2 \div [(+6) - (+8)]$

Solution

$(-6)^2 \div [(+6) - (+8)]$
$= (-6)(-6) \div [(+6) + (-8)]$
Do the operation in square brackets.
$= (-6)(-6) \div (-2)$
Do the multiplication.
$= (+36) \div (-2)$
Do the division.
$= -18$

Example 3 ....

The temperature of an ocean is recorded at several depths.
The temperatures are: +4°C, +4°C, −1°C, −1°C, −1°C
What is the mean temperature of the water?

Solution

To find the mean, add the temperatures and divide by how
many there are.
$[(+4) + (+4) + (-1) + (-1) + (-1)] \div 5$
Do the operations in square brackets.
$= (+5) \div 5$
$= +1$
The mean temperature is +1°C.

$+4\,^{\circ}C$

$+4\,^{\circ}C$

$-1\,^{\circ}C$

$-1\,^{\circ}C$

$-1\,^{\circ}C$

Working with Mathematics

Something to talk about

1. In each case, state the operations in the order in which they must be performed.
   a) $(+3)(+5) - (+7)$
   b) $(+3) - (+5)(+7)$
   c) $[(+3) - (+5)] \times (+7)$

2. Explain the statement: Multiplication and division are performed in order from left to right.

Practice

3. Find the mean temperature.
   a) $-4°C, -9°C, -8°C, -3°C$
   b) $-3°C, -9°C, +7°C, +1°C$
   c) $-14°C, +7°C, 0°C, +7°C, -4°C, -2°C$
   d) $+5°C, -3°C, -4°C, 0°C, +7°C$
   e) $-12°C, -16°C, +3°C, +5°C, -10°C$

4. Simplify.
   a) $(-1) + (-7) - (-3) - (-5)$
   b) $(+13) + (-12) - (+1) - (-10)$
   c) $(-17) - (+15) - (-25) - (-7)$
   d) $(+11) - (-11) + (-13) + (-8)$

5. Simplify.
   a) $(+3)(-5) + (-8)(-4)$
   b) $(-6)(-3) + (-4)(+5)$
   c) $(+12)(-2) + (+3)(-6)$
   d) $(+7)(-2) + (-10)(-3)$
   e) $(+6)(-3) - (-8)(+3)$
   f) $(-5)(+4) - (+4)(+6)$
   g) $(-10)(-4) - (+5)(-3)$
   h) $(-9)(+3) - (-2)(-5)$

Work together

6. Simplify.
   a) $(+7)[(+4) - (+6)] - (+5)$
   b) $(+2) - [(+3) + (-9)]$
   c) $[(+2) - (-5)] \div (+7)$
   d) $(+4) - (+10) \div (-2)$
   e) $[(+4) - (+10)] \div (-2)$
   f) $(-9) + (-6) \div (+3)$
   g) $[(-10) - (-4)] \div (-2)$
   h) $(-9) + (-12) \div (-3)$

7. Simplify.
   a) $(-10)^2 \div [(-7) + (-3)]$
   b) $(+4)^2 \div [(-1) - (-9)]$
   c) $(-8)^2 \div [(-12) - (+12) + (-8)]$
   d) $(+6)^2 \div [(-10) + (-4) - (+4)]$

8. Which expression simplifies to an integer?
   a) $(-4)(-5) \div (-6)$
   b) $(-5)(-8) \div (+4)$
   c) $(-2)(+6) \div (-9)$

9. Which of these expressions simplify to -16?
   a) $(-27) \div (+9) + (-13)$
   b) $(-4) - (+28) \div (+2)$
   c) $(+8) \times (-10) \div (-5)$
   d) $[(+6)(-3) - (+2)(+7)] \div (+2)$
   e) $(+2) \times (-2) - (+20)$
   f) $[(+8) - (-40)] \div (+3)$

10. Write an expression and then simplify.
    a) Add -6 to the product of -7 and -5.
    b) Add $+9$ to the quotient of -16 and $+8$.
    c) Subtract $+12$ from the sum of -14 and -6.
    d) Subtract -8 from the sum of -23 and -18.
    e) Add the square of -4 to the square of -3.

On your own

11. Complete the *Activity* on page 330 for the birthday of a friend or relative.

12. Find the mean temperature.
    a) $+9°C, +8°C, -2°C, -1°C, -4°C$
    b) $-12°C, +3°C, +2°C, +4°C, -7°C$
    c) $-9°C, +3°C, +5°C, -3°C, +9°C$

13. On one day in December, the temperatures of four western Canadian cities are as shown.

City	Temperature (°C)
Calgary	-12
Edmonton	-15
Regina	-18
Saskatoon	-19

   a) What is the mean temperature?
   b) Which cities have temperatures above the mean?

14. Simplify.
    a) $(+7)(-5) + (+7)(-3)$
    b) $(+4)(-1) + (+4)(-9)$
    c) $(-2)(-3) + (-2)(+8)$
    d) $(-2)[(-3) + (+8)]$
    e) $(+7)[(-5) + (-3)]$
    f) $(+4)[(-1) + (-9)]$

15. Match each expression with the corresponding number in the box below.
    a) $(-35) \div [(-8) + (+15)]$
    b) $(+20) \div [(+3) - (+8)]$
    c) $(-3)(-9) - (+5)$
    d) $(-4)^2 - (-3)(+3)$
    e) $(+77) \div [(+11) + (-18)]$
    f) $(+36) \div (-3) - (+15)$

	-5	-11
$+22$		-27
	$+25$	-4

16. Simplify.
    a) $(-7)[(+3) - (+9)]$
    b) $(+12) + (-6) \div (+3)$
    c) $[(-18) - (+4)] \div (-2)$
    d) $(-16) + (+12) \div (+4)$
    e) $(+6)(+9) + (-7)$
    f) $(-3)[(-19) + (-6) - (+13)]$
    g) $(+20) \div (-5) + (+1)$
    h) $(-8)[(+2) - (-5)]$
    i) $[(-17) + (+5)] \div (-3)$

17. Use a calculator to simplify.
    a) $[(+54) - (-30)] \div (-3)$
    b) $(+25) \div (-5) - (+10)$
    c) $(+54) \div [(-3) + (-15)]$
    d) $(-37) - [(+82) - (+25)]$

18. Write an expression, then simplify.
    a) Divide the sum of +24 and −16 by −8.
    b) Divide the sum of −9 and −12 by +7.
    c) Divide the product of +8 and −6 by −12.
    d) Subtract −4 from +11, then divide the result by −3.
    e) Divide the sum of +13 and −22 by −9.
    f) Subtract −18 from +30, then divide the result by +6.
    g) Divide the sum of −3, +16, and −24 by +11.

19. Simplify each expression as it is shown. Then insert one pair of brackets in each expression so it simplifies to −4.
    a) $(-20) \div (+2) - (-3)$
    b) $(-21) + (+9) \div (+3)$
    c) $(+72) \div (-9) \times (+2)$
    d) $(-8) + (+7) \times (+4)$
    e) $(+4)(+5) + (+20) \div (-10)$

Extend your thinking

20. Yuhua was born in August. When she applied the birthday formula, she entered −30 in Box C. On what day of the month was she born?

21. Using three −6s and any operations or brackets, write an expression that equals each number.
    a) −18   b) −6   c) 0
    d) −5   e) 7   f) 2

22. Use any four integers from the box and any operations or brackets.

$+2$		-6
	-5	
-4		$+8$

    Write an expression that equals each number.
    a) −10   b) +12   c) −2   d) +24

The Ideas

In your journal, explain why we need rules for the order of operations. Write an expression that has different answers depending on whether or not the order of operations is followed when the expression is simplified.

Comparing Winters

How can we tell if one winter is colder than another?

To compare the severity of winters, we use *degree days*.
A degree day tells how much the temperature is below 18°C.

The flow chart and example below show how to calculate
a degree day.

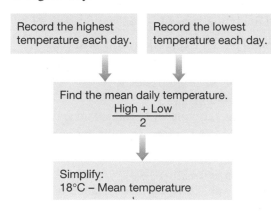

Record the highest temperature each day.   Record the lowest temperature each day.

Find the mean daily temperature.
$$\frac{High + Low}{2}$$

Simplify:
18°C – Mean temperature

Here is an example.

One day the highest temperature was +3°C. The lowest temperature was
−7°C. Calculate the degree day for that day.

Step 1
Calculate the mean temperature. $$\frac{(+3) + (-7)}{2} = \frac{-4}{2}$$ $$= -2$$

Step 2
Subtract from 18. $$(+18) - (-2) = (+18) + (+2)$$ $$= +20$$ The degree day for that day was +20.

To calculate the degree days for several days, add the results for those days.

1. The daily high and low temperatures for two weeks are given.

    a) Copy and complete the tables.   **b)** Which week was colder? How do you know?

WEEK 1

Day	S	M	T	W	T	F	S
High temperature (°C)	+4	+3	−2	0	−5	−1	+2
Low temperature (°C)	0	−3	−6	−8	−7	−7	−4
Mean temperature (°C)							
Degree day							

WEEK 2

Day	S	M	T	W	T	F	S
High temperature (°C)	−1	−3	+1	+5	+2	−4	0
Low temperature (°C)	−5	−5	−3	+1	−4	−8	−6
Mean temperature (°C)							
Degree day							

Mathematics & Science

Linking Ideas

Review

1. a) Which temperature is higher, −8°C or −5°C?

   b) Which integer is greater, −8 or −5? Explain.

2. Chinooks are warm winter winds that blow over western North America, rapidly raising temperatures. People who live in Calgary are happy when a Chinook blows and they can wear T-shirts and have barbecues for a day or two in the middle of winter. On a January day in Calgary, the temperature was −24°C at 8:00 a.m. By 11:00 a.m. the temperature was +15°C.

   a) Express the change in temperature as an integer.

   b) How long did it take for the temperature to change?

   c) Express as an integer how rapidly the temperature changed in degrees per hour.

3. Draw a number line and label it with integers from −10 to +10. Write the integer that is:

   a) 4 units more than −7

   b) 5 units less than +3

   c) half way between −9 and +5

   d) the mean of −5 and +7

4. The lowest temperature in Norris Point one day was 5°C less than the highest temperature of 2°C. What was the lowest temperature in Norris Point that day?

5. Describe each expression as a change in temperature. Calculate the final temperature.

   a) $(−11) + (−3)$ b) $(−7) − (+2)$

   c) $(+3) − (+8)$ d) $(−4) − (−3)$

   e) $(+7) − (+11)$ f) $(+4) − (+3)$

   g) $(+15) − (−9)$ h) $(−8) − (−13)$

6. Simplify.

   a) $(+15) + (−11)$ b) $(−27) + (+21)$

   c) $(−13) + (−18)$ d) $(+14) − (+26)$

   e) $(+23) − (−16)$ f) $(−17) − (+29)$

   g) $(−25) − (−37)$ h) $(−11) − (+22)$

   i) $(−31) + (+17)$ j) $(+16) − (−9)$

7. Christy has money in a savings account. This is her bank statement for August.

Description	Withdrawals	Deposits	Date	Balance
Balance forward			Aug 1	$237.00
Teller withdrawal	$50.00		Aug 3	
Teller withdrawal	$35.00		Aug 17	
Deposit		$28.00	Aug 25	
Final balance			Aug 31	

   a) i) What did Christy do with the account on August 3?

   ii) How can you write this as an integer?

   b) i) What did Christy do with the account on August 25?

   ii) How can you write this as an integer?

   c) What was Christy's final balance on August 31?

8. Simplify.

   a) $(+4) × (−5)$ b) $(+7) × (−6)$

   c) $(−8) × (−3)$ d) $(−9) × (−2)$

   e) $0 × (−3)$ f) $(−4) × (+7)$

   g) $(+2) × (+2)$ h) $(−2) × (−2)$

9. Explain why parts g and h of exercise 8 have the same result.

10. Simplify.

   a) $(−72) ÷ (+8)$ b) $(+45) ÷ (−9)$

   c) $(−49) ÷ (−7)$ d) $(+36) ÷ (+12)$

   e) $(+51) ÷ (−17)$ f) $(−52) ÷ (−13)$

   g) $(+12) ÷ (−3)$ h) $(−12) ÷ (+3)$

11. Explain why parts g and h of exercise 10 have the same result.

12. Write each product as an integer.

   a) $(−3)(−2)(+5)$ b) $(+2)(−6)(+5)$

   c) $(−4)(−4)(−4)$ d) $(−2)(+4)(−7)$

   e) $(−2)(−2)(−1)(+2)(−2)(−1)$

   f) $(−2)(−2)(−1)(+2)(−2)(−1)(−1)$

13. Describe a short cut for finding the result of part f of exercise 12 once the result of part e is known.

14. a) Two positive numbers and three negative numbers are all multiplied together. Is the final result positive or negative? Explain.

b) Two positive numbers and four negative numbers are all multiplied together. Is the final result positive or negative? Explain.

15. You own a store. Model each situation using integers. For each situation, calculate the amount of money that flows into or out of your store.

a) Five people come into your store and each buys items worth $10.

b) Four bills for $20 each arrive in the mail.

c) A friend decides to do you a favour by taking the bills in part b away and paying them.

d) A supplier gives you $3 for each of the 12 cases of her product you have sold this month.

16. Find the mean temperature.

a) −3°C, −12°C, +2°C, −3°C
b) −13°C, −11°C, −17°C, +5°C
c) −4°C, −4°C, −4°C, −4°C
d) −4°C, −7°C, +3°C, −2°C, 0°C

17. Simplify.

a) (+2) − (+3) + (−7) − (−5)
b) (−6) + (−4) − (+5) − (−2)
c) (−11) − (−17) − (−9) − (−6)
d) (−7) + (+4) − (+5) − (−9)

18. Simplify.

a) (+2)(−3) + (−8)(+3)
b) (−4)(+4) − (+5)(−2)
c) (−6)(−2) − (+4)(+3)
d) (+7)(+6) − (+5)(−8)

e) (−9)(+4) + (−5)(−6)
f) (+10)(−2) + (−7)(+3)

19. Write an expression and then simplify.

a) Subtract −4 from the product of +3 and −7.
b) Add +8 to the quotient of −8 and −4.
c) Subtract +7 from the sum of −8 and +4.
d) Subtract −5 from the sum of −20 and +9.
e) Subtract the square of −3 from the sum of +2 and −6.

20. Simplify.

a) (+3) − [(+4) + (−3)]
b) (+3) − (+4) + (−3)
c) (−3)[(+5) − (+6)] − (+2)
d) (−3)(+5) − (+6) − (+2)
e) [(−6) + (+4)] ÷ (−2)
f) (−6) + (+4) ÷ (−2)

21. a) Explain why the results of parts a and b of exercise 22 are different.
b) Explain why the results of parts c and d of exercise 22 are different.
c) Explain why the results of parts e and f of exercise 22 are different.

22. Simplify.

a) (−9)(+4) ÷ (+6)
b) (+3)[(−3) − (+3)]
c) (−15) + (−6) ÷ (−3)
d) (−5)^2 + (−3)(−4)
e) (−4)^2 − (−3)^2
f) (−3)(+4)(−3) ÷ (−6)
g) (−32) ÷ [(−19) − (−11)]
h) (+5) − (−4)[(−2) + (−4)]

This pyramid of cans was constructed by ten students from Cedar Girls Secondary School in Singapore in 1993. Each layer is a square with side length one can less than the layer below it. The bottom layer has 22 cans along each side. The top layer has only 1 can. Calculate the total number of cans in the pyramid.

Graphing Population Shifts

An article entitled *Harvests of Ruin* was printed in Canadian Geographic in 1992. It described the decline of Saskatchewan's rural way of life. This graph appeared in the article.

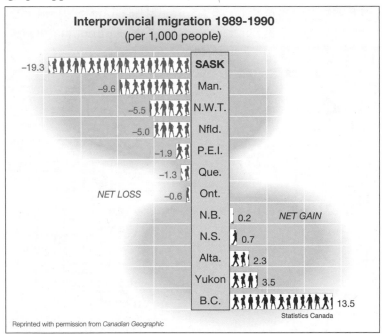

Interprovincial migration 1989-1990
(per 1,000 people)

−19.3	SASK
−9.6	Man.
−5.5	N.W.T.
−5.0	Nfld.
−1.9	P.E.I.
−1.3	Que.
−0.6	Ont.
	N.B. 0.2
	N.S. 0.7
	Alta. 2.3
	Yukon 3.5
	B.C. 13.5

NET LOSS

NET GAIN

Statistics Canada

Reprinted with permission from *Canadian Geographic*

The title of the graph, "Interprovincial migration", means the net change in the number of Canadians who move from one province to another.

ACTIVITY 1

This table shows how Canadians move from one province to another. The numbers are rounded to the nearest thousand people.

A positive number shows that more Canadians moved into that province than out of that province. A negative number shows that more Canadians moved out of that province than into that province.

Year	YT	NWT	BC	Alta	Sask	Man	Ont	Que	NB	NS	PEI	Nfld
1992	1	–1	41	–1	–8	–7	–3	–15	–2	–2	1	–4

Use the tables above and below. Calculate the interprovincial migration per 1000 people for each province in 1992.

POPULATION, 1992 (thousands of persons)			
YK	30	Ont	10 278
NWT	58	Que	6969
BC	3373	NB	926
Alta	2582	NS	904
Sask	990	PEI	132
Man	1096	Nfld	568

ACTIVITY 2

Use your results from *Activity 1* to construct a graph, like the one on the facing page, for 1992.

Compare your graph with the one on the facing page. Why are the provinces showing the greatest net loss and net gain not the same in both graphs?

ACTIVITY 3

From an almanac or some other source, determine the most recent figures you can for interprovincial migrations. Determine also the populations of the provinces. Use your data to draw a graph like the one on page 338 showing the changes per 1000 people.

The Ideas

Write a report to illustrate the results of these activities.

MEASUREMENT

AREA RADIUS²

Mathematics Files

Quest

Minds on Math Project

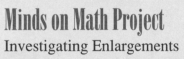

Start With What You Know

1. Estimate, using an appropriate metric unit.

a) the volume of a CD holder

b) the area of the top of a racing car
c) the volume of a racing car

d) the surface area of a tractor

e) the length, width, and height of a bicycle

f) the surface area of a fishing lure

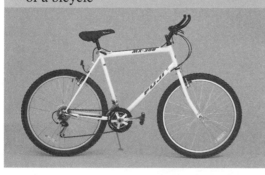

2. a) Estimate how long it would take the tractor in exercise 1d to spray 100 m² of soil. What could affect this time?

   b) About how long might it take the tractor to spray 1000 m²?

3. a) Estimate the maximum width of one wheel of the bicycle.

   b) Estimate the perimeter of the bicycle wheel.

4. Multiply.

   a) 5.4 × 10 000   **b)** 5.4 × 1000   **c)** 5.4 × 100

   d) 5.4 × 10   **e)** 5.4 × 1   **f)** 5.4 × 0.1

   g) 5.4 × 0.01   **h)** 5.4 × 0.001   **i)** 5.4 × 0.0001

5. Divide.

   a) 3500 ÷ 1000   **b)** 3500 ÷ 100   **c)** 3500 ÷ 10

   d) 3500 ÷ 1   **e)** 3500 ÷ 0.1   **f)** 3500 ÷ 0.01

6. Round to the nearest tenth.

   a) 5.74   **b)** 0.29   **c)** 17.92

   d) 87.05   **e)** 34.200   **f)** 0.035

7. Round to the nearest hundredth.

   a) 36.583   **b)** 8.075   **c)** 0.604

   d) 49.555   **e)** 63.9908   **f)** 30.999

8. Determine the area of each figure.

   a)

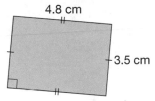

   4.8 cm   3.5 cm

   b)

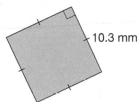

   10.3 mm

   c)

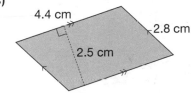

   4.4 cm   2.8 cm   2.5 cm

   d)

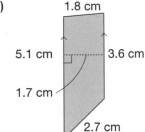

   1.8 cm   5.1 cm   3.6 cm   1.7 cm   2.7 cm

   e)

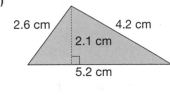

   2.6 cm   4.2 cm   2.1 cm   5.2 cm

9. Sketch an example of each figure below with an area of 36 cm². Label each figure with the measurements needed to calculate the area.

   a) square   **b)** rectangle   **c)** parallelogram

   d) triangle   **e)** trapezoid

10. Compare your answers to exercise 9 with those of a classmate. Explain why your answers may be different.

Work in group or with a partner. You will need measuring tapes or rulers.

11. a) Choose an object shaped like a rectangular prism.

   b) Measure the length and width of the base. Calculate the area of the base.

   c) Measure the height of the prism. Calculate the volume of the prism.

7.1 ESTIMATING THE CIRCUMFERENCE OF A CIRCLE

Developing the Ideas

▶ ▶ *Through Instruction*

The cross section of a tree approximates a circle. To measure the diameter of a tree, a forester uses a special tape measure called a *diameter tape*. It gives the diameter directly from a measurement of the distance around the tree.

The distance around a circle is called its *circumference*.

The *diameter* is the distance across a circle, measured through the centre.

The *radius* is the distance from the centre of a circle to any point on the circumference.

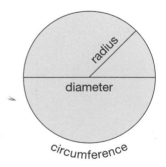

You can measure the circumference of a circular object by placing string around it, then measuring the string.

Work with a partner or in a group. You will need several circular objects, a calculator, a ruler, and a tape measure or string.

Step 1

Choose one circular object.
a) Which do you think is greater: the distance around the object or the distance across it?
b) How many times as great do you think it is?

Step 2

Measure and record the distance around each object (its circumference), to the nearest millimetre.

Step 3

Measure and record the distance across each object (its diameter). How can you be sure you have measured the diameter?

1. Repeat Steps 2 and 3 for the other objects. Record your results in a table. Include the results of your partner or other group members.

Object	Diameter (cm)	Circumference (cm)

2. a) Compare the numbers in the *Circumference* column with those in the *Diameter* column. About how many times as great as each diameter does each circumference appear to be?
   b) To check your answer, include another column in your table. Use your calculator to determine the numbers in this column. Round the numbers to one decimal place.

Object	Diameter (cm)	Circumference (cm)	Circumference / Diameter

3. What conclusion can you make about the circumference of a circle and its diameter?

▶▶ *Using a Computer*

In exercise 2, page 345, you can use a spreadsheet to calculate the values of $\dfrac{\text{Circumference}}{\text{Diameter}}$.

Start a new document in a spreadsheet program.

Input the following information. It assumes that you measured 10 objects.

If you measured more or fewer objects, amend the spreadsheet to show this.

TEMPLATE DISK

	A	B	C	D
1	Circle	Diameter	Circumference	Circumference/Diameter
2	1			=C2/B2
3	2			=C3/B3
4	3			=C4/B4
5	4			=C5/B5
6	5			=C6/B6
7	6			=C7/B7
8	7			=C8/B8
9	8			=C9/B9
10	9			=C10/B10
11	10			=C11/B11

In columns B and C, input the data from your table.

▶▶ *Through Guided Examples*

In the preceding *Activity*, you probably discovered that the circumference of a circle is approximately 3 times the diameter.

We think: The distance around a circle is about 3 times the distance across it.

We write: Circumference of circle $\doteq 3 \times$ diameter

This result applies for all circles, even ones that nobody has measured.

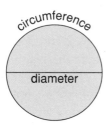

Example 1

The diameter of a bicycle wheel is 66 cm. Estimate its circumference.

Solution

Circumference $\doteq 3 \times$ diameter
$= 3 \times 66$ cm
$= 198$ cm

The circumference of the bicycle wheel is approximately 198 cm.

Example 2

The circumference of Canada's largest tree is 12 m. Estimate its diameter.

Solution

The circumference is approximately 3 times the diameter.

Since the circumference is 12 m, the diameter is approximately $\dfrac{12 \text{ m}}{3} = 4$ m

Working with Mathematics

Something to talk about

1. Suppose you know the diameter of a circular object. How could you estimate its circumference?

2. Suppose you know the radius of a circular object. How could you estimate its circumference?

3. a) How does the diameter of Canada's largest tree compare with the width of your classroom?

   b) How does its circumference compare with the width of your classroom?

4. In this diagram, all the line segments have the same length.

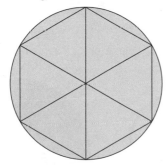

   a) i) How many segments are needed to form the diameter of the circle?

   ii) How many are needed to form the perimeter of the hexagon?

   iii) How many times as great as the diameter is the perimeter of the hexagon?

   b) Explain how this diagram shows that the circumference of a circle is not exactly 3 times its diameter.

   c) Is the circumference of a circle slightly more than 3 times its diameter or slightly less? Explain your answer.

5. a) In *Example 1*, is the circumference of the wheel a little more than 198 cm or a little less than 198 cm?

   b) In *Example 2*, is the diameter of the tree a little more than 4 m or a little less than 4 m? Explain your answer.

Practice

6. Each measurement is the diameter of a circle. Estimate the circumference of the circle to the nearest centimetre.

   a) 12 cm   b) 20 cm   c) 42 cm
   d) 35 cm   e) 7.8 cm   f) 100 cm
   g) 57 cm   h) 161 cm   i) 24.5 cm

7. Each measurement is the circumference of a circle. Estimate the diameter of the circle to the nearest centimetre.

   a) 12 cm   b) 64 cm   c) 72 cm
   d) 165 cm   e) 80 cm   f) 157 cm
   g) 200 cm   h) 142 cm   i) 360 cm

8. Copy and complete the table.

	Diameter	Circumference
a)	25 m	■
b)	■	96 cm
c)	■	135 mm
d)	248 m	■

Work together

9. A dream catcher has a diameter of 12 cm.

   a) What is the radius of the dream catcher?
   b) Estimate the circumference of the dream catcher.

10. In dressage, a horse and its rider have to execute circles of different circumferences. These exercises can be performed trotting or cantering. The smaller the circumference, the more difficult the exercises are to

perform. Estimate the diameter of each
dressage circle with given circumference.
Give the answers to the nearest metre.

a) 62.8 m   **b)** 47.1 m   **c)** 31.4 m

d) 25.1 m   **e)** 18.8 m

11. In curling, the diameters of the rings are
1.22 m, 2.44 m, and 3.66 m.

    a) Estimate the circumference of each ring.

    b) Make a table showing the diameters and
the circumferences of the rings.

    c) Use the data in the table to draw a graph.
Describe the graph.

    d) How would the table and the graph
change if you used the radii of the circles
instead of the diameters?

12. Is the relationship between the diameter and
the circumference of a circle a proportional
situation? Give reasons for your answer.

13. Get a can that you did not use in the
Activity on page 345.

    a) Use string to measure its circumference.

    b) Estimate the diameter of the can.

    c) Measure the diameter of the can to check
your estimate.

On your own

14. Estimate the circumference of each object.

    a)

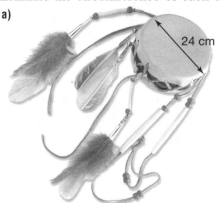

24 cm

b)

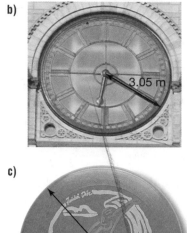

3.05 m

c)

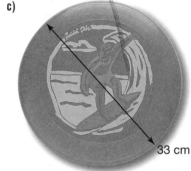

33 cm

15. Estimate the diameter of each object.

    a) 38 cm   **b)** 94 cm

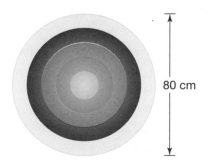

16. An archery target has an outside diameter
of 80 cm. The target face is divided into
five colour zones by circles with diameters
16 cm, 32 cm, 48 cm, and 64 cm.

80 cm

a) Estimate the circumference of each circle.

b) Make a table showing the diameters and the circumferences of the circles.

c) Use the data in the table to draw a graph.

d) How would the table and the graph change if you used the radii of the circles instead of the diameters?

17. **a)** Use string to measure the circumference of a tree.

b) Estimate the diameter of the tree.

c) Suppose the tree grows until its circumference is twice as great as it is now.

  i) How many times as great will its diameter be?

  ii) How many times as great will its radius be?

18. **a)** Estimate the circumference of each ball.

	Sport	Diameter of ball (cm)
i)	Baseball	7.4
ii)	Basketball	24.4
iii)	Golf	4.3
iv)	Soccer	22.2
v)	Squash	4.0
vi)	Table tennis	3.7
vii)	Tennis	6.5

b) Use your answers to part a to draw a graph.

Extend your thinking

19. Earth is approximately 150 000 000 km from the sun. Its orbit is approximately a circle. About how far does Earth travel in its orbit around the sun in each time?

a) one year   **b)** one day   **c)** one hour

d) one minute   **e)** one second

20. Refer to the description on page 344 of how foresters measure trees.

a) Suppose you had a forester's diameter tape. In what way would it be different from a regular measuring tape?

b) You can make a diameter tape from a piece of heavy string or twine. Tie knots in the string so that you could use it to measure the approximate diameter of a tree. How far apart should you make the knots?

c) Use your diameter tape to measure the diameters of some trees.

The Ideas

In your journal, explain how to estimate the circumference of a circle if you know:

a) its diameter   **b)** its radius

Use examples to illustrate your explanations.

BOGGLE YOUR **MIND**

The Great Wall of China is one of the most ambitious engineering projects ever attempted. Parts of it were built 3000 years ago. Since then, parts were rebuilt and others added, particularly during the Han Dynasty (206 B.C.–A.D. 220) and the Ming Dynasty (1368–1644). If branches from the main wall are included, the total length is about $\frac{1}{6}$ of Earth's circumference. Estimate the total length of the Great Wall. You will have to find the radius or the diameter of Earth from a resource book or a database.

Refining the Estimate of the Circumference of a Circle

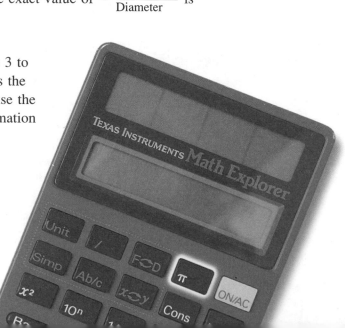

Earlier in this chapter, you discovered that the circumference of a circle is about 3 times its diameter. We will now refine this estimate to determine the circumference more accurately.

Work in a group or with a partner. Refer to the table you completed in exercise 2 on page 345.

1. a) Write the values of $\dfrac{\text{Circumference}}{\text{Diameter}}$ you calculated for as many different objects as possible.

   b) Determine the mean of these values. Round the mean to two decimal places.
   If you used the spreadsheet on page 346, you can extend it to calculate the mean.
   In cell C13, input Mean.
   In ClarisWorks, in cell D13, input =AVERAGE(D2..D11)
   In Microsoft Works, in cell D13, input =AVERAGE(D2:D11)

   c) Compare your mean with those of other students. Did everyone get approximately the same result?

2. To two decimal places, the value of $\dfrac{\text{Circumference}}{\text{Diameter}}$ is 3.14.
   a) Was your mean close to 3.14?
   b) Your mean may not have been exactly 3.14 to two decimal places. Can you think of a reason for this?

The value of $\dfrac{\text{Circumference}}{\text{Diameter}}$ has been determined very accurately. To ten decimal places, it is 3.141 592 653 6. The exact value of $\dfrac{\text{Circumference}}{\text{Diameter}}$ is represented by the Greek letter π (pi).

Circumference = π × diameter

Use your calculator to complete exercises 3 to 10. If your calculator has a π key, such as the *TEXAS INSTRUMENTS Math Explorer*, use the π key. Otherwise, use 3.14 as an approximation for π.

3. Calculate the circumference of the bicycle wheel in *Example 1* on page 346, to the nearest centimetre.

4. Calculate the circumference of each object, to one decimal place.

a)

7.8 m

b)

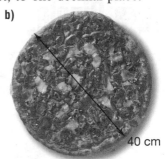

40 cm

c)

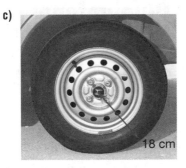

18 cm

5. a) A face-off circle in ringette has a diameter of 9 m. Calculate its circumference.

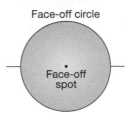

Face-off circle

Face-off
spot

b) The face-off spot has a radius of 30 cm. Calculate its circumference.

6. In exercise 16 on page 348, you estimated the circumferences of the circles on an archery target.

a) Use your calculator to obtain an estimate that is closer to the circumference of each circle.

b) How would the graph you drew in exercise 16 change if you drew it again using the closer estimates?

7. The diameter of Tamika's bicycle wheel is 36 cm.

a) How far will Tamika's bicycle go in one revolution?

b) The diameter of her older sister's bicycle wheel is 51 cm. Since her bicycle wheel is larger than Tamika's, how much farther will her bicycle travel in one revolution?

8. Marcus is sewing a tablecloth for a round table. He will decorate the edge of the cloth with a fringe. The diameter of the table is 45 cm. The tablecloth should be large enough that 10 cm of fabric overhang the table.

a) What length of fringe does Marcus need?

b) The store sells the fringe only in lengths that are multiples of 10 cm. What length should Marcus buy?

9. a) Use compasses to try to draw a circle with each circumference.

i) 9 cm   **ii)** 17 cm   **iii)** 28 cm

b) Measure the radius of each circle you drew in part a. Calculate each circumference. In each case, how close were you to the required circumference?

7.2 *ESTIMATING THE AREA OF A CIRCLE*

Developing the Ideas

For visitors from another planet approaching Earth, what signs of intelligent life might be visible? Some of the first signs might be certain circular patterns on the ground in western North America. Each circle is made by an irrigation system. A long pipe sprays water as it turns about the centre.

Only the part of a field that is watered by this system can produce a crop. So, farmers need to know how to calculate the area covered by the water.

In the activities below you will investigate how to estimate the area of a circle if you know its radius or diameter.

▶▶ *Through Activities*

Work with a partner or in a group. You will need some cans, a ruler, scissors, 1-cm grid paper, compasses, a protractor, and a calculator.

ACTIVITY 1

Relating the area of a circle to its radius
Carry out the following steps for each can.

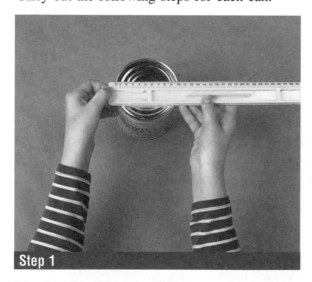

Step 1

Measure the diameter of the can and calculate its radius. Record the result to the nearest tenth of a centimetre.

Step 2

Use the can to draw a circle on the grid paper.

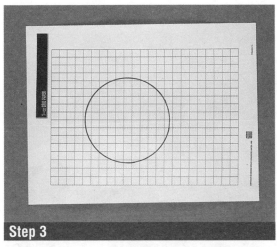

Step 3

Devise a plan for estimating the total number of squares enclosed by the circle. Use your plan to determine the area of the circle as accurately as you can. Record the result.

1. Repeat Steps 1 to 3 for the other cans. Record your results in a table. Include the results of your partner or other group members. For each circle, enter the radius in the second column and the area in the fourth column. The third column is included because we use square units when we work with area. To obtain the numbers in this column, multiply each radius by itself.

Description of can	Radius (cm)	Radius squared (cm²)	Area (cm²)

2. **a)** Compare the numbers in the *Area* column with those in the *Radius squared* column. About how many times as great do they appear to be?

   b) To check your answer, include another column in your table. Use your calculator to determine the numbers in this column. Round the numbers to one decimal place.

Description of can	Radius (cm)	Radius squared (cm²)	Area (cm²)	$\dfrac{Area}{(Radius)^2}$

3. What conclusion can you make about the area of a circle and the square of its radius?

Rearranging parts of a circle

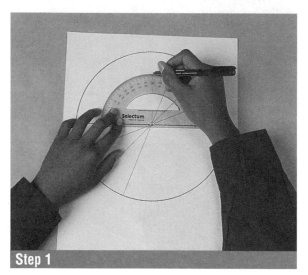

Step 1

Step 2

Use compasses to draw a large circle on a piece of heavy paper or cardboard. Use a protractor to divide the circle into equal sectors.

Cut out the circle. Cut out the sectors and rearrange them so that they appear to form a parallelogram.

1. Imagine that the figure formed by the rearranged parts is a parallelogram.
   a) How is the height of the parallelogram related to the circle? What is the height?
   b) How is the base of the parallelogram related to the circle? What is the base?
   c) What is the area of the parallelogram?
   d) How is the area of the circle related to the area of the parallelogram?

▶ ▶ *Using a Computer*

TEMPLATE DISK

In exercise 2 of *Activity 1*, you can use a spreadsheet to calculate the values of r^2 and $\dfrac{\text{Area}}{(\text{Radius})^2}$.

Start a new document in a spreadsheet program.

Input the following information. It assumes that you measured 5 cans. If you measured more or fewer cans, amend the spreadsheet to show this. In columns B and D, input the data from your table.

	A	B	C	D	E	F
1	Can	Radius	Radius^2	Area	Area/(Radius^2)	
2	1		=B2^2		=D2/C2	
3	2		=B3^2		=D3/C3	
4	3		=B4^2		=D4/C4	
5	4		=B5^2		=D5/C5	
6	5		=B6^2		=D6/C6	

▶ ▶ *Through a Guided Example*

In the preceding activities you probably discovered that the area of a circle is approximately 3 times the square of the radius.

We think: The area of a circle is approximately 3 times the square of the radius.

We write: Area of circle $\doteq$ 3 × (radius)²

This result applies for all circles, even ones that nobody has measured.

Example ....

Estimate the area of lawn watered by each sprinkler.

a)

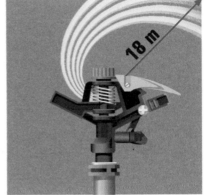

18 m

b)

◄── 4 m ──►

Solution

a) The radius is 18 m.

Area $\doteq$ 3 × (radius)²
$= 3 \times (18 \text{ m})^2$
$= 3 \times 324 \text{ m}^2$
$= 972 \text{ m}^2$

The area watered is approximately 972 m².

b) The diameter is 4 m.

The radius is $\frac{4 \text{ m}}{2} = 2$ m

Area $\doteq$ 3 × (radius)²
$= 3 \times (2 \text{ m})^2$
$= 3 \times 4 \text{ m}^2$
$= 12 \text{ m}^2$

The area watered is approximately 12 m².

BOGGLE YOUR MIND

The human circulatory system has some remarkable measurements. Here are two examples.

a) The inside surface of your blood vessels covers an area of about 800 m². How does this compare with the area of the floor in your classroom?

b) The total length of your blood vessels is about 100 000 km. How does this compare with the circumference of Earth?

Working with Mathematics

Something to talk about

1. Suppose you know the radius of a circular object. How could you estimate its area?

2. Suppose you know the diameter of a circular object. How could you estimate its area?

3. In *Activity 2*, suppose you had used smaller angles when you divided the circle into equal sectors.
   a) How would the parallelogram change?
   b) Would there be any changes in your answers to *Activity 2*, exercise 1?

4. In the diagrams below, O is the centre of the large square, and B is the midpoint of one side.
   a) Suppose you know the length of OB. How could you calculate the area of the shaded square?

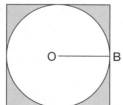

   b) Suppose you know the length of OB. How could you calculate the area of the white square?

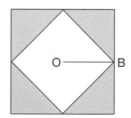

   c) Suppose you know the length of OB. How could you estimate the area of the circle?

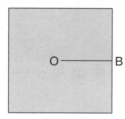

Practice

5. Estimate the area of the circle with each radius.
   a) 20.0 mm   b) 1.2 m   c) 13.0 cm
   d) 114.0 mm   e) 11.0 cm   f) 0.95 m

6. What is the radius of the circle with each diameter?
   a) 18 cm   b) 23 mm   c) 0.22 m
   d) 444 mm   e) 0.06 m   f) 50 cm

7. Estimate the area of each circle in exercise 6.

8. Estimate the radius and diameter of the circle with each area.
   a) 108.0 cm^2 b) 18.75 m^2 c) 1875.0 mm^2
   d) 45.63 m^2 e) 9408.0 mm^2 f) 1083.0 cm^2

9. Copy and complete this table.

	Diameter	Radius	Estimated area
a)	13 cm		
b)		90 mm	
c)			265.08 m^2
d)	27 cm		

Work together

10. One circle in the photograph on page 352 has a radius of 40 m. Estimate the area of the circle.

11. These four questions are designed to help you compare the circumference and area of a circle with the perimeter and area of a square. Find as many patterns as you can in the results.
    a) A and B are the midpoints of two sides of a square. Suppose you know the length of AB. How could you determine the perimeter of the square?

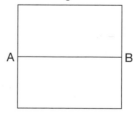

    b) AB is a diameter of the circle. Suppose you know the length of AB. How could you estimate the circumference of the circle?

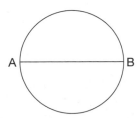

c) O is the centre of the square. Suppose you know the length of OB. How could you determine the area of the square?

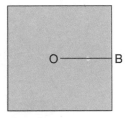

d) O is the centre of the circle. Suppose you know the length of OB. How could you estimate the area of the circle?

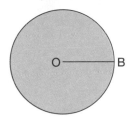

On your own

12. Farmers have been surprised to discover circular patterns of flattened plants in their fields. The crop circle below has a radius of 9 m. Estimate the area of the circle.

13. Two of Canada's largest craters are shown below. They are both in Quebec. Estimate the area of each crater, in square kilometres.
a) Manicouagan Crater, radius 35 km

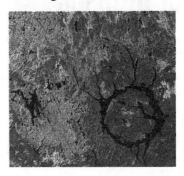

b) Crater Lake, diameter 3.2 km

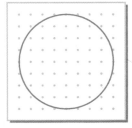

Extend your thinking

14. In *Activity 1*, instead of a grid of squares, Raji used a grid of dots spaced 1 cm apart horizontally and vertically. She claims that she can estimate the area of a circle simply by counting the number of dots inside it. Is Raji correct? Explain your answer.

The Ideas

In your journal, explain how to estimate the area of a circle if you know:
a) its radius   **b)** its diameter   **c)** its circumference

Use examples to illustrate your explanations.

Refining the Estimate of the Area of a Circle

In the preceding section, you discovered that the area of a circle is *about* 3 times the square of its radius.

Area $\doteq 3 \times (\text{radius})^2$

We will now refine this estimate so we can determine the area more accurately.

Area of a Circle

Work in a group or with a partner. Refer to the table you completed in exercise 2 on page 353.

TEMPLATE DISK

1. **a)** Write the values of $\dfrac{\text{Area}}{(\text{Radius})^2}$ you calculated for as many different circles as you can.

   b) Determine the mean of these values. Round the mean to two decimal places.
   If you used a spreadsheet on page 354, you can extend it to calculate the mean.
   In cell C13, input Mean.
   In ClarisWorks, in cell D13, input =AVERAGE(D2..D11)
   In Microsoft Works, in cell D13, input =AVERAGE(D2:D11)

   c) Compare your mean with those of other students.
   Did everyone get approximately the same result?

2. To two decimal places, the value of $\dfrac{\text{Area}}{(\text{Radius})^2}$ is 3.14.

   a) Was your mean close to 3.14?

   b) Your mean may not have been exactly 3.14 to two decimal places. Can you think of a reason for this?

We can use 3.14 to obtain an estimate that is closer to the area of a circle than when we used 3.

Area $\doteq 3.14 \times (\text{radius})^2$

3. Calculate the area of each item. Give the answers to 1 decimal place.

   a) A large pizza has a diameter of 40 cm.

   b) A car's hubcap has a radius of 14.2 cm.

   c) A compact disc has a diameter of 12.1 cm.

   d) The face of the clock in a clock tower has a radius of 3.05 m.

   e) The face-off circle in ringette has a diameter of 9 m.

   f) A small pizza has a radius of 11.5 cm.

4. Use your calculator to obtain an estimate that is closer to the area of lawn watered by each sprinkler in the *Example* on page 355.

5. The radii of circles on sports playing fields are shown in the table. Calculate the area of each circle.

Sport	Radius
a) Basketball, centre circle	1.8 m
b) Baseball, pitcher's mound	2.8 m
c) Soccer, centre circle	4.6 m

6. Two hundred computer chips are manufactured on a silicon wafer 10 cm in diameter. Calculate the approximate area of one chip.

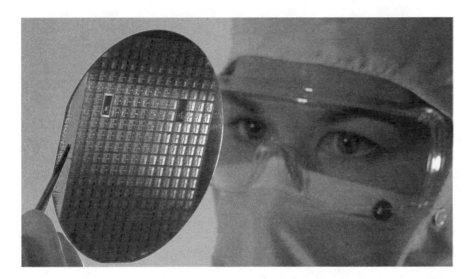

7. The photograph shows the recording surface of one side of a computer disk. Calculate the area of the recording surface.

8. Calculate each area shown in colour, rounded to the nearest tenth.

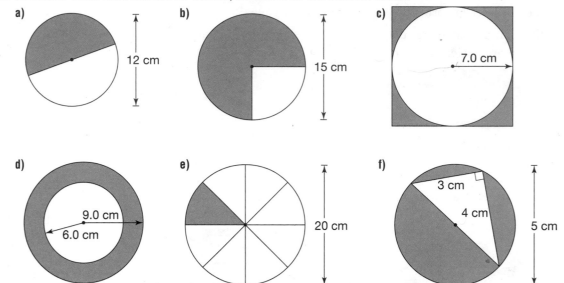

a) 12 cm

b) 15 cm

c) 7.0 cm

d) 9.0 cm 6.0 cm

e) 20 cm

f) 3 cm 4 cm 5 cm

9. a) On 1-cm grid paper, use compasses to try to draw a circle with each area.

 i) 100 cm^2 **ii)** 50 cm^2 **iii)** 25 cm^2

b) Measure the radius of each circle you drew in part a. Calculate each area. In each case, how close were you to the required area?

The value of $\dfrac{\text{Area}}{(\text{Radius})^2}$ has been determined very accurately. To ten decimal places, it is 3.141 592 653 6. The exact value of $\dfrac{\text{Area}}{(\text{Radius})^2}$ is represented by the Greek letter π (pi). Recall that π is also used to calculate the circumference of a circle.

Area $= \pi \times (\text{radius})^2$

For most calculations involving circles, it is sufficient to use 3.14 as an approximate value of π. The *TEXAS INSTRUMENTS Math Explorer* calculator has a π key. You can use this instead of 3.14.

BOGGLE YOUR **MIND**

In 1987, π was calculated to more than 100 million decimal places. If you wrote one digit each second, how long would it take you to write π to this many decimal places?

MATHEMATICS F I L E

Changing Cubic Units

The cube in the photograph
has edges 1 m long.

Since 1 m = 100 cm,
the edges are also 100 cm long.

We can express the volume of the cube in cubic metres or in cubic centimetres.

Volume in cubic metres

Volume = (area of base) × height
$$= (1 \text{ m} \times 1 \text{ m}) \times 1 \text{ m}$$
$$= 1 \text{ m}^3$$

The volume of the cube is 1 m³.

Volume in cubic centimetres

Volume = (area of base) × height
$$= (100 \text{ cm} \times 100 \text{ cm}) \times 100 \text{ cm}$$
$$= 1\ 000\ 000 \text{ cm}^3$$

The volume of the cube is 1 000 000 cm³.

$$1 \text{ m}^3 = 1\ 000\ 000 \text{ cm}^3$$

To change from cubic metres to cubic
centimetres, multiply by 1 000 000.

$$3 \text{ m}^3 = 3 \times 1\ 000\ 000 \text{ cm}^3$$
$$= 3\ 000\ 000 \text{ cm}^3$$

To change from cubic centimetres to cubic
metres, divide by 1 000 000.

$$2\ 500\ 000 \text{ cm}^3 = \frac{2\ 500\ 000}{1\ 000\ 000} \text{ m}^3$$
$$= 2.5 \text{ m}^3$$

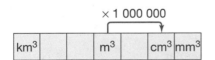

1. Suppose you filled one cubic metre completely with centimetre cubes.
   How many would you need?

2. Change to cubic centimetres.
   a) 4 m³   **b)** 50 m³   **c)** 2.4 m³   **d)** 0.5 m³

3. Change to cubic metres.
   a) 2 000 000 cm³   **b)** 1 500 000 cm³
   c) 500 000 cm³   **d)** 50 000 cm³

4. An aquarium is 60 cm long, 40 cm wide, and 40 cm high. What is the
   volume of the aquarium in cubic centimetres and in cubic metres?

7.3 *SURFACE AREA OF A TRIANGULAR PRISM*

Developing the Ideas

▶ ▶ *Using Manipulatives*

Work with a partner or in a group. You will
need 1-cm grid paper, scissors, and tape.

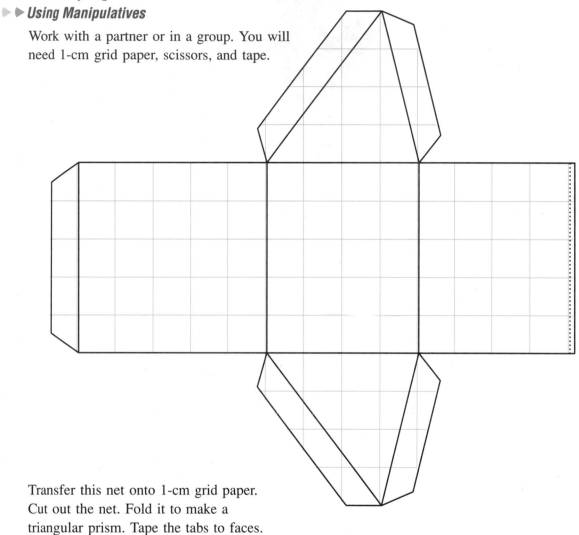

Transfer this net onto 1-cm grid paper.
Cut out the net. Fold it to make a
triangular prism. Tape the tabs to faces.

1. **a)** How many triangular faces does the prism have? How many whole
   squares can you count on each triangular face? How many part
   squares can you count on each? Estimate the area of each triangular
   face in square centimetres.

   b) How many rectangular faces does the prism have? How many
   whole squares can you count on each rectangular face? How many
   part squares can you count on each? Estimate the area of each
   rectangular face in square centimetres.

   c) *Surface area* is the area of the surface of the prism. What is the
   approximate surface area of the triangular prism?

2. In exercise 1, you found the surface area by counting squares. Explain
   how you could calculate the area of each face and the surface area of
   the triangular prism.

Example 1···

Determine the surface area of the prism.

Solution

There are three rectangular faces 30.5 cm long and 6.0 cm wide.

The area of each one is 30.5 cm × 6.0 cm = 183 cm²

The total area of these three faces is 3 × 183 cm² = 549 cm²

There are two triangular faces, each with base 6.0 cm and height 5.2 cm.

The area of each face is $\dfrac{\text{base} \ \times \ \text{height}}{2} = \dfrac{6.0 \text{ cm} \times 5.2 \text{ cm}}{2}$

$= 15.6 \text{ cm}^2$

The total area of these two faces is 2 × 15.6 cm² = 31.2 cm²

The total surface area of the prism is 549 cm² + 31.2 cm² = 580.2 cm²

To the nearest 10 cm², the surface area is 580 cm².

• • • • • • • • •

The surface area of a triangular prism is given by this formula.

Surface area = the sum of the areas of the faces

Example 2···

Find the surface area
of the play house.

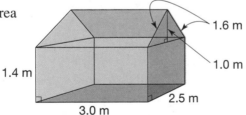

Solution

The house comprises a triangular prism on top of a rectangular prism.
Calculate the areas of the four vertical faces of the rectangular prism.

The areas are

(2 × 2.5 m × 1.4 m) + (2 × 3.0 m × 1.4 m) = 7.0 m² + 8.4 m²

$= 15.4 \text{ m}^2$

Calculate the areas of four faces of the triangular prism.

The areas are

$(2 \times \frac{1}{2} \times 2.5 \text{ m} \times 1.0 \text{ m}) + (2 \times 1.6 \text{ m} \times 3.0 \text{ m}) = 2.5 \text{ m}^2 + 9.6 \text{ m}^2$

$= 12.1 \text{ m}^2$

The surface area of the play house is 15.4 m² + 12.1 m² = 27.5 m²

Working with Mathematics

Something to talk about

1. In *Example 1* we included the areas of all the faces of the polyhedron, but in *Example 2* we did not. In a given problem, how can you tell whether to include the areas of all the faces or just some of them?

2. In *Example 2*, why did we not include the areas of the top face of the rectangular prism, and the bottom face of the triangular prism?

Practice

3. Find the area of each figure.

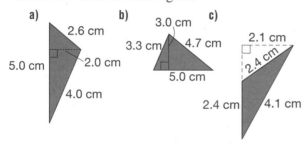

a) 2.6 cm, 5.0 cm, 2.0 cm, 4.0 cm

b) 3.0 cm, 3.3 cm, 4.7 cm, 5.0 cm

c) 2.1 cm, 2.4 cm, 2.4 cm, 4.1 cm

4. Suppose each triangle in exercise 3 were the base of a triangular prism with a height of 8.0 cm. What would be the surface area of each prism?

Work together

5. Draw a net for each prism. Estimate its surface area. Calculate its surface area.

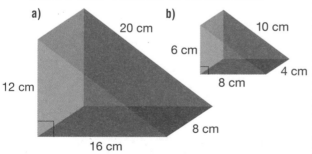

a) 20 cm, 12 cm, 16 cm, 8 cm

b) 10 cm, 6 cm, 8 cm, 4 cm

6. a) What do you notice about the surface areas in exercise 5a and b?

b) Use the measurements of the triangular prisms to explain your observation in part a.

7. Suppose you have two identical prisms like that in exercise 5b. The prisms are glued together at their rectangular faces to form a rectangular prism.

a) Sketch the rectangular prism and label it with its dimensions.

b) Calculate the surface area of the rectangular prism. Explain your method.

8. Each triangular prism below is made by stacking pattern blocks. Each triangular face of a pattern block is an equilateral triangle with side length 3.3 cm and area 4.7 cm^2. A pattern block is 0.9 cm high.

a) What is the surface area of each triangular prism?

b) Is the surface area of the larger prism twice the surface area of the smaller prism? Explain.

9. Set up a spreadsheet document. Design a spreadsheet that will calculate the surface area of any triangular prism. Use a prism in exercise 5 to check your spreadsheet. Compare your spreadsheet with that on page 377.

On your own

10. Each skeleton of a triangular prism was constructed from pipe cleaners 5 cm and 10 cm long. Calculate the area of paper needed to cover each prism.

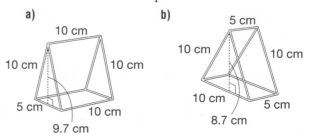

a) 10 cm, 10 cm, 10 cm, 5 cm, 10 cm, 9.7 cm

b) 5 cm, 10 cm, 10 cm, 10 cm, 5 cm, 8.7 cm

11. Calculate the surface area of this prism.

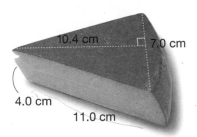

12. These pieces of cardboard will be taped together to make a triangular prism with an isosceles triangle base. Draw a net for this prism. What is the surface area of this prism?

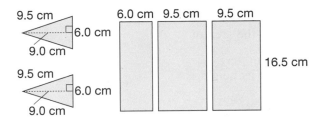

13. Calculate the surface area of this doorstop.

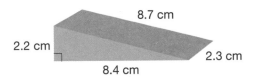

14. The diagram represents a garage with a small office attached. The diagram is not to scale.

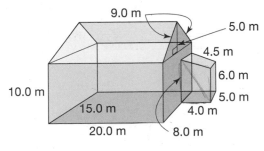

a) Estimate the surface area of the building.

b) Calculate the surface area of the building.

c) Twelve windows, each 2 m by 1.5 m, are to be installed. What percent of the wall area will the windows occupy? Give the answer to 1 decimal place.

d) A roofing sealer is applied to the roof of the garage and the office. A 20-L container will cover 50 m² of roof. How many containers must be purchased?

Extend your thinking

15. The base of a triangular prism is an equilateral triangle, with side length 3 m and area approximately 4 m². The surface area of the prism is 35 m².

a) What is the height of the prism? Explain how you calculated it.

b) What is the shape of each non-triangular face?

16. Create and solve a problem about the surface area of this object. Copy the diagram and label it with measurements that fit your problem.

Trade problems with a few classmates and compare solutions.

Explain what you learned by solving your classmates' problems.

Explain what you learned by reading your classmates' solutions for your problem.

COMMUNICATING

The Ideas

In your journal, describe how you calculate the surface area of a prism if you know its measurements. Illustrate your description with some examples.

7.4 *VOLUME OF A TRIANGULAR PRISM*

Developing the Ideas

▶▶ *Through Instruction*

Recall from earlier work that you calculated the volume of a rectangular prism by filling it with layers of centimetre cubes.

The number of cubes, including part cubes, needed to fill the prism is a measure of its volume.

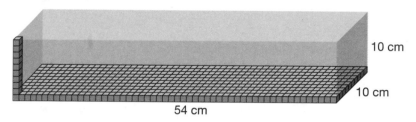

The volume of a rectangular prism is equal to the product of the area of its base and its height.

In the rectangular prism above, the base area is 540 cm^2 and its height is 10 cm.

The volume is 540 cm^2 × 10 cm = 5400 cm^3.

Imagine this rectangular prism cut in half vertically along one diagonal. This forms two congruent triangular prisms.

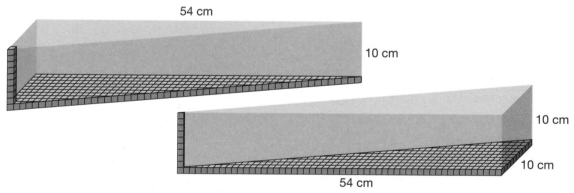

The triangular prisms have equal volumes.

The volume of each triangular prism
= $\frac{1}{2}$(base area of rectangular prism) × height
= base area of triangular prism × height

This illustrates that the volume of a triangular prism is calculated the same way as the volume of a rectangular prism.

• • • • • • • • •

Volume of a triangular prism = base area × height

Example 1

Determine the volume of concrete needed to make this wheelchair ramp.

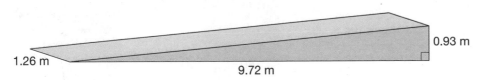

1.26 m

9.72 m

0.93 m

Solution

The ramp is a triangular prism.

The volume of the prism = base area × height

The triangular side of the ramp is the base of the prism.

The area of the triangle is $\dfrac{\text{base} \times \text{height}}{2} = \dfrac{9.72 \text{ m} \times 0.93 \text{ m}}{2}$

$\doteq 4.520 \text{ m}^2$

The height of the prism is the width of the ramp.

The volume of the ramp is $4.520 \text{ m}^2 \times 1.26 \text{ m} \doteq 5.70 \text{ m}^3$

To the nearest tenth of a cubic metre, the volume is 5.7 m^3.

Example 2

The volume of a triangular prism is 48 cm^3.

Sketch a prism with this volume. In your sketch, show the measurements of the prism.

Solution

Work backward.

The volume of a triangular prism = base area × height

Since the volume is 48 cm^3, find two numbers whose product is 48; for example, 6 and 8.

The base area could be 6 cm^2 and the height could be 8 cm.

The base of the prism is a triangle. Find the base and height of a triangle with area 6 cm^2.

The triangle could be a right triangle. Its base could be 4 cm and its height 3 cm.

Sketch the prism.

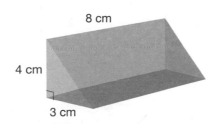

8 cm

4 cm

3 cm

Working with Mathematics

Something to talk about

1. For the prism in *Example 2*, suppose its base area is 8 cm² and its height is 6 cm. Sketch the prism.

2. For *Example 2*, describe different triangular prisms with volume 48 cm³. How many prisms are there? Explain.

3. When you determine the volume of a triangular prism, does it matter which face is taken to be the base? Explain your answer.

4. Do you think the formula for the volume of any prism is base area times height? Explain.

5. a) Each of three different triangular prisms has a volume of 36 cm³. What are some possible measurements for these prisms?
   b) Sketch two prisms from part a. Label each prism with its measurements.

Practice

6. Find the volume of each prism. Round the volumes to 1 decimal place where necessary.

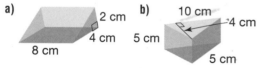

a)   2 cm   4 cm   8 cm

b)   10 cm   4 cm   5 cm   5 cm

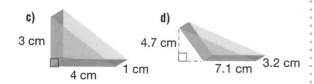

c)   3 cm   4 cm

d)   4.7 cm   1 cm   7.1 cm   3.2 cm

7. Suppose the height of each prism in exercise 6 is doubled. Sketch each prism with its new height. Calculate the volume of each prism.

8. Use the results from exercise 7. What happens to the volume of a triangular prism when its height is doubled?

9. For each height, calculate the volume of a triangular prism with base area 48 cm².
   a) 20 cm   b) 50 cm
   c) 100 cm   d) 1000 cm

Work together

10. Determine the volume of each prism.

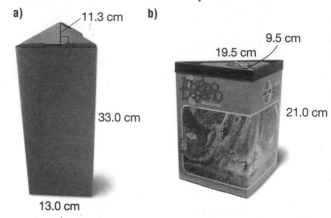

a)   11.3 cm   33.0 cm   13.0 cm

b)   9.5 cm   19.5 cm   21.0 cm

c)   3.5 cm   20.7 cm   3.0 cm

11. A barn has the dimensions shown. What is its volume?

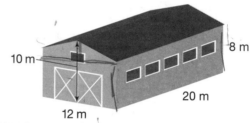

10 m   8 m   20 m   12 m

On your own

12. Each of three different triangular prisms has a volume of 120 cm³.
   a) Determine some possible dimensions for the prisms.
   b) What is the surface area of each prism in part a?
   c) Sketch three prisms from part a.

13. This diagram represents a tent. The triangles are congruent.

1.1 m   1.2 m   2.4 m

   a) Estimate the volume of air in the tent.
   b) Calculate the volume of air. How close was your estimate to the actual volume?

14. Sketch two different tents with the same volume of air as the tent in exercise 13.

15. This is one layer of a triangular prism constructed by linking small triangular prisms. The base of each small prism is a right isosceles triangle with equal sides 2 cm long. The height of each small prism is 2 cm.

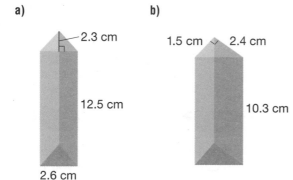

2 cm

a) Calculate the volume of one layer in this triangular prism.

b) What is the volume of a triangular prism with 8 layers? 16 layers?

16. For each height, calculate the volume of a triangular prism with base area 20 cm².

a) 15 cm   **b)** 30 cm

c) 60 cm   **d)** 120 cm

17. Determine the volume of each prism.

a)

2.3 cm

12.5 cm

2.6 cm

b)

1.5 cm   2.4 cm

10.3 cm

c)

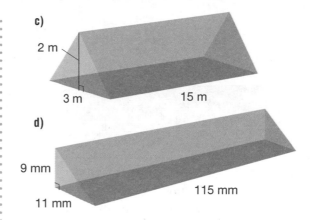

2 m

3 m   15 m

d)

9 mm

11 mm   115 mm

Extend your thinking

18. This is a graph of height against base area for triangular prisms with volume 1000 cm³. Use the graph to complete the exercise.

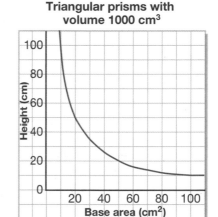

Triangular prisms with volume 1000 cm³

a) What happens to the base area when the height increases? decreases?

b) Estimate the height for each base area.

    i) 25 cm²   **ii)** 50 cm²   **iii)** 100 cm²

c) What happens to the height when the base area is doubled?

d) Estimate the base area for each height.

    i) 20 cm   **ii)** 40 cm   **iii)** 80 cm

e) What happens to the base area when the height is doubled?

f) Sketch two prisms represented by points on the graph.

The Ideas

In your journal, explain how to calculate the volume of a triangular prism.

How Much Space Is Yours?

You will need a tape measure.

Problem 1

Suppose all the floor space in your classroom were divided equally among the people in the room. How much floor space would there be per person?

Problem 2

Suppose all the space in your home were divided equally among the people who live there. How much floor space would there be per person?

Understand the problem

- What does "divided equally" mean?
- What does "per person" mean?
- What are you asked to do?

- What are you asked to do?

Think of a strategy

- You could calculate the area of the floor in your classroom and divide by the number of people.

- You could calculate the total floor area of your home and divide by the number of people who live in your home.

Carry out the strategy

- Measure the floor in your classroom.
- Calculate the area of the floor in square metres.
- How many people are there in your classroom?
- Divide the area of the floor by the number of people.
- How much floor space is there per person? This is the population density.

- Measure the floors in your home.
- Calculate the total area of all the floors in your home.
- Divide the total area of the floors by the number of people who live in your home.
- How much floor space is there per person? This is the population density.

Look back

- How would your floor space change if one more person entered the room?
- How would your floor space change if one person left the room?

- Find out the area and the population of the town or region where you live. How much space is there per person?

Communicating the Ideas

In your journal, write a description of this problem and your solution. Include an explanation of how to calculate population density.

7.5 *VOLUME IN CAPACITY UNITS*

Developing the Ideas

Many products are sold in packages marked in litres or millilitres. To find how these units of volume are related to cubic centimetres, complete the following activity.

▶▶ *Through an Activity*

Work with a partner. You will need a large box of juice and a ruler.

1. **a)** Measure the length, width, and height of the box.
   b) Calculate its volume in cubic centimetres.

2. Compare the volume in cubic centimetres with the volume in millilitres marked on the box.
   a) How do you think millilitres and cubic centimetres are related?
   b) How do you think litres and cubic centimetres are related?

▶▶ *Through Instruction*

Litres and millilitres are units of volume called capacity units. Capacity units are used for volumes of liquids and gases.

One millilitre is the same as one cubic centimetre.
One litre is 1000 times as large.
Hence, one litre is the same as one thousand cubic centimetres.

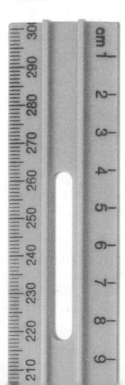

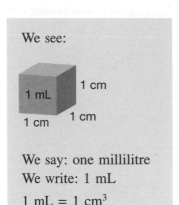

We see:

1 mL

1 cm
1 cm
1 cm

We say: one millilitre
We write: 1 mL

$1 \text{ mL} = 1 \text{ cm}^3$

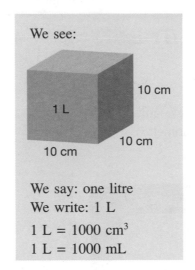

We see:

1 L

10 cm
10 cm
10 cm

We say: one litre
We write: 1 L

$1 \text{ L} = 1000 \text{ cm}^3$
$1 \text{ L} = 1000 \text{ mL}$

▶ ▶ **Through a Guided Example**

Example ···

a) Change to millilitres: 3 L   1.8 L
b) Change to litres: 2500 mL   450 mL

Solution

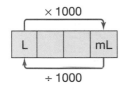

× 1000

| L | | | mL |

÷ 1000

a) *Changing to a smaller unit:*

3 L = 3000 mL   ◄ Multiplying by 1000
1.8 L = 1800 mL   ◄ Multiplying by 1000

b) *Changing to a larger unit:*

2500 mL = 2.5 L   ◄ Dividing by 1000
450 mL = 0.45 L   ◄ Dividing by 1000

BOGGLE YOUR **MIND**

If all the fresh water on Earth were collected, it would fill a cube with edges about 289 km. Almost all of this is ice. If all the ice were collected, it would fill a cube with edges about 287 km. On Earth, how much fresh water is there that is not ice?

Working with Mathematics

Something to talk about

1. On packages of food, give some reasons why the volume in cubic centimetres is not equal to the number of millilitres.

2. Which unit (litre or millilitre) would you use to describe each volume?
   a) shampoo in a bottle
   b) water in a swimming pool
   c) juice in a glass
   d) air in a hot-air balloon

3. Which unit would make each estimate reasonable?
   a) volume of milk in a carton, 250 ■
   b) volume of juice in a can, 1.36 ■
   c) volume of oil in a teaspoon, 5 ■
   d) volume of water in a hot tub, 1000 ■

Practice

4. Convert each volume to millilitres.
   a) 24 cm^3 b) 9.7 cm^3
   c) 1 L   d) 2 L
   e) 0.1 L   f) 0.4 L
   g) 0.35 L   h) 0.21 L
   i) 1.8 L   j) 4.18 L

5. Convert each volume to litres.
   a) 3000 mL   b) 8000 mL
   c) 300 mL   d) 900 mL
   e) 1500 mL   f) 2900 mL
   g) 246 mL   h) 68 mL
   i) 158 cm^3 j) 29 cm^3

6. Convert each volume to cubic centimetres.
   a) 1400 mL   b) 1800 mL
   c) 5 L   d) 9 L
   e) 0.24 L   f) 0.38 L
   g) 0.029 L   h) 0.066 L
   i) 1.6 L   j) 2.5 L

Work together

7. Express each volume in millilitres and in cubic centimetres.

   a)   b)

8. Express each volume in litres and in cubic centimetres.

   a)   b)

   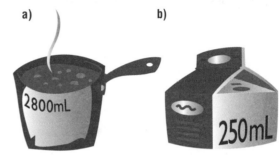

9. Choose the best estimate of each volume.
   a) the volume of liquid in a bowl
      20 L   200 mL   2 L

   b) the volume of oil in a tablespoon
      1 mL   10 mL   100 mL

   c) the volume of pop in a can of cola
      280 mL   2.8 L   28 mL
   d) the volume of fuel in a car's tank
      4 L   400 mL   40 L

10. An Olympic swimming pool has the dimensions shown.

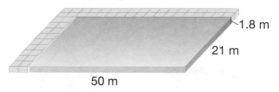

a) How many litres of water will fill the pool?

b) How long would it take to pump the water from the pool at 60 L/min?

11. Discuss how you would determine the volumes of objects like these: a rock, a light bulb, a pencil eraser, a marker, a roll of tape, and a tube of toothpaste. Obtain some objects like these and determine their volumes.

On your own

12. Copy and complete.

a) 3 L = ▮ mL   b) 2000 mL = ▮ L

c) 500 mL = ▮ L   d) 4.5 L = ▮ mL

e) 0.25 L = ▮ mL   f) 3200 mL = ▮ L

13. Copy and complete.

a) 150 mL = ▮ cm³   b) 375 mL = ▮ cm³

c) 2 L = ▮ cm³   d) 750 cm³ = ▮ mL

e) 1200 cm³ = ▮ mL   f) 525 cm³ = ▮ L

14. A bowl containing 6 L of punch is shared equally among 15 people. How many millilitres is each person's share?

15. Estimate each volume in millilitres or litres.

a)   b)

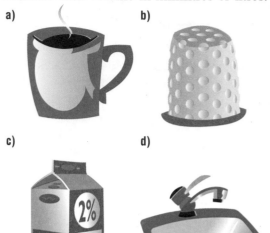

c)   d)

16. How many 250-mL glasses can be filled from a bowl containing 4.5 L of punch?

17. Some juice drinks come in 250-mL boxes.

a) Measure a drink box like this one.

b) Calculate its volume in cubic centimetres.

c) Does the result confirm that the box holds 250 mL of juice?

18. How many litres of water are needed to fill an aquarium that is 60 cm long, 30 cm wide, and 35 cm high?

Extend your thinking

19. a) Suppose 10 L of water were poured into the empty aquarium in exercise 18. How high will the water level rise?

b) How high will the water level rise if 20 L of water are poured in?

COMMUNICATING

The Ideas

In your journal, explain how cubic units and capacity units are related.

Review

1. A round table has a diameter of 1.4 m.
   a) Estimate the circumference of the table.
   b) Calculate the circumference of the table. How close was your estimate?

2. A plate has a circumference of 66 cm.
   a) Estimate the diameter of the plate.
   b) Calculate the diameter of the plate. How close was your estimate?

3. Earth's radius is about 6400 km.
   a) Calculate the diameter of Earth.
   b) Estimate the circumference of Earth.

4. Calculate the diameter and estimate the circumference of each planet.

	Planet	Radius (km)
a)	Mercury	2450
b)	Venus	6050
c)	Mars	3400
d)	Jupiter	69 950
e)	Saturn	58 300
f)	Uranus	25 350
g)	Neptune	24 600
h)	Pluto	1150

5. Find the circumference of each wheel.
   a) with 15 cm radius
   b) with 11 cm radius
   c) with 22.4 cm radius

6. Calculate the circumference of a circle with each diameter.
   a) 28.26 cm   b) 17.27 cm   c) 10.2 cm

7. A circular racetrack has a diameter of 0.36 km. Cherie drove her go-kart 12 laps of the track. Calculate the distance she covered, rounded to the nearest tenth of a metre.

8. Calculate the circumference of the circle with each diameter.
   a) 3 cm   b) 5.5 m   c) 2.8 km   d) 3.7 mm

9. Calculate the area of the circle with each diameter.
   a) 4 m   b) 11.1 cm   c) 13.5 km   d) 27.2 mm

10. Find the area of each coloured region, rounded to the nearest tenth of a square centimetre.

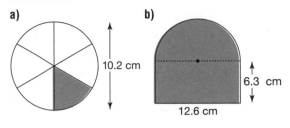

a)   b)

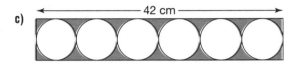

c)

11. The four walls of a bedroom are to be painted. The bedroom is 5.6 m long, 4.2 m wide, and 2.3 m high.
    a) Calculate the total area of the walls.
    b) From the total area, subtract 3.6 m² for the doors and 2.5 m² for the windows. The remaining area will be painted.
    c) One litre of paint covers 10 m². How much paint is needed for two coats?

12. Find the surface area of each solid.

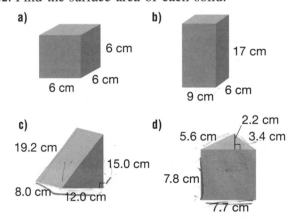

13. A storage room has length 7.4 m, width 3.9 m, and height 3.1 m.
    a) Find the surface area of the four walls.
    b) One sheet of panelling covers 3 m². How many sheets are needed to cover the walls?

14. a) Find the edge length of a cube with each surface area.

   i) 24 cm²   **ii)** 54 cm²   **iii)** 600 cm²

   b) If you know the surface area of a cube, how can you find its edge length?

15. The area of the base and the height of each prism are given. Calculate its volume.

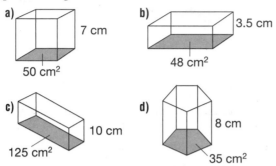

a) 7 cm, 50 cm²

b) 3.5 cm, 48 cm²

c) 10 cm, 125 cm²

d) 8 cm, 35 cm²

16. Calculate the volume of each prism.

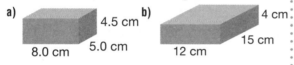

a) 4.5 cm, 8.0 cm, 5.0 cm

b) 4 cm, 12 cm, 15 cm

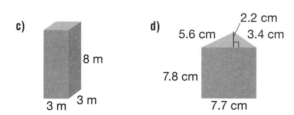

c) 8 m, 3 m, 3 m

d) 2.2 cm, 5.6 cm, 3.4 cm, 7.8 cm, 7.7 cm

17. An excavation for the foundation of a building measures 40 m by 25 m by 12 m. How many truckloads of earth must be removed if each truck holds 4.5 m³?

18. Find the volume of each oven.

   a) microwave: 60.0 cm by 40.0 cm by 44.5 cm

   b) toaster: 45.0 cm by 20.0 cm by 23.5 cm

19. How many different rectangular prisms can you find with natural number dimensions and a volume of 24 cm³?

20. You will need some masking tape and enough metre sticks to make a cubic metre like the one in the photograph on page 361.

   a) How many metre sticks do you need? Using masking tape to hold the ends of the metre sticks together, make your cubic metre.

   b) Find out how many students can fit inside the cubic metre.

   c) Suppose your classroom were filled with students from the floor to the ceiling. Measure your classroom. Use your answer to part b to estimate how many students would fill the space in your classroom.

21. Change to cubic centimetres.

   a) 3 m³   **b)** 8000 mm³
   c) 6.7 mm³   **d)** 7500 mm³
   e) 84 500 mm³   **f)** 0.56 m³
   g) 1.25 m³   **h)** 550 mm³

22. Change to cubic metres.

   a) 63 000 cm³   **b)** 127 000 cm³
   c) 8 km³   **d)** 9.2 km³
   e) 0.72 km³   **f)** 3 500 000 cm³
   g) 0.04 km³   **h)** 5.03 km³

23. Find each volume in cubic centimetres and in cubic millimetres.

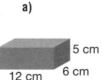

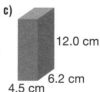

a) 5 cm, 12 cm, 6 cm

b) 20 mm, 20 mm, 20 mm

c) 12.0 cm, 6.2 cm, 4.5 cm

24. What unit (litre or millilitre) would you use to describe each volume?

   a) a large can of paint
   b) toothpaste in a tube
   c) a teacup
   d) water in an aquarium
   e) an oil drum
   f) perfume in a bottle

Surface Area on a Spreadsheet

We shall use a spreadsheet to investigate what happens to the surface area when the dimensions of a prism change.

Set up a spreadsheet document. Enter the information shown below.

TEMPLATE DISK

	A	B	C	D	E
1	Surface area of a rectangular prism				
2					
3	Length				
4	Width				
5	Height				
6	Area of base	=B3*B4			
7	Area of front	=B4*B5			
8	Area of end	=B3*B5			
9	Surface area	=2*B6+2*B7+2*B8			

1. Look at the formulas in cells B6 to B9. What does each formula tell the computer to do?

2. Choose a rectangular prism.
   a) Measure its length. Enter that number in cell B3.
   b) Measure its width. Enter that number in cell B4.
   c) Measure its height. Enter that number in cell B5.

3. Put the mouse in cell B3. Hold down the button and drag the mouse to cell E9. With all the cells from B3 to E9 highlighted, select Fill Right. Explain what happened.

4. Explore what happens to the surface area when one dimension is doubled.
   a) In cell C3, type =B3*2
   What happened to the areas in rows 6 to 9? Explain.
   b) In cell D4, type =B4*2
   What happened to the areas in rows 6 to 9? Explain.
   c) In cell E5, type =B5*2
   What happened to the areas in rows 6 to 9? Explain.

5. Explore what happens to the surface area if two dimensions are doubled.

6. Explore what happens to the surface area if all three dimensions are doubled.

7. Based on your observations, predict what will happen to the surface area if one, two, or three dimensions are tripled. Use the spreadsheet to check your prediction.

8. Change the spreadsheet to calculate the surface area of a triangular prism. Find out what happens to the surface area when you change one, two, or three dimensions of the prism.

Investigating Enlargements of Photographs

Photo finishers still use inches to describe the sizes of photographs. When you have a film developed, you can often choose 4" by 6" prints or $3\frac{1}{2}$" by 5" prints. When you have an enlargement made, it is made from a negative, not a print.

Kara wanted an enlargement of one of her favourite photographs. She took the negative to the photo-finishing store and ordered an 8" by 10" enlargement. When she got it back she noticed that it was not exactly the same as the original photograph. Parts of the photograph were missing at the top and the bottom.

In this project you will investigate different sizes of enlargements and find out how much of a photograph is missing when you get an enlargement.

ACTIVITY 1

- On page 378, measure the length and width of the negative.
- Visualize the negative growing in size until its width covers the entire width of an 8" by 10" enlargement. Calculate how long the photograph should be.
- From paper, cut one rectangle the size of the enlarged negative and one the size of the print Kara ordered. Place one on top of the other. What do you notice?
- Calculate the percent of the photograph that is missing when the enlargement is made from the negative.
- Why is it not possible to make an enlargement of the negative fit on the 8" by 10" photographic paper?

ACTIVITY 2

To do this activity you will need to gather some data.
- Get a negative and measure its length and width.
- Visit a photo-finishing store and find out the sizes of enlargements that are available.
- Repeat Activity 1 for each size of enlargement.
- For which enlargement is no part of the photograph chopped off?

ACTIVITY 3

On page 378, parts of the photograph are missing at the top and the bottom. Sometimes, parts of a photograph may be missing at the sides.
- Suppose you know the dimensions of the negative and the dimensions of the enlargement. How can you tell whether parts of the photograph will be missing at the top and bottom, or at the sides, or not at all?

The Ideas

Prepare a report or a display to illustrate the results of your investigations. Include an explanation of why you think the length to width ratios of some enlargements are not necessarily equal to the length to width ratios of negatives.

Cumulative Review

1. A school's basketball team sponsored a "Thanksgiving Turkey Shoot" to raise money. Each student paid $1.00 to shoot 25 foul shots. The student with the best score was awarded a prize. Here are the scores for the grade 8 students who participated.

12	18	21	8	16	11	14	4
9	8	13	17	23	7	12	5
14	12	6	13	18	17	22	

   a) Draw a stem-and-leaf diagram to display these data.
   b) Find the mean and the median scores.
   c) Determine the range and the quartiles.
   d) Draw a box-and-whisker plot.
   e) Display these data graphically.

2. Use the circle graph on page 112. What fraction of the world's total land area are:
   a) Asia and Africa together?
   b) Asia, Africa, and North America together?

3. Replace each ▆ by a number so that the quotient is close to 1.5.
   $$\frac{\blacksquare}{3} \div \frac{\blacksquare}{7}$$

4. Oil spilled from a supertanker covers two-thirds of a bay. The area of the bay is 4.5 km².
   a) Find the area of the oil spill.
   b) Clean-up crews reduce the area of the oil spill by one-third.
      i) What fraction of the bay is still covered by oil?
      ii) What area of the bay is still covered by oil?

5. Use your fraction strips and number lines to add.
   a) $\frac{1}{3} + \frac{1}{3}$ b) $\frac{1}{6} + \frac{1}{3}$ c) $\frac{3}{5} + \frac{1}{2}$
   d) $\frac{1}{3} + \frac{1}{4}$ e) $\frac{2}{5} + \frac{3}{10}$ f) $\frac{5}{8} + \frac{1}{2}$
   g) $\frac{3}{4} + \frac{5}{6}$ h) $\frac{1}{4} + \frac{3}{8} + \frac{1}{2}$ i) $\frac{1}{3} + \frac{3}{4} + \frac{3}{2}$

6. In a survey about cheddar cheese, $\frac{2}{5}$ of the people preferred mild cheddar, $\frac{1}{4}$ preferred medium, and $\frac{3}{10}$ preferred old.

The remaining people did not like any type of cheddar cheese.
   a) What fraction of the people surveyed liked cheddar cheese?
   b) What fraction of the people surveyed preferred medium or old cheddar cheese?
   c) What fraction of the people surveyed did not like any type of cheddar cheese?

7. Use your fraction strips and number lines to subtract.
   a) $\frac{1}{4} - \frac{1}{6}$ b) $\frac{11}{12} - \frac{1}{2}$ c) $\frac{3}{2} - \frac{1}{3}$
   d) $1 - \frac{7}{8}$ e) $\frac{7}{10} - \frac{3}{5}$ f) $2 - \frac{5}{6}$
   g) $\frac{11}{6} - \frac{5}{3}$ h) $2 - \frac{5}{4}$ i) $\frac{3}{2} - \frac{2}{3} - \frac{1}{6}$

8. Chris needs a total of 10 m of ribbon to complete a rug. She already has the following lengths: $1\frac{1}{2}$ m gold, $1\frac{1}{4}$ m red, $2\frac{1}{5}$ m blue, $\frac{3}{4}$ m orange, and $1\frac{2}{5}$ m green.
   a) What is the total length of ribbon Chris has?
   b) Chris wants to complete the rug with yellow ribbon. How much yellow ribbon does she need?

9. Use your fraction strips and number lines to multiply.
   a) $\frac{1}{4} \times 4$ b) $\frac{1}{12} \times 15$ c) $1 \times \frac{1}{6}$
   d) $2 \times \frac{2}{3}$ e) $\frac{3}{4} \times \frac{1}{2}$ f) $\frac{5}{4} \times \frac{4}{5}$
   g) $\frac{3}{2} \times \frac{1}{3}$ h) $\frac{1}{2} \times \frac{7}{6}$ i) $\frac{3}{2} \times \frac{2}{5}$

10. Three statements about the product of two numbers are given. Decide whether each statement is true or false. Illustrate your answer with examples.
   a) The product can sometimes be greater than both numbers.
   b) The product can sometimes be less than both numbers.
   c) The product can sometimes be greater than one number and less than the other number.

11. A hard fast-ball thrown by a top pitcher can exceed a speed of 150 km/h. How long would it take for a ball thrown at that speed to travel the 18 m from the pitcher's mound to home plate?

12. Abdul is a marathon runner. He can average a distance of 1 km every 5 min.
    a) At this speed, how far would he run in 2 h?
    b) How long would it take him to run 30 km?
    c) What is his average speed in kilometres per hour?
    d) Make a table showing how far Abdul can run for times up to 5 h.
    e) Use the data in the table to draw a graph.
    f) Write a formula to determine how far Abdul could run if you know the time he took. Test your formula using some of the number pairs in your table.
    g) Write a formula to determine the time Abdul took to run if you know the distance. Test your formula using some of the number pairs in the table.
    h) Would it be realistic to extend the pattern of the table or graph endlessly? Explain.

13. A quality-control inspector examines 120 cans of paint. She finds 6 cans substandard.
    a) What percent is substandard?
    b) What percent is acceptable?

14. The circle graph on page 246 shows that northern cod was about two-thirds of the total fish caught off the shores of Newfoundland in 1988. The table below shows the masses of the other fish caught—the remaining one-third of the total fish caught.

Redfish	76 000 t
Flatfsh	59 000 t
Pollock	43 000 t
Haddock	30 000 t
Halibut	13 000 t
Miscellaneous	6000 t

a) Construct a graph to illustrate these data.
b) Of the fish that are not cod, what fraction is:
   i) flatfish?
   ii) redfish and flatfish combined?
   iii) haddock, halibut, and pollock combined?
c) Make up your own question about the graph you drew. Give it to a classmate to answer.

15. A spinner is constructed as shown. The pointer is spun.

a) List the possible outcomes. How many different outcomes are there?
b) Are all the outcomes equally likely? Explain.
c) What is the probability of the pointer landing on 2?
d) What is the probability of the pointer landing on 3?

16. Simplify.
    a) $(+3) + (+2) + (+1)$ b) $(-3) + (-4) + (-7)$
    c) $(-5) + (+3) + (-2)$ d) $(+9) - (+4) - (-7)$
    e) $(-3) - (+4) - (+1)$ f) $(-2)(-1)(-2)$
    g) $(-1)(-1)(-1)$ h) $(-13)(-2)$
    i) $(8)(-3)$ j) $(-14) \div (-2)$
    k) $\frac{-54}{18}$ l) $\frac{120}{-30}$

17. An airplane is at an altitude of 800 m. It descends 100 m, climbs 300 m, then descends another 400 m. What is its altitude now?

18. Suppose you are 35 m from your school. You walk 20 m toward the school, then walk 8 m away from the school, then walk another 15 m from the school. What is your distance from the school?

ALGEBRA

Minds on Math Project

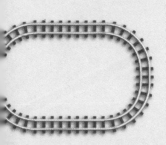

Start With What You Know

Work with a partner or in a group.

1. Look at the pattern of rectangles below. Suppose the pattern were continued.

1

2

3

a) Draw the next three rectangles in the pattern.

b) Copy and complete this table.

Diagram number	Number of green squares	Number of purple squares
1	1	1
2	2	4
3	3	9

c) What pattern do you see in the number of green squares? In the number of purple squares?

d) In the 10th diagram, how many squares are green? How many are purple?

e) In any diagram, how can you find the number of purple squares if you know the number of green squares?

2. Look at this photograph taken in the quality control department of a bakery.

a) How many buns are in each tray?

b) Copy and complete this table. Describe the pattern in the number of buns.

Number of trays	1	2	3	4	5
Number of buns					

c) If you know how many trays there are, how can you determine the number of buns?

d) Let t represent the number of trays. Write an expression to describe the number of buns.

3. Look at each number pattern on the facing page.

a) Describe each pattern in words.

b) What will be the 10th number in each pattern?

c) What will be the 30th number in each pattern?

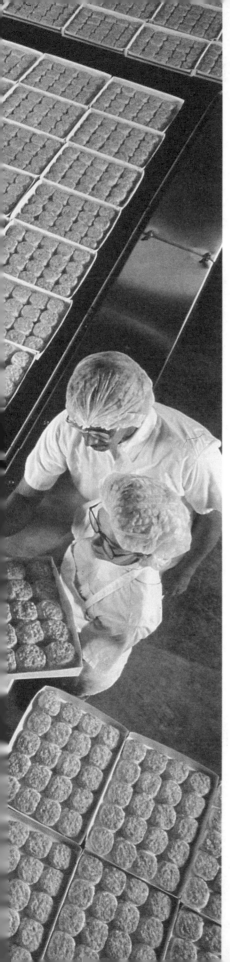

d) Write an expression to describe the nth number in each pattern.
  i) 7, 14, 21, 28, 35,…
  ii) 5, 6, 7, 8, 9,…
  iii) 11, 22, 33, 44, 55,…

4. By substituting the values 1, 2, 3, and so on, into each expression in parts i to iv below we obtain a pattern.
  a) For each pattern, make a table like the one below. Write the first 6 numbers in each pattern.

Counter	1	2	3	4	5	6
Number						

  b) The number 32 appears in each pattern. Use an equation to determine the counter for 32 in each pattern.
    i) $x + 2$ **ii)** $4p$ **iii)** $40 - s$ **iv)** $\dfrac{y}{2}$

5. a) Write two different expressions for 15, such as 3×5 or $18 - 3$.
  b) Write these expressions as opposite sides of an equation. How do you know the equation is true?
  c) Replace one of the numbers in your equation by a variable. Ask a classmate to determine the value of the variable in your equation.
  d) Repeat parts a to c for the numbers 36 and 21.

6. Look at the pattern of figures. Suppose the pattern were continued.

  a) On grid paper, draw the next three figures in this pattern.
  b) The length of one small square on the grid is 1 unit. Find the perimeter of each of the six figures in the pattern. Copy and complete the table below.

Length of side (units)	1	2	3	4	5	6
Perimeter of figure (units)						

  c) If you know the side length of a figure in the pattern, how can you calculate its perimeter?
  d) Let s represent the side length of a figure in the pattern and let P represent its perimeter. Write an equation to calculate P if you know s.
  e) Use your equation from part d to determine the perimeter of a figure with side length 10 units.
  f) Use your equation from part d to determine the side length of a figure with perimeter 52 units.

8.1 *SUBSTITUTING INTO FORMULAS*

Developing the Ideas

▶ ▶ *Through Discussion*

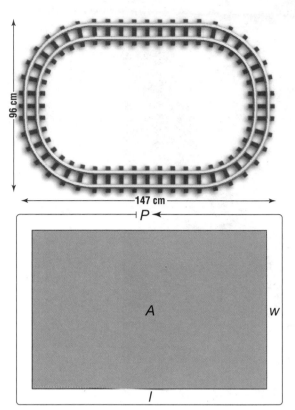

The Bui family is setting up a new model train set. The model includes an oval train track with a width of 96 cm and a length of 147 cm. The family is building a rectangular plywood base just large enough to hold the train set. The base will be painted and edged with wooden moulding. The Buis want to know the area of the surface they will have to paint and the amount of moulding they will have to buy.

The smallest rectangular base that will hold the train set has a width of 96 cm and a length of 147 cm.

The area of a rectangle is equal to the product of its length and width. We can write this as a *formula*. A mathematical formula is a rule or statement expressed in symbols.

$$\text{area} = \text{length} \times \text{width}$$

We can write this formula using single letters to represent the variables.

$$A = l \times w$$

The moulding is placed around the base. To determine how much they need, the Buis must calculate the perimeter of the rectangular base.

The perimeter of a rectangle is equal to the sum of twice its length and twice its width. We can write this as a formula.

$$\text{perimeter} = 2 \times \text{length} + 2 \times \text{width}$$

We can write this formula using single letters to represent the variables.

$$P = 2 \times l + 2 \times w$$

We do not need to write the multiplication signs in a formula.
$A = lw$ and $P = 2l + 2w$

1. **a)** Calculate the area of the plywood base in square centimetres. How many square metres is this?
   b) The Buis have half a can of green craft paint left over from an earlier project. According to the label, a full can of paint will cover 4 m². Is there enough paint left in the can to cover the top of the plywood base with one coat?

2. **a)** Calculate the perimeter of the plywood base.
   b) The Buis' local hardware store sells moulding in 2-m lengths. How many pieces should they buy?
   c) How much will the moulding cost if each piece costs $3.95?

In the preceding chapter, you reviewed or learned the formulas below. In each formula we use single letters to represent the variables.

Rectangle

Area = length × width
$A = lw$

Parallelogram
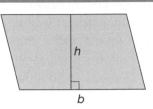
Area = base × height
$A = bh$

Triangle
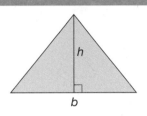
Area = $\dfrac{\text{base} \times \text{height}}{2}$
$A = \dfrac{bh}{2}$

Trapezoid
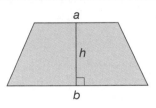
Area = $\dfrac{(\text{sum of parallel sides}) \times \text{height}}{2}$
$A = \dfrac{(a + b) \times h}{2}$

Circle

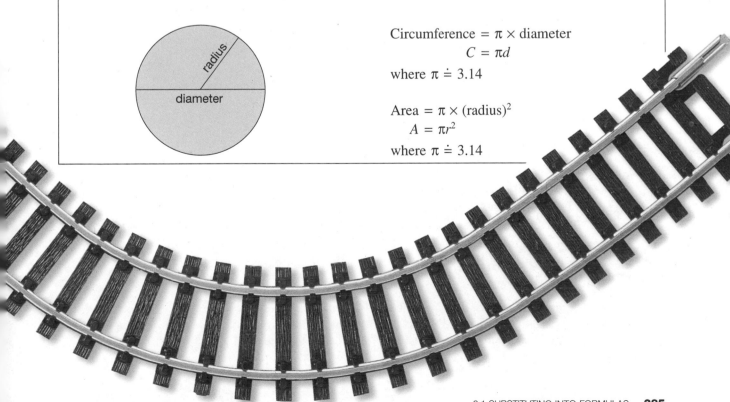

Circumference = π × diameter

$$C = \pi d$$

where $\pi \doteq 3.14$

Area = π × (radius)^2

$$A = \pi r^2$$

where $\pi \doteq 3.14$

Through Guided Examples

Example 1

Determine the area and the circumference of a circle with radius 8 cm.

Solution

The formula for the circumference of a circle is $C = \pi d$, where d is its diameter. Since the radius is 8 cm, the diameter is 16 cm. Substitute 3.14 for π and 16 for d in the formula.

$$\begin{aligned} C &= \pi d \\ &\doteq 3.14 \times 16 \\ &\doteq 50.24 \end{aligned}$$

The circumference of the circle is about 50 cm.

The formula for the area of a circle is $A = \pi r^2$, where r is its radius. Substitute 3.14 for π and 8 for r in the formula.

$$\begin{aligned} A &= \pi r^2 \\ &\doteq 3.14 \times 8^2 \\ &\doteq 3.14 \times 64 \\ &\doteq 200.96 \end{aligned}$$

The area of the circle is about 201 cm^2.

If you have a π key on your calculator, you can use it instead of 3.14 in calculations involving π.

Example 2

A triangle has an area of 24 cm^2. Its base is 6 cm. Calculate its height.

Solution

The formula for the area of a triangle is $A = \frac{bh}{2}$, where b is its base and h is its height. Substitute 24 for A and 6 for b in the formula.

$$A = \frac{bh}{2}$$

$$24 = \frac{6 \times h}{2}$$

To find the value of h, we think: What number multiplied by 6, then divided by 2 gives 24?
We know that $6 \times 8 = 48$, and $48 \div 2 = 24$. So, $h = 8$
The height of the triangle is 8 cm.

BOGGLE YOUR MIND

On average, at every Toronto Blue Jays home game, 25 baseballs end up in the stands because of home runs or foul balls. How many balls would this be in a typical season? Each ball costs \$12. How much would the team spend on lost baseballs in a season?

Example 3

Tameika sells computer and electronics equipment. She earns $550 per week, plus a 2% commission on all her sales. Her weekly earnings, E dollars, can be represented by the formula $E = 550 + 0.02s$, where s dollars is her weekly sales.

a) Calculate Tameika's earnings for these weekly sales.

  i) $7250   ii) $11 600

b) What would Tameika's sales have to be for her to earn $850?

c) Draw a graph to show how the amount of money Tameika earns is related to the amount of merchandise she sells. Describe the graph.

d) Use the graph to estimate Tameika's earnings for weekly sales of $8500. Use the graph to estimate her weekly sales if her earnings are $1000.

Solution

a) i) Substitute 7250 for s in the formula.

$E = 550 + 0.02s$
$\quad = 550 + 0.02(7250)$
$\quad = 550 + 145$
$\quad = 695$
Tameika earns $695.

ii) Substitute 11 600 for s in the formula.

$E = 550 + 0.02s$
$\quad = 550 + 0.02(11\ 600)$
$\quad = 550 + 232$
$\quad = 782$
Tameika carns $782.

b) Substitute a value for s in the formula. Compare the resulting value of E to $850. Adjust the value of s accordingly. Repeat until E is equal to $850.
Tameika would have to sell $15 000 worth of merchandise to earn $850.

s	$550 + 0.02s$	Equal to 850?
13 000	810	No; try a greater value of s.
16 000	870	No; try a smaller value of s.
15 000	850	Yes

c) Use the data from parts a and b.
Create a table of values and draw a graph.

Weekly sales ($)	Weekly earnings ($)
0	550
7 250	695
11 600	782
15 000	850

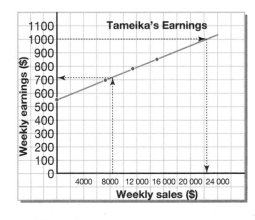

The graph is a straight line passing through (0, 550).
The graph leans upwards to the right.

d) Starting from $8500 on the *Weekly sales* axis, draw a vertical line to intersect the graph. From there, draw a horizontal line to the *Weekly earnings* axis. This indicates weekly earnings of slightly more than $700.
Starting from $1000 on the *Weekly earnings* axis, draw a horizontal line to intersect the graph. From there, draw a vertical line to the *Weekly sales* axis. This indicates weekly sales of about $22 500.

Working with Mathematics

Something to talk about

1. Identify all the variables in the formulas for the perimeter and area of a rectangle.

2. What does "substitute for a variable in a formula" mean?

3. Determine the area of a rectangle with each pair of measurements.
   a) length 8 cm, width 6 cm
   b) length 16 m, width 5 m
   c) length 12 m, width 2.5 m

Practice

4. Use the formula $P = 2l + 2w$ to calculate the perimeter of each rectangle.
   a) $l = 4$ m, $w = 2$ m
   b) $l = 6$ km, $w = 3$ km
   c) $l = 7$ km, $w = 10$ km

5. Use the formula $A = bh$ to calculate the area of each parallelogram.
   a) $b = 3.8$ cm, $h = 2.9$ cm
   b) $b = 5.7$ km, $h = 1.9$ km
   c) $b = 4.6$ m, $h = 1.3$ m

6. Use the formula $A = \dfrac{bh}{2}$ to calculate the area of each triangle.
   a) $b = 3$ cm, $h = 5$ cm
   b) $b = 9$ cm, $h = 7$ cm
   c) $b = 2.5$ cm, $h = 3.5$ cm

7. Use the formula $A = \pi r^2$ to calculate the area of each circle. Give the answers to 1 decimal place.
   a) $r = 2$ cm   b) $r = 3.5$ cm   c) $r = 0.2$ cm

8. Use the formula $C = \pi d$ to calculate the circumference of each circle in exercise 7. Give the answers to 1 decimal place.

9. Use the formula $A = \dfrac{(a + b) \times h}{2}$ to calculate the area of each trapezoid.
   a) $a = 5.0$ cm, $b = 6.3$ cm, $h = 1.9$ cm
   b) $a = 2.3$ cm, $b = 1.2$ cm, $h = 5.4$ cm
   c) $h = 12.3$ m, $a = 14.6$ m, $b = 10.4$ m
   d) $b = 8.7$ m, $h = 9.6$ m, $a = 11.5$ m

Work together

10. One measure of tree size used by foresters is the diameter at breast height, or DBH. Breast height is about 1.3 m above the ground. A tree has a DBH of 51 cm.
    a) What is the tree's circumference at this height?
    b) Suppose you were to cut the tree at this height. What would be the area of the exposed surface?

11. Determine the width of the rectangle with each pair of measurements.
    a) length 9 cm, area 63 cm^2

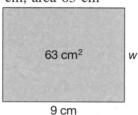

    b) length 14 cm, area 70 cm^2

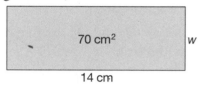

    c) length 10 cm, perimeter 28 cm
    d) length 7 cm, perimeter 20 cm

12. The salesperson at CarpetsRUs estimates that the amount of carpet remaining on a roll is 24 m^2. The width of the roll of carpet is 4 m. What is the length of the carpet on the roll?

13. A child's mass is usually much less than that of an adult. Because of this, children usually require smaller doses of medication. A nurse who knows the adult dose of a medication can use a formula called Clark's Rule to calculate a child's dose. Clark's Rule states that the child's dose, d, can be calculated using the formula $d = \dfrac{m}{68} \times a$, where m is the child's mass in kilograms and a is the adult dose in milligrams. Suppose the adult dose of a particular medication were 60 mg.

a) Calculate the dose, to the nearest milligram, for a child with each mass.
   i) 10 kg   ii) 18 kg   iii) 34 kg   iv) 40 kg

b) Draw a graph to show how a child's dose of this medication is related to the child's mass. Describe the graph.

c) Use the graph to estimate the dose for a 25-kg child.

TEMPLATE DISK

14. When a bungee jumper takes off, gravity causes her speed to increase until the bungee cord slows her down. The jumper's speed up to that point, s metres per second, t seconds after jumping, can be calculated using the formula $s = 9.8t$.

a) Explain to your partner how you would calculate the speed of the jumper if you knew the number of seconds that she had been falling.

b) Start a new spreadsheet document and enter the text and formulas shown below. What do the formulas in cells A3 and B3 tell the computer to do? Explain how the formula in cell C3 calculates the speed in kilometres per hour.

	A	B	C
1	Number of seconds	Speed (m/s)	Speed (km/h)
2	0.5	=9.8*A2	=B2*3600/1000
3	=A2+0.5	=9.8*A3	=B3*3600/1000

c) Copy the formulas in row 3 down to about row 20. Use the spreadsheet to find the speed of the jumper after each time, assuming there is no air resistance.
   i) 2 s   ii) 3 s   iii) 4 s   iv) 5 s

d) The speed limit for cars in cities and towns is usually 50 km/h. How many seconds does it take the bungee jumper to reach this speed? How does her speed after 5 s compare with this speed?

On your own

15. Calculate the height of a triangle with each pair of measurements.
   a) base 10 cm, area 20 cm^2
   b) base 4 cm, area 12 cm^2

16. a) Find the area of a trapezoid with parallel sides of lengths 12.5 cm and 7.6 cm and a height of 5.8 cm.
   b) Find the height of a trapezoid if its parallel sides are 10 cm and 15 cm long, and its area is 100 cm^2.

17. Nick works in a clothing store. He earns $395 per week, plus a 4% commission on all his sales. His weekly earnings, E dollars, can be represented by the formula $E = 395 + 0.04s$, where s dollars is his weekly sales.
   a) Calculate Nick's earnings for these weekly sales.
      i) $1675   ii) $1800   iii) $2050
   b) What would Nick's sales have to be for him to earn $510?
   c) Draw a graph to show how Nick's earnings are related to his weekly sales. Describe the graph.

Extend your thinking

18. You began this section by discussing how the Bui family would set up its train set. The Buis decided to build a table to hold the rectangular base and to give them an additional 48 cm of space along each side. What will be the area of the table top?

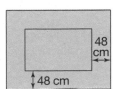

COMMUNICATING

The Ideas

Your friend phones you and wants to know how to use the formula for the area of a triangle to determine the height of a triangle. Explain how she can do this.

How Many Targets Were Missed?

The biathlon is a sport that combines cross-country skiing and target shooting. In the women's 15-km Olympic biathlon, the athletes make four stops during the 15-km route to shoot a total of 20 targets. For each target she misses, an athlete must ski a 150-m penalty lap. The total distance an athlete skis, D metres, can be represented by the formula $D = 15\,000 + 150t$, where t is the number of missed targets.

At the 1994 Olympic Winter games, the athlete who finished 44th had to ski 16 350 m. How many targets did she miss?

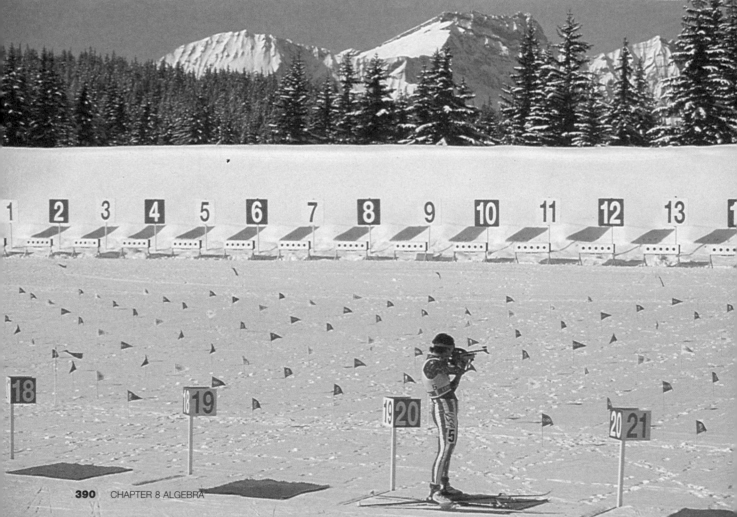

Understand the problem

- How far must an athlete ski in this event if she doesn't miss any targets? If she misses one target?
- What are you asked to find?

Think of some strategies

- Use the given formula. Find the value of t for which D is equal to 16 350. There are several ways to do this: guess and check, make a table, or work backwards.

Carry out the strategies

Choose one of these methods.

Guess and check

- Guess a value of t. Substitute it into the given formula.
- Is the result greater or less than 16 350? Was your guess for t too great or too small?
- Revise your guess for the value of t until the result is equal to 16 350.

Make a table

- In your notebook, copy and complete a table like the one on the right.

Number of targets missed	Distance skied
0	15 000
1	15 150

- Find 16 350 in the second column of the table. What is the corresponding value for t?

Work backwards

- Draw a flow chart showing the steps you would follow to work forwards through the formula if you knew the value of t. Reverse the steps.

Forwards

t targets were missed ➔ multiply by 150 ➔ add 15 000 ➔ the result is 16 350

Backwards

distance skied is 16 350 ➔ subtract 15 000 ➔ divide by 150 ➔ the result is t

Look back

- Compare your solution with those of students who used different methods. Which of the three methods do you think is easiest?
- Why do you think the athletes are penalized for missing targets?
- Will the fastest skier always win the gold medal? Explain.

Communicating the Ideas

In your journal, describe how you can determine the number of targets a biathlon competitor missed when you know the distance she skied.

8.2 THE LANGUAGE OF ALGEBRA

Developing the Ideas

In the previous section, you worked with formulas. A formula is a shorthand way of writing an English sentence about a mathematical situation.

One formula you used was for the perimeter of a rectangle.

We write in words: The perimeter of a rectangle is twice the length plus twice the width.

As a formula, we write: $P = 2l + 2w$

We can also use a mathematical shorthand to represent an English phrase about a mathematical situation. It is called an *algebraic expression*, or simply an expression.

▶ ▶ *Through Activities*

Work with a partner or in a group to complete the following activities.

ACTIVITY 1

For each phrase, choose a variable to represent "a number."
Write an algebraic expression that describes the phrase.

1. 4 more than a number

2. 5 less than a number

3. a number subtracted from 12

4. 3 times a number

5. the product of a number and 8

6. 12 divided by a number

7. 7 more than double a number

8. 6 times a number, decreased by 5

9. the sum of a number and −4

Compare your algebraic expressions with those of another group. For each phrase, did you all write the same expression? If not, how did the expressions differ?

ACTIVITY 2

When we see an algebraic expression, how can we read it?
Write a phrase for each expression.

1. $n + 8$ **2.** $8 + n$ **3.** $y - 3$ **4.** $3 - y$

5. $6p$ **6.** $3m + 2$ **7.** $\frac{a}{3}$ **8.** $5 - 9x$

Compare your phrases with those of other groups. For each expression, did you all write the same phrase? If not, were the phrases equivalent?

ACTIVITY 3

Look back at your answers to *Activities 1* and *2*. Make a list of words and phrases that appear to indicate either addition or subtraction. Make another list of words and phrases that appear to indicate either multiplication or division.

Example 1 ·····································

  a) Find the value in dollars of two $10 bills, of six $10 bills, and of
  n $10 bills.

  b) Find the number of days in 3 weeks, in 5 weeks, and in k weeks.

  c) Find the number of days in 48 h, in 120 h, and in p hours.

Solution

  a) We know that each $10 bill has a value of $10.
  Therefore, we multiply the number of bills by $10 to
  determine their value.

  The value of two $10 bills is $10 × 2, or $20.

  Similarly, the value of six $10 bills is $10 × 6, or $60.

  The value of n $10 bills is $10 × n, or 10n$.

  b) We know that each week contains 7 days.
  Therefore, we multiply the number of weeks by 7 to
  determine the number of days.

  There are 7 × 3 days, or 21 days in 3 weeks.

  Similarly, there are 7 × 5 days, or 35 days in 5 weeks.

  There are 7 × k, or 7k days in k weeks.

  c) We know that there are 24 h in one day.
  Therefore, we divide the number of hours by 24 to
  determine the number of days.

  There are $\frac{48}{24}$ days, or 2 days in 48 h.

  Similarly, there are $\frac{120}{24}$ days, or 5 days in 120 h.

  There are $\frac{p}{24}$ days in p hours.

Example 2 ·····································

  Rosie earns $7.50 per hour cutting grass.

  a) If you know the number of hours she worked, how can you find her
  total earnings?

  b) Write an expression to describe her total earnings.

Solution

  a) To find her total earnings, multiply the number of hours Rosie worked
  by her hourly rate.

  b) Let n represent the number of hours Rosie worked. We know she earns
  $7.50 for every hour worked.

  Thus, her earnings are $7.50 × n, or 7.5n$.

Working with Mathematics

Something to talk about

1. Does it matter what letter you use as a variable? Explain.

2. Choose the correct expression for each phrase.
   a) 3 times a number
   $$3p \qquad p + 3 \qquad 3 - p$$
   b) the product of a number and 5
   $$\frac{r}{5} \qquad 5 + r \qquad 5r$$
   c) 10 decreased by a number
   $$x - 10 \qquad 10 - x \qquad \frac{10}{x}$$
   d) 6 less than a number
   $$6 - n \qquad n - 6 \qquad \frac{6}{n}$$

3. From the box below, choose the correct phrase for each expression.
   a) $k + 7$ b) $c - 4$ c) $6 - m$ d) $\frac{w}{7}$

   > 7 less than a number
   > the sum of a number and 7
   > 4 more than a number
   > 6 more than a number
   > a number decreased by 4
   > a number decreased by 7
   > a number subtracted from 6
   > a number divided by 7

4. The fine for an overdue library book at the Woody Point Public Library is 10¢ per day.
   a) If you know the number of days a book is overdue, how can you calculate the fine?
   b) Which expression describes the fine in cents for a book that is d days overdue?
   $$10 + d \qquad \frac{10}{d} \qquad d - 10 \qquad 10d$$

Practice

5. Write an expression to represent each phrase.
   a) 1 less than a number
   b) a number decreased by 11
   c) a number subtracted from 18
   d) the sum of a number and 20
   e) 8 decreased by a number
   f) the product of a number and 10
   g) the quotient of a number divided by −5
   h) 6 divided by a number
   i) a number divided by 12
   j) 3 more than triple a number

6. Write a phrase to describe each expression.
   a) $t + 16$ b) $m - 5$ c) $24 - x$
   d) $7 + n$ e) $4p$ f) $\frac{s}{17}$
   g) $11y - 9$ h) $2t + 3$ i) $15 - 2k$

Work together

7. a) Find the value, in cents, of 2 quarters, of 5 quarters, and of n quarters.
   b) Find the value, in dollars, of three $5 bills, of seven $5 bills, and of p $5 bills.
   c) Find the number of minutes in 3 h, in 5 h, and in m hours.
   d) Find the number of metres in 100 cm, in 1000 cm, and in b centimetres.
   e) Find the number of hours in 4 days, in 10 days, and in d days.

8. a) Write an expression to represent the number of years in n days.
   b) Open the *Mammals of Canada* database. Look through the records. Notice the gestation period field. It shows the number of days for a mammal's young to develop from the time of conception to birth. How would you convert this to a time in years? Create a new calculated field in the database to display the gestation period in years.
   c) Sort the database by the new field. How many Canadian mammals have gestation periods of one year or longer? To what two groups do these mammals belong?

DATA DISK

9. To measure a patient's pulse rate, a nurse counts the number of beats in 10 s and multiplies by 6. Choose a variable to represent the number of beats in 10 s. Write an expression for the pulse rate in beats per minute.

10. A printer tells a student council that the total cost of producing a school yearbook is $1500 plus $7 for each yearbook ordered.
   a) If you know the number of yearbooks ordered, how can you find the total cost to produce the book?
   b) Write an expression to describe the total cost in dollars of producing a school yearbook when p copies are ordered.

On your own

11. Write an expression to represent each phrase.
   a) a number subtracted from 7
   b) the product of a number and 15
   c) a number divided by 3
   d) 7 times a number, decreased by 8

   Compare your expressions with those of other students. For each phrase, did you all write the same expression? Did you all use the same variable? Does it matter?

12. Write a phrase to describe each expression.
   a) $\dfrac{x}{9}$ b) $100m$ c) $4 - y$
   d) $p - 16$ e) $2b + 27$ f) $20 - 4z$

   Compare your phrases with those of other students. For each expression, did you all write the same phrase?

13. Write an expression to represent each quantity.
   a) the number of seconds in m minutes
   b) the number of grams in k kilograms
   c) the value in cents of n nickels
   d) the value in dollars of t $20 bills
   e) the number of hours in d minutes
   f) the distance in metres of c centimetres

14. Abdul has 35 coins. They are dimes and quarters. Let x represent the number of dimes. Write an expression to represent:
   a) the number of quarters
   b) the total value of the coins

15. Heidi bought some fabric at $6.49 per metre. If you know the number of metres of material Heidi purchased, how can you find the total cost?

16. A worker earns $500 per week, plus $20 for each hour of overtime.
   a) If you know the number of overtime hours worked, how can you find the total earnings in a week?
   b) Write an expression to describe the total weekly earnings when a person worked y hours overtime.

Extend your thinking

17. The worker in exercise 16 has a 35-h work week. Any time worked after 35 h is considered overtime.
   a) Write an expression to describe the total weekly earnings when w hours are worked in a week. Assume that w is greater than or equal to 35.
   b) In part a, is your expression correct if w is less than 35? Describe two different ways the worker might be paid if she works fewer than 35 h in a week. Compare your answers with those of other students. How many different possibilities did your class come up with?

18. A square has sides of unknown length. Let s metres represent the side length. Write an expression for:
   a) the perimeter of the square in centimetres
   b) the area of the square in square centimetres

The Ideas

The phrase "7 more than a number" can be written as $n + 7$ and also as $7 + n$. Can the phrase "7 less than a number" be written as $n - 7$ and also as $7 - n$? Explain.

How Long Can You Talk for $25?

When you make an overseas phone call, the amount you are charged depends on the country you are calling and how long you talk. Most telephone companies offer discounts for calls made during off-peak periods. Many local phone directories include a list of rates for calls to different countries made during different rate periods. The length of your call will be rounded up to the next whole number of minutes.

Gita lives in Ottawa, Ontario. Every month, she phones her cousin Afshar, who lives in Tehran, Iran. She always calls between 10 p.m. and midnight, Ottawa time. The company that provides Gita's long-distance service charges $2.79 for the first minute and $1.86 for each additional minute for calls to Iran made between 6 p.m. and 1 a.m. The cost of Gita's call, C dollars, can be modelled by the formula $C = 2.79 + 1.86(t - 1)$, where t represents the length of the call, in minutes.

1. Gita is phoning Afshar on his birthday. She has $25 to spend on the phone call and cannot spend more. For how long can the two talk?

   Use a spreadsheet to help you answer this question.

   Start a new spreadsheet document. Enter the text and formulas shown below. Format column B to display numbers as currency.

TEMPLATE DISK

	A	B	C
1	Cost of a phone call from Ottawa to Tehran		
2	Minutes talked	Cost	
3	1	=2.79+1.86*(A3−1)	
4	=A3+1	=2.79+1.86*(A4−1)	

   a) What does each formula in row 4 tell the computer to do?
   b) Copy the formulas in row 4 down to row 15. What does the computer display in column B?
   c) Use the spreadsheet to determine how long Gita and Afshar can talk for $25. How much money will Gita have left?

2. Use the spreadsheet you created in exercise 1 to answer these questions.
   a) How long could Gita and Afshar talk for $15? For $20?
   b) How much would it cost Gita to talk to Afshar for 5 min?

3. Gita always phones between 10 p.m. and midnight, Ottawa time. The local time in Tehran is 9.5 h ahead of the time in Ottawa. What time is it in Tehran when Gita phones?

4. Why do you think the telephone company charges more for the first minute of an overseas call?

5. Julian lives in Saskatoon, Saskatchewan. His grandmother lives in Bermuda. Julian is charged $1.47 for the first minute, and $0.98 for each additional minute for calls he makes to Bermuda between 7 a.m. and 11 p.m.

   a) Write a formula to represent the cost of calls from Saskatoon to Bermuda.

   b) Revise the spreadsheet from exercise 1 to calculate the cost of a call from Saskatoon to Bermuda.

   c) Use your revised spreadsheet to determine how long Julian can talk to his grandmother for $25.

   d) Use the spreadsheet to determine how much it would cost Julian to talk to his grandmother for 10 min.

   e) Use an atlas and the time zone map on page 321 to determine the time in Bermuda when it is between 7 a.m. and 11 p.m. in Saskatchewan. What do you think would be a good time for Julian to phone his grandmother?

6. a) If your local telephone directory includes a list of costs for overseas calls, choose a country from the list. Determine the local time in that country during each of the rate periods listed in the directory. Choose a rate period that would be convenient for you and the person you are calling. Record the cost for the first minute and each additional minute.

   b) Write a formula that represents the cost of a phone call from your area to that country, dialed during the rate period you chose in part a.

   c) Revise the spreadsheet you used in exercise 1 to calculate the cost of a call from your area to the country you chose.

   d) Use your revised spreadsheet to determine how long you could speak to someone in that country for $25.

   e) How much would it cost to talk to someone in that country for 15 min?

8.3 *EVALUATING EXPRESSIONS*

Developing the Ideas

▶▶ *Through Guided Examples*

You can substitute a number for each variable in an expression in the same way that you do for each variable in a formula. This is called *evaluating the expression*.

Example 1..

Evaluate each expression when x is 18 and y is −3.

a) $x + 16$ **b)** $\frac{x}{3}$ **c)** $24 - 2x$

d) $2(x - 5)$ **e)** $x - y$ **f)** $2x + 3y$

Solution

Substitute 18 for x and −3 for y in each expression and simplify.

a) $x + 16 = 18 + 16$
$\qquad = 34$

b) $\frac{x}{3} = \frac{18}{3}$
$\qquad = 6$

c) $24 - 2x = 24 - 2(18)$
$\qquad\quad = 24 - 36$
$\qquad\quad = -12$

d) $2(x - 5) = 2(18 - 5)$
$\qquad\quad\ = 2(13)$
$\qquad\quad\ = 26$

e) $x - y = 18 - (-3)$
$\qquad\quad = 18 + 3$
$\qquad\quad = 21$

f) $2x + 3y = 2(18) + 3(-3)$
$\qquad\quad\ = 36 + (-9)$
$\qquad\quad\ = 36 - 9$
$\qquad\quad\ = 27$

Example 2..

Raji is participating in a Walk-A-Thon to raise money for a charity. She has pledges totalling $8.25 for every kilometre she walks.

a) Write an expression to determine the amount of money Raji raises if you know the distance she walks.

b) Raji walked 15 km. Use your expression from part a to determine how much money Raji raised.

Solution

a) Let n kilometres represent the distance Raji walks.
For every kilometre, she raises $8.25.
Thus, the amount of money she raises is $8.25n$.

b) Substitute 15 for n in the expression from part a.

$8.25n = 8.25(15)$
$\qquad = 123.75$

Raji raised $123.75 in the Walk-A-Thon.

Working with Mathematics

Something to talk about

1. What does "evaluate an expression" mean?

2. Between 8 a.m. and 6 p.m., Monday to Friday, it costs 48¢ per minute for a phone call from Saint John to Vancouver. The total cost in cents can be represented by the expression $48t$, where t is the number of minutes the call lasts. Calculate the cost of a call that lasts:

   a) 8 min   **b)** 15 min   **c)** 23 min

Practice

3. Evaluate each expression when x is 4.

   a) $x + 4$ **b)** $x - 3$ **c)** $x - 7$

   d) $2x$ **e)** $4x$ **f)** $-5x$

   g) $16 + x$ **h)** $\frac{x}{2}$ **i)** $\frac{24}{x}$

4. Evaluate each expression when x is 3.

   a) $2x + 1$ **b)** $3x + 5$ **c)** $8 - 2x$

   d) $5 - 3x$ **e)** $-2x - 8$ **f)** $-3x + 4$

   g) $\frac{x}{3} - 2$ **h)** $\frac{x + 5}{2}$ **i)** $\frac{2x + 4}{-5}$

5. Evaluate each expression when n is 12.

   a) $n + 5$ **b)** $19 - n$ **c)** $\frac{n}{12}$

   d) $\frac{n}{4}$ **e)** $3n$ **f)** $6n - 25$

6. Evaluate each expression when m is -5.

   a) $m + 7$ **b)** $21 - m$ **c)** $m - 3$

   d) $\frac{15}{m}$ **e)** $8m$ **f)** $4m + 30$

7. Evaluate each expression when p is 8 and q is 3.5.

   a) $3p - 2q$ **b)** $p + 3q$

   c) $5p - 6q$ **d)** $2p + 10q$

Work together

8. Which expressions have the same value when m is 4?

   a) $3m - 2$ **b)** $30 - 5m$

   c) $2m + 3$ **d)** $\frac{m}{2} + 8$

   e) $21 - 2m$ **f)** $\frac{5(m + 2)}{3}$

   g) $8m - 5m - 1$ **h)** $3m - m + 2$

9. Evaluate the expression $2x + y$ for each pair of values.

   a) $x = 1.2; y = -3.7$ **b)** $x = 4.1; y = 2.3$

   c) $x = 5.1; y = 12.4$ **d)** $x = 30.5; y = -20.6$

   e) $x = -2.5; y = 1.2$ **f)** $x = 3.5; y = 2.4$

10. Evaluate each expression.

    a) $5x - 2y$ when $x = -2.8$ and $y = 1.7$

    b) $3x - 5y$ when $x = -3.2$ and $y = -3.2$

    c) $\frac{x + 4}{y}$ when $x = 5$ and $y = 3$

    d) $\frac{2x + 3}{3y}$ when $x = 5$ and $y = -2$

11. The Seneca Scouts are playing in a volleyball tournament. Two points are awarded to a team for each win and 1 point for each tie.

    a) Let w represent the number of wins and t the number of ties. Write an expression to describe a team's total points.

    b) The Scouts won 10 games in the tournament and tied 3. How many points do they have?

12. The win and tie records for three other teams in the volleyball tournament are given. Use your expression from exercise 11a to calculate each team's points.

    a) Cougars — 7 wins, 2 ties

    b) Huskies — 12 wins, no ties

    c) Phantoms — 5 wins, 1 tie

13. The cost of printing a roll of film at a photo shop is $4.98 to develop the film plus 35¢ for each photograph printed.

    a) Let n be the number of photographs on a roll of film. Write an expression to represent the total cost to develop and print the roll.

    b) Use your expression to determine the cost to develop a roll of 24 photographs.

14. Luis charges $4.50 for each hour he babysits, chargeable by the half hour.

    a) What does "chargeable by the half hour" mean?

    b) Let n represent the number of hours Luis babysits.

i) Based on your answer to part a, what can you say about the possible values of n?

ii) Write an expression to describe how much Luis earns for babysitting n hours.

c) Start a new spreadsheet file like the one below. What does the formula in cell A3 do? Copy this formula down to row 17. What does column A show?

TEMPLATE DISK

	A	B
1	Hours	Money earned
2	0.5	
3	=A2+0.5	

d) Format column B to show numbers as currency. Suppose Luis babysat for the number of hours shown in cell A2. Enter a formula in cell B2 to calculate how much Luis will earn. Copy this formula down to row 17. What does column B show?

e) Use the spreadsheet to answer these questions.

i) How much will Luis earn for 3 h of babysitting?

ii) How much will Luis earn for 7 h of babysitting?

iii) How many hours must Luis babysit to earn at least $20?

On your own

15. Evaluate each expression.
    a) $x + 4$ when x is 7.5
    b) $w - 10$ when w is 27.3
    c) $m + 1.5$ when m is 3.5
    d) $a - 2.5$ when a is 10.5

16. Evaluate each expression when x is $\frac{3}{4}$.
    a) $3x$ b) $2x - 1$
    c) $4x + 3$ d) $12 + 5x$

17. Evaluate each expression in exercise 16 when x is −1.5.

18. Evaluate each expression when a is 3.5 and b is 7.2.
    a) $5a - 2b$ b) $7a + b$
    c) $3a + 5b$ d) $2a - 3b$

19. Evaluate each expression in exercise 18 when a is 2.3 and b is −5.7.

20. Devon and Anna have part-time jobs working for a banquet hall. The hall has tables that each seat 8 people. The morning a banquet is to be held, their boss tells them how many people will attend. Devon and Anna have to determine how many tables will be needed and set them with linen, dishes, and cutlery.

    a) Let p represent the number of people attending the banquet. Write an expression to determine how many tables are needed.

    b) Suppose Devon and Anna use your expression from part a and get a decimal in the result. What should they do?

    c) Use your expression from part a to determine how many tables are needed for each number of people.

    i) 120   ii) 200   iii) 150   iv) 194

21. Brenda works in a warehouse. She is preparing an order of books to be shipped to a customer. Let x represent the number of books ordered.

    a) The cost to ship the books will depend on their total mass. Each book has a mass of 675 g. Write an expression to calculate the total mass of the shipment.

    b) Only 24 copies of the book will fit in each box. Write an expression to calculate the number of boxes Brenda will need.

    c) Use your expressions from parts a and b to determine the total mass and the number of boxes needed for a shipment of 360 books.

22. You are allowed 1 h of free parking in the hospital parking lot when visiting a relative. The charge for each additional hour or part hour is $1.50. The parking cost in dollars can be calculated using the expression $1.50(n - 1)$, where n is the number of hours parked to the next full hour.

a) Find the charge for parking from:

   i) 08:00 to 12:00   **ii)** 09:30 to 16:30

   iii) 07:30 to 15:00

b) What is the longest time you can park for $12.00?

Extend your thinking

23. Sometimes expressions are written to describe the relationship among variables in one case, but the expression may not be true for all cases. For example, a bricklayer wanted to know if there is a relationship between the total number of bricks needed for a wall, the length of the wall, and the height of the wall. She observed that when the length of the wall was 10 m and the height was 3 m, 1950 bricks were used. When she divided the number of bricks by the product of the length and height, she got 65. So in this case, the number of bricks can be represented by the expression $65lh$, where l and h are the length and height of the wall, respectively. Describe some reasons why this expression may not be true for all walls.

24. The dimensions of an ice hockey rink are shown. The distance from the goal line to the end boards varies in different rinks. Let x metres represent this distance. Assume that the shape of the rink is a rectangle.

  a) Write expressions for the rink's:

    i) length   **ii)** perimeter   **iii)** area

  b) Evaluate each expression in part a when the distance x is 1.5 m.

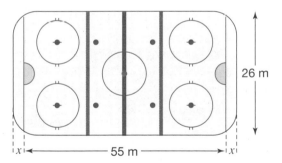

COMMUNICATING

The Ideas

Two students, José-France and Katie-Lyn, used their calculators to determine the perimeter of a rectangle with length 6 cm and width 4 cm. Each student substituted these values in the expression $2l + 2w$. José-France's answer was 56 cm while Katie-Lyn's answer was 20 cm. Which student is correct? What error do you think the other girl made?

Mind-Bending Math!

In the summer of 1991, the makers of Chiclets gum launched a new radio advertising campaign. Each commercial featured a character named Chuck who posed a mind-bending trick or puzzle for the listener to try.

THEME PLAYED ON CHICLETS BOX KAZOO

And now here's Chuck with another Chiclets mindbender.

Hey, I'm here at the 40 Winks Motel where I have learned from the great master the Bogey Yogi – nice name incidentally – how to read minds. But first, we must join our minds on the astral plane, and will that be coach or first class? OK let's get serious. Pop a Chiclets into your mouth.

RUMBLING, EARTHQUAKE

Whoa, I feel your vibration or is that the furnace on the fritz? Anyway, pick a number of Chiclets between 1 and 10 but don't tell me what it is. Actually, you can tell me but I won't hear you cause I'm on the radio and you're out there somewhere. Now, double that number, add 28, eat half of them and subtract your original number. How many Chiclets are you left with?

PERCUSSIVE CHICA CHICA OF CHICLETS BOX

I will now read your mind. You're thinking fourteen Chiclets. Hey how do you do it? I'm amazing that's how. And for my next amazing feat, I will make your mouth water through the radio but don't drool in the cords because of the electrical thing.

Chiclets in spearmint, peppermint, pepsin, cinnamon, wild cherry and assorted fruit. Mindbending flavour.

1. **a)** Try the trick several times with different starting numbers. What number do you get at the end?
   b) Talk to other students about their results. What do you notice?

2. Choose a variable to represent the number between 1 and 10 that you picked in the first step. Using the variable, write an expression to describe what you do in each step of the trick. What expression do you end up with after the last step? Why does the trick work?

3. Suppose you were to pick a number greater than 10 in the first step. Do you think the trick would still work? Explain.

4. Modify the trick so that the number you end up with is 11.

5. Modify the trick so that the number you end up with is the number you picked in the first step.

6. Make up a similar number trick of your own and share it with a friend.

8.4 *USING MODELS TO SOLVE EQUATIONS*

Developing the Ideas

▶ ▶ *Through Activities*

Recall the two-pan balance you studied in *Minds on Math 7*. Each balance contained one or more bags. Each bag contained an unknown number of candies. When there was more than one bag in a picture, the bags contained the same number of candies. All the candies had the same mass. The bags containing the candies were light enough not to affect the balance. There were also some loose candies in the pans, which were identical to those in the bags.

You used these balances to model *equations*. Recall that an equation is a number sentence that indicates two expressions are equal. Every equation has one equals sign. Each equation contains one variable.

You will use two-pan balances for further investigation of equations.

ACTIVITY 1

Work with a partner.

1. For each picture below, let *x* represent the number of candies in a bag.
   i) Write an equation relating the number of candies in each pan.
   ii) What is the value of *x*? Explain how you know.
   iii) How could you check your answer?

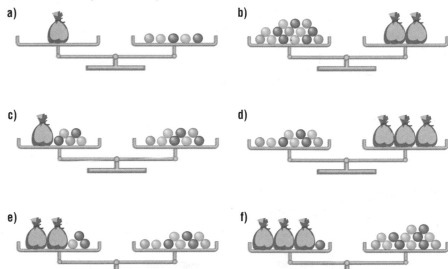

2. Check your results with other students. Did all of you get the same answers? If your answer is no, do you see where the errors occurred?

When you found the value for *x* that made both sides of the equation equal, you solved the equation for *x*. We say that the value of *x* satisfies the equation.

In *Minds on Math 7*, you also used algebra tiles to model and solve equations. With these tiles, you can model equations when some terms and solutions are negative. Recall these algebra tiles.

This tile represents 1. ■

This tile represents −1. ■

We call these *unit* tiles.

This tile represents one variable. For example, if you are using x, you can call this a $1x$-tile, or simply an x-tile.

This tile represents the opposite of $1x$, or $−1x$. We simply say it is a $−x$-tile.

We call these *variable* tiles.

To model the algebraic expression $2x + 5$, you need two x-tiles and five 1-tiles.

In your integer work in *Minds on Math 7*, the number zero was modelled by an equal number of tiles of each colour. This is true for both unit tiles and variable tiles.

For example, three 1-tiles (+3) and three −1-tiles (−3) model zero. Similarly, four x-tiles (+4x) and four $−x$-tiles (−4x) also model 0.

We can write a number sentence for each situation:
$+3 + (−3) = 0$ and $+4x + (−4x) = 0$

We call this the *Zero Principle*.

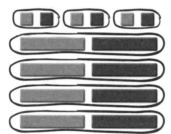

Recall the *Balance Principle*. When you solve an equation using algebra tiles, you use a work chart. You can add the same tiles to each side of the work chart and still maintain equality. You can remove the same tiles from each side of the work chart and still maintain equality.

ACTIVITY 2

Work with a partner.

1. For each picture below, let t represent the variable.
   i) Write an equation that the algebra tiles represent.
   ii) Use algebra tiles to model, then solve the equation.
   iii) What is the value of t?
   iv) How could you check your answer?

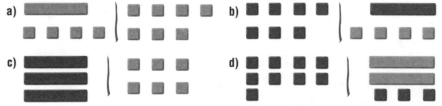

2. Check your results with other students. Did all of you get the same answers? If your answer is no, do you see where the errors occurred?

Example 1 ···

Let *n* represent the number of candies in a bag. Write an equation relating the number of candies in each pan. Solve the equation to find the value of *n*. Check your answer.

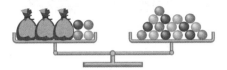

Solution

There are $n + n + n + 4$, or $3n + 4$ candies in the pan on the left.
There are 16 candies in the pan on the right.
The equation is $3n + 4 = 16$.
To solve the equation, we first remove 4 candies from each pan.
We then have $3n = 12$.
We then divide the candies in the pan on the right into 3 equal groups.
Each group contains 4 candies. This means that each bag contains 4 candies.
$n = 4$
To check, replace each bag in the pan on the left with 4 candies.

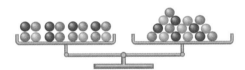

Since there are 16 candies in each pan, the pans are balanced.
The solution $n = 4$ is correct.

Recall that there is another principle you may use when solving an equation using algebra tiles. The *Sharing Principle* states that when two numbers are equal, you can divide each of them by the same number and maintain equality. Similarly, when two sets of tiles are equal, and you can divide both sets into the same number of groups, all these groups will be equal.

Example 2

Use algebra tiles and symbols to solve the equation $5 - 4x = -7$.

Solution

Using algebra tiles	Using symbols

Using algebra tiles

Step 1

Start with

Step 2

You want all the 1-tiles on the right side. Add five −1-tiles to each side.

According to the Zero Principle, this is the same as

Step 3

Each side can be arranged into 4 equal groups. Each group on the left contains one −x-tile. Each group on the right contains three −1-tiles. According to the Sharing Principle, you need only use one group from each side and still maintain equality.

We can flip all the tiles.

From the tiles, $x = 3$.

Using symbols

Step 1

Start with

$$5 - 4x = -7$$

Step 2

Add −5 to each side.

$$5 - 4x - 5 = -7 - 5$$
$$-4x = -12$$

Step 3

We divided the tiles on each side of the work chart into 4 equal groups, then flipped the tiles. This is the same as dividing each side of the equation by −4.

$$\frac{-4x}{-4} = \frac{-12}{-4}$$
$$x = 3$$

Working with Mathematics

Something to talk about

1. Why is it not possible to solve an equation like the one in *Example 2* using a two-pan balance?

2. In the activities and guided examples, all the numbers in the equations were integers. Would you be able to use a two-pan balance or algebra tiles to model, then solve an equation such as $2x - 3.2 = 5.7$? Explain.

3. Describe the steps you would take to model, then solve the equation $4 + 3n = 13$:
   a) using a two-pan balance
   b) using algebra tiles

4. a) Write an equation that could be solved using a two-pan balance as well as algebra tiles.
   b) Write an equation that could be solved using algebra tiles, but not a two-pan balance.
   c) Are there equations that could be solved using a two-pan balance, but not algebra tiles?

5. How can you check your solution when you solve an equation using algebra tiles?

Practice

6. Use a two-pan balance to solve. Check your answers.
   a) $t + 1 = 2$ b) $c + 2 = 5$ c) $5 + w = 10$
   d) $13 = y + 8$ e) $2 + h = 15$ f) $7 = x + 1$
   g) $4a = 12$ h) $2s = 4$ i) $2l = 10$
   j) $10n = 50$ k) $9x = 72$ l) $8a = 48$
   m) $18 = 3x$ n) $35 = 5n$ o) $11 = 3 + a$

7. Use algebra tiles to solve. Check your answers.
   a) $n + 1 = 3$ b) $q + 2 = 4$ c) $2 - s = 3$
   d) $x + 2 = -1$ e) $1 - d = -2$ f) $-3 - n = -5$
   g) $-2h = 6$ h) $3t = -9$ i) $-4y = -8$
   j) $6b = -42$ k) $-11x = 55$ l) $5n = 50$
   m) $-49 = -7x$ n) $-56 = 8x$ o) $3 = 12 + n$
   p) $3 = -12 - n$ q) $28 = -7a$ r) $40 = 8b$

Work together

8. For each picture below:
   i) Write an equation relating the number of candies in each pan.
   ii) Solve the equation.
   iii) How many candies are in each bag?
   a)
   b)

   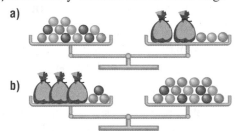

9. Each variable represents a bag with an unknown number of candies. The numbers represent candies. Draw a two-pan balance to represent each equation. Solve the equation.
   a) $3x + 4 = 13$ b) $12 = 4x + 8$
   c) $3 + 2x = 17$ d) $26 = 11 + 5x$

10. The cost of a ferry trip for one vehicle is $10, plus $2 for each passenger. One vehicle is charged $22 for the trip. Let x represent the number of people in the car. Write an equation to represent the cost of this ferry trip. Draw a two-pan balance to represent the equation. Solve the equation. How many people were in the car?

11. For each picture below, let p represent the variable.
   i) Write an equation represented by the algebra tiles.
   ii) Use algebra tiles to model, then solve the equation. What is the value of p?
   iii) Check your answer.
   a)   b)

   c)   d)

   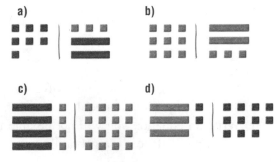

12. Kelly went to a fall harvest fair. She paid $4 for admission and $2 for each ride. Kelly spent $18 at the fair. Let r represent the number of rides Kelly went on. Write an equation to represent the total cost of Kelly's day at the fair. Use algebra tiles to solve the equation. How many rides did Kelly go on?

13. Explain what each equation represents.
    a) $x + 5 = 18$ b) $x - 5 = 18$ c) $5 - x = 18$
    d) $5x = 20$ e) $5x + 8 = 18$ f) $5x - 7 = 18$

14. Use algebra tiles or a two-pan balance to solve each equation in exercise 13.

On your own

15. Each variable represents a bag with an unknown number of candies. The numbers represent candies. Draw a two-pan balance to represent each equation. Solve the equation.
    a) $5 + 2n = 17$ b) $18 = 4x + 2$
    c) $28 = 3 + 5x$ d) $3n + 5 = 17$

16. Lesley made 36 sausage rolls for a meeting. Eight sausage rolls were left over. Let s represent the number of sausage rolls eaten. Write an equation to represent this situation. Draw a two-pan balance to represent the equation. Solve the equation. How many sausage rolls were eaten?

17. Write an equation to represent each sentence. Solve the equation.
    a) A number increased by 7 is 15.
    b) A number decreased by 4 is 7.
    c) A number tripled is 18.
    d) A number doubled is 12.

e) A number doubled and decreased by 5 is 15.
f) Three more than double a number is 29.
g) Fifty-two decreased by triple a number is 31.
h) A number doubled and increased by 8 is 20.
i) Two less than 4 times a number is 26.

18. Explain what each equation represents.
    a) $4 + n = 16$ b) $4 - n = 16$ c) $n - 4 = 16$
    d) $4n = 16$ e) $4n + 5 = 21$ f) $5 - 4n = 15$

19. Madhu had 6 sports cards. She bought 4 packs of sports cards. Each pack had the same number of cards. Madhu now has a total of 34 sports cards. Let p represent the number of cards in each pack. Write an equation to represent this situation. Use algebra tiles to solve the equation. How many sports cards were in each pack?

Extend your thinking

20. In the diagram below, the first two scales are balanced. Which block(s) will balance the block on the third scale? Explain the steps you used to get your answer.

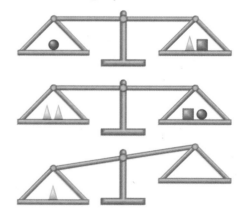

The Ideas

In your journal:
    a) Write an equation you could solve with a two-pan balance.
    b) Write an equation you could solve with algebra tiles.
    c) Write an equation you will not be able to solve with either a two-pan balance or algebra tiles.

Networks

This diagram is an example of a *network*.

In this network, there are:

4 regions   8 vertices   11 segments

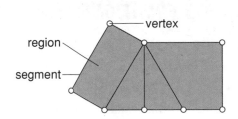

1. How many regions, vertices, and segments are there in each network?

   a) 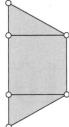   **b)** 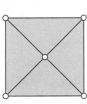   **c)** 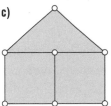   **d)**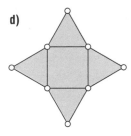

2. Draw an example of a network that has:

   a) 1 region, 3 vertices, 3 segments   **b)** 1 region, 4 vertices, 4 segments

   c) 2 regions, 4 vertices, 5 segments   **d)** 2 regions, 6 vertices, 7 segments

   Compare your networks with those of other students.

3. Let *R* represent the number of regions, *V* the number of vertices, and *S* the number of segments.

   a) Copy and complete a table like that below for the networks in exercises 1 and 2.

   b) For each network, compare the value of *S* with the value of $R + V$. What do you notice?

S	R	V	R + V

4. **a)** Use the result of exercise 3 to write an expression that you can use to find the number of segments if you know the numbers of regions and vertices.

   b) Check your expression using these networks.

   i)   **ii)** 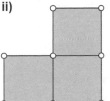   **iii)** 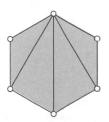   **iv)**

.......8.5 *SOLVING EQUATIONS ALGEBRAICALLY*

Developing the Ideas

▶▶ *Through Guided Examples*

In the previous section, you modelled the solutions of equations using two-pan balances and algebra tiles. Some equations cannot be represented easily using two-pan balances or algebra tiles. But you can write and solve many of these equations algebraically.

To solve some of the equations using the balance, you simplified them by removing equal numbers of candies from each pan. You were placing all the bags in one pan and all the loose candies in the other pan.

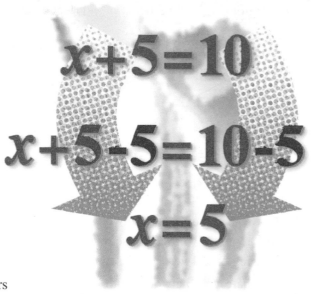

You simplified the equations with the algebra tiles by placing all the variable tiles on one side of the work chart and all the unit tiles on the other side.

In a similar way, you can simplify equations algebraically by adding or subtracting equal numbers from each side before solving. You want to place all the variables on one side of the equals sign, and the numbers on the other side.

Example 1 ....

Solve each equation.

a) $s + 4 = 7$ **b)** $4y + 15 = 9$ **c)** $\frac{s}{7} = 12$ **d)** $3y = 22$ **e)** $\frac{x}{4} + 5 = 18$

Solution

a) $s + 4 = 7$
Subtract 4 from each side.
$s + 4 - 4 = 7 - 4$
$s = 3$

b) $4y + 15 = 9$
Subtract 15 from each side.
$4y + 15 - 15 = 9 - 15$
$4y = -6$
Divide each side by 4.
$\frac{4y}{4} = \frac{-6}{4}$
$y = \frac{-3}{2}$, or $-1\frac{1}{2}$, or -1.5

c) $\frac{s}{7} = 12$
Multiply each side by 7.
$7 \times \frac{s}{7} = 12 \times 7$
$s = 84$

d) $3y = 22$
Divide each side by 3.
$\frac{3y}{3} = \frac{22}{3}$
$y = \frac{22}{3}$, or $7\frac{1}{3}$, or $7.\overline{3}$

e) $\quad \frac{x}{4} + 5 = 18$

Subtract 5 from each side.

$\frac{x}{4} + 5 - 5 = 18 - 5$

$\qquad\qquad \frac{x}{4} = 13$

Multiply each side by 4.

$\qquad 4 \times \frac{x}{4} = 13 \times 4$

$\qquad\qquad\quad x = 52$

Earlier in this chapter, you solved problems involving formulas by guessing and checking, making tables, or working backwards. Now you can solve problems like these algebraically.

Example 2

Recall from the Quest on page 390 that the distance, D metres, an athlete skis in the 15-km Olympic biathlon can be represented by the formula $D = 15\ 000 + 150t$, where t is the number of targets she misses. The winner of the gold medal in this event at the 1994 Olympic Winter Games was Myriam Bedard of Quebec. Myriam skied 15 300 m. How many targets did she miss?

Solution

Substitute 15 300 for D in the formula for the distance skied. Solve the resulting equation.

$$D = 15\ 000 + 150t$$
$$15\ 300 = 15\ 000 + 150t$$

Subtract 15 000 from each side.

$$15\ 300 - 15\ 000 = 15\ 000 - 15\ 000 + 150t$$
$$300 = 150t$$

Divide each side by 150.

$$\frac{300}{150} = \frac{150t}{150}$$
$$2 = t$$

Myriam missed 2 targets in the race.

When you have solved an equation, you can check your answer by following these steps:

- Substitute your answer for the variable in the original equation.
- Simplify both sides of the equation separately. If both sides simplify to the same number, your answer is correct.

You can use equations to represent many situations in the world around you.

Example 3

Jacques works at a hotel. One of his jobs is to help set up for meetings. Jacques has to prepare a room for 550 people who will sit at round tables. Each table seats 10 people. How many tables will Jacques need?

a) Write an equation to model this situation.

b) Explain how the equation models the situation.

c) Solve the equation and answer the question.

Solution

a) Let t represent the number of tables. There are 10 people at each table. There are 550 people all together. The equation is $10t = 550$

b) The equation is "Ten times the number of tables are equal to the number of people." That is, we multiply the number of tables by the number of people who sit at a table to get the total number of people.

c) $10t = 550$

$$\frac{10t}{10} = \frac{550}{10}$$ ◄ Dividing each side by 10

$$t = 55$$

Jacques needs 55 tables.

Example 4

Refer to *Example 3*. Two days before the meeting, Jacques is told that 8 guests will sit at a rectangular table. The total number of people is still 550. How many round tables does Jacques need?

a) Write an equation to model this situation.

b) Solve the equation and answer the question.

Solution

a) Let n represent the number of round tables.
There are 10 people at each round table, and 8 people at a rectangular table. There are 550 people all together.
The equation is $10n + 8 = 550$

b) $10n + 8 = 550$

$10n + 8 - 8 = 550 - 8$ ◄ Subtracting 8 from each side

$$10n = 542$$
$$\frac{10n}{10} = \frac{542}{10}$$ ◄ Dividing each side by 10
$$n = 54.2$$

It does not make sense to say that Jacques needs 54.2 tables. He could use 54 tables and have 1 extra person at two of these tables, or he could use 55 tables. If he uses 55 tables, he could move the people around so that one table does not have only 2 people.

Working with Mathematics

Something to talk about

1. a) Why would it be difficult to represent and solve equations like those in *Example 1* on a two-pan balance?

   b) Which equations in *Example 1* would be difficult to solve using algebra tiles?

Practice

2. Solve.

   a) $x + 2 = 5$ b) $y + 9 = 15$
   c) $a - 3 = 8$ d) $c - 5 = -3$
   e) $n + 4 = -3$ f) $t + 3 = -1$
   g) $q + 1 = 4$ h) $w - 2 = 5$
   i) $s - 3 = -1$ j) $h - 2 = -11$
   k) $k - 1 = -5$ l) $b - 2 = -4$
   m) $y + 8 = 30$ n) $x + 3 = 10$
   o) $k + 15 = 8$ p) $s - 17 = 12$
   q) $r - 9 = 2$ r) $t + 9 = 12$

3. Solve.

   a) $4t = 8$ b) $-3w = -9$
   c) $-3h = 6$ d) $2q = -8$
   e) $3a = 5$ f) $-2y = 3$
   g) $-4s = 7$ h) $5k = -9$
   i) $-10t = 48$ j) $5t = -23$
   k) $-4t = -7$ l) $9t = -81$

4. Solve.

   a) $\frac{s}{3} = 2$ b) $\frac{t}{2} = 3$
   c) $\frac{a}{7} = -1$ d) $\frac{m}{4} = -1$
   e) $\frac{q}{-4} = -3$ f) $\frac{b}{-5} = -5$
   g) $\frac{t}{10} = -1$ h) $\frac{-x}{5} = 4$
   i) $\frac{-n}{4} = -6$ j) $\frac{a}{7} = 3$
   k) $\frac{n}{-6} = -2$ l) $\frac{m}{8} = -2$
   m) $\frac{n}{2} = 70$ n) $\frac{m}{4} = 9$

Work together

5. Solve each equation.

   a) $3k + 5 = 11$ b) $3m - 20 = 1$
   c) $9x + 14 = 8$ d) $2m - 9 = 13$
   e) $4x + 19 = 29$ f) $6n + 23 = 8$

6. Solve. Check by substituting in the equation.

   a) $\frac{w}{3} = -2$ b) $x - 5 = 8$
   c) $3q = -2$ d) $\frac{t}{-5} = -2$
   e) $c + 6 = -3$ f) $2y = -11$
   g) $\frac{a}{3} - 1 = 4$ h) $-4 = 1 + \frac{a}{2}$
   i) $15 = 2 - \frac{x}{3}$ j) $-11 = \frac{n}{3} + 3$

7. Solve and check.

   a) $2q + 1 = 7$ b) $3r + 4 = 10$
   c) $3s - 2 = 6$ d) $5n - 1 = 9$
   e) $4a + 2 = -2$ f) $2y + 4 = -2$
   g) $-3c - 2 = -5$ h) $-2k - 8 = -14$
   i) $\frac{d}{2} + 1 = 3$ j) $\frac{p}{3} - 4 = -3$

8. For each sentence, write an equation, then solve it algebraically to find the number.

   a) Two times a number is equal to 18.

   b) Eight times a number is equal to 32.

   c) A number divided by 7 is equal to 2.

   d) A number divided by 5 is equal to 4.

   e) Six more than 2 times a number is equal to 20.

   f) Eight more than 3 times a number is equal to 20.

   g) Three less than 4 times a number is equal to 11.

   h) One more than a number divided by 3 is equal to 2.

   i) One less than a number divided by 2 is equal to 2.

9. For each situation, write an equation. Solve the equation, then answer the question.

   a) A farmer has 8 more pigs than cows. She has 12 cows. How many pigs does she have? Let n represent the number of pigs.

   b) A parking lot has 3 more cars than trucks. It has 5 cars. How many trucks does it have? Let n represent the number of trucks.

   c) In a bag, there are 3 times as many donuts as muffins. There are 2 muffins. How many donuts are in the bag? Let n represent the number of donuts.

d) In a box, there are 4 times as many nails as bolts. There are 24 nails. How many bolts are in the box? Let n represent the number of bolts.

For each of exercises 10 to 16, write an equation. Solve the equation to answer the question. Check your answer.

10. There are 5 eggs in the fridge. Two dozen eggs are placed inside. How many eggs are there all together?

11. A large basket contains 20 oranges. Yesterday, it contained 4 oranges. How many oranges were placed in the basket since yesterday?

12. Jolyn bought 5 video games on sale. She paid $149.75. What was the cost of 1 video game?

13. A dump truck can hold 8 t of gravel. How many trips will be required to transport 188 t?

14. Eighteen people lined up for the bus. After the bus left, 3 people were still at the bus stop. How many people got on the bus?

15. A carpet store has 50 m² of carpet on a roll. A customer bought carpet for 3 rooms, each with the same floor area. The roll still contains 5 m² of carpet. How much did the customer purchase for each room?

16. Tyler had $60 in the bank. He made 4 equal deposits. His account now has a balance of $140. What was the amount of each deposit?

For each of exercises 17 and 18, use the information to write a problem that can be solved by writing and solving an equation. Exchange problems with a classmate. Solve your classmate's problems.

17. Yarmouth is 302 km from Halifax, Nova Scotia. Liverpool is approximately halfway between these two towns. Mei Lin drives her car at 80 km/h. Lucien drives his car at 70 km/h.

18. A catalogue lists these items: slippers $5.95 per pair; pillow $11.95; soap dish $4.95; shower curtain $2.95; and blanket $18.95. Sarah has $40 to spend on these items. Abdhul has $45 to spend.

19. Erin works 10 h per week selling magazine subscriptions. She earns $75.00 per week, plus a 3% commission on all her sales. Her weekly earnings E dollars can be represented by the formula $E = 75.00 + 0.03s$, where s dollars is her weekly sales. Calculate Erin's weekly sales for her to earn:
a) $94.47   **b)** $96.45   **c)** $104.94

On your own

20. Solve each equation.
a) $s + 11 = 16$ **b)** $z + 20 = 6$
c) $d - 16 = 4$ **d)** $b - 5 = 1$
e) $r + 8 = 4$ **f)** $q + 21 = 7$

21. Solve each equation.
a) $2k + 9 = 11$ **b)** $3p - 16 = -1$
c) $7y + 41 = 6$ **d)** $2d - 15 = 8$
e) $5x + 9 = 49$ **f)** $6b - 14 = -5$

22. Solve each equation.
a) $\frac{r}{8} = 7$ **b)** $\frac{t}{3} = 21$ **c)** $\frac{s}{13} = 5$
d) $\frac{b}{5} = 20$ **e)** $\frac{k}{9} = 12$ **f)** $\frac{m}{6} = 4$

23. For each sentence, write an equation, then solve it algebraically to find the number.
a) Three more than a number is equal to 5.
b) Eight more than a number is equal to 12.
c) A number decreased by 2 is equal to 4.
d) A number decreased by 12 is equal to 16.
e) Eight decreased by a number is equal to 3.
f) Twenty decreased by a number is equal to 5.

For each of exercises 24 to 28, write an equation. Solve the equation to answer the question. Check your answer.

24. There are 8 oranges in a bag. In the fridge, there are 5 oranges. Three bags are placed in the fridge. How many oranges will there be all together? Let n represent the number of oranges.

25. A fridge now contains 31 eggs. Yesterday, it contained 7 eggs. How many dozens of eggs were placed in the fridge since yesterday?

26. A roll of fabric has 20 m² of cloth. A customer bought 2 identical lengths. This left 13 m² of cloth on the roll. What was the size of each length?

27. Vicki rented skis for $18. The chair lift cost $1.00 each time. Vicki spent $28 all together. How many times did she use the chair lift?

28. Half the team's supply of pucks was taken from the dressing room to the bench. During the game, the team lost 8 pucks. At the end of the game, there were 14 pucks left on the bench. What was the original number of pucks in the dressing room?

29. Mei Lin and Thomas are planning their wedding reception. Including all taxes, it will cost them $750 to rent the hall plus $30 for each dinner guest.
   a) Write a formula to represent the total cost of the reception when *n* guests attend.
   b) Use your formula to determine how many guests Mei Lin and Thomas could invite if they spend:
      i) $2250   ii) $3450   iii) $4500

For each of exercises 30 and 31, use the information to write a problem that can be solved by writing and solving an equation. Exchange problems with a classmate. Solve your classmate's problems.

30. The walls of a room have a total area of 40 m² (excluding windows and doors). One litre of paint costs $10.50, and can cover 16 m². A paint roller and pan together cost $8.50.

31. A pickup truck has a mass of 1800 kg. A crate of apples has a mass of 40 kg. The loaded truck has a mass of 2000 kg.

32. The cost of renting a truck for 1 day (excluding fuel) is $45. There is an additional charge of $0.20/km. The cost, *C* dollars, of renting the truck and driving it *k* kilometres is given by $C = 45 + 0.2k$.
   a) The truck is driven 70 km. Find the total cost.
   b) Mr. Atkinson rented the truck. He paid a total of $65. How far was the truck driven?
   c) Mrs. Whiffen rented the truck. She paid a total of $58.20. How far did she drive the truck?
   d) Choose a few more values for the distance driven. Calculate the cost for each distance. Draw a graph to show how the cost is related to the distance driven. Describe the graph.

Extend your thinking

33. Solve each equation.
   a) $5(3x + 1) = -21 + 2x$
   b) $-3(n + 2) = 10 + n$
   c) $-3(2x - 1) = -3(x + 7)$
   d) $2(x + 3) = 6$
   e) $7(y - 6) = 14$
   f) $3(z + 9) = 12$
   g) $4(d - 2.5) = 26$
   h) $3(x + 1) = 2x$
   i) $4(t + 1) = 2t + (1 - t)$
   j) $6(w - 2) = 3w + 2(w + 1)$
   k) $7.2x - 7.5 - 1.7x = 4.6 + 4.4x$
   l) $15(0.3 - z) + 14.5z = 2(0.5z - 10)$
   m) $-1.03 - 0.62m = 0.71 - 0.22m$
   n) $0.125w - 8(3.75 - 0.375w) = -0.875w$

The Ideas

For two equations you have solved, explain to a friend how you know that you have the correct answer.

Review

1. When people exercise, their pulse rate increases. The recommended maximum pulse rate depends on the person's age. For people between the ages of 18 and 50, the maximum recommended pulse rate, P, is given by $P = 220 - A$, where A is the person's age in years. Find the recommended maximum pulse rate for a person of each age.
   a) 18 years   b) 38 years   c) 50 years
   d) 10 years older than you
   e) twice your age

2. Use the formula in exercise 1 to determine the age of a person with each maximum recommended pulse rate.
   a) 200   b) 170   c) 185   d) 179

3. Use the data from exercises 1 and 2 to draw a graph to show how a person's maximum recommended pulse rate is related to age. Describe the graph. What happens to the maximum recommended pulse rate as a person gets older? Why do you think this happens?

4. A store is advertising $12 off all shirts.
   a) If you know the regular price of a shirt, how can you calculate the sale price?
   b) Write an expression to describe the sale price of a shirt with a regular price of p dollars.
   c) Use your expression from part b to determine the sale price of each shirt.
      i) $24   ii) $34   iii) $50
   d) Calculate the percent discount on each shirt in part c.

5. This table shows the 1995 Bell Canada rates for phone calls from Canada to France.

Time of day	Cost for first minute ($)	Cost for each additional minute ($)
9 a.m. to 1 p.m.	1.28	0.85
1 p.m. to 6 p.m.	1.16	0.77
6 p.m. to 9 a.m.	0.96	0.64

a) The cost, C dollars, of a call made between 9 a.m. and 1 p.m. that lasts t minutes can be expressed with the formula $C = 1.28 + 0.85(t - 1)$. Write a formula to express the cost of a call lasting t minutes dialed in each of the other time periods.
b) Use the time zone map on page 321 to determine the local times in France when it is 9 a.m., 1 p.m., and 6 p.m. in your region.
c) Which time period do you think is the best to make a phone call to France? Explain your answer.

6. Use your formulas from exercise 5 to determine the cost of each phone call from Canada to France.
   a) A call made at 10 a.m. that lasted 5 min.
   b) A call made at 11 a.m. that lasted 9 min.
   c) A call made at 3 p.m. that lasted 5 min.
   d) A call made at 5 p.m. that lasted 10 min.
   e) A call made at 7 p.m. that lasted 5 min.
   f) A call made at 9 p.m. that lasted 11 min.

7. A door-to-door vacuum cleaner salesperson earns a salary of $200 per week plus $40 for every vacuum cleaner she sells.
   a) If you know the number of vacuum cleaners sold, how can you calculate her salary for the week?
   b) Write an equation to represent the total weekly earnings E dollars when v vacuum cleaners are sold.
   c) Calculate her salary when she sells 3 vacuum cleaners in a week, and when she sells 8 vacuum cleaners in a week.
   d) Calculate how many vacuum cleaners she sells in a week when her salary is $400 and when her salary is $640.
   e) Draw a graph to show how the salary is related to the number of vacuum cleaners sold. Describe the graph.

8. Evaluate each expression when x is 7.
   a) $x - 2$ b) $x + 11$ c) $4x - 9$
   d) $15 - 2x$ e) $\frac{x}{2} - 3$ f) $\frac{4 - x}{3}$

9. Evaluate each expression in exercise 8 when x is -2.

10. Concetta and her family own a fruit farm. They sell peaches to a local distributor, who then sells them all over the province. The distributor pays Concetta $8.50 per box for Number 1 Grade peaches, and $4.75 per box for Number 2 Grade peaches.
    a) Let x represent the number of boxes of Number 1 Grade peaches, and y the number of boxes of Number 2 Grade peaches. Write an expression to represent the total amount the distributor pays Concetta for the peaches.
    b) Calculate how much the distributor pays Concetta for each shipment.

	No. 1 Grade	No. 2 Grade
i)	17	9
ii)	34	8
iii)	85	11
iv)	68	23

11. Write an equation to represent each sentence. Solve the equation.
    a) 7 more than a number is 41.
    b) A number decreased by 5 is 19.
    c) 3 times a number, subtracted from 35 is 26.
    d) A number divided by 2 is 18.

12. These pictures show two-pan balances. Let x represent the number of candies in a bag. Write and solve an equation to find the value of x.
    a)

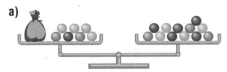

    b)

c)

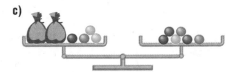

13. What equation does each group of algebra tiles represent? Use algebra tiles to model the solution to each equation. Record each solution in symbols. Check your answers.
    a)

    b)

    c)

14. Use algebra tiles to model the solution to each equation. Record each solution in symbols. Check your answers.
    a) $a + 8 = 3$ b) $5d + 4 = -11$
    c) $2x + 5 = 3$ d) $4y - 3y = -1$
    e) $3b + 2b = 15$ f) $4e + 7 = 3$

15. Solve each equation algebraically. Check your answers.
    a) $a - 3 = 10$ b) $2b + 9 = 5$
    c) $\frac{c}{6} = 8$ d) $\frac{d}{12} = 3$
    e) $2e + 6 = 20$ f) $3f - 21 = -6$

16. A truck can hold 60 crates. It has a maximum capacity of 5000 kg. The truck can be safely loaded in 20 min. The people who load the truck are paid $13.50/h.
    a) Make up two problems based on the above information.
    b) Write an equation for each problem. Solve the equations to solve the problems you wrote.

A Balanced Diet = A Healthy Diet

Do you think you are a healthy eater? This project can help you find out.

The chart below is taken from *Canada's Food Guide*. This document was prepared by Health and Welfare Canada. It helps you plan your meals to ensure your diet is healthy. The data apply to people aged four years and over. The guide divides the food we eat into four main groups. It shows how many servings from each group you should eat each day. These groups are grain products, vegetables and fruit, milk products, and meat and alternatives. You will use mathematics to explore different ways to examine the information in *Canada's Food Guide*.

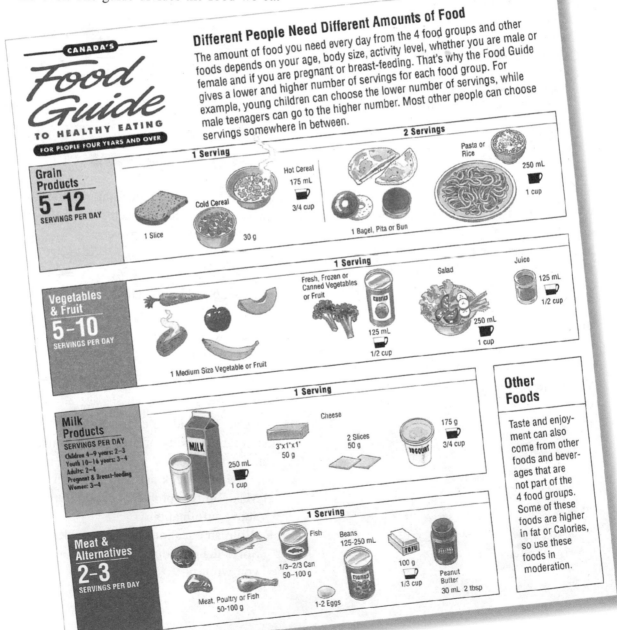

ACTIVITY 1

TEMPLATE DISK

1. Start a new spreadsheet document and input the headings below. Find the minimum and maximum recommended number of servings of each food group for someone your age. Input these numbers in the appropriate cells. Use the spreadsheet's charting options to draw two circle graphs: one showing the minimum number of servings from each group someone your age should eat and the other showing the maximum.

	A	B	C	D	E
1		Grain products	Vegetables and fruit	Milk products	Meat and alternatives
2	Youth minimum				
3	Youth maximum				
4	My consumption				

2. Increase the number of servings of grain products in cell B2 by 1. Do not change any of the other numbers. How does the circle graph change? Repeat this until you reach the maximum number of servings of grain products. Describe the changes in the graph as you increased the number of servings. When you have completed this, set the number in cell B2 back to the minimum value.

3. Estimate the number of servings you ate yesterday from each of the four groups. Enter your estimates in cells B4 to E4. Use the spreadsheet's charting options to draw a circle graph of your daily food consumption. How does it compare with the graphs you drew in exercise 1?

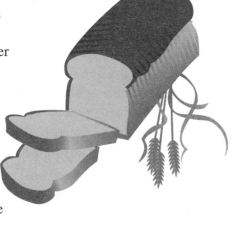

4. a) What are some foods that do not fit into any of the four groups? Did you eat any foods like these yesterday? If you did, estimate the number of servings of these foods you ate yesterday. Explain how you estimated the number of servings.

b) Why do you think these foods are not included in *Canada's Food Guide*?

c) Think of a name to describe these foods. Add this to your spreadsheet as a new food group. Construct a circle graph of your consumption that includes this fifth group.

d) Determine the ratio of the number of servings of food included in *Canada's Food Guide* to the number of servings of food in this fifth group.

5. Based on your answers to exercises 3 and 4, would you classify yourself as a healthy eater? Explain.

ACTIVITY 2

1. Why do you think *Canada's Food Guide* gives a range for the recommended number of servings rather than a specific number?

2. Observe that the ratio of the maximum number of servings of grain products to the maximum number of servings of meat and alternatives is 12 : 3, or 4 : 1. That is, if you decide to eat the maximum number of servings from both groups, for every 4 servings of grains, you should eat 1 serving of meat and alternatives.

a) Write a ratio that compares the minimum number of servings of grain products to the minimum number of servings of meat and alternatives.

b) Write at least three other ratios that compare a number of servings of grain products to a number of servings of meat and alternatives that fall within the recommended ranges.

c) Express each ratio in parts a and b with a second term of 1. Order these ratios from least to greatest.

3. Choose a different pair of food groups. Repeat exercise 2 for these groups.

ACTIVITY 3

Use *g* to represent the number of servings of grain products, *v* to represent the number of servings of vegetables and fruits, *m* to represent the number of servings of milk products, and *a* to represent the number of servings of meat and alternatives.

1. Write an algebraic expression that describes the total number of servings of food a person eats in one day.

2. Suppose a 15-year-old person eats the minimum number of servings in each category. What are the values of *g*, *v*, *m*, and *a*? Substitute these values for the variables in your expression in exercise 1.

3. Repeat exercise 2, but suppose that the 15-year-old person eats the maximum number of servings in each category.

4. In *Activity 1*, you estimated the number of servings you ate in a day from each of the food groups. What were your values of *g*, *v*, *m*, and *a* for that day? Substitute these values for the variables in your expression in exercise 1.

The Ideas

Prepare a poster to promote healthy eating. On your poster, describe *Canada's Food Guide* and list the number of servings it recommends a youth eat from each food group. Include the graphs you drew in exercises 1 and 3 of *Activity 1*. Explain what the graphs show about your eating habits.

Cumulative Review

1. A map scale is 1 cm represents 150 km. Find the map distance for each actual distance.
   - **a)** 300 km
   - **b)** 1500 km
   - **c)** 675 km
   - **d)** 1425 km
   - **e)** 750 km
   - **f)** 1687.5 km

2. On a map, two cities are 3.5 cm apart. Suppose the map had the following scales. What would the actual distance be between the two cities?
   - **a)** 1 cm represents 20 km.
   - **b)** 1 cm represents 1.5 km.
   - **c)** 1 cm represents 50 km.
   - **d)** 1 cm represents 1500 km.
   - **e)** 1 cm represents 250 km.
   - **f)** 1 cm represents 100 km.

3. **a)** What is the scale of this drawing?
   b) How high is the tree?

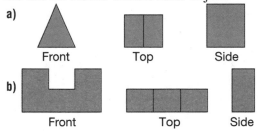

angle of elevation
29°
50 m

4. The front, top, and side views of two objects are shown below. Sketch each object.

   a) Front   Top   Side

   b) Front   Top   Side

5. Write each number in expanded form.
   - **a)** 13 054
   - **b)** 8674
   - **c)** 3 237 920
   - **d)** 24.85
   - **e)** 103.092
   - **f)** 1.407

6. Arrange each set of numbers in order from least to greatest. Explain your reasoning.
   - **a)** $4.9 \times 10^3, 4.4 \times 10^3, 4.5 \times 10^3$
   - **b)** $6.3 \times 10^6, 6.3 \times 10^8, 6.3 \times 10^5$
   - **c)** $8.42 \times 10^5, 8.56 \times 10^5, 8.53 \times 10^5$
   - **d)** $7.013 \times 10^9, 7.92 \times 10^8, 7.113 \times 10^9$

7. Express each power as a product and as a numeral.
   - **a)** 10^3
   - **b)** 3^2
   - **c)** 5^4
   - **d)** 10^5
   - **e)** 1.5^2
   - **f)** 7^3
   - **g)** 12^2
   - **h)** 8^4

8. Write each number in scientific notation.
   - **a)** 327 450 000
   - **b)** 92 086
   - **c)** 5 720 000
   - **d)** 771 496
   - **e)** 1.7 billion
   - **f)** 486 million

9. Replace each ■ with <, >, or =.
   - **a)** $\frac{2}{7}$ ■ $\frac{1}{2}$
   - **b)** $\frac{3}{4}$ ■ $\frac{8}{9}$
   - **c)** $\frac{4}{5}$ ■ $\frac{7}{12}$
   - **d)** $\frac{2}{3}$ ■ $\frac{10}{15}$
   - **e)** 0.55 ■ $\frac{4}{9}$
   - **f)** $\frac{8}{6}$ ■ 1.5
   - **g)** $\frac{3}{10}$ ■ 0.28
   - **h)** 5.8 ■ 6.1
   - **i)** 10.05 ■ 4.9

10. Add by expressing the fractions in decimal form.
    - **a)** $\frac{1}{2} + \frac{3}{5}$
    - **b)** $\frac{3}{7} + \frac{1}{4}$
    - **c)** $\frac{1}{6} + \frac{2}{9}$
    - **d)** $\frac{3}{5} + \frac{1}{8}$
    - **e)** $\frac{3}{2} + \frac{7}{10}$
    - **f)** $\frac{5}{3} + \frac{2}{7}$
    - **g)** $\frac{4}{3} + \frac{5}{8} + \frac{1}{7}$
    - **h)** $\frac{5}{9} + \frac{2}{3} + \frac{1}{10}$
    - **i)** $\frac{6}{7} + \frac{7}{11} + \frac{4}{9}$

11. Use your fraction strips and number lines to divide.
    - **a)** $\frac{1}{4} \div 2$
    - **b)** $\frac{1}{4} \div 1$
    - **c)** $\frac{1}{4} \div \frac{1}{2}$
    - **d)** $\frac{1}{4} \div \frac{1}{4}$
    - **e)** $\frac{1}{4} \div \frac{1}{8}$
    - **f)** $\frac{1}{4} \div \frac{3}{8}$

12. In a class of 32 students, $\frac{5}{8}$ of the students are girls.
    - **a)** How many girls are in the class?
    - **b)** Two-fifths of the girls attended the football game. How many girls attended the football game?
    - **c)** Five-sixths of the boys attended the football game. How many boys attended the game?

13. Milena bought 1000 shares of Global Inc. for $10⅞ per share. Three months later, she sold half of them for $12¼.
    - **a)** How much profit did Milena earn per share?
    - **b)** How much profit did she earn altogether?

14. a) Which of these provinces consumes the most energy?

Province	Fraction of Canadian energy consumption	Fraction of Canadian population
British Columbia	$\frac{1}{10}$	$\frac{3}{25}$
Ontario	$\frac{1}{3}$	$\frac{10}{27}$
Quebec	$\frac{1}{5}$	$\frac{1}{4}$

b) What fraction of the total Canadian energy consumption do the three provinces consume together?

c) What fraction do the other provinces and territories consume together?

d) Compare the fraction of energy consumption with the fraction of Canadian population. Which fraction is larger for each province?

e) Why do you think the fractions in part d for each province are different?

15. A salesperson earns a monthly salary of $1000 plus 3.5% commission on all goods sold. If she sells more than $30 000, she receives a bonus of $500. In a certain month, the salesperson sells $40 000 worth of goods. Calculate her total earnings for that month.

16. A computer costs $3000, taxes included. Clara estimates it will take her 1 year to save to buy one. The system is currently on sale at 20% off. Clara is considering borrowing money to buy the computer now.

a) Calculate the discount and sale price.

b) A loan for the cost of the computer can be obtained for 1 year at 12% interest. Calculate the interest and the total amount Clara will have to pay back.

c) Is it cheaper for Clara to borrow and purchase the computer at the sale price, or to wait until she has saved enough to buy the computer at the regular price?

17. A quality-control inspector randomly removes items from the production line to test their durability. Some results for various products are given below. For each item, determine which measure of central tendency best describes the data.

	Name	Time before failure (weeks)
a)	headlight	2 2 2 4 3 4 26
b)	tail-light	13 18 19 22 33 33 109
c)	household bulb	27 29 29 31 31 33 36

18. A spinner has 3 congruent sectors labelled A, B, and C. The pointer is spun and a regular die is rolled.

a) What is the probability of spinning A and rolling 1?

b) What is the probability of spinning A and rolling an odd number?

c) What is the probability of spinning A or B and rolling 1 or 2?

19. At a basketball game, a random sample of 500 students were asked to fill in this questionnaire.

Do you think booing should be allowed during a game?					Of which team are you a fan?	
Strongly agree	No opinion	Strongly disagree			Home Team	Visiting Team
2	1	0	−1	−2	☐	☐

The results were sorted. All the home team ballots were placed in one hat. All the visitors' ballots were placed in another hat. Fifty ballots were then removed from each hat. The scores were added. The results are shown in the graph below.

a) What does a negative score indicate about booing?

b) What is the visiting team supporter's opinion on booing?

c) Are home team fans in favour of booing? Explain.

20. A die is labelled A, B, C, D, E, and F. Two people play a game. They each roll the die in turn for a total of 5 turns. The scoring is as follows: A counts as −2, B counts as +2, C counts as −1, D counts as +1, E counts as −3, and F counts as +3. The person with the lowest score wins. The results from one game are shown.

Turn	Brendan	Alexander
1	F	A
2	B	A
3	B	E
4	A	F
5	C	D

a) What were the scores?
b) Which player won?

21. A multiple-choice test has 25 items. A score of +4 is given for each correct answer. A score of −1 is given for each incorrect answer. A student has 17 items correct. What is his score?

22. A student plans a 3-day bicycle trip. On the first day, she travelled 64.2 km. On the second day, she travelled 72.8 km. The total journey is 182.6 km. How far will she have to travel on the third day?

23. A mechanic completes repairs on a car. The work order is shown in the table.

Repair	Time (h)
replace cylinder head gasket	5.3
replace CV joint	1.6
tune and adjust transmission	2.6
repair brake lines	0.8

The mechanic works an 8-h day. If she is required to work more than 8 h, she is paid extra.

a) Estimate the time taken for the repairs.
b) Calculate the time taken. Did the job involve overtime? If so, how much?

24. A clown costume is to be sewn for a play. The pattern requires 3.2 m² of cloth, 1.35 m of various ribbons and trim, and 14 buttons. The prices of these items at two stores are shown.

Item	Cloth World	Stitch Ville
cloth	$6.95/m²	$6.59/m²
ribbons and trim	$3.24/m	$4.51/m
buttons	$0.04 each	$0.05 each

a) Calculate the total cost at each store.
b) From which store should the items be bought?

25. Let l represent the length of a piece of paper. Write an expression to describe the length of each paper.
   a) a piece 6 cm longer
   b) a piece 3 cm shorter
   c) a piece twice as long
   d) a piece half as long
   e) a piece four times as long
   f) a piece two-thirds as long

26. For each picture below:
   i) Write an equation relating the number of candies in each pan.
   ii) Solve the equation.
   iii) How many candies are in each bag?

   a)

   b)

   c)

   d)

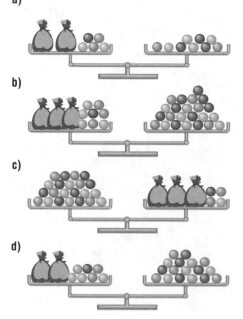

TWO-DIMENSIONAL GEOMETRY

WHAT'S COMING UP?

DEPARTMENTS

9

Start With What You Know

John Hancock Center

Fazlur Khan

The innovative, 100-storey John Hancock Center opened in Chicago in 1970. Its exterior diagonal braces provide support and stability. Each diagonal beam spans 18 storeys. Engineer Fazlur Kahn played a vital role in the building's design.

1. Describe each of these items in your own words. Then find an example of each item in the photographs on these pages. If you have questions about any of these items, check the glossary at the end of this book.
   a) parallel lines
   b) perpendicular lines
   c) an acute angle
   d) an obtuse angle
   e) a right angle
   f) a straight angle
   g) a reflex angle
   h) a rectangle
   i) a square
   j) a parallelogram
   k) a rhombus
   l) a trapezoid

2. Draw an example of each of these triangles. Find an example of each kind of triangle in the photographs on these pages.
   a) equilateral
   b) isosceles
   c) scalene
   d) right

3. Determine the value of x that makes each of these equations true. Describe each step you make.
   a) $x = 23 - 11$
   b) $x + 52 = 180$
   c) $37 = 90 - x$
   d) $18 = 3x$
   e) $2x = 126$

4. Use the photographs and information on these pages to make up an exercise for a classmate to answer. Prepare a solution to your exercise so the person can check her or his answer.

I.M. Pei

Bank of China

The Bank of China in Hong Kong is a dramatic structure which rises over 350 m. Architect I.M. Pei and engineer Leslie Robertson used a triangular glass and metal grid instead of a traditional interior steel frame. The bank required 40% less steel than most buildings of this height.

National Gallery of Canada

Moshe Safdie

The National Gallery of Canada, in Ottawa, was completed in 1988. This striking building contains great works of art from around the world. It was designed by architect Moshe Safdie. From the Great Hall, visitors can look out to the city of Ottawa or enter the galleries.

9.1 *USING A VARIETY OF TOOLS FOR CONSTRUCTIONS*

Developing the Ideas

We use many tools to make geometric constructions. Some of these tools are shown below.

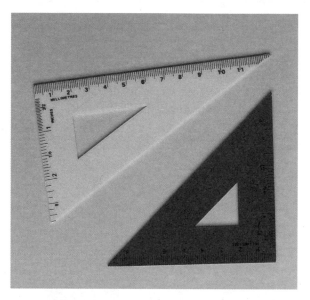

Plastic triangles are used to construct angles of 30°, 45°, 60°, and 90°.

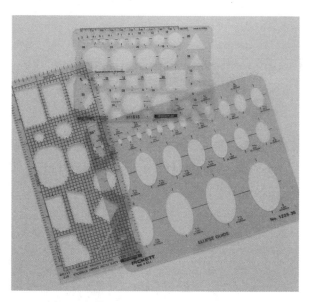

Templates can be used to draw certain figures quickly and accurately.

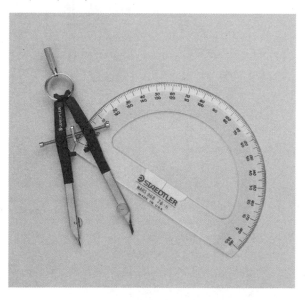

Protractors are used to construct and measure angles. *Compasses* are used to draw circles.

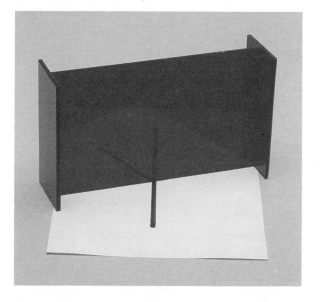

Transparent mirrors can be used to construct lines of symmetry and perpendicular lines.

We can also use simple ideas, like paper folding, to construct lines of symmetry. Tracing paper can be used to copy a diagram or part of a diagram.

Work in a group. Some groups complete the activities by using Method 1. The others use Method 2.

ACTIVITY 1

Follow the steps to construct an angle and then draw the line that divides the angle into two equal parts. This line is called the *bisector* of the angle.

Method 1 Using a plastic triangle
Step 1
Draw any acute angle, ∠ABC.
Step 2
Place the triangle with one angle at B and one edge along BC. Draw a line.

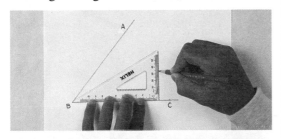

Step 3
Place the triangle with the same angle at B and the same edge along AB. Draw a line.

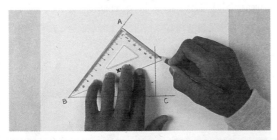

Step 4
Label M where the lines you drew intersect. Join BM. BM is the bisector of ∠ABC.

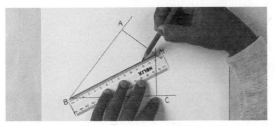

Method 2 By paper folding
Step 1
Draw any acute angle, ∠XYZ.
Step 2
Fold the paper so that XY lies along ZY. Crease along the fold line.

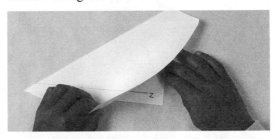

Step 3
Open the paper. The fold line is the bisector of ∠XYZ.

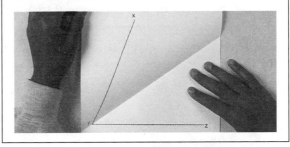

- Show another group of students how you completed your construction. Listen while the other group explains its method. Ensure that you understand how it was done.

Follow the steps to construct a perpendicular to a line at a point on the
line. Recall that a perpendicular to a line intersects the line at 90°.

Method 1 Using a transparent mirror	Method 2 Using a plastic triangle
Step 1	**Step 1**
Draw any line. Label it VW. Mark a point N on the line.	Draw any line. Label it EF. Mark a point P on the line.
Step 2	**Step 2**
Place the mirror on the line so that it passes through N. Adjust the mirror so that the line coincides with itself when you look in the mirror.	Place the triangle so that the 90° angle is at P, and one side of the triangle lies along the line.
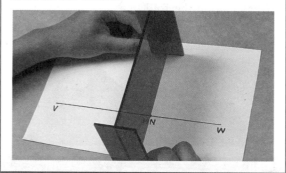	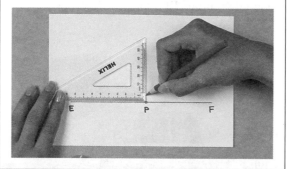
Step 3	**Step 3**
Draw a line along the edge of the mirror, through N. This line is perpendicular to VW.	Draw a line along the side of the triangle, through P. This line is perpendicular to EF.
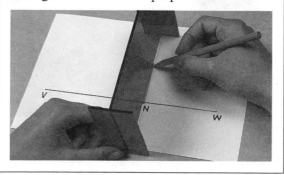	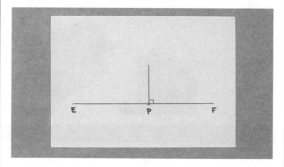

• Show another group of students how you completed your construction.
  Listen while the other group explains its method. Ensure that you
  understand how it was done.

Follow the steps to construct a line that is perpendicular to a line segment and divides the line segment into two equal parts. This line is called the *perpendicular bisector* of the line segment.

Method 1 By paper folding

Step 1

Draw a line segment any length. Label it AB.

Step 2

Fold the paper so that point A lies on point B. Crease along the fold.

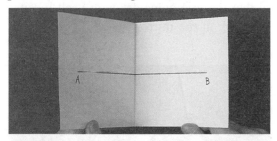

Step 3

Open the paper. The fold line is the perpendicular bisector of AB.

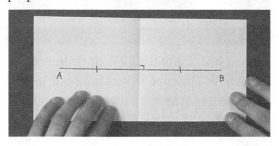

- Show another group of students how you completed your construction. Listen while the other group explains its method. Ensure that you understand how it was done.

Method 2 Using both sides of a ruler

Step 1

Draw a line segment any length. Label it PQ.

Step 2

Place the ruler so that P is on one side and Q is on the other. Draw lines on both sides.

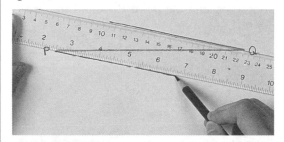

Step 3

Repeat Step 2 with the ruler placed the other way.

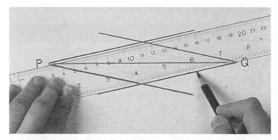

Step 4

Label S and T where the lines you drew intersect. Join ST. ST is the perpendicular bisector of PQ.

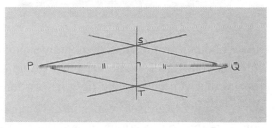

Follow the steps to construct a perpendicular to a line through a point that is not on the line.

Method 1 Using a ruler and protractor
Step 1
Draw any line. Label it EF. Mark a point P above the line.
Step 2
Place the protractor on the line. The line should coincide with 0° and 180° on the protractor, and the point P should lie on the 90° line. Mark a point C at the 90° mark.
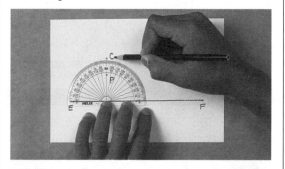
Step 3
Join CP. Extend CP to meet the line EF. CP is perpendicular to EF.
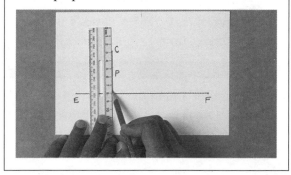

Method 2 Using a transparent mirror
Step 1
Draw any line. Label it RS. Mark a point Y above the line.
Step 2
Place the mirror across the line, so that the mirror passes through Y. Adjust the mirror so that the line coincides with itself when you look in the mirror.

Step 3
Draw a line along the edge of the mirror, through Y. This line is perpendicular to RS.
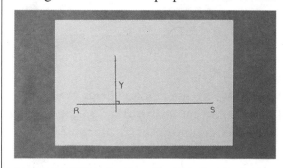

- Show another group of students how you completed your construction. Listen while the other group explains its method. Ensure that you understand how it was done.

In the following exercises, you will have opportunities to use other tools to complete the constructions in *Activities 1* to *4*.

Working with Mathematics

Something to talk about

1. Look around you. Give examples of perpendicular line segments.

2. Explain what is meant by each term:
   a) the midpoint of a line segment
   b) the bisector of an angle
   c) the perpendicular bisector of a line segment

3. Several different line segments can be drawn from point P to line AB.

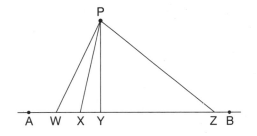

Which line segment represents the distance between P and the line AB? Explain.

Practice

4. Measure this angle.

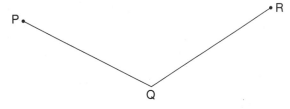

Use a protractor and ruler to construct another angle the same size.

5. Draw any obtuse angle PQR. Use a transparent mirror to bisect the angle. Measure the two parts of the angle. Are they equal?

6. Draw any line segment MN. Mark a point on the segment. Use paper folding to construct the perpendicular at that point.

7. Mark a point X. Use compasses to draw all the points that are 4 cm from X.

Work together

8. a) Draw any line segment PQ. Use a ruler and protractor to construct the perpendicular bisector of PQ.
   b) Choose a point on the perpendicular bisector. Measure its distance from P and from Q. What do you notice?
   c) Choose a different point on the perpendicular bisector and repeat part b.
   d) Compare your conclusion with those of other students. Explain how a point on the perpendicular bisector of a line segment is related to the ends of the segment.

9. Draw any line segment TU. Mark a point below the segment. Use a plastic triangle to construct the perpendicular to the segment through the point.

10. Draw any line segment AB that is less than 10 cm long.
    a) Use compasses to mark the points that are 5 cm from A.
    b) Use compasses to mark the points that are 5 cm from B.
    c) How many points are there that are 5 cm from both A and B? Join these points.
    d) Label the point C where the line you drew in part c intersects AB. Measure AC and CB. What do you notice? What is the measure of the angle at C?

11. Draw any triangle DEF. Construct the perpendicular from D to the side EF. If △DEF is obtuse, you may need to extend the side EF. Label the point G where the perpendicular from D intersects EF. The line segment DG is called an *altitude* of △DEF. How many altitudes can you draw for your triangle?

12. a) Draw any triangle GHI. Construct the perpendicular bisector of each side of the triangle. What do you notice? Check your result with those of other students.
    b) Write a rule about the perpendicular bisectors of the sides of a triangle.

13. a) Draw any triangle JKL. Construct the bisector of each angle. What do you notice? Check your result with those of other students. Do all of you agree?

    b) Write a rule about the angle bisectors of a triangle.

14. To help boats navigate the rocky areas of a harbour, the coast guard installed two buoys 800 m apart. A boat uses radar to travel a path so that the boat is always the same distance from both buoys.

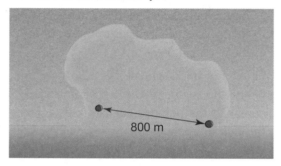

800 m

    a) Choose a scale to represent the distance in metres. Draw a line segment PS to represent the buoys, and the distance between them.

    b) Use compasses to mark the possible positions of the boat when it is at these distances from P and from S.
       i) 600 m   ii) 500 m   iii) 450 m

    c) Join the points you marked in part b. This represents the path of the boat.

    d) How does the path of the boat relate to line segment PS? How could you verify this?

On your own

15. Measure this angle.

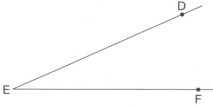

    Use tracing paper and a ruler to construct another angle the same size.

16. Draw any acute angle ABC. Use a ruler and protractor to bisect the angle. Measure the two parts of the angle. Are they equal?

17. Draw any line segment CD. Mark a point on the segment. Use a ruler and protractor to construct the perpendicular at that point.

18. Draw any line segment JK. Mark a point above the segment. Use paper folding to construct the perpendicular to the segment through that point.

19. Draw any line segment XY. Use a transparent mirror to construct the perpendicular bisector of XY.

20. To measure the distance across a river, the angle to a tree T on the opposite bank was measured from two points A and B. The distance between A and B and the measures of the angles are shown in this diagram.

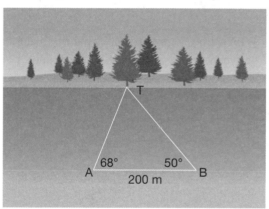

T

68°   50°

A   200 m   B

Complete this exercise to construct a scale drawing to measure the shortest distance across the river from T.

    a) Choose a scale to represent the distance in metres. Using this scale, how long will the line segment AB be?

    b) Construct △ABC using the measurements in the diagram.

    c) Construct the altitude from T to AB. Measure the altitude.

    d) What is the shortest distance across the river at T?

21. To find the height of a mound of sugar, measurements were made from point A at the base of the mound to point B at the top. The measure of ∠A and the length AB are shown on the photograph below. Construct a scale drawing. Calculate the approximate height of the mound of sugar.

22. Use any of the constructions in *Activities 1 to 4* on pages 429 to 432.
   a) Construct a rectangle with length 10 cm and width 7 cm.
   b) Construct a square with sides 8 cm.

23. **a)** Mark a point. Use it as the centre of a circle. Draw a circle with radius 4.5 cm.
   b) Mark and label two points A and B. Draw a circle, centre A, so that B lies on the circle.
   c) Mark and label two points C and D. Draw a circle that has CD as its diameter.
   d) Mark and label two points E and F. Draw a circle through E and F so that EF is not a diameter.
   e) Mark and label 3 points A, B, and C, not in a straight line. Draw a circle through A, B, and C.

Extend your thinking

24. A ski chalet approximates an isosceles triangle. The height of the chalet is 10 m. The sloping roofs measure 12 m from the base to the peak. Construct a scale drawing. What is the width of the chalet at its base?

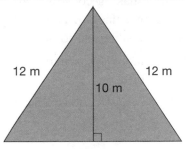

25. A and B are two vertices of a square.

Copy these dots on paper. Draw as many squares as you can that have A and B as two vertices.

COMMUNICATING

The Ideas

In your journal, explain each term in your own words. Draw a diagram where necessary.
   a) the bisector of an angle
   b) the perpendicular bisector of a line segment
   c) an altitude of a triangle

BOGGLE YOUR MIND

Hertz Corporation is the world's largest car rental company. In March 1995, Hertz announced that it would buy 520 000 new vehicles for its worldwide fleet. Estimate how far these cars would stretch if they were parked end-to-end. How large a parking lot would they fill if they were parked side-by-side?

Making Constructions Using a Draw Program

 You have been making constructions using compasses for circles and a ruler for straight lines. A Draw program has some interesting tools built in, which enable you to do constructions on the screen.

We shall use ClarisWorks. Start the program and choose Drawing. Turn Autogrid off.

For most of the constructions, you only need to use the Arc tool; the one that looks like this

and makes a figure that looks like this:

You will also need the Flip Horizontal and Flip Vertical commands from the Arrange menu.

Constructing the perpendicular bisector of a line segment

1. Make a horizontal segment in the middle of your screen.

2. Use the Arc tool to make an arc big enough to cover more than one-half of the segment. Drag the arc so that the arc centre is exactly on one end of the segment. Colour the arc to find its centre.

3. Select Duplicate from the Edit menu. Select Flip Horizontal from the Arrange menu. Drag the duplicate so that its centre is on the other end of the segment.

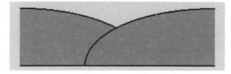

4. Select both arcs (click on one, shift-click on the other). Duplicate both arcs. Flip the duplicates vertically and drag them so that their centres are on each end of the segment.

5. Change the shading of all four arcs to transparent so you can see where the arcs cross.

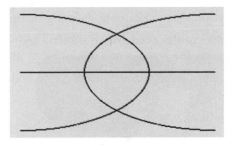

6. Draw a segment that passes through the points where the arcs intersect.

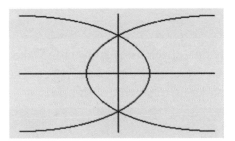

7. Delete the arcs. You have drawn the perpendicular bisector of the original segment.

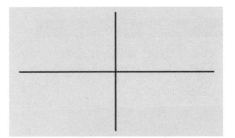

8. Repeat the construction on paper, using ruler and compasses. The compasses will produce arcs of circles. The computer program produces arcs of ovals. These arcs work just as well if you duplicate the same arc for all four parts.

Constructing the perpendicular from a point to a line

Use the preceding construction as a guide. Develop the steps to draw a perpendicular from a point to a line using the Arc tool. This is how you can start.

1.

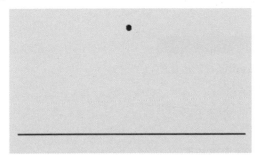

2.

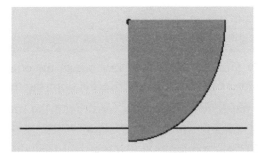

Mathematics & Technology

Linking Ideas

9.2 THE ANGLE MEASURES OF A TRIANGLE

Developing the Ideas

▶ ▶ *Through Activities*

ACTIVITY 1

Work in a group. You'll need paper, a ruler, and scissors.

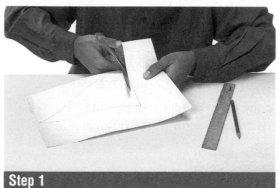

Step 1

Use a ruler to draw a large, acute scalene triangle. Be sure all the sides have different lengths. Cut out the triangle.

Step 2

Fold one side of the triangle in half. Make a small crease at the edge of the paper. The crease marks the midpoint of the side.

Step 3

Repeat the previous step to find the midpoint of another side of the triangle. Join the two midpoints with a ruler.

Step 4

Fold the paper along the line segment you drew. Where does the vertex at the top of the triangle end up?

Step 5

Carefully fold the triangle so that one of the other vertices ends up at the same point as the first vertex. Repeat with the third vertex.

1. What happened to the three vertices of the triangle? What does this tell you about the sum of the angle measures in the triangle?

2. Repeat your exploration using a right triangle, an isosceles triangle, or an equilateral triangle. What do you discover about the sum of its angle measures?

ACTIVITY 2

1. Draw a large triangle.

2. Use a protractor to measure the angles of the triangle.

3. Record these measures and calculate their sum.

4. Repeat Steps 1 to 3 for two different large triangles.

5. Compare your answers with those of five students. List the sum of the angle measures for each of the 18 triangles.

6. Calculate the mean and the median for the sum of the angle measures of a triangle.

7. Write a statement about the sum of the measures of the angles of a triangle.

8. Try to construct a triangle whose angle measures have a sum different from that in Step 7.

▶ ▶ **Through Guided Examples**

In the previous activities, you should have discovered this fact.

• • • • • • • •

The sum of the measures of the angles of a triangle is 180°.

We can use this fact to find the measure of an angle of a triangle if we know the measures of the other two angles.

Example 1 ....

Find the measure of ∠P.

Solution

The sum of the angle measures is 180°.
∠P + ∠Q + ∠R = 180°
∠P + 18° + 114° = 180°
∠P + 132° = 180°
We want the number that is added to 132° to make 180°.
This is 180° − 132° = 48°
∠P = 48°

BOGGLE YOUR MIND

According to Statistics Canada, Canadians spend an average of 20 min daydreaming every day. The life expectancy of a Canadian female is 79 years. The life expectancy of a Canadian male is 73 years. Does a typical Canadian spend more or less than one year daydreaming in her or his lifetime?

Example 2···

Find the measure of the angles marked *x*.

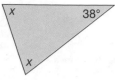

Solution

The two angles marked *x* have equal measure.
The sum of the angle measures is 180°.
$x + x + 38° = 180°$
$\quad 2x + 38° = 180°$
$2x$ is the number that is added to 38° to make 180°.
This is $180° - 38° = 142°$
$2x = 142°$
$\quad x = \dfrac{142°}{2}$
$\quad\quad = 71°$

Example 3··

Find the measure of the angle marked *x*.

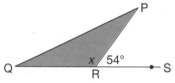

Solution

We do not know the measures of any angles in △PQR.
We cannot use the sum of the angle measures to find *x*.
We know that ∠QRS is a straight angle.
$\quad ∠QRS = 180°$
$x + 54° = 180°$
x is the number that is added to 54° to make 180°.
This is $180° - 54° = 126°$
$x = 126°$

Example 3 illustrates supplementary angles.

• • • • • • • • •

Two angles are *supplementary* if their sum is 180°.

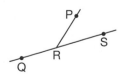

∠QRP and ∠PRS are supplementary angles.

Example 4

Find the measure of the angle marked *a*.

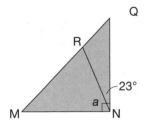

Solution

We do not know the measures of the angles in △MNR. We cannot use the sum of the angle measures to find *a*. We do know that ∠QNM is a right angle.

∠QNM = 90°

$a + 23° = 90°$

a is the number that is added to 23° to make 90°.

This is $90° − 23° = 67°$

$a = 67°$

Example 4 illustrates complementary angles.

• • • • • • • • •

Two angles are *complementary* if their sum is 90°.

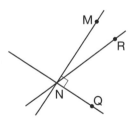

∠MNR and ∠RNQ are complementary angles.

Arrange three toothpicks to form an equilateral triangle, as in the photograph. Add three more toothpicks to the figure so that at least four equilateral triangles are formed.
Can you think of more than one way to do this?

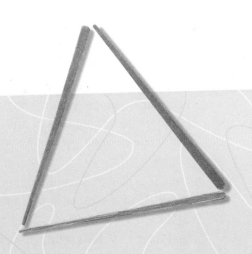

Working with Mathematics

Something to talk about

1. **a)** What is the sum of the measures of the angles in a triangle?

   b) Is it possible for a triangle to contain two right angles? Why or why not?

   c) Explain why a triangle cannot have more than one obtuse angle.

   d) Is there a right triangle that has an obtuse angle?

2. The three angles of an equilateral triangle have equal measure. What is the measure of each angle?

3. A certain right triangle has two angles of equal measure. What are the measures of the angles of that triangle?

Practice

4. Two angles of a triangle are given. State the measure of the third angle.

   a) 50°, 110°   **b)** 45°, 90°

   c) 130°, 25°   **d)** 27°, 71°

5. Name two pairs of complementary angles and two pairs of supplementary angles in the diagram below. Measure one angle in each pair, then calculate the measure of the second angle. Check your calculation by measuring.

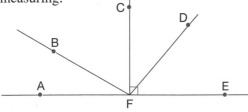

6. Find one pair of complementary angles and one pair of supplementary angles in the photographs on pages 426 and 427. Measure one angle in each pair. Draw each pair of angles.

7. One of a pair of supplementary angles is given. Find the other supplementary angle.

   a) 30°   **b)** 40°   **c)** 72°

   d) 85°   **e)** 111°   **f)** 159°

8. One of a pair of complementary angles is given. Find the other complementary angle.

   a) 87°   **b)** 73°   **c)** 65°

   d) 24°   **e)** 18°   **f)** 2°

Work together

9. Find the measure of each angle marked x.

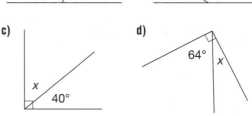

10. Draw any triangle. Label the vertices A, B, and C. Cut out the triangle, then tear each angle from the triangle as shown. Try to arrange the angles to show that the sum of their measures is 180°.

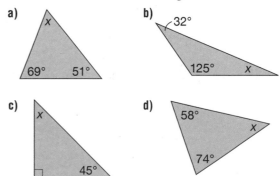

11. Find the measure of each angle marked x.

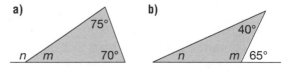

12. Find the measures of the angles marked m and n.

    a)   **b)**

c)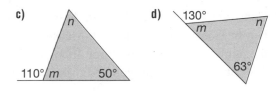

d)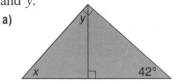

13. Find the measures of the angles marked *x* and *y*.

a)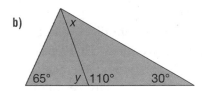

b)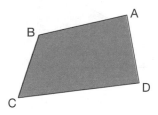

14. a) Is it possible for two angles in a triangle to be supplementary? If your answer is yes, what kind of triangle is it? If your answer is no, explain.

b) Is it possible for two angles in a triangle to be complementary? If your answer is yes, what kind of triangle is it? If your answer is no, explain.

15. Draw a quadrilateral like that shown.

Draw the diagonal AC.

a) What is the sum of the measures of the angles of △ABC?

b) What is the sum of the measures of the angles of △ADC?

c) What is the sum of the measures of the angles of quadrilateral ABCD?

d) Is the result for part c true for all quadrilaterals? Explain.

e) Draw several different quadrilaterals. Measure the angles in each one. Does each sum agree with your answer to part c?

16.

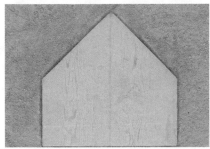

Home plate on a baseball diamond has the shape of a pentagon. Draw a pentagon like the home plate shown in the photograph. Use the method of exercise 15 to divide the pentagon into triangles.

a) How many triangles did you draw?

b) What is the sum of the angle measures of a pentagon?

On your own

17. For each angle, state the measure of the angle that is complementary to it, and the measure of the angle that is supplementary to it.

a) 12°   **b)** 24°   **c)** 47°   **d)** 63°   **e)** 89°

18. Find the measure of the third angle in each triangle.

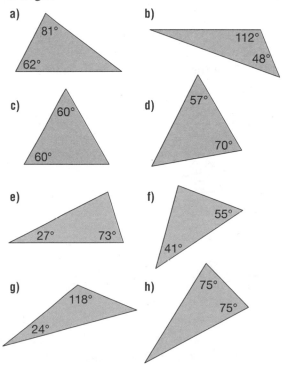

19. Find the measure of each angle marked *e*.

a)

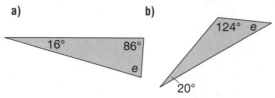

16°   86°
e

b)

124° e

20°

c)

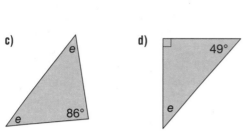

e

e   86°

d)

49°

e

20. Find the measures of the angles marked *r* and *s*.

a)

s r   36°

87°

b)

72°
r   34°

s

c)

121°
r
67°

s

d)

138°
s   r

44°

21. Find the measures of the angles marked *w* and *x*.

a)

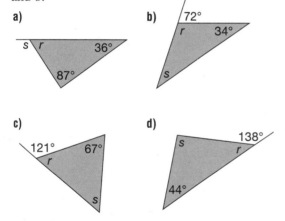

37°

44°

w   x

b)

x w

53°

22. Construct a right triangle ABC like that below. Construct altitude AD. Measure the angles in each of the three triangles. Describe any patterns you discover.

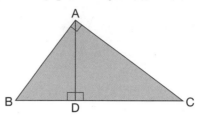

A

B   D   C

Extend your thinking

23. Kelly and Sook-Yin were discussing the triangle below. Kelly said, "That's neat. One angle is double another, and one angle is triple another. This must only be true for a triangle with angles of 30°, 60°, and 90°." After thinking for a moment, Sook-Yin replied, "No, that's not true. I can draw a triangle with different angles from this one that has this same property." Is Sook-Yin correct? If so, what are the measures of the angles in her triangle? If not, explain how you know she is wrong.

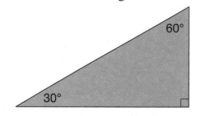

60°

30°

In your journal, draw diagrams and explain how we use the sum of the angle measures of a triangle to find the sum of the angle measures of a quadrilateral, and of a pentagon.

9.3 *ISOSCELES AND EQUILATERAL TRIANGLES*

Developing the Ideas

▶▶ *Through an Activity*

You can use paper triangles like the ones you made earlier to investigate some properties of isosceles and equilateral triangles. You'll need paper, scissors, a ruler and a protractor.

Step 1

Follow *Step 1* on page 438 to make a triangle. Mark the midpoints of two sides.

Step 2

Draw a perpendicular line from the third side of the triangle to one of the midpoints.

Step 3

Fold along the line you have drawn. Draw a line along the edge of the folded piece.

Step 4

Unfold the paper. The line you have drawn forms a triangle with two sides of the large triangle.

1. **a)** What kind of triangle have you drawn?
   b) What special properties does it have? How does your triangle illustrate those properties?

2. Fold and draw another triangle of the same kind on your paper triangle. Does it have the same properties?

3. Repeat the investigation using a right triangle, an isosceles triangle, or an equilateral triangle. Did you get the same results? Describe any differences or special cases that you see. Share your discoveries when all the groups have finished their investigations.

In an isosceles triangle, the angles opposite the equal sides are equal.

In an equilateral triangle, all three angles are equal. Since the sum of the angle measures is 180°, each angle measures 60°.

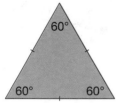

Example

Determine the angle measure indicated by *y*.

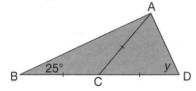

Solution

Since △ABC is isosceles, ∠BAC = 25°
Since the sum of the angle measures in △ABC is 180°,
25° + 25° + ∠BCA = 180°
    50° + ∠BCA = 180°
∠BCA is the angle that is added to 50° to make 180°.
∠BCA = 130°

Since ∠BCA and ∠ACD are supplementary, ∠ACD
is the angle that is added to 130° to make 180°.
∠ACD = 50°

Since the sum of the angle measures in △ACD is 180°,
50° + ∠CAD + ∠CDA = 180°
    ∠CAD + ∠CDA = 130°
Since △ACD is isosceles, ∠CAD = ∠CDA, so ∠CAD + ∠CDA = 2*y*.
2*y* = 130°
 y = $\frac{130°}{2}$
 y = 65°

Working with Mathematics

Something to talk about

1. Take turns explaining how to find the angle measure indicated by each letter. You may make sketches or rough calculations if you wish.

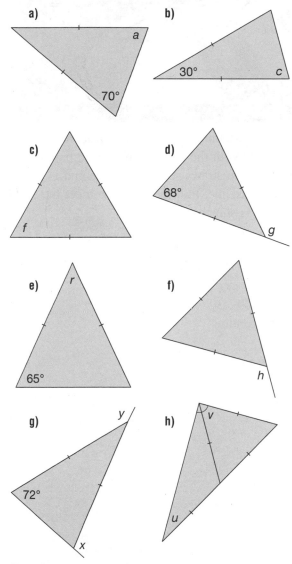

a)

b)

c)

d)

e)

f)

g)

h)

Practice

2. The measures of two angles in a triangle are given. Determine the measure of the third angle. State whether each triangle is isosceles.

   a) 40°, 60°   b) 20°, 85°   c) 38°, 100°

   d) 49°, 71°   e) 36°, 108°   f) 59°, 62°

   g) 45°, 90°   h) 22°, 79°   i) 20°, 128°

On your own

3. Determine the angle measure indicated by each letter.

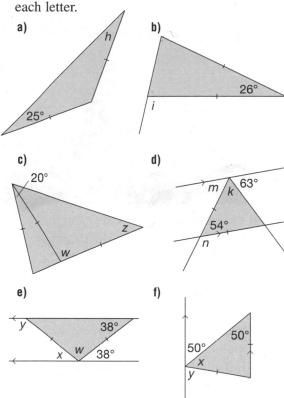

a)

b)

c)

d)

e)

f)

Work together

4. In a certain isosceles triangle, one angle is double another angle. What are the measures of the angles in this triangle?

5. There are two different isosceles triangles, each of which has a 30° angle. What are the measures of the other two angles in each triangle?

6. There are two different isosceles triangles, each of which has one angle that is 30° greater than another angle. What are the measures of all the angles in these triangles?

7. Do you think that it is possible to have each kind of triangle? Give reasons for your answers.

   a) an isosceles right triangle
   b) an isosceles obtuse triangle
   c) an isosceles acute triangle
   d) an isosceles scalene triangle

Extend your thinking

8. You'll need a straw, a length of string, cardboard, a protractor, and some tape.

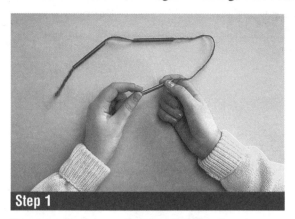

Step 1

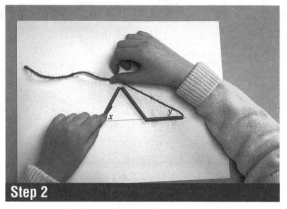

Step 2

Cut the straw into three equal lengths. Thread the string through the straws. Tape the string at one end and pull the extra string to the other end. This hinges the straw pieces.

Draw a baseline on a piece of cardboard. Tape the straw with the extra string to the baseline. Arrange the straws so that the free end is also on the baseline. Pull the string to meet the top vertex, as shown.

Look at the angles marked *x* and *y* in *Step 2*. Move the free end of the straw along the baseline and observe how the angles change. You will need to adjust the string each time so it meets the vertex.

a) Determine the value of *y* for each value of *x*: 70°, 65°, 40°, 30°, 15°.

b) If you know a value of *x*, how can you find the corresponding value of *y*?

c) Determine an equation relating *x* and *y*.

d) Use your model to show the largest possible value of *x*. What is the corresponding value of *y*?

e) Use your model to show the smallest possible value of *x*. What is the corresponding value of *y*?

f) Draw a graph showing how the value of *y* depends on the value of *x*.

COMMUNICATING

The Ideas

Suppose you know the measure of one angle in an isosceles triangle. In your journal, describe how to calculate the measures of the other two angles.

Calculating Angles in House Construction

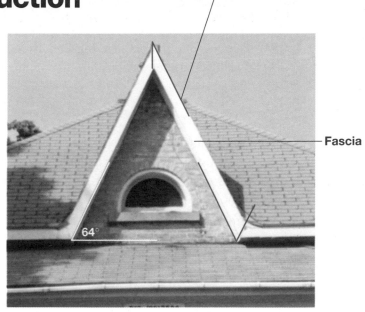

Dormer

Fascia

64°

A dormer is a small structure that projects from a sloping roof and has a window set into its outer wall.

The dormer roof of this cottage is inclined at an angle of 64°, as shown. To construct the fascia boards around the dormer, the builder needs to know the measures of the two angles indicated. You can use your knowledge of isosceles triangles to calculate these angles.

Understand the problem

- What kind of triangle is formed by the dormer roof and the baseline? How do you know this?
- How are the angles to be cut related to the angles in the triangle?

Think of a strategy

- Without measuring, can you find a way to calculate the measures of the other angles in the triangle?
- How are the angles in the triangle related to the angles the builder needs to know to make the fascia boards?

Carry out the strategy

- What are the measures of the angles the builder requires?

Look back

- Compare this problem with exercise 1b on page 447. In both cases, the measure of one angle of an isosceles triangle is given. Explain the differences in the ways that you determined the other two angles.
- In this problem, you determined the measures of some angles without measuring them. Why do you think a person would need to do this when the angles could be measured with a protractor?

Communicating the Ideas

In your journal, write a description of this problem and your solution. Someone reading your solution should be able to use your ideas to solve similar problems with different angles for the dormer roofs.

Patterns in the Angles in Isosceles Triangles

Work in a group to complete this activity. All groups will be investigating the relationships among angles in isosceles triangles.

Group 1

Copy this table. For each isosceles triangle on pages 446 and 447, record the measures of its angles in the table. Then use the data to draw a graph on a grid like the one shown on the right.

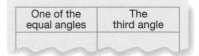

One of the equal angles	The third angle

1. Describe the pattern formed by the plotted points. Try to explain why this pattern occurs.

2. Let x represent the measures of the angles in the first column of your table. Let y represent the measures of the angles in the second column.
   a) Determine an equation relating x and y.
   b) What are the possible values of x and y in your equation?

3. Compare your graph and your equation with those of Group 2.

Angles in an isosceles triangle

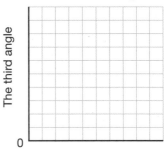

The third angle

One of the equal angles

Group 2

Copy this table. For each isosceles triangle on pages 446 and 447, record the measures of its angles in the table. Then use the data to draw a graph on a grid like the one shown on the right.

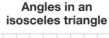

The smallest angle	The largest angle

1. Describe the patterns formed by the plotted points. Try to explain why these patterns occur.

2. Let x represent the measures of the angles in the first column of your table. Let y represent the measures of the angles in the second column.
   a) Determine an equation relating x and y for each part of your graph.
   b) What are the possible values of x and y in each equation?

3. Compare your graph and your equations with those of Group 1.

Angles in an isosceles triangle

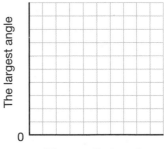

The largest angle

The smallest angle

Angles and Intersecting Lines

Work with a partner to explore some properties of intersecting lines.
You'll need a piece of waxed paper and a protractor.

Step 1

Fold the paper along a slanted line. Unfold it to show a crease.

Step 2

Fold the paper along a line that intersects the first one. Unfold the paper to show two creases.

1. Four angles are formed by the creases.
   a) Which of these angles are equal?
   b) Check your answers by measuring with a protractor or folding the paper. Then use your paper model to explain why the angles are equal. These pairs of equal angles are called *opposite angles*. Some people call these angles *vertically opposite angles*.

2. Name the pairs of opposite angles and supplementary angles in the diagram at the right. Suppose you know that *a* = 145°. Explain how to determine the values of *b*, *c*, and *d*.

3. Determine the value of *x* and of *y* in each diagram.

a)

110°
x
y

b)

x / 48°
y

c)

121° *x*
y

d)

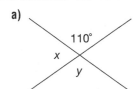

70°
x *y*
60°

e)

140°
95°
x
y

f)

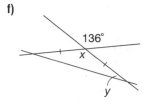

136°
x
y

9.4 ANGLES AND PARALLEL LINES

Developing the Ideas

▶ ▶ *Through Activities*

ACTIVITY 1

You can use paper triangles to investigate some properties of parallel lines. You will need paper, scissors, a ruler, and a protractor.

Step 1

Get the triangle you used on page 438 or follow the steps on that page to make another triangle.

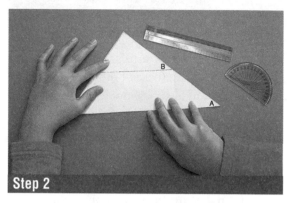

Step 2

Look at the angles shown above. How do you think their measures compare? Check your prediction. Mark the angles on your triangle to show what you have discovered.

1. The base of the triangle and the line joining the midpoints are *parallel lines*. The side of the triangle is a *transversal*. The marked angles are called *corresponding angles*.

   a) When a transversal intersects two parallel lines, what do you think is true about the corresponding angles?

   b) Find another pair of corresponding angles. Mark these angles.

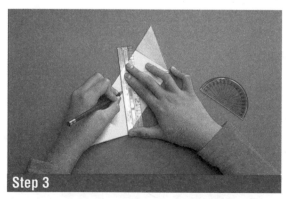

Step 3

Fold the triangle along the line joining the midpoints, so that the top vertex lies on the base. Draw a line along each edge of this folded portion.

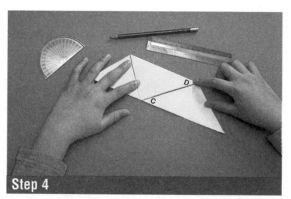

Step 4

Look at the angles shown above. How do you think their measures compare? Check your prediction. Mark the angles on your triangle to show what you have discovered.

2. The marked angles are called *interior alternate angles*.

   a) When a transversal intersects two parallel lines, what do you think is true about the interior alternate angles?

   b) Find another pair of interior alternate angles. Mark these angles.

3. Repeat your exploration using a right triangle, an isosceles triangle, or an equilateral triangle. Did you get the same results? Describe any differences or special cases that you see. Share your discoveries when all the groups have finished their investigations.

ACTIVITY 2

1. Draw a pair of parallel lines by tracing along each edge of a ruler. Draw a transversal that crosses both lines. Label the angles, as shown in the diagram.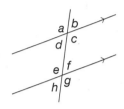

2. a) Angles *a* and *g* are called *exterior alternate angles*. How do you think their measures compare? Check your prediction by measuring.

   b) Find another pair of exterior alternate angles in the diagram. How do their measures compare?

3. a) Angles *d* and *e* are called *interior angles on the same side of the transversal*. What is the sum of their measures?

   b) Find another pair of interior angles on the same side of the transversal. How does the sum of their measures compare to your answer in part a?

4. a) Angles *a* and *h* are called *exterior angles on the same side of the transversal*. What is the sum of their measures?

   b) Find another pair of exterior angles on the same side of the transversal. How does the sum of their measures compare to your answer in part a?

5. Compare the results of your investigation with those of other groups. Did drawing different diagrams affect your results?

▶ ▶ *Through a Guided Example*

The diagrams show related angles. The lines do not have to be parallel.

- Angles forming a Z-pattern are called *interior alternate angles*. See the diagrams below left.

- Angles forming an F-pattern are called *corresponding angles*. See the diagrams above right.

- Angles on opposite sides of the transversal and outside the lines are called *exterior alternate angles*.

- Angles on the same side of the transversal and between the lines are called *interior angles on the same side of the transversal*. See the diagrams below left.

- Angles on the same side of the transversal and outside the lines are called *exterior angles on the same side of the transversal*. See the diagrams above right.

When a transversal intersects two *parallel* lines:
- The interior alternate angles are equal.
- The corresponding angles are equal.
- The exterior alternate angles are equal.
- The interior angles on the same side of the transversal are supplementary.
- The exterior angles on the same side of the transversal are supplementary.

Example

Determine the angle measure indicated by x.

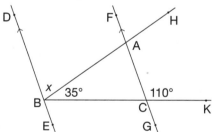

Solution

Since $\angle BCA$ and $\angle ACK$ are supplementary,

$\angle BCA + 110° = 180°$
$\quad\quad \angle BCA = 70°$

Since FG ∥ DE and $\angle EBC$ and $\angle BCA$ are interior alternate angles,

$\angle EBC = \angle BCA$
$\quad\quad = 70°$

Since $\angle DBE$ is a straight angle,

$x + 35° + 70° = 180°$
$\quad\quad\quad x = 75°$

Working with Mathematics

Something to talk about

1. In this figure:

a) name two pairs of interior alternate angles

b) name four pairs of corresponding angles

c) name two pairs of exterior alternate angles

d) name two pairs of interior angles on the same side of the transversal

e) name two pairs of exterior angles on the same side of the transversal

f) name four pairs of opposite angles

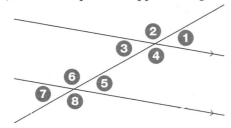

2. Find at least two sets of parallel lines and transversals in each photograph on pages 426 and 427. In each example, point out which lines are parallel, which line is the transversal, one pair of corresponding angles, and one pair of interior alternate angles.

3. In the *Example*, the angle measure indicated by *x* can be determined in many different ways. Find as many of these ways as you can.

Practice

4. Work with a partner. Take turns explaining how to find the angle measures indicated by *x*, *y*, and *z*. You may make sketches or rough calculations if you wish.

a)

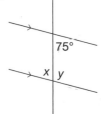

b)

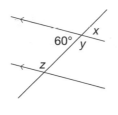

c)

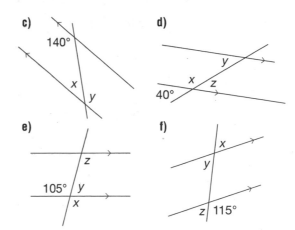

d)

e)

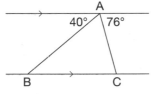

f)

On your own

5. Determine the measures of the three angles in △ABC.

a)

b)

c)

6. Determine the angle measure indicated by each letter.

a)

b)

c)

d)

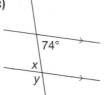

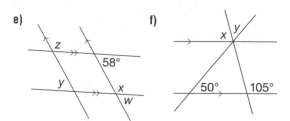

e) f)

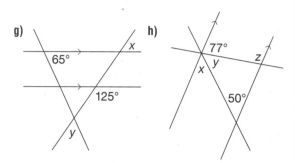

g) h)

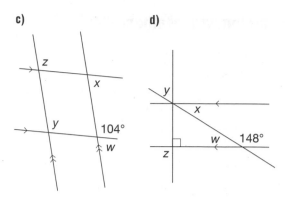

c) d)

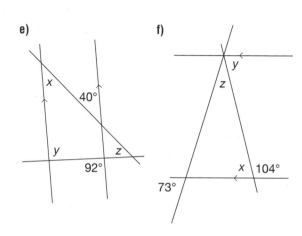

e) f)

7. Make up an exercise involving angles and parallel lines like those in exercises 4 to 6. Exchange exercises with a classmate. Complete the exercise you receive. Explain your reasoning to the person who wrote the exercise.

Work together

8. In the diagram in exercise 1, if ∠**❷** = 112°, determine the measure of each other angle. Explain each calculation.

9. In the diagram below, determine the measure of each angle. Explain each calculation.

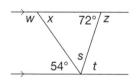

10. Determine the angle measure indicated by each letter.

a) b)

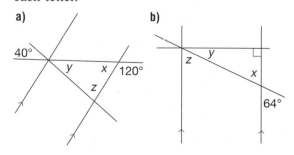

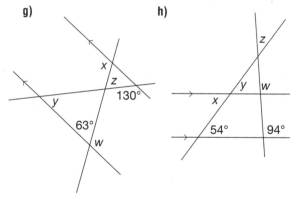

g) h)

11. Make up an exercise involving angles and parallel lines like those in exercise 10. Exchange exercises with another group. Answer the exercise you receive. Explain your reasoning to the group that wrote the exercise.

12. Do you think that two intersecting lines can both be parallel to a third line? Draw a diagram to support your answer.

13. Do you think that two intersecting lines can both be perpendicular to a third line? Draw a diagram to support your answer.

Extend your thinking

14. Two lines can intersect in 0 points or 1 point, as shown below.

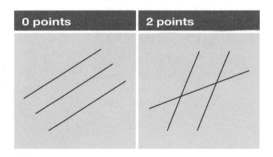

Two possibilities for three lines are also shown.

a) What other possibilities are there for three lines? Draw diagrams to support your answer.

b) What is the greatest number of points in which four lines can intersect? What is the least number? Try to find examples of four lines intersecting in all the possible numbers of points from the least to the greatest.

c) What is the greatest number of points in which five lines can intersect? Six lines can intersect?

d) If you know the number of lines, how can you find the greatest number of points in which they can intersect?

The Ideas

A transversal intersects two lines that are not parallel. Do you think any of the pairs of angles formed are equal? Record your ideas in your journal.

Arrange 12 toothpicks as shown. Then try to complete each of these challenges.

1. Create 4 identical diamonds by moving 4 toothpicks.

2. Create 3 equilateral triangles by moving 4 toothpicks.

9.5 *THE PYTHAGOREAN THEOREM*

Developing the Ideas

Over 4000 years ago, the ancient Egyptians built pyramids such as the pyramid at Cheops.

The base of the pyramid is a square. The Egyptian engineers had a method for marking 90° corners that did not require a protractor or compasses. It is believed by some that the engineers tied knots to divide a rope into 12 equal parts. The rope was then shaped into a triangle with sides of lengths 3, 4, and 5 equal parts. The engineers knew that the angle between the sides with 3 parts and 4 parts is 90°.

This triangle has a right angle opposite the longest side, which is called the *hypotenuse*. Recall that a triangle with a right angle is a *right triangle*.

Is it possible to construct a triangle with sides of lengths 3 cm, 4 cm, and 5 cm that is not a right triangle? You will investigate this in *Activity 1*.

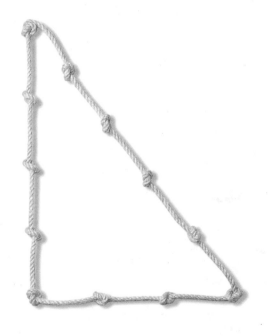

Work in a group. You will need 8 straws, a ruler, scissors, a protractor, and 1-cm grid paper.

ACTIVITY 1

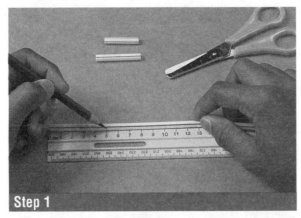

Step 1

Cut two straws so you have lengths of 3 cm, 4 cm, and 5 cm.

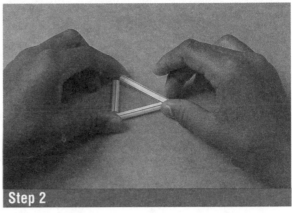

Step 2

Arrange the straws so they form the sides of a triangle. Is this a right triangle?

Can you arrange these straws to create a triangle that is not a right triangle?

Step 3

Cut out squares of side lengths 3 cm, 4 cm, and 5 cm. Place each square on the corresponding side of the triangle, as shown in the photo.

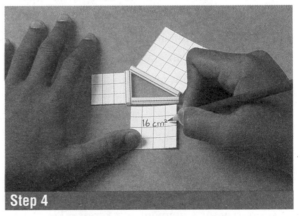

Step 4

Write on each paper square its area in square centimetres. Look at the three areas.

1. Write a sentence to describe any relationship you notice among the areas of the squares on the sides of the triangle.

ACTIVITY 2

1. Cut two straws so you have lengths of 5 cm, 12 cm, and 13 cm.

2. Repeat Step 2 of *Activity 1*.

3. Cut out squares of side lengths 5 cm, 12 cm, and 13 cm. Place the squares beside your triangle.

4. Repeat Step 4 of *Activity 1*.

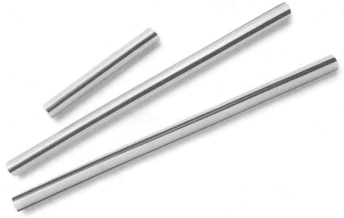

ACTIVITY 3

1. Cut two straws so you have lengths of 7 cm, 9 cm, and 10 cm.

2. Repeat the steps of *Activity 1*, but cut out squares to fit on this triangle. Classify the triangle.

3. Cut two straws so you have lengths of 4 cm, 7 cm, and 10 cm.

4. Repeat the steps of *Activity 1*, but cut out squares to fit on this triangle. Classify the triangle.

5. What relationship did the areas of the squares on the sides of a right triangle seem to have?

6. Does this relationship exist among the squares on the sides of an acute or obtuse triangle?

7. Write a statement about a relationship among the areas of the squares on the sides of a right triangle.

8. Construct a triangle with side lengths 2.8 cm, 9.6 cm, and 10.0 cm. Is this a right triangle? Use your calculator to find the area of the square you would place on each side. Does this triangle support your statement in exercise 7?

The relationship that you may have discovered in these activities is an ancient theorem called the Pythagorean Theorem.

• • • • • • • • •

The Pythagorean Theorem

The area of the square on the hypotenuse of a right triangle is equal to the sum of the areas of the squares on the other two sides.

When we know the areas of the squares on two sides of a right triangle, we can use the Pythagorean Theorem to find the area of the square on the third side.

Example 1

Find the area of the square on side AC.

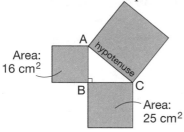

Area: 16 cm²

A hypotenuse

B

C

Area: 25 cm²

Solution

AC is the hypotenuse.

The areas on the two shorter sides are 16 cm² + 25 cm² = 41 cm²

The area of the square on AC is 41 cm².

Example 2

Find the area of the square on XY.

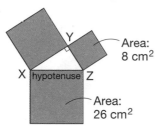

Y

Area: 8 cm²

X hypotenuse Z

Area: 26 cm²

Solution

XY is one of the shorter sides.

The area of the square on XY + 8 cm² = 26 cm²

The area of the square on XY = 26 cm² − 8 cm²

= 18 cm²

Working with Mathematics

Something to talk about

1. Explain what is meant by each term.
   a) right triangle   **b)** hypotenuse

2. State the Pythagorean Theorem in your own words.

3. **a)** Is the largest angle in a triangle always opposite the longest side?
   b) How could you use this fact to conclude that the hypotenuse is always opposite the right angle?

Practice

4. Name the hypotenuse in each triangle.

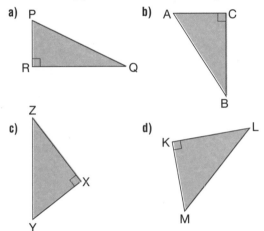

a) P, R, Q
b) A, C, B
c) Z, X, Y
d) K, L, M

5. For each triangle, write the area of the square on the third side.

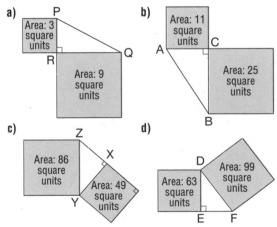

a) P, R, Q — Area: 3 square units, Area: 9 square units
b) A, C, B — Area: 11 square units, Area: 25 square units
c) Z, X, Y — Area: 86 square units, Area: 49 square units
d) D, E, F — Area: 99 square units, Area: 63 square units

Work together

6. In a right triangle, the areas of the squares on the two shortest sides are 18 cm² and 12 cm². What is the area of the square on the hypotenuse?

7. The area of the square on the hypotenuse of a right triangle is 40 cm². The area of the square on one of the other sides is 24 cm². What is the area of the square on the third side?

8. The areas of the squares on two sides of a right triangle are 12 cm² and 8 cm². What are the possible areas for the square on the third side?

9. Each triangle is an isosceles triangle. Find the area of the square on XY.

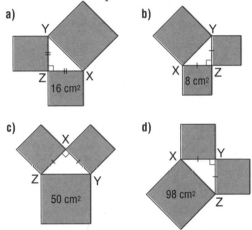

a) Y, Z, X — 16 cm²
b) Y, X, Z — 8 cm²
c) X, Z, Y — 50 cm²
d) X, Y, Z — 98 cm²

On your own

10. For each triangle, is side RS the hypotenuse of △RST?

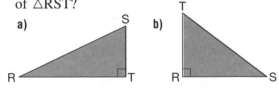
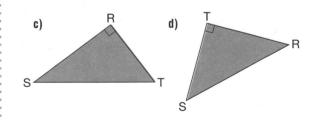

a) R, S, T
b) T, R, S
c) R, S, T
d) T, R, S

11. The areas of the squares on two sides of △ABC are given. Find the area of the square on AC.

a)

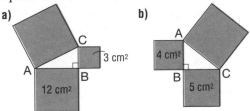

b)

12. For each triangle, calculate the area of the square on the third side.

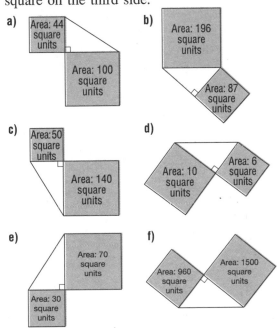

a) Area: 44 square units / Area: 100 square units

b) Area: 196 square units / Area: 87 square units

c) Area: 50 square units / Area: 140 square units

d) Area: 10 square units / Area: 6 square units

e) Area: 70 square units / Area: 30 square units

f) Area: 960 square units / Area: 1500 square units

13. If you have access to a computer and *The Geometer's Sketchpad* software, load the sketch entitled Shear Pythagoras (Macintosh version) or shear.gsp (Windows version), which comes with the program. Follow the instructions on the screen to see a visual demonstration of the Pythagorean Theorem. Try some of the other Pythagorean sketches that come with the program.

COMMUNICATING
The Ideas

Research Pythagoras for whom the Pythagorean Theorem is named. In your journal, write a few sentences about Pythagoras, and how he contributed to mathematics.

14. For each diagram, which expression represents the area of the square on side AC?

a) i) $3 \times 3 + 2 \times 2$
   ii) $3 \times 3 - 2 \times 2$

b) i) $5 \times 5 + 1 \times 1$
   ii) $5 \times 5 - 1 \times 1$

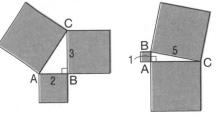

15. Find the area of the square on AC.

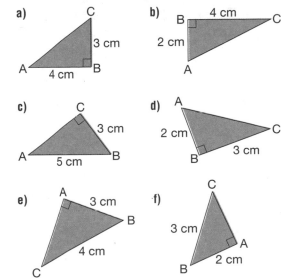

a) C, 3 cm, A, 4 cm, B

b) B, 4 cm, C, 2 cm, A

c) C, 3 cm, A, 5 cm, B

d) A, 2 cm, C, B, 3 cm

e) A, 3 cm, B, 4 cm, C

f) C, 3 cm, A, 2 cm, B

16. The area of the square on one side of a right isosceles triangle is 50 cm². What are the possible areas for the squares on the other two sides?

Extend your thinking

17. The sides of a triangle are such that the area of the square on the longest side is equal to the sum of the areas of the squares on the other two sides. Does it follow from the Pythagorean Theorem that the triangle is a right triangle? Explain your answer.

Investigating the Pythagorean Theorem Using *The Geometer's Sketchpad*

Over 2000 years ago, a Greek mathematician named Pythagoras discovered how the lengths of the sides of a right triangle are related. This relationship was also known by the ancient Babylonians during the period 1900 B.C. to 1600 B.C. The Chinese knew the Pythagorean relationship as early as A.D. 400. Follow these steps to see if you can discover the Pythagorean relationship.

Step 1 Constructing a right angle

Start the program. Select the Line tool. Draw a line.

Choose the Selection tool. The line you drew has 2 points marked with small circles. Hold the shift key down and click on one of these circles. Both the line and the point should be selected. Choose Perpendicular Line from the Construct menu. The computer will draw a new line that passes through the point you chose and is perpendicular to the line you drew.

Step 2 Constructing a right triangle

Choose the Selection tool. Click on the perpendicular line you created in Step 1.

Choose Point On Object from the Construct menu. This will create a point somewhere on the line you created in Step 1.

Use the Text tool to label one point on each line and the point where the two lines meet. If necessary, change the labels to A, B, and C, as shown in the diagram. Select the Line Segment tool.

Use the Selection tool to shift-click the points A, B, and C. Choose Segment from the Construct menu.

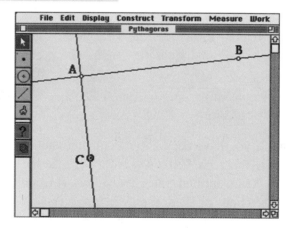

The computer will draw a triangle joining the three points.

Click on one of the lines you drew in Step 1.

Shift-click on the other line you drew in Step 1. Be sure to click on portions of the lines that are not part of the triangle. Choose Hide Lines from the Display menu.

You should now see right triangle ABC on your screen.

Label the sides of the triangle a, b, and c, as shown.

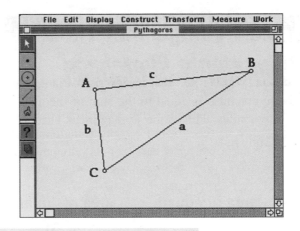

Choose the Selection tool.

Drag any vertex of △ABC. Is △ABC always a right triangle?

Step 3 Looking for a relationship

Click on line segment a. Select Length from the Measure menu. The length of this line segment is displayed on the screen. Similarly, measure and display the lengths of sides b and c.

Use the Text tool. Double-click the measure of line segment a. Type a = in the box that appears and click OK. This shortens the length statement. Repeat for line segments b and c.

Use the Selection tool to move the measures so they appear next to the sides.

Click on the measure of line segment a. Select Calculate from the Measure menu. A box like the one on the right will appear.

Click on a.
Click on ∗ (the multiplication symbol).
Click on a again. Click OK.

The computer calculates and displays the square of the length of line segment a.

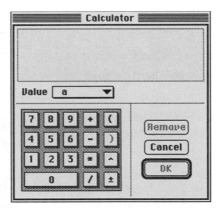

Repeat for line segments b and c.

What relationship can you find among the values?

Drag one of the vertices to change the triangle. The measures that are displayed will also change. Does the relationship you discovered still hold?

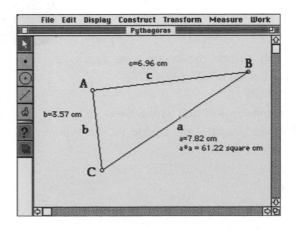

......9.6 *APPLYING THE PYTHAGOREAN THEOREM*

▶▶ *Through Discussion*

In the preceding section, you learned that in any right triangle, the area of the square on the hypotenuse is equal to the sum of the areas of the squares on the other two sides. This is the Pythagorean Theorem.

For the right triangle shown,

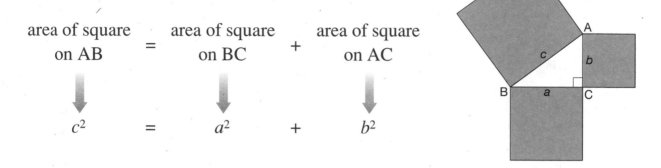

area of square on AB	=	area of square on BC	+	area of square on AC
⬇		⬇		⬇
c^2	=	a^2	+	b^2

If you know the lengths of two sides of a right triangle, you can use the Pythagorean Theorem to calculate the length of the third side.

▶▶ *Through Guided Examples*

Example 1 ....

The size of a television screen is the length of its diagonal. A television screen is 56 cm wide and 40 cm high. Calculate the length of its diagonal to the nearest centimetre.

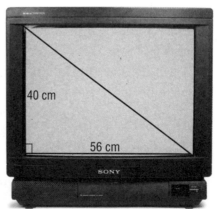

Solution

Let d centimetres represent the length of the diagonal. According to the Pythagorean Theorem,

$$d^2 = 56^2 + 40^2$$
$$= 3136 + 1600$$
$$d^2 = 4736$$

To find the value of d, we find the square root. That is, which number multiplied by itself gives 4736?
We know that $d^2 = 4736$.
This is the area of the square on the hypotenuse.
The length d is the side length of the square on the hypotenuse.
This is the square root of 4736.

$$d = \sqrt{4736}$$
$$\doteq 68.8186$$

The length of the diagonal is approximately 69 cm.

Example 2

In △RST, calculate the length of RS to the nearest millimetre.

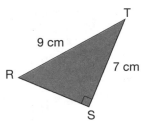

Solution

Triangle RST is a right triangle. We can use the Pythagorean Theorem.
Let t centimetres represent the length of RS.

$$9^2 = 7^2 + t^2$$
$$81 = 49 + t^2$$
$$81 - 49 = t^2$$
$$t^2 = 32$$
$$t = \sqrt{32}$$
$$\doteq 5.6568$$

RS is approximately 5.7 cm.

Example 3

Anna and Lim are on a hike. They come to a corner of a rectangular field
that measures 750 m by 400 m. Anna decides to take a shortcut and walk
diagonally across the field. Lim walks around two sides of the field.

a) Who walks farther?

b) How much farther does that person walk?

Solution

Draw a diagram.

a) Anna follows the path AC.
Lim walks along AB and BC.
Use the Pythagorean Theorem in △ABC.
Let b represent the length of AC.

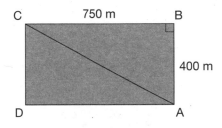

$$b^2 = 750^2 + 400^2$$
$$= 562\ 500 + 160\ 000$$
$$= 722\ 500$$
$$b = \sqrt{722\ 500}$$
$$= 850$$

Anna walks 850 m.
Lim walks 400 m + 750 m = 1150 m.
Lim walks farther.

b) Subtract to find out how much farther Lim walks.
1150 m − 850 m = 300 m
Lim walks 300 m farther.

Working with Mathematics

Something to talk about

1. In *Example 1*, the areas of the squares were added, but in *Example 2*, they were subtracted. When you use the Pythagorean Theorem, how can you tell whether to add or subtract the areas of the squares on the sides of the right triangle?

2. Which expression represents the area of the square on side AC?

a) i) $3^2 + 2^2$
   ii) $3^2 - 2^2$

b) i) $5^2 + 1^2$
   ii) $5^2 - 1^2$

c) i) $2^2 + 2^2$
   ii) $2^2 - 2^2$

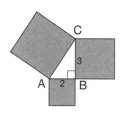
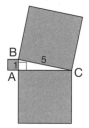
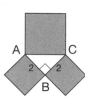

Practice

3. For each triangle below, calculate the area of the square on side AC. Use your knowledge of square roots to calculate the length of side AC, to the nearest millimetre.

a)
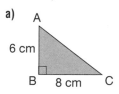

b)
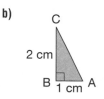

c)
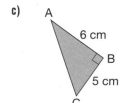

d)
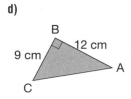

e)
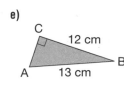

f)
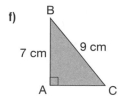

g)
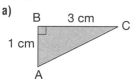

h)
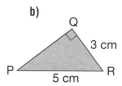

4. Calculate the length of the third side of each triangle, to the nearest millimetre.

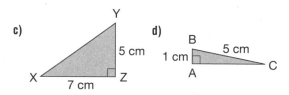

a) B   3 cm   C, 1 cm, A

b) Q   3 cm, P, 5 cm, R

c) Y, 5 cm, X, 7 cm, Z

d) B, 5 cm, 1 cm, A, C

Work together

5. a) Refer to exercise 5 on page 462. Determine the lengths of all three sides of each triangle, to 1 decimal place.
   b) Refer to exercise 9 on page 462. Determine the lengths of all three sides of each triangle, to 1 decimal place.

6. The world's smallest and lightest colour TV set was introduced in 1992. It has a screen measuring about 28 mm by 21 mm. Calculate the length of its diagonal.

7. Calculate the length of the rafters for a building. It is 12.0 m wide and has the peak of the roof 3.0 m above the ceiling. Give the answer to the nearest centimetre.

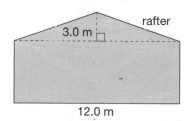

On your own

8. Find the length of each side XY. Give the answers to the nearest millimetre.

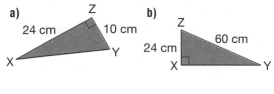

a)

Z, 24 cm, 10 cm, X, Y

b)

Z, 24 cm, 60 cm, X, Y

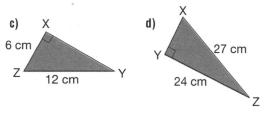

c)

X, 6 cm, Z, 12 cm, Y

d)

X, 27 cm, Y, 24 cm, Z

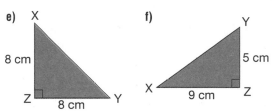

e)

X, 8 cm, Z, 8 cm, Y

f)

Y, 5 cm, X, 9 cm, Z

9. A road goes up a hill. A map indicates that the horizontal distance from the foot of the hill to the top is 1.6 km. A car's odometer indicates that the distance from the foot of the hill to the top is 2.4 km. Draw a diagram. Use it to find the height of the hill.

10. A ramp is to be built from one level of one parking garage to another. Calculate the length of the ramp, to the nearest centimetre.

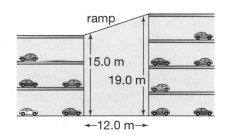

ramp
15.0 m
19.0 m
←12.0 m→

11. The world's largest TV screen was a Jumbotron constructed for an exhibition in Japan in 1985. It measured 45.7 m by 24.4 m. Calculate the length of its diagonal.

12. A boat travels due west for 1 h at 12 km/h. It then turns due north and travels in that direction for another 1.5 h. Draw a diagram. Use it to find the distance travelled by the boat from its starting point.

Extend your thinking

13. An equilateral triangle has sides 4.0 cm long. Calculate the area of the triangle to the nearest tenth of a square centimetre.

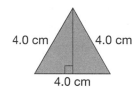

4.0 cm, 4.0 cm, 4.0 cm

14. Calculate the length of the diagonal of each rectangular prism. Give the answers to 1 decimal place.

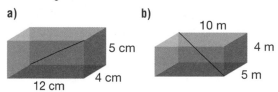

a)

5 cm, 12 cm, 4 cm

b)

10 m, 4 m, 5 m

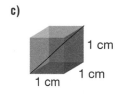

c)

1 cm, 1 cm, 1 cm

d)

1.4 m, 0.8 m, 0.6 m

The Ideas

Suppose you know the lengths of two sides of a right triangle. In your journal, write an explanation of how you could calculate the length of the third side. Include two examples with your explanation.

Review

1. Classify each triangle in two ways.

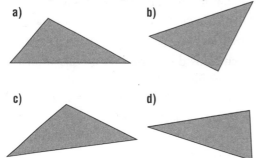

a)

b)

c)

d)

2. Use a ruler and protractor to construct an angle of measure 80°. Use any method to bisect the angle. Explain your method.

3. Draw any line segment AB. Mark a point P on the line. Use a transparent mirror to construct a line that passes through P, and is perpendicular to AB. Explain your method.

4. Draw a line segment 8 cm long. Use any method to draw the perpendicular bisector of the line segment. Explain your method.

5. Draw any line segment. Mark a point X below the line. Construct a perpendicular from the point to the line. Explain your method.

6. a) Construct ∠ABC of measure 120°.

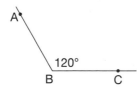

A

120°

B   C

   b) Draw the bisector of ∠ABC.
   c) Pick a point on the bisector that is at least 3 cm from B. Label this point D. Draw a line through D that is perpendicular to BC. Label the point where these two lines intersect E.
   d) Draw a line through D that is perpendicular to AB. Label the point where these two lines intersect F.
   e) Measure the distances DE and DF. What do you notice?

f) Measure ∠FDB and ∠EDB. What do you notice?

g) Measure the distances FB and EB. What do you notice?

7. a) Construct a rectangle. Decide the lengths of its sides. Draw the diagonals of the rectangle.
   b) Measure the diagonals. What do you notice?
   c) Measure the lengths of the parts of the diagonals from their point of intersection. What do you notice?
   d) Compare your answers to parts b and c with those of other students. Did all of you reach the same conclusions?

8. To determine the height of a mountain, the following angle and distance measurements were made. The length of CD cannot be measured directly since it is inside the mountain. Follow the instructions below to make a scale drawing to determine the height of the mountain.

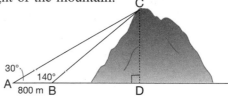

30°
140°
A 800 m B   D

   a) Choose a scale to represent the distance in metres. Use this scale to determine the length of the line segment AB.
   b) Draw the scale diagram of △ABC.
   c) Extend AB to the right. Draw the perpendicular from C to the line through AB. Mark the point D where the perpendicular intersects the line.
   d) Measure the length of CD on your diagram. What is the height of the mountain in metres?

9. The measures of two angles in a triangle are given. Determine the measure of the third angle, then classify each triangle.
   a) 59°, 31°   b) 81°, 18°   c) 42°, 85°
   d) 47°, 86°   e) 18°, 144°   f) 60°, 90°

10. a) Explain what it means for a pair of angles to be complementary or supplementary. Include diagrams with your explanations.

b) For each angle, state the measure of the angle that is complementary to it, and the measure of the angle that is supplementary to it.

    i) 8°   **ii)** 39°   **iii)** 52°

    iv) 67°   **v)** 74°   **vi)** 81°

11. Determine the angle measure indicated by each letter. Explain your calculations.

a)
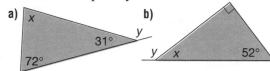

b)
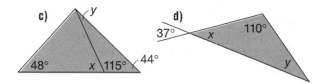

c)
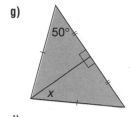

d)
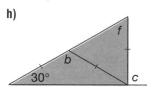

e)
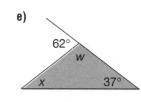

f)
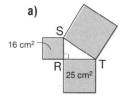

g)
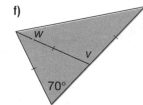

h)
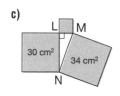

i)
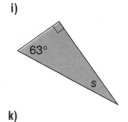

j)
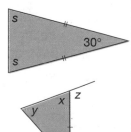

k)
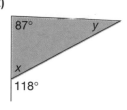

l)
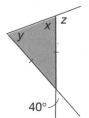

12. In the diagram below:

a) Identify six pairs of equal angles. Explain how you know the angles in each pair are equal.

b) Identify four pairs of angles that are supplementary. Explain how you know the angles are supplementary.

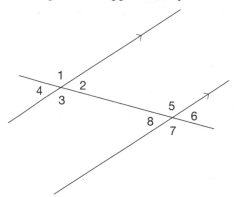

13. For each triangle, calculate the area of the square on the third side.

a)
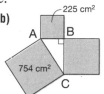

b)
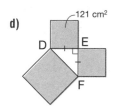

c)
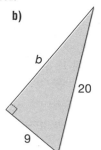

d)
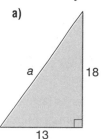

14. Find the length, to 1 decimal place, indicated by each letter.

a)
b)

Geometry on Earth's Surface

The geometry in this chapter is called *plane geometry* because the figures are all drawn on a plane. Geometry on the surface of Earth is called *spherical geometry* because the figures are drawn or visualized on a sphere. In this project you will investigate some of the differences between spherical geometry and plane geometry. You will need a globe, tape, thread, a ruler, and a protractor.

ACTIVITY 1

Investigating the distance between two points

The distance between two points can be represented by joining them with a thread. On a plane, this is a straight line.

On a globe, the distance between two points is an arc of a *great circle* — the circle formed when a plane passes through the two points and Earth's centre.

The shortest distance between two cities is an arc of a great circle, but it does not look that way on most maps. On this map the straight line joining Winnipeg and Bombay crosses the Atlantic Provinces and North Africa. This route, however, is actually much longer than the great-circle route which passes near the North Pole. Similarly, the shortest route from Winnipeg to Hong Kong is the great-circle route along the north coast of Alaska.

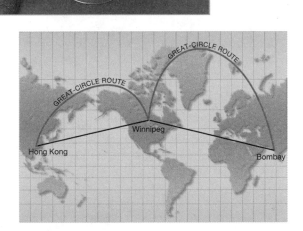

1. On a globe, using tape and thread, show the great-circle routes from Winnipeg to Hong Kong and Bombay. Compare your routes with those shown on the map. Then measure the lengths of the threads in centimetres.

2. Establish a scale for your globe by measuring its diameter as accurately as you can. Then, from a reference book, determine the diameter of Earth. How many kilometres on Earth are represented by 1 cm on the globe?

3. Combine the results of exercises 1 and 2 to calculate the great-circle distances from Winnipeg to Hong Kong and Bombay.

ACTIVITY 2

Investigating the sum of the angle measures in a triangle

When you draw a triangle on a plane, you know that its three sides are line segments. However, when you draw a triangle on a sphere, its three sides are arcs of great circles. The triangle is called a *spherical triangle*.

1. On a globe, with tape and thread, show the spherical triangles with vertices at the following cities. Measure their angles with a protractor. What is the sum of the angle measures in each spherical triangle? Do you notice anything unusual about the results?

   a) St. John's, Vancouver, Miami

   b) Winnipeg, Cairo, Rio de Janeiro

   c) Honolulu, Caracas, Nairobi

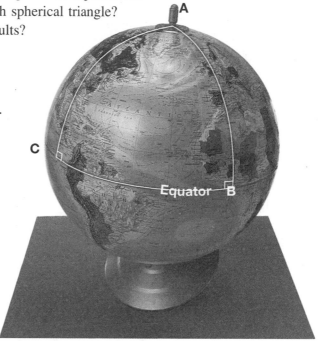

2. Let A represent the North Pole on your globe. Locate the 0° longitude line, which passes near London, England. Follow this line to where it meets the Equator, just south of Ghana in Africa. Let B represent this point. Locate the 90°W longitude line. Follow it to point C on the Equator, near the Galapagos Islands in the Pacific Ocean. Examine spherical △ABC on your globe carefully. What are the measures of its three angles? What is the sum of the measures of these angles? What kind of triangle is spherical △ABC?

3. a) In exercise 2, suppose A and B are fixed and C moves along the Equator. What happens to the sum of the angle measures in spherical △ABC? What is the minimum sum of the angle measures in this triangle? What is the maximum sum?

   b) Suppose B is fixed and C moves along the Equator to the 180°W longitude line. Suppose A moves along the 90°E longitude line through Russia towards the Equator. What happens to the sum of the angle measures in spherical △ABC? What is the maximum sum?

   c) State a conclusion about the minimum and maximum sums of the angle measures in a spherical triangle.

The Ideas

Prepare a report or a display to illustrate the results of your investigations. Include a comparison of geometric properties on a plane and on Earth's surface.

Cumulative Review

1. What units would you use to measure each item?
   a) the length of a pen
   b) the length of a river
   c) the length of a snake
   d) the distance around a running track
   e) the length of an ant

2. Make each equation true by replacing ■ with a number.
   a) $8400 = 8.4 \times 10^{■}$
   b) $211\,000\,000 = 2.11 \times 10^{■}$
   c) $31\,040\,000 = 3.104 \times 10^{■}$
   d) $670\,000 = 6.7 \times 10^{■}$
   e) $1\,980\,000 = 1.98 \times 10^{■}$
   f) $43\,000 = 4.3 \times 10^{■}$

3. List all the possible digits that could replace each ■ so the number is divisible by 4. Use a calculator to check your answers.
   a) $5■$ b) $24■$ c) $386■$
   d) $25\,79■$ e) $19■4$ f) $641\,18■$

4. Multiply or divide.
   a) 4.2×7.5 b) 12.08×6.9
   c) 0.7×21.6 d) 27.4×18.2
   e) 125.6×5.8 f) 13.4×13.7
   g) $25 \div 6.25$ h) $86.8 \div 12.4$
   i) $16.2 \div 5.4$ j) $37 \div 7.4$
   k) $21.75 \div 8.7$ l) $73.96 \div 8.6$

5. Write each fraction as a decimal and as a percent.
   a) $\frac{1}{2}$ b) $\frac{3}{4}$ c) $\frac{4}{5}$ d) $\frac{7}{10}$
   e) $\frac{3}{8}$ f) $\frac{2}{9}$ g) $\frac{8}{15}$ h) $\frac{5}{12}$

6. Calculate the percent increase or decrease in price.

	Old price ($)	New price ($)
a)	9.99	11.79
b)	13.99	9.39
c)	9.39	13.99
d)	29.99	26.74
e)	69.99	49.99
f)	25.99	20.24

7. The table lists the percent of households in each province that own an air conditioner.

Province	Households with an air conditioner (%)
Newfoundland and Labrador	2
Prince Edward Island	2
Nova Scotia	5
New Brunswick	8
Quebec	15
Ontario	48
Manitoba	48
Saskatchewan	38
Alberta	8
British Columbia	9

   a) Display the information on a graph. Explain how you decided which type of graph to draw.
   b) Describe the shape of your graph.
   c) Based on your graph, predict which parts of Canada have the warmest and the coolest summer temperatures. Do some research on summer temperatures. Were your predictions correct?

8. a) Write a set of 5 numbers with a mean of 14 and a median of 11.
   b) Write a set of 6 numbers with a mean of 14 and a median of 11.
   c) Write a set of 7 numbers with a mean of 25 and a mode of 21.

9. Use an integer to describe each situation.
   a) A swimmer dives to a depth of 3 m.
   b) Terry travelled 153 km farther on Tuesday than on Monday.
   c) The temperature was 8°C colder on Saturday than on Friday.
   d) After paying for a CD, Claire has $12 less in her wallet.

10. Use a number line. Write the integer that is:
   a) 7 units to the right of −3
   b) 4 units to the left of +4
   c) 8 units to the right of 0
   d) 12 units to the right of −9
   e) 15 units to the left of −7

11. For each number pattern below:
   a) Describe the pattern.
   b) What is the 15th number in the pattern?
   c) What is the 20th number in the pattern?
   d) Use a variable to describe any number in the pattern.
      i) 6, 12, 18, 24, 30, 36, …
      ii) 9, 10, 11, 12, 13, 14, …
      iii) 29, 28, 27, 26, 25, 24, …
      iv) 100, 50, $\frac{100}{3}$, 25, 20, $\frac{100}{6}$, …
      v) 180, 90, 60, 45, 36, 30, …

12. Write an equation to represent each sentence. Find the value of the variable that makes each equation true.
   a) 5 more than a number is 21.
   b) A number divided by 3 is 10.
   c) A number subtracted from 8 is −7.
   d) Double a number is 36.
   e) A number increased by 12 is 19.

13. Write each equation in words. Find the value of the variable that makes each equation true.
   a) $a + 7 = 18$ **b)** $3b = -21$
   c) $15 - c = 6$ **d)** $15 = \frac{d}{3}$
   e) $\frac{e}{4} = -2$ **f)** $-8 = f + 4$
   g) $-2 = g - 11$ **h)** $10 = h + 3$

14. Use a two-pan balance or algebra tiles to represent each situation. Find the answer to each question.
   a) Anouk has 5 magazines. After Lesley gives her some, Anouk has 12. How many magazines did Lesley give Anouk?
   b) Michael has some loonies in a piggy-bank. His mother puts 7 more loonies in the bank. Michael then has 11 loonies. How many loonies were in the bank before the 7 loonies were added?
   c) One spring morning, the temperature increased 7°C from 5 a.m. to 10 a.m. The temperature at 10 a.m. was 4°C. What was the temperature at 5 a.m.?

15. Draw any line segment AB. Use compasses and ruler to construct the perpendicular bisector of AB. Check your work using a ruler and protractor.

16. Determine the angle measure indicated by each letter. Explain your answers.

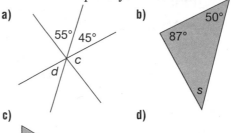

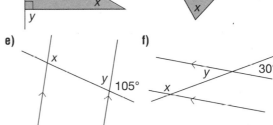

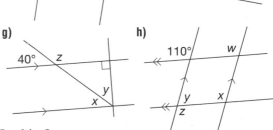

17. In this figure:
   a) name four pairs of corresponding angles
   b) name two pairs of exterior alternate angles
   c) name four pairs of opposite angles
   d) name two pairs of interior angles on the same side of the transversal

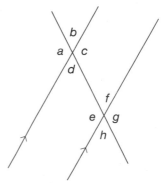

ANSWERS

INTRODUCTION: MODELLING

Start With What You Know, page 24

1. Answers may vary. The giraffe is about 1.6 times as tall, but the elephant is about 2.8 times as heavy.
2. The short, wide container would hold more liquid.
3. Answers may vary. Merle Keagle had more hits and more home runs, but Faye Dancer had a better batting average.
4. Ottawa

Numerical Models

Developing the Ideas, page 26

1. Answers may vary.
2. Answers may vary. If only 1 judge were used, the opinion of 1 person from 1 country would decide the winner and that is not fair. If 10 judges were used, there might be more ties.
3. a)

	1	2	3	4	5	6	7	8	9
Baiul	11.4	11.7	11.8	11.7	11.7	11.6	11.6	11.4	11.6
Kerrigan	11.7	11.6	11.7	11.6	11.6	11.7	11.7	11.5	11.6

   b) Four
4. Oksana Baiul
5. a) Nancy Kerrigan　　　　b) Answers may vary.
6. Answers may vary.　　　7. Wayne Gretzky
8. Mario Lemieux　　　　9. Wayne Gretzky
10. Answers may vary.

Working with Mathematics, page 29

1. Answers may vary.
   a) 10　　　　　　　b) 5 to 6
2. Answers may vary. It is easier to compare and tally opinions when people use the same numerical scale to describe their opinions.
3. a) People express their opinions about a party or candidate by voting.
   b) The candidate who receives the most votes wins.
4., 5. Answers may vary.
6. a) No, since 4 was the median you know that most of them did not like the movie.
   b) Make some changes to the movie.
7. a) *Home Alone*: $140 099 000; *Dances with Wolves*: $81 537 971
   b) *Home Alone*: 0; *Dances with Wolves*: 7
   c) Answers may vary, depending on whether you think critical acclaim or box office earnings are more important.
8. a) $126.20　b) $252.40　c) $100　d) $200
9. a) Roger Maris　　　　b) Babe Ruth
   c) Babe Ruth　　　　d) Answers may vary.
10. Answers may vary.

11. a) Superburger; fish sandwich　b) Superburger; fish sandwich
    c) Superburger; fish sandwich　d) Answers may vary.
12. a) 240 min, or 4 h
    b) i) You　　　　　　　　ii) 3 times
    c) Because the amount of time you can stay in the sun depends on several factors, including your skin type and the time of day.
13. a) 130 db　　　b) 120 db　　　c) 10 times
    d) 100 times　　e) , f) 10 000 times　　g) 100 times

Linking Ideas: Mathematics and Technology

Rank by Sorting in Spreadsheets and Databases, page 32

1. a) The data are sorted in alphabetical order according to the park name.
   b) The data are sorted in reverse alphabetical order according to the park name.
   c) Ascending
   d) Ascending; Banff, Yoho, Glacier, Waterton Lakes, Jasper, Elk Island, Mount Revelstoke, St. Lawrence Islands
2. Jasper, Banff, Glacier, Yoho, Waterton Lakes, Mount Revelstoke, Elk Island, St. Lawrence Islands
3. Have the computer perform an ascending sort according to the data in column B.
4. a) The blue whale, which has a mass of 120 000 kg
   b) The Gaspé shrew, which has a mass of 0.0037 kg
5. a) The blue whale (2362 cm) is the longest. The eastern small-footed bat (7.7 cm) is the shortest.
   b) The sperm whale has the longest gestation period (473 days). The Virginia opossum has the shortest gestation period (12 days).
6. a) *E.T. the Extra-Terrestrial*, which earned $228 618 939
   b) *From Here to Eternity*, *Gone With the Wind*, *Mary Poppins*, and *Who's Afraid of Virginia Woolf?* each received 13 Academy Award nominations.
   c) *Ben-Hur* and *West Side Story* each received 11 Academy Awards.
7. Warner Bros., which has 43 movies in the database

Statistical Models

Working with Mathematics, page 37

1. 55 is the median. 30 is the lowest mark in the class and 80 is the highest mark. 45 is the lower quartile and 75 is the upper quartile. The range is 50.
2. The range is 18 cm. The mean is 174 cm. The median is 172 cm. The lower quartile is 168 cm and the upper quartile is 176 cm. The shortest student is 164 cm and the tallest student is 182 cm.
3. a) i) 5　　ii) 6　　iii) 2　　iv) 8　　v) 1, 8　　vi) 7
   b) i) 8　　ii) 6　　iii) 3　　iv) 10　　v) 3, 20　　vi) 17
   c) i) 17　　ii) 15　　iii) 13　　iv) 21　　v) 12, 23　　vi) 11

4. a) i) 23   ii) 25   iii) 16   iv) 34   v) 12, 34   vi) 22
   b) i) 43   ii) 45   iii) 35   iv) 50   v) 30, 53   vi) 23
5. a) i) 16   ii) 14   iii) 12   iv) 21   v) 10, 25   vi) 15
   b) i) 55   ii) 59   iii) 52   iv) 61   v) 31, 63   vi) 32
7. a) i) 41   ii) 40   iii) 35   iv) 48   v) 30, 58   vi) 28
   b) i) $220.0\overline{6}$ ii) 223   iii) 212   iv) 229   v) 201, 230   vi) 29

8. a), c)

Group	Mean	Median	Lower quartile	Upper quartile	Range
A	16	16	14	19	12
B	11.5	11	9.5	13.5	13
A and B	13.8	14	11	17	15

9. Answers may vary. For example:
   a) 32, 50, 50, 50, 70, 70, 70, 70, 74, 80, 80, 80, 91, 91, 92
   b)

```
3 | 2
4 |
5 | 000
6 |
7 | 00004
8 | 000
9 | 112
```

10. a) i) Phillies   ii) Phillies   iii) Phillies   iv) Phillies   v) Blue Jays
    b) Answers may vary. Yes
13. a) 50th, 25th, 75th   b) 22%

Geometric Models

Developing the Ideas, page 41

Answers may vary.

Working with Mathematics, page 42

1. Answers may vary. Maps allow us to see a large area in a small amount of space.
2. 30 km   3. 1 cm to 10 m
4. a), b) Answers may vary.
   c) 2 mm to 1 mm
5. a) 40 km   b) 200 km   c) 60 km   d) 110 km
   e) 74 km   f) 48 km   g) 178 km   h) 126 km
6. a) 2 cm   b) 2.5 cm   c) 5.85 cm   d) 18 cm
   e) 7.7 cm   f) 1.65 cm   g) 3.95 cm   h) 22.05 cm
7. a) 1 cm represents 50 km.   b) 1 cm represents 30 km.
   c) 1 cm represents 100 km.   d) 1 cm represents 40 km.
   e) 1 cm represents 50 km.   f) 1 cm represents 150 km.
8. a) 3 cm   b) 27 cm   c) 1 cm to 9 m   d) About 38 m
9. a) 1 cm to 20 m   b) About 90 m
10., 11. Answers may vary.
13. a) ii   b) iv   c) i   d) iii
14. The paper strip remains as one piece but becomes longer and thinner.
15. a) 1 cm to 5 m   b) About 13.5 m
16. b) 15
17. a) 1 cm represents 6 cm.   b) 108 cm
18. a) 264 m   b) 236 m
19. a) 1 cm represents 50 m.   b) 100 m
20. c) Yes
21. a) 4.8 cm   b) 3.4 cm   c) 3.9 cm   d) 2.8 cm
    e) About 2 times as great

Quest: Can You Visualize the Hidden Faces of a Cube?, page 45

The second photo does not belong to the set.

Review, page 46

1. a) An alphabetical scale is used. The highest possible rating is AAA, the lowest is D.
   b) Credit ratings use a scale to rate the state of a country's or province's economy. These ratings use letters rather than numbers.
2. a) From most people under 15 to least: China, Canada, Chile, Congo
   b) Canada: 0.21; Chile: 0.31; China: 0.27; Congo: 0.44
   c) From largest fraction to smallest: Congo, Chile, China, Canada
   d) Congo; almost half of the people in this country are under 15 years old.
3. a) $263.20   b) About $400.00
4. a) Dislike   b) 2.3, 2
   c) Neither measure would indicate popularity.
   d) Either measure
5. a) i) 12   ii) 10.5   iii) 10   iv) 14   v) 9, 19   vi) 10
   b) i) 117   ii) 116   iii) 105   iv) 126   v) 101, 132   vi) 31
8. a) ii   b) iv   c) i   d) iii
9. 1 cm represents 4 km.
10. a) 8 cm   b) 0.8 m   c) 5.2 m
11. a) 1 cm represents 32 m.   b) 64 m
12. 450 km
13. a) 1 cm to 20 m   b) 54 m
14. a) i) Cylinder   ii) Square pyramid
    b) i) Cube   ii) Triangular prism or square pyramid

CHAPTER 1 REPRESENTING WHOLE NUMBERS

Start With What You Know, page 53

1. a) 10^2 b) 10^4 c) 10^6 d) 10^4 e) 10^5 f) 10^7
2. One trillion: 1 000 000 000 000, 10^{12}; one quadrillion: 1 000 000 000 000 000, 10^{15}
3. a) Australia, Canada, Italy, Nigeria, Brazil, China
   b) Brazil: 10^8; Canada: 10^7; China 10^9; Italy 10^8; Nigeria: 10^8
   c) Brazil   d) China
   e) No, explanations may vary.
4. a) About 21%   b) 10^{10}
5. a) 45   b) 450   c) 4500
   d) 45 000   e) 450 000   f) 4 500 000
   g) 382.57   h) 3825.7   i) 38 257
   j) 382 570   k) 3 825 700   l) 38 257 000
6. a) The second number in each product is a power of 10. In each of parts a to f and h to e the second number is 10 times as great as the second number in the preceeding part.
   b) Each answer in parts b to f and h to l is 10 times as great as the preceding answer.
7. a) The only factors of the number are 1 and the number itself.
   b) The number has at least 3 factors.
   c) The numbers in i, iv, and vi are composite. The numbers in ii, iii, and v are prime.

Quest: Forming Expressions with 1, 4, 8, and 9, page 54

Expressions may vary.

1.1 Expressing Numbers in Expanded Form

Developing the Ideas

Using Manipulatives, page 55

1. b) $(1 \times 10^3) + (3 \times 10^2) + (2 \times 10) + 4$; $(7 \times 10^2) + (4 \times 10) + 2$

2. a) $(5 \times 10) + 7$
   b) $(3 \times 10^2) + (6 \times 10) + 2$
   c) $(4 \times 10^2) + 6$
   d) $(3 \times 10^3) + (5 \times 10^2) + (4 \times 10) + 2$
   e) $(9 \times 10^3) + (7 \times 10)$

3. a) 2; 2×10^3 b) 2; 2×10^2 c) 4; 4×10 d) 6; 6
   e) $(2 \times 10^3) + (2 \times 10^2) + (4 \times 10) + 6$; 2246

4. a) $(3 \times 10^3) + (4 \times 10^2) + 5$; 3405
   b) $(5 \times 10^2) + (3 \times 10) + 7$; 537
   c) $(4 \times 10^3) + (3 \times 10^2) + (6 \times 10)$; 4360
   d) $(1 \times 10^3) + (9 \times 10^2) + (2 \times 10) + 5$; 1925

5. Australia: $(1 \times 10^7) + (7 \times 10^6) + (5 \times 10^4) + (2 \times 10^3)$
   Brazil: $(1 \times 10^8) + (5 \times 10^7) + (3 \times 10^5) + (6 \times 10^4)$
   Canada: $(2 \times 10^7) + (6 \times 10^6) + (5 \times 10^5) + (2 \times 10^4) + (1 \times 10^3)$
   China: $(1 \times 10^9) + (1 \times 10^8) + (3 \times 10^7) + (9 \times 10^6) + (9 \times 10^5) + (6 \times 10^4)$
   Italy: $(5 \times 10^7) + (7 \times 10^6) + (6 \times 10^5) + (2 \times 10^4)$
   Nigeria: $(1 \times 10^8) + (8 \times 10^6) + (5 \times 10^5) + (4 \times 10^4) + (2 \times 10^3)$

Working with Mathematics, page 57

1. Expanded form is a way of writing a number that shows the value of each digit in the number.

2. Yes, explanations may vary.

3. A power of 10 is the product when several 10s are multiplied. Powers of 10 allow you to write a number like 1 000 000 000 as 10^9, which saves time.

4. a) 80   b) 800   c) 800 000
   d) 8 000 000   e) 80 000   f) 8000

5. a) $(6 \times 10^2) + (2 \times 10) + 4$; six hundred twenty-four, 624
   b) $(4 \times 10^3) + (1 \times 10^2) + (3 \times 10) + 8$; four thousand one hundred thirty-eight, 4138
   c) $(2 \times 10^3) + (5 \times 10) + 3$; two thousand fifty-three, 2053

6. a) $(8 \times 10) + 7$; eighty-seven
   b) $(3 \times 10^2) + (6 \times 10)$; three hundred sixty
   c) $(7 \times 10^2) + (2 \times 10) + 5$; seven hundred twenty-five
   d) $(1 \times 10^3) + (3 \times 10^2) + (7 \times 10) + 7$; one thousand three hundred seventy-seven
   e) $(5 \times 10^3) + (2 \times 10^2) + 6$; five thousand two hundred six
   f) $(7 \times 10^3) + (4 \times 10^2) + (3 \times 10) + 8$; seven thousand four hundred thirty-eight

7. a) 44 533   b) 97 029   c) 506 282
   d) 2 356 000   e) 741 258   f) 8 609 307

8. a) 800   b) 2   c) 70 000
   d) 91 600   e) 90   f) 4 058 020

9. a) one thousand; $10 \times 10 \times 10$; 10^3
   b) ten thousand; $10 \times 10 \times 10 \times 10$; 10^4
   c) ten million; $10 \times 10 \times 10 \times 10 \times 10 \times 10 \times 10$; 10^7
   d) one billion; $10 \times 10 \times 10 \times 10 \times 10 \times 10 \times 10 \times 10 \times 10$; 10^9
   e) ten billion; $10 \times 10 \times 10 \times 10 \times 10 \times 10 \times 10 \times 10 \times 10 \times 10$; 10^{10}
   f) one hundred billion; $10 \times 10 \times 10 \times 10 \times 10 \times 10 \times 10 \times 10 \times 10 \times 10 \times 10$; 10^{11}

10. a) 7×10^3 b) 8×10^4 c) 5×10^6 d) 8×10^5
    e) 9×10^4 f) 5×10^2 g) 3×10^9 h) 4×10^4

11. For exercise 7:
    a) $(4 \times 10^4) + (4 \times 10^3) + (5 \times 10^2) + (3 \times 10) + 3$
    b) $(9 \times 10^4) + (7 \times 10^3) + (2 \times 10) + 9$
    c) $(5 \times 10^5) + (6 \times 10^3) + (2 \times 10^2) + (8 \times 10) + 2$
    d) $(2 \times 10^6) + (3 \times 10^5) + (5 \times 10^4) + (6 \times 10^3)$
    e) $(7 \times 10^5) + (4 \times 10^4) + (1 \times 10^3) + (2 \times 10^2) + (5 \times 10) + 8$
    f) $(8 \times 10^6) + (6 \times 10^5) + (9 \times 10^3) + (3 \times 10^2) + 7$

    For exercise 8:
    a) $(6 \times 10^4) + (3 \times 10^3) + (8 \times 10^2) + (1 \times 10) + 9$
    b) $(4 \times 10^3) + (9 \times 10^2) + 2$
    c) $(8 \times 10^5) + (7 \times 10^4) + (2 \times 10^3) + (1 \times 10^2)$
    d) $(9 \times 10^4) + (1 \times 10^3) + (6 \times 10^2)$
    e) $(3 \times 10^3) + (8 \times 10^2) + (9 \times 10) + 8$
    f) $(4 \times 10^6) + (5 \times 10^4) + (8 \times 10^3) + (2 \times 10)$

12. a) $(1 \times 10^4) + (9 \times 10^3) + (6 \times 10^2) + 4$
    b) $(1 \times 10^5) + (2 \times 10^4) + (7 \times 10^3) + (3 \times 10^2)$
    c) $(5 \times 10^6) + (8 \times 10^4) + (4 \times 10^3)$
    d) $(6 \times 10^5) + (4 \times 10) + 9$
    e) $(9 \times 10^4) + (2 \times 10^3) + (7 \times 10^2) + (3 \times 10) + 8$
    f) $(3 \times 10^8) + (2 \times 10^7) + (8 \times 10^6) + (9 \times 10^5) + (2 \times 10^4) + (3 \times 10^3) + (5 \times 10^2)$
    g) $(3 \times 10^9) + (7 \times 10^8) + (5 \times 10^7)$
    h) $(2 \times 10^{10}) + (1 \times 10^9) + (4 \times 10^8) + (9 \times 10^7) + (5 \times 10^6)$

13. a) 97 060   b) 2 008 004   c) 603 090   d) 3201
    e) 620 600   f) 5808   g) 60 206 000   h) 9 050 070

14. a) 10 000 000; 1×10^7
    b) 412 000; $(4 \times 10^5) + (1 \times 10^4) + (2 \times 10^3)$; 196 000, $(1 \times 10^5) + (9 \times 10^4) + (6 \times 10^3)$
    c) 600 000 000 000; 6×10^{11}
    d) 14 000 000 000; $(1 \times 10^{10}) + (4 \times 10^9)$

15. a) 9210   b) 7543   c) 76 532
    d) 764 200   e) 8 652 211   f) 98 654 310

16. a) $(4 \times 10) + 5$; forty-five
    b) $(9 \times 10^2) + (2 \times 10) + 1$; nine hundred twenty-one
    c) $(3 \times 10^2) + (3 \times 10)$; three hundred thirty
    d) $(2 \times 10^3) + (8 \times 10^2) + (7 \times 10) + 7$; two thousand eight hundred seventy-seven
    e) $(4 \times 10^3) + (3 \times 10^2) + 3$; four thousand three hundred three
    f) $(6 \times 10^3) + (5 \times 10) + 9$; six thousand fifty-nine

17. a) $(3 \times 10^5) + (1 \times 10^4) + (5 \times 10^3) + (7 \times 10) + 5$
    b) $(9 \times 10^4) + (1 \times 10^3) + (4 \times 10^2) + (2 \times 10) + 6$
    c) $(1 \times 10^6) + (2 \times 10^5) + (3 \times 10^4) + (9 \times 10^3)$
    d) $(8 \times 10^5) + (9 \times 10^4) + (7 \times 10^3) + (4 \times 10^2) + (8 \times 10) + 4$
    e) $(4 \times 10^7) + (1 \times 10^6) + (6 \times 10^5) + (9 \times 10^4) + (3 \times 10^2)$
    f) $(1 \times 10^8) + (2 \times 10^7) + (6 \times 10^6) + (4 \times 10^5) + (5 \times 10^4) + (2 \times 10^3) + (9 \times 10^2) + (1 \times 10) + 8$

18. a) \$3 400 000, $(3 \times 10^6) + (4 \times 10^5)$
    b) 5 900 000 000, $(5 \times 10^9) + (9 \times 10^8)$
    c) 48, $(4 \times 10) + 8$; 1 900 000, $(1 \times 10^6) + (9 \times 10^5)$

19. a) 938 231 900 km   b) 937 221 900 km

20. a) 2 000 000 000 000; 2×10^{12}
    b) 30 000 000 000 000; 3×10^{13}

c) 5 000 000 000 000 000; 5×10^{15}
d) 7 000 000 000 000 000 000; 7×10^{18}

21. a) i) 4, 2^2 **ii)** 8, 2^3 **iii)** 16, 2^4 **iv)** 32, 2^5
    b) i) $8 + 4$, or $2^3 + 2^2$ **ii)** $16 + 4 + 1$, or $2^4 + 2^2 + 1$
    iii) $16 + 8 + 2$, or $2^4 + 2^3 + 2$ **iv)** $32 + 4 + 2$, or $2^5 + 2^2 + 2$
    v) $32 + 16 + 4 + 2$, or $2^5 + 2^4 + 2^2 + 2$

1.2 Estimating with Large Numbers
Developing the Ideas, page 59

1. Estimates may vary.   **2.** Answers may vary.

3. a) Answers may vary. Most households and businesses have more telephones than telephone books.
    b) Estimates may vary.

4. , 5. , 6. Estimates may vary.

7. Answers may vary.

Page 60

1. a) Between 4 and 5   **b)** Yes

Page 61

2. Answers may vary.
    a) A standard business envelope is about 24 cm long.
    b) 2.88×10^9 cm, or 28 800 000 m
    c) This is almost three-quarters of Earth's circumference.
    d) Yes

Working with Mathematics, page 62

1. a) 320 500   **b)** 350 km/h   **c)** 104 000   **d)** 1 150 000 000
    e) 26 000 000   **f)** 8890 km   **g)** 807 m   **h)** 9 900 000

2. 2 million

3. a) 7; 28, 30, or 31, depending on the month; 365
    b) 2100 mL or 2.1 L; for a month with 30 days 9000 mL, or 9 L; 109 500 mL, or 109.5 L.

4. a) 60, 1440, 525 600   **b)** 9000, 216 000, 78 840 000

5. , 6. , 7. , 8. Answers may vary.

9. Estimates may vary.

10. a) Answers may vary. 10 000 characters fill three to four pages in size 12 type.
    b) Answers may vary.

11. a) No
    b) 30 ha per minute is almost 16 million ha per year, which is much greater than the second rate. Explanations may vary.
    c) Answers may vary.

Mathematics File: How Big Is One Billion?, page 64

1. Estimates may vary.

2. a) 3600   **b)** 86 400   **c)** 31 536 000

3. Yes. It takes about 11.5 days to reach 1 million seconds.

4. Estimates may vary.

5. It takes almost 32 years to equal 1 billion seconds.

6. The number 1 000 000 would be $\frac{1}{1000}$ of the distance along the line, which is 0.1 mm from the left end.

7. No, the claim is not reasonable. To speak 7 billion words in 35 years, you would have to speak 200 000 000 words each year. Even if you spoke 24 hours a day, every day, this would be almost 381 words every minute, or over 6 words every second.

1.3 Positive Exponents
Developing the Ideas
Activity 1, page 65

4.

Number of folds	Number of sections	Sections as power of 2
1	2	2^1
2	$4 = 2 \times 2$	2^2
3	$8 = 2 \times 2 \times 2$	2^3
4	$16 = 2 \times 2 \times 2 \times 2$	2^4
5	$32 = 2 \times 2 \times 2 \times 2 \times 2$	2^5
6	$64 = 2 \times 2 \times 2 \times 2 \times 2 \times 2$	2^6

5. Each time you fold the paper, the number of sections doubles.

6. If you could fold the paper 10 times you would create 2^{10}, or 1024, sections.

Activity 2, page 66

2. b) 4; $2^2 = 4$

3. b) 8; $2^3 = 8$

4. b) 3 rows; 3; $3^2 = 9$ **c)** 3 layers; 9; $3^3 = 27$

5. You would need 4 rows in the model for 4×4, with 4 cubes in each row. You would need 4 layers in the model for $4 \times 4 \times 4$, with 16 cubes in each layer.

6. a) Because you can model the number it represents with a square
    b) Because you can model the number it represents with a cube

7. Models may vary. The number of cubes in each model is given here.
    a) 16   **b)** 32   **c)** 64

Working with Mathematics, page 67

1. a) $10 \times 10 \times 10 \times 10$ **b)** 4×4
    c) $6 \times 6 \times 6$ **d)** 13×13

2. a) 10^4: the base is 10 and exponent is 4; 4^2: the base is 4 and exponent is 2; 6^3: the base is 6 and exponent is 3; 15^2: the base is 15 and the exponent is 2
    b) The exponent tells how many copies of the base number are to be multiplied.
    c) Whatever the exponent is, write the base that number of times, then multiply.

3. a) 10 000   **b)** 16   **c)** 216   **d)** 169

4. a) 4^2 **b)** 6^2 **c)** 7^2

5. a) 5^7 **b)** 100^5 **c)** 116^4 **d)** 67^5 **e)** 825^3 **f)** 1^8

6. a) $10 \times 10 \times 10 \times 10 \times 10 \times 10 \times 10$; 10 000 000
    b) $11 \times 11 \times 11$; 1331   **c)** $2 \times 2 \times 2 \times 2 \times 2 \times 2$; 64
    d) $1 \times 1 \times 1 \times 1 \times 1 \times 1 \times 1 \times 1 \times 1$; 1
    e) $5 \times 5 \times 5 \times 5$; 625   **f)** 25×25; 625

7. i) a) 2×2 **b)** 2   **c)** $2 \times 2 \times 2$; 2^3
    ii) a) 6×6 **b)** 6   **c)** $6 \times 6 \times 6$; 6^3

8. a) 343   **b)** 169   **c)** 625   **d)** 1728

9. 18^2 cm^2, or 324 cm^2 **10.** $8 250 000

11. Answers may vary.

12. a) 100 000   **b)** 27   **c)** 64   **d)** 28 561   **e)** 512

13. a) The formula multiplies the number in cell A1 by 2.
    b) The powers of 2
    c) The formula to enter in cell B2 is =B1∗3.
    d) The formula to enter in cell C2 is =C1∗5.

e) The row number and the exponents of the powers in that row are equal.

14. a) 2^6 **b)** 3^4 **c)** 4^5 **d)** 6^8 **e)** 3^7 **f)** 9^{10}

15. It is less than 1000 m^2.

16. a) $4.50   **b)** $18.00

17. a) 42.875 cm^3 **b)** 343 cm^3 **c)** 8 times   **d)** 2744 cm^3
e) The volume is eight times as great.

18. 100^3, or 1 000 000

19. a) i) 2^1 **ii)** 2^5 **iii)** 2^{10}
b) i) $2   **ii)** $32   **iii)** $1024
c) About 10 years   **d)** About 20 years

20. 10^4 m^2

Quest: Can You Out-Think Your Calculator?, page 69

The pattern in the last digit is 7, 9, 3, 1, 7, 9, 3, 1 …
The last digits are as follows: 7^{12}: 1; 7^{16}: 1; 7^{20}: 1; 7^{22}: 9

1.4 Scientific Notation
Developing the Ideas, page 70

1. More than 50 000 000 000   **2.** More than 50 billion

3. Calculator displays may vary.   **4.** 58 000 000 km

5. The dinosaurs first appeared on Earth 2 600 000 years ago.

6. No, 2.5×10^7 years ago are longer ago than 2.6×10^6, which is when dinosaurs first appeared.

Working with Mathematics, page 73

1. The first number is between 1 and 10, and the second number is a power of 10.

2. a) 1×10^3 **b)** 1×10^6 **c)** 1×10^9
d) 1×10^4 **e)** 1×10^7 **f)** 1×10^{10}

3. a) Yes
b) No, because the second number is not a power of 10.
c) Yes   **d)** Yes
e) No, because 0.8 is not between 1 and 10.
f) No, because 24.1 is greater than 10.

4. a) 3   **b)** 5   **c)** 6   **d)** 6   **e)** 7   **f)** 9

5. a) 9.4   **b)** 4.0   **c)** 7.02
d) 549 000   **e)** 6.7   **f)** 131 100 000

6. a) 8; 590 000 000   **b)** 4; 63 500   **c)** 6; 9 010 000
d) 3; 1120   **e)** 5; 830 000   **f)** 11; 459 200 000 000

7. a) 1.47×10^6 **b)** 6.8×10^5 **c)** 3.175×10^7
d) 1.18×10^4 **e)** $9.587\ 02 \times 10^7$ **f)** 4.6985×10^9

8. a) 130 000   **b)** 39 700   **c)** 2 175 000 000
d) 3 000 000   **e)** 79 400 000   **f)** 930 000 000

9. a) Earth: 150 000 000 km,
5 976 000 000 000 000 000 000 t
Mercury: 58 000 000 km,
330 000 000 000 000 000 000 000 t
Neptune: 4 500 000 000 km,
102 000 000 000 000 000 000 000 t
Saturn: 1 430 000 000 km,
569 000 000 000 000 000 000 000 t
Earth: $(1 \times 10^8) + (5 \times 10^7)$,
$(5 \times 10^{21}) + (9 \times 10^{20}) + (7 \times 10^{19}) + (6 \times 10^{18})$
Mercury: $(5 \times 10^7) + (8 \times 10^6)$, $(3 \times 10^{23}) + (3 \times 10^{22})$
Neptune: $(4 \times 10^9) + (5 \times 10^8)$, $(1 \times 10^{23}) + (2 \times 10^{21})$
Saturn: $(1 \times 10^9) + (4 \times 10^8) + (3 \times 10^7)$,

$(5 \times 10^{23}) + (6 \times 10^{22}) + (9 \times 10^{21})$
b) Mercury, Earth, Saturn, Neptune
c) Earth, Neptune, Mercury, Saturn
d) Answers may vary. Because the numbers are so great, it is awkward to write them as numerals.

10. a) $(1 \times 10^{22}) + (2 \times 10^{21})$, $(5 \times 10^9) + (9 \times 10^8)$
1.2×10^{22} kg, 5.9×10^9 km
b) Multiply by 1000. 12 000 000 000 000 000 000 000 000 g, or 1.2×10^{25} g
c) Multiply by 1000. 5 900 000 000 000 m, or 5.9×10^{12} m

11. a) 8×10^6 cm^2, 1×10^5 km   **b)** 100 000 000 m, or 1×10^8 m

12. a) 751 000   **b)** 2.81×10^5
c) 4 600 000 000 years   **d)** 1 650 000 km^2
e) 3.847×10^5 km   **f)** 5 976 000 000 000 000 000 000 t

13. *Mona Lisa* has a higher value.

14. a) 5.2×10^4, 5.4×10^4, 5.5×10^4
b) 2.7×10^7, 2.79×10^7, 2.9×10^7
c) 3.6×10^5, 3.62×10^5, 3.68×10^5
d) 7.21×10^9, 7.211×10^9, 7.215×10^9
e) 6.7×10^4, 6.9×10^4, 6.9×10^5
f) 5.24×10^7, 5.42×10^7, 4.25×10^8

15. The final spreadsheet should look like this:

	A	B	C
1	1	1.00e+0	
2	10	1.00e+1	
3	100	1.00e+2	
4	1000	1.00e+3	thousand
5	10000	1.00e+4	
6	100000	1.00e+5	
7	1000000	1.00e+6	million
8	10000000	1.00e+7	
9	100000000	1.00e+8	
10	1000000000	1.00e+9	billion
11	10000000000	1.00e+10	
12	100000000000	1.00e+11	
13	1000000000000	1.00e+12	trillion
14	10000000000000	1.00e+13	
15	100000000000000	1.00e+14	
16	1000000000000000	1.00e+15	quadrillion

16. a) 7.5×10^5 **b)** 8.5×10^6
c) 2.76×10^7 **d)** 7.81×10^8

17. a) 5.9×10^7 **b)** 6.228×10^9
c) 1.4×10^{12} **d)** 4.351×10^{12}
e) 1.4×10^{10} **f)** 4×10^{13}
g) 4×10^4 **h)** 4×10^5

18. a) 171 000 000   **b)** 4.7×10^7 **c)** 725 000
d) 7×10^8 **e)** 26 500 000 000

19. The movies are listed from least money earned to most. *Dick Tracy*: $60 610 000; *Sister Act*: $62 420 000; *The Fugitive*: $92 600 000; *Mrs. Doubtfire*: $109 800 000; *Jurassic Park*: $208 000 000

21.

Province	Population	Area (ha)	Total farm income
Alberta	2.5×10^6	6.61×10^7	1.41×10^8
British Columbia	3.2×10^6	9.48×10^7	1.29×10^8
Manitoba	1.1×10^6	6.5×10^7	1.0×10^8
New Brunswick	7.0×10^5	7.3×10^6	2.4×10^7
Newfoundland	6.0×10^5	4.06×10^7	5.0×10^6
Nova Scotia	9.0×10^5	5.5×10^6	5.0×10^7
Ontario	9.9×10^6	1.069×10^8	3.25×10^8
Prince Edward Island	1.0×10^5	6.0×10^5	3.2×10^7
Quebec	6.8×10^6	1.541×10^8	6.89×10^8
Saskatchewan	1.0×10^6	6.52×10^7	4.12×10^8

22. a) 9×10^6 km²   b) i) 100   ii) 9×10^8 ha

23. a) 4.52×10^5 b) 7.65×10^4 c) 8.24×10^6 d) 9.31×10^5

Linking Ideas: Mathematics and Science

In July 1994, Did We See What Destroyed the Dinosaurs?, page 76

1. 65 million years: 6.5×10^7 years; 175 million years: 1.75×10^8 years; 143 000 km: 1.43×10^5 km; 12 756 km: 1.2756×10^4 km; 216 000 km/h: 2.16×10^5 km/h; 965 km: 9.65×10^2 km; 200 000 megatonnes: 2×10^5 megatonnes

2. Answers may vary.

3. a) About 11.2 times   b) 5 times

4. Because 10^{27} is 1000 times as great as 10^{24}

5. a) 216 000 km/h   b) 4320 times   c) 60 km/s

6. 2×10^{11} t

1.5 Divisibility Rules

Developing the Ideas, page 78

Activity 1

1. Any number that is divisible by 2 is a multiple of 2.

2. Every second column of numbers is coloured.

3. 2, 4, 6, 8, 0, 2, 4, 6, 8, 0, 2, 4, 6, 8, 0; there are only five different last digits, four of these are multiples of 2, the last is 0.

4. Yes, any number that is divisible by 2 has a last digit of 2, 4, 6, 8, or 0.

5. A number is divisible by 2 if its last digit is 0 or is divisible by 2.

Activity 2

1. b) Any number that is divisible by 9 is a multiple of 9.

2. Except for 90, the coloured numbers lie in a diagonal line.

3. a) 9
   b) A number less than 100 is divisible by 9 if the sum of its digits is 9.

4. a) No; for example, 729 is divisible by 9 but the sum of its digits is 18.
   b) The sum of the digits is always a multiple of 9.
   c) A number is divisible by 9 if the sum of its digits is

divisible by 9.

Activity 3

1. Any number that is divisible by 3 is a multiple of 3.

2. The coloured numbers lie in diagonal lines, with one diagonal that is not coloured between each pair.

3. a) 3, 6, 9, 3, 6, 9, 3, 6, 9, 3, 6, 9, 12, 6, 9; all the sums are multiples of 3.
   b) A number is divisible by 3 if the sum of its digits is divisible by 3.

4. Yes, the rule works for numbers greater than 100.

Working with Mathematics, page 80

1. a) Nine divides evenly into 1638, with no remainder. Yes, this is true since $1638 \div 9 = 182$.
   b) There is a whole number that gives a product of 1638 when multiplied by 9. Yes, this is true since $9 \times 182 = 1638$.

2. No; explanations may vary.

3. a) If the last digit of the number is 0 or is divisible by 2, the number is even.
   b) If the last digit of the number is not 0 and not divisible by 2, the number is odd.

4. a) 28
   b) Add the digits of the number in part a. If the sum is 9 or a multiple of 9, the number is divisible by 9.

5. No; explanations may vary.   6. 1

7. The numbers in parts b, d, g, and h are divisible by 2.

8. Answers may vary. You could increase or decrease each number by 1.

9. a) Answers may vary. Some examples are 546, 554, and 562.
   b) Answers may vary. The odd numbers are 18 749, 18 751, 18 753, and 18 755.

10. The numbers in parts c, e, g, and h are divisible by 3.

11. The numbers in parts e and h are divisible by 9.

12. a) No, the sum of the digits is 12, which is not divisible by 9.

13. a) 2, 5238   b) 3, 23 634   c) 5, 59 067
    d) 0, 7065   e) 6, 90 486   f) 6, 875 466

14. b) The last column is coloured.
    c) A number is divisible by 10 if the last digit is 0.
    d) A number is divisible by 5 if the last digit is 5 or 0.

15. a) The number in part g is divisible by 10.
    b) The numbers in parts f and g are divisible by 5.

16. b) No   c) No
    d) A number is divisible by 6 if its last digit is 0, 2, 4, 6, or 8, and the sum of its digits is divisible by 3.

17. The numbers in parts g and h are divisible by 6.

18. b)

Number	Divisible by 4?	Last two digits	Divisible by 4?
2 367	no	67	no
4 982	no	82	no
34 592	yes	92	yes
15 674	no	74	no
34 690	no	90	no
236 876	yes	76	yes
54 864	yes	64	yes

c) The numbers in the 2 columns are the same.
d) A number is divisible by 4 if the last 2 digits are divisible by 4.

19. The numbers in parts b, d, and h are divisible by 4.

20. 60

21. a) 30   **b)** No, because 30 is divisible by 2.

22. 18   **23.** 111, 18, 27, 99, 10 563

24. 24 714   **25.** 20 175, 24 714

26. Answers may vary; any multiple of 45

27. a) Yes, each child would receive 16 cookies.
   b) There are only 46 cookies left, and 46 is not divisible by 3. The children could receive 15 cookies each and leave 1 cookie in the bag.

28. Answers may vary.

29. Answers may vary.
   a) 2, 5, or 8   **b)** 3, 6, or 9   **c)** 2, 5, or 8

1.6 Expressing Numbers as Products of Powers of Primes

Developing the Ideas

Activity 1, page 82

4. The multiples of 4 are already crossed out because they are also multiples of 2.

The prime numbers up to 100 are 2, 3, 5, 7, 11, 13, 17, 19, 23, 29, 31, 37, 41, 43, 47, 53, 59, 61, 67, 71, 73, 79, 83, 89, and 97.

Activity 2, page 83

1. a) $18 = 2 \times 3^2$ **b)** $24 = 2^3 \times 3$ **c)** $100 = 2^2 \times 5^2$

2. a) $28 = 2^2 \times 7$ **b)** $66 = 2 \times 3 \times 11$ **c)** $91 = 7 \times 13$

Working with Mathematics, page 84

1. A prime number has exactly two different factors, 1 and itself; a composite number has at least three different factors.

2. When a number is expressed as the product of several natural numbers, each of the natural numbers in the product is a factor of the number.

3. Two; the number itself and 1.

4. No; since 2056 is even, it has 2 as a factor.

5. No; since $3 \times 19 = 57$, 3 and 19 are factors of 57.

6. No; because a prime number has no factors except itself and 1, you cannot draw a factor tree for a prime number.

7. a) 1, 5, 25
   b) 1, 2, 4, 8, 16, 32
   c) 1, 7, 49
   d) 1, 2, 3, 4, 5, 6, 10, 12, 15, 20, 30, 60
   e) 1, 2, 4, 8, 16, 32, 64
   f) 1, 3, 5, 15
   g) 1, 2, 3, 4, 6, 9, 12, 18, 36
   h) 1, 2, 3, 6, 9, 18, 27, 54
   i) 1, 71
   j) 1, 2, 4, 10, 25, 50, 100

8. a) $63 = 3^2 \times 7$ **b)** $75 = 3 \times 5^2$ **c)** $99 = 3^2 \times 11$
   d) $50 = 2 \times 5^2$ **e)** $54 = 2 \times 3^3$

9. a) $16 = 2^4$ **b)** $42 = 2 \times 3 \times 7$ **c)** $85 = 5 \times 17$
   d) $96 = 2^5 \times 3$ **e)** $120 = 2^3 \times 3 \times 5$ **f)** $74 = 2 \times 37$
   g) $108 = 2^2 \times 3^3$ **h)** $125 = 5^3$ **i)** $176 = 2^4 \times 11$
   j) $400 = 2^4 \times 5^2$

10. A number may have factor trees with different branching patterns, but the prime numbers in the last row of each tree will be the same.

11. Answers may vary; some examples are 60, 100, 210.

12. A number may have several different factor trees, but the prime numbers in the last row of each tree will be the same. Therefore, there is a unique way to express each number as a product of prime factors.

13. a) 98   **b)** 216   **c)** 225

14. 90, which can be written as $2 \times 3^2 \times 5$

15. a) For exercise 7:
   a) 3   **b)** 6   **c)** 3   **d)** 12   **e)** 7   **f)** 4   **g)** 9   **h)** 8   **i)** 2   **j)** 7
   b) The numbers with an odd number of factors are 25, 49, 64, 36, and 100; they are all perfect squares.
   c) Yes; examples may vary.

16. a) $98 = 2 \times 7^2$ **b)** $60 = 2^2 \times 3 \times 5$ **c)** $81 = 3^4$

17. a) $45 = 3^2 \times 5$ **b)** $56 = 2^3 \times 7$ **c)** $102 = 2 \times 3 \times 17$
   d) $144 = 2^4 \times 3^2$ **e)** $200 = 2^3 \times 5^2$

18. a) 36   **b)** 200   **c)** 392   **d)** 1764

19. The twin primes between 1 and 100 are: 3 and 5; 5 and 7; 11 and 13; 17 and 19; 29 and 31; 41 and 43; 59 and 61; 71 and 73

20. 61 is the greatest possible prime factor of a number between 120 and 130. 127 is the only prime number between 120 and 130.

21. a) $2^2 = 4$, $2^3 = 8$, $2^5 = 32$; none of these numbers is prime since they are all even.
   b) The numbers in the last column are 3, 7, 31, and 127. All of these numbers are prime.
   c) No; for example, 11 is a prime number that cannot be written as a Mersenne prime.

1.7 Order of Operations with Exponents

Working with Mathematics, page 88

1. We follow the order of operations so that two people who simplify an expression involving several operations do the steps in the same order.

2. a) i) Calculate the power, then add 1 to the result.
   ii) Add 4 and 1, then calculate the power.
   b) When brackets are used, the sum is calculated before the power.

3. Answers may vary. For all numbers between 1 and 9, the result in part b is greater than the result in part a.

4. a) 34, 10
   b) No, the brackets mean that the subtraction is completed before the division.

5. a) 5   **b)** 3   **c)** 9   **d)** 1   **e)** 8   **f)** 14   **g)** 36   **h)** 4   **i)** 0

6. a) 18   **b)** 24   **c)** 36   **d)** 216   **e)** 1   **f)** 32   **g)** 4   **h)** 8   **i)** 0.5

7. Answers may vary. For all numbers between 1 and 20, the result in part b is greater than the result in part a.

8. a) 23   **b)** 64   **c)** 98   **d)** 9   **e)** 64   **f)** 152

9. a), b)

Column A	Column B	Column A – Column B
16	10	6
25	13	12
36	20	16
64	34	30

   c) The number in the third column is twice the product of the two numbers being added in column A.

d) 340

10. a) 1.2225　　　**b)** 5624.952　　　**c)** 0.327 027

11. a) $6^2 + 3 + 2^4 = 84$　　　**b)** $(4 + 3)^2 - 5^2 = 24$
　　c) $(8 \div 2)^2 + 7^2 = 65$

12. You can get 6 different answers:
　　$4^3 + (2 \times 3^2) - 7 = 75$; $(4^3 + 2) \times 3^2 - 7 = 587$;
　　$4^3 + 2 \times (3^2 - 7) = 68$; $4^3 + (2 \times 3)^2 - 7 = 93$;
　　$(4^3 + 2) \times (3^2 - 7) = 132$; $(4^3 + 2 \times 3)^2 - 7 = 4893$

13. a) 44　　　**b)** 114　　　**c)** 56　　　**d)** 48
　　e) 31　　　**f)** 3　　　**g)** 20　　　**h)** 101

14. $1^2 + 2^2 + 3^2 = 14$; $(1 + 2 + 3)^2 = 36$; the second expression is greater.

15. a) 52　　　**b)** 25　　　**c)** 1600　　　**d)** 20

16. a) 3^2, 6^2
　　b) i) 10^2, or 100　　　**ii)** 15^2, or 225

17. a) 2^3, 3^3, 4^3
　　b) i) 5^3, or 125　　　**ii)** 6^3, or 216

18. a) $2 + 3^2 \times (5 - 1)$　　　**b)** $36 \div (4 + 2^2 + 1)$
　　c) $10 + (5 + 3^3) \div 4$　　　**d)** $(2 + 3^2) \times (7 - 4)$

19. Answers may vary.

20. a) i) 69　　　**ii)** 48　　　**iii)** 147
　　b) Variables may differ.
　　　i) $(x + 13)^2$　　　**ii)** $(x + 9)^3 \div 6$
　　　iii) $[(x + 3)(x - 3) \div 3]^2$
　　c) Answers may vary. It is a much shorter way to describe a series of operations.
　　d) Answers may vary.

1.8 Square Roots

Developing the Ideas, page 91

Activity 1

1. a) Yes　　　**b)** 5 units by 5 units　　　**c)** 5

2. 3, 7

Activity 2

Step 1 — 5 units by 5 units, 5

1. 5.5; 5.48; very close　　　**2.** 5.5; 5.57

Working with Mathematics, page 94

1. A square root is a number which, when multiplied by itself, results in a given number.

2. Perfect squares have square roots that are natural numbers.

3. a) 8 cm　　　**b)** 8

4. Yes; explanations may vary.

5. Explanations may vary; $\frac{2}{3}$

6. a) 2　　　**b)** 6　　　**c)** 8　　　**d)** 10

7. Yes

8. Estimates may vary.
　　a) 4.5; 4.47　　**b)** 4.5; 4.58　　**c)** 6.5; 6.48　　**d)** 6.5; 6.56
　　e) 7.5; 7.48　　**f)** 7.5; 7.55　　**g)** 8.5; 8.49　　**h)** 11.5, 11.49

9. b) $\sqrt{34}$ and **c)** $\sqrt{26}$ are between 5 and 6.

10. Estimates may vary; the calculated square roots are given here to the nearest tenth.
　　a) 3.6　**b)** 4.4　**c)** 5.3　**d)** 6.4　**e)** 7.2　**f)** 7.9　**g)** 8.4　**h)** 9.2

11. a) F　　**b)** E　　**c)** B　　**d)** G　　**e)** A　　**f)** C　　**g)** D　　**h)** H

12. a) Estimates may vary. About 3.5 m.
　　b) Estimates may vary. About 6.9 m.

c) The square in part b has side length double that of the square in part a; its area is 4 times as great.

13. a) Explanations may vary. When you multiply the square root of a number by the same square root, the product is the original number.

14. a) 4.1　　　**b)** 8.5　　　**c)** 10.9　　　**d)** 31.6

15. a) $\frac{1}{2}$　　　　　　　　**b)** $\frac{3}{4}$

16. a) 30 m　　　　　　　**b)** 120 m

17. a) 30 cm　　　　　　　**b)** 2

18. a) 5.4　　　**b)** 12.2　　　**c)** 15.8　　　**d)** 18.9

19. a) The formula in cell A5 tells the computer to square the number you enter in cell A2. The formula in cell A6 tells the computer to calculate the difference between the original number and the square of your estimate.
　　b) Estimates may vary. The calculated square roots are given here to the nearest hundredth.
　　　i) 6.56　　　**ii)** 10.82　　　**ii)** 13.53　　　**iv)** 23.37

20. a) 32 m²　　　**b)** About 5.6 m　　　**c)** 23 m

21. a) 2　　　**b)** 3　　　**c)** 5　　　**d)** 4

22. a) 5 cm　　　**b)** 25 cm²　　　**c)** 150 cm²

23. About 29.2 cm

Review, page 96

1. a) 600　　　　　　**b)** 1　　　　　　**c)** 478 263
　　d) 107 040　　　**e)** 6000　　　　**f)** 609 832

2. a) 8　　**b)** 200 000　　**c)** 6　　**d)** 60 000　　**e)** 7　　**f)** 7

3. a) 76 985　　　　　**b)** 30 465
　　c) 20 401 001　　**d)** 5 096 807

4. a) $(2 \times 10^3) + (5 \times 10^2) + (4 \times 10) + 7$
　　b) $(3 \times 10^4) + (9 \times 10^3) + (6 \times 10^2) + (7 \times 10) + 5$
　　c) $(3 \times 10^5) + (5 \times 10^4) + (8 \times 10^3) + (2 \times 10^2)$
　　d) $(8 \times 10^4) + (6 \times 10^2) + 3$
　　e) $(7 \times 10^5) + (8 \times 10^4) + (5 \times 10^3) + (4 \times 10^2) + (2 \times 10) + 6$
　　f) $(1 \times 10^7) + (6 \times 10^5) + (7 \times 10^4) + (4 \times 10^3) + (9 \times 10^2)$

5. a) 16×16; 256　　　　　**b)** $5 \times 5 \times 5$; 125
　　c) $6 \times 6 \times 6 \times 6$; 1296　　**d)** $7 \times 7 \times 7 \times 7$; 2401
　　e) $10 \times 10 \times 10 \times 10 \times 10 \times 10$; 1 000 000
　　f) $9 \times 9 \times 9 \times 9 \times 9$; 59 049

6. a) Predictions may vary.
　　b) $8^4 = 4096$; $4^8 = 65\ 536$; 4^8 is greater.

7. a) 25 cm²　　**b)** 100 cm²　　**c)** 225 cm²　　**d)** 400 cm²
　　c)

Side length (cm)	Area (cm²)	side length / original side length	area / original area
5	25	1	1
10	100	2	4
15	225	3	9
20	400	4	16

When the side length of a square is doubled, the area of the new square is 4 times as great as that of the original. When the side length of a square is tripled, the area of the new square is 9 times as great as that of the original. When the side length of a square is multiplied by 4, the area of the new square is 16 times as great as that of the original.

8. a) $1.80　　　**b)** $7.20

9. a) 6　　　**b)** 4　　　**c)** 5　　　**d)** 7

10. a) 4.235×10^6　　**b)** 1.4×10^5　　**c)** 1.37×10^4

d) 1.971×10^7 e) 6.08×10^5 f) 8.136×10^9

11. a) 290   b) 3 720 000
   c) 430 600 000   d) 700 000 000 000
   e) 57 940   f) 9 510 000 000

12. a) 4.4×10^3, 4.5×10^3, 4.9×10^3
   b) 6.3×10^5, 6.3×10^6, 6.3×10^8
   c) 8.42×10^5, 8.53×10^5, 8.56×10^5
   d) 7.92×10^8, 7.013×10^9, 7.113×10^9
   e) 6.4×10^5, 6.4×10^6, 4.8×10^7

13. 2 million years: 2×10^6 years; 200 million years: 2×10^8 years; 140 million years: 1.4×10^8 years; 65 million years: 6.5×10^7 years; 30 million species: 3×10^7

14. a) 4.85×10^8 b) 100 000 000   c) 1 840 000 000
   d) 9.5×10^7 e) 1×10^8 f) 15 000 000
   The crater in Sudbury is the oldest.

15. a) 1 887 000 coins, 48 100 m
   b) 250 000 000 000 coins, 41 600 m
   c) 24 700 000 loonies, 642 000 m

16. The numbers in parts c, d, and f are divisible by 2.

17. a) Only when replaced by 8   b) Only when replaced by 7
   c) Only when replaced by 7   d) Only when replaced by 6
   e) Only when replaced by 7   f) Only when replaced by 8

18. Answers may vary. The digits you could use are listed.
   a) 0, 3, 6, or 9   b) 2, 5, or 8   c) 1, 4, or 7
   d) 0, 3, 6, or 9   e) 4   f) 2, 5, or 8

19. a) 0 or 9   b) 7   c) 1   d) 5   e) 1   f) 3

20. Yes, since the last 2 digits of this number are divisible by 4, the number is divisible by 4. There will be 86 foursomes.

21. a) $40 = 2^3 \times 5$ b) $32 = 2^5$

22. a) $92 = 2^2 \times 23$ b) $90 = 2 \times 3^2 \times 5$
   c) $110 = 2 \times 5 \times 11$ d) $126 = 2 \times 3^2 \times 7$
   e) $65 = 5 \times 13$ f) $88 = 2^3 \times 11$
   g) $136 = 2^3 \times 17$ h) $175 = 5^2 \times 7$

23. a) 196   b) 100   c) 441   d) 3528

Cumulative Review, page 100

1. a) i) 139   ii) 136   iii) 132
   iv) 141   v) 128, 166   vi) 38
   b) i) 28.8   ii) 27   iii) 23
   iv) 37   v) 13, 49   vi) 36

3. Answers may vary.

4. b) No, you may not be able to tell some objects apart by looking at them from only one view.

5. a) 62 495   b) 8 508 073   c) 741 258   d) 1 230 790
   e) 4 070 308   f) 20 060 904   g) 130 250

6. a) 3000   b) 30 000   c) 30
   d) 3 000 000   e) 30 000 000   f) 300 000

7. a) $9 \times 9 \times 9$; 729   b) $2 \times 2 \times 2 \times 2 \times 2 \times 2$; 64
   c) $3 \times 3 \times 3 \times 3 \times 3$; 243   d) 15×15; 225
   e) $11 \times 11 \times 11 \times 11 \times 11$; 161 051
   f) 13×13; 169   g) $5 \times 5 \times 5$; 125
   h) $1 \times 1 \times 1 \times 1 \times 1 \times 1 \times 1 \times 1$; 1

8. a) 3^5 b) 2^9 c) 4^6 d) 3^8

9. a) 16 cm^2 b) 64 cm^2 c) 4 cm^2

10. a) 6   b) 4   c) 5   d) 7

11. a) 2×10^5 b) 3.98×10^4 c) 1.13×10^7

---

d) 8.79×10^6 e) 1.704×10^7 f) 1.06×10^{10}
g) 3.35×10^4 h) 9.61×10^6

12. a) 221 000   b) 8020   c) 9 000 000
   d) 451 000 000   e) 73 700   f) 10 630 000
   g) 1 050 000 000 000   h) 3 200 000

13. a) 2.5×10^3, 2.2×10^4, 2.3×10^4
   b) 1.05×10^7, 1.052×10^7, 1.06×10^7
   c) 5.65×10^6, 5.49×10^8, 5.5×10^8
   d) 9.133×10^5, 9.311×10^5, 9.131×10^6

14. a) 7.618×10^8 b) 922 100 000   c) 1 827 000
   d) 3.66×10^5 e) 99 000   f) 1.003×10^7
   g) 3.392×10^6

15. The numbers in parts c and f are divisible by 3.

16. a) No   b) Yes   c) Only if replaced by 4
   d) No   e) Yes   f) Only if replaced by 4

17. a) 15   b) 188   c) 17   d) 32   e) 32   f) 58

18. a) $15 - 2^2 \times 3 + 8 = 11$
   b) Answers may vary. Two examples are:
     $(8 + 2)^2 \div 4 - 9 = 16$, or $(8 - 2)^2 \times 4 \div 9 = 16$

19. Estimates may vary. 3.2   20. $\frac{4}{7}$

CHAPTER 2 FRACTIONS

Start With What You Know, page 104

1. Answers may vary; for example, $\frac{1}{2}$, $\frac{2}{4}$, $\frac{3}{6}$, $\frac{4}{8}$, $\frac{6}{12}$. They are called equivalent fractions because they have the same value.

2. a) $\frac{2}{3}$ b) $\frac{3}{4}$ c) $\frac{4}{3}$ d) $\frac{3}{2}$

3. Find a decimal on the tenths line or hundredths line that lines up with the fraction.

4. a) 0.25   b) 0.66   c) 1.5   d) 3.62

5. Divide the numerator by the denominator.

6. a) 0.4285…   b) 1.4285…   c) 0.555…   d) 2.111…

7. a) <   b) >   c) >   d) <   e) <   f) >

8. a) The tenths line; 0.5, 0.4   b) 0.9

9. a) $\frac{5}{4}$ b) $\frac{9}{6}$, or $\frac{3}{2}$ c) $\frac{7}{12}$

10. a) The twelfths line; $\frac{15}{12}$, $\frac{8}{12}$ b) $\frac{7}{12}$

11. a) $\frac{5}{8}$ b) $\frac{3}{10}$ c) $\frac{7}{5}$

2.1 Computing with Fractions in Decimal Form
Working with Mathematics, page 111

1. a) 5480 million; $\frac{3}{5}$
   b) Multiply 5480 million by $\frac{3}{5}$. The answer is 3288 million, which is close to the population given in the table.

2. a) 740 million
   b) $\frac{740}{5480} \doteq 0.13$, which is close to the answer calculated in *Example 2*.

3. a) The answers are 1.11, 0.54, 0.24, and 2.86, respectively.
   b) The answers are 1.12, 0.55, 0.24, and 2.91, respectively.

4. a) 1.12   b) 0.55   c) 0.24   d) 2.92

5. Answers may vary.

6. a) 0.5   b) 0.25   c) 0.2   d) 0.1   e) 0.75
   f) 0.6   g) 0.4   h) 0.8   i) 0.7   j) 0.4

7. a) 0.33   b) 0.83   c) 0.38   d) 0.22   e) 0.67

f) 0.27   **g)** 0.71   **h)** 0.58   **i)** 0.31   **j)** 0.56

8. a) 0.79   **b)** 0.43   **c)** 1.78   **d)** 0.18   **e)** 0.10
    f) 0.37   **g)** 0.20   **h)** 3.60   **i)** 0.29

9. a) $\frac{11}{14}$ **b)** $\frac{13}{30}$ **c)** $\frac{16}{9}$, or $1\frac{7}{9}$ **d)** $\frac{5}{28}$ **e)** $\frac{1}{10}$
    f) $\frac{41}{110}$ **g)** $\frac{11}{56}$ **h)** $\frac{18}{5}$, or $3\frac{3}{5}$ **i)** $\frac{2}{7}$

10. a) 1.08   **b)** 0.63   **c)** 0.19   **d)** 3.86   **e)** 1.47
     f) 0.61   **g)** 0.24   **h)** 0.80   **i)** 0.48

11. a) $\frac{68}{63}$, or $1\frac{5}{63}$ **b)** $\frac{40}{63}$ **c)** $\frac{12}{63}$, or $\frac{4}{21}$ **d)** $\frac{27}{7}$, or $3\frac{6}{7}$
     e) $\frac{22}{15}$, or $1\frac{7}{15}$ **f)** $\frac{17}{28}$ **g)** $\frac{10}{42}$, or $\frac{5}{21}$ **h)** $\frac{12}{15}$, or $\frac{4}{5}$ **i)** $\frac{10}{21}$

12. Newfoundland and Labrador: 609 000; Prince Edward Island: 139 000; Nova Scotia: 975 000; New Brunswick: 770 000; Quebec: 7 312 000; Ontario: 10 833 000; Manitoba: 1 170 000; Saskatchewan: 1 045 000; Alberta: 2 742 000; British Columbia: 3 510 000; Yukon: 30 000; Northwest Territories: 62 000

13. a) The population of Canada, 29 248 100
    b) Approximate
    c) i) 0.998   **ii)** 29 197 000

14. a) 0.06   **b)** 0.17

15. a) 1.05   **b)** 0.20   **c)** 0.27
     d) 1.46   **e)** 0.54   **f)** 0.54
     g) 0.29   **h)** 2.85   **i)** 0.58

16. a) $\frac{59}{56}$, or $1\frac{3}{56}$ **b)** $\frac{11}{56}$ **c)** $\frac{15}{56}$
     d) $\frac{35}{24}$, or $1\frac{11}{24}$ **e)** $\frac{13}{24}$ **f)** $\frac{13}{24}$
     g) $\frac{15}{52}$ **h)** $\frac{77}{27}$, or $2\frac{23}{27}$ **i)** $\frac{21}{36}$, or $\frac{7}{12}$

17. a) Slacks: $11.25; Jacket: $39.25; Shirt: $13.00; Shoes: $9.19
    b) Slacks: $22.50; Jacket: $39.25; Shirt: $6.50; Shoes: $36.76

18. a) 51
    b) USA: $\frac{10}{51}$; SOV: $\frac{7}{51}$; AUT: $\frac{7}{51}$; SWE: $\frac{5}{51}$; GBR: $\frac{4}{51}$; GER: $\frac{4}{51}$; GDR: $\frac{3}{51}$; CAN: $\frac{2}{51}$; FRA: $\frac{2}{51}$; BEL: $\frac{1}{51}$; CZE: $\frac{1}{51}$; FIN: $\frac{1}{51}$; HOL: $\frac{1}{51}$; NOR: $\frac{1}{51}$

19. Asia: 44 million km^2; North America: 25 million km^2; Antarctica: 13 million km^2; Australia: 8 million km^2; Africa: 30 million km^2; South America: 18 million km^2; Europe: 11 million km^2; Pacific Islands: less than 1 million km^2

20. , 21. Answers may vary.

Quest: How Was the Inheritance Divided?, page 113

The eldest daughter received 9 rings, the second daughter 6 rings, and the youngest 2 rings.

Linking Ideas: Mathematics and Music
Fractions and Musical Notes, page 114

Answers may vary.

2.2 Adding and Subtracting Fractions in Fraction Form
Working with Mathematics, page 118

1. a) 20, 30, 40, …; 10 is the least common multiple.
    b) 24, 36, 48, …; 12 is the least common multiple.

2. No; sometimes one denominator is a multiple of the other.

3. a) 1   **b)** $\frac{1}{2}$ **c)** 1   **d)** $\frac{4}{5}$ **e)** 1
     f) $\frac{3}{2}$, or $1\frac{1}{2}$ **g)** 2   **h)** $3\frac{2}{3}$ **i)** 2

4. a) $\frac{1}{3}$ **b)** $\frac{2}{3}$ **c)** $\frac{1}{2}$ **d)** $\frac{2}{3}$ **e)** 1
    f) 1   **g)** $\frac{8}{7}$, or $1\frac{1}{7}$ **h)** $1\frac{1}{2}$ **i)** $1\frac{4}{5}$

5. a) $\frac{3}{4}$ **b)** $\frac{1}{2}$ **c)** $\frac{5}{6}$ **d)** $\frac{2}{9}$ **e)** $\frac{9}{8}$, or $1\frac{1}{8}$
    f) $2\frac{7}{9}$ **g)** $3\frac{3}{10}$ **h)** $1\frac{3}{4}$ **i)** $2\frac{5}{8}$

6. a) $\frac{5}{2}$, or $2\frac{1}{2}$ **b)** $\frac{4}{3}$, or $1\frac{1}{3}$ **c)** $\frac{1}{4}$ **d)** $\frac{1}{2}$

7. a) $\frac{6}{7}$ **b)** $\frac{2}{3}$ **c)** $\frac{7}{9}$
    d) $\frac{1}{2}$ **e)** $\frac{13}{16}$ **f)** $1\frac{1}{3}$
    g) $\frac{11}{10}$, or $1\frac{1}{10}$ **h)** $4\frac{1}{12}$ **i)** $5\frac{4}{15}$

8. a) $\frac{3}{5}$ **b)** $\frac{1}{3}$ **c)** $\frac{1}{6}$
    d) $\frac{7}{8}$ **e)** $1\frac{1}{14}$ **f)** $\frac{9}{20}$
    g) $\frac{9}{25}$ **h)** $4\frac{1}{20}$ **i)** $1\frac{5}{24}$

9. a) $\frac{7}{8}$ **b)** $\frac{23}{12}$, or $1\frac{11}{12}$ **c)** $\frac{4}{15}$ **d)** $\frac{1}{3}$

10. 0.1, 0.11, 0.111; $\frac{1}{10} + \frac{1}{100} + \frac{1}{1000} + \frac{1}{10\,000} = 0.1111$; $\frac{1}{10} + \frac{1}{100} + \frac{1}{1000} + \frac{1}{10\,000} + \frac{1}{100\,000} = 0.111\,11$

11. 5

12. a) $\frac{1}{2}$ **b)** $1\frac{1}{2}$ **c)** $\frac{11}{15}$ **d)** $\frac{17}{21}$ **e)** $\frac{7}{9}$
     f) $1\frac{3}{5}$ **g)** $\frac{1}{2}$ **h)** $8\frac{11}{12}$ **i)** $7\frac{13}{20}$

13. a) $\frac{3}{4}$ **b)** $\frac{1}{2}$ **c)** $\frac{3}{10}$ **d)** $\frac{7}{18}$ **e)** $2\frac{1}{6}$
     f) $\frac{7}{8}$ **g)** $\frac{1}{75}$ **h)** $5\frac{1}{18}$ **i)** $2\frac{9}{40}$

14. a) $\frac{19}{20}$ **b)** $\frac{17}{18}$ **c)** $\frac{13}{30}$
     d) $\frac{41}{24}$, or $1\frac{17}{24}$ **e)** $\frac{5}{12}$ **f)** $\frac{22}{27}$
     g) $\frac{13}{36}$ **h)** $\frac{7}{60}$ **i)** $\frac{19}{30}$

15. a) 1   **b)** $1\frac{3}{4}$ **c)** $\frac{29}{12}$, or $2\frac{5}{12}$ **d)** $\frac{31}{24}$, or $1\frac{7}{24}$

16. a) Veneer and plywood   **b)** $\frac{3}{4}$ **c)** $\frac{1}{4}$

17. a) i) $\frac{3}{16}$ **ii)** $\frac{1}{6}$ **iii)** $\frac{1}{4}$
     b) $\frac{3}{16}$
     c) i) $\frac{15}{16}$ **ii)** $\frac{7}{12}$
     d) Answers may vary.
        i) Comedy, Suspense/Thriller, Drama, and Westerns
        ii) Comedy, Suspense/Thriller, and Action
        iii) Comedy and Horror

18. $\frac{1}{6}$, $\frac{1}{2}$; $\frac{1}{3}$

19. a) $\frac{3}{4}$, $\frac{1}{8}$ **b)** $\frac{5}{8}$

20. $\frac{5}{8}$ **21.** 2 L

22. b) $\frac{1}{5}$ **c)** $\frac{1}{5}$, $\frac{1}{20}$, $\frac{1}{30}$, $\frac{1}{20}$, $\frac{1}{5}$

2.3 Using Patterns to Multiply with Decimals
Developing the Ideas, page 120

Activity 1

1. a) 28, 280, 2800, 28 000
    b) 36.7, 367, 3670, 36 700

2. a) 0.28, 0.028, 0.0028, 0.000 28
    b) 0.367, 0.0367, 0.003 67, 0.000 367

3. a) Larger   **b)** Smaller

4. To multiply a number by 10, 100, 1000, or 10 000, move the decimal point 1, 2, 3, or 4 places to the right. To multiply a number by 0.1, 0.01, 0.001, or 0.0001, move the decimal point 1, 2, 3, or 4 places to the left.

5. a) 57   **b)** 6134   **c)** 0.72   **d)** 8740

Activity 2

1. **a)** 5400, 540, 54, 5.4
   b) The second number is one-tenth the second number in the line above it.
   c) The product is one-tenth the product in the line above it.

2. **a)** 5400, 540, 54, 5.4
   b) The first number is one-tenth the first number in the line above it.
   c) The product is one-tenth the product in the line above it.

3. **a)** 966
   b) i) The first number is one-tenth the first number in part a; the second numbers are equal.
   ii) 96.6
   c) i) The second number is one-tenth the second number in part b; the first numbers are equal.
   ii) 9.66

4. **a)** 828, 82.8, 8.28   **b)** 4000, 400, 40

Working with Mathematics, page 123

1. The products in parts b, c, and e are less than 24.5.

2. **a)** 142.56 **b)** 790.54 **c)** 666.12 **d)** 84.288 **e)** 17.045 **f)** 5.568

3. **a)** The products in parts i and v are greater than 2000.
   b) The products in parts iii, vi, and viii are less than 1000.

4. Answers may vary.

5. **a)** 57   **b)** 6134   **c)** 0.72   **d)** 8740
   e) 4250   **f)** 8.7   **g)** 0.035   **h)** 0.0025
   i) 4800   **j)** 12 430   **k)** 0.63   **l)** 0.053
   m) 23.8   **n)** 75   **o)** 0.0129   **p)** 0.000 45

6. **a)** 918, 91.8, 9.18   **b)** 4352, 435.2, 43.52
   c) 468, 46.8, 4.68   **d)** 5187, 518.7, 51.87
   e) 11 392, 1139.2, 113.92   **f)** 2255, 225.5, 22.55
   g) 3948, 394.8, 39.48

7. **a)** 10   **b)** 1000   **c)** 0.01   **d)** 1   **e)** 0.001   **f)** 0.1

8. The products in parts a and c will be greater than 64.8.

9. About 46.6 km/s   **10.** About 12 000 km

11. 25 times in 10 s; 250 times in 100 s

12. **a)** $2.8 \times 3.8 = 10.64$
    b) $2.8 \times 7.2 = 20.16$
    c) $3.8 \times 7.9 = 30.02$

13. Estimates may vary. Calculated products are shown to the nearest cent.
    a) $127.60   **b)** $391.73   **c)** $42.32
    d) $671.42   **e)** $76.18   **f)** $63.77

14. **a)** 82.4   **b)** 100.8   **c)** 5.53
    d) 54.6   **e)** 8.288   **f)** 284.375

15. 34 mm   **16.** $20.48   **17.** $24 857.25

18. **a)** Estimates may vary. She has enough money.
    b) $2.10

19. **a)** $18.50   **b)** Answers may vary.

20. $89.90

21. **a)** 13.28   **b)** 1130.4   **c)** 64.2   **d)** 6.208
    e) 1152   **f)** 105.78   **g)** 0.774   **h)** 2.183

22. **a)** 600   **b)** 50   **c)** 1300
    d) 300   **e)** 600   **f)** 1300

23. 10.494 kg

24. **a)** Estimates may vary. She does not have enough money.
    b) $5.49

25. 10.15 kg   **26.** $433.13

27. 332.15 m; reasons may vary

28. **a)** 92 cm, 36.8 cm, 14.72 cm, 5.888 cm
    b) After 6 bounces, the height is just under 1 cm.

29. **a)** 10.5 m
    b) Answers may vary. The extra distance allows the athletes to reach a high speed before they jump over the first hurdle.

Mathematics File: Forms of Answers, page 126

1. **a) i)** One   **ii)** One   **iii)** At least three

2. **a)** If it is rounded to the nearest tenth, the answer is 1.4.
   If it is rounded to the nearest hundredth, the answer is 1.42.
   If it is rounded to the nearest thousandth, the answer is 1.417.
   b) The form of the fraction may vary depending on how it will be used in further calculations.

3. **a)** Because it was an improper fraction
   b) Yes   **c)** Yes   **d)** Yes, for example $\frac{34}{24}, \frac{51}{36}$

2.4 Multiplying with Fractions
Developing the Ideas, page 127

1. **a)** $\frac{6}{5}$
   b) i) $\frac{4}{5}$ **ii)** $\frac{8}{5}$ **iii)** $\frac{10}{5}$, or 2

2. **a)** $\frac{3}{3}$, or 1   **b)** $\frac{6}{3}$, or 2   **c)** $\frac{12}{3}$, or 4
   d) $\frac{5}{3}$, or $1\frac{2}{3}$ **e)** $\frac{20}{3}$, or $6\frac{2}{3}$ **f)** $\frac{10}{3}$, or $3\frac{1}{3}$

Working with Mathematics, page 131

1. Answers may vary. The first number in each product is not a natural number.

2. **a)** Greater; less   **b)** $\frac{5}{4} \times \frac{1}{2}$ **c)** $\frac{3}{2} \times \frac{3}{2}$

3. **a)** $\frac{1}{8}$ **b)** $\frac{1}{12}$ **c)** $\frac{3}{8}$ **d)** $\frac{2}{4}$, or $\frac{1}{2}$ **e)** $\frac{1}{10}$
   f) $\frac{2}{3}$ **g)** $\frac{14}{16}$, or $\frac{7}{8}$ **h)** $\frac{9}{5}$, or $1\frac{4}{5}$ **i)** $\frac{1}{12}$

4. **a)** $\frac{15}{8}$, or $1\frac{7}{8}$ **b)** $\frac{6}{6}$, or 1   **c)** $\frac{12}{12}$, or 1   **d)** $\frac{3}{10}$
   e) $\frac{5}{12}$ **f)** $\frac{6}{10}$, or $\frac{3}{5}$ **g)** $\frac{7}{12}$ **h)** $\frac{5}{6}$ **i)** $\frac{3}{12}$, or $\frac{1}{4}$

5. **a)** $\frac{1}{4} \times \frac{1}{2} = \frac{1}{8}$ **b)** $\frac{1}{2} \times \frac{1}{2} = \frac{1}{4}$ **c)** $\frac{3}{4} \times \frac{1}{2} = \frac{3}{8}$
   d) $1 \times \frac{1}{2} = \frac{1}{2}$ **e)** $\frac{5}{4} \times \frac{1}{2} = \frac{5}{8}$ **f)** $\frac{3}{2} \times \frac{1}{2} = \frac{3}{4}$

6. **a)** $\frac{3}{4}$ **b)** $\frac{4}{3}$ **c)** $\frac{1}{5}$ **d)** $\frac{1}{6}$ **e)** $\frac{3}{5}$ **f)** 1

7. Reasons may vary.
   a) $\frac{3}{2} \times 2 = 3$ **b)** $\frac{3}{8} \times 2 = \frac{3}{4}$

8. Reasons may vary.
   a) $\frac{1}{4} \times \frac{4}{3} = \frac{1}{3}$ **b)** $\frac{1}{4} \times \frac{1}{3} = \frac{1}{12}$

9. **a)** $\frac{3}{5}$ **b)** $\frac{3}{8}$ **c)** $\frac{1}{3}$

10. **a) i)** 1   **ii)** 1   **iii)** 1   **iv)** 1   **v)** 1   **vi)** 1
    b) 3, $\frac{1}{3}$; $\frac{1}{4}$, 4; 2, $\frac{1}{2}$; $\frac{1}{10}$, 10; $\frac{1}{8}$, 8; 5, $\frac{1}{5}$

11.

×	$\frac{1}{4}$	$\frac{1}{2}$	$\frac{3}{4}$	1	$\frac{5}{4}$	$\frac{3}{2}$
$\frac{1}{4}$	$\frac{1}{16}$	$\frac{1}{8}$	$\frac{3}{16}$	$\frac{1}{4}$	$\frac{5}{16}$	$\frac{3}{8}$
$\frac{1}{2}$	$\frac{1}{8}$	$\frac{1}{4}$	$\frac{3}{8}$	$\frac{1}{2}$	$\frac{5}{8}$	$\frac{3}{4}$
$\frac{3}{4}$	$\frac{3}{16}$	$\frac{3}{8}$	$\frac{9}{16}$	$\frac{3}{4}$	$\frac{15}{16}$	$\frac{9}{8}$
1	$\frac{1}{4}$	$\frac{1}{2}$	$\frac{3}{4}$	1	$\frac{5}{4}$	$\frac{3}{2}$
$\frac{5}{4}$	$\frac{5}{16}$	$\frac{5}{8}$	$\frac{15}{16}$	$\frac{5}{4}$	$\frac{25}{16}$	$\frac{15}{8}$
$\frac{3}{2}$	$\frac{3}{8}$	$\frac{3}{4}$	$\frac{9}{8}$	$\frac{3}{2}$	$\frac{15}{8}$	$\frac{9}{4}$

12. Answers may vary. $\frac{2}{4}$ does not have 3 equal parts.

13. a) 6   b) 3   c) 18   d) 9   e) 8   f) 39

14. a) $\frac{1}{2} \times \frac{1}{3} = \frac{1}{6}$ b) $\frac{1}{2} \times \frac{2}{3} = \frac{1}{3}$ c) $\frac{1}{2} \times 1 = \frac{1}{2}$
d) $\frac{1}{2} \times \frac{4}{3} = \frac{2}{3}$ e) $\frac{1}{2} \times \frac{5}{3} = \frac{5}{6}$ f) $\frac{1}{2} \times 2 = 1$

15. a) $\frac{1}{2}$ b) $\frac{24}{12}$, or 2

16. a) $\frac{9}{4}$, or $2\frac{1}{4}$ b) $\frac{9}{16}$

17. a) i) 1   ii) 1   iii) 1   iv) 1   v) 1   vi) 1
b) They are reciprocals because each product is 1.

18. a) $\frac{15}{8}$, or $1\frac{7}{8}$ b) $\frac{9}{20}$ c) 2

19. a) =A1*B1   b) , c) Answers may vary.

20. a) $\frac{1}{4}$ b) 15 min

21. a) $\frac{2}{4}$, or $\frac{1}{2}$; yes
b) Answers should equal those in the solutions. Answers may vary.
c) Answers may vary.

22. Explanations may vary.

2.5 Multiplying Fractions in Fraction Form
Developing the Ideas, page 133

2. a) $\frac{1}{8}$ b) $\frac{3}{10}$ c) 1   d) $\frac{5}{4}$ e) 1   f) $\frac{4}{9}$

3. The numerator is the product of the numerators and the denominator is the product of the denominators.

4. a) $\frac{5}{12}$ b) $\frac{15}{8}$ c) $\frac{15}{24}$, or $\frac{5}{8}$

Working with Mathematics, page 134

1. $\frac{4}{5} = 0.8$, $\frac{3}{2} = 1.5$, $0.8 \times 1.5 = 1.2$, $1.2 = \frac{12}{10}$

2. No; for example, $2 \times \frac{1}{4} = \frac{1}{2}$; $\frac{1}{2}$ is less than 2

3. a) Less than $\frac{5}{4}$ b) Greater than $\frac{2}{9}$

4. a) $\frac{1}{14}$ b) $\frac{1}{7}$ c) $\frac{3}{14}$ d) $\frac{2}{7}$ e) 1
f) $\frac{3}{7}$ g) $\frac{1}{2}$ h) $\frac{4}{7}$ i) $\frac{9}{14}$

5. a) 1   b) $\frac{1}{9}$ c) $\frac{3}{8}$ d) $\frac{1}{3}$ e) $\frac{10}{9}$, or $1\frac{1}{9}$
f) $\frac{1}{2}$ g) 1   h) 2   i) $\frac{1}{12}$

6. a) 1   b) 1   c) $\frac{1}{4}$ d) 2   e) $\frac{1}{2}$
f) 1   g) 3   h) $\frac{2}{3}$ i) $\frac{7}{2}$, or $3\frac{1}{2}$

7. a) $\frac{1}{20}$ b) $\frac{1}{10}$ c) $\frac{3}{20}$ d) $\frac{1}{5}$ e) $\frac{1}{4}$ f) $\frac{3}{10}$

8. a) $\frac{8}{9}$ b) $\frac{1}{10}$ c) 9
d) $\frac{20}{8}$, or $2\frac{1}{2}$ e) $\frac{5}{9}$ f) $\frac{15}{4}$, or $3\frac{3}{4}$
g) $\frac{2}{7}$ h) $\frac{3}{10}$ i) $\frac{7}{5}$

9. a) $\frac{1}{2}$, $\frac{1}{3}$, $\frac{1}{4}$
b) $\frac{1}{2} \times \frac{2}{3} \times \frac{3}{4} \times \frac{4}{5} = \frac{1}{5}$; $\frac{1}{2} \times \frac{2}{3} \times \frac{3}{4} \times \frac{4}{5} \times \frac{5}{6} = \frac{1}{6}$
c) $\frac{1}{11}$

10. a) i) $\frac{1}{61}$ ii) $\frac{1}{427}$ iii) $\frac{3}{488}$
b) $\frac{8}{1525}$

11. a) i) 21; $\frac{21}{60}$, or $\frac{7}{20}$ ii) $10.10   iii) $3.54
b) Answers may vary.

12. a) $20   b) $10

13. a) Less
b) Less than $\frac{1}{3}$; explanations may vary: $\frac{1}{2}$ of $\frac{2}{3}$ is $\frac{1}{3}$, so $\frac{1}{4}$ of $\frac{2}{3}$ will be less than $\frac{1}{3}$

14. a) $\frac{1}{4}$ b) $\frac{1}{2}$ c) $\frac{3}{4}$
d) 1   e) $\frac{5}{4}$, or $1\frac{1}{4}$ f) $\frac{3}{2}$, or $1\frac{1}{2}$

15. a) $\frac{1}{4}$ b) $\frac{1}{4}$ c) $\frac{10}{3}$, or $3\frac{1}{3}$
d) $\frac{11}{2}$, or $5\frac{1}{2}$ e) $\frac{9}{25}$ f) $\frac{9}{7}$, or $1\frac{2}{7}$
g) $\frac{1}{4}$ h) $\frac{5}{8}$ i) $\frac{3}{7}$

16. See the answers for pages 141 and 142, exercises 11 and 16.

17. a) $10.00   b) $14.00   c) $12.00
d) $24.80   e) $28.80   f) $37.50

18. i) a) 24, 12, 6, 3, $\frac{3}{2}$
b) The second number in each row is half the second number in the preceding row. The answer in each row is half the answer in the preceding row.
c) $4 \times \frac{3}{16} = \frac{3}{4}$, $4 \times \frac{3}{32} = \frac{3}{8}$, $4 \times \frac{3}{64} = \frac{3}{16}$
ii) a) $\frac{3}{2}$, $\frac{3}{4}$, $\frac{3}{8}$, $\frac{3}{16}$, $\frac{3}{32}$
b) The first number in each row is half the first number in the preceding row. The answer in each row is half the answer in the preceding row.
c) $\frac{1}{8} \times \frac{3}{8} = \frac{3}{64}$, $\frac{1}{16} \times \frac{3}{8} = \frac{3}{128}$, $\frac{1}{32} \times \frac{3}{8} = \frac{3}{256}$

19. a) About $\frac{1}{3}$ b) About $\frac{1}{2}$

20. a) $\frac{3}{2}$, $\frac{4}{2}$, $\frac{5}{2}$
b) $\frac{3}{2} \times \frac{4}{3} \times \frac{5}{4} \times \frac{6}{5} = \frac{6}{2}$, $\frac{3}{2} \times \frac{4}{3} \times \frac{5}{4} \times \frac{6}{5} \times \frac{7}{6} = \frac{7}{2}$
c) $\frac{12}{2}$, or 6

21. $\frac{1}{2}$

22. a) $\frac{1}{24}$ b) $\frac{1}{4}$ c) $\frac{5}{2}$, or $2\frac{1}{2}$
d) $\frac{8}{9}$ e) $\frac{25}{32}$ f) $\frac{27}{64}$

23. a) $\frac{3}{4}$, $\frac{8}{9}$, $\frac{15}{16}$; $\frac{4}{5} \times \frac{6}{5} = \frac{24}{25}$, $\frac{5}{6} \times \frac{7}{6} = \frac{35}{36}$, $\frac{6}{7} \times \frac{8}{7} = \frac{48}{49}$
b) Answers may vary. The numerator is always 1 less than the denominator. The denominator is always a perfect square.

Quest: Will You Ever Cut off All the String?, page 136

You must make 7 cuts to have less than 0.01 m remaining.
You must make 10 cuts to have less than 0.001 m remaining.
You must make 23 cuts to have about 0.000 000 1 m of string remaining.

2.6 Using Patterns to Divide with Decimals
Developing the Ideas, page 138
Activity 1

1. a) 42.5, 4.25, 0.425, 0.0425
   b) 1.8, 0.18, 0.018, 0.0018

2. a) 4250, 42 500, 425 000, 4 250 000
   b) 180, 1800, 18 000, 180 000

3. a) Smaller   b) Greater

4. To divide a number by 10, 100, 1000, or 10 000, move the decimal point 1, 2, 3, or 4 places to the left. To divide a number by 0.1, 0.01, 0.001, or 0.0001, move the decimal point 1, 2, 3, or 4 places to the right.

5. a) 8.4   b) 4.253   c) 3400   d) 435

Activity 2

1. a) 2, 2, 2, 2, 2
   b) In each line, the dividend is one-tenth the dividend in the line above it. The divisor is also one-tenth the divisor in the line above it. So, the fractions are equivalent.

2. a) 3.24, 3.24, 3.24, 3.24
   b) See the answer to exercise 1b.

3. a) 2
   b) i) Each number is one-tenth the corresponding number in part a.
      ii) They should be the same.
      iii) 2
   c) i) Each number is one-tenth the corresponding number in part b.
      ii) They should be the same.
      iii) 2

4. a) 3, 3, 3   b) 5.5, 5.5, 5.5

Working with Mathematics, page 141

1. The quotients in parts b, c, and e are greater than 32.6.

2. Estimates may vary.
   a) Between 10 and 10.5   b) Almost 16
   c) Just over 55   d) Just under 45

3. Answers may vary.

4. a) 0.65   b) 0.324   c) 47   d) 2340
   e) 0.85   f) 0.0053   g) 2900   h) 6.2
   i) 9.4   j) 940   k) 0.94   l) 9400
   m) 0.7   n) 0.023   o) 42   p) 6450

5. 16¢   6. 0.112 s   7. 0.586 s

8. The quotients in parts b, d, and f are greater than 24.

9. a) $8\overline{)361.6}$, 45.2   b) $13\overline{)113.1}$, 8.7
   c) $34\overline{)666.4}$, 19.6   d) $75\overline{)393}$, 5.24
   e) $49\overline{)73.5}$, 1.5   f) $53\overline{)64.66}$, 1.22

10. a) 17.9   b) 7.4   c) 13.1   d) 1.3

11. a) 7.80   b) 44.08   c) 1.22   d) 3.77

12. She can buy 7 fish.   13. Just over 27 weeks

14. 512   15. 8.95   16. 94¢   17. 0.28 kg

18. a) 25.56 kg
    b) 6.39 kg It might not be possible to divide the mass equally since an item like an axe cannot be divided.
    c) Answers may vary. Here is one possible arrangement. Person A carries the food (5.95 kg); Person B carries the axe, cooking utensils, and 1 sleeping bag (6.39 kg); Person C carries both tents and 1 sleeping bag (6.54 kg); Person D

carries the stove and fuel, 2 sleeping bags, the first-aid kit, and water filler (6.68 kg).
    d) By the end of the trip, there will be less food and less fuel for the stove. Each of the other people could give 1 item to the person carrying the food.

19. a) 42.9   b) 12.53   c) 43.17   d) 55.7
    e) 166   f) 4.13   g) 4.53   h) 8.21

20. a) 0.04   b) 1.17   c) 0.39   d) 0.09
    e) 4.91   f) 346.67   g) 0.76   h) 94.19

21. a) $8.8 \div 2.8 \doteq 3.14$ b) $2.8 \div 8.8 \doteq 0.32$ c) $8.8 \div 2.8 \doteq 3.14$

22. Tuna: $18.96; juice: $11.88; cereal: $23.92

23. 3300   24. 13 weeks   25. About 5.2 times as fast

26. a) i) 15 years   ii) About 5.26 years   iii) About 52.6 years
    b) Answers may vary.

2.7 Dividing with Fractions
Developing the Ideas, page 143

1. a) $\frac{1}{4}$; no
   b) i) $\frac{1}{2}$ ii) $\frac{1}{8}$ iii) $\frac{1}{4}$

2. a) 4; halves; no
   b) i) 2   ii) 3   iii) 6

3. a) $\frac{1}{8}$ b) $\frac{1}{4}$ c) 6
   d) 4   e) 12   f) $\frac{12}{8}$, or $\frac{3}{2}$, or $1\frac{1}{2}$

4. Answers may vary.

Working with Mathematics, page 147

2. Answers may vary.

3. a) $\frac{1}{2}$ b) $\frac{1}{3}$ c) $\frac{2}{6}$, or $\frac{1}{3}$ d) $\frac{1}{12}$ e) $\frac{1}{8}$
   f) $\frac{3}{6}$, or $\frac{1}{2}$ g) $\frac{2}{12}$, or $\frac{1}{6}$ h) $\frac{10}{6}$, or $\frac{5}{3}$ i) $\frac{20}{8}$, or $\frac{5}{2}$

4. a) $\frac{2}{5}$ b) 2   c) $4\frac{1}{2}$ d) $1\frac{1}{2}$ e) $\frac{7}{3}$, or $2\frac{1}{3}$
   f) 3   g) 4   h) 8   i) $\frac{7}{5}$, or $1\frac{2}{5}$

5. a) 10   b) 9   c) 3   d) 12   e) 21
   f) 10   g) $5\frac{1}{2}$ h) $3\frac{1}{2}$ i) 14

6. a) $2 \div 4 = \frac{2}{4}$, or $\frac{1}{2}$ b) $2 \div 2 = 1$ c) $2 \div 1 = 2$
   d) $2 \div \frac{1}{2} = 4$ e) $2 \div \frac{1}{4} = 8$ f) $2 \div \frac{1}{8} = 16$

7. a) $\frac{1}{8}$ b) $\frac{3}{4}$ c) 3
   d) 6   e) $\frac{5}{2}$, or $2\frac{1}{2}$ f) $\frac{3}{2}$, or $1\frac{1}{2}$

8. Reasons may vary.
   a) $\frac{3}{2} \div 2 = \frac{3}{4}$ b) $\frac{3}{8} \div 2 = \frac{3}{16}$

9. a) 4   b) 16

10. a) $\frac{5}{3}$, or $1\frac{2}{3}$ b) $\frac{6}{15}$, or $\frac{2}{5}$ c) $\frac{9}{10}$

11. a) i) 50   ii) $0.5 \div 0.01 = 50$
    b) i) 125   ii) $\frac{5}{4} \div \frac{1}{100} = 125$
    c) i) 75   ii) $\frac{3}{4} \div \frac{1}{100} = 75$

12.

÷	1	$\frac{5}{6}$	$\frac{4}{6}$	$\frac{3}{6}$	$\frac{2}{6}$	$\frac{1}{6}$
1	1	$\frac{5}{6}$	$\frac{4}{6}$	$\frac{3}{6}$	$\frac{2}{6}$	$\frac{1}{6}$
$\frac{5}{6}$	$\frac{6}{5}$	1	$\frac{4}{5}$	$\frac{3}{5}$	$\frac{2}{5}$	$\frac{1}{5}$
$\frac{4}{6}$	$\frac{6}{4}$	$\frac{5}{4}$	1	$\frac{3}{4}$	$\frac{2}{4}$	$\frac{1}{4}$
$\frac{3}{6}$	$\frac{6}{3}$	$\frac{5}{3}$	$\frac{4}{3}$	1	$\frac{2}{3}$	$\frac{1}{3}$
$\frac{2}{6}$	$\frac{6}{2}$	$\frac{5}{2}$	$\frac{4}{2}$	$\frac{3}{2}$	1	$\frac{1}{2}$
$\frac{1}{6}$	$\frac{6}{1}$	$\frac{5}{1}$	$\frac{4}{1}$	$\frac{3}{1}$	$\frac{2}{1}$	1

13. a) $\frac{1}{2} \div 4 = \frac{1}{8}$ **b)** $\frac{1}{2} \div 2 = \frac{1}{4}$ **c)** $\frac{1}{2} \div 1 = \frac{1}{2}$

d) $\frac{1}{2} \div \frac{1}{2} = 1$ **e)** $\frac{1}{2} \div \frac{1}{4} = 2$ **f)** $\frac{1}{2} \div \frac{1}{8} = 4$

14. a) $\frac{1}{3}$ **b)** $\frac{1}{6}$ **c)** 4

d) 6   **e)** 2   **f)** $\frac{7}{2}$, or $3\frac{1}{2}$

15. Reasons may vary.

a) $\frac{8}{3} \div \frac{2}{3} = 4$ **b)** $\frac{2}{3} \div \frac{2}{3} = 1$ **c)** $\frac{2}{3} \div \frac{1}{3} = 2$

16. a) $\frac{9}{4}$, or $2\frac{1}{4}$ **b)** $\frac{9}{16}$

17. a) $= A1/B1$ **b)** , **c)** , **d)** Answers may vary.

18. a) $\frac{7}{4}$, or $1\frac{3}{4}$ **b)** $\frac{35}{8}$, or $4\frac{3}{8}$ **c)** $\frac{8}{3}$, or $2\frac{2}{3}$

19. a) i) 150   **ii)** $1.5 \div 0.01 = 150$

b) i) 60   **ii)** $0.60 \div 0.01 = 60$

c) i) 180   **ii)** $\frac{9}{5} \div \frac{1}{100} = 180$

20. Diagrams may vary. 12 days

21. Diagrams may vary. $\frac{3}{16}$

22. a) $\frac{2}{3} \div \frac{1}{4} = \frac{8}{3}$, or $2\frac{2}{3}$ **b)** $\frac{1}{4} \div \frac{2}{3} = \frac{3}{8}$

c) $\frac{3}{4} \div \frac{1}{3} = \frac{9}{4}$, or $2\frac{1}{4}$ **d)** $\frac{1}{3} \div \frac{3}{4} = \frac{4}{9}$

23. 1512 m

Linking Ideas: Mathematics and the Consumer
Estimating Sale Prices, page 149

1. Estimates may vary. Land of Illusion: $20.00; Aladdin: $30.00; Baseball: $22.50; Jurassic Park: $35.00; NBA Action: $42.50; Sonic Chaos: $39.00

2. Estimates may vary. In-line skates: $70.00 (Adult), $55.00 (Youth); Running shoes: $20.00 to $60.00; Baseball gloves: $10.00 to $45.00; Bicycle helmets: $17.00 (Infant/Child), $24.00 (Youth), $38.00 (Adult); Mountain bikes: $185.00 (Adult), $100.00 (Youth)

3. Estimates may vary. Tents: $360.00; Sleeping bags: $95.00; Day packs: $30.00; Hiking boots: $110.00

2.8 Dividing Fractions in Fraction Form
Developing the Ideas, page 150

2. a) 8   **b)** 2   **c)** $\frac{3}{8}$ **d)** 2   **e)** $\frac{1}{6}$ **f)** 4

3. The numerator of the answer is the product of the numerator of the first fraction and the denominator of the second. The denominator is the product of the denominator of the first fraction and the numerator of the second.

4. a) 6   **b)** $\frac{24}{10}$, or $2\frac{2}{5}$ **c)** $\frac{3}{4}$

Working with Mathematics, page 152

1. False, for example, $2 \div \frac{1}{4} = 8$; 8 is greater than both 2 and $\frac{1}{4}$.

2. Greater than $\frac{9}{10}$

3. a) 5   **b)** 7   **c)** $\frac{5}{3}$ **d)** $\frac{2}{3}$ **e)** $\frac{1}{4}$ **f)** 10

4. a, b, and d

5. Yes, the number 1 is equal to its reciprocal.

6. a) 2   **b)** $\frac{7}{2}$ **c)** 9   **d)** $\frac{5}{4}$ **e)** $\frac{1}{3}$

f) $\frac{2}{5}$ **g)** $\frac{1}{5}$ **h)** 4   **i)** $\frac{4}{7}$

7. a, c, d, f, h, i

8. a) $\frac{1}{3}$ **b)** $\frac{2}{3}$ **c)** 1   **d)** $\frac{4}{3}$, or $1\frac{1}{3}$ **e)** $\frac{5}{3}$, or $1\frac{2}{3}$

f) $\frac{7}{3}$, or $2\frac{1}{3}$ **g)** $\frac{8}{3}$, or $2\frac{2}{3}$ **h)** 3   **i)** $\frac{10}{3}$, or $3\frac{1}{3}$

9. a) 1   **b)** $\frac{1}{4}$ **c)** 8   **d)** $\frac{1}{3}$ **e)** $\frac{25}{4}$, or $6\frac{1}{4}$

f) $\frac{1}{10}$ **g)** $\frac{1}{2}$ **h)** $\frac{5}{2}$, or $2\frac{1}{2}$ **i)** $\frac{36}{5}$, or $7\frac{1}{5}$

10. a) $\frac{2}{5}$ **b)** $\frac{4}{5}$ **c)** $\frac{6}{5}$, or $1\frac{1}{5}$

d) $\frac{8}{5}$, or $1\frac{3}{5}$ **e)** 2   **f)** $\frac{12}{5}$, or $2\frac{2}{5}$

11. a) 12   **b)** 160   **c)** $\frac{1}{12}$

d) $\frac{7}{15}$ **e)** $\frac{80}{9}$, or $8\frac{8}{9}$ **f)** 6

g) $\frac{3}{20}$ **h)** $\frac{1}{12}$ **i)** $\frac{7}{18}$

12. Examples may vary.
a) Reciprocal becomes smaller and smaller.
b) Reciprocal is halved.

13. 7

14. a) 4   **b)** 6   **c)** 10

15. a) 20   **b)** 15
c) More seats; since $\frac{3}{8}$ is less than $\frac{3}{5}$, more seats will fit in the same length of row.
d) 32; 24

16. 60

17. a) No; two positive numbers that are both less than 1 will have a product that is less than 1.
b) No; two positive numbers that are both greater than 1 will have a product that is greater than 1.

18. a) $\frac{10}{3}$, or $3\frac{1}{3}$ **b)** $\frac{5}{3}$, or $1\frac{2}{3}$ **c)** $\frac{10}{9}$, or $1\frac{1}{9}$

d) $\frac{5}{6}$ **e)** $\frac{2}{3}$ **f)** $\frac{5}{9}$

19. a) 27   **b)** $\frac{16}{3}$, or $5\frac{1}{3}$ **c)** $\frac{5}{6}$

d) $\frac{5}{12}$ **e)** $\frac{7}{6}$, or $1\frac{1}{6}$ **f)** $\frac{10}{7}$, or $1\frac{3}{7}$

g) $\frac{11}{9}$, or $1\frac{2}{9}$ **h)** $\frac{3}{10}$ **i)** $\frac{1}{36}$

20. i) a) 1, 2, 4, 8, 16
b) The dividend stays the same, the divisor is halved, and the answer doubles.
c) $4 \div \frac{1}{8} = 32$, $4 \div \frac{1}{16} = 64$, $4 \div \frac{1}{32} = 128$

ii) a) 16, 8, 4, 2, 1
b) The dividend is halved, the divisor stays the same, and the answer is halved.
c) $\frac{1}{8} \div \frac{1}{4} = \frac{1}{2}$, $\frac{1}{16} \div \frac{1}{4} = \frac{1}{4}$, $\frac{1}{32} \div \frac{1}{4} = \frac{1}{8}$

21. The graph in part b; as a number increases, its reciprocal decreases. This decrease is most dramatic for small numbers. For example, consider $\frac{1}{2}$, 1, $\frac{3}{2}$. The difference between each number and the next is $\frac{1}{2}$. Their reciprocals are 2, 1, and $\frac{2}{3}$. The difference between the first two reciprocals is 1, the difference between the next two is only $\frac{1}{3}$.

22. 24 days

23. a) 12 times   **b)** 6 times   **c)** 4 times

24. 12 glasses   **25.** 2.4 m

Quest: Why Does 0.9999999…= 1?, page 154

Descriptions and solutions may vary.

2.9 Applications of Fractions
Working with Mathematics, page 158

1. One was taken from 24, converted to quarters, and added to the $\frac{1}{4}$ to make $\frac{5}{4}$. This is similar to taking one ten in subtraction problems involving natural numbers, and converting it to ten ones.

2. Answers may vary.

3. $24.25 - 17.875 = 6.375$, or about $6.38

4. a) $\frac{8}{9}$ **b)** $\frac{5}{14}$ **c)** $\frac{19}{12}$, or $1\frac{7}{12}$ **d)** $2\frac{1}{4}$
   e) $2\frac{3}{10}$ **f)** $1\frac{1}{4}$ **g)** $15\frac{5}{8}$ **h)** $9\frac{1}{3}$ **i)** $135\frac{7}{11}$

5. a) 4   **b)** 36   **c)** $\frac{3}{2}$, or $1\frac{1}{2}$ **d)** $\frac{27}{8}$, or $3\frac{3}{8}$
   e) 250   **f)** 40   **g)** $\frac{1}{70}$ **h)** 48   **i)** 30

6. a) $2\frac{7}{8}$ **b)** $9\frac{1}{4}$ **c)** $\frac{13}{3}$, or $4\frac{1}{3}$ **d)** $\frac{8}{11}$
   e) 1   **f)** $14\frac{5}{8}$ **g)** $19\frac{1}{9}$ **h)** 180   **i)** 144

7. a) $^3/_8$ cup
   b) $^2/_3$ cup shortening
      $3^1/_2$ cups sifted cake flour
      $1^1/_2$ cups sugar
      5 teaspoons baking powder
      1 teaspoon salt
      2 eggs
      $1^1/_2$ cups milk
      3 teaspoons vanilla

9. a) Decrease by $^1/_4$ **b)** $13.88, $11.38, $12.00   **c)** $2.38

10. l) a) $2.50   **h)** $250.00   **c)** $625.00
   ii) a) $7.63   **b)** $762.50   **c)** $1906.25
   iii) a) $22.75   **b)** $2275.00   **c)** $5687.50

11. a) $\frac{3}{14}$ **b)** $\frac{27}{14}$, or 1.93
   c) Because 9 innings is the standard length of a baseball game

12. a) 2, 5, 10, 20, 50   **b)** 1913   **c)** $1100

13. a) 8, 6, 2, 8   **b)** $\frac{1}{3}$

14. a) 75 mL shortening
      425 mL sifted cake flour
      175 mL sugar
      12 mL baking powder
      2 mL salt
      1 egg
      175 mL milk
      7 mL vanilla
   b) 1 tsp. = 4 mL; The measurements are approximate.
   c) 1.25 mL; $\frac{1}{2}$ tsp. = 2.5 mL
   d) 1 cup = 225 mL, $^1/_2$ cup = 113 mL, $^2/_3$ cup = 150 mL, $^1/_4$ cup = 56 mL, $^3/_4$ cup = 169 mL

Review, page 160

1. a) $\frac{2}{3}$ **b)** $\frac{2}{5}$ **c)** $\frac{4}{9}$ **d)** $\frac{5}{7}$
2. a) 0.2   **b)** 0.666…   **c)** 1.25   **d)** 0.375
   e) 0.571 428…   **f)** 0.6363…   **g)** 1.625   **h)** 0.479 166 6…
3. a) The fraction with the greater numerator is greater.

b) The number with the smaller denominator is greater.

4. a) 0.2666…
   b) i) 2.666…   **ii)** 26.666…   **iii)** 0.0266…   **iv)** 0.002 66…
5. a) i) 0.142 857, 0.285 714, 0.428 571
      ii) 0.857 142, 0.714 285, 0.571 428
      iii) 0.428 571, 0.5, 0.6
      iv) 0.375, 0.333, 0.3
   b) i) Increases   **ii)** Decreases
6. a) $\frac{2}{10}$, or $\frac{1}{5}$ **b)** $\frac{6}{5}$, or $1\frac{1}{5}$ **c)** $\frac{5}{4}$, or $1\frac{1}{4}$
   d) $\frac{7}{12}$ **e)** $\frac{19}{10}$, or $1\frac{9}{10}$ **f)** About 0.78
7. a) $3\frac{5}{6}$ **b)** $8\frac{1}{4}$ **c)** $8\frac{5}{8}$ **d)** $8\frac{11}{12}$
8. a) 0.7   **b)** 1.625   **c)** 2.35   **d)** 0.575
9. a) $\frac{19}{12}$, or $1\frac{7}{12}$ **b)** $\frac{53}{63}$
   c) $\frac{428}{165}$, or $2\frac{98}{165}$ **d)** $\frac{157}{36}$, or $4\frac{13}{36}$
10. Answers may vary. $\frac{5}{7} + \frac{3}{11}$
11. a) $\frac{2}{5}$ **b)** $\frac{1}{8}$ **c)** $\frac{3}{4}$
   d) $\frac{1}{12}$ **e)** $\frac{11}{10}$, or $1\frac{1}{10}$ **f)** $\frac{1}{12}$
12. a) $2\frac{3}{6}$, or $2\frac{1}{2}$ **b)** $2\frac{1}{4}$ **c)** $2\frac{1}{8}$ **d)** $4\frac{1}{12}$
13. a) 0.3   **b)** 0.875   **c)** 0.75   **d)** 1.05
14. a) $\frac{7}{12}$ **b)** $\frac{17}{63}$ **c)** $\frac{287}{165}$, or $1\frac{122}{165}$ **d)** $\frac{43}{36}$, or $1\frac{7}{36}$
15. Answers may vary. $\frac{2}{3} - \frac{9}{13}$ **16.** $\frac{1}{10}$
17. a) 6   **b)** 4   **c)** $\frac{3}{10}$
   d) $\frac{4}{8}$, or $\frac{1}{2}$ **e)** $\frac{10}{12}$, or $\frac{5}{6}$ **f)** $\frac{6}{6}$, or 1
18. a) $\frac{6}{12}$, or $\frac{1}{2}$ **b)** $\frac{6}{10}$, or $\frac{3}{5}$ **c)** $\frac{16}{15}$, or $1\frac{1}{15}$
   d) $\frac{1}{8}$ **e)** $\frac{10}{3}$, or $3\frac{1}{3}$ **f)** $\frac{40}{60}$, or $\frac{2}{3}$
19. Answers may vary. $\frac{8}{5} \times \frac{1}{7}$
20. a) $\frac{6}{12}$, or $\frac{1}{2}$ **b)** 15
21. a) 10   **b)** 5   **c)** 15
22. a) 1.27   **b)** 0.30   **c)** 24.29
   d) 0.18   **e)** 1.38   **f)** 0.18
   g) 0.47   **h)** 1.30   **i)** 1.87
23. a) $\frac{19}{15}$, or $1\frac{4}{15}$ **b)** $\frac{23}{77}$ **c)** $\frac{340}{14}$, or $24\frac{2}{7}$
   d) $\frac{8}{45}$ **e)** $\frac{62}{45}$ **f)** $\frac{8}{45}$
   g) $\frac{21}{45}$, or $\frac{7}{15}$ **h)** $\frac{35}{27}$, or $1\frac{8}{27}$ **i)** $\frac{28}{15}$, or $1\frac{13}{15}$
24. a) i) $15.00   **ii)** $9.94   **iii)** $25.00   **iv)** $18.49
   b) i) $29.99   **ii)** $29.83   **iii)** $99.98   **iv)** $18.49
25. a) 10   **b)** 12   **c)** 20   **d)** 24   **e)** 36   **f)** 30
26. a) $\frac{6}{5}$, or $1\frac{1}{5}$ **b)** $\frac{9}{11}$ **c)** $\frac{13}{24}$
   d) $\frac{7}{9}$ **e)** $\frac{19}{24}$ **f)** $\frac{33}{30}$, or $1\frac{1}{10}$
   g) $\frac{23}{21}$, or $1\frac{2}{21}$ **h)** $\frac{19}{45}$ **i)** $4\frac{11}{36}$
27. a) $\frac{3}{7}$ **b)** $\frac{3}{9}$, or $\frac{1}{3}$ **c)** $\frac{1}{9}$
   d) $\frac{4}{12}$, or $\frac{1}{3}$ **e)** $\frac{11}{40}$ **f)** $\frac{19}{60}$
   g) $\frac{1}{10}$ **h)** $\frac{2}{21}$ **i)** $1\frac{11}{24}$
28. a) $\frac{32}{60}$, or $\frac{8}{15}$ **b)** $\frac{28}{60}$, or $\frac{7}{15}$
29. a) $\frac{37}{28}$, or $1\frac{9}{28}$ **b)** $\frac{11}{36}$ **c)** $\frac{27}{35}$
   d) $\frac{89}{30}$, or $2\frac{29}{30}$ **e)** $3\frac{1}{8}$ **f)** $5\frac{4}{15}$
30. a) $\frac{12}{6}$, or 2   **b)** $\frac{11}{12}$

c) $\frac{15}{12}$, or $1\frac{1}{4}$ d) $\frac{35}{24}$, or $1\frac{11}{24}$

31. 3 t

32. a) $\frac{3}{50}$ **b) i)** $\frac{4}{5}$ **ii)** $\frac{33}{50}$

c) Answers may vary. Sample answers are provided here.
   i) Chocolate and Vanilla
   ii) Chocolate, Vanilla, Butterscotch ripple, Rocky road, and Chocolate chip

33. a) $\frac{1}{6}$ **b)** $\frac{6}{20}$, or $\frac{3}{10}$ **c)** $\frac{8}{9}$

d) $\frac{10}{3}$, or $3\frac{1}{3}$ **e)** $\frac{20}{35}$, or $\frac{4}{7}$ **f)** $\frac{180}{200}$, or $\frac{9}{10}$

g) $\frac{210}{63}$, or $3\frac{1}{3}$ **h)** $\frac{63}{100}$ **i)** $\frac{12}{10}$, or $1\frac{1}{5}$

34. a) $19.00   **b)** $58.00   **c)** $57.00

d) $25.80   **e)** $45.00   **f)** $63.70

35. 58.5 m

36. a) $3\frac{1}{8}$, or $3.125   **b)** $3125.00

37. a) i) 40 L   **ii)** 32 L   **iii)** 25.6 L
b) 8 weeks

38. a) 7   **b)** $\frac{3}{2}$ **c)** $\frac{1}{5}$ **d)** $\frac{10}{4}$

39. a) $\frac{2}{3}$ **b)** 40   **c)** $\frac{35}{27}$, or $1\frac{8}{27}$

d) $\frac{20}{48}$, or $\frac{5}{12}$ **e)** $\frac{45}{120}$, or $\frac{3}{8}$ **f)** $\frac{84}{72}$, or $1\frac{1}{6}$

g) $\frac{112}{420}$, or $\frac{4}{15}$ **h)** $\frac{66}{63}$, or $1\frac{1}{21}$ **i)** $\frac{5}{18}$

40. a) 1   **b)** 9   **c)** $\frac{2}{6}$, or $\frac{1}{3}$

d) $\frac{4}{3}$, or $1\frac{1}{3}$ **e)** $\frac{6}{4}$, or $1\frac{1}{2}$ **f)** $\frac{1}{24}$

41. a) The result in part b is larger. When you multiply a number by a number less than 1, the product is smaller than the original number; but when you divide by a number less than 1, the quotient is larger than the original number.

b) The result in part d is larger. The explanation is the same as that for part a.

c) The result in part e is larger. When you multiply a number by a number larger than 1, the product is larger than the original number; but when you divide by a number larger than 1, the quotient is smaller than the original number.

Linking Ideas: Mathematics and Science
Paper Chromatography, page 166

Answers may vary.

CHAPTER 3 THINKING PROPORTIONALLY

Start With What You Know, page 170
Activity 1

Answers may vary.

Activity 2

Answers may vary.

Activity 3

Answers may vary.

3.1 Working with Rates of Pay
Developing the Ideas, page 172

1. $5/h

2. a) $10   **b)** $15   **c)** $20   **d)** $30   **e)** $35

3. See page 173.

4. Answers may vary. In any row, if we divide the earnings by the number of hours we always get 5. If the number of hours doubles, the earnings also double.

5. See page 174.

6. Answers may vary. The points lie on a straight line that passes through the origin.

7. a) $E = 5n$

Page 174
Problem 1: $48

Problem 2: $35

Problem 3: $80

Problem 4: About $64.17

1. Answers may vary. They all deal with rates of pay. The rates of pay are different.

2. , 3. , 4. Answers may vary.

Working with Mathematics, page 175

1. a) The first column would not change. The second column would be: 6, 12, 18, 24, 30, 36, 42
b) The first column would not change. The second column would be: 4, 8, 12, 16, 20, 24, 28

2. a) Yes, reasons may vary.
b) i) The graph would be steeper.
   ii) The graph would be less steep.

3. Yes

4. Estimates may vary.
a) $6, $12, $15   **b)** 6 h
c) 4.5 h, $13.50   **d)** $3
e) Variables may differ. $E = 3n$

5. i) a) $6/h   **b)** $36
  ii) a) $5/h   **b)** $30
  iii) a) $7/h   **b)** $42

6. a) i) $3/h   **ii)** $8/h   **iii)** $5/h   **iv)** $11/h   **v)** $7/h
b) i, iii, v, ii, iv
c) i) $15   **ii)** $40   **iii)** $25   **iv)** $55   **v)** $35

7. a) $4.50/h   **b)** $9.35/h   **c)** $6.75/h
d) $6.50/h   **e)** $7.15/h

8. a) $27   **b)** $56.10   **c)** $40.50   **d)** $39   **e)** $42.90

9. Estimates in parts c and d may vary.
a)

Number of hours	Amount earned ($)
1	7
4	28
5	35
9	63

b) Descriptions may vary. The points lie on a straight line that passes through the origin.
c) $42, $59.50, $77
d) 7 h, 4.5 h
e) Variables may differ. $E = 7n$

10. Estimates in parts c and d may vary.

a)

Number of hours	Amount earned ($)
1	6.50
3	19.50
6	39.00
9	58.50
10	65.00

b) Descriptions may vary. The points lie on a straight line that passes through the origin.

c) $13, $45.50, $78

d) 5 h, 8 h

e) Variables may differ. $E = 6.5n$

11. a) $48.00, $72.00   **b)** $50.00, $75.00   **c)** $16.80, $39.20

12. Answers may vary.

13. a) $35 for 6 h   **b)** $40 for 7 h

14. Explanations may vary. $30

15. a) Multiplication and division

b) Answers may vary. We divide to find the pay for 1 h, then multiply to find the pay for several hours.

16. Estimates in parts d and e may vary.

a) $24

b)

Number of hours	Amount earned ($)
1	4
2	8
3	12
4	16
5	20
6	24
7	28
8	32
9	36
10	40

c) Descriptions may vary. The points lie on a straight line that passes through the origin.

d) $18, $48   **e)** 6.5 h, 9.5 h

f) Variables may differ. $E = 4h$

17. a) $25.50   **b)** $46.75

c) i) $127.50   **ii)** $153.00   **iii)** $170.00

d) =A2*5.65

e) i) $45.20   **ii)** $84.75

18. a) $32.00   **b)** $84.00   **c)** $88.00   **d)** $67.20

19. a) $58.00, $43.50   **b)** $60.00, $45.00   **c)** $52.80, $39.60

20. $150.00   **21.** Yes

22. a) 5   **b)** $75

c) Answers may vary. The lawns are the same size and Bahi works at the same pace.

Quest: Which Is the Best Buy?, page 178

The 675-g box of cereal and the whole watermelon

3.2 Working with Unit Prices

Developing the Ideas, page 180

1. 45¢

2. a) 54¢   **b)** $1.08   **c)** 90¢   **d)** 81¢

3. See page 181.

4. Answers may vary. In any row, the cost of the sticks divided by the number of sticks is 9. If the number of licorice sticks doubles, the cost also doubles.

5. See page 190.

6. a) Estimates may vary. 63¢, $1.35   **b)** 11

7. a) $C = 9n$

Page 182

Problem 1: $4.50

Problem 2: 30¢

Problem 3: $2.18

Problem 4: $3.31

1. Answers may vary. They all deal with items that are bought. They all have different prices.

2. , 3. , 4. , 5. Answers may vary.

Working with Mathematics, page 183

1. a) The first column would not change. The second column would be: 30, 10, 50, 60, 120, 100, 90

b) The first column would not change. The second column would be: 24, 8, 40, 48, 96, 80, 72

2. a) Answers may vary. If the number of sticks is 0, the cost is $0.

b) For exercise 1a, the graph would be steeper. For exercise 1b, the graph would be less steep.

3. a) i) $5.00   **ii)** $2.10   **iii)** $8.00   **iv)** 56¢   **v)** 96¢   **vi)** $3.47

b) i) $10.00   **ii)** $4.20   **iii)** $16.00   **iv)** $1.12   **v)** $1.92   **vi)** $6.94

4. a) Cans   **b)** 750 mL   **c)** 800 g   **d)** 4 L   **e)** 250 g

5. a) 15¢

b)

Number of popsicles	Cost (¢)
1	15
2	30
4	60
5	75
10	150
13	195

c) Descriptions may vary. The points lie on a straight line that passes through the origin.

d) Estimates may vary. $1.05, $2.25, $2.70

e) 6, 20   **f)** Variables may differ. $c = 15n$

6. a) 32.5¢, 28.1¢, 35.4¢, 40.6¢

b) Answers may vary. We don't want to buy colours we don't use.

7. a) =B4/A4; answers may vary. They should.

b) $7.80, $3.90, $2.60

8. $3.00   **9.** Yes

10. a) 42¢

b)

Number of pieces	Cost (¢)
1	7
3	21
6	42
8	56
12	84

c) Descriptions may vary. The points lie on a straight line that passes through the origin.

d) Estimates may vary. 28¢, 49¢, 70¢

e) Variables may differ. $C = 7n$

11. a) 5/$1.29   **b)** $3.21 for 2.5 kg   **c)** $2.35 for 5 kg

12. a) $3.60   **b)** $1.05

13. a) 250 sheets, 200 sheets, 100 sheets, 50 sheets

14. Answers may vary.
   a) Large size: paper plates, paper cups, serviettes; giant size fruit drink
   b) $17.47

Linking Ideas: Mathematics and Science
Heartbeats, Breathing, and Lifetimes, page 185

1. Yes, about 840 000 000   **2.** Yes, about 850 000 000

3. About 850 000 000

4. Use the value from exercise 3. The heartbeats are rounded to the nearest 10. Squirrel: 160; domestic cat: 130; polar bear: 60; gorilla: 40

5. Humans: their average heartbeat is about 70 times per minute.

6. a) This is approximately the same.
   b) About 210 000 000
   c) Shrew: 200; elephant: 6; squirrel: 40; domestic cat: 33; polar bear: 15; gorilla: 10

3.3 Working with Speed
Developing the Ideas, page 186

1. About 28 000 km

2. a) About 14 000 km   **b)** About 42 000 km
   c) About 56 000 km   **d)** About 70 000 km
   e) About 84 000 km

3.

Time in hours	Distance in kilometres
0	0
0.5	14 000
1.0	28 000
1.5	42 000
2.0	56 000
2.5	70 000
3.0	84 000

4. Answers may vary. In any row, if we divide the distance by the time we get 28 000.

5. See page 190.

6. a) $d = 28\,000t$

Page 187

Problem 1: 3200 km

Problem 2: 1400 km

Problem 3: 375 km

Problem 4: About 3.3 km

1. Answers may vary. They all deal with speeds. The speeds are all different.

2. , 3. , 4. , 5. Answers may vary.

6. Each speed remains constant — this is unlikely in practice.

Working with Mathematics, page 188

1. a) The first column would not change. The second column would be: 0, 17 500, 35 000, 52 500, 70 000, 87 500, 105 000
   b) The first column would not change. The second column would be: 0, 10 000, 20 000, 30 000, 40 000, 50 000, 60 000

2. a) Answers may vary. The pairs of numbers are proportional and in 0 h, the shuttle has travelled 0 km. The distance travelled is proportional to the time spent.
   b) About 1.75 h   **c)** About 60 000 km
   d) For exercise 1a, the graph would be steeper. For exercise 1b, the graph would be less steep.

3. a) i) 60 km/h   **ii)** About 167 km/h
   iii) About 667 km/h   **iv)** 18 km/h   **v)** 30 000 km/h
   b) i) 360 km   **ii)** 1000 km   **iii)** 4000 km
   iv) 108 km   **v)** 180 000 km

4. Estimates in parts d and e may vary.
   a) 17 km/h
   b)

Time in hours	Distance in kilometres
1	17
2	34
5	85
8	136

   c) Descriptions may vary. The points lie on a straight line that passes through the origin.
   d) About 50 km, about 120 km, about 150 km
   e) About 3.5 h, about 6.5 h **f)** Variables may differ. $D = 17t$

5. a) 240 km, 480 km   **b)** 255 km, 510 km
   c) About 317 km, about 443 km   **d)** Answers may vary.

6. a) 30 km in 8 min   **b)** 8 km in 5 min

7. a) About 11 min 25 s   **b)** About 9 min 38 s

8. 480 km   **9.** Yes

10. a) 480 km   **b)** 400 km   **c)** 500 km   **d)** 540 km

11. a) 10 m; 30 m
   b)

Time in seconds	Distance in metres
0	0
5	10
10	20
15	30
20	40
25	50
30	60
35	70
40	80
45	90
50	100
55	110
60	120

   c) Descriptions may vary. The points lie on a straight line that passes through the origin.
   d) Estimates may vary. 56 m, 86 s
   e) Variables may differ. $d = 2t$

12. a) i) 48 m   **ii)** 108 m   **b)** About 163 m

13. 7500 km

14. a) 4800   **b)** About 8.3 m

15. Answers may vary.

3.4 Recognizing Proportional and Non-Proportional Situations

Developing the Ideas, page 191

Group 1

1.

Distance (km)	Cost ($)
1	2.25
2	2.50
3	2.75
4	3.00
5	3.25
6	3.50
7	3.75
8	4.00
9	4.25
10	4.50

3. It is not a proportional situation because a line drawn through the plotted points would not pass through the origin.

Group 2

1.

Number of eggs	Number of slices
1	1.5
2	3.0
3	4.5
4	6.0
5	7.5
6	9.0
7	10.5
8	12.0
9	13.5
10	15.0

3. This is a proportional situation because the plotted points lie on a straight line that passes through the origin, and the graph leans upwards to the right.

Group 3

1.

Number of hours	Cost ($)
1	0
2	2
3	4
4	6
5	8
6	10
7	12
8	14
9	16
10	18

3. This is not a proportional situation because a line drawn through the plotted points would not pass through the origin.

Group 4

1.

Number of litres of gas	Distance (km)
10	90
20	180
30	270
40	360
50	450
60	540
70	630
80	720
90	810
100	900

3. This is a proportional situation because the plotted points lie on a straight line that passes through the origin, and the graph leans upwards to the right.

Working with Mathematics, page 192

1. Explanations may vary.
   a) This is a proportional situation.
   b) This is not a proportional situation.
   c) This is not a proportional situation.
   d) This is not a proportional situation.
   e) This is a proportional situation.

2. This is a proportional situation. 16 orbits

3. This is a proportional situation. $42 Can

4. This is not a proportional situation. 25 laps

5. This is a proportional situation. 4 acres

6. This is not a proportional situation. 45 L

7. This is a proportional situation. 84 beats/min

8. This is not a proportional situation. $1.20

9. This is a proportional situation. 8

10. This is not a proportional situation. 48 years old

11. This is a proportional situation. 12 mg

12. a) No, reasons may vary.
    b) Probably not   c) 0; 100 W

13. a) $1 217 250
    b) About 0.8¢; answers may vary; probably agree
    c) Both a and b

Quest: For How Long Must You Exercise to Burn the Energy in Food?, page 194

About 20 min bicycling; about 16 min climbing stairs; about 14 min cross-country skiing; about 9 min running; about 38 min ironing, about 16 min swimming; about 17 min tennis; about 24 min walking

Linking Ideas: Mathematics and the Consumer
Unit Prices at the Donut Shop, page 196

1. a) 6 for $3.15 and 3 @ 60¢ each
   b) Answers may vary. Joanne could have bought 12 donuts for only $4.49.
   c) Joanne could buy 12 donuts, but she may not want that many.

2. a), 3. a)

Number of donuts	Total price ($)	Unit price ($)
1	0.60	0.60
2	1.20	0.60
3	1.80	0.60
4	2.40	0.60
5	3.00	0.60
6	3.15	0.53
7	3.75	0.54
8	4.35	0.54
9	4.49	0.50
10	4.49	0.45
11	4.49	0.41
12	4.49	0.37
13	5.09	0.39
14	5.69	0.41
15	6.29	0.42
16	6.89	0.43
17	7.49	0.44
18	7.64	0.42
19	8.24	0.43
20	8.84	0.44
21	8.98	0.43
22	8.98	0.41
23	8.98	0.39
24	8.98	0.37
25	9.58	0.38
26	10.18	0.39
27	10.78	0.40
28	11.38	0.41
29	11.98	0.41
30	12.13	0.40

2. c) No, explanations may vary.

3. c) No, explanations may vary.

4. Answers may vary.

3.5 Solving Problems in Proportional Situations
Working with Mathematics, page 199

1. We can calculate the answer only if the rate remains constant.

2. 45 s   **3.** About 57 s

4. Explanations may vary.
   a) For every $5 profit, Mrs. Adams got $3 and Mr. Singh got $2.
   b) Out of every 12 students in class, 7 are girls and 5 are boys.
   c) Out of 10 people, 3 are smokers and 7 are non-smokers.

5. Answers may vary.
   a) 4 : 10, 6 : 15, 8 : 20   **b)** 8 : 6, 12 : 9, 16 : 12
   c) 14 : 8, 21 : 12, 28 : 16   **d)** 6 : 16, 9 : 24, 12 : 32
   e) 8 : 2, 12 : 3, 16 : 4   **f)** 2 : 10, 3 : 15, 4 : 20
   g) 20 : 6, 30 : 9, 40 : 12   **h)** 10 : 14, 15 : 21, 20 : 28
   i) 4 : 22, 6 : 33, 8 : 44   **j)** 2 : 1, 4 : 2, 6 : 3
   k) 12 : 10, 18 : 15, 24 : 20   **l)** 1 : 5, 2 : 10, 4 : 20

6. a) 1 : 3   **b)** 7 : 6   **c)** 2 : 3   **d)** 3 : 7   **e)** 4 : 9   **f)** 9 : 7
   g) 2 : 3   **h)** 4 : 1   **i)** 52 : 71   **j)** 29 : 8   **k)** 8 : 11   **l)** 13 : 2

7. a) 7 : 20, 2 : 5, 1 : 4, 1 : 5
   b) 8 : 7, 8 : 5, 2 : 1   **c)** 4 : 7, 1 : 2, 4 : 5

8. a) Ratio, 1 : 2   **b)** Rate, $5/h
   c) Ratio, 7 : 6   **d)** Rate, 56¢/100 g, or 0.56¢/g
   e) Rate, 95 km/h

9. 80   **10.** 60   **11.** About 130

---

12. a) 2.5   **b)** 2.0   **c)** 3.0; Nadine, Amy, and Elio

13. Car B

14. a) 1620 kJ   **b)** 4260 kJ   **c)** 2520 kJ
   d) 2880 kJ   **e)** 1020 kJ   **f)** 2010 kJ

15. a) About 57   **b)** Answers may vary.

16. Answers will depend on the rate used. Answers are given here with the rate in the exercise.
   a) i) Adds $5 to the amount in cell A2.
    ii) Multiplies the amount in cell A2 by 1.3725.
    iii) Multiplies the amount in cell A3 by 1.3725.
   b) $27.45
   c) i) $274.50   **ii)** $2745   **iii)** $2.75
   d) i) $89.21   **ii)** $109.80
   e) Descriptions may vary.
   f) The numbers in column B would decrease. The graph would be a straight line below the previous graph.
   g) Yes, explanations may vary.

17. About 467 m

18. a) 9   **b)** 30   **c)** Between 11 and 12

19. 60   **20.** 480 min   **21.** Sharon

22. a) 40   **b)** 900   **c)** 45   **d)** 150   **e)** 75

23. a) 2 : 1   **b)** 2 : 5   **c)** 4 : 3
   d) 9 : 7   **e)** 3 : 2   **f)** 11 : 15

24. a) Cat and chipmunk; dog and chipmunk; horse and squirrel; chipmunk and mouse
   b) Cat and deer; cow and squirrel; dog and deer
   c) Horse and cow; deer and chipmunk
   d) Cow and mouse

25. a) 1 : 3   **c)** 15 : 45   **e)** 6 : 18   **f)** 2 : 6   **h)** 5 : 15

26. 20 rolls, assuming all customers bought 2 and got 1 free

27. No, explanations may vary. 6 measures of coffee to 7 cups of water is the strongest. 4 measures of coffee to 5 cups of water is the weakest.

28. Answers may vary.
   a) The mass of the body is 200 times the mass of the heart. The mass of the lungs is twice the mass of the heart.
   b) 1 : 100

Review, page 202

1. a) i) $7/h   **ii)** $5.50/h   **iii)** $8.50/h
   b) Kajsa   **c)** $70, $55, $85

2. a) $8/h
   b)

Number of hours	Oonagh's earnings ($)
1	8
5	40
8	64
13	104
14	112
20	160

   c) Descriptions may vary. The points lie on a straight line that passes through the origin.
   d) Estimates may vary. $48, $96, $136
   e) Variables may differ. $E = 8n$

3. a) $36, $42, $30, $62, $82, $102, $72
   b) Answers may vary.   **c)** Answers may vary.

4. a) i) =A2∗4.75   **ii)** =A2∗6

b) i) Raji   ii) $13.75
c) i) Paloma   ii) $5.25
d) $4.40/h   e) About $6.48/h

5. a) $1.99 for 1.35 kg
b) One dozen for $2.49
c) $4.99 per kilogram

6. a) $8.91   b) Answers may vary.   c) 19.8¢, 17.8¢
d) i) 70   ii) 56

7. a) i) 85 km/h   ii) 4 km/h   iii) 72 km/h   iv) 180 km/h
b) i) 340 km   ii) 16 km   iii) 288 km   iv) 720 km

8. a) i) 190 km   ii) 95 km/h   b) i) 255 km   ii) 85 km/h

9. a) 10 m/s   b) 3600   c) 36 km
d) 36 km/h   e) 20 km/h   f) Explanations may vary.

10. a) Proportional situations: i and iii; explanations may vary.
b) Explanations may vary.

11. i) 14   iii) 2340

12. a) i) $36   ii) $42   iii) $48   iv) $60   v) $90
b) 1 print job of 1000 pages   c) No, explanations may vary.

13. a) 2 : 1   b) 1 : 4   c) 1 : 8

Cumulative Review, page 204A

1. i) 78   ii) 77   iii) 74   iv) 83   v) 72, 85   vi) 34

3. a) 1.5 km   b) 3.75 km   c) 5.5 km
d) 2.25 km   e) 0.75 km   f) 3.3 km

4. a) 1 cm represents 10 m.   b) About 20.2 m

5. a) i) Top and side   ii) Top and side   iii) Front and side
b) Front of i and ii, and top of iii

6. a) $10 \times 10 \times 10$; 1000   b) 9×9; 81
c) $2 \times 2 \times 2 \times 2 \times 2$; 32   d) 25×25; 625
e) $3 \times 3 \times 3 \times 3$; 81

7. a) 17 100   b) 30 560 000   c) 2 975 000 000
d) 883 000   e) 9040   f) 5 420 000

8. The numbers in parts d, e, and f are divisible by 9.

9. a) Two and seventy-four hundredths, $(2 \times 1) + \left(7 \times \frac{1}{10}\right) +$
$\left(4 \times \frac{1}{100}\right)$; one hundred fifty-six and five tenths,
$(1 \times 100) + (5 \times 10) + (6 \times 1) + \left(5 \times \frac{1}{10}\right)$
b) Five and seven tenths, $(5 \times 1) + \left(7 \times \frac{1}{10}\right)$; one and six
tenths, $(1 \times 1) + \left(6 \times \frac{1}{10}\right)$
c) Eleven thousand and two hundred seventy-seven,
$(1 \times 10\ 000) + (1 \times 1000) + (2 \times 100) + (7 \times 10) + (7 \times 1)$
d) One billion five hundred million, $(1 \times 10^9) + (5 \times 10^8)$

10. a) $78 = 2 \times 3 \times 13$ b) $72 = 2^2 \times 3^2$

11. a) $30 = 2 \times 3 \times 5$ b) $44 = 2^2 \times 11$
c) $84 = 3 \times 4 \times 7$ d) $128 = 2^7$

12. a) 189   b) 1225   c) 675   d) 900

13. a) 6 cm   b) 8 cm   c) 9 cm   d) 11 cm

14. Estimates may vary.
a) 5.6   b) 8.1   c) 9.1   d) 9.7

15. a) $3.056\ 91 \times 10^{79}$ b) 80 digits

16. Estimates may vary.
a) 4.2   b) 5.9   c) 9.2
d) 10.2   e) 12.2   f) 14.5

17. a) $\frac{11}{9}$, or $1\frac{2}{9}$ b) $\frac{15}{14}$, or $1\frac{1}{14}$ c) $\frac{23}{12}$, or $1\frac{11}{12}$
d) $\frac{16}{12}$, or $1\frac{1}{3}$ e) $1\frac{5}{8}$ f) $2\frac{13}{16}$

g) $5\frac{11}{12}$ h) $\frac{20}{6}$, or $3\frac{1}{3}$ i) $\frac{51}{24}$, or $2\frac{1}{8}$

18. a) $\frac{4}{9}$ b) $\frac{7}{12}$ c) $\frac{17}{12}$, or $1\frac{5}{12}$ d) $\frac{17}{8}$, or $2\frac{1}{8}$
e) $\frac{5}{4}$, or $1\frac{1}{4}$ f) $2\frac{1}{7}$ g) $7\frac{1}{4}$ h) $\frac{1}{3}$ i) $\frac{1}{10}$

19. a) $\frac{1}{8}$ b) 6   c) 1   d) $\frac{1}{4}$ e) 10   f) $\frac{11}{20}$ g) $\frac{2}{3}$ h) $\frac{1}{15}$ i) $\frac{3}{10}$

20. a) $\frac{5}{6}$ b) 4   c) $\frac{16}{3}$, or $5\frac{1}{3}$ d) $\frac{3}{20}$ e) $\frac{1}{12}$
f) $\frac{9}{16}$ g) $\frac{1}{12}$ h) $\frac{7}{6}$, or $1\frac{1}{6}$ i) 16

21. c; examples may vary.

22. a) i) $2.00   ii) $2.10   iii) $2.20
b) i) $0.20   ii) $1.00   iii) $2.00   iv) $10.00
c) The basic fare calculation is not a proportional situation.
The charge for waiting is a proportional situation.
Explanations may vary.

23. a) About 23 s   b) Time taken would be less   c) About 13 s

CHAPTER 4 PERCENT

Start With What You Know, page 208

1. a) 100%   b) 25%   c) 50%   d) 75%   e) $66\frac{2}{3}$%   f) $33\frac{1}{3}$%

2. Estimates may vary.
a) 25%   b) 40%   c) 25%   d) 10%

3. The sum should be 100% since these 4 categories cover all the possibilities.

4. a) 0.05   b) 0.50   c) 0.35   d) 0.72   e) 0.40   f) 1.00

5. Atlantic Provinces: $4 324 107; Quebec: $7 350 981; Ontario: $21 620 534; Manitoba and Saskatchewan: $2 162 053; Alberta: $3 459 285; British Columbia: $4 324 107

6. a) 0.625   b) 0.6   c) 0.35   d) 0.26

7. a) 45%   b) 3%   c) 64%   d) 1%

8. a) In 1990, 56% of the people receiving a bachelor's degree from Canadian universities were women.
b) According to the 1991 census, 30% of Canadians were fluent in two or more languages.
c) In 1851, only 13% of Canadians lived in urban areas. In 1992, 75% of Canadians lived in urban areas.
d) In 1991, 80% of Canadians who were 100 years of age or older were women.

9. a) 32 800   b) 3.28   c) 750   d) 0.075
e) 43   f) 0.0043   g) 7   h) 0.0007

10. a) When multiplying by 100, move the decimal two places to the right.
b) When dividing by 100, move the decimal two places to the left.

11. a) Smaller   b) Larger

12. a) 46.88   b) 77.46   c) 79.66

Linking Ideas: Mathematics and the Consumer
Estimating Sales Tax, page 210

1. Estimates may vary. The exact provincial sales tax in dollars for each item in each province is given here, using the 1997 rates.

Province	Radio	Shoes	Pants	Camera
Alberta	0.00	0.00	0.00	0.00
British Columbia	15.75	3.15	2.59	10.43
Manitoba	15.75	3.15	2.59	10.43
New Brunswick	33.75	6.75	5.55	22.35
Newfoundland	33.75	6.75	5.55	22.35
Northwest Territories	0.00	0.00	0.00	0.00
Nova Scotia	33.75	6.75	5.55	22.35
Ontario	18.00	3.60	2.96	11.92
Prince Edward Island	22.50	4.50	3.70	14.90
Quebec	16.88	3.38	2.77	11.18
Saskatchewan	15.75	3.15	2.59	10.43
Yukon	0.00	0.00	0.00	0.00

Estimates may vary. The exact GST on each item is given here, using the 1997 rate of 7%. Radio: $15.75; shoes: $3.15; pants: $2.59; camera: $10.43

2. Estimates may vary. The exact total cost of each item in dollars including provincial and federal sales tax is given here, using the 1997 sales tax rates.

Province	Phone	Bicycle	Puzzle	Shirt
Alberta	31.98	102.72	9.36	15.72
British Columbia	34.07	109.44	9.97	16.75
Manitoba	34.07	109.44	9.97	16.75
New Brunswick	34.37	110.40	10.06	16.89
Newfoundland	34.37	110.40	10.06	16.89
Northwest Territories	31.98	102.72	9.36	15.72
Nova Scotia	34.37	110.40	10.06	16.89
Ontario	34.37	110.40	10.06	16.90
Prince Edward Island	34.97	112.32	10.24	17.19
Quebec	34.38	110.42	10.06	16.90
Saskatchewan	34.07	109.44	9.97	16.75
Yukon	31.98	102.72	9.36	15.72

4.1 Percent and Proportion
Developing the Ideas, page 211

Group 1

Answers will vary depending on your province. These sample answers refer to Saskatchewan and Manitoba, with a 7% sales tax rate in 1997.

1. a) $0.14 b) $0.28 c) $0.42 d) $0.56 e) $0.70
2. The total costs are: $0.00, $2.14, $4.28, $6.42, $8.56, $10.70.
3. Both the graphs represent proportional situations. Each graph is a straight line passing through the origin and leaning upwards to the right.
4. a) $S = P \times \frac{7}{100}$, or $S = 0.07P$　　b) $T = 1.07P$

Group 2

1. , 2. The amounts by which the items are reduced are: $50, $100, $200, $700. The sale prices are $150, $300, $600, $2100.
3. Both graphs represent proportional situations. Each graph is a straight line passing through the origin and leaning upwards to

the right.

4. a) $D = R \times \frac{25}{100}$, or $D = 0.25R$　　b) $S = 0.75R$

Group 3

1. , 2. a) 54 g b) 72 g c) 90 g d) 108 g e) 126 g
3. The graph represents a proportional situation. The graph is a straight line passing through the origin and leaning upwards to the right.
4. $W = A \times \frac{90}{100}$, or $W = 0.90A$

Group 4

1. , 2. a) 147 cm b) 168 cm c) 189 cm d) 210 cm
3. The graph represents a proportional situation. It is a straight line passing through the origin and leaning upwards to the right.
4. $L = 1.05h$

Working with Mathematics, page 214

1. a) Compare pairs of numbers in the columns. Suppose a number in the first column were twice as great as another number in that column. The same relationship should exist between the corresponding numbers in the second column.
   b) The graph is a straight line passing through the origin and leaning upwards to the right.
   c) The variables in the formula are related by multiplication or division.

2. a) The numbers in the second columns of the tables would increase. The graphs would still be straight lines passing through the origin, but they would lean more steeply upwards to the right. In the formula, P would be multiplied by a greater number.
   b) The numbers in the second columns of the tables would decrease. The graphs would still be straight lines passing through the origin, but they would lean less steeply upwards to the right. In the formula, P would be multiplied by a smaller number.

3. a) The amounts by which the items are reduced would be greater and the sale prices would be lower. Both graphs will still be straight lines passing through the origin. The graph for amounts by which the items are reduced would lean more steeply upwards to the right. The graph for sale prices would lean less steeply upwards to the right. The formulas would be $D = 0.5R$ and $S = 0.5R$.
   b) The amounts by which the items are reduced would be slightly greater and the sale prices slightly lower. The graphs would still be straight lines passing through the origin. The formulas would be $D = 0.3R$ and $S = 0.7R$.

4. a) The numbers in the *Mass of water* column would decrease. The graph would still be a straight line passing through the origin but it would lean less steeply upwards to the right. The formula would be $W = 0.8A$.
   b) The numbers in the *Mass of water* column would be greater. The graph would still be a straight line passing through the origin but it would lean more steeply upwards to the right. The formula would be $W = 0.95A$.

5. The numbers in the *Ski length* column would be greater. The graph would still be a straight line passing through the origin, but it would lean more steeply upwards to the right. The formula would be $L = 1.15h$.

6. a) 0.5 b) 0.05 c) 5.0 d) 0.2

e) 0.02   f) 0.09   g) 0.255   h) 0.3175
i) $0.\overline{6}$ j) 1.0   k) 0.75   l) 0.63
m) 0.6   n) 0.01   o) $0.\overline{3}$ p) 0.06

7. a) 15%   **b)** 4%   **c)** 37%   **d)** 99%
e) 86%   **f)** 1%   **g)** 62.5%   **h)** 100%
i) 87.5%   **j)** 22.5%   **k)** 27.5%   **l)** 5.5%
m) 10.75%   **n)** $33\frac{1}{3}$%   **o)** $66\frac{2}{3}$%   **p)** $99.\overline{9}$%

8. a) $10   **b)** $20   **c)** $15   **d)** $8   **e)** $12.50   **f)** $50

9. a) 1 cm   **b)** 4 cm   **c)** 1.5 km   **d)** 2.5 m
e) 0.29 km   **f)** 0.185 cm   **g)** 0.525 cm   **h)** 4.95 km

10. a) 9 kg   **b)** 18 kg   **c)** 180 kg   **d)** 108 kg
e) 33.75 g   **f)** 48.87 kg   **g)** 97.74 kg   **h)** 4.32 g

11. a) $0.70   **b)** $4.90   **c)** $1400   **d)** $8400
e) $0.14   **f)** $0.63   **g)** $1.26   **h)** $0.07

12. a) 8 cm   **b)** 16 cm   **c)** 24 cm   **d)** 32 cm   **e)** 40 cm
f) 10 cm   **g)** 20 cm   **h)** 30 cm   **i)** 13.33 cm   **j)** 26.67 cm

13. a) Each answer would be half as large since 20 cm is half of 40 cm.
  b) Each answer would be one-quarter as large since 10 cm is one-quarter of 40 cm.
  c) Each answer would be three-quarters as large since 30 cm is three-quarters of 40 cm.
  d) Each answer would be one-and-a-half times as large since 60 cm is one-and-a-half times as large as 40 cm.

14. a)

Province	Sales tax ($)	Total cost ($)
Alberta	0	39.99
British Columbia	2.80	42.79
Manitoba	2.80	42.79
New Brunswick	6.00	45.99
Newfoundland	6.00	45.99
Northwest Territories	0	39.99
Nova Scotia	6.00	45.99
Ontario	3.20	43.19
Prince Edward Island	4.00	43.99
Quebec	3.00	42.99
Saskatchewan	2.80	42.79
Yukon	0	39.99

b)

Sales tax rate (%)	Sales tax ($)
0	0.00
7.5	3.00
7	2.80
8	3.20
10	4.00
15	6.00

Sales tax rate (%)	Total cost ($)
0	39.99
7.5	42.99
7	42.79
8	43.19
10	43.99
15	45.99

c) Only the first graph represents a proportional situation. The *Total cost* graph does not pass through the origin, so it does not represent a proportional situation.
d) $S = 40 \times \frac{r}{100}$; $T = 40 + S$

15. a) 4 kg   **b)** 5.6 kg

16. $3.14

17. a) $12   **b)** $24   **c)** $36   **d)** $48   **e)** $60
f) $15   **g)** $30   **h)** $45   **i)** $20   **j)** $40

18. a) Each answer would be twice as great since $120 is twice as great as $60.
  b) Each answer would be four times as great since $240 is four times as great as $60.

c) Each answer would be half as great since $30 is half of $60.
d) Each answer would be one-quarter as great since $15 is one-quarter of $60.

19. a) Amount: $10.50; sale price: $24.49
  b) Amount: $12.49; sale price: $37.46
  c) Amount: $0.55; sale price: $2.22

20. 76.3 cm

21. a) 20%
  b) Answers may vary. For example, 44 squares: 18.2%, 54 squares: 16.7%, 65 squares: 15.4%.
  c) No

Linking Ideas: Percent and Data Management
What Do We Throw Away?, page 216

1. 0.664 t, or 664 kg

2. Industrial, commercial, and institutional: 55%; residential: 45%

3. a) 540 800 t   **b)** 118 300 t   **c)** 202 800 t   **d)** 169 000 t

4. 151 424 t   **5.** About 11.5%

6. , 7. , 8. Answers may vary.

4.2 Solving Problems Using Percent
Working with Mathematics, page 219

1. a) The percent would increase.
  b) The percent would decrease.

2. a) The amount earned would be greater.
  b) The amount earned would be greater.

3. a) 45%   **b)** 2.5%   **c)** 24.4%   **d)** 60%   **e)** 51%   **f)** 60%
g) 75%   **h)** 25%   **i)** 40%   **j)** 60%   **k)** 55%   **l)** $83.\overline{3}$%

4. a) 0.45   **b)** 0.95   **c)** 0.325   **d)** 0.145   **e)** 0.0525   **f)** 0.0975

5. a) 10 g   **b)** $35   **c)** 24 books
d) 72 cars   **e)** $3   **f)** $3

6. a) 4   **b)** 10   **c)** 10   **d)** 10   **e)** 8   **f)** 20

7. 12 students

8. a) $63.74   **b)** $36.25   **c)** 36.25%

9. $4.49

10. a) 75%, 80%, 60%, 50%   **b)** 66.25%

11. Terry

12. a) 40   **b)** 45   **c)** 50   **d)** 120

13. 36 students

14. a) 40 cm   **b)** 150 m   **c)** $40
d) $200   **e)** 16 g   **f)** 16 g

15. a) $21   **b)** $14.40   **c)** $29.99   **d)** $53.99

16. a) 12   **b)** 30   **c)** 28

17. a) i) 4.5 kg   **ii)** 45 g   **iii)** 4.5 g   **iv)** 450 g
  b) Groundhog: 4.3 kg or 4300 g, 215 g (heart); yellownose vole: 43 g, 2.15 g (heart); northern long-eared bat: 4.3 g, 0.215 g (heart)

18. Dresses and coats

19. a) 80%   **b)** 70%   **c)** 67%   **d)** 75%   **e)** 72%

20. 75%

21. Estimates may vary. About 60 billion

22. Animals: 140 000 000; Plants: 50 000 000

23. a) 25 squares, 39%
  b) i) From any square along the edge of the board the queen

controls only 21 squares, or about 33% of the board.

ii) From any of the centre four squares the queen controls 27 squares, or about 42% of the board.

Quest: How Can You Get a 50% Reduction on a Copy Machine?, page 221

It is not possible to get a reduction that is 50% of the original. You can get a copy that is 49.92% of the original by making a 64% copy followed by a 78% copy, or vice versa.

4.3 Discount
Developing the Ideas, page 222

1. Answers may vary. $\frac{20}{100}$ of the original price has been deducted to get the sale price.

2. Reduced by 20¢; you would pay 80¢.

3.

Original price	Discount	Sale price
$4.99	$1.00	$3.99
$9.99	$2.00	$7.99
$29.99	$6.00	$23.99
$46.99	$9.40	$37.59
$84.99	$17.00	$67.99

Working with Mathematics, page 223

1., 2. Answers may vary.

3. a) $4.85 b) $3.75

4. a) $50.80 b) $8.95

5. a) Answers may vary. b) Hawkeye
   c) Delete the words "Up to". Change the sale prices to: $19.60, $15.00, $15.60, and $27.80
   d) Answers may vary; yes.

6. PST and total cost will vary. Sale price and GST:
   a) $14.00, $0.98 b) $21.00, $1.47
   c) $28.80, $2.02 d) $65.80, $4.61

7. Answers may vary.
   a) Yes, because 40% off $280 should be $168
   b) No, the reductions are 20%.

8. 25%

Linking Ideas: Mathematics and the Consumer
Discount Coupons, page 224

1. PST will vary. Total: $210.87; Discount: $10.00; Subtotal: $200.87; GST: $14.06

2. PST will vary. Subtotal: $131.16; GST: $9.18

3. USave:
   a) $30.00 b) $50.00 c) $10.00 d) $80.00
   Scratch'n'Save:
   a) $32.00 b) $48.00 c) $16.00 d) $72.00

4. $50

4.4 Percent Increase and Decrease
Developing the Ideas, page 225

1. 33% of 60 is 20 and 33% of 90 is 30

2. 90, 135 3. 75, 113 4. 20% 5. $66\frac{2}{3}$%

Working with Mathematics, page 227

1. a) 10% of 10 is 1 b) 25%

2. a) $48 is the original price. b) $30 is the original price.

3. a) 16% b) 40% c) 25%
   d) 5% e) 12.5% f) 6.6%

4. a) 25% b) 25% c) 20%
   d) 25% e) 15%

5. 8.3%, 10%

6. a) 6; 50% b) 6; 33%
   c) The percent increase in part a is greater than the percent decrease in part b because the original amount is smaller in part a.

7. Explanations may vary. The classmate did not realize that the original amount was 150 in the first case, but 200 in the second. A decrease from 200 to 150 is a 25% decrease.

8. About 750 ml 9. 9.6%

10. a) 20% b) 20% c) $33\frac{1}{3}$%

11. a) 5.6% b) 20% c) 10%

12. a) $24.29 b) $27.99 c) $11.04

13. 95%

14. a) 28.6% b) Yes; 57.1%
   c) Even though the amount of extra shampoo is the same, it is not as great a percent. 22.2%

15. a) 13.6%
   b) Answers may vary. c) Answers may vary.

16. a) $990.00 b) It has decreased by 1%.

17. a) In cell B2, enter =A2−.1∗A2 or =.9∗A2. In cell C2, enter =.1∗B2+B2 or =1.1∗B2.
   b) Less
   c) An 11.1% increase was needed. The formula is =B2+0.111∗B2.
   d) Yes

4.5 Interest and Commission
Working with Mathematics, page 231

1. a) Yes b) Yes

2. Estimates may vary.
   a) $6.18 b) $4.78 c) $18.34 d) $60.94

3. a) $10 470 b) $164 030

4. a) $60 b) $25 c) $1200 d) $6300 e) $39 f) $138
   g) $2205 h) $7000 i) $16 j) $17.50 k) $38.75 l) $45
   m) $5.40 n) $27.50 o) $19.50 p) $58

5. a) $70 b) $1070

6. a) $124 b) $924

7. $800

8. $1046.22

9. September: $2103.50; October: $2085.50; November: $1977.50; December: $2270.00

10. a)

Interest rate (%)	Interest earned after one year ($)	Interest rate (%)	Total amount after one year ($)
0	0	0	250
2	5	2	255
4	10	4	260
6	15	6	265
8	20	8	270
10	25	10	275

b) The graph of interest earned represents a proportional situation. It is a straight line, passing through the origin and leaning upwards to the right. The other graph does not pass through the origin.

11. Answers may vary.

12. a) $220   **b)** 10%

13. a) $8.00   **b)** $600.00   **c)** $7950.00

14. a) $1 310 000   **b)** $14.41 million

15. $262.50

16. a) $180.00   **b)** $1191.02
c) Nasmin received $11.02 more interest.

Quest: Should Sales Tax Be Applied before or after a Discount?, page 233

a) Any method   **b)** Method 1   **c)** Method 2

4.6 Percents Greater than 100% and Less than 1%
Working with Mathematics, page 235

1. a) Decimals greater than 1, such as 1.2, 1.04, 2.0, and so on
b) Decimals less than 0.01, such as 0.008, 0.005, 0.0001, and so on

2. a) 1.0   **b)** 1.2   **c)** 1.6   **d)** 1.8   **e)** 2.0
f) 0.004   **g)** 0.006   **h)** 0.008   **i)** 0.01

3. a) 130%   **b)** 145%   **c)** 270%   **d)** 150%   **e)** 125%
f) 0.5%   **g)** 0.3%   **h)** 0.1%   **i)** 2.5%

4. a) 20%   **b)** 200%   **c)** 0.2%   **d)** 48.5%   **e)** 0.5%   **f)** 0.35%
g) 148%   **h)** 400%   **i)** 700%   **j)** 860%   **k)** $0.\overline{3}$%   **l)** 1000%
m) $3.\overline{3}$%   **n)** 10 000%   **o)** 75%   **p)** $66.\overline{6}$%

5. a) 2%   **b)** 0.2%   **c)** 200%   **d)** 300%   **e)** 400%   **f)** 125%
g) $166.\overline{6}$%   **h)** 0.6%   **i)** $0.\overline{3}$%   **j)** $0.0\overline{6}$%   **k)** 1%   **l)** 250%
m) 0.1%   **n)** 0.01%   **o)** $0.\overline{6}$%   **p)** 1000%

6. a) 3.0   **b)** 9.0   **c)** 1.05   **d)** 1.1   **e)** 0.001   **f)** 0.009
g) 0.0035   **h)** 1.0875   **i)** 2.9437   **j)** 0.003   **k)** 1.33   **l)** 0.0005
m) 1.66   **n)** 0.0008   **o)** 2.5   **p)** 0.0025

7. a) 0.005   **b)** 0.0025   **c)** $0.00\overline{3}$ **d)** $0.00\overline{6}$ **e)** $6.\overline{6}$ **f)** $1.\overline{3}$
g) 0.006   **h)** 1.08   **i)** 0.001   **j)** 1.3725   **k)** 1.055   **l)** 0.002
m) 0.0075   **n)** 1.001   **o)** $0.001\overline{6}$ **p)** $0.00\overline{1}$

8. a) 140 kg   **b)** 55 s   **c)** $10.70   **d)** $53.50   **e)** 140 cm   **f)** 6
g) 114.4   **h)** $1705   **i)** 20.35 mL   **j)** $490.\overline{6}$ cm^2
k) $526.08   **l)** 1 km   **m)** 375.375   **n)** 200 cm   **o)** 0.3 g   **p)** $0.90

9. a) i) 50   **ii)** $\frac{50}{100}$; 50%
b) i) 25   **ii)** $\frac{25}{100}$; 25%
c) i) 12.5   **ii)** $\frac{12.5}{100}$; 12.5%
d) i) 6.25   **ii)** $\frac{6.25}{100}$; 6.25%
e) i) 3.125   **ii)** $\frac{3.125}{100}$; 3.125%

---

f) The number was half the preceding number.

10. a) One 100-square and the red squares
b) Two 100-squares and the blue squares
c) One 100-square and the yellow squares
d) Two 100-squares and the green squares
e) One 100-square and the black squares
f) Two 100-squares
g) Two 100-squares and the yellow squares
h) One 100-square and the green squares

11. a) About $1.48   **b)** $2.95

12. a) $48   **b)** $60   **c)** $100   **d)** $0.20   **e)** $0.28   **f)** $0.36

13. $42   **14.** 125%   **15.** 6

16. The diameters listed here are rounded to the nearest kilometre. Saturn: 119 883 km; Jupiter: 142 688 km; Pluto: 2293 km

17. a) i) $33\frac{1}{3}$ **ii)** $\frac{33.\overline{3}}{100}$; $33\frac{1}{3}$%
b) i) $66\frac{2}{3}$ **ii)** $\frac{66.\overline{6}}{100}$; $66\frac{2}{3}$%
c) i) The green squares   **ii)** The red squares
iii) Two 100-squares and the red squares
iv) One 100-square and the green squares

18. a) $\frac{8}{8}$ **b)** $\frac{16}{8}$
c) The numerator of the fraction for 200% is twice as great.
d) $\frac{24}{8}$ **e)** $\frac{12}{12}, \frac{24}{12}, \frac{36}{12}$
f) The number in cell A2 should be 25, the formula in cell A3 should be =A2+25.

19. $966.24   **20.** $72

21. a) 27.5 cm   **b)** 30 cm   **c)** 50 cm
d) 0.125 cm   **e)** 0.05 cm   **f)** 0.025 cm

22. a) 79.8 m   **b)** 22.2 m

23. 180%   **24.** $30.96   **25.** 2

26. Newfoundland and Labrador: 399 728 km^2; New Brunswick: 79 946 km^2; Nova Scotia: 59 960 km^2; Prince Edward Island: 5996 km^2

27. 1 068 210 men and 14 510 women

28. 3 mg   **29.** 2 : 1

Mathematics File: What Percent of a Newspaper Is Advertising?, page 238

Answers may vary.

Review, page 239

1. a) 6 cm   **b)** 12 cm   **c)** 18 cm   **d)** 24 cm   **e)** 36 cm
f) 48 cm   **g)** 15 cm   **h)** 30 cm   **i)** 45 cm   **j)** 60 cm

2. a) Each answer would be half as great.
b) Each answer would be twice as great.
c) Each answer would be one-quarter as great.
d) Each answer would be one-and-a-half times as great.

3. a)

Leather coat	120.00	479.99
Ski jacket	60.00	239.99
Ski pants	40.00	159.99
Toque	4.00	15.99

c) Both graphs represent proportional situations. They both are straight lines passing through the origin and leaning upwards to the right.

d) Variables may differ. $D = 0.2R$; $S = 0.8R$

4. a) $10.00, $39.99   **b)** $38.99, $90.96   **c)** $28.00, $51.99

5. a), **b)** Answers may vary, depending on the sales tax rate.
c) No, the final price is the same.

6. 120

7. a) 44 girls; 36 boys
b) 24 walk; 28 ride the bus; 16 get rides from parents; 12 use other methods.
c) 64 eat at school; 16 eat at home.
d) 74 like to watch movies at the theatre.
e) 30 prefer hockey; 18 prefer baseball; 32 prefer other sports.

8. a) $33\frac{1}{3}$%   **b)** 60%   **c)** $6\frac{2}{3}$%

9. a) 90%, 85%, 44%, 80%, 76%   **b)** 75%

10. a) 28%, 30%, 40%
b) i) 25 hits, 75 at bats   **ii)** $33\frac{1}{3}$%
c) 28.6%, 30%, 37.5%
d) Each player had a batting average of 30% on the next 10 at bats. Because this was higher than Alina's previous average, her average increased; because it was the same as Sophia's previous average, her average did not change; because it was less than Dominique's previous average, her average decreased.

11. a) Gold earrings: 83.3%; gold ring: 75.0%; gold bracelet: 58.3%; gold necklace: 41.7%
b) 24K: 100%; 20K: 83.3%; 18K: 75%; 14K: 58.3%; 10K: 41.7%
c) Yes, it represents a proportional situation.
d) Variables may differ. $P = \frac{k}{24} \times 100$

12. The maximum mass is 300 kg. This is much less than the mass of many large mammals such as whales, seals, and walrus. Even a fish such as the sturgeon can reach a mass of 225 kg.

13. 80 kg

14. a) 25%   **b)** 25%   **c)** 37.5%   **d)** 12.5%

15. $5000   **16.** $17 500   **17.** $147.40

18. a) $18.00   **b)** $12.00   **c)** $15.05   **d)** $32.45
e) $30.00   **f)** $14.00   **g)** $20.31   **h)** $6.52

19. a) $127.50   **b)** $1627.50

20. a) 1.3   **b)** 0.76   **c)** 1.51   **d)** 0.148
e) 0.0179   **f)** 0.0045   **g)** $0.00\overline{6}$ **h)** $0.001\,\overline{428\,57}$
i) 0.2225   **j)** 0.0575   **k)** $0.08\overline{6}$ **l)** $1.07\overline{3}$

21. a) 53%   **b)** 7%   **c)** 0.4%   **d)** 390%
e) 1820%   **f)** 140%   **g)** $0.\overline{3}$%   **h)** 0.52%
i) 292%   **j)** 0.02%   **k)** 488.7%   **l)** 0.975%

22. a) $84.00   **b)** $70.20   **c)** 48¢   **d)** 9¢

23. Approximately 1.127 m^2 **24.** $114 798

CHAPTER 5 DATA MANAGEMENT

Start With What You Know, page 246

1. Cod

2. Estimates may vary. The actual percents are given here.
a) 67%   **b)** 11%   **c)** 8.5%

3. Estimates may vary. The calculated amounts are given here.
a) 75 687 t   **b)** 58 485 t   **c)** 92 888 t

Answers to exercises 4, 5, and 6 may vary, depending on approximations made from the graph.

4. a) i) 275 000 t   **ii)** 175 000 t   **iii)** 100 000 t
b) 64%

5. a) i) 600 000 t   **ii)** 75 000 t   **iii)** 525 000 t
b) 12.5%

6. a) i) 175 000 t   **ii)** 150 000 t   **iii)** 25 000 t
b) 86%

7. 24 000 t

8. 1960: 500 000 t; 1970: 600 000 t; 1980: 200 000 t
a) 433 333 t   **b)** 500 000 t
c) The mean; explanations may vary.

Linking Ideas: Mathematics and Technology
Using Data for Investigations, page 248

1. a) Lyudmila Belousova and Oleg Protopopov
b) Answers may vary. In ClarisWorks, use the Find feature and enter Figure Skating - Pairs and 1968. In Microsoft Works, use a filter or query using the same information. Other possibilities are to find the Figure Skating - Pairs records, then scroll to find 1968; or find the 1968 events, then scroll through the records to find Figure Skating - Pairs.
c) More information is given than is required. For example, if 1968 is given, then Grenoble is not required.

2. Answers may vary.

3. a) Puma, cougar, or mountain lion (78 cm); 3 (river otter, 43 cm; beaver, 46 cm; grey wolf, 47 cm)
b) Answers may vary. Sort the database by tail length. Lengths could be sorted from longest to shortest, or shortest to longest. Scan the sorted data to find mammals with a tail length between 40 cm and 50 cm. Alternatively, use the Find feature for tail lengths 40 cm, 41 cm, 42 cm, and so on to 50 cm. This method is time-consuming.
c) Sorting gives enough information to find the mammal with the longest tail. However, scan through the sorted data to find the mammals with tail lengths 40 cm to 50 cm.

4. Answers may vary.

5. No; *Ghostbusters* made the most money ($130 211 324) of all Columbia's movies in the database, but did not win any Academy Awards. *Lawrence of Arabia* made much less money ($19 000 000), but it won 7 Academy Awards.

6. Answers may vary.   **7.** 41 moons

8. a) 5.75×10^9 km   **b)** 9.2×10^7 km

9. About $4\frac{1}{2}$ days   **10.** About 4 times   **11.** Closer to the sun

12. No; Saturn has the most moons but Jupiter is the largest planet.

13. Answers may vary.

5.1 Constructing Graphs
Developing the Ideas, page 250

1.

Population by region					
Region	**Year**				
Western and Northern	3 000 000	4 000 000	4 900 000	6 200 000	6 900 000
Central	9 800 000	12 700 000	14 900 000	16 200 000	18 100 000
Eastern	1 700 000	1 900 000	2 100 000	2 200 000	2 300 000

4. Central Canada

5. Yes; the difference between the heights of the first and last points is greatest for this region.

6. a) $\frac{18.1}{9.8}$, or about 1.85   b) 185%
   c) A 200% increase would represent a doubling of the population. Since 185% is close to 200%, the population almost doubled.

7. $\frac{6.9}{3}$, or 2.3

8. Yes; the population of Western and Northern Canada more than doubled during the 40-year period, which represents a greater rate of increase than those of the other regions.

Working with Mathematics, page 255

1. Answers may vary. Many people find it easier to see the changes in data when the data are presented as a graph.

2. Examples may vary.
   a) A double-bar graph shows two sets of data by using horizontal or vertical bars whose lengths are proportional to the numbers they represent.
   b) A broken-line graph shows data by using points joined by line segments.
   c) A double broken-line graph is two broken-line graphs on the same axes.
   d) A circle graph uses a circle divided into parts whose areas are proportional to the numbers the parts represent.

3. a) 5000   b) 186 000   c) 20 000   d) 400 000   e) 1 400 000

4. a) $\frac{1}{2}$ b) $\frac{1}{4}$ c) $\frac{1}{5}$ d) $\frac{10}{17}$ e) $\frac{7}{8}$ f) $\frac{114}{203}$

5. a) $23.\overline{3}\%$ b) 12.5%   c) 40%   d) 18%   e) 35.5%   f) 10.5%

6. a) 40%   b) 17%   c) 41%   d) 22.5%   e) 25%   f) 20%

7. a) The total number of recordings purchased increased from 1988 to 1992.
   b) To the nearest percent, the answers are:
      i) 29%   ii) 61%   iii) 10%
   c) To the nearest percent, the answers are:
      i) 1%   ii) 54%   iii) 45%
   d) CDs had a much larger share of the market in 1992 than in 1988.
   e) CD
   f) You would need to know the price of each product in each year.

8. a) The number of CDs sold was increasing dramatically. Usually, when you can manufacture a greater quantity of an item, the cost to produce each item is lower.
   b) 1988: $325 494 000; 1990: $416 227 000; 1992: $567 945 000
   c) More
   d) Questions and answers may vary.

9. a) The table provides information about the world population and the amount of grain produced in four different years.
   b) The numbers with asterisks are predictions.
   c) There arc 1000 million in 1 billion.
      1950: 500 000 million kg; 1980: 1 400 000 million kg; 2010: 2 000 000 million kg; 2040: 1 900 000 million kg
   d) 1950: 198.6 kg; 1980: 318.2 kg; 2010: 277.8 kg; 2040: 197.9 kg
   f) The graph suggests that the supply of grain will be greatly reduced from the current level.

10. b) 1989: $486 691 630; 1990: $443 959 164; 1991: $392 797 870; 1992: $396 059 083; 1993: $552 338 181
    c) Answers may vary, depending on the type of graph drawn.
    d) Answers may vary. You might want to know the names of

the top 5 movies from 1994.

11. c) Estimates may vary. The winning times were 9.95 s for the men's race and 11.08 s for the women's race.
    d) The women's performance has improved more than the men's.
    e) Answers may vary.

12. b) Dancing and gardening   c) Jogging
    d) The data suggest that Canadians were more active in 1988 than in 1981.

13. b) Manitoba   c) Yukon Territory
    d) Because the population of the Yukon was so small in 1952, even a small increase in the number of people living there represents a large percent increase.

14. b) Western and Northern Canada's share of the population has been increasing. Central and Eastern Canada's shares have decreased.

15. a) Dances, sports teams and drama club (same amount), winter carnival, class trips
    b) $2000; $1200

16. a) $17 185.44   b) 19.6 L   c) 15.2 kg
    d) $7.14   e) $1.67

17. a)

Year	World grain production (billions of kg)	World population (millions)	Grain per person (kg/person)
1950	500	2518	198.6
1980	1400	4400	318.2
2010	3000	5040	595.2
2040	2850	6720	424.1

b) The graph suggests that although the grain supply per person decreases after 2010, it will be adequate for at least the first half of the century.

5.2 Collecting Data
Developing the Ideas, page 259

Answers may vary.

Page 261

1. Answers may vary.
   a) The following data were probably collected using a sample: the amount of sleep per night, type, colour, and age of car, and length of drive to the office for the average Canadian female; the number of TV sets and time TV is on each day for the average Canadian family.
   b) This information is not available from tax form data or census data collected by the Canadian government and it would be difficult for any person or organization other than the government to collect data about all Canadians.

2. Answers may vary.
   a) The following data were probably collected on the entire population: the age of the average Canadian female; the size and age of home and the amount spent on shelter for the average Canadian family.
   b) This information is available on almost all Canadians from census data or tax form data.

3. Answers may vary.
   Mode: most popular type and colour of car, number of TV sets
   Median: age of average female, age of car, age of house, portion of income spent on shelter, length of time TV on

Mean: hours of sleep per night, number of rooms in house

4. Answers may vary. Probably each part of this statement is true, but the combination of the three conditions may not be. That is, the most common colour of a car is white, the most common type of a car is compact, and the most common age of a car is 7 years; but "white, compact, 7-years old" may not be the most common description of women's cars.

Working with Mathematics, page 262

1. Samples are used to gather information about a population because it is often difficult or even impossible to gather information from every member of a population.

2. a) People from Vancouver are more likely to pick a team from their area.
   b) People from different age groups will probably like different TV programs.
   c) This survey excludes Canadians not listening to the program. Since the show's audience may have common beliefs, the survey will not represent a wide variety of viewpoints.
   d) Some people may not purchase as many shoes as other people, either by choice or because stores do not carry enough shoes in their size.
   e) The researcher should record travellers using other methods of transportation, such as car, bus, train, or boat.

3. Answers may vary. They try to make sure their sample is not biased.

4. a) From Statistics Canada Census data
   b) 75%   c) 25%
   d) Yes; it includes all residents of Canada.

5. a) to c) Answers may vary.
   d) i) Spring   ii) Winter
   iii) Answers may vary.
   e) Answers may vary. Generally, spring records the most births.
   f) A graph for all students in the school would be a larger sample than a class graph. Therefore, a graph for all students in the school is more likely to resemble the graph for all Canadians.

6. a) Women
   b) Watching TV is the most popular recreational activity for all age groups and for both sexes.
   c) Answers may vary.   d) Answers may vary.

7. Answers may vary. a) iii   b) iii

8. a) Answers may vary. Players whose teams have a high attendance at games may have an advantage.
   b) Answers may vary.

9. In a door-to-door survey, people would probably claim to brush their teeth more frequently.

10. Answers may vary. There could be many people who were not satisfied but did not or could not return the game.

11. No; it could be that students in one group had better mathematics skills to begin with. The researcher should have tested the students' mathematics skills at the beginning and checked which group showed the most improvement.

Mathematics File: The Poggendorf Effect, page 265

Answers may vary.

5.3 Misuses of Statistics

Developing the Ideas, page 267

Answers may vary.

Activity 1, page 267

1. Billions

2. a) 1.7 cm   b) 0.0083 cm   c) 2.0 cm

3. 2.4 cm; it is taller than it should be.

4. a) 3.5 cm   b) 0.7 cm; it is much shorter than it should be.

5. Answers may vary.

Activity 2, page 268

1. a) Canada   b) Equal   c) United States

2. Unemployed—Canada: 3 186 000, 11.8%;
   United States: 17 420 000, 6.7%
   Budget deficit—Canada: $45.7 billion, $1692.59 per capita;
   United States: $234 billion, $900 per capita

3. a) The percent
   b) Because the total populations are so different; the U.S. population is almost 10 times as great as the Canadian population.

4. a) The total deficits are compared.
   b) When the deficits are compared on a per capita basis, Canada's deficit is much greater than that of the United States.

5. Answers may vary.

Working with Mathematics, page 269

1. a) A question you ask to try to understand better what a statement means to help you find out if the statement is misleading.
   b) Answers may vary.

2. Answers may vary.
   a) What brand? What does "up to" mean?
   b) How was this determined? Do most teenagers purchase their own beverages or drink the beverages the family buys?
   c) What is meant by cost of living? Is the 14% an increase from the previous year or from many years ago?
   d) More vigorously than what? How was the study conducted?
   e) Who was surveyed? Did the sample include people without a driver's licence?
   f) Compared to what? How was this determined?
   g) Is the flight free or only the car rental? Are there other conditions that have to be met?

3. Answers may vary.

4. a) Answers may vary. People are more likely to answer yes to the first question even if they are not concerned for their own safety.

5. b) The second graph; the differences in heights between the points are greater.
   c) The second graph; the vertical scale does not start at 0.

6. a) Unoccupied space   b) Occupied space
   c) Estimates may vary. About 40%
   d) The amount of unoccupied space on the graph is about double the stated percent.
   e) There is a break in the vertical scale where it jumps from 0 to 90 000.

7. Answers may vary, depending on the year chosen. Answers given here are for 1985.
   a) i) $16 000   ii) $13 000   iii) 81.25%

Just over 80% of a person's income remains after taxes.

b) i) 4.7 cm   **ii)** 2.4 cm   **iii)** 51.06%

Just over 50% of a person's income appears to remain after taxes.

c) The vertical scale starts at $10 000 rather than 0. The answer in part a is correct.

8. a) Yes   **b)** No

c) Answers may vary. Some people with no preference may say no.

d) The conclusion may not be valid because the wording of the question does not take into account people who do not like either product.

9. Although the heights of the bags are proportional to the profits, the areas of the bags representing the second and third years are much greater than they should be.

10. a) 730   **b)** 1961: 237; 1975: 701

c) The number of murders is increasing.

d) The number of murders per 100 000 people decreased from 3.09 in 1975 to 2.7 in 1992.

e) Answers may vary.

Linking Ideas: Mathematics and Science
Contaminants in the Great Lakes, page 272

1. a) Taking all the eggs may harm the gull population if the birds do not lay new eggs to replace those taken.

b) To be able to compare contaminant levels in different locations

2. 1 000 000 cm equal 10 000 m, or 10 km.

3. a) Mugg's Island/Leslie St.

b) There is a lot of industry near this location.

4. a) Mugg's Island and Big Sister Island

b) The decreases occurred in the late 1970s and early 1980s. This follows the regulation of the use of PCBs in the U.S. and Canada.

5. The contamination levels were lower to begin with because PCBs were not dumped directly into the lake. The rate of decrease in contamination would be slower than in lakes where direct dumping was suddenly stopped.

5.4 Measures of Central Tendency
Working with Mathematics, page 277

1. Answers may vary.
a) Mean   **b)** Median   **c)** Mean   **d)** Mean   **e)** Mean   **f)** Mode

2. No, explanations may vary. Doubling the sample size does not double the mean value.

3. No, to calculate the mean the student must add the marks for 4 exams, then divide by 4.

4. 40.1, 40.5, there are four modes: 23, 32, 41, 54

5. a) 5.8, 4   **b)** 7.7, 6   **c)** 13.3, 13   **d)** 48, 55
   e) 16, 16   **f)** 3.4, 4   **g)** 10.3, 10

6. a) 3   **b)** Answers may vary. 2, 2, 2, 4, 5; 1, 2, 2, 4, 6

7. 66.8%

8. a) 1, 5, 5, 5, 5, 5, 5, 6, 9, 9, 10, 10, 10, 10, 10

b) The mean increases. The median increases. There are now two modes: 5 and 10.

9. a) Sum of heights of plants (cm): 26 cm, 38 cm, 28 cm; Total number of plants: 5; Total height: 92 cm

b) 18.4 cm

10. a) 6.125, 6, 2   **b)** 12.25, 12, 4   **c)** All are doubled.
d) 18.375, 18, 6   **e)** All are tripled.   **f)** 10.125, 10, 6
g) They increase by the amount added to each number.

11. a) $8771

b) Answers may vary. It may be unreasonable, but many more people shop on Saturday than any other day of the week, so she might make it.

12. $15.88, $14.99   **13.** 18   **14.** Answers may vary.

15. a) The mean and median both increase by 5.

b) The mean and median both double.

c) The mean and median do not change.

d) The mean more than triples. The median increases slightly.

e) The mean decreases more than the median decreases.

16. 99%

17. Answers may vary. 1 m, 1 m, 1 m, 3 m, 14 m, 15 m, 20 m

18. 74.1

19. a) The mean is $50 571.43. The median is $55 000. The modes are $55 000 and $33 000.

b) Answers may vary. The median and mean most fairly represent the pay structure. There are 8 out of 14 people who earn at least these amounts.

20. a) Answers may vary. 24%, 55%, 63%, 64%, 64%, 72%, 72%, 72%, 72%, 82%

b) Answers may vary. For the marks in part a, the mean increases, the median increases, the mode is not affected.

21. Answers may vary. The mode, because we assume the greatest number of people did not use incorrect units.

22. a) There are different numbers of people in each group.
b) $16 700

23. Answers may vary.
a) 9, 10, 18, 19, 20   **b)** 1, 62, 63, 64, 67, 79
c) 18, 19, 20, 21, 22, 46, 46   **d)** 8, 9, 9, 9, 9, 9, 9, 10
e) 6, 6, 6, 6, 6, 6, 7   **f)** 4, 4, 4, 4, 4, 4   **g)** 5, 5, 5, 5, 5

24. a) $55.90, $59.80   **b)** 63, 69

25. Answers may vary.
a) 6, 8, 10, 13, 14, 15, 18   **b)** 41, 63, 64, 65, 66, 67, 68
c) 0, 5, 5, 10, 11, 12, 13   **d)** 7, 8, 9, 12, 15, 15, 39

5.5 Calculating Relative Frequency
Developing the Ideas, page 280

2., 4. The frequency and relative frequency of each letter are as follows.

a: 52, 0.079; **b:** 8, 0.012; **c:** 12, 0.018; **d:** 39, 0.059; **e:** 81, 0.122; **f:** 22, 0.033; **g:** 21, 0.032; **h:** 47, 0.071; **i:** 56, 0.085; **j:** 1, 0.002; **k:** 8, 0.012; **l:** 31, 0.047; **m:** 14, 0.021; **n:** 54, 0.082; **o:** 46, 0.069; **p:** 8, 0.012; **q:** 0, 0; **r:** 30, 0.045; **s:** 29, 0.044; **t:** 56, 0.085; **u:** 13, 0.020; **v:** 6, 0.009; **w:** 17, 0.026; **x:** 0, 0; **y:** 11, 0.017; **z:** 0, 0

3. There are 662 letters in the poem.

5. The letter e, which has a relative frequency of 0.122

6. About 122 times

Working with Mathematics, page 282

1. a) The number of times a letter is used in a given passage is called the frequency of the letter.

b) $\frac{18}{100}$, or 0.18   **c)** 90 times

2. $\frac{6}{29}$, or 0.207

No; this is greater than the relative frequency of the letter in the entire poem. Because there were only 29 letters in the sample, a word like Seventeenth, with 4 **e**, has a great effect on the relative frequency.

3. The relative frequency in the second book should be close to that in the first book although it may not be exactly the same.

4. **a)** , **b)** First two verses — **a**: 21, 0.70; **e**: 34, 0.114; **s**: 17, 0.057; **t**: 27, 0.090

 third and fourth verses — **a**: 31, 0.90; **e**: 43, 0.125; **s**: 11, 0.032; **t**: 26, 0.075

 c) No; since the total number of characters in each part is fairly small, a few extra occurrences of a letter in one part have a great effect on the relative frequency.

 d) You would expect the relative frequencies to be closer in a long poem because the number of characters in each half of the poem is greater.

5. **a)** **a**: 60; **e**: 107; **s**: 66; **t**: 78

 b) **a**: 0.069; **e**: 0.123; **s**: 0.076; **t**: 0.090

 c) The relative frequencies of **e**, **t**, and **a** are within 0.01 of each other. The relative frequencies of **s** differ more noticeably. It is not surprising that there are some differences since both poems are fairly short.

6. **a)** **a**: 112; **e**: 188; **s**: 95; **t**: 134

 b) **a**: 0.073; **e**: 0.123; **s**: 0.062; **t**: 0.088

7. Answers may vary.

8. **a)** 2, 3, 4, 5, 6, 7, 8, 9, 10, 11, 12

 b) to **e)** Answers may vary.

9. **a)** No. Some letters are much more frequently used and will therefore sell much faster.

 b) , **c)** , **d)** Answers may vary.

10. **a)** Answers may vary. **e**: 10 553; **t**: 8862; **s**: 4834

 b) No; because the relative frequencies are rounded to 3 decimal places you cannot calculate the exact value.

5.6 Probability
Developing the Ideas, page 284

1. 30; 0.75   2. , 3. Answers may vary.

4. Answers may vary. The greater the number of spins, the closer you would expect the frequency to be to the predicted value.

Page 285

1. 100   2. 300

3. Red: $\frac{1}{4}$, or 0.25; green: $\frac{3}{4}$, or 0.75

Working with Mathematics, page 287

1. When the outcomes of an experiment are equally likely, the probability of an event is the number of outcomes favourable to the event divided by the total number of outcomes.

2. The probability is based on a prediction of how often you think an outcome would occur if an experiment were done; the relative frequency is determined using the results of an experiment.

3. You can use probability when you want to make a prediction about whether or not a particular event will occur.

4. **a)** Landing on: blue, purple, red, yellow, green
 b) Yes

5. **a)** Heads, tails; 2   **b)** $\frac{1}{2}$

6. **a)** Rolling: A, B, C; 3   **b)** $\frac{1}{3}$

7. **a)** 1, 1; 1, 2; 1, 3; 1, 4; 1, 5; 1, 6; 2, 2; 2, 3; 2, 4; 2, 5; 2, 6;

3, 3; 3, 4; 3, 5; 3, 6; 4, 4; 4, 5; 4, 6; 5, 5; 5, 6; 6, 6
(This assumes that, for example, 2, 1 is the same outcome as 1, 2.); 21
 b) No

8. **a)** 52   **b)** Yes

9. **a)** 1, 2, 3, 4, 5, 6, 7   **b)** Yes

 c) **i)** $\frac{1}{7}$ **ii)** $\frac{3}{7}$ **iii)** $\frac{3}{7}$ **iv)** $\frac{2}{7}$ **v)** $\frac{3}{7}$

10. **a)** Blue, yellow

 b) No; because there are different numbers of blue and yellow balls in the jar.

 c) **i)** $\frac{4}{7}$ **ii)** $\frac{3}{7}$ **iii)** 1   **iv)** 0

11. Answers may vary.

 f) The manufacturer could make only a small number of some of the items in the set.

12. **a)** 12   **b)** $\frac{12}{52}$, or $\frac{3}{13}$

13. **a)** 1, 2, 3, 4, 5, 6, 7, 8, 9, 10   **b)** Yes

 c) **i)** $\frac{1}{10}$ **ii)** $\frac{3}{10}$ **iii)** $\frac{5}{10}$, or $\frac{1}{2}$ **iv)** $\frac{2}{10}$, or $\frac{1}{5}$ **v)** $\frac{8}{10}$, or $\frac{4}{5}$

14. **a)** Selecting: purple, white, green   **b)** No

 c) **i)** $\frac{3}{8}$ **ii)** $\frac{2}{8}$, or $\frac{1}{4}$ **iii)** $\frac{3}{8}$ **iv)** $\frac{6}{8}$, or $\frac{3}{4}$ **v)** $\frac{3}{8}$

15. **a)** 4   **b)** $\frac{4}{52}$, or $\frac{1}{13}$

16. Answers may vary.

17. Assuming that there is 1 correct answer to each question on the test, the probabilities are:

 a) $\frac{1}{5}$ **b)** $\frac{4}{5}$

18. Answers may vary. Experiments in which the outcomes are not equally likely

Quest: Is Anita's Idea Fair?, page 289

No, the idea is not fair. Mitra will be twice as likely to go first since there are 2 ways the coins could land 1H and 1T — HT or TH.

Linking Ideas: Mathematics and Technology
Using Simulations to Calculate Probability, page 290

1. No

2. Two girls and 1 boy or 2 boys and 1 girl are most likely.

3. $\frac{1}{8}$ 4. $\frac{1}{4}$ 5. Answers may vary. 0.28 or 28%

6. Toss 3 coins many times. Keep a tally of how many times they are tossed. Keep a tally each time 3 heads show. These represent 3 girls. After repeating the experiment many times (at least 100 times), divide the number of times 3 heads showed by the total number of times the coins were tossed. This is the probability that the children are girls.

7. This is similar to exercise 6. Toss 4 coins many times. Tally the number of times 3 tails and 1 head show. After many repetitions, divide the number of times this combination showed by the total number of times the coins were tossed.

5.7 Probability of Compound Independent Events
Developing the Ideas, page 294

1. 2   2. 6   3. 12

5. **a)** $\frac{1}{12}$ **b)** $\frac{1}{4}$ **c)** $\frac{1}{3}$ **d)** $\frac{1}{4}$

Working with Mathematics, page 295

1. A compound event consists of two single events.

2. a) $\frac{1}{2}$ **b)** No   **c)** No

3. H, H; H, T; T, T

4. 1, 1; 1, 2; 1, 3; 1, 4; 1, 5; 1, 6; 2, 2; 2, 3; 2, 4; 2, 5; 2, 6; 3, 3; 3, 4; 3, 5; 3, 6; 4, 4; 4, 5; 4, 6; 5, 5; 5, 6; 6, 6

5. H1, H2, H3, H4, H5, H6, T1, T2, T3, T4, T5, T6

6. 52 cards can be selected, and for each one the coin can show heads or tails; there are 104 outcomes.

7. 52 cards can be selected, and for each one the die can show 1, 2, 3, 4, 5, 6; there are 312 outcomes.

8. a) RY, RB, GY, GB; yes   **b)** $\frac{1}{4}$

9. 1, 2, 3, 4, 6, 9; no

10. a) R Black, RW, RY, Blue Black, Blue W, Blue Y, G Black, GW, GY; yes

    b) $\frac{1}{3}$ **c)** $\frac{1}{3}$ **d)** $\frac{1}{9}$ **e)** $\frac{1}{9}$

11. a) A Red, A Blue, A Yellow, A Green, B Red, B Blue, B Yellow, B Green, C Red, C Blue, C Yellow, C Green

    b) $\frac{1}{3}$ **c)** $\frac{1}{4}$ **d)** $\frac{1}{12}$ **e)** $\frac{2}{3}$ **f)** $\frac{1}{6}$ **g)** $\frac{1}{3}$

12. a) $\frac{5}{36}$ **b)** $\frac{1}{36}$ **c)** $\frac{1}{6}$ **d)** $\frac{1}{12}$ **e)** $\frac{31}{36}$

13. a) Final branches: GB; GG; BB; BG   **b)** $\frac{1}{4}$

14. a) Final branches: GGGG; GGGB; GGBG; GGBB; GBGG; GBGB; GBBG; GBBB; BGGG; BGGB; BGBG; BGBB; BBGG; BBGB; BBBG; BBBB

    b) $\frac{1}{16}$

15. a) $\frac{1}{6}$ **b)** $\frac{1}{6}$ **c)** $\frac{1}{9}$

    d) Answers may vary. The points which correspond to the same total lie on a straight line.

16. a) 9, 12, 15, 18, 21, 16, 20, 24, 28, 25, 30, 35, 36, 42; answers may vary

    b) No, several combinations of factors produce the same outcome.

    c) i) $\frac{1}{20}$ **ii)** $\frac{6}{20}$, or $\frac{3}{10}$ **iii)** $\frac{14}{20}$, or $\frac{7}{10}$ **iv)** 0   **v)** 1

17. a) 312   **b)** $\frac{1}{312}$ **c)** $\frac{1}{78}$ **d)** $\frac{1}{8}$ **e)** $\frac{1}{13}$

18. a) 24   **b)** $\frac{1}{24}$ **c)** $\frac{1}{8}$ **d)** $\frac{1}{12}$ **e)** $\frac{1}{4}$

19. a) 0.25   **b)** 0.1875   **c)** 0.5625

Quest: Can You Calculate the Number of Black Jellybeans in a Jar?, page 297

There are approximately 300 black jellybeans. In *Look back*, there are approximately 200 red jellybeans; there are approximately 175 yellow jellybeans; there are approximately 270 pennies.

Review, page 298

1. a) 299 000   **b)** 57 500   **c)** 23 000

    d) Estimates may vary. If you choose a number of rides in the middle of each range, multiply it by the number of people who chose that range, and add the results you will get a weekly ridership of between 800 000 and 900 000.

2. Answers may vary.

3. a) The readers who take large doses of vitamin C probably do so because they believe this helps them to avoid colds. Since this is the group who have been asked to write in, you are more likely to hear from people who say they have had fewer colds.

    b) It will generate a biased sample, as explained in part a.

4. a) The spending increased greatly from 1993 to 1994.

    b) Because the vertical axis jumps from 0 to 100, the bar for 1994 is 10 times as tall as the bar for 1993, even though the amount spent was only about 1.1 times as great.

5. a) a: 0.035; **c:** 0.193; **d:** 0.105; **f:** 0.018; **h:** 0.105; **i:** 0.018; **k:** 0.070; **l:** 0.035; **m:** 0.018; **o:** 0.193; **u:** 0.123; **w:** 0.088

    b) No, this tongue twister contains an unusually great number of **w**, **c**, and **o**.

6. a) i) $\frac{1}{6}$ **ii)** $\frac{3}{6}$, or $\frac{1}{2}$

    b) i) 5 times   **ii)** 15 times

    c) i) Answers may vary.   **ii)** Answers may vary.

    iii) The experimental probability may be quite different from the predicted probability, particularly when the experiment is repeated only 30 times.

7. a: 11, 0.057; **e:** 22, 0.113; **s:** 15, 0.080; **t:** 22, 0.113

8. a) $\frac{1}{10}$ **b)** $\frac{2}{10}$, or $\frac{1}{5}$ **c)** $\frac{7}{10}$ **d)** $\frac{7}{10}$ **e)** $\frac{5}{10}$, or $\frac{1}{2}$ **f)** 0

9. a) $\frac{1}{20}$ **b)** $\frac{2}{20}$, or $\frac{1}{10}$ **c)** $\frac{7}{20}$ **d)** $\frac{17}{20}$ **e)** $\frac{15}{20}$, or $\frac{3}{4}$ **f)** $\frac{10}{20}$, or $\frac{1}{2}$

10. a) 3; H, T; T, T; H, H   **b)** No   **c)** $\frac{1}{4}$ **d)** $\frac{1}{2}$

11. a) $\frac{1}{52}$ **b)** $\frac{1}{13}$ **c)** $\frac{1}{4}$

12. a) No   **b)** $\frac{1}{7}$ **c)** $\frac{6}{7}$

13. a) 4

    b) Yes, explanations may vary; each number occurs twice.

    c) $\frac{1}{4}$

Cumulative Review, page 300A

1. a) i) 5   **ii)** 5   **iii)** 3   **iv)** 7   **v)** 1, 9   **vi)** 8

    b) i) 193.8 **ii)** 192 **iii)** 184 **iv)** 206 **v)** 181, 207 **vi)** 26

3. a) 100 km   **b)** 62.5 km   **c)** 205 km

    d) 170 km   **e)** 80 km   **f)** 127.5 km

4. a) 1 cm represents 1 m.   **b)** 2.9 m   **c)** 2.5 m

6. a) $0.\overline{2}$ **b)** $0.3\overline{57\ 142\ 8}$ **c)** $1.58\overline{3}$ **d)** 0.5   **e)** $14.58\overline{3}$

    f) 1.125   **g)** $0.3\overline{13\ 852\ 81}$ **h)** $0.3\overline{65\ 079}$ **i)** 5.75

7. a) $\frac{1}{4}$ **b)** 4   **c)** 5

    d) $\frac{4}{3}$, or $1\frac{1}{3}$ **e)** $\frac{5}{6}$ **f)** $\frac{15}{16}$

8. a) 8.4×10^3 **b)** 2.11×10^8 **c)** 3.104×10^7

    d) 6.7×10^5 **e)** 1.98×10^6 **f)** 4.3×10^4

9. a) 2, 6   **b)** 0, 4, 8   **c)** 0, 4, 8

    d) 2, 6   **e)** 0, 2, 4, 6, 8   **f)** 0, 4, 8

10. a) 31.5   **b)** 83.352   **c)** 15.12   **d)** 498.68

    e) 728.48   **f)** 183.58   **g)** 4   **h)** 7

    i) 3   **j)** 5   **k)** 2.5   **l)** 8.6

11. Answers are rounded to the nearest percent.

    a) 20% increase   **b)** 20% decrease

    c) 25% increase   **d)** 25% decrease

    e) 35% decrease   **f)** 15% decrease

12. 7560

13. Basketball: 48; volleyball: 32

14. a) 20   **b)** 8   **c)** 12

15. a) $800   **b)** 2 800 000   **c)** $12 950   **d)** 33 250 kg

16. a) 45%   **b)** 15%   **c)** 12%   **d)** 45%

18. Answers may vary.

    a) One person's opinion is insufficient to make a conclusion about the average Canadian.

    b) One class is not a random sample; the sample should

consider all age groups.

c) Only people sufficiently interested will receive a completed questionnaire — the sample is not random.

d) This random sample is too small.

19. Answers may vary. The first and last numbers could be: 9, 16; 8, 17; 7, 18; 6, 19; 5, 20; 4, 21; 3, 22; 2, 23; 1, 24. The middle numbers are 10, 10, 11, 14, 14.

20. $136 000

21. **a)** $44 533, $42 000, $21 000
    b) Answers may vary; the median

22. **a)** 2, 3, 4, 5, 6 **b)** 4 **c)** $\frac{1}{9}$ **d)** $\frac{2}{9}$

23. **a)** 3; A, B, C **b)** No
    c) i) $\frac{1}{2}$ **ii)** $\frac{1}{3}$ **iii)** $\frac{1}{6}$

CHAPTER 6 OPERATIONS WITH INTEGERS

Start With What You Know, page 304

1. Answers and examples may vary.
   a) Integers that have 5 as a factor; they end in 5 or 0
   b) The product of an integer multiplied by itself
   c) An indicated quotient of two quantities
   d) Any of the numbers…−2, −1, 0, 1, 2…
   e) The value of 2^n where n is an integer
   f) Integers where each one is 1 more than (or 1 less than) the preceding integer
   g) A number whose only factors are itself and 1

2. 1, 2, 3, 5, 6, 10   3. 7, 56, 392; 2, 6, 12

4. 9, 3   5. 81

6. 8, $\frac{1}{8}$; 2, $\frac{1}{2}$ 7. 90

8. Answers may vary.

6.1 Modelling with Integers
Developing the Ideas, page 306

1. The score for *strongly disagree* would probably be −2 because *strongly agree* has a score of +2.

2. The score for *agree* would probably be +1 because *disagree* has a score of −1.

3. Either students had no opinion or equal numbers of students had opposite opinions.

4. **a)** In graph 1, a positive score means that the students in the countries think that mathematics is easy.
   b) In graph 2, a positive score means that the students in the countries think that mathematics is fun.

5. **a)** In graph 1, a negative score means that the students in the countries think that mathematics is not easy.
   b) In graph 2, a negative score means that the students in the countries think that it is no fun doing mathematics.

6. **a)** Canada, Hungary, the United States, and Sweden
   b) Canada, Hungary, Hong Kong, and Sweden

7. Japan and the United States

8. Answers may vary.

Working with Mathematics, page 307

1. −5 is greater.

2. , 3. Answers may vary.

4. **a)** Hungary   **b)** Hong Kong and the United States

c) Canada, Hungary, and Sweden

5. Never: −2; infrequently: −1; no opinion: 0; frequently: +1; always: +2

6. **a)** −8   **b)** −12   **c)** 0   **d)** −9

7. Answers may vary.

8. **a)** A *quarter* means three months.
   b) The net earnings in millions of dollars
   c) Because the net earnings were negative (the company lost money)
   d) January, February, and March
   e) Answers may vary. The company lost about $65 million.
   f) i) The fourth quarter of 1993
   ii) October, November, and December
   iii) Answers may vary. About $160 million

9. **a)** >   **b)** >   **c)** >   **d)** <

10. **a)** Her birth   **b)** The death of her dog
    c) i) −4   **ii)** −6   **iii)** Moving to a new house
    d) Answers may vary.   **e)** Answers may vary.

11. **a)** Brandie Burton and Betsy King   **b)** Vicki Fergon
    c) 277 strokes   **d)** −14

12. **a)** Abu Dhabi, Caracas, and Sydney; the cost of rent decreased from 1982 to 1994
    b) Bangkok, Bombay, Copenhagen, Geneva, London, Manila, Montreal, Singapore, and Tokyo; the cost of rent increased from 1982 to 1994.
    c) Abu Dhabi, Tokyo

13. **a)** Doug Gilmour; he had the greatest +/− statistic. While Gilmour was on the ice his team scored 16 more goals than the opposing teams.
    b) More likely to be scored on   **c)** 19

6.2 Adding and Subtracting Integers
Developing the Ideas, page 310

1. **a)** The temperature is +5°C. It warms up 9°C.
   c) +14°C

2. **a)** The temperature is +5°C. It cools down 9°C.
   d) −4°C

3. See the answers for exercise 2.

4. See the answers for exercise 1.

5. **a)** The temperature is −5°C. It warms up 9°C.
   c) +4°C

6. **a)** The temperature is −5°C. It cools down 9°C.
   b) −14°C

7. See the answers for exercise 6.

8. See the answers for exercise 5.

Working with Mathematics, page 313

1. Winter or early spring; the predicted temperatures are fairly low and snow is expected in several cities.

2. Vancouver   3. Winnipeg   4. 9°C   5. Regina   6. −21°C

7. **a)** −12°C   **b)** −12°C   **c)** −10°C   **d)** −14°C
   e) +23°C   **f)** +20°C   **g)** +42°C   **h)** +14°C

8. **a)** +23   **b)** −9   **c)** +17   **d)** −12   **e)** +16   **f)** −20   **g)** +13
   h) +2   **i)** −12   **j)** +10   **k)** −21   **l)** +37   **m)** −32   **n)** −22

9. Elevation at shore: −400 m; depth: −328 m; depth relative to sea level: −728 m

10. Depth at surface of lake: −66 m; depth of lake: −84 m; depth

of lake from ground level: −150 m

11. a) +183, +176, +176, +174, +75
b) −405, −281, −229, −64, −224
c) −222, −105, −53, +110, −149

12. a) 3:00 p.m.   **b)** 10:00 a.m.   **c)** 8:00 a.m.
d) i) 3:00 p.m.   **ii)** 10:30 p.m.

13. a) +7°C   **b)** −16°C   **c)** +8°C   **d)** −19°C
e) +22°C   **f)** −15°C   **g)** +19°C   **h)** −11°C

14. a) +13   **b)** +30   **c)** +25   **d)** +25   **e)** −20   **f)** −18   **g)** −31   **h)** −16

15. a) +44   **b)** −5   **c)** −16   **d)** −52   **e)** −21   **f)** −1   **g)** +2   **h)** −11

16.

+1	+2	−3
−4	0	+4
+3	−2	−1

17. a) Gerl Gld: 42¢; Booker Gld: 220¢; Greshm Rs: 125¢
b) i) Gerl Gld: $\frac{-7}{42}$, or $-\frac{1}{6}$; Booker Gld: $\frac{-15}{220}$, or $-\frac{3}{44}$;
Greshm Rs: $\frac{19}{125}$
ii) Gerl Gld: −16.7%; Booker Gld: −6.8%;
Greshm Rs: +15.2%
iii) Gerl Gld: −17; Booker Gld: −7; Greshm Rs: +15
c) Gerl Gld, which had a 16.7% decrease in value

18. a) +33   **b)** +26   **c)** +4   **d)** +59   **e)** +25   **f)** −4

6.3 Multiplying Integers

Developing the Ideas, page 315

1. a) $(+3) \times (-4) = -12$ **b)** $(+4) \times (-3) = -12$
c) $(+3) \times (+4) = +12$ **d)** $(+4) \times (+3) = +12$
e) $(+4) \times (+2) = +8$ **f)** $(+2) \times (-5) = -10$
g) $(+6) \times (-2) = -12$ **h)** $(+5) \times (+3) = +15$

3. The product of two positive integers is a positive integer.

4. The product of a positive integer and a negative integer is a negative integer.

Page 316

1. The second number, +3   **2.** It decreases by 1.

3. It decreases by 3.   **4.** The product is a positive integer.

5. The numbers to complete the pattern are: −3, −6, −9, −12. The product is a negative integer.

6. The second number, −3   **7.** It decreases by 1.

8. It increases by 3.   **9.** The product is a negative integer.

10. The numbers to complete the pattern are: +3, +6, +9, +12. The product is a positive integer.

Page 317

1. a) Adds 1 to the number in cell A1.
b) Multiplies the numbers in cells A1 and B1.

2. a) i) Negative   **ii)** No sign, zero   **iii)** Positive
b) i) Positive   **ii)** No sign, zero   **iii)** Negative

Working with Mathematics, page 318

1. a) Negative   **b)** Negative   **c)** Positive   **d)** Positive

2. Zero

3. To complete and extend the pattern:

a) −5, −10, −15, −20, $(+5) \times (-5) = -25$, $(+5) \times (-6) = -30$, $(+5) \times (-7) = -35$
b) +4, +8, +12, +16, +20, $(-4) \times (-6) = +24$, $(-4) \times (-7) = +28$, $(-4) \times (-8) = +32$
c) 0, +7, +14, +21, $(+7) \times (+4) = +28$, $(+7) \times (+5) = +35$, $(+7) \times (+6) = +42$
d) +6, 0, −6, −12, −18, $(-6) \times (+4) = -24$, $(-6) \times (+5) = -30$, $(-6) \times (+6) = -36$

4. a) +20   **b)** −20   **c)** +14   **d)** 0   **e)** +21
f) −48   **g)** +36   **h)** −72   **i)** +9   **j)** 0

5. Explanations may vary.
a) True   **b)** False   **c)** True   **d)** True

6. a) +33   **b)** −1   **c)** +24   **d)** −8   **e)** +30   **f)** −49

7. a) Multiply the preceding number by +4 to obtain the next number. −256, −1024, −4096
b) Multiply the preceding number by −3 to obtain the next number. +243, −729, +2187
c) Multiply the preceding number by +5 to obtain the next number. −1250, −6250, −31 250
d) Multiply the preceding number by −1 to obtain the next number. −3, +3, −3
e) Multiply the preceding number by −7 to obtain the next number. +4802, −33 614, +235 298
f) Multiply the preceding number by +6 to obtain the next number. +1296, +7776, +46 656
g) Multiply the preceding number by −10 to obtain the next number. +100 000, −1 000 000, +10 000 000

8. a) +6   **b)** −6   **c)** +6   **d)** −6   **e)** +6   **f)** +6   **g)** +6   **h)** −6

9. a) −15°C   **b)** −21°C

10. a) +18   **b)** −27   **c)** −44   **d)** 0   **e)** −60   **f)** +63

11. a) −40   **b)** −42   **c)** +32   **d)** −54   **e)** +72   **f)** +65

12. Explanations may vary.
a) If the first integer is negative, the product is negative. If the first integer is positive, the product is positive.
b) If the first integer is negative, the product is positive. If the first integer is positive, the product is negative.

13. a) $(+3) \times (-7) = -21$ **b)** $(-4) \times (-13) = +52$
c) $(+5) \times (+16) = +80$ **d)** $(-16) \times (-7) = +112$
e) $(-13) \times (+3) = -39$ **f)** $(+14) \times (-7) = -98$

14. a) +12   **b)** +12   **c)** −12   **d)** +20   **e)** −20   **f)** +20

15. a) −1, +24; +1, −24; −2, +12; +2, −12; −3, +8; +3, −8; −4, +6; +4, −6
b) −24, −12, −8, −6, −4, −3, −2, −1, +1, +2, +3, +4, +6, +8, +12, +24

16. Answers may vary.
a) 20, 0   **b)** −5

Quest: When It Is Breakfast Time in Moscow, What Time Is It in Vancouver?, page 320

It is 7:00 p.m. in Vancouver when it is 6:00 a.m. in Moscow.
It is 5:00 p.m. in Moscow when it is 6:00 a.m. in Vancouver.
It is 7:00 a.m. in Tokyo when it is noon in Honolulu.
There are 24 time zones. Since 360° is divisible by 24, you can divide Earth into 24 equal sections. This works well since there are 24 h in a day.
Integers are used so that the table can be used for all times of day.

Mathematics File: Modelling the Multiplication of Integers, page 322

1. a) −6   **b)** +6   **2.** No

6.4 Dividing Integers

Developing the Ideas, page 324

1. $(+6) \div (+3) = +2$; $(+6) \div (+2) = +3$

2. a) $(+12) \div (+3) = +4$; $(+12) \div (+4) = +3$
   b) $(+48) \div (+6) = +8$; $(+48) \div (+8) = +6$
   c) $(+120) \div (+12) = +10$; $(+120) \div (+10) = +12$

3. All quotients are positive. The result of dividing two positive integers is always a positive number.

4. When two positive integers are divided, the quotient is positive.

5. $(+6) \div (-2) = -3$; $(+6) \div (-3) = -2$

6. a) $(+12) \div (-3) = -4$; $(+12) \div (-4) = -3$
   b) $(+48) \div (-6) = -8$; $(+48) \div (-8) = -6$
   c) $(+120) \div (-12) = -10$; $(+120) \div (-10) = -12$

7. All quotients are negative. The result of dividing a positive integer by a negative integer is always a negative number.

8. When a positive integer is divided by a negative integer, the quotient is negative.

9. $(-6) \div (-3) = +2$; $(-6) \div (+2) = -3$

10. $(-6) \div (-2) = +3$; $(-6) \div (+3) = -2$

11. a) $(-12) \div (-3) = +4$, $(-12) \div (+4) = -3$
   b) $(-48) \div (+6) = -8$, $(-48) \div (-8) = +6$
   c) $(-120) \div (+12) = -10$, $(-120) \div (-10) = +12$
   d) $(-20) \div (-5) = +4$, $(-20) \div (+4) = -5$

12. Some of the signs are positive; some are negative. The result of dividing a negative integer by a positive integer is always a negative number. The result of dividing two negative integers is always a positive number.

13. When a negative integer is divided by a positive integer, the quotient is negative.

14. When two negative integers are divided, the quotient is positive.

Page 326

1. a) −3   **b)** +3

2. Answers may vary. The boxes represent the divisors. When the divisor is negative, we use a red box and any tiles inserted change colour. When the divisor is positive, we use a yellow box.

Working with Mathematics, page 327

1. a) Negative   **b)** Negative   **c)** Positive   **d)** Positive

2. Zero

3. a) −5   **b)** +5   **c)** +5   **d)** −5   **e)** +4   **f)** −4
   g) −4   **h)** +4   **i)** +2   **j)** −2   **k)** −2   **l)** +2

4. a) $(+32) \div (+4) = +8$, $(+32) \div (+8) = +4$
   b) $(+72) \div (+8) = +9$, $(+72) \div (+9) = +8$
   c) $(+21) \div (+3) = +7$, $(+21) \div (+7) = +3$
   d) $(+28) \div (-4) = -7$, $(+28) \div (-7) = -4$
   e) $(+54) \div (-6) = -9$, $(+54) \div (-9) = -6$
   f) $(-24) \div (+4) = -6$, $(-24) \div (-6) = +4$
   g) $(-15) \div (-5) = +3$, $(-15) \div (+3) = -5$
   h) $(-40) \div (+8) = -5$, $(-40) \div (-5) = +8$
   i) $(-10) \div (-10) = +1$, $(-10) \div (+1) = -10$

5. a) $(+4) \times (-2) = -8$ **b)** $(-7) \times (+3) = -21$
   c) $(+8) \times (+4) = +32$ **d)** $(-6) \times (-5) = +30$
   e) $(-3) \times (+6) = -18$ **f)** $(+6) \times (-7) = -42$
   g) $(-5) \times (-8) = +40$ **h)** $(+2) \times (+9) = +18$
   i) $(+30) \times (-1) = -30$

6. a) −6   **b)** −7   **c)** +9   **d)** +13
   e) +9   **f)** +7   **g)** −34   **h)** −7
   i) +36   **j)** −15   **k)** +12   **l)** −29

7. a) −5   **d)** −5   **e)** −6   **f)** −7   **g)** −12

8. a) $(+52) \div (-13) = -4$ **b)** $(-96) \div (-12) = +8$
   c) $(+108) \div (+6) = +18$ **d)** $(-135) \div (+9) = -15$
   e) $(-112) \div (-7) = +16$ **f)** $(+126) \div (-14) = -9$

9. a) 4 h   **b)** 7 h

10. a) Divide the preceding number by +2 to obtain the next number. +8, +4, +2
   b) Divide the preceding number by −3 to obtain the next number. −9, +3, −1
   c) Divide the preceding number by +2 to obtain the next number. +20, +10, +5
   d) Divide the preceding number by +3 to obtain the next number. +36, +12, +4
   e) Divide the preceding number by −4 to obtain the next number. −64, +16, −4
   f) Divide the preceding number by −2 to obtain the next number. −48, +24, −12
   g) Divide the preceding number by −10 to obtain the next number. −100, +10, −1

11. a) $(+56) \div (+7) = +8$ **b)** $(-20) \div (-4) = +5$
   c) $(+60) \div (+4) = +15$ **d)** $(+96) \div (-12) = -8$
   e) $(-90) \div (+6) = -15$ **f)** $(-48) \div (-4) = +12$

12. a) −11   **b)** +6   **c)** −51   **d)** +11
   e) −24   **f)** −9   **g)** +9   **h)** +25

13. a) +7   **b)** −7   **c)** +7   **d)** −6
   e) −7   **f)** +11   **g)** −8   **h)** +6

14. a) +6   **b)** +18   **c)** +6   **f)** +17   **g)** +12   **h)** +11

15. a) $(-16) \div (+4) = -4$ **b)** $(+49) \div (-7) = -7$
   c) $(-56) \div (-8) = +7$ **d)** $(+45) \div (-3) = -15$
   e) $(-72) \div (-8) = +9$ **f)** $(+169) \div (-13) = -13$
   g) $(+180) \div (-12) = -15$

16. a) Divide the preceding number by +5 to obtain the next number. −25, −5, −1
   b) Divide the preceding number by −2 to obtain the next number. −512, +256, −128
   c) Divide the preceding number by +8 to obtain the next number. −64, −8, −1
   d) Divide the preceding number by +2 to obtain the next number. +28, +14, +7
   e) Divide the preceding number by −3 to obtain the next number. −18, +6, −2

17. a) $(+20) \div (-4) = -5$ **b)** $(+63) \div (-7) = -9$
   c) $(-72) \div (-12) = +6$ **d)** $(+75) \div (+5) = +15$
   e) $(-72) \div (+9) = -8$ **f)** $(-144) \div (-12) = +12$

18. −3, +3, +6; −6, +3, +9; −9, +9, +6; 0, +9, −3

19. a) +4, −2; +2, −1; −2, +1   **b)** +3, +4
   c) −2, −1   **d)** +4, −1

Quest: Operations with Integers, page 329

When we divide two integers, the result is not always an integer. The result is a fraction or decimal.

6.5 Order of Operations with Integers
Working with Mathematics, page 333

1. a) Multiply +3 by +5, then subtract +7; the final result is +8.
   b) Multiply +5 by +7, then subtract the result from +3; the final result is −32.
   c) Subtract +5 from +3, then multiply the result by +7; the final result is −14.

2. Explanations may vary. Multiplication and division are performed in the order in which they appear in the expression.

3. a) −6°C   b) −1°C   c) −1°C   d) +1°C   e) −6°C

4. a) 0   b) +10   c) 0   d) 1

5. a) +17   b) −2   c) −42   d) +16   e) +6   f) −44   g) +55   h) −37

6. a) −19   b) +8   c) +1   d) +9   e) +3   f) −11   g) +3   h) −5

7. a) −10   b) +2   c) −2   d) −2

8. b) (−5)(−8) ÷ (+4) = +10

9. The expressions in parts a and d simplify to −16.
   b) −18   c) +16   e) −24   f) +16

10. a) (−7)(−5) + (−6); +29   b) (−16) ÷ (+8) + (+9); +7
    c) (−14) + (−6) − (+12); −32   d) (−23) + (−18) − (−8); −33
    e) (−4)^2 + (−3)^2; +25

11. Answers may vary.   12. a) +2°C   b) −2°C   c) +1°C

13. a) −16°C   b) Calgary and Edmonton

14. a) −56   b) −40   c) −10   d) −10   e) −56   f) −40

15. a) −5   b) −4   c) +22   d) +25   e) −11   f) −27

16. a) +42   b) +10   c) +11   d) −13   e) +47
    f) +114   g) −3   h) −56   i) +4

17. a) −28   b) −15   c) −3   d) −94

18. a) [(+24) + (−16)] ÷ (−8) = −1   b) [(−9) + (−12)] ÷ (+7) = −3
    c) (+8) × (−6) ÷ (−12) = +4   d) [(+11) − (−4)] ÷ (−3) = −5
    e) [(+13) + (−22)] ÷ (−9) = +1   f) [(+30) − (−18)] ÷ (+6) = +8
    g) [(−3) + (+16) + (−24)] ÷ (+11) = −1

19. a) −13; (−20) ÷ [(+2) − (−3)] = −4
    b) −18; [(−21) + (+9)] ÷ (+3) = −4
    c) −16; (+72) ÷ [(−9) × (+2)] = −4
    d) +20; [(−8) + (+7)] × (+4) = −4
    e) +18; [(+4)(+5) + (+20)] ÷ (−10) = −4

20. August 5th

21. a) (−6) + (−6) + (−6)   b) (−6) ÷ (−6) × (−6)
    c) [(−6) − (−6)] × (−6) or [(−6) − (−6)] ÷ (−6)
    d) (−6) + [(−6) ÷ (−6)]   e) (−6) ÷ (−6) − (−6)
    f) [(−6) + (−6)] ÷ (−6)

22. Answers may vary. One expression is given for each part.
    a) [(−4) + (+2)] × (+8) − (−6)   b) (−5)(+8) ÷ (−4) + (+2)
    c) (−4)(+8) + (−5)(−6)   d) (−6) × (+8) ÷ [(−4) + (+2)]

Linking Ideas: Mathematics and Science
Comparing Winters, page 335

1. a) Week 1

Day	S	M	T	W	T	F	S
High temperature (°C)	+4	+3	−2	0	−5	−1	+2
Low temperature (°C)	0	−3	−6	−8	−7	−7	−4
Mean temperature (°C)	+2	0	−4	−4	−6	−4	−1
Degree day	+16	+18	+22	+22	+24	+22	+19

Total number of degree days for week 1 = +143

Week 2

Day	S	M	T	W	T	F	S
High temperature (°C)	−1	−3	+1	+5	+2	−4	0
Low temperature (°C)	−5	−5	−3	+1	−4	−8	−6
Mean temperature (°C)	−3	−4	−1	+3	−1	−6	−3
Degree day	+21	+22	+19	+15	+19	+24	+21

Total number of degree days for week 2 = +141
   b) The first week was colder, because it has the higher total degree days.

Review, page 336

1. a) −5°C   b) −5

2. a) +39   b) 3 h   c) +13

3. a) −3   b) −2   c) −2   d) +1

4. −3°C

5. a) The temperature is −11°C. It cools down 3°C. The final temperature is −14°C.
   b) The temperature is −7°C. It cools down 2°C. The final temperature is −9°C.
   c) The temperature is +3°C. It cools down 8°C. The final temperature is −5°C.
   d) The temperature is −4°C. It warms up 3°C. The final temperature is −1°C.
   e) The temperature is +7°C. It cools down 11°C. The final temperature is −4°C.
   f) The temperature is +4°C. It cools down 3°C. The final temperature is +1°C.
   g) The temperature is +15°C. It warms up 9°C. The final temperature is +24°C.
   h) The temperature is −8°C. It warms up 13°C. The final temperature is +5°C.

6. a) +4   b) −6   c) −31   d) −12   e) +39
   f) −46   g) +12   h) −33   i) −14   j) +25

7. a) i) She withdrew $50.00   ii) −50
   b) i) She deposited $28.00   ii) +28
   c) $180.00

8. a) −20   b) −42   c) +24   d) +18
   e) 0   f) −28   g) +4   h) +4

9. The only difference between the integers in parts g and h is that their signs are opposites. Since the product of these two negative integers or two positive integers is positive, the results are the same.

10. a) −9   b) −5   c) +7   d) +3
    e) −3   f) +4   g) −4   h) −4

11. The only difference between the integers in parts g and h is that their signs are opposites. Since the quotient of a negative integer and a positive integer is negative, both results are the same.

12. a) +30   b) −60   c) −64
    d) +56   e) −16   f) +16

13. Since the numbers being multiplied are the same, except for the additional −1 in part f, you can just multiply the result from part e by −1.

14. a) Negative; the product of a group of numbers of which exactly 3 are negative is negative.
    b) Positive; the product of a group of numbers of which exactly 4 are negative is positive.

15. a) $(+5) \times (+10) = +50$; $50 flow into the store.
  b) $(+4) \times (-20) = -80$; $80 flow out of the store.
  c) $(-1) \times (-80) = +80$; $80 flow into the store.
  d) $(+12) \times (+3) = +36$; $36 flow into the store.

16. a) $-4°C$ **b)** $-9°C$ **c)** $-4°C$ **d)** $-5°C$

17. a) -3 **b)** -13 **c)** $+21$ **d)** $+1$

18. a) -30 **b)** -6 **c)** 0 **d)** $+82$ **e)** -6 **f)** -41

19. a) $(+3) \times (-7) - (-4)$; -17
  b) $(-8) \div (-4) + (+8)$; $+10$
  c) $(-8) + (+4) - (+7)$; -11
  d) $(-20) + (+9) - (-5)$; -6
  e) $(+2) + (-6) - (-3)^2$; -13

20. a) $+2$ **b)** -4 **c)** $+1$ **d)** -23 **e)** $+1$ **f)** -8

21. a) In part a, +4 and −3 are added and the sum is subtracted from +3. In part b, +4 is subtracted from +3, and −3 is then added to the sum.
  b) In part c, +6 is subtracted from +5 and the result is multiplied by −3. In part d, only +5 is multiplied by −3 and +6 is subtracted from the result.
  c) In part e, the sum of −6 and +4 is divided by −2. In part f, only +4 is divided by −2 and the result is then added to −6.

22. a) -6 **b)** -18 **c)** -13 **d)** $+37$
  e) $+7$ **f)** -6 **g)** $+4$ **h)** -19

CHAPTER 7 MEASUREMENT

Start With What You Know, page 342

1. , 2. , 3. Estimates may vary.

4. a) 54 000 **b)** 5400 **c)** 540 **d)** 54 **e)** 5.4
  f) 0.54 **g)** 0.054 **h)** 0.0054 **i)** 0.000 54

5. a) 3.5 **b)** 35 **c)** 350
  d) 3500 **e)** 35 000 **f)** 350 000

6. a) 5.7 **b)** 0.3 **c)** 17.9
  d) 87.1 **e)** 34.2 **f)** 0.0

7. a) 36.58 **b)** 8.08 **c)** 0.60
  d) 49.56 **e)** 63.99 **f)** 31.00

8. a) 16.8 cm^2 **b)** 106.09 mm^2 **c)** 11.0 cm^2
  d) 7.395 cm^2 **e)** 5.46 cm^2

9. Sketches may vary. **10.** Explanations may vary.

11. Answers may vary.

7.1 Estimating the Circumference of a Circle

Developing the Ideas, page 345

1. Tables may vary.

2. a) About 3 times

3. The circumference of a circle is about 3 times its diameter.

Working with Mathematics, page 347

1. Multiply the diameter by 3. **2.** Multiply the radius by 6.

3. Answers may vary.

4. a) i) 2 **ii)** 6 **iii)** 3 times
  b) Answers may vary. Since the hexagon is inside the circle, and the perimeter of the hexagon is 3 times the diameter, the circumference is different from this, but close to it.
  c) The circumference is slightly more than 3 times the diameter since it is outside the hexagon and hence greater than the perimeter of the hexagon.

5. a) Little more
  b) Little less; explanations may vary. We should divide 12 m by a number greater than 3, so the quotient will be less than 4 m.

6. a) 36 cm **b)** 60 cm **c)** 126 cm
  d) 105 cm **e)** 23 cm **f)** 300 cm
  g) 171 cm **h)** 483 cm **i)** 74 cm

7. a) 4 cm **b)** 21 cm **c)** 24 cm
  d) 55 cm **e)** 27 cm **f)** 52 cm
  g) 67 cm **h)** 47 cm **i)** 120 cm

8. a) 75 m **b)** 32 cm **c)** 45 mm **d)** 744 m

9. a) 6 cm **b)** About 36 cm

10. a) About 21 m **b)** About 16 m **c)** About 10 m
  d) About 8 m **e)** About 6 m

11. a) About 3.66 m, about 7.32 m, about 10.98 m
  b)

Diameter (m)	Circumference (m)
1.22	3.66
2.44	7.32
3.66	10.98

  c) The points appear to lie on a straight line that passes through the origin.
  d) The table would need an extra column. The numbers in this column would be one-half the numbers in the diameter column. The points would still appear to lie on a straight line, but it would be steeper.

12. Yes, explanations may vary.

13. Answers may vary.

14. a) 72 cm **b)** 18 m **c)** 99 cm

15. a) 12 cm **b)** 30 cm

16. a) 48 cm, 96 cm, 144 cm, 192 cm, and 240 cm
  b)

Diameter (cm)	Circumference (cm)
16	48
32	96
48	144
64	192
80	240

  d) The table would need an extra column. The numbers in this column would be one-half the numbers in the diameter column. The points would still appear to lie on a straight line but it would be steeper.

17. a) , b) Answers may vary.
  c) i) Twice as great **ii)** Twice as great

18. a) i) About 22.2 cm **ii)** About 73.2 cm
  iii) About 12.9 cm **iv)** About 66.6 cm
  v) About 12.0 cm **vi)** About 11.1 cm
  vii) About 19.5 cm

19. a) About 900 000 000 km
  b) About 2 500 000 km **c)** About 100 000 km
  d) About 1700 km **e)** About 29 km

20. a) It would have markings about every 3 cm, not every centimetre.
  b) About 3 cm

Mathematics File: Refining the Estimate of the Circumference of a Circle, page 350

1., 2. Answers may vary.

3. About 207 cm

4. a) 49.0 m   **b)** 125.7 cm   **c)** 113.1 cm

5. a) About 28.3 m   **b)** About 188.5 cm

6. a) About 50 cm, about 100 cm, about 151 cm, about 201 cm, about 251 cm

   b) Answers may vary. The points would still lie on a straight line, but each point would be slightly higher.

7. a) About 113 cm   **b)** About 47 cm

8. a) Round up to the next whole centimetre. 205 cm

   b) 210 cm

9. Answers may vary.

7.2 Estimating the Area of a Circle
Developing the Ideas, page 353

Activity 1

2. a) About 3 times as great

3. The area of a circle is approximately 3 times the square of its radius.

Activity 2

1. a) The height of the parallelogram is equal to the radius of the circle.

   b) The base of the parallelogram is equal to one-half the circumference of the circle.

   c) Answers may vary.

   d) The area of the circle is equal to the area of the parallelogram.

Working with Mathematics, page 356

1. Multiply the radius by itself, then multiply by 3.

2. Divide the diameter by 2 to get the radius. Multiply the radius by itself, then multiply by 3.

3. a) The base would be closer to a straight-line segment.

   b) No

4. a) Multiply OB by 2, then multiply the result by itself.

   b) The white square is one-half the shaded square. Multiply OB by 2, then multiply the result by itself, then divide by 2. This is the same as multiplying OB by itself, then multiplying the result by 2.

   c) Multiply OB by itself, then multiply the result by 3.

5. Estimates may vary.

   a) 1200 mm^2 **b)** 4.32 m^2 **c)** 500 cm^2

   d) 39 000 mm^2 **e)** 360 cm^2 **f)** 3 m^2

6. a) 9 cm   **b)** 11.5 mm   **c)** 0.11 m

   d) 222 mm   **e)** 0.03 m   **f)** 25 cm

7. Estimates may vary.

   a) 240 cm^2 **b)** 400 mm^2 **c)** 0.04 m^2

   d) 148 000 mm^2 **e)** 0.003 m^2 **f)** 1875 cm^2

8. Estimates may vary.

   a) 6 cm, 12 cm   **b)** 2.5 m, 5 m   **c)** 25 mm, 50 mm

   d) 4 m, 8 m   **e)** 56 mm, 112 mm   **f)** 19 cm, 38 cm

9. Estimates may vary.

   a) 6.5 cm, 130 cm^2 **b)** 180 mm, 24 300 mm^2

   c) 18.8 m, 9.4 m   **d)** 13.5 cm, 550 cm^2

10. About 4800 m^2

11. a) Multiply AB by 4.   **b)** Multiply AB by 3.

   c) Multiply OB by 2, then multiply the result by itself.

   d) Multiply OB by itself, then multiply the result by 3.

12. About 243 m^2

13. a) About 3675 km^2 **b)** About 8 km^2

14. Yes; explanations may vary.

Mathematics File: Refining the Estimate of the Area of a Circle, page 358

1. Answers may vary.   **2.** Answers may vary.

3. a) 1256.6 cm^2 **b)** 633.5 cm^2 **c)** 115.0 cm^2

   d) 29.2 m^2 **e)** 63.6 m^2 **f)** 415.5 cm^2

4. a) About 1017 m^2 **b)** About 12.6 m^2

5. a) About 10.2 m^2 **b)** About 24.6 m^2 **c)** About 66.4 m^2

6. About 0.4 cm^2

7. About 51 cm^2

8. a) About 56.5 cm^2 **b)** About 132.5 cm^2

   c) About 42.1 cm^2 **d)** About 141.3 cm^2

   e) About 39.3 cm^2 **f)** About 13.6 cm^2

9. a) Circles may vary.

   b) Radii may vary.

   Sample radii:

   i) 5.6 cm   **ii)** 4.0 cm   **iii)** 2.8 cm

Mathematics File: Changing Cubic Units, page 361

1. 1 000 000

2. a) 4 000 000 cm^3 **b)** 50 000 000 cm^3

   c) 2 400 000 cm^3 **d)** 500 000 cm^3

3. a) 2 m^3 **b)** 1.5 m^3

   c) 0.5 m^3 **d)** 0.05 m^3

4. 96 000 cm^3, 0.096 m^3

7.3 Surface Area of a Triangular Prism
Developing the Ideas, page 362

1. a) 2; 3; 10; estimates may vary, 8 cm^2

   b) 3; 25, 20, 20; 0, 0, 5; estimates may vary, 25 cm^2, 20 cm^2, 21 cm^2

   c) Estimates may vary. 82 cm^2

2. Explanations may vary. Measure the edges of the prism. Calculate the area of each triangular face using the formula for the area of a triangle. Calculate the area of each rectangular face using the formula for the area of a rectangle. Add the areas of the faces.

Working with Mathematics, page 364

1. Answers may vary. If the object is portable, include the areas of all the faces.

2. Answers may vary. These faces coincide and do not form part of the surface area.

3. a) 5 cm^2 **b)** 7.5 cm^2 **c)** 2.52 cm^2

4. a) 102.8 cm^2 **b)** 119 cm^2 **c)** 76.24 cm^2

5. a) 576 cm^2 **b)** 144 cm^2

6. a) The surface area of the larger prism is 4 times as great as the surface area of the smaller prism.

   b) Each dimension of the smaller prism was multiplied by 2 to get the corresponding dimension in the larger prism. Since area is a product of two dimensions, the area is 4 times as great.

7. b) Explanations may vary. 208 cm^2

8. a) 36.13 cm^2, 62.86 cm^2
   b) No, because not every dimension of the larger prism is double the corresponding dimension of the smaller prism.

9. Spreadsheets may vary.

10. a) 298.5 cm^2 **b)** 237 cm^2

11. Approximately 190 cm^2 **12.** 466.5 cm^2

13. Approximately 63 cm^2

14. a) Estimates may vary.
   b) 1203.5 m^2 **c)** 4.8%   **d)** 8

15. a) Explanations may vary. 3 m   **b)** Square

16. Problems may vary.

7.4 Volume of a Triangular Prism
Working with Mathematics, page 368

1. Answers may vary. The base is a triangle. If it were a right triangle, its base and height could be 8 cm and 2 cm, or 4 cm and 4 cm, or 1 cm and 16 cm, and so on.

2. Descriptions of different prisms may vary. There is an infinite number of prisms with this volume.

3. Yes; the base must be the triangular face.

4. Yes; explanations may vary.

5. a) Answers may vary; for example: 1 cm by 1 cm by 36 cm, 1 cm by 3 cm by 12 cm, 1 cm by 4 cm by 9 cm, 1 cm by 6 cm by 6 cm, 2 cm by 2 cm by 9 cm, 2 cm by 4 cm by 4.5 cm, 2 cm by 5 cm by 3.6 cm, 6 cm by 2 cm by 3 cm, 3 cm by 3 cm by 4 cm, 18 cm by 2 cm by 1 cm

6. a) 32 cm^3 **b)** 100 cm^3 **c)** 6 cm^3 **d)** 53.4 cm^3

7. a) 64 cm^3 **b)** 200 cm^3 **c)** 12 cm^3 **d)** 106.8 cm^3

8. The volume is doubled.

9. a) 960 cm^3 **b)** 2400 cm^3 **c)** 4800 cm^3 **d)** 48 000 cm^3

10. a) 2424 cm^3 **b)** 1945 cm^3 **c)** 108.7 cm^3

11. 2160 m^3

12. Answers may vary.
   a) 1 cm by 1 cm by 120 cm; 2 cm by 2 cm by 30 cm; 4 cm by 4 cm by 7.5 cm
   b) 482 cm^2, 248 cm^2, 152 cm^2

13. a) Estimates may vary. About 1.5 m^3 **b)** 1.584 m^3

14. Sketches may vary.

15. a) 100 cm^3 **b)** 800 cm^3, 1600 cm^3

16. a) 300 cm^3 **b)** 600 cm^3 **c)** 1200 cm^3 **d)** 2400 cm^3

17. a) 37.4 cm^3 **b)** 18.5 cm^3 **c)** 45 m^3 **d)** 5693 mm^3

18. a) Decreases; increases
   b) i) 40 cm   **ii)** 20 cm   **iii)** 10 cm
   c) The height is halved.
   d) i) 50 cm^2 **ii)** 25 cm^2 **iii)** 12.5 cm^2
   e) The base area is halved.
   f) Sketches may vary.

Quest: How Much Space Is Yours?, page 370

Descriptions and solutions may vary.

7.5 Volume in Capacity Units
Developing the Ideas, page 371

1. Answers may vary.

2. a) 1 mL = 1 cm^3 **b)** 1 L = 1000 cm^3

Working with Mathematics, page 373

1. Answers may vary. The volume in cubic centimetres is the volume of the container. It might not be full of the contents, whose volume is in millilitres.

2. a) millilitre   **b)** litre   **c)** millilitre   **d)** litre

3. a) mL   **b)** L   **c)** mL   **d)** L

4. a) 24 mL   **b)** 9.7 mL   **c)** 1000 mL   **d)** 2000 mL   **e)** 100 mL
   f) 400 mL   **g)** 350 mL   **h)** 210 mL   **i)** 1800 mL   **j)** 4180 mL

5. a) 3 L   **b)** 8 L   **c)** 0.3 L   **d)** 0.9 L   **e)** 1.5 L
   f) 2.9 L   **g)** 0.246 L   **h)** 0.068 L   **i)** 0.158 L   **j)** 0.029 L

6. a) 1400 cm^3 **b)** 1800 cm^3 **c)** 5000 cm^3 **d)** 9000 cm^3 **e)** 240 cm^3
   f) 380 cm^3 **g)** 29 cm^3 **h)** 66 cm^3 **i)** 1600 cm^3 **j)** 2500 cm^3

7. a) 4000 mL, 4000 cm^3 **b)** 1500 mL, 1500 cm^3

8. a) 2.8 L, 2800 cm^3 **b)** 0.25 L, 250 cm^3

9. a) 2 L   **b)** 10 mL   **c)** 280 mL   **d)** 40 L

10. a) 1 890 000 L   **b)** About 3 weeks

11. Answers may vary.

12. a) 3 L = 3000 mL   **b)** 2000 mL = 2 L
   c) 500 mL = 0.5 L   **d)** 4.5 L = 4500 mL
   e) 0.25 L = 250 mL   **f)** 3200 mL = 3.2 L

13. a) 150 mL = 150 cm^3 **b)** 375 mL = 375 cm^3
   c) 2 L = 2000 cm^3 **d)** 750 cm^3 = 750 mL
   e) 1200 cm^3 = 1200 mL   **f)** 525 cm^3 = 0.525 L

14. 400 mL

15. Estimates may vary.
   a) 250 mL   **b)** 2 mL   **c)** 1 L or 2 L   **d)** 15 L

16. 18 glasses   **17.** Answers may vary.   **18.** 63 L

19. a) About 5.6 cm   **b)** About 11.1 cm

Review, page 375

1. a) Estimates may vary. About 4.2 m   **b)** About 4.4 m

2. a) Estimates may vary. About 22 cm   **b)** About 21 cm

3. a) About 12 800 km   **b)** About 38 400 km

4. **a)** 4900 km, 14 700 km   **b)** 12 100 km, 36 300 km
   c) 6800 km, 20 400 km   **d)** 139 900 km, 419 700 km
   e) 116 600 km, 349 800 km   **f)** 50 700 km, 152 100 km
   g) 49 200 km, 147 600 km   **h)** 2300 km, 6900 km

5. a) About 94 cm   **b)** About 69 cm   **c)** About 140.7 cm

6. a) 88.78 cm   **b)** 54.26 cm   **c)** 32.0 cm

7. 13.5717 km

8. a) About 9 cm   **b)** About 17.3 m
   c) About 8.8 km   **d)** About 11.6 mm

9. a) About 13 m^2 **b)** About 96.8 cm^2
   c) About 143.1 km^2 **d)** About 581.1 mm^2

10. a) 13.6 cm^2 **b)** 141.7 cm^2 **c)** 63.1 cm^2

11. a) About 45 m^2 **b)** About 39 m^2 remain   **c)** About 8 L

12. a) 216 cm^2 **b)** 618 cm^2 **c)** 549.6 cm^2 **d)** 147.2 cm^2

13. a) About 70 m^2 **b)** About 24 sheets

14. a) i) 2 cm   **ii)** 3 cm   **iii)** 10 cm
   b) Divide the surface area by 6, then find which number,

multiplied by itself is equal to the quotient.

15. a) 350 cm³ **b)** 168 cm³ **c)** 1250 cm³ **d)** 280 cm³

16. a) 180.0 cm³ **b)** 720 cm³ **c)** 72 m³ **d)** 66.1 cm³

17. About 2667 truck loads

18. a) 106 800 cm³ **b)** 21 150 cm³

19. Answers may vary. 1 cm by 1 cm by 24 cm, 1 cm by 2 cm by 12 cm, 1 cm by 3 cm by 8 cm, 1 cm by 4 cm by 6 cm, 2 cm by 2 cm by 6 cm, 2 cm by 3 cm by 4 cm

20. a) 12 **b) , c)** Answers may vary.

21. a) 3 000 000 cm³ **b)** 8 cm³ **c)** 0.0067 cm³ **d)** 7.5 cm³ **e)** 84.5 cm³ **f)** 560 000 cm³ **g)** 1 250 000 cm³ **h)** 0.55 cm³

22. a) 0.063 m³ **b)** 0.127 m³ **c)** 8 000 000 000 m³ **d)** 9 200 000 000 m³ **e)** 720 000 000 m³ **f)** 3.5 m³ **g)** 40 000 000 m³ **h)** 5 030 000 000 m³

23. a) 360 cm³, 360 000 mm³ **b)** 8 cm³, 8000 mm³ **c)** 334.8 cm³, 334 800 mm³

24. a) litre **b)** millilitre **c)** millilitre **d)** litre **e)** litre **f)** millilitre

Linking Ideas: Mathematics and Technology
Surface Area on a Spreadsheet, page 377

1. B6: Multiply the length by the width;
B7: Multiply the width by the height;
B8: Multiply the length by the height

2. Answers may vary.

3. The computer filled cells from B6 to E9 with area values.

4. a) The areas in C6 and C8 doubled. The area in C9 increased.
b) The area in D6 quadrupled. The area in D7 doubled. The area in D9 increased.
c) The areas in E7 and E8 quadrupled. The area in E9 doubled.

5. These results are shown with how cell B9 compares with cell D9. The surface area increases.

6. These results are shown with how cell B9 compares with cell E9. The surface area is 4 times the original area.

7. The surface area increases if one or two dimensions are tripled. The new surface area is 9 times the original area if three dimensions are tripled.

8. Answers may vary. Similar results should occur.

Cumulative Review, page 378A

1. a)
```
0 | 4567889
1 | 1222334467788
2 | 123
```

b) 13, 13 **c)** 19; 8, 17

2. a) $\frac{1}{2}$ **b)** $\frac{2}{3}$

3. Answers may vary. $\frac{2}{3} \div \frac{3}{7}$

4. a) 3 km² **b) i)** $\frac{4}{9}$ **ii)** 2 km²

5. a) $\frac{2}{3}$ **b)** $\frac{1}{2}$ **c)** $\frac{11}{10}$, or $1\frac{1}{10}$ **d)** $\frac{7}{12}$ **e)** $\frac{7}{10}$ **f)** $\frac{9}{8}$, or $1\frac{1}{8}$ **g)** $\frac{19}{12}$, or $1\frac{7}{12}$ **h)** $\frac{9}{8}$, or $1\frac{1}{8}$ **i)** $\frac{31}{12}$, or $2\frac{7}{12}$

6. a) $\frac{19}{20}$ **b)** $\frac{11}{20}$ **c)** $\frac{1}{20}$

7. a) $\frac{1}{12}$ **b)** $\frac{5}{12}$ **c)** $\frac{7}{6}$, or $1\frac{1}{6}$ **d)** $\frac{1}{8}$ **e)** $\frac{1}{10}$ **f)** $1\frac{1}{6}$ **g)** $\frac{1}{6}$ **h)** $\frac{3}{4}$ **i)** $\frac{2}{3}$

8. a) 7.1 m **b)** 2.9 m

9. a) 1 **b)** $\frac{5}{4}$, or $1\frac{1}{4}$ **c)** $\frac{1}{6}$ **d)** $\frac{4}{3}$, or $1\frac{1}{3}$ **e)** $\frac{3}{8}$ **f)** 1 **g)** $\frac{1}{2}$ **h)** $\frac{7}{12}$ **i)** $\frac{3}{5}$

10. a) True **b)** True **c)** True

11. About 0.4 s

12. a) 24 km **b)** 2.5 h **c)** 12 km/h

d)

Time (h)	Distance run (km)
0	0
1	12
2	24
3	36
4	48
5	60

f) Variables may differ. $D = 12t$
g) $t = \frac{D}{12}$
h) No, Abdul could not keep running at the same pace without resting.

13. a) 5% **b)** 95%

14. b) i) $\frac{59}{227}$, or about 0.26 **ii)** $\frac{135}{227}$, or about 0.59 **iii)** $\frac{86}{227}$, or about 0.38
c) Questions and answers may vary.

15. a) 1, 2, 3, 4, 5; 5
b) No, the outcome 3 is twice as likely as any of the other outcomes.
c) $\frac{1}{6}$ **d)** $\frac{1}{3}$

16. a) +6 **b)** −14 **c)** −4 **d)** +12 **e)** −8 **f)** −4 **g)** −1 **h)** +26 **i)** −24 **j)** +7 **k)** −3 **l)** −4

17. 600 m **18.** 38 m

CHAPTER 8 ALGEBRA

Start With What You Know, page 382

1. b)

Diagram number	Number of green squares	Number of purple squares
1	1	1
2	2	4
3	3	9
4	4	16
5	5	25
6	6	36

c) The number of green squares is the same as the diagram number; it increases by 1 with each step. The number of purple squares is the square of the diagram number.
d) 10, 100
e) Square the number of green squares.

2. a) 20
b)

Number of trays	1	2	3	4	5
Number of buns	20	40	60	80	100

The numbers of buns are multiples of 20.
  c) Multiply the number of trays by 20.
  d) $20t$

3. i) a) Multiples of 7   b) 70
    c) 210   d) $7n$
  ii) a) The pattern starts with 5, and each number is one greater
       than the previous number.
    b) 14   c) 34   d) $4 + n$
  iii) a) Multiples of 11   b) 110
    c) 330   d) $11n$

4. i) a)

Counter	1	2	3	4	5	6
Number	3	4	5	6	7	8

  b) 30
  ii) a)

Counter	1	2	3	4	5	6
Number	4	8	12	16	20	24

  b) 8
  iii) a)

Counter	1	2	3	4	5	6
Number	39	38	37	36	35	34

  b) 8
  iv) a)

Counter	1	2	3	4	5	6
Number	$\frac{1}{2}$	1	$\frac{3}{2}$	2	$\frac{5}{2}$	3

  b) 64

5. a) Answers may vary; some examples are $10 + 5$, 5×3, $19 - 4$.
  b) The equation is true because each side is equal to the same number, 15.
  c) Answers may vary.   d) Answers may vary.

6. b)

Length of side (units)	1	2	3	4	5	6
Perimeter of figure (units)	4	8	12	16	20	24

  c) Multiply the side length by 4.
  d) $P = 4s$ e) 40 units   f) 13 units

8.1 Substituting into Formulas
Developing the Ideas, page 384

1. a) 14 112 cm^2, or about 1.4 m^2
  b) Yes, there is enough paint to cover 2 m^2 with one coat.
2. a) 486 cm   b) 3   c) $11.85

Working with Mathematics, page 388

1. P (perimeter), A (area), l (length), w (width)
2. To substitute for a variable in a formula, replace the variable with a number.
3. a) 48 cm^2 b) 80 m^2 c) 30 m^2
4. a) 12 m   b) 18 km   c) 34 km
5. a) 11.02 cm^2 b) 10.83 km^2 c) 5.98 m^2
6. a) 7.5 cm^2 b) 31.5 cm^2 c) 4.375 cm^2
7. a) 12.6 cm^2 b) 38.5 cm^2 c) 0.1 cm^2
8. a) 12.6 cm   b) 22.0 cm   c) 1.3 cm

9. a) 10.7 cm^2 b) 9.5 cm^2 c) 153.8 m^2 d) 97.0 m^2
10. a) 160 cm   b) 2043 cm^2
11. a) 7 cm   b) 5 cm   c) 4 cm   d) 3 cm
12. 6 m
13. a) i) 9 mg   ii) 16 mg   iii) 30 mg   iv) 35 mg
  b) The graph is a straight line passing through the origin. The graph leans upwards to the right.
  c) Estimates may vary. About 20 mg
14. a) Multiply the number of seconds by 9.8.
  b) The formula in cell A3 adds 0.5 s to the time. The formula in cell B3 calculates the speed in metres per second by multiplying the number of seconds by 9.8. The formula in cell C3 multiplies the speed in metres per second by the number of seconds in an hour, then divides the result by the number of metres in one kilometre.
  c) i) 19.6 m/s, or 70.56 km/h   ii) 29.4 m/s, or 105.84 km/h
    iii) 39.2 m/s, or 141.12 km/h   iv) 49 m/s, or 176.4 km/h
  d) Just under 1.5 s; after 5 s, her speed would be about 3.5 times as great as this speed
15. a) 4 cm   b) 6 cm
16. a) 58.29 cm^2 b) 8 cm
17. a) i) $462   ii) $467   iii) $477
  b) $2875
18. 46 656 cm^2, or about 4.7 m^2

Quest: How Many Targets Were Missed?, page 390

The athlete who finished 44th missed 9 targets.
The fastest skier will not always win. A person who skis very quickly but misses many targets may finish after a slower skier who hits all the targets and does not have to ski any penalty laps.

8.2 The Language of Algebra
Developing the Ideas, page 392

Activity 1

Variables may differ.

1. $n + 4$ 2. $x - 5$ 3. $12 - s$
4. $3p$ 5. $8y$ 6. $\frac{12}{m}$
7. $2t + 7$ 8. $6r - 5$ 9. $q + (-4)$, or $q - 4$

Activity 2

Some phrases may vary.

1., 2. 8 more than a number
3. 3 less than a number   4. A number subtracted from 3
5. 6 times a number   6. 3 times a number, increased by 2
7. A number divided by 3   8. 9 times a number, subtracted from 5

Activity 3

Phrases that indicate addition or subtraction: more than, less than, increased by, decreased by, subtracted from
Phrases that indicate multiplication or division: times, divided by

Working with Mathematics, page 394

1. No; explanations may vary.
2. a) $3p$ b) $5r$ c) $10 - x$ d) $n - 6$
3. a) The sum of a number and 7
  b) A number decreased by 4

c) A number subtracted from 6

d) A number divided by 7

4. a) Multiply the number of days by 10 to determine the fine, in cents.

 b) $10d$

5. Variables may differ.

 a) $a - 1$ **b)** $b - 11$ **c)** $18 - c$ **d)** $d + 20$ **e)** $8 - e$
 f) $10f$ **g)** $\frac{g}{-5}$ **h)** $\frac{6}{h}$ **i)** $\frac{i}{12}$ **j)** $3j + 3$

6. Some phrases may vary.

 a) A number increased by 16 **b)** 5 less than a number

 c) A number subtracted from 24

 d) The sum of 7 and a number

 e) 4 times a number **f)** A number divided by 17

 g) 11 times a number, decreased by 9

 h) 2 times a number, increased by 3

 i) 2 times a number, subtracted from 15

7. a) 50¢, 125¢, 25n¢ **b)** $15, $35, $5p

 c) 180 min, 300 min, 60m minutes

 d) 1 m, 10 m, $\frac{b}{100}$ metres **e)** 96 h, 240 h, 24d hours

8. a) $\frac{n}{365}$ **b)** Divide the time in days by 365.

 c) 12; they are all in the *Whales, dolphins, and porpoises*, or *Seals and sea lions* groups.

9. Variables may differ. $6b$

10. a) Multiply by $7 and add the result to $1500.

 b) $1500 + 7p$

11. Variables may differ.

 a) $7 - w$ **b)** $15x$ **c)** $\frac{y}{3}$ **d)** $7z - 8$

12. Some phrases may vary.

 a) A number divided by 9

 b) A number multiplied by 100

 c) A number subtracted from 4

 d) 16 less than a number

 e) 2 times a number, increased by 27

 f) 4 times a number, subtracted from 20

13. a) 60m seconds **b)** 1000k grams **c)** 5n¢

 d) $20t **e)** $\frac{d}{60}$ hours **f)** $\frac{c}{100}$ metres

14. a) $35 - x$ **b)** $[10x + (35 - x) \times 25]$¢

15. Multiply the number of metres by $6.49.

16. a) Multiply by $20, and add the result to $500.

 b) $500 + 20y$

17. a) $500 + 20(w - 35)$

 b) No, answers may vary. The worker may still be paid $500 if the time missed is due to illness, or she may be paid at an hourly rate of about $14.28 per hour.

18. a) $400s$ **b)** 10 000s²

Linking Ideas: Mathematics and Technology
How Long Can You Talk for $25?, page 396

1. a) The formula in cell A4 adds 1 to the number of minutes talked. The formula in cell B4 calculates the cost of the call.

 b) The spreadsheet lists the costs of calls from Ottawa to Tehran for times from 1 min to 13 min.

 c) Gita and Afshar can talk for 12 min. Gita will have $1.75 left.

2. a) 7 min; 10 min **b)** $10.23

3. Between 7:30 a.m. and 9:30 a.m.

4. Answers may vary.

5. a) $C = 1.47 + 0.98(t - 1)$

 c) 27 min **d)** $8.33

 e) It is between 8 a.m. and midnight. Answers may vary.

6. Answers may vary.

8.3 Evaluating Expressions
Working with Mathematics, page 399

1. To evaluate an expression, substitute a number for each variable and determine the value of the expression.

2. a) $3.84 **b)** $7.20 **c)** $11.04

3. a) 8 **b)** 1 **c)** −3 **d)** 8 **e)** 16
 f) −20 **g)** 20 **h)** 2 **i)** 6

4. a) 7 **b)** 14 **c)** 2 **d)** −4 **e)** −14
 f) −5 **g)** −1 **h)** 4 **i)** −2

5. a) 17 **b)** 7 **c)** 1 **d)** 3 **e)** 36 **f)** 47

6. a) 2 **b)** 26 **c)** −8 **d)** −3 **e)** −40 **f)** 10

7. a) 17 **b)** 18.5 **c)** 19 **d)** 51

8. The expressions in a, b, d, f, and h are all equal to 10; the expressions in c and g are both equal to 11.

9. a) −1.3 **b)** 10.5 **c)** 22.6 **d)** 40.4 **e)** −3.8 **f)** 9.4

10. a) −17.4 **b)** 6.4 **c)** 3 **d)** −2.1$\overline{6}$

11. a) $2w + t$ **b)** 23

12. a) 16 **b)** 24 **c)** 11

13. a) $4.98 + 0.35n$ **b)** $13.38

14. a) Luis rounds the time he babysits up to the next half-hour.

 b) i) n will be a multiple of 0.5. **ii)** $4.50n$

 c) The formula in cell A3 adds one-half hour to the time. Column A shows times in half-hour intervals from 0.5 h to 8 h.

 d) The formula to enter in cell B2 is =4.5*A2. Column B shows the amount Luis should charge for times of up to 8 h.

 e) i) $13.50 **ii)** $31.50

 iii) When Luis babysits 4.5 h, he will earn $20.25.

15. a) 11.5 **b)** 17.3 **c)** 5.0 **d)** 8.0

16. a) $\frac{9}{4}$, or $2\frac{1}{4}$ **b)** $\frac{2}{4}$, or $\frac{1}{2}$ **c)** 6 **d)** $\frac{63}{4}$, or $15\frac{3}{4}$

17. a) −4.5 **b)** −4 **c)** −3 **d)** 4.5

18. a) 3.1 **b)** 31.7 **c)** 46.5 **d)** −14.6

19. a) 22.9 **b)** 10.4 **c)** −21.6 **d)** 21.7

20. a) $\frac{p}{8}$

 b) Answers may vary. Suppose the answer Devon and Anna get is 12.25. Since $0.25 \times 8 = 2$, they need 12 tables of 8 and 2 extra places. They could set 12 full tables and one table with only 2 places; they could set 13 full tables and some places will remain empty; they could set 12 full tables and squeeze in 1 extra setting at 2 of the tables.

 c) i) 15 **ii)** 25
 iii) 19 **iv)** 25

21. a) $675x$ grams **b)** $\frac{x}{24}$
 c) 243 000 g, or 243 kg; 15 boxes

22. a) i) $4.50 **ii)** $9.00 **iii)** $9.75
 b) 9 h

23. Answers may vary. The number of bricks needed would be affected by the size of brick used, the number of windows in the wall, and any pattern desired in the brickwork.

24. a) i) $55 + 2x$ **ii)** $162 + 4x$ **iii)** $1430 + 52x$
 b) i) 58 m **ii)** 168 m **iii)** 1508 m²

Mathematics File: Mind-Bending Math!, page 402

1. a) 14   **b)** Everyone gets the same answer.

2. Variables may differ. The steps and expressions are as follows. Pick a number between 1 and 10: x; multiply the number by 2: $2x$; add 28 to the result: $2x + 28$; divide by 2: $\frac{2x + 28}{2}$, or $x + 14$; subtract the original number: $x + 14 - x$, or 14.

3. Yes, explanations may vary.

4. In the third step, add 22 instead of 28.

5. In the last step, subtract 14 instead of the original number.

6. Answers may vary.

8.4 Using Models to Solve Equations

Developing the Ideas

Activity 1, page 403

1. Explanations may vary.
- **a) i)** $x = 5$ **ii)** 5
  - **iii)** Replace the bag with 5 candies.
- **b) i)** $14 = 2x$ **ii)** 7
  - **iii)** Replace each bag with 7 candies.
- **c) i)** $x + 5 = 8$ **ii)** 3
  - **iii)** Replace each bag with 3 candies.
- **d) i)** $9 = 3x$ **ii)** 3
  - **iii)** Replace each bag with 3 candies.
- **e) i)** $2x + 3 = 9$ **ii)** 3
  - **iii)** Replace each bag with 3 candies.
- **f) i)** $3x + 1 = 13$ **ii)** 4
  - **iii)** Replace each bag with 4 candies.

Activity 2, page 404

1. a) i) $t + 4 = 7$ **iii)** 3
  - **iv)** Replace the t-tile with three 1-tiles.
- **b) i)** $-7 = -t + 4$ **iii)** 11
  - **iv)** Replace the $-t$-tile with eleven 1-tiles.
- **c) i)** $-3t = 6$ **iii)** -2
  - **iv)** Replace each $-t$-tile with two 1-tiles.
- **d) i)** $-9 = 2t - 3$ **iii)** -3
  - **iv)** Replace each t-tile with three -1-tiles.

Working with Mathematics, page 407

1. We cannot represent a negative number of candies or a negative number of bags.

2. No

3. a) Place 4 candies and 3 bags on one pan, and 13 candies on the other pan. Remove 4 candies from each pan to leave 3 bags in one pan and 9 candies in the other pan. Since there are 3 bags, divide the 9 candies into 3 groups. Each group contains 3 candies. So, 1 bag has 3 candies, or $n = 3$.
- **b)** Place 4 green 1-tiles and 3 green n-tiles on one side of a work chart. Place 13 green 1-tiles on the other side of the work chart. Remove 4 green 1-tiles from each side of the chart to leave 3 green n-tiles on one side and 9 green 1-tiles on the other side. Since there are 3 green n-tiles, divide the 9 green 1-tiles into 3 groups. Each group contains three green 1-tiles. So, 1 green n-tile equals 3 green 1-tiles, or $n = 3$.

4. Answers may vary.
- **a)** $2x + 3 = 17$ **b)** $2x - 3 = 17$ **c)** No

5. Replace each variable tile with the number of 1-tiles equal to the variable. There should be the same number of 1-tiles on each side of the work chart.

6. a) 1   **b)** 3   **c)** 5   **d)** 5   **e)** 13
- **f)** 6   **g)** 3   **h)** 2   **i)** 5   **j)** 5
- **k)** 8   **l)** 6   **m)** 6   **n)** 7   **o)** 8

7. a) 2   **b)** 2   **c)** -1 **d)** -3 **e)** 3   **f)** 2
- **g)** -3 **h)** -3 **i)** 2   **j)** -7 **k)** -5 **l)** 10
- **m)** 7   **n)** -7 **o)** -9 **p)** -15 **q)** -4 **r)** 5

8. a) i) $13 = 2x + 3$ **ii)** $x = 5$ **iii)** 5
- **b) i)** $3c + 3 = 15$ **ii)** $c = 4$ **iii)** 4

9. a) 3   **b)** 1   **c)** 7   **d)** 3

10. $22 = 2x + 10$; 6

11. a) i) $-7 = -2p + 3$ **ii)** 5
- **b) i)** $9 = 2p + 3$ **ii)** 3
- **c) i)** $-4p + 4 = 16$ **ii)** -3
- **d) i)** $3p - 2 = -11$ **ii)** -3

12. $18 = 2r + 4$; 7

13. a) Five added to a number is 18.
- **b)** Five subtracted from a number is 18.
- **c)** A number subtracted from 5 is 18.
- **d)** Five times a number is 20.
- **e)** Five times a number, increased by 8 is 18.
- **f)** Five times a number, decreased by 7 is 18.

14. a) 13   **b)** 23   **c)** -13 **d)** 4   **e)** 2   **f)** 5

15. a) 6   **b)** 4   **c)** 5   **d)** 4

16. $36 = s + 8$; 28

17. a) $x + 7 = 15$; 8   **b)** $x - 4 = 7$; 11   **c)** $3x = 18$; 6
- **d)** $2x = 12$; 6   **e)** $2x - 5 = 15$; 10   **f)** $2x + 3 = 29$; 13
- **g)** $52 - 3x = 31$; 7   **h)** $2x + 8 = 20$; 6   **i)** $4x - 2 = 26$; 7

18. a) Four more than a number is 16.
- **b)** A number subtracted from 4 is 16.
- **c)** Four subtracted from a number is 16.
- **d)** Four times a number is 16.
- **e)** Four times a number, increased by 5 is 21.
- **f)** Four times a number, subtracted from 5 is 15.

19. $34 = 4p + 6$; 7   **20.** 2 square blocks

Mathematics File: Networks, page 409

1. a) 3, 6, 8   **b)** 4, 5, 8   **c)** 3, 7, 9   **d)** 5, 8, 12

2. Networks may vary.

3. a)

S	R	V	R + V
8	3	6	9
8	4	5	9
9	3	7	10
12	5	8	13
3	1	3	4
4	1	4	5
5	2	4	6
7	2	6	8

- **b)** The value of S is 1 less than the value of $R + V$.

4. a) $S = R + V - 1$
- **b) i)** $6 = 2 + 5 - 1$ **ii)** $10 = 3 + 8 - 1$
- **iii)** $9 = 4 + 6 - 1$ **iv)** $15 = 6 + 10 - 1$

8.5 Solving Equations Algebraically
Working with Mathematics, page 413

1. a) Because some of the equations involve negative numbers and decimals, which are difficult to represent on a two-pan balance

b) The equation in part a, which involves decimals; the equation in part c, which involves division; the equation in part d, which involves a large number

2. a) 3   **b)** 6   **c)** 11   **d)** 2   **e)** -7 **f)** -4
g) 3   **h)** 7   **i)** 2   **j)** -9 **k)** -4 **l)** -2
m) 22   **n)** 7   **o)** -7 **p)** 29   **q)** 11   **r)** 3

3. a) 2   **b)** 3   **c)** -2 **d)** -4 **e)** $\frac{5}{3}$ **f)** -1.5
g) $-\frac{7}{4}$ **h)** -1.8 **i)** -4.8 **j)** -4.6 **k)** $\frac{7}{4}$ **l)** -9

4. a) 6   **b)** 6   **c)** -7 **d)** -4 **e)** 12
f) 25   **g)** -10 **h)** -20 **i)** 24   **j)** 21
k) 12   **l)** -16 **m)** 140   **n)** 36

5. a) 2   **b)** 7   **c)** $-\frac{2}{3}$
d) 11   **e)** $\frac{5}{2}$, or 2.5   **f)** $-\frac{5}{2}$, or -2.5

6. a) -6 **b)** 13   **c)** $-\frac{2}{3}$
d) 10   **e)** -9 **f)** $-\frac{11}{2}$, or -5.5
g) 15   **h)** -10 **i)** -39 **j)** -42

7. a) 3   **b)** 2   **c)** $\frac{8}{3}$, or $2\frac{2}{3}$ **d)** 2   **e)** -1
f) -3 **g)** 1   **h)** 3   **i)** 4   **j)** 3

8. a) $2x = 18; 9$ **b)** $8x = 32; 4$ **c)** $\frac{x}{7} = 2; 14$
d) $\frac{x}{5} = 4; 20$ **e)** $6 + 2x = 20; 7$ **f)** $8 + 3x = 20; 4$
g) $4x - 3 = 11; 3.5$ **h)** $1 + \frac{x}{3} = 2; 3$ **i)** $\frac{x}{2} - 1 = 2; 6$

9. a) $12 + 8 = n; 20$ **b)** $5 + 3 = n; 8$
c) $3(2) = n; 6$ **d)** $24 = 4n; 6$

10. $x = 5 + 2(12); 29$ **11.** $20 - x = 4; 16$

12. $149.75 = 5x; \$29.95$ **13.** $188 = 8t; 24$

14. $x + 13 = 18; 15$ **15.** $50 = 5 + 3x; 15 \text{ m}^2$

16. $60 + 4x = 140; \$20$ **17., 18.** Answers may vary.

19. a) $649.00   **b)** $715.00   **c)** $998.00

20. a) 5   **b)** -14 **c)** 20
d) 6   **e)** -4 **f)** -14

21. a) 1   **b)** 5   **c)** -5
d) $\frac{23}{2}$, or 11.5   **e)** 8   **f)** $\frac{3}{2}$, or 1.5

22. a) 56   **b)** 63   **c)** 65
d) 100   **e)** 108   **f)** 24

23. a) $x + 3 = 5; 2$ **b)** $8 + x = 12; 4$ **c)** $x - 2 = 4; 6$
d) $x - 12 = 16; 28$ **e)** $8 - x = 3; 5$ **f)** $20 - x = 5; 15$

24. $n = 5 + 8(3); 29$ **25.** $12n + 7 = 31; 2$ dozen

26. $13 + 2x = 20; 3.5 \text{ m}^2$ **27.** $1x + 18 = 28; 10$

28. $\frac{x}{2} = 14 + 8; 44$

29. a) $C = 750 + 30n$
b) i) 50   **ii)** 90   **iii)** 125

30., 31. Answers may vary.

32. a) $59   **b)** 100 km   **c)** 66 km

33. a) -2 **b)** -4 **c)** 8   **d)** 0   **e)** 8   **f)** -5 **g)** 9
h) -3 **i)** -1 **j)** 14   **k)** 11   **l)** $16.\overline{3}$ **m)** -4.35 **n)** 7.5

Review, page 416

1. a) 202   **b)** 182   **c)** 170
d) Answers may vary.   **e)** Answers may vary.

2. a) 20   **b)** 50   **c)** 35   **d)** 41

3. The graph is a straight line leaning downwards to the right. As a person's age increases, the maximum recommended pulse rate decreases. This is to avoid placing too much stress on the heart muscles.

4. a) Subtract $12 from the regular price.   **b)** $p - 12$
c) i) $12   **ii)** $22   **iii)** $38
d) i) 50%   **ii)** About 35%   **iii)** 24%

5. a) From 1 p.m. to 6 p.m.: $C = 1.16 + 0.77(t - 1)$
From 6 p.m. to 9 a.m.: $C = 0.96 + 0.64(t - 1)$
b) Answers may vary, depending on your region. The time in France is 9 h ahead of Pacific time, 8 h ahead of Mountain time, 7 h ahead of Central time, 6 h ahead of Eastern time, 5 h ahead of Atlantic time, and 4.5 h ahead of Newfoundland time.
c) Answers may vary. Rates are cheapest between 6 p.m. and 9 a.m. However, in some parts of Canada it may not be convenient to call during this period.

6. a) $4.68   **b)** $8.08   **c)** $4.24
d) $8.09   **e)** $3.52   **f)** $7.36

7. a) Multiply the number of vacuum cleaners sold by $40 and add the result to $200.
b) $E = 200 + 40v$ **c)** $320, $520   **d)** 5, 11

8. a) 5   **b)** 18   **c)** 19
d) 1   **e)** $\frac{1}{2}$, or 0.5   **f)** -1

9. a) -4 **b)** 9   **c)** -17 **d)** 19   **e)** -4 **f)** 2

10. a) $8.50x + 4.75y$
b) i) $187.25   **ii)** $327.00
iii) $774.75   **iv)** $687.25

11. Variables may differ.
a) $x + 7 = 41; 34$ **b)** $y - 5 = 19; 24$
c) $35 - 3z = 26; 3$ **d)** $18 = \frac{n}{2}; 36$

12. Variables may differ.
a) $a + 7 = 12; 5$ **b)** $3b + 1 = 7; 2$ **c)** $2c + 4 = 6; 1$

13. Variables may differ.
a) $a - 3 = 7; 10$ **b)** $3b + 7 = -2; -3$ **c)** $3c = 6; 2$

14. a) -5 **b)** -3 **c)** -1 **d)** -1 **e)** 3   **f)** -1

15. a) 13   **b)** -2 **c)** 48   **d)** 36   **e)** 7   **f)** 5

16. Answers may vary.

Cumulative Review, page 421

1. a) 2 cm   **b)** 10 cm   **c)** 4.5 cm   **d)** 9.5 cm   **e)** 5 cm   **f)** 11.25 cm

2. a) 70 km   **b)** 5.25 km   **c)** 175 km
d) 5250 km   **e)** 875 km   **f)** 350 km

3. a) 1 cm represents 10 m.   **b)** About 28 m

5. a) $(1 \times 10\ 000) + (3 \times 1000) + (5 \times 10) + (4 \times 1)$
b) $(8 \times 1000) + (6 \times 100) + (7 \times 10) + (4 \times 1)$
c) $(3 \times 1\ 000\ 000) + (2 \times 100\ 000) + (3 \times 10\ 000) + (7 \times 1000) + (9 \times 100) + (2 \times 10)$
d) $(2 \times 10) + (4 \times 1) + (8 \times \frac{1}{10}) + (5 \times \frac{1}{100})$
e) $(1 \times 100) + (3 \times 1) + (9 \times \frac{1}{100}) + (2 \times \frac{1}{1000})$
f) $(1 \times 1) + (4 \times \frac{1}{10}) + (7 \times \frac{1}{1000})$

6. a) $4.4 \times 10^3, 4.5 \times 10^3, 4.9 \times 10^3$
b) $6.3 \times 10^5, 6.3 \times 10^6, 6.3 \times 10^8$
c) $8.42 \times 10^5, 8.53 \times 10^5, 8.56 \times 10^5$
d) $7.92 \times 10^8, 7.013 \times 10^9, 7.113 \times 10^9$

7. a) $10 \times 10 \times 10; 1000$ **b)** $3 \times 3; 9$

c) $5 \times 5 \times 5 \times 5$; 625   d) $10 \times 10 \times 10 \times 10 \times 10$; 100 000

e) 1.5×1.5; 2.25   f) $7 \times 7 \times 7$; 343

g) 12×12; 144   h) $8 \times 8 \times 8 \times 8$; 4096

8. a) 3.2745×10^8 **b)** 9.2086×10^4

c) 5.72×10^6 **d)** $7.71\ 496 \times 10^5$

e) 1.7×10^9 **f)** 4.86×10^8

9. a) $\frac{2}{7} < \frac{1}{2}$ **b)** $\frac{3}{4} < \frac{8}{9}$ **c)** $\frac{4}{5} > \frac{7}{12}$

d) $\frac{2}{3} = \frac{10}{15}$ **e)** $0.55 > \frac{4}{9}$ **f)** $\frac{8}{6} < 1.5$

g) $\frac{3}{10} > 0.28$ **h)** $5.8 < 6.1$ **i)** $10.05 > 4.95$

10. a) 1.1   **b)** 0.68   **c)** 0.39   **d)** 0.73   **e)** 2.2

f) 1.95   **g)** 2.10   **h)** 1.32   **i)** 1.94

11. a) $\frac{1}{8}$ **b)** $\frac{1}{4}$ **c)** $\frac{1}{2}$ **d)** 1   **e)** 2   **f)** $\frac{2}{3}$

12. a) 20   **b)** 8   **c)** 10

13. a) $1.38   **b)** $687.50

14. a) Ontario   **b)** $\frac{19}{30}$ **c)** $\frac{11}{30}$

d) British Columbia: population; Ontario: population; Quebec: population

e) Answers may vary. They suggest that people conserve energy.

15. $2900

16. a) $600, $2400   **b)** $288, $2688

c) Cheaper to borrow and buy it now

17. Answers may vary.

a) Mode or median   **b)** Median

c) Median, mode, or mean

18. a) $\frac{1}{18}$ **b)** $\frac{1}{6}$ **c)** $\frac{2}{9}$

19. a) People disagree with booing.

b) Strongly disagree   **c)** Slightly disagree

20. a) +4; −3   **b)** Alexander

21. 60   **22.** 45.6 km

23. a) Estimates may vary. 11 h   **b)** 10.3 h; yes, 2.3 h

24. a) $27.17; $27.88   **b)** Cloth World

25. a) $(l + 6)$ centimetres   **b)** $(l - 3)$ centimetres

c) $2l$ centimetres   **d)** $\frac{1}{2}l$ centimetres

e) $4l$ centimetres   **f)** $\frac{2}{3}l$ centimetres

26. a) i) $5 + 2x = 9$ **ii)** $x = 2$ **iii)** 2

b) i) $3x + 8 = 23$ **ii)** $x = 5$ **iii)** 5

c) i) $22 = 4 + 3x$ **ii)** $x = 6$ **iii)** 6

d) i) $2x + 7 = 17$ **ii)** $x = 5$ **iii)** 5

CHAPTER 9 TWO-DIMENSIONAL GEOMETRY

Start With What You Know, page 426

1. , 2. Answers may vary.

3. a) $x = 12$ **b)** $x = 128$ **c)** $x = 53$

d) $x = 6$ **e)** $x = 63$

4. Questions and answers may vary.

9.1 Using a Variety of Tools for Constructions
Working with Mathematics, page 433

1. Answers may vary.

2. a) The point that divides a line segment into two equal sections

b) The line that divides an angle into two equal angles

c) The line that divides a line segment into two equal sections

and is perpendicular to the line segment

3. PY   **4.** $\angle PQR = 119°$

7. A circle with centre X and radius 4 cm

8. d) Points on the perpendicular bisector are equidistant from P and Q.

10. c) There are 2 points that are 5 cm from both A and B.

d) AC and CB have the same length. The angle at C has measure 90°. So, the line we draw is the perpendicular bisector of AB.

11. You can draw 3 altitudes.

12. b) The perpendicular bisectors of the sides of a triangle intersect at a point inside the triangle.

13. b) The angle bisectors of a triangle intersect at a point inside the triangle.

14. a) Scales may vary.

d) The path is the perpendicular bisector of PS. You can verify this by measuring the angle of intersection of the path and PS and the length of each segment of PS.

15. $\angle DEF = 24°$

20. a) Scales may vary. For a scale of 1 cm to 25 m, AB will be 8 cm long.

c) For a scale of 1 cm to 25 m, the altitude is 6.4 cm.

d) About 160 m

21. 5.6 m

24. To one decimal place, the width of the chalet is 13.3 m.

25. There are 3 such squares.

9.2 The Angle Measures of a Triangle
Developing the Ideas, page 438

Activity 1

1. The vertices meet at one point and form a straight angle. The sum of the angles in the triangle was 180°.

2. The sum of the angles in any triangle is 180°.

Working with Mathematics, page 442

1. a) 180°

b) No; the sum of two right angles is 180°, so the third angle would have measure 0°.

c) Because the sum of two obtuse angles is greater than 180°

d) No; the sum of a right angle and an obtuse angle is greater than 180°.

2. 60°   **3.** 45°

4. a) 20°   **b)** 45°   **c)** 25°   **d)** 82°

5. Complementary: $\angle BFA$ and $\angle BFC$, $\angle CFD$ and $\angle DFE$; supplementary: $\angle AFB$ and $\angle BFE$, $\angle AFC$ and $\angle CFE$, $\angle DFE$ and $\angle DFA$; $\angle AFB = 28°$, $\angle BFC = 62°$, $\angle CFD = 40°$, $\angle DFE = 50°$

6. Answers may vary.

7. a) 150°   **b)** 140°   **c)** 108°   **d)** 95°   **e)** 69°   **f)** 21°

8. a) 3°   **b)** 17°   **c)** 25°   **d)** 66°   **e)** 72°   **f)** 88°

9. a) 113°   **b)** 32°   **c)** 50°   **d)** 26°

11. a) 60°   **b)** 23°   **c)** 45°   **d)** 48°

12. a) 35°, 145°   **b)** 115°, 25°   **c)** 70°, 60°   **d)** 50°, 67°

13. a) 48°, 42°   **b)** 40°, 70°

14. a) No, if two angles had a sum of 180°, the third angle would have measure 0°.

b) Yes, in a right triangle, the two other angles are complementary.

15. a) 180°   **b)** 180°   **c)** 360°
d) Yes, all quadrilaterals can be divided into two triangles by a diagonal.

16. a) Three   **b)** 540°

17. Complementary:
a) 78°   **b)** 66°   **c)** 43°   **d)** 27°   **e)** 1°

Supplementary:
a) 168°   **b)** 156°   **c)** 133°   **d)** 117°   **e)** 91°

18. a) 37°   **b)** 20°   **c)** 60 °   **d)** 53°
e) 80°   **f)** 84°   **g)** 38°   **h)** 30°

19. a) 78°   **b)** 36°   **c)** 47°   **d)** 41°

20. a) 57°, 123°   **b)** 108°, 38°   **c)** 59°, 54°   **d)** 42°, 94°

21. a) 46 °, 53°   **b)** 37°, 53°

22. ∠ABD = ∠CAD and ∠BAD = ∠ACD

23. Sook-Yin is correct; the angle measures in the triangle are 20°, 40°, and 120°, or 18°, 54°, and 108°.

9.3 Isosceles and Equilateral Triangles

Developing the Ideas, page 445

1. a) Isosceles
b) Two sides have equal length. The angles opposite the equal sides are equal.

2. Yes   **3.** Answers may vary.

Working with Mathematics, page 447

1. a) 70°   **b)** 75°   **c)** 60°   **d)** 136°
e) 50°   **f)** 120°   **g)** 108°, 144°   **h)** 30°, 90°

2. a) 80°; no   **b)** 75°; no   **c)** 42°; no
d) 60°; no   **e)** 36°; yes   **f)** 59°; yes
g) 45°; yes   **h)** 79°; yes   **i)** 32°; no

3. a) 25°   **b)** 103°   **c)** 100°, 40°
d) 63°, 54°, 126°   **e)** 104°, 38°, 142°   **f)** 50°, 80°

4. There are 2 triangles that satisfy these conditions. Their angles are 45°, 45°, 90° and 36°, 72°, 72°.

5. 30°, 120° or 75°, 75°   **6.** 40°, 70°, 70° or 50°, 50°, 80°

7. a) Yes, an isosceles right triangle will have angles 45°, 45°, 90°.
b) Yes, for example, a triangle with angles 120°, 30°, 30° is isosceles and obtuse.
c) Yes, for example, a triangle with angles 70°, 70°, 40° is isosceles and acute.
d) No. If a triangle is scalene it has no equal sides and therefore cannot be isosceles.

8. a) 35°, 32.5°, 20°, 15°, 7.5°
b) Divide by 2.   **c)** $y = \frac{x}{2}$
d) When $x = 90°$, $y = 45°$ **e)** When $x = 0°$, $y = 0°$

Quest: Calculating Angles in House Construction, page 449

The carpenter must cut the boards for the peak of the roof at an angle of 26°, and the boards for the baseline at an angle of 58°.

Linking Ideas: Algebra and Geometry

Patterns in the Angles in Isosceles Triangles, page 450

Group 1

1. The points appear to lie along a straight line sloping down to the right. For every 5° increase or decrease in the measure of one of the equal angles, there is a corresponding 10° decrease or increase in the measure of the third angle.

2. a) $y = 180° - 2x$
b) x must be between 0° and 90°, y will be between 180° and 0°.

Group 2

1. There are two groups of points. The points in each group appear to lie on lines sloping down to the right, but with different slopes. The lines meet at (60°, 60°). The more steeply sloped line represents the case when the third angle is the largest, the other line represents the case when the equal angles are the largest.

2. When the third angle is largest:
a) $y = 180° - 2x$
b) x must be between 0° and 60°, y will be between 180° and 60°.

When the equal angles are largest:
a) $y = \frac{180° - x}{2}$
b) x must be between 0° and 60°, y will be between 90° and 60°.

Mathematics File: Angles and Intersecting Lines, page 451

1. a) The angles opposite each other are equal.
b) Explanations may vary.

2. Opposite angles: a and c, b and d; supplementary angles: b and a, a and d, d and c, b and c
When $a = 145°$, $b = 35°$, $c = 145°$, and $d = 35°$

3. a) 70°, 110°   **b)** 132°, 132°   **c)** 121°, 59°
d) 70°, 50°   **e)** 85°, 55°   **f)** 136°, 22°

9.4 Angles and Parallel Lines

Developing the Ideas

Activity 1, page 452

1. a) The corresponding angles have equal measure.

2. a) The interior alternate angles have equal measure.

Activity 2, page 453

2. a) They are equal.   **b)** They are equal.

3. a) 180°   **b)** It is the same, 180°.

4. a) 180°   **b)** It is the same, 180°.

5. No, the results are the same for all diagrams.

Working with Mathematics, page 455

1. a) 4 and 6, 3 and 5
b) 1 and 5, 4 and 8, 2 and 6, 3 and 7
c) 2 and 8, 1 and 7
d) 4 and 5, 3 and 6
e) 2 and 7, 1 and 8
f) 1 and 3, 2 and 4, 6 and 8, 5 and 7

2. Examples may vary.   **3.** Answers may vary.

4. a) 75°, 105°   **b)** 60°, 120°, 120°

c) 40°, 140° **d)** 140°, 40°, 40°

e) 105°, 75°, 105° **f)** 65°, 65°, 65°

5. a) $\angle ABC = 40°$, $\angle ACB = 76°$, $\angle BAC = 64°$
   b) $\angle ABC = 92°$, $\angle BAC = 38°$, $\angle BCA = 50°$
   c) $\angle ACB = 90°$, $\angle CAB = 43°$, $\angle ABC = 47°$

6. a) 110° **b)** 63°, 117° **c)** 74°, 106°
   d) 35° **e)** 58°, 122°, 58°, 122°
   f) 75°, 55° **g)** 55°, 60° **h)** 50°, 53°, 103°

7. Exercises may vary.

8. When angle 2 has measure 112°, angles 4, 6, and 8 all have measure 112°; angles 1, 3, 5, and 7 all have measure 68°.

9. $x = 54°$, $t = 72°$, $s = 54°$, $w = 126°$, $z = 108°$

10. a) 60°, 40°, 80° **b)** 64°, 26°, 64°
   c) 76°, 76°, 104°, 104° **d)** 32°, 32°, 58°, 90°
   e) 40°, 92°, 48° **f)** 76°, 76°, 31°
   g) 117°, 117°, 50°, 67° **h)** 94°, 54°, 54°, 40°

11. Exercises may vary. **12.** No. Diagrams may vary.

13. No, not in the same plane. Diagrams may vary.

14. a) Three lines can also intersect in 1 or 3 points.
   b) The greatest number of points in which four lines can intersect is 6, the least is 0. There are also examples of four lines intersecting in 1, 3, 4, and 5 points, but not in 2 points.
   c) The greatest number of points in which five lines can intersect is 10; for 6 lines, the greatest number of points is 15.
   d) The greatest number of points in which n lines can intersect is $\frac{n(n-1)}{2}$.

9.5 The Pythagorean Theorem
Developing the Ideas, page 460

Activity 3

5. For a right triangle, the sum of the areas of the squares on the shorter sides is equal to the area of the square on the hypotenuse.

6. No **7.** See exercise 5.

8. Yes; $2.8^2 = 7.84$, $9.6^2 = 92.16$, and $7.84 + 92.16 = 100$

Working with Mathematics, page 462

1. a) A triangle with a 90° angle
   b) The side opposite the 90° angle in a right triangle

2. Answers may vary.

3. a) Yes
   b) In a right triangle, the 90° angle is the largest angle.

4. a) PQ **b)** AB **c)** ZY **d)** LM

5. a) 12 square units **b)** 36 square units
   c) 135 square units **d)** 36 square units

6. 30 cm^2 **7.** 16 cm^2

8. 20 cm^2 (if the third side is the hypotenuse), 4 cm^2 (if the side with a square of area 12 cm^2 is the hypotenuse)

9. a) 32 cm^2 **b)** 16 cm^2 **c)** 25 cm^2 **d)** 49 cm^2

10. a) Yes **b)** No **c)** No **d)** Yes

11. a) 15 cm^2 **b)** 9 cm^2

12. a) 144 square units **b)** 109 square units
   c) 190 square units **d)** 16 square units
   e) 100 square units **f)** 2460 square units

14. a) i **b)** ii

15. a) 25 cm^2 **b)** 20 cm^2 **c)** 16 cm^2 **d)** 13 cm^2 **e)** 7 cm^2 **f)** 5 cm^2

16. 50 cm^2 and 100 cm^2 (if the side with a square of area 50 cm^2 is one of the equal sides); 25 cm^2 and 25 cm^2 (if the other two sides are the equal sides)

17. Yes; explanations may vary.

Linking Ideas: Mathematics and Technology
Investigating the Pythagorean Theorem Using *The Geometer's Sketchpad*, page 464

In a right triangle, the square of the length of the hypotenuse is equal to the sum of the squares of the lengths of the two shorter sides.

9.6 Applying the Pythagorean Theorem
Working with Mathematics, page 468

1. Answers may vary. If I am calculating the area on a leg, I subtract. If I am calculating the area on the hypotenuse, I add.

2. a) i **b)** ii **c)** i

3. a) 100 cm^2; 10.0 cm **b)** 5 cm^2; 2.2 cm
   c) 61 cm^2; 7.8 cm **d)** 225 cm^2; 15.0 cm
   e) 25 cm^2; 5.0 cm **f)** 32 cm^2; 5.7 cm
   g) 279 cm^2; 16.7 cm **h)** 56 cm^2; 7.5 cm

4. a) 3.2 cm **b)** 4.0 cm **c)** 8.6 cm **d)** 4.9 cm

5. a) 1.7, 3.0, 3.5; 3.3, 5.0, 6.0; 9.3, 7.0, 6.1; 7.9, 9.9, 6.0
   b) 4.0 cm, 4.0 cm, 5.7 cm; 2.8 cm, 2.8 cm, 4.0 cm; 7.1 cm, 5.0 cm, 5.0 cm; 9.9 cm, 7.0 cm, 7.0 cm

6. 35 mm **7.** 6.71 m

8. a) 26.0 cm **b)** 55.0 cm **c)** 10.4 cm
   d) 12.4 cm **e)** 11.3 cm **f)** 10.3 cm

9. 1.8 km **10.** 12.65 m **11.** 51.8 m **12.** 21.6 km **13.** 6.9 cm^2

14. a) 13.6 cm **b)** 11.9 m **c)** 1.7 cm **d)** 1.7 m

Review, page 470

1. a) Obtuse, scalene **b)** Right, isosceles
   c) Obtuse, isosceles **d)** Acute, scalene

6. e) They are equal. **f)** They are equal. **g)** They are equal.

7. b) Their lengths are equal.
   c) The point of intersection is the midpoint of each diagonal.
   d) Yes

8. a) Scales may vary. **d)** About 1400 m

9. a) 90°; right **b)** 81°; acute isosceles
   c) 53°; acute scalene **d)** 47°; acute isosceles
   e) 18°; obtuse isosceles **f)** 30°; right

10. a) A pair of angles is complementary if the sum of their measures is 90°. A pair of angles is supplementary if the sum of their measures is 180°.
   b) Complementary:
      i) 82° **ii)** 51° **iii)** 38°
      iv) 23° **v)** 16° **vi)** 9°
      Supplementary:
      i) 172° **ii)** 141° **iii)** 128°
      iv) 113° **v)** 106° **vi)** 99°

11. a) 77°, 149° **b)** 38°, 142° **c)** 65°, 21° **d)** 37°, 33°
   e) 118°, 25° **f)** 110°, 35° **g)** 40° **h)** 120°, 90°, 60°
   i) 27° **j)** 75° **k)** 62°, 31° **l)** 70°, 70°, 110°

12. Answers may vary.
  a) 2 and 4, 1 and 3, 5 and 7, 6 and 8, 2 and 6, 1 and 5, 3 and 7, 4 and 8, 2 and 8, 3 and 5, 4 and 6, 1 and 7
  b) 1 and 2, 3 and 4, 1 and 4, 2 and 3, 5 and 6, 6 and 7, 7 and 8, 5 and 8, 2 and 5, 3 and 8, 1 and 6, 4 and 7

13. a) 41 cm^2 **b)** 592 cm^2 **c)** 4 cm^2 **d)** 242 cm^2

14. a) 22.2   **b)** 17.9

Cumulative Review, page 474

1. a) centimetres   **b)** kilometres   **c)** centimetres
  d) metres   **e)** millimetres

2. a) 8.4×10^3 **b)** 2.11×10^8 **c)** 3.104×10^7
  d) 6.7×10^5 **e)** 1.98×10^6 **f)** 4.3×10^4

3. a) 2, 6   **b)** 0, 4, 8   **c)** 0, 4, 8
  d) 2, 6   **e)** 0, 2, 4, 6, 8   **f)** 0, 4, 8

4. a) 31.5   **b)** 83.352   **c)** 15.12   **d)** 498.68
  e) 728.48   **f)** 183.58   **g)** 4   **h)** 7
  i) 3   **j)** 5   **k)** 2.5   **l)** 8.6

5. The repeating decimals are rounded to 2 decimal places.
  a) 0.5; 50%   **b)** 0.75; 75%
  c) 0.8; 80%   **d)** 0.7; 70%
  e) 0.375; 37.5%   **f)** 0.22; 22%
  g) 0.53; 53%   **h)** 0.42; 42%

6. Answers are rounded to the nearest percent.
  a) 18% increase   **b)** 33% increase
  c) 49% increase   **d)** 11% decrease
  e) 29% decrease   **f)** 22% decrease

7. a) Graphs may vary. A bar graph would be suitable.
  b) Descriptions may vary. The graph is bell-shaped.
  c) Based on the shape of the graph, one would predict that the Maritime provinces have the coolest summer temperatures, and Ontario and Manitoba have the warmest summer temperatures.

8. Answers may vary.
  a) A set of 2 numbers less than or equal to 11, 2 numbers greater than or equal to 11, and the number 11, such that the sum of all 5 numbers is 70
  b) A set of 6 numbers, such that when arranged in order from least to greatest, the 3rd and 4th numbers have a sum of 22, and the sum of all 6 numbers is 84
  c) A set of 7 numbers with a sum of 175, such that the number that occurs most often is 21

9. a) -3 **b)** $+153$ **c)** -8 **d)** -12

10. a) $+4$ **b)** 0   **c)** $+8$ **d)** $+3$ **e)** -22

11. i) a) Each number is a multiple of 6.
  b) 90   **c)** 120   **d)** $6n$
  ii) a) Each number is 1 more than the preceding number. Each is the sum of 8 and a number.
  b) 23   **c)** 28   **d)** $8 + n$
  iii) a) Each number is 1 less than the preceding number. Each is the difference between 30 and a number.
  b) 15   **c)** 10   **d)** $30 - n$
  iv) a) Each number is equal to 100 divided by a number.
  b) $\frac{100}{15}$, or $\frac{20}{3}$ **c)** 5   **d)** $\frac{100}{n}$
  v) a) Each number is equal to 180 divided by a number.
  b) 12   **c)** 9   **d)** $\frac{180}{n}$

12. a) $a + 5 = 21; a = 16$ **b)** $\frac{b}{3} = 10; b = 30$
  c) $8 - c = -7; c = 15$ **d)** $2d = 36; d = 18$
  e) $e + 12 = 19; e = 7$

13. Some sentences may vary.
  a) A number increased by 7 is 18; $a = 11$
  b) 3 times a number is -21; $b = -7$
  c) 15 decreased by a number is 6; $c = 9$
  d) A number divided by 3 is 15; $d = 45$
  e) A number divided by 4 is -2; $e = -8$
  f) A number increased by 4 is -8; $f = -12$
  g) A number decreased by 11 is -2; $g = 9$
  h) A number increased by 3 is 10; $h = 7$

14. a) 7   **b)** 4   **c)** $-3°$C

16. a) 80°, 45°   **b)** 43°   **c)** 30°, 90°   **d)** 70°, 118°
  e) 105°, 75°   **f)** 150°, 30°
  g) 40°, 50°, 140°   **h)** 110°, 110°, 70°, 110°

17. a) b and f, c and g, a and e, d and h
  b) b and h, a and g
  c) a and c, b and d, e and g, f and h
  d) c and f, d and e

acute angle: an angle measuring less than 90°

acute triangle: a triangle whose three angles are each less than 90°

algebraic expression: a mathematical expression containing a variable; for example, $6x - 4$ is an algebraic expression

alternate angles: angles that are between two lines and are on opposite sides of a transversal that cuts the two lines

Angles 1 and 3 are alternate angles.
Angles 2 and 4 are alternate angles.

altitude: the perpendicular distance from the base of a figure to the opposite side or vertex

angle: the figure formed by two rays from the same endpoint

angle bisector: the line that divides an angle into two equal parts

approximate: close to the exact value; the symbol $\doteq$ means "is approximately equal to"

arc: part of a circle
AB is an arc of the circle, centre O.

area: the number of square units needed to cover a region

array: an arrangement in rows and columns

ascending order: arranged in order from least to greatest

average: a single number that represents a set of numbers; see *mean*, *median*, and *mode*

balance: the result when money is added to or subtracted from an original amount; a scale that uses two pans on the ends of a pivoting rod to measure mass

Balance Principle: when the same number is added to or subtracted from two equal expressions, the results will be equal

bar graph: a graph that displays data by using horizontal or vertical bars whose lengths are proportional to the numbers they represent

bar notation: the use of a horizontal bar over decimal digits to indicate that they repeat; for example, $1.\overline{3}$ means 1.333 333 …

bar scale: a ruler that shows the scale for a map or diagram

0   200   400   600   800   1000 km

base: the side of a polygon or the face of a solid from which the height is measured; the factor repeated in a power; the number that forms the basic unit of a number system

bias: an emphasis on characteristics that are not typical of the entire population

bisector: a line that divides a line segment in two equal parts

The broken line is a bisector of AB.

box-and-whisker plot: a diagram in which data are plotted horizontally and values between the upper and lower quartiles are enclosed in a box

broken-line graph: a graph that displays data by using points joined by line segments

capacity: the amount a container can hold

centroid: the point where the three medians of a triangle intersect

chevron: a V-shaped bar

circle: a closed curve, all of whose points are the same distance from a point called the centre

circle graph: a diagram that uses parts of a circle to display data

circumcentre: the point where the perpendicular bisectors of the sides of a triangle intersect

circumcircle: a circle drawn through each of the vertices of a triangle and with its centre at the circumcentre of the triangle

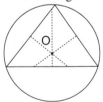

circumference: the distance around a circle, and sometimes the circle itself

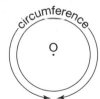

clinometer: an instrument that measures the angle of elevation of objects from a base level, such as eye level

commission: money earned by sales people on items they sell; a percent of the price of items sold

common denominator: a number that is a multiple of each of the given denominators; for example, 12 is a common denominator for the fractions $\frac{1}{3}, \frac{5}{4}, \frac{7}{12}$

common factor: a number that is a factor of each of the given numbers; for example, 3 is a common factor of 15, 9, and 21

compasses: an instrument for drawing circles and arcs

complementary angles: two angles whose sum is 90°

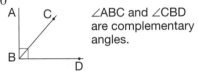

∠ABC and ∠CBD are complementary angles.

composite number: a number with three or more factors; for example, 8 is a composite number because its factors are 1, 2, 4, and 8

compound event: a combination of two or more events

compound interest: when the interest for one time period is added to the principal, and the interest for the next time period is calculated on that sum

congruent: figures that have the same size and shape, but not necessarily the same position

conjecture: a statement that someone believes to be true and may appear to be true, but has not yet been proved

consecutive numbers: integers that come one after the other without any integers missing; for example, 34, 35, 36 are consecutive numbers, so are −2, −1, 0, and 1

Consumer Price Index: the change in the costs of goods and services, based on their costs on a set date

continuous-line graph: a graph that shows the value of one variable corresponding to the value of another variable, for all values over a given interval

coordinate grid: a two-dimensional surface on which a coordinate system has been set up

coordinates: the numbers in an ordered pair that locate a point on a grid by telling the point's distance and direction from the *x*-axis and the *y*-axis

corresponding angles: angles that are on the same side of a transversal that cuts two lines and on the same side of each line
   Angles 1 and 3 are corresponding angles.
   Angles 2 and 4 are corresponding angles.
   Angles 5 and 7 are corresponding angles.
   Angles 6 and 8 are corresponding angles.

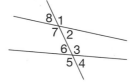

cube: a solid with six congruent, square faces that meet at right angles

cube root: a number which, when three of them are multiplied, results in a given number; for example, 2 is the cube root of 8 because $2 \times 2 \times 2 = 8$

cubic units: units that measure volume

cylinder: a solid with two parallel, congruent, circular bases

data: facts or information

database: facts or information supplied by computer software

decibel: a measure of the intensity of sound

decimal: a numeral that shows fractional amounts by using digits to the right of a dot called the decimal point; for example, 0.7 is a decimal for $\frac{7}{10}$

deficit: a debt caused by spending more money than is taken in

denominator: the term below the line in a fraction; the denominator tells the number of parts into which the whole has been divided

descending order: arranged in order from greatest to least

diagonal: a line segment that joins two vertices of a figure, but is not a side

diameter: the distance across a circle, measured through the centre; a line segment through the centre of a circle whose end points are on the circle

difference: the result when one number is subtracted from another

digit: any of the symbols 0, 1, 2, 3, 4, 5, 6, 7, 8, 9 used to write numbers

dimensions: measurements, such as length, width, and height

discount: the amount by which a price is reduced

distortion: a change in the shape of a figure

dividend: a number to be divided by another number

divisor: the number by which another number is to be divided; a number that divides another without a remainder

double-bar graph: a bar graph that shows two sets of data

double broken-line graph: broken-line graphs that show two sets of data

edge: the line segment where two faces of a solid meet

enlargement: a copy of a figure that is larger than the original figure, but has the same shape

equation: a mathematical statement that two expressions are equal; for example, $2 + 4x = 14$

equidistant: the same distance apart

equilateral triangle: a triangle with three equal sides

equivalent: having the same value; for example, $\frac{2}{3}$ and $\frac{6}{9}$ are equivalent fractions, $1 : 2$ and $5 : 10$ are equivalent ratios

estimate: to make a careful guess that is close to the actual value, without calculating it exactly

evaluate: to substitute a value for each variable in an expression

even number: an integer that has 2 as a factor; for example, 2, 4, −2, and −4 are even numbers

event: any set of outcomes of an experiment

expanded form: a way of writing a number so that the place value of each digit is shown; for example, 4679 in expanded form is $(4 \times 1000) + (6 \times 100) + (7 \times 10) + 9$

exponent: a symbol that is placed to the right of and above another symbol

expression: a meaningful combination of symbols

exterior alternate angles: angles that are outside two lines and are on opposite sides of a transversal that cuts the two lines

Angles *a* and *g* are exterior alternate angles.
Angles *b* and *h* are exterior alternate angles.

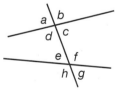

exterior angle: the angle created outside a triangle when one of the sides of the triangle is extended

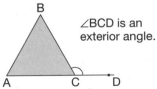

∠BCD is an exterior angle.

extremes: the highest and lowest values in a set of numbers

face: a flat surface of a solid

factor: to factor means to write as a product; a factor is any of the natural numbers used to form a product; for example, 2 and 4 are factors of 8

factor tree: a way to find the prime factors of a composite number

first-hand data: data gathered by oneself

formula: a rule that is expressed as an equation

fraction: a number that represents part of a whole or part of a set

frequency: the number of times a particular value occurs in a set of data; the number of times an outcome or event occurs

geodesic sphere: a ball-like construction whose framework is made up of triangular sections

greatest common factor (GCF): the greatest natural number that divides into each number in a set; for example, 5 is the greatest common factor of 10 and 15

Greek cross: a geometric figure that resembles an addition sign

hand span: the distance between the tips of the outstretched thumb and little finger of one hand

hectare: a unit of area represented by a square with sides 100 m

height: the perpendicular distance from the base of a figure to the opposite vertex or side (if it is parallel to the base); the perpendicular distance from the base of a pyramid to the opposite vertex; the perpendicular distance between congruent faces in a prism

hexagon: a six-sided polygon

hexagonal prism: a prism whose bases are six-sided polygons

histogram: a graph that uses bars, where each bar represents a range of values, and the data are continuous

hypotenuse: the side opposite the right angle in a right triangle

hypotenuse

image: the figure that results from a transformation

imperial units: units in the British system of measurement based on natural objects such as the foot

independent events: when the outcome of one event does not affect the outcome of another event

inference: a conclusion drawn from factual evidence or data

integer: any of the numbers …−3, −2, −1, 0, +1, +2, +3,…

interior alternate angles: angles that are between two lines and are on opposite sides of a transversal that cuts the two lines

Angles *d* and *f* are interior alternate angles.
Angles *c* and *e* are interior alternate angles.

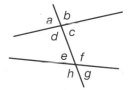

interest: money paid for the use of money

intersect: meet or cross

intersecting lines: lines that meet or cross; lines that have one point in common

inverse operation: an operation that reverses the result of another operation; for example, subtraction is the inverse of addition, and division is the inverse of multiplication

irregular polygon: a polygon that is not a regular polygon

isosceles acute triangle: a triangle with two equal sides and all angles less than 90°

isosceles obtuse triangle: a triangle with two equal sides and one angle greater than 90°

isosceles right triangle: a triangle with two equal sides and a 90° angle

isosceles triangle: a triangle with at least two equal sides

kilojoule: a measure of energy

kite: a quadrilateral with two pairs of equal adjacent sides

least common multiple: the smallest number that is a multiple of a set of numbers; for example, 24 is the least common multiple of 6 and 8

legs: the sides of a right triangle that form the right angle

light-year: a unit for measuring astronomical distances; one light-year is the distance light travels in one year

line: a set of points in a straight path extending infinitely in both directions

line segment: a part of a line between two points on the line

line symmetry: a figure that coincides with itself when it is reflected in a line is said to have line symmetry; for example, line *l* is the line of symmetry for figure ABCD

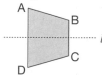

lower quartile: the number at the one-quarter point when data are arranged in increasing order

lowest terms: a ratio is in lowest terms when the only factor that the terms have in common is 1

mass: the amount of matter in an object

mean: the sum of a set of numbers divided by the number of numbers in the set; for example, 38 is the mean for the set of numbers 30, 40, 44

measure of central tendency: a single value that represents a set of data; see *mean, median,* and *mode*

median: the middle number or value when data are arranged in numerical order; for example, 11 is the median for the set of numbers 6, 10, 11, 20, 42

median of a triangle: a line segment from one vertex to the midpoint of the opposite side

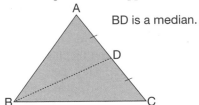

BD is a median.

metric units: units in a system of measurement based on the decimal system, related by 10, 100, 1000, and so on

midpoint: the point that divides a line segment into two equal parts

minimal: the least value or amount

mixed number: a number consisting of a whole number and a fraction

mode: the number that occurs most often in a set of numbers

model: a set of data or a diagram that describes an object, opinion, or situation

multiple: the product of a given number and a natural number; for example, some multiples of 8 are 8, 16, 24, …

natural numbers: the set of numbers 1, 2, 3, 4, 5, …

negative integer: any of the numbers −1, −2, −3, −4, …

negative number: a number less than 0

net: a pattern for a solid

network: a diagram made up of line segments that meet, forming vertices and regions

numeral: the written form of a number; for example, X is the Roman numeral for ten, while 10 is the Arabic numeral for ten

numerator: the term above the line in a fraction; the numerator tells how many parts are being talked about

obtuse angle: an angle measuring more than 90° and less than 180°

obtuse triangle: a triangle with one angle greater than 90°

octagon: an eight-sided polygon

octahedron: a solid that has eight faces

odd number: an integer that does not have 2 as a factor; for example, 1, 3, and −7 are odd numbers

operation: a mathematical process or action such as addition, subtraction, multiplication, or division

opposite angles: the equal angles that are formed by two intersecting lines

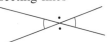

opposite number: a number whose sum with a given number is 0; for example, 3 and −3 are opposites

opposites: two numbers whose sum is zero; each number is the opposite of the other

Opposites Principle: when two equal expressions are multiplied by −1, the results will be equal

order of operations: the rules about which operations to do first when simplifying or evaluating an expression

ordinal: a number indicating position in a series; for example, *first, second,* and *third*

origin: the point where the *x*-axis and the *y*-axis intersect

orthocentre: the point at which the altitudes of a triangle intersect

outcome: a possible result of an experiment or a possible answer to a survey question

palindromic number: a number that reads the same in both directions; for example, 314413

parallel lines: lines in the same plane that do not intersect

parallelogram: a quadrilateral with both pairs of opposite sides parallel

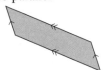

pentagon: a five-sided polygon

pentagonal prism: a prism whose bases are five-sided polygons

pentagonal numbers: a natural number that can be represented by arranging objects in a pentagon; for example, 5 and 12 are pentagonal numbers

pentagonal pyramid: a pyramid whose base is a five-sided polygon

per annum: per year

per capita: for each person

percent: the number of parts per 100; the numerator of a fraction with denominator 100

percent decrease: the decrease divided by the original amount, expressed as a percent

percent increase: the increase divided by the original amount, expressed as a percent

percentiles: hundredths of the data when they are arranged in order

perfect square: a number that is the square of a whole number; for example, 1, 4, 9, 16, and 25 are perfect squares (sometimes called square numbers)

perimeter: the distance around a closed figure

perpendicular: intersecting at right angles

perpendicular bisector: the line that is perpendicular to a line segment and divides the line segment into two equal parts

perspective: a view in which objects on a flat surface appear to have depth

pi (π): the ratio of the circumference of a circle to its diameter; $\pi \doteq 3.1416$

pictograph: a graph in which a symbol represents a certain amount, and repetitions of the symbol illustrate the data

place value system: a number system in which the position of a digit tells its value; for example, in our decimal system, the 3 in the numeral 4389 means 3 hundreds

polygon: a closed figure that consists of line segments; for example, triangles, squares, and quadrilaterals are polygons

polyhedron (plural, **polyhedra**): a three-dimensional solid that has only flat faces that are polygons; for example, pyramids and prisms are polyhedra

population: the set of all the things or people being considered

positive integer: any of the numbers +1, +2, +3, +4, …

positive number: a number greater than 0

power: a representation of a number as the product of equal factors; for example, 64, or $4 \times 4 \times 4$, can be expressed as the power 4^3

power of 10: a product in which all the factors are 10; for example, 10^2 and 10^3 are powers of 10

prediction: a statement of what you think will happen

prime factor: a factor that is a prime number

prime number: a whole number with exactly two different factors, itself and 1; for example, 3, 5, 7, and 11 are prime numbers; 1 is not considered to be a prime number

principal: the amount of money invested

probability: the likelihood of a particular event; if the outcomes of an experiment are equally likely, then the probability of an event is the ratio of the number of outcomes favourable to the event to the total number of outcomes

product: the result when two or more numbers are multiplied

proportional situation: a situation in which two quantities are related by multiplication or division

proportional thinking: the ability to see how one quantity is related to another quantity, when they are related by multiplication or division

protractor: an instrument for measuring angles in degrees

pyramid: a solid whose base is a polygon and whose other faces are triangles that meet at a common vertex

Pythagorean Theorem: the rule that states that, for any right triangle, the area of the square drawn on the hypotenuse is equal to the sum of the areas of the squares drawn on the other two sides

quadrant: one of the four regions into which coordinate axes divide a plane

quadrilateral: a four-sided polygon

quartiles: quarters of the data when they are arranged in order

quotient: the result when one number is divided by another

radius (plural, **radii**): the distance from the centre of a circle to any point on the circumference; a line segment joining the centre of a circle to any point on the circumference

random sample: a sample in which all members of the population have an equal chance of being selected

range: the difference between the highest and lowest values (the *extremes*) in a set of data

rate: a certain quantity or amount of one thing considered in relation to a unit of another thing

ratio: a comparison of two or more quantities with the same unit; for example, in the following diagram, the ratio of coloured squares to white squares is 2 to 3

ray: part of a line, extending without end in one direction only

reciprocals: two numbers whose product is 1; for example, $\frac{3}{4}$ and $\frac{4}{3}$ are reciprocals, so are 2 and $\frac{1}{2}$

rectangle: a quadrilateral that has four right angles

rectangular prism: a prism whose faces are rectangles

rectangular pyramid: a pyramid whose base is a rectangle

reduction: a copy of a figure that is smaller than the original figure, but has the same shape

reflection: a transformation that matches every point P with an image point P′ such that P and P′ are equidistant from the mirror line, and line PP′ is perpendicular to the mirror line

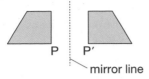

reflex angle: an angle between 180° and 360°

regular hexagon: a polygon that has six equal sides and six equal angles

regular octagon: a polygon that has eight equal sides and eight equal angles

regular polygon: a polygon whose sides are equal and whose angles are equal

regular polyhedron: a polyhedron with faces that are congruent regular polygons

relative frequency: the ratio of the number of times a particular outcome or event occurred to the total number of times the experiment was conducted

repeating decimal: a decimal in which one or more digits repeat endlessly

rhombus: a parallelogram with four equal sides

right angle: an angle measuring 90°

right triangle: a triangle with one 90° angle

rotation: a transformation in which a figure is turned about a fixed point

rotational symmetry: a figure that coincides with itself in less than one full turn is said to have rotational symmetry; for example, a square has rotational symmetry about its centre O

sample/sampling: a representative portion of a population

scale: the ratio of the distance between two points on a map, model, or diagram to the actual distance between the locations

scale drawing: a reproduction that may be larger or smaller than the original, but is the same shape

scale model: a smaller version of an object that has the same proportions

scalene triangle: a triangle with no equal sides

scientific notation: a number expressed as the product of a number greater than −10 and less than −1 or greater than 1 and less than 10, and a power of 10; for example, 4700 is written as 4.7×10^3

second-hand data: data not collected by oneself, but by others; data found in sources such as books, databases, newspapers, encyclopedias, and atlases

semicircle: half a circle

shares: a way of owning part of a company

Sharing Principle: when two equal expressions are divided by the same number, the results will be equal

sieve of Eratosthenes: a method of finding prime numbers by crossing out multiples

similar: having the same shape, but not necessarily the same size

simplest form: a faction is in simplest form when the only common factor of the numerator and denominator is 1; a ratio is in simplest form when the only common factor of the terms is 1

skeleton: a model showing only the edges and vertices of a solid

solid: a three-dimensional object whose interior is completely filled; for example, a sphere, a cube, and a pyramid are solids

spreadsheet: a computer-generated arrangement of data in rows and columns, where a change in one value can result in appropriate changes in the other values

square: a rectangle with four equal sides

square number: a natural number that can be represented by arranging objects in a square; for example, 4 and 9 are square numbers

square of a number: the product of a number multiplied by itself; for example, 25 is the square of 5

square pyramid: a pyramid whose base is a square

square root: a number which, when multiplied by itself, results in a given number; for example, 5 is a square root of 25, so is −5

statistics: the branch of mathematics that deals with the collection, organization, and interpretation of data

stem-and-leaf diagram: a way to represent data; for two-digit values, the tens digits are shown as the stem and the ones digits as the leaves

stock market: a place where shares of companies are bought and sold

straight angle: an angle measuring 180°

straightedge: a strip of wood, metal, or plastic with a straight edge, but no markings

sum: the result when two or more numbers are added

supplementary angles: two angles whose sum is 180°

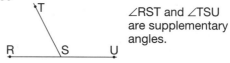

∠RST and ∠TSU are supplementary angles.

surface area: the total area of all the surfaces of an object

symmetrical: possessing symmetry; see *line symmetry* and *rotational symmetry*

tally: a record that uses stroke marks to record the frequency of data

template: a firm, thin sheet with cutouts of figures, used to trace outlines of these figures

term: of a fraction is the numerator or the denominator of the fraction; when an expression is written as the sum of several quantities, each quantity is called a term of the expression

terminating decimal: a decimal with a limited number of digits; a decimal that is complete after a certain number of digits, with no repetition

tetrahedron: a solid with four triangular faces

three-dimensional: having length, width, and depth or height

tiling pattern: a pattern made up of congruent tiles that do not overlap and that leave no gaps

transformation: a reproduction of a figure that results in a change in position, shape, or size of the figure; for example, slides, flips, and turns are transformations

translation: a transformation that moves a point or a figure in a straight line to another position in the same plane

transversal: a line crossing two or more lines

trapezium: a quadrilateral with no parallel sides

trapezoid: a quadrilateral that has only one pair of parallel sides

tree diagram: a branching diagram used to show all possible outcomes of an experiment

triangle: a three-sided polygon

triangular number: a natural number that can be represented by arranging objects in a triangle; for example, 3 and 10 are triangular numbers

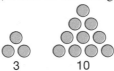

triangular prism: a prism whose bases are triangles

triangular pyramid: a pyramid whose base is a triangle

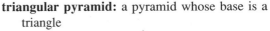

twin primes: consecutive odd numbers that are prime numbers; for example, 5 and 7

two-dimensional: having length and width, but no thickness, height, or depth

unit fraction: a fraction that has a numerator of 1

unit price: the price of one item, or the price for a particular mass or volume of an item

unit rate: the quantity associated with a single unit of another quantity; for example, 6 m in 1 second is a unit rate

upper quartile: the number at the three-quarter point when data are arranged in increasing order

variable: a letter or symbol representing a quantity that can vary

verify: prove something is true

vertex (plural, **vertices**): the corner of a figure or a solid

volume: the amount of space occupied by an object

whole numbers: the set of numbers 0, 1, 2, 3, 4, …

***x*-axis:** the horizontal number line on a coordinate grid

***x*-coordinate:** the first number of an ordered pair; the *x*-coordinate represents the distance and direction from zero along the horizontal number line

***y*-axis:** the vertical number line on a coordinate grid

***y*-coordinate:** the second number of an ordered pair; the *y*-coordinate represents the distance and direction from zero along the vertical number line

Zero Principle: the sum of opposites is zero

INDEX

PHOTO CREDITS AND ACKNOWLEDGMENTS

The publisher wishes to thank the following sources for photographs, illustrations, articles, and other materials used in this book. Care has been taken to determine and locate ownership of copyright material used in this text. We will gladly receive information enabling us to rectify any errors or omissions in credits.

p. 24 (left) Frans Lanting/First Light/ p. 24 (right) Mitch Reardon/Tony Stone Images/ p. 25 (top left) UPI/Corbis-Bettmann/ p. 25 (top right) UPI/Corbis-Bettmann/ p. 25 (bottom left) Philip & Karen Smith/Tony Stone Images/ p. 25 (bottom middle) Ron Watts/First Light/ p. 25 (bottom right) Doug Armand/Tony Stone Images/ p. 26 (top) Richard Martin/Allsport/ p. 26 (bottom) Shaun Botterill/Allsport/ p. 27 "Almost a Fairy Tale" reprinted by permission of the Canadian Press/ p. 27 Richard Martin/Allsport/ p. 28 David Michael Allen/ p. 29 Everett Collection/ p. 30 (top and bottom)UPI/Corbis-Bettmann/ p. 32 (top) Darwin Wiggett/First Light/ p. 32 (middle) Philip & Karen Smith/Tony Stone Images/ p. 32 (bottom) Darwin Wiggett/First Light/ p. 33 (top) Art Wolfe/Tony Stone Images/ p. 33 (bottom) Harry Engels/Animals Animals/ p. 34 (top) Joe M. McDonald/Animals Animals/ p. 34 (bottom left) Gerard Lacz/Animals Animals/ p. 34 (bottom right) Johnny Johnson/Animals Animals/ p. 38 Canapress/ p. 39 (top) David Michael Allen/ p. 39 (bottom) Ian Crysler/ p. 40 (top) Ian Crysler/ p. 40 (bottom) David Michael Allen/ p. 41 David Michael Allen/ p. 44 David Michael Allen/ p. 48 (top) NATIONAL ARCHIVES OF CANADA/NMC 15033/ p. 52–53 Miles Ertman/Masterfile/ p. 52 (inset top) Travelpix/Masterfile/ p. 52 (inset bottom) Y.C.L.-TCL/Masterfile/ p. 59 David Michael Allen/ p. 60 Canada Post Corporation/ p. 62 Donna Aitkenhead/Animals Animals/ p. 63 Jacques Jangoux/Tony Stone Images/ p. 64 (left) The Toronto Star/ p. 64 (right) David Michael Allen/ p. 66 Tony Stone Images/ p. 69 Joe Lepiano/ p. 70 David A. Hardy/S.P.L./Photo Researchers/ p. 70 (inset) Biophoto Associates/Photo Researchers/ p. 71 (top) Jean-Philippe Varin/Photo Researchers/ p. 71 (bottom) Ken Lucas-TCL/Masterfile/ p. 72 Pronk&Associates/ p. 74 Giraudon/Art Resource/ p. 77 NASA p. 86 "The Far Side" cartoon by Gary Larson is reprinted by permission of Chronicle Features, San Francisco, CA. All Rights reserved./ p. 91 Ian Crysler/ p. 92 Ian Crysler/ p. 105 Ian Crysler/ p. 108 Tony Stone Images/ p. 139 (top) First Light/ p. 109 (bottom) Joe Lepiano/ p. 110 Tony Stone Images/ p. 114 David Michael Allen/ p. 115 David Michael Allen/ p. 125 Courtesy of the Charlottetown Guardian/ p. 126 "Math Quiz Answer Was Improper" reprinted with permission—The Toronto Star Syndicate/ p. 126 "Three Equally Valid Answers Can Be Given for Math Question" reprinted with permission of Wallace Krawczyk/ p. 127 Pronk&Associates/ p. 130 David Michael Allen/ p. 136 Dave Starrett/ p. 146 David Michael Allen/ p. 149 Dave Starrett/ p. 155 Pronk&Associates/ p. 156 David Michael Allen/ p. 157 Pronk&Associates/ p. 163 Pronk&Associates// p. 170 Ian Crysler/ p. 171 Ian Crysler/ p. 172 David Michael Allen/ p. 178 David Michael Allen/ p. 179 Joe Lepiano/ p. 180 David Michael Allen/ p. 181 David Michael Allen/ p. 185 (top left) Nicholas Parfitt/Tony Stone Images/ p. 185 (top right) Bill Ivy/Tony Stone Images/ p. 185 (bottom) Tom Kitchin/First Light/ p. 186 NASA/ p. 193 "Superbowl Ads Snapped Up at $900,000 for 30 Seconds" reprinted with permission from Associated Press/ p. 194 (left) David Madison/Tony Stone Images/ p. 194 (right) Greg Vaughn/First Light/ p. 195 (left) Rick Rusing/Tony Stone Images/ p. 195 (right) Tom Stewart/First Light/ p. 197 Ian Crysler/ p. 198 Joe Lepiano/ p. 200 exercise 18 from "Research Ideas for the Classroom: Middle Grades Mathematics," National Council of Teachers of Mathematics/ p. 201 Pronk&Associates/ p. 204 David Michael Allen/ p. 205 David Michael Allen/ p. 209 David Michael Allen/ p. 211 David Michael Allen/ p. 212 David Michael Allen/ p. 213 Ian Crysler/ p. 216 Nick Vedros/Tony Stone Images/ p. 217 (top) Johan Elzenga/Tony Stone Images/ p. 217 (bottom) Joe Lepiano/ p. 218 Christoph Burki/Tony Stone Images/ p. 220 Leonard Lee Rue III/Animals Animals/ p. 221 David Michael Allen/ p. 224 David Michael Allen/ p. 225 David Michael Allen/ p. 226 Albert Lee/Atlantic Stock Images/ p. 227 David Michael Allen/ p. 228 David Michael Allen/ p. 230 David Michael Allen/ p. 234 Ian Crysler/ p. 237 (left) Gray Mortimore/Allsport/ p. 237 (right) Bill Staley/Tony Stone Images/ p. 238 (top) David Michael Allen/ p. 238 (bottom) Rate card courtesy of the Winnipeg Free Press Advertising Department/ p. 239 Art Wolfe/Tony Stone Images/ p. 242 David Michael Allen/ p. 243 David Michael Allen/ p. 246 "Northern Cod Catch" chart reprinted with permission—The Toronto Star Syndicate/ p. 247 (top left) Labat-Lanceau/Jacana/Photo Researchers/ p. 247 (top right) Stephen Homer/First Light/ p. 247 (middle right) Bryn Campbell/Tony Stone Images/ p. 247 (bottom right) Greg Locke/First Light/ p. 251 Rainer Grosskopf/Tony Stone Images/ p. 253 Ian Crysler/ p. 254 (left) Peter D'Angelo/Tony Stone Images/ p. 254 (middle) Ron Watts/First Light/ p. 254 (right) Alan Marsh/First Light/ p. 264 David Michael Allen/ p. 267 "The Debt Treadmill" chart published by the Ministry of Finance, Canada from 200% of Nothing by A.K. Dewdney. Copyright © 1993 A.K. Dewdney. Reprinted by permission of John Wiley & Sons, Inc./ p. 268 "Comparing Economies" chart reprinted with permission—The Toronto Star Syndicate/ p. 269 "Metro's Office Vacancies" chart reprinted with permission—The Toronto Star Syndicate/ p. 270 "B.C. Personal Per Capita Income" chart reprinted from the Vancouver Sun/ p. 271 "Perception Crime Is Epidemic Blamed on Misuse of Statistics" by Doug Fischer, Southam News and Neal Hall, Vancouver Sun/ p. 272 "PCB Concentrations in Herring Gull Eggs" reprinted with permission from the Canadian Wildlife Service, Environment Canada/ p. 272 Tony Stone Images/ p. 273 Henry Ausloos/Animals Animals/ p. 273 (inset) Don Standfield/First Light/ p. 275 Terry Vine/Tony Stone Images/ p. 276 Tony Stone Images/ p. 279 Kevin Morris/Tony Stone Images/ p. 280 "Fifteen" from Stories that Could Be True by William Stafford. Reprinted with permission of Dorothy Stafford./ p. 282 "To the Mothers and Fathers Who Hover" from When the Pie Was Opened. Copyright © 1968 by Jean Little. Reprinted by permission of the author./ p. 284 Ian Crysler/ p. 286 David Michael Allen/ p. 289 David Michael Allen/ p. 292 © Fred Lyon/Photo Researchers/ p. 293 David Michael Allen/ p. 294 David Michael Allen/ p. 297 Dave Starrett/ p. 298 "Weekly Trips" chart reprinted with permission of the Edmonton Journal/ p. 299 "Music" from From the Heart © Mario Pietrantoni. East End Literacy Press/ p. 300 "Have Large Feet, Will Travel South" courtesy of Joan Hardwicke/ p. 301 David Michael Allen/ p. 306 "I think mathematics is easy" and "I think mathematics is fun" charts courtesy of the Board of Trustees of the University of Illinois/ p. 307 "I think mathematics is important" chart courtesy of the Board of Trustees of the University of Illinois/ p. 308 "Avenor Inc." chart reprinted with permission of the Financial Post/ p. 309 David Cannon/Allsport/ p. 310 Dave Starrett/ p. 310 (inset) Archive Photos/ p. 310 "Today's Skies across Canada" © Meteorological Technologies Inc./ p. 311 David Michael Allen/ p. 312 David Michael Allen/ p. 320 (left) Dallas & John Heaton/First Light/ p. 320 (right) Philip & Karen Smith/Tony Stone Images/ p. 331 David Michael Allen/ p. 332 Peter David/Masterfile/ p. 335 Don Enger/Earth Scenes/ p. 337 Courtesy Marina Jaycees/ p. 342 (top left, middle left and right) Dave Starrett, (top right) Jon Eisberg/Masterfile, (bottom) Michael Hart/Masterfile/ p. 344 (left) Bill Gabriel/BioGraphics/ p. 344 (right) Doug Nealy/Tony Stone Images/ p. 345 Ian Crysler/ p. 347 David Michael Allen/ p. 348 exercise 14 a) and c) David Michael Allen

b) Joe Lepiano; exercise 15 Joe Lepiano/p. **349** R. Ian Lloyd/First Light/ p. **350** David Michael Allen/p. **351** (left) Dennis McColeman/Tony Stone Images/p. **351** (middle) David Michael Allen/p. **351** (right) Joe Lepiano/ p. **352** (top) Mike Andrews/Earth Scenes/p. **352** (bottom) Ian Crysler/ p. **353** (left) Ian Crysler/p. **353** (right) Joe Lepiano/p. **354** Ian Crysler/ p. **357** (left) Canapress/p. **357** (right) Canada Centre for Remote Sensing/p. **359** (top) Bruce Ando/Tony Stone Images/p. **359** (bottom) David Michael Allen/p. **361** Ian Crysler/p. **363** David Michael Allen/p. **364** (top right) Dave Starrett/p. **365** (left) David Michael Allen/p. **368** exercise 10 David Michael Allen/p. **369** (top left) Dave Starrett/p. **371** (top) David Michael Allen/p. **371** (bottom) Joe Lepiano/p. **372** David Michael Allen/ p. **374** David Michael Allen/p. **378** Tosca Radigonda/The Image Bank/ p. **382–383** David Joel/Tony Stone Images/p. **384–385** David Michael Allen/p. **390** (top) Canapress/p. **390** (bottom) Richard Martin/Allsport/ p. **396** Dave Starrett/Jun Park/p. **398** Canapress/p. **401** M. Layton/The Image Bank/p. **402** Joe Lepiano/p. **411** Canapress/p. **418** *Canada's Food Guide* © Minister of Supply and Services Canada/p. **426** (top) Skidmore, Owings & Merrill/p. **426** (bottom) Kunio Owaki/Masterfile/p. **427** (top left) Phil Huber/Black Star/p. **427** (bottom left) Leslie E. Robertson & Associates/p. **427** (top right) Aliza Auerbach/p. **427** (bottom right) J.A. Kraulis/Masterfile/p. **428** David Michael Allen/p. **429** Ian Crysler/p. **430** Ian Crysler/p. **431** Ian Crysler/p. **432** Ian Crysler/p. **435** The Toronto Star Syndicate/p. **438** Ian Crysler/p. **439** Ian Crysler/p. **441** David Michael Allen/p. **443** Joe Lepiano/p. **445** Ian Crysler/p. **448** Ian Crysler/p. **449** Bob Alexander/p. **451** Ian Crysler/p. **452** Ian Crysler/p. **457** David Michael Allen/p. **458** (top) Hugh Sitton/Tony Stone Images/p. **458** (bottom) David Michael Allen/p. **459** Ian Crysler/p. **460** (top) Dave Starrett/p. **460** (bottom) Ian Crysler/p. **464** *The Geometer's Sketchpad*, Key Curriculum Press, P.O. Box 2304, Berkeley, CA 94702, 1-800-995-MATH/p. **466** L.J. Lozano/p. **472** Pronk&Associates/p. **473** Pronk&Associates

ILLUSTRATIONS

Steve Attoe **31**, **90**, **91**, **116**, **144**, **146**, **148**, **151** (bottom), **174**, **182**, **187**, **229**, **241**, **258**, **260**, **261**, **262**, **267**, **274**, **300**, **306**, **314**, **327**, **350**, **355** (bottom), **358**, **397**, **439**
Graham Bardell **211**
Justin Diggle **248–249**
Michel Garneau **330**
Kevin Ghiglione **250**, **259**
Mike Herman **87**, **126**, **133**, **151** (top), **280**, **281**, **329**, **355** (top), **372**, **392**, **393**, **410**
Brian Hughes **186**, **223**, **224** (bottom), **324**, **373**, **374**, **419**, **420**
Stephen MacEachern **40**, **82**, **98**, **141**, **142**, **197**, **316**
Martha Newbigging **48**, **54**, **60**, **61**, **111**, **194**, **195**, **196**, **208**, **210**, **215**, **224** (top), **228**, **232**, **237**, **239**, **246**, **252**
Jun Park **45**, **107**, **129**, **143**, **173**, **315**, **322**, **332**
Kent Smith **76**, **113**, **157**, **191**, **360**
Tracy Walker **35**
Technical art by Pronk&Associates unless otherwise stated.